Kant to Wittgenstein and Sartre

Contents of *A History of Western Philosophy,* SECOND EDITION

W. T. JONES
Pomona College

Kant to Wittgenstein and Sartre

A History of Western Philosophy

SECOND EDITION

Harcourt, Brace & World, Inc.

NEW YORK   CHICAGO   SAN FRANCISCO   ATLANTA

LIST OF COPYRIGHTS AND ACKNOWLEDGMENTS

The author records his thanks for the use of the selections reprinted in this book by permission of the following publishers and copyright holders:

GEORGE ALLEN & UNWIN LTD. for excerpts from *Logical Atomism* by Bertrand Russell, in *Contemporary British Philosophy*, edited by J. H. Muirhead; from *Introduction to Mathematical Philosophy* by Bertrand Russell; and from *The Phenomenology of Mind* by G. W. F. Hegel, translated by J. B. Baillie, marketed in the United States by Humanities Press, Inc.

BASIL BLACKWELL, PUBLISHER, OXFORD, for excerpts from *Philosophical Investigations* by Ludwig Wittgenstein, translated by G. E. M. Anscombe.

CAMBRIDGE UNIVERSITY PRESS for excerpts from *An Enquiry Concerning the Principles of Natural Knowledge* by Alfred North Whitehead.

THE CLARENDON PRESS, OXFORD, for excerpts from *Philosophy of Right* by G. W. F. Hegel, translated by T. M. Knox; from *Encyclopedia of the Philosophical Sciences*, Chapters VII and VIII, translated by W. Wallace; and from *Religion and Science* by Bertrand Russell. Reprinted by permission of the Clarendon Press, Oxford.

DOUBLEDAY & COMPANY, INC., for excerpts from *The Birth of Tragedy and The Genealogy of Morals* by Friedrich Nietzsche, translated by F. Golffing. Copyright © 1956 by Doubleday & Company, Inc. Reprinted by permission of the publisher.

ALEXANDER DRU for excerpts from *The Journals of Kierkegaard*, translated by Alexander Dru.

FARRAR, STRAUS & GIROUX, INC., for excerpts from *The Transcendence of the Ego* by Jean-Paul Sartre, translated by F. Williams and R. Kirkpatrick. Copyright © 1957 by The Noonday Press, Inc. Reprinted with the permission of Farrar, Straus & Giroux, Inc.

HARCOURT, BRACE & WORLD, INC., for an excerpt from "The Love Song of J. Alfred Prufrock," in *Collected Poems 1909–1962* by T. S. Eliot.

HARPER & ROW, PUBLISHERS, INC., for excerpts from *Phenomenology and the Crisis of Philosophy* by Edmund Husserl, translated by Q. Lauer. Reprinted by permission of Harper & Row, Publishers, Inc.

D. C. HEATH AND COMPANY for excerpts from *How We Think* by John Dewey. Copyright © 1933 by John Dewey. Published by D. C. Heath & Co., a Division of Raytheon Education Co., Boston, Mass.

SIMON & SCHUSTER, INC., for excerpts from *Our Knowledge of the External World* by Bertrand Russell. Copyright © 1945 by Bertrand Russell. Reprinted by permission of Simon & Schuster, Inc.

THE VIKING PRESS, INC., for excerpts from *The Portable Nietzsche,* translated by Walter Kaufmann. Copyright 1954 by The Viking Press, Inc. Reprinted by permission of The Viking Press, Inc.

C. A. WATTS & CO. LTD. for excerpts from *Karl Marx: Early Writings,* translated and edited by T. B. Bottomore.

GEORGE WEIDENFELD & NICOLSON LTD. for excerpts from *Progress of the Human Mind* by Marquis de Condorcet, translated by J. Barraclough.

Preface

The changes incorporated into this revision of A *History of Western Philosophy* reflect what I have learned, in the seventeen years since the book was first published, about the history of philosophy, the nature of the philosophical enterprise itself, and the role that philosophy plays in the general culture. They also reflect a good deal of thought about what characteristics make a textbook useful.

The most noticeable innovation is the division of the book into four separate volumes: *I. The Classical Mind; II. The Medieval Mind; III. Hobbes to Hume;* and *IV. Kant to Wittgenstein and Sartre*. This division has provided space for expansion of the text, especially in the fourth volume. It also conforms to the way in which courses in the history of philosophy are now organized and enables the reader to choose the periods on which he wishes to concentrate.

In my revision I have been able to condense and at the same time clarify the exposition materially. In addition, I have greatly simplified the elaborate system of subheadings used in the first edition, for I believe that today's generation of students no longer needs such a complex set of guideposts. The condensation of material and the elimination of superfluous heads have allowed me to expand the discussions of a number of thinkers and to add discussions of many others who were omitted from the earlier edition. For instance, in Volume I, I have added a short section on axiomatic geometry and a longer section on Greek Scepticism, with extracts from the writings of Sextus Empiricus. In Volume II, I have added a discussion of Gnosticism and have balanced this with a section on physical theory in the late Middle Ages, illustrated by quotations from John Buridan. It is Volume IV, however, that contains the most extensive additions. The sections on Hegel, Marx, and Nietzsche have been completely rewritten and greatly expanded; there are entirely new chapters on Kierkegaard, Wittgenstein, Husserl, and Sartre.

There are also a great many changes—some of them major—in my interpretation and evaluation of individual thinkers and their theories. For instance, I have softened my criticisms of Greek Atomism and of Augustine, and in the sections on St. Paul and on the author of the Fourth Gospel I have taken account of recent scholarship. There is, indeed, hardly a page that has not undergone extensive revision. This edition is a thoroughgoing and rigorous updating of the first version.

Despite all these alterations, my point of view remains basically the same. In revising, as in originally writing, this history, I have been guided by four principles—concentration, selectivity, contextualism, and the use of original sources.

An historian of philosophy can either say something, however brief, about everyone who philosophized, or he can limit himself to giving a reasonably consecutive account of a number of representative thinkers, omitting discussion of many second- and third-flight philosophers. I have chosen the latter approach, for two reasons. First, many works based on the first approach are already available, and I see no good reason for adding to their number. Second, such works are likely to be unintelligible to the beginning student. I still recall my own bewilderment as an undergraduate in seeking to understand a complicated theory that some expositor had "boiled down" to a summary. The principle of concentration rests on the thesis that it is better to understand a few theories than to be superficially acquainted with a great many.

But concentration implies selectivity, and I can hardly hope that even those who accept the principle of concentration will approve all my selections. There will probably be no difference of opinion about the great figures of the remote past. Everyone will surely agree that Plato and Aristotle are the masters of their age. And perhaps there will be general agreement that Augustine and Thomas occupy similar positions in the Middle Ages—that Augustine demands more attention than, say, Boethius, and Thomas more attention than Duns Scotus. But how is one to choose among philosophers of more recent times? Here one must try to anticipate the judgment of time. To some extent, I have simply avoided the issue by dealing with more philosophers in the modern period. The result is that, whereas the first two volumes cover more than two millenia, the last two focus on hardly more than four hundred years.

Even so, I have been forced to be selective by my determination that here, as in the earlier periods, I would not mention a philosopher unless I could deal with his views in some detail. Thus I have repressed a natural desire at least to mention Fichte and Schelling, in order to provide extended analyses of Hegel and Schopenhauer. All these thinkers represent reactions to Kantianism, and although they differ among themselves in many ways, it is better, I believe, to select and concentrate on a few than to attempt to give a complete enumeration.

Also underlying the writing of this history is the generally recognized but seldom adopted principle that philosophers are men, not disembodied spirits. Some histories of philosophy treat theories as if they were isolated from everything except other philosophical theories. But all the great philosophers have actually been concerned with what may be called "local" problems. To be understood, their theories must be seen as expressions—doubtless at a highly conceptualized level—of the same currents of thought and feeling that were moving the poets and the statesmen, the theologians and the playwrights, and the ordinary men, of the age. Otherwise, how could their philosophies ever have been accepted? These philosophers furnished satisfactory answers only because they were alert to the problems that were exercising their contemporaries and because they were harassed by the same doubts. The cultural milieu in which a given philosophy emerges can be ignored only at the risk of making the philosophy seem a detached (and so meaningless and inconsequential) affair.

In carrying out this principle I have begun my account of Greek philosophy by describing the state of affairs in Athens at the end of the Peloponnesian War, and I have drawn on the plays of Euripides and Aristophanes to illustrate the mood of the times. This, I believe, is a necessary setting for Plato, because his central thesis—the theory of forms—was an attempt to answer the scepticism and cynicism of his age. Plato's insistence on the existence of "absolute" standards for conduct and for knowledge is understandable only as a reflection of the social, economic, and political chaos and the moral and religious collapse that occurred at the end of the fifth century.

Similarly, my discussion of medieval philosophy is prefaced with an account of the dissolving Roman Empire, and I have tried to indicate the rich and diversified cultural background within which Christian philosophy developed. In discussing the theories of Augustine and Thomas I have kept in mind that, whereas Augustine expressed the eschatological fervor of a new sect fighting for its life, Thomas embodied the serenity of an imperial and universal religion whose piety had been softened by a new sense of responsibility for "that which is Caesar's."

Finally, in discussing the development of early modern philosophy I have tried to show the many factors—exploration and discovery, the rise of money

power, Humanism, the Reformation, and above all the new scientific method—
that combined to overthrow the medieval synthesis and to create new problems
that philosophy even today is struggling to resolve. In a word, I have conceived
the history of philosophy to be a part of the general history of culture and hence
to be intelligible only in its cultural context.

The fourth principle is my conviction that in philosophy—or in any discipline, for that matter—nothing takes the place of a direct, patient, and pains-
taking study of a great and subtle mind. For this reason there is much to be
said for the use of a source book. But a source book alone has serious limitations, because its selections are apt to be discontinuous and difficult to follow.
The advantage of a text is that it can explicate obscure passages and draw
comparisons. Even so, explication and interpretation are not substitutes for the
documents themselves. Therefore, each of the volumes in this series stands
halfway between textbook and source book and tries to combine the advantages
of both: I have set out a philosopher's thought in his own words by a careful
selection of key passages and have bound these together with my own comment and criticism. The quoted passages constitute about one third of the contents.

To undertake to give an account of the history of philosophy in its cultural
context is a formidable and perhaps presumptuous task for a single expositor.
In this undertaking I have received help from a wide variety of sources. In
addition to those who have read and commented on the first edition, whose names
I shall not repeat here, I wish to thank many friends and colleagues who have
called my attention to points that needed correction: Stanley M. Daugert,
Stewart C. Easton, Robert L. Ferm, John H. Gleason, Douglas Greenlee, Ray-
mond Lindquist, Edwin L. Marvin, James A. McGilvray, Philip Merlan, John E.
Smith, Robert T. Voelkel, Culver G. Warner, Rev. S. Y. Watson, S.J., and R. M.
Yost, Jr. I am much indebted to Robert J. Fogelin, from whom I learned a great
deal during the years we taught a joint course on nineteenth-century philosophy,
and to Clark Glymour, who has sent me extensive notes, especially on the history
of science. My greatest appreciation is due to Cynthia A. Schuster, who read the
revised version of Volumes I, II, and III and commented in immense—and
immensely helpful—detail, and to Stephen A. Erickson, on whom I have constantly leaned for advice about matters small as well as great and whose detailed
comments both on the first edition and on successive drafts of the revision have
been invaluable. These readers have saved me from many errors of fact and interpretation; for errors that remain I must be responsible, and I shall be grateful if
any that come to notice are pointed out to me.

I am obliged to the many publishers and copyright holders (listed on pages
iv–vi) through whose cooperation the quotations used in these volumes appear.
Since I have followed the style of the various writers and translators I have
quoted, there is some variation in spelling, capitalization, and punctuation in
the reprinted passages. Full bibliographical notes, keyed to the text by letters
rather than numbers, appear at the end of each volume.

For the secretarial work on the manuscript I am chiefly indebted to Helen Armstrong, Dorothy Overaker, Catherine Tramz, and Judith Strombotne, who divided the typing. I am also grateful to Paul Cabbell, who checked all references in the first three volumes and made many helpful suggestions, to Joan McGilvray, who performed a similar function for the last volume, and to my good friend Margaret L. Mulhauser, who generously allowed me to impose on her the onerous task of proofreading.

W. T. Jones

Contents

6

7

8

9

Introduction

The eighteenth-century *philosophes* were persuaded that they lived in the best of all possible worlds. Because nature seemed to them beneficent—"Whatever is, is right"—and because men seemed rational, they concluded that progress was inevitable. But this optimism soon suffered a series of heavy blows. The French Revolution, which was supposed to mark the overthrow of tyranny, only ushered in a more formidable tyrant—Napoleon. The Industrial Revolution, instead of bringing peace and plenty, resulted in urban overcrowding and misery. And Hume's use of Locke's empirical criterion of meaning proved to have undermined—even more than Hume himself realized—both the concept of nature and the concept of reason. As a result a countermovement began to emerge—a movement hostile to science, sceptical of progress, opposed to prosperity, and increasingly alienated from the long-dominant values of rationality, self-consciousness, objectivity, and detachment. (Chapter 1.)

Some of the complex interactions between formal philosophical theory and the two divergent currents of thought and feeling described above can be seen in the philosophy of Kant. Kant recognized the destructive potential of Hume's critique; one of the main drives that animated his thought was the desire to answer Hume's criticisms of the claims of science and to show that an a priori knowledge of nature is possible. (Chapter 2.) A second main drive of his philosophy, however, was to limit scientific knowledge in order to make a place for feeling, for what he called "faith." (Chapter 3.) Both of these aims were accomplished in a single stroke by what Kant called his "Copernican revolution" in the theory of knowledge. Abandoning the traditional view that minds are the essentially passive contemplators of independently existing objects, Kant held that objects are constructs in which the activity of minds plays an essential part.

Many important consequences followed from this revolution. Indeed, philosophy since Kant has been largely a series of modulations of, and reactions against, his formulations. Kant maintained first that since cognition involves construction, things into which this constructive activity has not entered are literally unknowable, and second that there is a realm of reality that is inaccessible to human minds because they have not participated in its construction. Post-Kantian philosophy has divided into two main streams, depending on which part of this double thesis was accepted and which part rejected. Some philosophers agreed with Kant that knowledge is limited to the spatiotemporal world but rejected his unknowable things-in-themselves as mere vestiges of an outmoded metaphysics; as a result they concentrated their attention on this world and its problems. Other philosophers agreed with Kant that there is a reality independent of human minds but did not want to admit that this reality is unknowable. Accordingly, since these philosophers accepted Kant's contention that reason is limited to the spatiotemporal world, they had to rely on some other mode of access to the reality they believed lay behind the phenomena. The result was a reaffirmation of metaphysics, but in an antirational (or at least arational) form very different from the pre-Kantian rationalistic metaphysics.

Hegel and Schopenhauer represented these two tendencies in nineteenth-century thought. Hegel rejected Kant's things-in-themselves; reality, he argued, is "for" minds. But he greatly expanded the role of mind in the construction of reality (or "experience"). Whereas Kant had limited that role to a few standard syntheses that are common to all human minds everywhere, Hegel held that mind itself undergoes development; it passes through successive stages, each of which includes the lower stages while superseding them. Schopenhauer adopted the other alternative. Kant's spatiotemporal world, he held, is the appearance of an underlying reality that becomes accessible in intuition, that is, when we free ourselves from the constructions of sense perception and of science. Intuition, which is direct, unmediated apprehension, discloses this reality to be a blind, insatiable will from which the only escape is a universal asceticism. (Chapter 4.)

Though Schopenhauer's view had affinities with the Romantic rejection of reason and of science, the predominant world view for many decades descended more or less directly from the Enlightenment's optimism, meliorism, and confidence. The difference was that the instrument of progress was no longer "pure" reason; it was now reason informed by the methods of empirical science. Since these scientifically oriented philosophers rejected Kant's things-in-themselves, and since they saw that the industrialization and urbanization of Europe were creating grave economic and social problems, their attention shifted from metaphysics to social philosophy. The British Utilitarians, the Comtians, and the Marxists were all representative of these developments. (Chapter 5.)

But the philosophers of the countermovement, as it has just been called, were not only suspicious of science as a cognitive enterprise; they were also contemptuous of the concentration of attention on the improvement of social conditions and on material welfare. Instead, they concentrated on existential problems—above all, on finding what Kierkegaard called "a focus and a center" for their own lives, something that would give meaning to what they felt to be an otherwise meaningless existence. This search led Kierkegaard himself to reject reason and to repudiate evidence. At best they yield only "approximations," but he demanded absolute certainty. He found this certainty, paradoxically, in the passionate affirmation of the "absurdity" that God became incarnate as man and died on the Cross for our sins. Nietzsche's solution to this existential problem was completely antithetical to Kierkegaard's. God is dead, he said. It follows that there can be no absolute values or criteria to guide our choices. The man who is strong enough to face these truths and to create values for himself is rare. Indeed, he is an overman, sharply distinguished from those who slavishly conform to the ethic of their society or who, like Kierkegaard, make a cowardly leap of faith. (Chapter 6.)

One of the critical turning points in nineteenth-century thought was Darwin's *Origin of Species*, even though long before its publication many thinkers (among them, Hegel) had anticipated the new emphasis on process. Bergson, Dewey, and Whitehead all shared this vision of a fecund and evolving universe. Like Schopenhauer, Bergson held that reality is disclosed in intuition, but he believed reality to be a fruitful and productive *élan vital*, not a blind and insatiable will. Hence his view of man and of man's relation to the universe was far more optimistic than Schopenhauer's. Dewey agreed with Bergson that intellect is instrumental to will and that "truth" is whatever satisfies the will, but he rejected both Bergson's intuition and his metaphysical tendencies. For Dewey, philosophy was not an inquiry into the nature of the universe; it was a way of making our traffic with nature and with other men more viable. In contrast to Bergson and Dewey, Whitehead was a rationalist. But his rationalism was very different from the traditional ideal of a complete deductive system. Rather, he worked out an open-ended "categoreal" scheme that was designed to bridge the chasm between the world of ordinary experience and that of the physical and biological sciences. (Chapter 7.)

The theories of Bergson, Dewey, and Whitehead dominated philosophy during much of the first half of the twentieth century, but by the end of World War II two other schools, or movements, had largely superseded them. One of these is called in the text the analytical tradition. It has its roots in certain more or less implicit assumptions about the nature of the world and of philosophical inquiry that can be traced back to Hume, and beyond Hume to Hobbes. Among these assumptions is the belief that most philosophical problems are linguistic in origin and that ordinary language is so seriously inadequate that it must be purified for philosophical use. The account presented in the text concentrates first on Russell, who gave a classic formulation of the analytical position, and then on Wittgenstein, who, although he accepted many of the basic tenets of the tradition, developed a view of language that emphasized use rather than meaning and that defended ordinary usage. Wittgenstein's innovations not only revolutionized the analytical tradition; they also deeply influenced philosophers who are not a part of this tradition. (Chapter 8.)

What is called in the text the phenomenological tradition is the second main movement that dominated postwar philosophical thinking. Like many other post-Kantians, the phenomenologists concluded that reality consists in things-as-they-appear. But, unlike the Hegelians, they also rejected the constructivist view of mind that Kant had introduced into philosophy. In their view, consciousness does not make a world; it merely displays the world. Accordingly, the task of philosophy is to describe the world that consciousness displays—including those acts of consciousness in which this world is displayed. The two representatives of this tradition discussed in this volume are Husserl, commonly regarded as the founder of the movement, and Sartre, who sought to combine the ontological and epistemological theories of phenomenology with his personal existential insights. (Chapter 9.)

Ah, what a dusty answer gets the soul
When hot for certainties in this our life!

GEORGE MEREDITH

Turning and turning in the widening gyre
The falcon cannot hear the falconer;
Things fall apart; the center cannot hold.

W. B. YEATS

CHAPTER 1

The Age of Reason

The Mood of the Enlightenment

If one had to characterize the seventeenth and eighteenth centuries by a single word, that word would be "optimistic." It is not surprising that the Age of Reason—or the Enlightenment, as it is also called—was optimistic. Europe had finally emerged from a long period of superstition and bigotry. The new science was revealing that the universe, appearances to the contrary, is a vast but fundamentally simple mechanism. As a part of this orderly universe man's behavior should be subject to prediction, and hence to control, in the interests of improving his material and social well-being. Great progress had already been made in this respect. There seemed to be no reason why continued, indeed unlimited, progress was not possible.

A characteristic expression of these widely held beliefs is found in Condorcet's[1] *Sketch for a Historical Picture of the Progress of the Human Mind:*

> If man can, with almost complete assurance, predict phenomena when he knows their laws, . . . why, then, should it be regarded as a fantastic undertaking to sketch, with some pretence to truth, the future destiny of man on the basis of his history? The sole foundation for belief in the natural sciences is this idea, that the general laws directing the phenomena of the universe, known or unknown, are necessary and constant. Why should this principle be any less true for the development of the intellectual and moral faculties of man than for the other operations of nature? . . .
>
> Our hopes for the future condition of the human race can be subsumed under three important heads: the abolition of inequality between nations, the progress of equality within each nation, and the true perfection of mankind. . . .
>
> Is there on the face of the earth a nation whose inhabitants have been debarred by nature herself from the enjoyment of freedom and the exercise of reason?
>
> Are those differences which have hitherto been seen in every civilized country in respect of the enlightenment, the resources, and the wealth enjoyed by the different classes into which it is divided . . . [an inevitable] part of civilization itself, or are they due to the present imperfections of the social art? . . . In other words, will men approach a condition in which everyone will have the knowledge necessary to conduct himself in the ordinary affairs of life, according to the light of his own reason, to preserve his mind free from prejudice, to understand his rights and to exercise them in accordance with his conscience and his creed . . . ?
>
> In answering these . . . questions we shall find in the experience of the past, in the observation of the progress that the sciences and civilization have already made, in the analysis of the progress of the human mind and of the development of its faculties, the strongest reasons for believing that nature has set no limit to the realization of our hopes. . . .
>
> The time will therefore come when the sun will shine only on free men who know no other master but their reason; when tyrants and slaves, priests and their stupid or hypocritical instruments will exist only in works of history and on the stage; and when we shall think of them only . . . to learn how to recognize and so to destroy, by force of reason, the first seeds of tyranny and superstition, should they ever dare to reappear amongst us. . . .
>
> New instruments, machines and looms can add to man's strength and can improve at once the quality and the accuracy of his productions, and can diminish the time and labour that has to be expended on them. The obstacles still in the way of this progress will disappear, accidents will be foreseen and prevented, the insanitary conditions . . . will be eliminated. . . .

---

1 Condorcet (1743–94) was a mathematician who made important contributions to the study of probability theory. Although he was a strong supporter of the French Revolution, he was proscribed by the radical Jacobins because he opposed them. He wrote the *Sketch* while in hiding and died before finishing it.

So not only will the same amount of ground support more people, but everyone will have less work to do, will produce more, and satisfy his wants more fully. . . .

Organic perfectibility or deterioration amongst the various strains in the vegetable and animal kingdom can be regarded as one of the general laws of nature. This law also applies to the human race. No-one can doubt that, as preventitive medicine improves and food and housing become healthier . . . the average length of human life will be increased. . . . It is reasonable to hope that all other diseases may likewise disappear as their distant causes are discovered. Would it be absurd then to suppose that this perfection of the human species might be capable of indefinite progress; that the day will come when death will be due only to extraordinary accidents[;] . . . and that ultimately the average span between birth and decay will have no assignable value? . . .

Finally may we not extend such hopes to the intellectual and moral faculties? . . .

How consoling for the philosopher who laments the errors, the crimes, the injustices which still pollute the earth and of which he is often the victim is this view of the human race, emancipated from its shackles, released from the empire of fate and from that of the enemies of its progress, advancing with a firm and sure step along the path of truth, virtue and happiness![a]

What Condorcet projected in his *Sketch* was a secular, this-worldly heaven: His belief in the inevitability of progress was not an empirical hypothesis, despite the form in which it is cast and the language used to describe it. More akin to religious belief, it was an article of faith, immune to negative empirical evidence because it sustained Condorcet in the trials and defeats he encountered.

The key ideas that underpin Condorcet's optimistic faith are nature and reason. These two concepts were indeed central to almost all the thinking of the eighteenth century. Doubtless, they meant rather different things to different people; yet, because men agreed on what was unnatural and irrational, it is possible to get at the mood of the Enlightenment by examining what the writers of the eighteenth century excluded from nature and reason. Whether they were thinking of time past or of time present, whether of physical nature or of human nature, they excluded the unpredictable and miraculous, especially the possibility of intervention by supernatural forces from outside the closed system of nature. Accordingly, although few Enlightenment thinkers were explicit atheists, they were, at most, very tepid Deists. They envisaged a God who, having created an orderly universe, left it strictly alone.

Opinion varied through a broad spectrum—from that of a relative sceptic like Voltaire, who held that if God did not exist He would have to be invented, to that of Rousseau, who regarded himself as a Christian but who was certainly far from orthodox.

It is not in my power to believe that passive and dead matter can have brought forth living and feeling beings. . . . I believe, therefore, that the world is governed by a wise and powerful will; I see it or rather I feel it, and it is a great thing to know this. But has this same world always existed, or has it been created? Is there one source of all things? Are there two or many? What is their nature? I know not; and what concern is it of mine? . . . I see God everywhere in his works; I feel him within myself; I behold him all around me; but if I try to ponder him himself, if I try to find out where he is, what he is, what is his substance, he escapes me. . . .[b]

Furthermore, most eighteenth-century thinkers, whether sceptics or believers, drew a sharp distinction between the few simple truths of natural religion, on which they held all men could agree, and the complex theological doctrines that divided the various "high" religions into hostile camps.[2] The *philosophes* had nothing but contempt for Christianity, regarded either as a body of formal philosophical beliefs or as an institution wielding political power. Edward Gibbon's[3] attitude, for instance, was coldly supercilious:

A candid but rational inquiry into the progress and establishment of Christianity may be considered as a very essential part of the history of the Roman empire. While that great body was invaded by open violence, or undermined by slow decay, a pure and humble religion gently insinuated itself into the minds of men, grew up in silence and obscurity, derived new vigour from opposition, and finally erected the triumphant banner of the cross on the ruins of the Capitol. . . .

Our curiosity is naturally prompted to inquire by what means the Christian faith obtained so remarkable a victory over the established religions of the earth. To this inquiry, an obvious but satisfactory answer may be returned; that it was owing to the convincing evidence of the doctrine itself, and to the ruling providence of its great Author. But, as truth and reason seldom find so favourable a reception in the world, and as the wisdom of Providence frequently condescends to use the passions of the human heart, and the general circumstances of mankind, as instruments to execute its purpose; we may still be permitted, though with becoming submission, to ask not indeed what were the first, but what were the secondary causes of the rapid growth of the Christian church? . . .

When the promise of eternal happiness was proposed to mankind, on condition of adopting the faith and of observing the precepts of the gospel, it is no wonder that so advantageous an offer should have been accepted by great numbers of every religion, of every rank, and of every province in the Roman empire. The ancient Christians were animated by a contempt for their present existence, and by a just confidence of immortality, of which the doubtful and imperfect faith of modern ages cannot give us any adequate

2 In *The Social Contract*, for instance, Rousseau distinguished between "the religion of man" and the Christianity of his own day. The former, which he identified with the teachings of the Gospels, is "holy, sublime, and true." The latter, he felt, "clouds the true worship of Divinity with vain ceremonies."

3 Gibbon (1737–94) was the author of *Decline and Fall of the Roman Empire*, one of the great monuments of historical scholarship.

notion. In the primitive church, the influence of truth was very powerfully strengthened by an opinion which, however it may deserve respect for its usefulness and antiquity, has not been found agreeable to experience. It was universally believed that the end of the world and the kingdom of Heaven were at hand. The near approach of this wonderful event had been predicted by the apostles; the tradition of it was preserved by their earliest disciples, and those who understood in their literal sense the discourses of Christ himself were obliged to expect the second and glorious coming of the Son of Man in the clouds, before that generation was totally extinguished, which had beheld his humble condition upon earth, and which might still be witness of the calamities of the Jews under Vespasian or Hadrian. The revolution of seventeen centuries has instructed us not to press too closely the mysterious language of prophecy and revelation; but, as long as, for wise purposes, this error was permitted to subsist in the church, it was productive of the most salutary effects on the faith and practice of Christians, who lived in the awful expectation of that moment when the globe itself, and all various race of mankind, should tremble at the appearance of their divine Judge.[c]

Gibbon made it clear that he regarded the triumph of this "pure and humble" religion as a major catastrophe.[4] He believed, however, that the age in which he lived was freeing mankind from this incubus; hence he faced the future with confidence, expecting posterity to build a new world on rational lines, freed from the prejudice, superstition, and ignorance with which the Church had so long bound men's minds.[5]

It is also obvious, even in this short passage, that Gibbon was determined to treat Christianity as a social and cultural phenomenon. Whatever may be thought about its supernatural origin, Christianity has a natural history and is just as much a neutral object of study as are the pagan cults, the barbarian invasions, or the criminal insanity of Caligula. Suppose, for instance, that the "philosophical historian" wishes to inquire about the reliability of a particular document. Does he ask whether the author was a devout Christian? He does indeed; but instead of taking this devotion as a guarantee of the truthfulness of the report, he becomes suspicious of the information that the document contains. For the author was an interested party, and the historian knows enough about human nature to recognize the bias that personal loyalties create. We read of miracles and prodigies. Are we to accept them? On the contrary; we must "conclude that . . . the eyes of the spectators have sometimes been deceived by fraud [and] the understanding of the readers . . . much more frequently . . . insulted by fiction." In every case our rule must be to accept only those claims that are "agreeable to experience." In adopting this criterion, Gibbon applied

---

4 In summarizing his account of the Middle Ages, Gibbon said, "I have described the triumph of barbarism and religion."
5 It was always convenient for the "Protestant and philosophic" historian to talk about the evils of the Catholic Church while intending his readers to understand the evils of religion.

to historical inquiry one of the same criteria that Newton applied to physics. In this sense Gibbon's history was scientific.

Indeed, it is fair to say that the Enlightenment rejected the concept of divine intervention in the world and relegated God to the role of spectator. This it did in order to be able to deal with a closed, completely regular system. Whatever differences existed among eighteenth-century views of the nature of "nature," a common feature of these views was the notion of order.

This theme was clearly sounded by Montesquieu (1689–1755) in the opening lines of his great work on social anthropology: "Laws, in their most general signification, are the necessary relations arising from the nature of things. In this sense all beings have their laws: the Deity His laws, the material world its laws, the intelligences superior to man their laws, the beasts their laws, man his laws." Montesquieu recognized that the study of human nature is more difficult than the study of physical nature, not because it is less subject to laws, but because its laws are more complex.

> The intelligent world is far from being so well governed as the physical. For though the former has also its laws, which of their own nature are invariable, it does not conform to them so exactly as the physical world. This is because, on the one hand, particular intelligent beings are of a finite nature, and consequently liable to error; and on the other, their nature requires them to be free agents. Hence they do not steadily conform to their primitive laws; and even those of their own instituting they frequently infringe.[e]

This passage has a medieval sound, but whereas a medieval theologian would have followed it with a disquisition on sin, grace, and salvation, Montesquieu at once launched into an analysis of the factors that produce this variability in human conduct. Consider, for instance, the conclusion of his famous study of climate: "If it be true that the temper of the mind and the passions of the heart are extremely different in different climates, the laws ought to be in relation both to the variety of those passions and to the variety of those tempers."[f] In other words, there are underlying regularities (in Montesquieu's assumption) that can be discovered in the midst of the superficial diversities of human character and conduct, and these regularities should be taken into account in political science, that is, in the adjustment of constitutions and systems of government to the needs and capacities of different peoples. This empirical and pragmatic interest dominated Montesquieu's whole work. Observation, for instance, showed the following:

> Cold air constringes the extremities of the external fibres of the body; this increases their elasticity. . . . On the contrary, warm air relaxes and lengthens the extremes of the fibres [and so] diminishes their force and elasticity.
>
> People are therefore more vigorous in cold climates . . . ; the blood moves more freely towards the heart, and reciprocally the heart has more power. This [in its turn] must produce various effects; for instance, a greater boldness . . . , a greater sense of superiority . . . ; a greater opinion of security. . . .[g]

It follows that the kind of government suitable for men living in hot climates (despotism) is entirely inappropriate for men living in the temperate zone. Montesquieu buttressed his conclusions with pages of supporting evidence—observations on differing audience reactions in England and Italy to the same operas, conclusions inferred from experiments on a frozen sheep's tongue, and so on. We may smile at some of his evidence and at the facility with which he made sweeping generalizations concerning complex causal relationships, but to do so is to miss his achievement. Montesquieu's thesis was that stable governments depend (at least in part) on adjustment to the psychological makeup of the governed; that psychological traits depend (at least in part) on physiological characteristics; and that physiological characteristics depend (at least in part) on environmental factors like climate. Thus, even though human nature is more complex than physical nature, Montesquieu nevertheless believed that there are laws that determine human conduct. Furthermore, these laws are to be discovered by an essentially empirical method, and, once discovered, the knowledge of them can be utilized to resolve social conflicts and thus to make life better in every respect.

So much for nature. As for reason—the other leading idea of the age—despite considerable diversity of opinion, a similar core of common meaning can be detected in the work of eighteenth-century thinkers. Though these thinkers equated reason with anything from common sense to strict logical deduction on a geometric model, they generally agreed that there exists an innate intellectual power, which is equal, or nearly equal, in all men. They reasoned that all men have what Descartes had called *bon sens*. Consequently, given adequate education, men will be able to solve all the problems that arise in the course of their lives. Reason will demonstrate—reason was already demonstrating in the work of the physicists, in the work of anthropologists like Montesquieu, and in the work of historians like Gibbon—that nature is orderly, that the universe, though a mighty maze, is nonetheless not without a plan. Reason will demonstrate that each man's long-range interests dovetail with those of other men, and thus men can work together in peace and harmony, each pursuing his own good.

Because men are, by and large, capable of running their own affairs, laws can be kept at a minimum. *Laissez-faire* political and economic systems and moral theories based on self-respect, decency, and the dignity of man are the logical outcomes of this line of thought. Americans are familiar with it in the form it took in the organization of the United States; but this spirit of reasonableness, sanity, democracy, and optimism about the capacities of human nature was not confined to one nation. It can, therefore, be illustrated from many sources. Since, however, we shall shortly be concerned with the philosophical theories of Kant, let us examine a little essay of his called, characteristically, *What Is Enlightenment?*[h]

Enlightenment is man's release from self-imposed tutelage. Tutelage is the inability to use one's natural powers without direction from another. This tutelage is called "self-imposed" because its cause is not any absence of rational competence but simply a lack of courage and resolution to use one's reason without direction from another. *Sapere aude!*—Dare to reason! Have the courage to use your own minds!—is the motto of enlightenment.

Since Kant took it for granted that reason is an adequate power in most men, he held that bringing it to bear on the solution of social, moral, and other problems was merely a matter of having the courage to use it.

Laziness and cowardice explain why so many men . . . remain under a life-long tutelage and why it is so easy for some men to set themselves up as the guardians of all the rest. . . . If I have a book which understands for me, a pastor who has a conscience for me, a doctor who decides my diet, I need not trouble myself. If I am willing to pay, I need not think. Others will do it for me. . . .

Do we now live in an *enlightened* age? No; but we live in an age of *enlightenment.* Though certainly much is lacking, the obstacles to the general enlightenment are gradually being reduced. Men are releasing themselves from self-imposed tutelage and learning to deal freely with religious and other matters.

This discussion has been primarily devoted to religious enlightenment, because . . . religious tutelage is not only the most harmful but the most degrading of all. But with regard to civil liberties, however, there should be room for every man to extend himself to his full capacities. As the use of reason gradually spreads and develops it will first have an effect on the character so that men become more capable of managing their freedom. Eventually it will have an effect on the principles of government, for rulers will find it to their own advantage to treat men in accordance with their dignity as rational creatures.

To this may be appended a sentence from Kant's essay on *Perpetual Peace:*

The problem of establishing a state . . . is solvable for a race of devils if only they are intelligent. The problem is, given a group of rational beings who require universal laws for their preservation, but each of whom is secretly inclined to exempt himself from them; to organize a constitution in such a way that, although their private purposes conflict, they check each other, with the result that their public conduct is the same as if they had no such evil purposes.[i]

If the political problem can be solved by intellectual analysis and for a race of devils, it can surely be solved for a race of men, who are endowed not only with intellects but with sentiments of benevolence, friendship, and humanity.

Thus Kant, and the whole century along with him, agreed with Pope that "the proper study of mankind is man"—not the particularity and variability of individual men, but the abiding human nature that could be confidently assumed a possible and legitimate object of study. The reason in us that was presently exploring the external universe could turn within and, discovering its own essential nature, fashion a social order that would reflect the rationality of the cosmos.

The Collapse of Confidence

The basic assumption of the Enlightenment was that the universe is rational in all its aspects and in every detail. Because the physical universe is rational, there are a number of "rational principles" at work in it; it therefore has a simple orderly pattern. Because the human intellect is rational, it has the capacity to discover these principles, to understand the pattern. Because the human will is rational, it is capable of acting in the light of this knowledge. Given these beliefs, it is not surprising that the age was optimistic.

But such optimism could not last. Hardly had these beliefs been accepted when they began to be challenged. The application of science to technology, a process that was supposed to result in unlimited improvement of material conditions, actually led to urban slums, in which the lot of the workers was far worse than that of the peasants of "unenlightened" feudal times.[6] The French Revolution, which had promulgated the rights of man and which had been held by its supporters to herald a new age of reason and of democratic freedom, collapsed into a reign of terror. This was followed by an absolutism even more formidable, because it was more efficient, than the regime that the Revolution had overthrown.[7] Far from being rational creatures able to control their destinies, men seemed driven by their hates and fears—moved less by enlightened self-interest or by cool benevolence than by irrational and destructive aggressions against one another and even against themselves.

The type of man who emerged in the nineteenth century was thus very different from the new-model man who had appeared during the Renaissance and who had dominated Europe for two centuries. That man had been self-con-

6 See p. 163.
7 To appreciate the disillusionment caused by the failure of the Revolution, it is necessary to understand the inordinate hopes that its outbreak had occasioned. In A Decade of Revolution (New York, 1934), pp. 65–66, Crane Brinton quotes some contemporary enthusiasm. For instance, the German historian A. L. Schlozer stated: "One of the greatest nations in the world, the greatest in general culture, has at last thrown off the yoke of tyranny. . . . Without doubt God's angels in heaven have sung a Te Deum." Then, after citing Wordsworth, Goethe, and other literary figures, Brinton adds, "Perhaps most impressive is the description [Henrik] Steffens gives [he was fifteen years old at the time] of how his father . . . gathered his sons about him, and with tears of joy told them that the Bastille had fallen, that a new era had begun, that if they were failures in life they must blame themselves, for henceforth 'poverty would vanish, the lowliest would begin' the struggles of life on equal terms with the mightiest, with equal arms, on equal ground.'"

fident and self-assured; though considering himself in harmony with his environment, he also believed himself capable of mastering it if need be. In contrast,
the new man of the nineteenth century was uneasy, anxious, alienated, and
introspective. He was increasingly unsure of himself—doubtful of the validity
of his values, of his ability to communicate in a meaningful way with others,
and of his ability even to know himself.

Dostoevsky's short story *Notes from Underground* contains one of the earliest—and also one of the most powerful—portraits of this new, anxious man.[8]
The opening of the story consists of a long monologue:

> I am a sick man. . . . I am a spiteful man. No, I am not a pleasant man
> at all. I believe there is something wrong with my liver. However, I don't
> know a damn thing about my liver; neither do I know whether there is
> anything really wrong with me. I am not under medical treatment, and never
> have been. . . . I refuse medical treatment out of spite. . . . I don't expect
> I shall be able to explain to you who it is I am actually trying to annoy in
> this case by my spite; I realise full well that I can't "hurt" the doctors by
> refusing to be treated by them; I realise better than any one that by all this
> I am only hurting myself and no one else. Still, the fact remains that if I
> refuse to be medically treated, it is only out of spite.
> . . . .
>
> I assure you, gentlemen, that to be too acutely conscious is a disease,
> a real, honest-to-goodness disease . . . not only too much consciousness, but
> any sort of consciousness is a disease. . . . Tell me this: why did it invariably
> happen that . . . I was not only conscious but also guilty of the most con-
> temptible actions which—well, which, in fact, everybody is guilty of, but
> which, as though on purpose, I only happened to commit when I was most
> conscious that they ought not to be committed? . . . I was ashamed (and
> quite possibly I still am ashamed); it got so far that I felt a sort of secret,
> abnormal, contemptible delight when, on coming home on one of the foulest
> nights in Petersburg, I used to realise intensely that again I had been guilty
> of some particularly dastardly action that day, and that once more it was
> no earthly use crying over spilt milk; and inwardly, secretly, I used to go
> on nagging myself, worrying myself, accusing myself, till at last the bitterness
> I felt turned into a sort of shameful, damnable . . . delight! Yes, into delight.
> Into delight! I'm certain of it. . . . Good Lord, I have talked a lot, haven't
> I? But have I explained anything? How is one to explain this feeling of
> delight? . . .
>
> Let me continue calmly about the people with strong nerves who do not
> understand the subtleties of the pleasure I have been speaking of. Though

---

8 Fyodor Dostoevsky (1821–81) was educated as an army engineer in Russia, but he soon resigned
his commission to concentrate on his writing. In 1849 he was convicted of "taking part in
criminal plots" against the Czarist regime; the sentence of death was commuted at the last
moment, and he was imprisoned in Siberia for several years. Subsequently, he became an
archconservative and reactionary. *Notes from Underground* was published in 1864.

on some occasions these gentlemen may roar at the top of their voices like
bulls, . . . they at once capitulate in face of the impossible. The impossible
is to them equivalent to a stone wall. What stone wall? Why, the laws of
nature, of course, the conclusions of natural science, mathematics. When,
for instance, it is proved to you that you are descended from a monkey, then
it's no use pulling a long face about it: you just have to accept it. When
they prove to you . . . that all the so-called virtues and duties and other
vain fancies and prejudices are, as a result of that consideration, of no
importance whatever, then you have to accept it whether you like it or not,
because twice-two—mathematics. Just try to refute that.

"Good Lord," they'll scream at you, "you can't possibly deny that: twice
two *is* four! Never does nature ask you for your opinion. . . . You are obliged
to accept her as she is and, consequently, all her results. A stone wall, that
is, is a stone wall, . . . etc., etc." But . . . what do I care for the laws of
nature and arithmetic if for some reason or other I don't like those laws of
twice-two? . . . I shall not reconcile myself to it just because I have to deal
with a stone wall and haven't the strength to knock it down.

As though such a stone wall were really the same thing as peace of
mind. . . .

You say that science itself will then teach man . . . that he himself
is nothing more than a sort of piano-key or organ-stop, and that, in addition,
there are the laws of nature in the world; so that whatever he does is not
done of his own will at all, but of itself, according to the laws of nature.
Consequently, as soon as these laws of nature are discovered, man will no
longer have to answer for his actions, . . . [and] everything will be calculated
and specified with such an exactness that there will be no more independent
actions or adventures in the world.

Then—it is still you who are saying this—new economic relations will be
established, . . . so that all sorts of problems will vanish in a twinkling simply
because ready-made solutions will be provided for all of them. It is then that
the Crystal Palace will be built.[9] . . . Everything will be so splendidly
rational. . . .

Quite right, but there's the rub! . . . Reason is only reason, and it can only
satisfy the reasoning ability of man, whereas volition is a manifestation of
the whole of life, I mean, of the whole of human life, including reason with
all its concomitant head-scratchings. And although our life, thus manifested,
very often turns out to be a sorry business, it is life none the less and not
merely extractions of square roots. . . . What does reason know? Reason only
knows what it has succeeded in getting to know . . . , whereas human nature
acts as a whole, with everything that is in it, consciously, and unconsciously,
and though it may commit all sorts of absurdities, it persists. . . . The whole
meaning of human life can be summed up in the one statement that man
only exists for the purpose of proving to himself every minute that he is a
man and not an organ-stop![j]

9 [The Crystal Palace was built in London to house the exhibition of 1851, which was designed
to demonstrate the progress of the sciences. Dostoevsky views it here as a symbol of everything
he disliked in contemporary culture—AUTHOR.]

This underground man, as Dostoevsky observes, has "all the characteristics of an anti-hero." He and his contemporaries "have lost all touch with life, we are all cripples, every one of us. . . . We are stillborn." k What a change from the self-confident optimist of the eighteenth century! Underground man is solitary: "I did have a sort of a friend once, but by that time I was already a tyrant at heart: I wanted to exercise complete authority over him." l He is masochistic: "My liver hurts me—well, let it damn well hurt—the more it hurts the better." m Underground man lives by feeling; he is profoundly pessimistic: "It is much better to do nothing at all! Better passive awareness!" n He is "passionately fond of destruction and chaos" o; he is endlessly introspective because he is convinced that no matter how deeply he probes, he can never find his real motive: "I had a noble loophole for every thing." p Most of all, underground man actually does not want to find his real motive—he is always hiding from himself: "There are certain things in a man's past which he does not divulge to everybody but, perhaps, only to his friends. Again there are certain things he will not divulge even to his friends; he will divulge them perhaps only to himself. . . . But, finally, there are things which he is afraid to divulge even to himself. . . ." q

Because *Notes from Underground* was published in 1864, discussion of it may seem to be out of place in a chapter on the end of the Enlightenment; after all, Kant's *Critique of Pure Reason*, which is examined in the following chapter, was written almost a hundred years earlier. But some of the changes that went into the formation of underground man were already in motion when Kant wrote, and his *Critique* was a response to them.

One of the major changes that led to this shift in values was Hume's discovery that there is no "necessary connection" among matters of fact. In most respects Hume was representative of this age—in his "mitigated" scepticism, his cool benevolence, his contempt for "enthusiasm," his irreligion. But as regards nature and reason—which, as we have seen, were the leading concepts of the Enlightenment and the bases for its optimism—Hume's views were revolutionary, far more revolutionary than he himself realized. Hume regarded reason as merely an instrument for detecting relations among ideas; reason can tell us nothing, he thought, about the real world. We do experience nature—the real world—as ordered. But there is no evidence, Hume maintained, that the order we find there is necessary: There is no rationale in nature to which the rational mind of man conforms. Hume in effect was driving a wedge between reason and nature. In doing so, he opened the way for a shift in beliefs and values that he would have deplored, for a shift to that whole complex of attitudes expressed in *Notes from Underground*—for instance, underground man's conviction that "you can't explain anything by reasoning and consequently it is useless to reason." r

Among Hume's contemporaries Kant was almost alone in recognizing the destructive force of this attack on reason. As is evident from *What Is Enlightenment?* Kant was deeply committed to the Enlightenment ideal.[10] Hence he was

10 See pp. 7–8.

deeply disturbed by Hume's argument. He realized that to answer Hume some compromise was necessary and in this compromise he proposed to save as much as he could. Ultimately, however, Kant made many more concessions to anti-rationalism than he realized: His *Critique* was not merely a response to the changes that marked the end of the Enlightenment; it was a working-out of the basic conceptual scheme in terms of which the new underground view of man later came to be expressed.

Kant's philosophy thus constitutes one of the fundamental turning points in the history of Western thought. In studying his theories, and those of the philosophers who followed him, we must look for the complex interactions between formal philosophical speculation and the deeper currents of thought and feeling that were to surface in such literary works as *Notes from Underground.*

CHAPTER 2

Kant: Theory of Knowledge

Immanuel Kant (1724–1804) was born in Königsberg in East Prussia (now incorporated in the Soviet Union) and lived all his life in that provincial city. His parents were lower middle class, industrious, and deeply religious. They were Pietists, members of one of the numerous sects on the Protestant left that held that the Reformation had bogged down in its own form of dogmatism. They believed that true religion was a matter of the inner life and emphasized simplicity and obedience to the moral law. Kant came to dislike the evangelical side of Pietism; he had as little use for "enthusiasm" (hymn-singing and other manifestations of "fervor") as Hume or Gibbon. But in contrast to Hume, whose religious background was not dissimilar, Kant remained all his life a deeply religious man.

Little need be said about the details of Kant's life; as one writer has remarked, it was like the most regular of regular verbs. Kant was educated at the University of Königsberg, where he studied classics and theology, and subsequently physics and philosophy. He had, of course, to earn his own living, and his first job was that of a tutor in a private family. Kant did not like the relationship that this entailed, and by 1755 he was back at the university, where he remained the rest of his active life. His lectures were very popular (it is worth emphasizing this in view of the difficulty of his published works), and without ever leaving Königsberg he became in time the best-known professor in Germany. Distinction brought comfort and security, and though he was full of those little eccentricities that students expect to find in their teachers, he was an excellent conversationalist and a charming host. Kant's principal work, the *Critique of Pure Reason* (1781), is concerned primarily with epistemology and metaphysics, but Kant also wrote on anthropology, esthetics, ethics, and law; early in his career he did original work in astronomy and physics.

The following examination of Kant's philosophy is divided into two main parts: (1) a discussion of his attempt to show how, despite Hume's attack on "necessary connection," real knowledge of matters of fact is possible and (2) an account of the values that he believed lay outside this field of scientific, matter-of-fact knowledge. Kant's version of the nature and limits of scientific knowledge is the concern of the present chapter, which discusses, first, the nature of the problem Kant believed he had inherited from Hume and his general solution to this problem, and, second, Kant's attempted validation of knowledge in mathematics and physics and his criticism of alleged metaphysical knowledge. The next chapter considers Kant's theory of value: first, his ethical theory, including his conception of duty and his solution to the problem of freedom, and, second, his conception of religion.

Kant's Hypothesis

In order to comprehend what Kant sought to do in his *Critique of Pure Reason*, it is necessary to understand that by the middle of the eighteenth century philosophy had got itself into a most embarrassing situation. Descartes' aim had been to put the new physics on a firm philosophical foundation. This meant providing a field in which physical inquiry could be carried on undisturbed by theological scruples and at the same time excluding mechanism from the realm of values (as Hobbes had failed to do). Descartes believed he had accomplished this by dividing reality into two metaphysically distinct substances, matter and mind. But subsequent attempts to straighten out these apparently reasonable assumptions had resulted in the most paradoxical solutions, solutions that, though different in many respects, were alike in unintentionally demolishing the intellectual basis for physical theory.

The Continental Rationalists pressed Descartes' rationalistic bias to its logical conclusion. They aimed at certainty; because they held that mathematical knowledge is certain, they regarded mathematics as the ideal of all knowledge. They quite failed to see that, as Hume pointed out, the indubitable knowledge so obtained consisted merely of implicatory relations holding among propositions. To obtain a knowledge of matters of fact they needed perception, but they had written off perception as mere confused thinking, that is, as no more than degenerate conception. Hence their theories remained only speculation, incapable of being verified or refuted.

Locke and his followers pursued an exactly opposite course, but they ended up with an equally frustrating conclusion. They were less concerned with certainty than with the actual world—the shoes, ships, and sealing wax of experience. They recognized, of course, that we have access to the actual world in sense perception, but they held that what we perceive are ideas caused in us by things outside us. Unfortunately, as Hume pointed out, if we start from the assumption that what people are aware of are their own mental states, this is precisely where we remain: We do not know an external world; we know only our own ideas. Thus, in a curious way, by following very different paths both the rationalists and the empiricists reached the same sceptical dead end: The former were confined to tracing out implicatory relations among ideas; the latter, to recording relations of coexistence and succession among ideas.

Meanwhile, the working scientists, unperturbed by philosophical doubts about the nature of their subject, had been making advance after advance, and the Hobbesian vision of a world that was thoroughly mechanistic seemed about to be fulfilled in detail. Hence Hobbes's challenge to the traditional religious and teleological view of the cosmos was more formidable than ever. It had begun to occur to scientists that they might get on very nicely without the hypothesis of a God; as regards morality, it seemed clear that in a completely deterministic universe obligation could be only a vain and chimerical delusion. It was therefore no longer necessary to protect the infant science of physics from the theologians. Indeed, the shoe was now on the other foot. It looked as if traditional values were becoming subjective illusions in a world of neutral fact.

KANT'S VIEW OF SCIENTIFIC METHOD

It was obvious to Kant, then, that the Cartesian compromise had failed. But exactly where had it gone wrong? It was clear, Kant thought, that Descartes had misunderstood the nature of scientific method, which involves both an empirical factor and a rational factor. Descartes' followers had alternatively emphasized each of these factors, with the disastrous results we have seen. None of his followers understood how the two factors combine in cognition; none succeeded in giving an intelligible account of knowledge. Accordingly, Kant undertook to make a much more rigorous and sophisticated analysis of the nature of scientific method than had yet been undertaken.

He began by emphasizing the striking contrast between natural science before and after Galileo. It seemed to him that everyone agreed that, since Galileo's time, physics had been on "the secure path of a science." This did not mean that every proposition in physics was infallibly certain; it meant that when physicists made conflicting assertions about nature they were able to agree on "a common plan of procedure" for settling their dispute. Formerly, natural science had deserved the appellation "science" only by courtesy; it had been a "merely random groping."

What had brought about this revolutionary change? Kant thought that the essence of scientific method could be grasped by concentrating attention on those novel features, introduced by Galileo and the other early seventeenth-century physicists, that had made physics for the first time an "objective science."

> Natural science . . . enter[ed] upon the highway of science . . . only about a century and a half [ago, when] Bacon, by his ingenious proposals, partly initiated this discovery, partly inspired fresh vigour in those who were already on the way to it. In this case also the discovery can be explained as being the sudden outcome of an intellectual revolution. . . .
>
> When Galileo caused balls, the weights of which he had himself previously determined, to roll down an inclined plane; when Torricelli made the air carry a weight which he had calculated beforehand to be equal to that of a definite volume of water; or in more recent times, when Stahl changed metal into lime, and lime back into metal, by withdrawing something and then restoring it, a light broke upon all students of nature. They learned that reason has insight only into that which it produces after a plan of its own, and that it must not allow itself to be kept, as it were, in nature's leading-strings, but must itself show the way with principles of judgment based upon fixed laws, constraining nature to give answer to questions of reason's own determining. Accidental observations, made in obedience to no previously thought-out plan, can never be made to yield a necessary law, which alone reason is concerned to discover. Reason, holding in one hand its principles, according to which alone concordant appearances can be admitted as equivalent to laws, and in the other hand the experiment which it has devised in conformity with these principles, must approach nature in order to be taught by it. It must not, however, do so in the character of a pupil who listens to everything that the teacher chooses to say, but of an appointed judge who compels the witnesses to answer questions which he has himself formulated. Even physics, therefore, owes the beneficent revolution in its point of view entirely to the happy thought, that while reason must seek in nature, not fictitiously ascribe to it, whatever as not being knowable through reason's own resources has to be learnt, if learnt at all, only from nature, it must adopt as its guide, in so seeking, that which it has itself put into nature. It is thus that the study of nature has entered on the secure path of a science, after having for so many centuries been nothing but a process of merely random groping.
>
> . . . .
>
> The examples of mathematics and natural science, which by a single and sudden revolution have become what they now are, seem to me sufficiently

remarkable to suggest our considering what may have been the essential features in the changed point of view by which they have so greatly benefited. . . . Hitherto it has been assumed that all our knowledge must conform to objects. But all attempts to extend our knowledge of objects by establishing something in regard to them *a priori*, by means of concepts, have, on this assumption, ended in failure. We must therefore make trial whether we may not have more success in the tasks of metaphysics, if we suppose that objects must conform to our knowledge. This would agree better with what is desired, namely, that it should be possible to have knowledge of objects *a priori*, determining something in regard to them prior to their being given. We should then be proceeding precisely on the lines of Copernicus' primary hypothesis. Failing of satisfactory progress in explaining the movements of the heavenly bodies on the supposition that they all revolved round the spectator, he tried whether he might not have better success if he made the spectator to revolve and the stars to remain at rest. A similar experiment can be tried in metaphysics, as regards the *intuition* of objects. If intuition must conform to the constitution of the objects, I do not see how we could know anything of the latter *a priori;* but if the object (as object of the senses) must conform to the constitution of our faculty of intuition, I have no difficulty in conceiving such a possibility. Since I cannot rest in these intuitions if they are to become known, but must relate them as representations to something as their object, and determine this latter through them, either I must assume that the *concepts*, by means of which I obtain this determination, conform to the object, or else I assume that the objects, or what is the same thing, that the *experience* in which alone, as given objects, they can be known, conform to the concepts. In the former case, I am again in the same perplexity as to how I can know anything *a priori* in regard to the objects. In the latter case the outlook is more hopeful. For experience is itself a species of knowledge which involves understanding; and understanding has rules which I must presuppose as being in me prior to objects being given to me, and therefore as being *a priori*. They find expression in *a priori* concepts to which all objects of experience necessarily conform, and with which they must agree. As regards objects which are thought solely through reason, and indeed as necessary, but which can never—at least not in the manner in which reason thinks them—be given in experience, the attempts at thinking them (for they must admit of being thought) will furnish an excellent test of what we are adopting as our new method of thought, namely, that we can know *a priori* of things only what we ourselves put into them.[a]

There are two main points in this passage. First, Kant notes that if (as everyone up to then had held) the test of truth is agreement of the mind with an external object, only particular truths can be known. We can watch a particular body and see that it gravitates; we can watch another and see that it gravitates; and so on. But we can never know that *all* bodies gravitate, because we can never observe all bodies to see whether or not they gravitate. Consequently, agreement of the mind with its objects cannot be the test of truth, at least as far as universal propositions are concerned. Why not, Kant asks, do what a scientist does when one of his hypotheses breaks down? Why not try another hypothesis? This is just what Copernicus did. After men had tried for centuries to work out a satisfactory astronomical theory on the hypothesis that the earth is the center of the planetary system, it occurred to Copernicus to try something else—to put the sun at the center of the system. This hypothesis was successful. And just as only prejudice had so long prevented men from trying the heliocentric hypothesis, so only prejudice had prevented men from trying a new epistemological hypothesis. It may seem "inevitable" that truth consists in the mind's agreement with its objects, but this "inevitability" is only the result of our having got used to thinking in these terms. The actual procedure of the scientist shows how inadequate the old conventional view really is.[1]

This brings us to Kant's second point, which concerns the crucial role that experiment plays in science. To make an experiment is to ask a question; unless we ask questions of nature we do not get answers. If a Gallup pollster silently hands blank pieces of paper to the housewives whose doorbells he rings, he will never find out their preferences in breakfast foods. Similarly, if Galileo had simply waited for bodies to fall in order to report their velocities, we would all still be in ignorance of this matter. In Kant's view, this consideration completely alters the conventional notion of the mind's relation to its objects. It means that the mind is not passive but active, and that Locke's metaphor of the blank tablet is profoundly mischievous.

In other words, examination of the nature of scientific knowledge shows that in scientific thinking truth does not consist merely in the agreement of the mind with an already existing state of affairs, for if this were all there were to it, the mind would never come to know any scientific truth at all. This led Kant to frame a new epistemological hypothesis that would conform with the way the mind actually proceeds when it thinks scientifically.

As will be seen, Kant's new hypothesis was a reversal of the old, rejected hypothesis (corresponding to the Copernican shift from a geocentric to a heliocentric system). It was originally assumed that the mind must agree with its objects; however, this assumption proved not only hopelessly inadequate to account for universal truths but a caricature of the nature of scientific thought. Thus Kant adopted the hypothesis that the mind's objects must agree with the mind. Let us see if this fared better.

DISTINCTION BETWEEN FORM AND CONTENT

Kant's hypothesis will seem absurd if we fail to distinguish between the form of a judgment and its content. Kant did not mean to suggest that in judgments like "Some roses are red" or "There is a centaur in my office," the objects judged about have to agree with the mind. For, obviously, the truth (or falsity) of such

---

1 Kant did not altogether reject a correspondence theory of truth. Rather, he held that it is inadequate as a complete account. See pp. 40–43.

judgments depends on the agreement (or disagreement) of the judgment with an external state of affairs. If there is a centaur in my office, the judgment is true; if there is not, it is false. And the way to find out is to go to the office and look.

But all the judgments we make fall into certain classes, depending on their form. For instance, they assert either that something has such-and-such a property ("This rose is red"), or that something is the cause of something else, or that something has such-and-such a degree of some quality, and so on. There is a kind of putting together that consists in attribution; there is another kind of putting together that consists in causation; and so on.

KNOWLEDGE A COOPERATIVE AFFAIR

Kant's hypothesis did not concern particular judgments (for example, "This rose is red"); rather, it concerned the various types of putting together (for example, attribution). According to his hypothesis, knowledge is a cooperative affair in which both mind and object make a contribution, and mind contributes the relations while objects contribute the relata. But mind does not, according to this hypothesis, contribute the *particular* relations of sense experience—not "on the table," "on the sofa," "on the desk." What it contributes is the spatial relationship common to all these situations, the relationship designated by the term "on"—the relationship of "superposition," if we want another term to describe it. Or take the judgment "This rose is red." What we are judging about here is, of course, something we see—a rose that is red. But an immense quantity of sense data of all kinds—visual, tactile, and olfactory experiences—is constantly streaming in upon us. Nonetheless, we are able to sort out from these data the experience of a rose that is red because, according to this hypothesis, attribution (the relation designated by the term "is") is one of the ways in which the mind organizes and structures the welter of experiences that it encounters.

To put this differently, attribution is one of the types of questions that the mind asks nature and in terms of which, accordingly, nature answers. Thus, all the particular questions (or experiments) that scientists ask take one or the other of certain basic forms. "Who killed President Kennedy?" the Warren Commission asked. This is a particular question, but it has a causation form. Now, if all the questions asked of nature were to have one or the other of certain basic forms, obviously all the answers given by nature would have these same forms, and there would then be some knowledge about nature that is independent of all particular experiences. Or, again, suppose the new hypothesis to be correct and that we know the *types* of judgment, that is, the basic ways in which the mind relates (or organizes) its experiences. We would then have absolutely certain knowledge, not about this particular experience ("This rose is red"), but about the form of all experience (ordered under the form "is"). In other words, it would not be necessary that the particular rose be red; Hume was correct about this—the rose might be white or yellow. But it would be necessary, if Kant's hypothesis is correct, that experience be organized into things-having-properties, for this way of perceiving things proves to be one of the universal forms of human experience. Hence, despite Hume's attack, there does exist a "necessary connection" among matters of fact—not a necessary connection between this particular fact A and that particular fact B, but a necessary connection, or structure, that organizes experience into an "A-is-B" type.

An example may help. Consider the process by which crude oil is refined into various petroleum products—kerosene, gasoline of various octane numbers, and so on. The refining process corresponds, in this analogy, to the standard forms of judgment in terms of which, according to Kant's hypothesis, experience is organized. If we know that such-and-such steps have been built into the refining process, we can say with confidence that gasoline of such-and-such an octane number will issue from the refinery. The "necessary connection" is not found in the crude oil; it is supplied by the refining process.

Similarly, suppose we have a machine for sorting oranges that consists of an inclined plane with holes of various sizes. Oranges rolling down the surface of the plane fall through the holes into boxes underneath. If one of the holes is, say, two and one-half inches in diameter, we can say that no orange in the box under this hole has a diameter greater than two and one-half inches; and the same applies to the other holes. Although there are many things about the oranges that we could not tell without examining them (for example, whether some are rotten or whether some are green), we can know that the oranges in a particular box cannot be larger than such-and-such a size. Here again we have discovered a necessary connection, namely, that between being in a particular box and having a maximum diameter of so many inches. We know this connection prior to measuring any of the oranges, because we know the nature of the sorting principle being employed.[2]

THE GENERAL PROBLEM OF PURE REASON

So far in this chapter Kant's hypothesis has been formulated in laymen's terms. Before we can proceed to Kant's attempt to prove his hypothesis, the argument must be reformulated in the highly technical language he himself used. In Kant's terminology the question is, "How are synthetical a priori judgments possible?" This, according to Kant, is "the general problem of pure reason." We must first understand how this question is related to the distinction, formulated by Kant in his study of the nature of scientific method, between the content of an experience and certain standard forms, or ways, of organizing that experience.

---

2 It must be borne in mind that this is only a mechanical metaphor. In Kant's view, the mind, which orders experience, is not at all *like* the machine, which "orders" oranges. The mind is not static like the machine; it is active. In fact, in Kant's view, it is *not* a thing at all; it is the ordering process itself. The example is intended to show only that if we know the nature of *an ordering principle* we can know a priori the characteristics of order imparted by it to the things it orders.

A judgment, according to Kant, is a movement of thought in which two items are brought together and combined. We judge whenever we say, "This house is large," "That dog is a Sealyham," or "The interior angles of a triangle equal two right angles." The mind brings the items together in judgment because it detects a connection between them. It is this connection that is the warrant, or basis, for the judgment. Now, the most obvious kind of evidence on which we base our judgments is experience: It is sense experience, for instance, that warrants our judging that a particular house is large. Such a judgment Kant called empirical, or "a posteriori." In contrast, there is a kind of judgment that is "independent of all experience." For instance, we do not have to measure the angles of a particular triangle to know that its interior angles equal two right angles; we know this as a result of a geometric proof—it follows from Euclid's definition of the nature of a triangle that the interior angles of any triangle equal two right angles. This kind of judgment Kant called pure, or "a priori." There are two characteristics of a priori judgments that enable us to distinguish them with certainty from a posteriori judgments.

> Experience teaches us that a thing is so and so, but not that it cannot be otherwise. First, then, if we have a proposition which in being thought is thought as *necessary*, it is an *a priori* judgment. . . . Secondly, . . . if, then, a judgment is thought . . . in such manner that no exception is allowed as possible, it is not derived from experience, but is valid absolutely *a priori*. . . . Necessity and strict universality are thus sure criteria of *a priori* knowledge, and are inseparable from each other.[b]

In addition to distinguishing between a posteriori and a priori judgments, Kant distinguished between analytical and synthetical judgments. In an analytical judgment the predicate is covertly contained in the subject and may be obtained by analysis of it. "Roses are flowers" is an example: That roses are flowers is a part of the definition of roses. In a synthetical judgment the predicate is *not* contained in its subject. "Some roses are red" is an example: Red is not a part of the definition of rose.

We thus have two pairs of judgments, a priori–a posteriori and analytical–synthetical. These pairs yield four logically possible classes of judgments, as follows:

	a posteriori	a priori
analytical	1 analytical a posteriori	2 analytical a priori
synthetical	3 synthetical a posteriori	4 synthetical a priori

But the class in the upper left quadrant (class 1) is obviously empty: There can be no analytical a posteriori judgments, since all analytical judgments are universal and necessary. Thus there are three classes of judgment to examine, and the question is, "What *kind* of evidence warrants each of these classes?" There is no problem about class 2. All judgments of this class are warranted by the law of contradiction. Since being a flower is a part of the definition of rose, we would contradict ourselves if we asserted that a rose is not a flower. The knowledge yielded by this type of judgment, it will be seen, is just what Hobbes called knowledge of the agreement and disagreement of names. Similarly, there is no problem about class 3. The warrant for synthetical a posteriori judgments is experience. The judgment "This rose is red" is warranted by the visual experience (under suitable light conditions) of the rose's redness.

But what about class 4? What warrant can there be for synthetical a priori judgments? The "principle," as Kant called it, of this type of judgment cannot be the law of contradiction, for judgments in this quadrant are synthetical—that is, their predicates are not contained covertly in their subjects. Nor can the principle be experience, for "experience teaches us only that a thing is so and so," and judgments in this quadrant, being a priori, assert a universal and necessary connection. Is there any third type of principle, other than experience or the law of contradiction, that might serve as a warrant for synthetical a priori judgments? Hume thought not. He pointed out, first, that there is never any logical impossibility in denying an assertion of a matter of fact (we do not contradict ourselves if we judge, "This rose is not red," whereas we contradict ourselves if we judge, "This rose is not a flower") and, second, that it is impossible to "collect" from any series of particulars, however numerous, universality and necessity. Accordingly, Hume's position, expressed in Kantian language, is this: All judgments are either synthetical a posteriori (judgments about what Hume called matters of fact) or analytical (judgments about what he called relations of ideas). This was the basis for Hume's scepticism regarding causality and inductive inference. He believed he had shown that there was no evidence—and *could be* no evidence—that because *a* had been associated with *b* in the past, it would continue to be associated with *b* in the future.

Kant, of course, wanted to show that there are judgments of the synthetical a priori type—judgments that are both "instructive," like synthetical a posteriori, matter-of-fact judgments, and universal and necessary, like analytical judgments. But, once again, what possible warrant can there be for such judgments? We are left therefore with the following situation regarding the principles of various classes of judgment:[3]

	a posteriori	a priori
analytical	1 null	2 warranted by law of contradiction
synthetical	3 warranted by experience	4 ?

3 Kant's system of classification does not take account of some judgments—for instance, contradictions: "Squares are round" is not analytical, according to Kant's definition, and it is certainly not synthetical.

The fourth quadrant, then, poses "the general problem of pure reason"—that is, "How are synthetical a priori judgments possible?" We shall not progress very far toward an answer until we narrow the question down. Kant pointed out that, rightly or wrongly, philosophers have believed judgments of the kind he called synthetical a priori to occur in three areas, namely, mathematics, natural science, and metaphysics. The general question "How are synthetical a priori judgments possible?" thus divides into three subquestions: (1) "How are synthetical a priori judgments possible in mathematics?" (2) "How are synthetical a priori judgments possible in natural science?" and (3) "Are synthetical a priori judgments possible in metaphysics?" Note the change in phrasing in the third question.

Kant agreed with Hume that synthetical a priori judgments are *not* possible in metaphysics, although he believed that our disposition to ask and to try to answer metaphysical questions points to the fact that reason has a "regulative" use. More will be said about this later in the chapter.

Kant agreed with Hume that mathematical judgments are universal and necessary, but he maintained that they are synthetical rather than analytical.[4] He also agreed with Hume that most judgments in natural science are a posteriori. But—and this is the crucial point, of course—he denied that all are a posteriori. Thus the proposition "Friction causes heat" is a posteriori because it is a generalization of experience. But the proposition "Every event has a cause" is a priori. In Kant's view, the fact that this and certain other basic propositions in physics are a priori means that inductive inference is validated. Hence the empirical proposition "Friction causes heat" is highly probable, not a wild shot in the dark, as Hume's view implied.

Kant's point can be illustrated by the game of guessing what card a dealer is going to turn up next. If, after an ordinary deck of fifty-two cards has been shuffled, we are invited to bet that the first card turned up will be the ace of spades, we would want odds of 52 to 1. Of course, after the first card has been drawn and removed from the deck, the odds would decrease. But suppose that, after each drawing, the card is reinserted in the deck and the deck is reshuffled. Then the odds would remain 52 to 1. Further, if the deck is increased in size, the odds would grow greater. And if it contained an infinite number of cards, we would refuse to bet, for the odds would be infinitely against us. There is no evidence, according to Hume, that the human situation is not like this: Every drawing of a card (every event that takes place) is an isolated occurrence, and we can make no inference from what has happened to what may happen.

But what if the dealer tells us (we shall have to assume that he can be trusted) that he has arranged the cards in a definite order? Then, suppose that the following sequence occurs: ace of spades, ace of hearts, ace of diamonds, ace of clubs, king of spades, king of hearts, king of diamonds, king of clubs, queen

---

4 Though Hume wavered about the status of geometry, when he held that it is synthetical, he said that it is not a priori; when he allowed that it is a priori, he insisted that it is analytical.

of spades, ... Most of us would probably bet that the next card will be the queen of hearts. If it is, we would probably take lower odds (that is, feel more confident) that the next card will be the queen of diamonds and the next the queen of clubs. In a word, on the assumption that there *is* an order, we begin to form hypotheses about what that order is (for example, that the dealer has arranged the cards in their order of value in bridge). Of course, any hypothesis we frame may be falsified—the next card after the queen of clubs may be the deuce of spades, for the order may be "three times round from the top of the deck, then three times round from the bottom of the deck." Hence, though we can never be *certain* of what the order is, our hypothesis can become increasingly probable, and after a sufficient number of correct predictions we may regard the hypothesis as "certain for all practical purposes." But all this depends, it will be seen, on the deck being well ordered; if it is not, all probabilities at once reduce to zero.

In this example, of course, we must rely without evidence on the honesty of the dealer. According to Kant's hypothesis, our confidence in the orderliness of the physical world rests on firmer grounds. It is derived from the fact that we know that every event necessarily has a cause. We can never be sure, with respect to any particular event a, that its cause is b. But because we know that there is *some* event that is the cause of a, we can become increasingly confident it is b.

All this holds only if the proposition that every event has a cause is, as Kant claimed, necessarily true. And that it is true is precisely what Hume denied. The concept "cause," Hume pointed out, cannot be derived analytically from the concept "event." Since it cannot be so derived, we cannot say that every event necessarily has a cause. Hence inductive inference is not validated. Does Kant's reply to Hume merely reaffirm what Hume denied? If so, it is surely a poor answer.

Those who criticize Kant on this score, however, miss his main point. It seemed to him that there is a *prima facie* case in favor of synthetical a priori judgments in mathematics and natural science. The only reason, he thought, for questioning them would be the suspicion aroused by Hume's attack. The situation must have seemed to Kant to be rather like that expressed in the legal maxim "A man is innocent until proved guilty." Suppose that circumstantial evidence suggests that a highly respectable citizen has committed a particularly revolting murder. If the evidence against him is shown to be misleading and incompetent, his reputation should be rehabilitated.

This is precisely the position Kant took with regard to synthetical a priori judgments in mathematics and natural science, and this is why he framed his question as he did. He did not ask *whether* such judgments are possible; he asked *how* they are possible. It did not seem to him that he was assuming the point at issue between himself and Hume, for he thought that Hume was disturbed by his own conclusion and would be delighted to be proved wrong. Although a man might be able to rest in "mitigated" scepticism, no man would *choose* to adopt this position. Hence, Kant thought, it was necessary only to show that Hume's suspicion of these judgments was based upon a mistake, namely, the mistaken belief that the only possible basis for making a connection in a synthetical judgment is experience. To "rehabilitate the reputation" of such a judgment, one had only to find the real connection that is operative.

At this point it will be helpful to translate back from the technical language Kant actually used into the form-and-content language that has been derived from Kant's analysis of scientific method. Kant's hypothesis, as formulated earlier, was that certain standard forms are contributed by the mind, in terms of which the content of experience is organized. These standard forms "sort" the content of experience into standard patterns. Though the materials that are thus organized into patterns are not necessary, the patterns themselves are necessary, for without them the variable contents would be only a chaotic jumble, not the well-ordered content we actually experience. Accordingly, if there are any standard forms, there is a kind of knowledge that is synthetical (because the predicate of the judgment is not contained in the subject) and that is also a priori (because it is contributed to experience by the mind and is therefore universal and necessary for all experience). Thus Kant's hypothesis can be rephrased to mean that there are, after all, judgments in the fourth quadrant, and that these judgments are warranted neither by experience nor by the law of contradiction but by an organizing principle of the mind.

If this hypothesis can be proved, the "problem of pure reason" is solved, and a correct combination of the empirical and rational elements in knowledge will have been found. If the hypothesis is correct, then "all our knowledge begins with experience," as Locke and the other empiricists had insisted. But it does not necessarily follow, as they supposed, "that it all arises out of experience." Indeed, if the hypothesis is correct, *all* knowledge, not just scientific knowledge, contains elements that are not drawn from experience but supplied by the mind itself. Such elements would be a priori in the sense required.

> But though all our knowledge begins with experience, it does not follow that it all arises out of experience. For it may well be that even our empirical knowledge is made up of what we receive through impressions and of what our own faculty of knowledge (sensible impressions serving merely as the occasion) supplies from itself. If our faculty of knowledge makes any such addition, it may be that we are not in a position to distinguish it from the raw material, until with long practice of attention we have become skilled in separating it.
>
> This, then, is a question which at least calls for closer examination, and does not allow of any offhand answer:—whether there is any knowledge that is thus independent of experience and even of all impressions of the senses. Such knowledge is entitled *a priori*, and distinguished from the *empirical*, which has its sources *a posteriori*, that is, in experience.[c]

So far, Kant has not *proved* that there is any necessary synthetical a priori knowledge. His position, in terms of the sorting-machine analogy, is as follows:

We could make a priori judgments about the size of oranges in boxes beneath the machine, providing we knew the dimensions of the holes in the machine's surface. Similarly, assuming that all the objects of knowledge were connected by certain basic types of putting together, we could know a priori several relational characteristics of all objects, providing we were able to discover what these basic types of putting together were. But that this is so remains to be proved.

Let us return to the three central questions that Kant hoped to answer: "How are synthetical a priori judgments possible in mathematics?" "How are they possible in physics?" and "Are they possible in metaphysics?" It will be seen that Kant proposed to answer the first two questions by showing that there are certain basic types of putting together that operate in these fields. As regards the third question, in Kant's view, the answers to the questions about mathematics and physics dispose of the possibility of there being knowledge of metaphysical objects.

The A Priori in Mathematics

Kant dealt with his first question—"How are synthetical a priori judgments possible in mathematics?"—in a section of the *Critique* called the "Transcendental Aesthetic." He called it "aesthetic" because he believed the basis for this kind of knowledge to be immediate, nondiscursive, and sensuous; he called it "transcendental" because he believed that such knowledge is not *in* experience but a necessary condition *for* experience. His first step was to try to show that mathematical knowledge is synthetical.

> *All mathematical judgments, without exception, are synthetic.* This fact, though incontestably certain and in its consequences very important, has hitherto escaped the notice of those who are engaged in the analysis of human reason. . . .
>
> We might, indeed, at first suppose that the proposition $7 + 5 = 12$ is a merely analytic proposition, and follows by the principle of contradiction from the concept of a sum of 7 and 5. But if we look more closely we find that the concept of the sum of 7 and 5 contains nothing save the union of the two numbers into one, and in this no thought is being taken as to what that single number may be which combines both. The concept of 12 is by no means already thought in merely thinking this union of 7 and 5; and I may analyse my concept of such a possible sum as long as I please, still I shall never find the 12 in it. We have to go outside these concepts, and call in the aid of the intuition[5] which corresponds to one of them, our five fingers,

---

5 [By "intuition" Kant meant "immediate and sensuous," as opposed to "discursive and reasoned." This was the point of his calling the whole section the "Transcendental Aesthetic"—AUTHOR.]

for instance, . . . adding to the concept of 7, unit by unit, the five given in intuition. For starting with the number 7, and for the concept of 5 calling in the aid of the fingers of my hand as intuition, I now add one by one to the number 7 the units which I previously took together to form the number 5, and with the aid of that figure [the hand] see the number 12 come into being. That 5 should be added to 7, I have indeed already thought in the concept of a sum = 7 + 5, but not that this sum is equivalent to the number 12. Arithmetical propositions are therefore always synthetic. This is still more evident if we take larger numbers. For it is then obvious that, however we might turn and twist our concepts, we could never, by the mere analysis of them, and without the aid of intuition, discover what [the number is that] is the sum.

Just as little is any fundamental proposition of pure geometry analytic. That the straight line between two points is the shortest, is a synthetic proposition. For my concept of *straight* contains nothing of quantity, but only of quality. The concept of the shortest is wholly an addition, and cannot be derived, through any process of analysis, from the concept of the straight line. Intuition, therefore, must here be called in; only by its aid is the synthesis possible.[d]

Those who agree with Hobbes that mathematical judgments are analytical will, of course, think that the "Transcendental Aesthetic" is a waste of time, for there is no problem, as Kant himself pointed out, about the necessity of analytical judgments. But for those who share Kant's view that mathematical judgments are synthetical, there is indeed a puzzle about how such judgments can be a priori. Hence the hypothesis put forward in the "Transcendental Aesthetic" is worth considering.

BASIS OF MATHEMATICAL CERTAINTY

Let us therefore proceed to the second stage in Kant's argument: Assuming that mathematics is synthetical, how can it be a priori? What, for example, is the basis of certainty in geometry, the science of the properties of space? We must first ask what space is. According to the Newtonian view, space is an absolute reality, independent of ourselves, a big box in which events occur. According to the Leibnizian view, space is not real (the monads are nonspatial) but relational, a structure produced by sense and imagination. Neither of these views, however, wholly satisfied Kant. For one thing, he was much impressed by the curious kind of spatial relationship obtaining between, for instance, right- and left-handed gloves. If space were merely relational, as Leibniz claimed, it would be possible to superimpose one glove on the other, for all the relationships between parts (for example, between thumb and forefinger in each glove) are identical. The gloves ought to be spatially identical, like two vases made from the same mold. The fact that they are not shows there is more to space than the relation of parts.

On the other hand, if space were Newtonian, how could we ever have the a priori knowledge of it claimed in geometry? We could know that in the part of space under inspection here and now triangles have interior angles equal to 180°, but how could we know that this is true, as geometry claims, in all space everywhere? It is the old problem, obviously, of the impossibility of explaining a priori knowledge on the usual assumption that the mind's objects are independent reals and that truth consists in bringing the mind into agreement with them.

Furthermore, Kant noted that although we grasp the difference between right-handed and left-handed gloves as soon as we see them, we are unable to give this difference a rational, discursive formulation. This suggested to Kant that the mind's apprehension of space is sensuous ("aesthetic") rather than intellectual.

Drawing all these considerations together Kant came to the conclusion that space is simply a mode of the mind's apprehension of its world. It is, in fact, one of the ways of putting together whose existence he had already hypothecated to account for our knowledge of objects. It is not a putting together *in judgment,* for (as we have seen) our experience of space is sensuous, not intellectual. But, like the types of putting together that occur in judgment, it is a way of relating and organizing experiences. And because it is contributed by the mind, we can be a priori certain that *all* the mind's objects have spatial characteristics. That is, the mind organizes its experiences spatially, just as, in the sorting-machine analogy, the machine spreads oranges out into different boxes.

> Space is not an empirical concept which has been derived from outer experiences. For in order that certain sensations be referred to something outside me (that is, to something in another region of space from that in which I find myself), and similarly in order that I may be able to represent them as outside and alongside one another, and accordingly as not only different but as in different places, the representation of space must be presupposed. The representation of space cannot, therefore, be empirically obtained from the relations of outer appearance. On the contrary, this outer experience is itself possible at all only through that representation.
>
> Space is a necessary *a priori* representation, which underlies all outer intuitions. We can never represent to ourselves the absence of space, though we can quite well think it as empty of objects. It must therefore be regarded as the condition of the possibility of appearances, and not as a determination dependent upon them. . . .
>
> Space is not a discursive or, as we say, general concept of relations of things in general, but a pure intuition. For, in the first place, we can represent to ourselves only one space; and if we speak of diverse spaces, we mean thereby only parts of one and the same unique space. Secondly, these parts cannot precede the one all-embracing space, as being, as it were, constituents out of which it can be composed; on the contrary, they can be thought only as *in* it. Space is essentially one; the manifold in it, and therefore the general

concept of spaces, depends solely on [the introduction of] limitations. Hence it follows that an *a priori*, and not an empirical, intuition underlies all concepts of space.[e]

This argument is directed chiefly against the empiricists, who held space to be an empirical concept derived from the perception of things as "outer" (as the concept "red" is derived from the perception of red objects). Kant's point here is that since the experience of "outer" already implies space, space cannot be derived from it. We can think of space without objects in it, but we cannot think of objects that are not in space. Hence our experience of space is prior to, and a condition of, our experience of objects. Kant assumed that, if objects are not a condition of our experience of space, space must be a condition of our experience of objects.

Next, Kant undertook to show that the apriority of space (which he believed himself to have established) validates the claim of geometry to be an a priori and synthetical science. Geometry is the science of space. According to Kant, space is not an independently existing entity but a way in which the human mind organizes its experience. Hence, what the geometrician investigates is not the properties of outer objects but the modes of our faculty of intuition (outer perception). Hence, again, any properties found to characterize a particular region of space (for example, that the space here and now is such that triangles formed in it have interior angles equal to 180°) will characterize space everywhere, for the geometric properties in question are a projection of the human mind. Since they are among the basic ways in which the mind organizes the objects of its experience, all objects that the mind experiences will have these properties.

> Geometry is a science which determines the properties of space synthetically, and yet *a priori*. What, then, must be our representation of space, in order that such knowledge of it may be possible? It must in its origin be intuition; for from a mere concept no propositions can be obtained which go beyond the concept—as happens in geometry. Further, this intuition must be *a priori*, that is, it must be found in us prior to any perception of an object, and must therefore be pure, not empirical, intuition. For geometrical propositions are one and all apodeictic, that is, are bound up with the consciousness of their necessity; for instance, that space has only three dimensions. Such propositions cannot be empirical or, in other words, judgments of experience, nor can they be derived from any such judgments.
>
> How, then, can there exist in the mind an outer intuition which precedes the objects themselves, and in which the concept of these objects can be determined *a priori*? Manifestly, not otherwise than in so far as the intuition has its seat in the subject only, as the formal character of the subject, in virtue of which, in being affected by objects, it obtains *immediate representation*, that is, *intuition*, of them; and only in so far, therefore, as it is merely the form of outer *sense* in general.
>
> Our explanation is thus the only explanation that makes intelligible the *possibility* of geometry, as a body of *a priori* synthetic knowledge.[f]

LIMITATIONS OF KANT'S VIEW

What are we to make of this "transcendental exposition" (or validation) of the synthetical a priori character of geometry? Since Kant's day, our notion of the object of geometric knowledge has radically altered as a result of, first, the development of non-Euclidean geometries and, subsequently, the discovery that there are parts of space (for example, the microspaces within an atom and the macrospaces of the galaxies) of which these other geometries appear to give better accounts than does Euclidean geometry. It looks, indeed, as if the various geometries (including Euclidean geometry) are so many logics rather than sciences of space. Whether or not any of these logics *is* relevant to the description of the spatial properties of bodies thus becomes an empirical, not an a priori, question. It just happens that Euclidean geometry is particularly relevant to ordinary perceptual space and to the problems of constructing buildings, surveying fields, and so on. This is why people thought for so long that it was per se the science of space. But as new kinds of experiences (say, those obtained by looking into high-powered telescopes) were obtained, it was found that the behavior thus observed could be more conveniently accounted for in terms of a non-Euclidean geometry. Thus the applicability of any given geometry is determined by the kind of experience it is applied to.

Where does this leave Kant's transcendental exposition? Though it seems clear that Kant was mistaken in believing that such-and-such specific forms of spatial putting together are a priori, it does not necessarily follow that he was mistaken about space being a form of the mind's apprehension of its world. Space might be a mode of ordering contributed by the mind, and the various geometries might be accounts of the various possible types of such ordering. Thus, to revert to the sorting-machine analogy, we might know a priori that the oranges were ordered (that is, sorted), but we might not know which of several possible sorting principles was being used. To determine the exact type of principle being used would require an empirical study of the machine. Though this type of determination would be much less than Kant wanted to prove (and much less than he thought he had proved), it would be a very important point to have established.

APPEARANCE AND REALITY

If space is a way in which the mind orders things, obviously things are not really (in themselves) spatial; and what they really are we cannot possibly imagine. For we can imagine things only as spread out in space—this is the only form of externality that minds like ours can conceive of.

> Space does not represent any property of things in themselves, nor does it represent them in their relation to one another. That is to say, space does not represent any determination that attaches to the objects themselves, and which remains even when abstraction has been made of all the subjective conditions of intuition. . . .
>
> It is, therefore, solely from the human standpoint that we can speak of

space, of extended things, etc. . . . This predicate can be ascribed to things only in so far as they appear to us, that is, only to objects of sensibility. The constant form of this receptivity, which we term sensibility, is a necessary condition of all the relations in which objects can be intuited as outside us; and if we abstract from these objects, it is a pure intuition, and bears the name of space. Since we cannot treat the special conditions of sensibility as conditions of the possibility of things, but only of their appearances, we can indeed say that space comprehends all things that appear to us as external, but not all things in themselves, by whatever subject they are intuited. . . . For we cannot judge in regard to the intuitions of other thinking beings, whether they are bound by the same conditions as those which limit our intuition and which for us are universally valid. . . . Our exposition therefore establishes the *reality*, that is, the objective validity, of space in respect of whatever can be presented to us outwardly as object, but also at the same time the *ideality* of space in respect of things when they are considered in themselves through reason, that is, without regard to the constitution of our sensibility.[g]

The "Transcendental Aesthetic" also contains an exposition of time, which can be treated more briefly because it is largely parallel to the exposition of space. According to Kant, time, like space, is a "pure form of intuition," that is, a mode of ordering (or of putting together) that is immediate and sensuous, not a matter of judgment. Just as our minds order our experiences spatially, as being above or below, to the right or left, of other experiences, so they order these experiences temporally, as being before, after, or simultaneous with other experiences. There is, of course, a felt difference, immediately recognizable and unmistakable, between time and space—between, for instance, before and after on the one hand and above and below on the other. And this felt difference is perceived by us as the difference between what is inner and what is outer. Whatever we experience as spatial, we hold to be a datum of "outer sense." This is true of the materials of the five senses, all of which have this character of externality. Regarded, however, as states of oneself, these same materials are experienced as having a temporal order, that is, as coming before, after, or simultaneous with other experiences we have. Hence, in contrast to space, "time is nothing but the form of inner sense, that is, of our awareness of ourselves and of our own inner state."

So far in his account of the a priori properties of experience, Kant has not reached anything like the level of ordinary human experience, which consists in a knowledge of objects, that is, of complex and relatively enduring structures. So far, that is, Kant has dealt merely with the spatiotemporal ordering of contents, for example, with experiences of colored patches succeeding one another. Kant's point is that *to have even this very elementary kind of experience* there must be certain synthetical ordering activities of the mind. Obviously, to have an experience of *objects*, still more complex types of putting together must occur. This brings us to the natural sciences, which, unlike mathematics, are concerned with the cognition of physical objects.

The A Priori in Physics

Kant's second question—"How are synthetical a priori judgments possible in physics?"—is discussed in a section of the *Critique* called the "Transcendental Logic." Kant called it "logic" because he was concerned with the kinds of putting together that occur in judgment (in contrast to the immediate, sensuous putting together discussed in the "Aesthetic"); he called it "transcendental" because, once again, he was concerned not with the content of experience but with the conditions that make an experience of objects possible.[6]

As we have seen, Kant did not maintain that *all* judgments in the natural sciences are synthetical a priori (as he held all mathematical judgments to be). But he did think that certain judgments must be synthetical a priori in order to provide an underpinning for the inductive procedures of the sciences.

Furthermore, Kant hoped to do more than merely show that there are *some* a priori elements in our experience of objects. In the "Aesthetic" he was not content merely to establish spatiality; he wanted to establish a particular kind of spatiality (namely, Euclidean spatiality). That is, he wanted to do more than reply to Hume in a general way, by showing how an objective world can exist and inductive inference can be possible. He wanted to show, specifically, that the concept employed in Newtonian physics (the particular kinds of order it presupposes) are a priori.

It is necessary, therefore, to distinguish two questions: (1) Can a case be made for the existence of *some* ordering elements contributed by the mind? (2) Can it be shown that these elements are those presupposed in Newtonian physics? The first question is relatively simple, and the answer seems to be in the affirmative. The second question is much more difficult, and it involved Kant in many complications.

THE TWO ELEMENTS IN JUDGMENT

Let us remind ourselves of what was said earlier about judgment.[7] To think is to judge; knowledge is the end product of judging, and judging is a kind of putting together. According to Kant, two different components are always involved in judging: a direct, sensuous component and a conceptual, structural component. The difference between these components is like the difference between "guidebook" knowledge of a city and direct experience of it. A man could sit at home with his Baedeker, memorizing a map of Rome and learning the names of various buildings and their dimensions. As a result, he might be able to tell us quite a lot about the dome of St. Peter's. But if he has never seen the basilica, if he has never looked at a dome, his knowledge is, in Kant's terminology, "empty."

6 The "Transcendental Logic" is in turn divided into two parts: the "Transcendental Analytic" and the "Transcendental Dialectic." The "Analytic" is concerned with what may be called the proper use of logic; the "Dialectic," with its improper use. Here we are concerned with the "Analytic"; for the "Dialectic," see pp. 51–58.

7 See pp. 24–25.

He has acquired a number of concepts ("dome," "lantern," "pendentive," "barrel vault"), but they lack the concrete filling of perception and feeling. At the other extreme is the tourist who rushes through Europe so fast that, though he has "seen" St. Peter's (in the sense of having looked in that direction as his bus sped by), his knowledge of it is, again in Kant's terms, "blind." He lacks the historical and architectural knowledge that would structure, organize, and focus the sensory experience.

Kant's first point then—and surely it is a good one—is that all effective knowledge must contain two elements—an experiential element (a concrete filling of sense data, perceptions, and feelings) and a structural or relational element (a conceptual ordering of the percepts and feelings). This double requirement is what Kant meant to insist on when he said that "thoughts without content are empty, intuitions without concepts are blind. It is just as necessary to make our concepts sensible, that is, to add the object to them in intuition, as to make our intuitions intelligible, that is, to bring them under concepts." [h] Even the most rudimentary kind of judgment, a judgment of identification (for example, "That was a clock striking three") is a case in point. Only when an experience (a noise) is "brought under" a concept ("clock striking") can it be identified, or known for what it is.

This is an extremely important distinction, and Kant was the first philosopher to formulate it unambiguously. Most rationalists, from Plato down to Descartes and his successors, had taken it for granted that cognitive processes form a continuum; they regarded perception as "confused thought"—that is, as the same sort of activity as reasoning, differing only in degree of adequacy. Although the empiricists, of course, had not maintained that perception is confused, neither had they drawn the Kantian distinction between percepts and concepts, for they had tended to treat concepts as fictions, or even (as with the extreme nominalists) as merely words. Hence they too failed to emphasize that there are two indispensable elements in human knowledge. Here, then, is another reason why Kant's theories can be regarded as a watershed in the history of philosophy. On the whole, most nineteenth- and twentieth-century philosophers have accepted Kant's distinction between percepts and concepts, with the limitations that this entails regarding direct, immediate knowledge of the self and its world. Those philosophers who did not nevertheless had to deal with the distinction Kant had drawn; philosophy could not return to its pre-Kantian course.

A PRIORI CONCEPTS

To return to the argument of the "Transcendental Logic": Obviously, most concepts, like the concept "clock striking," are what Kant called empirical. They are derived from experience. That their derivation requires complicated acts of thought is beside the point here. The question for Kant was whether there are any pure a priori concepts, that is, forms of thought (of judging) that correspond to space and time as pervasive forms of sensing.

The "clue" to the discovery of these pure a priori concepts lies in recognizing that all judgments whatsoever fall into one or the other of several types (categorical, hypothetical, affirmative, negative, and so forth). According to Kant, we could not make a judgment of any of these types unless we *understood* the "relationship" being asserted. By "relationship" Kant meant, not the particular relationship in a particular judgment ("All crows are black"), but the generic relationship ("All —— are ——"). To grasp the particular connection between "crow" and "black," sense experience is required, for the concept "crow" is an empirical concept like the concept "clock striking." But before *any* particular empirical judgment of this type can be made, it is necessary to understand the generic relationship "All —— are ——." Hence the concept "All —— are ——" is a pure a priori concept, antecedent to all experience and a condition of there being any specific judgments of this type and therefore any knowledge of this kind.

Kant believed that Aristotelian logic furnished a complete and exhaustive table of all possible types of judgment. Hence from this list he drew up a corresponding list of pure a priori concepts. Kant classified the various possible types of judgment as follows:

I. QUANTITY OF JUDGMENTS	II. QUALITY
Universal	Affirmative
Particular	Negative
Singular	Infinite

III. RELATION	IV. MODALITY
Categorical	Problematic
Hypothetical	Assertoric
Disjunctive	Apodeictic[i]

Since, in Kant's view, each form of judgment is an a priori concept (or "category") by means of which the mind orders its various particular judgings, there is a table of categories that corresponds exactly with the table of types of judgment:

I. OF QUÂNTITY	II. OF QUALITY
Unity	Reality
Plurality	Negation
Totality	Limitation

III. OF RELATION	IV. OF MODALITY
Of Inherence and Subsistence (*substantia et accidens*)	Possibility–Impossibility
Of Causality and Dependence (cause and effect)	Existence–Nonexistence
Of Community (reciprocity between agent and patient)	Necessity–Contingency[j]

It is important to see that, once Kant had discovered the all-important connection between the types of judgment and the a priori concepts (or forms of synthesis), the actual list of a priori concepts followed automatically, being guaranteed by the authority of Aristotle's logic.

> The same function which gives unity to the various representations *in a judgment* also gives unity to the mere synthesis of various representations *in an intuition;* and this unity, in its most general expression, we entitle the pure concept of the understanding. The same understanding, through the same operations by which in concepts, by means of analytical unity, it produced the logical form of a judgment, also introduces a transcendental content into its representations, by means of the synthetic unity of the manifold in intuition in general. On this account we are entitled to call these representations pure concepts of the understanding, and to regard them as applying *a priori* to objects—a conclusion which general logic is not in a position to establish.
>
> In this manner there arise precisely the same number of pure concepts of the understanding which apply *a priori* to objects of intuition in general, as . . . there have been found to be logical functions in all possible judgments. For these functions specify the understanding completely, and yield an exhaustive inventory of its powers. These concepts we shall, with Aristotle, call *categories.*[k]

THE METAPHYSICAL DEDUCTION

This is what Kant called the "metaphysical deduction" of the categories.[8] In it he purported to show that every judgment the mind makes ("Roses are red," "Crows are black," "Friction causes heat") presupposes one or the other of twelve different synthetical operations ("puttings together"), or categories. It is important to understand that a category is *not* a fixed pigeonhole into which experience is dumped. One of the unfortunately misleading aspects of the sorting-machine analogy is that it suggests this sort of static conception—as, for that matter, does Kant's own term, "category." On the contrary, the categories are transcendental concepts, or rules, that underlie and make possible those actual, empirical syntheses that occur every time we judge. In calling them "transcendental," Kant merely meant they are not empirically observable "puttings together," as are the judgments "Roses are red" and "That was a clock striking three." We can be sure that they occur because, if they did not, the actual judgments we make could not occur.

THE TRANSCENDENTAL DEDUCTION

From the metaphysical deduction, Kant went on to what he called the "transcendental deduction" of the categories. So far he had merely shown that

---

8 By "deduction" Kant meant proof, or justification. The metaphysical deduction corresponds to the "expositions" of space and time—that is, it validates the existence of pure a priori concepts.

pure a priori concepts, or categories, underlie all our acts of judging. The function of the transcendental deduction was to show that these same categories make possible the kind of world we live in, namely, a world in which self knows objects. In other words, to talk about "acts of judging" is to deal in abstractions. It is a *self* that judges, and what it judges about are *objects*. The transcendental deduction is thus an extension of the metaphysical deduction.

The main points of the argument of the transcendental deduction are as follows: (1) All experience, whatever else it involves, is of the succession of a variety of contents. (2) To be experienced at all, these successive data have to be combined, or held together in unity for a consciousness. (3) Unity of experience therefore implies unity of self. (4) This unity of self is as much an object of experience as anything else is. (5) It follows that experience of both the self and its objects rests on prior acts of synthesis, which, because they are the conditions of any experience at all, are not themselves experienced. (6) These prior syntheses are made possible by the categories.

Kant's argument may perhaps be made clearer by reference to Locke's rather facile remark that the mind somehow "collects" certain of its ideas. Among these, according to Locke, are some of our most important ideas, for example, the ideas of substance and causality. In a sense, Kant's transcendental deduction was an attempt to define Locke's "somehow" with precision. Kant saw, as Locke did not, that the concept "collection" undermines the empirical criterion of meaning. Unlike, for example, the idea "red," substance and cause do not have their sources in experience. On the contrary, they make possible the very experience that would explain them.

THE CONDITIONS THAT MAKE EXPERIENCE POSSIBLE

Human experience is an experience of *objects*, or, as they may be called, unified representations. Human experience, that is, does not consist merely in a subjective flow of sense data in a mind that claims all these data as its own. With such a flow, "objects" are to be contrasted: Objects occupy, or have, an *objective* order different from their place in one's individual mental life. But what is implied by the existence of such "objects of representation"?

> We have stated above that appearances are themselves nothing but sensible representations, which, as such and in themselves, must not be taken as objects capable of existing outside our power of representation. What, then, is to be understood when we speak of an object corresponding to, and consequently also distinct from, our knowledge? It is easily seen that this object must be thought only as something in general = x, since outside our knowledge we have nothing which we could set over against this knowledge as corresponding to it.
>
> Now we find that our thought of the relation of all knowledge to its object carries with it an element of necessity; the object is viewed as that which prevents our modes of knowledge from being haphazard or arbitrary, and which determines them *a priori* in some definite fashion. For in so far as they

are to relate to an object, they must necessarily agree with one another, that is, must possess that unity which constitutes the concept of an object.

But it is clear that, since we have to deal only with the manifold of our representations, and since that x (the object) which corresponds to them is nothing to us—being, as it is, something that has to be distinct from all our representations—the unity which the object makes necessary can be nothing else than the formal unity of consciousness in the synthesis of the manifold of representations. It is only when we have thus produced synthetic unity in the manifold of intuition that we are in a position to say that we know the object. But this unity is impossible if the intuition cannot be generated in accordance with a rule by means of such a function of synthesis as makes the reproduction of the manifold *a priori* necessary, and renders possible a concept in which it is united. . . .

All knowledge demands a concept, though that concept may, indeed, be quite imperfect or obscure. But a concept is always, as regards its form, something universal which serves as a rule. The concept of body, for instance, as the unity of the manifold which is thought through it, serves as a rule in our knowledge of outer appearances. But it can be a rule for intuitions only in so far as it represents in any given appearances the necessary reproduction of their manifold, and thereby the synthetic unity in our consciousness of them. The concept of body, in the perception of something outside us, necessitates the representation of extension, and therewith representations of impenetrability, shape, etc.

All necessity, without exception, is grounded in a transcendental condition. There must, therefore, be a transcendental ground of the unity of consciousness in the synthesis of the manifold of all our intuitions, and consequently also of the concepts of objects in general, and so of all objects of experience, a ground without which it would be impossible to think any object for our intuitions; for this object is no more than that something, the concept of which expresses such a necessity of synthesis.[1]

In Kant's view, self and object are not independent entities but reciprocal elements in experience. If we start from object, we are led to self; if we begin with self, we are led to object. The experience of either one involves the experience of the other, and the experience of both depends on the prior occurrence of certain synthetical acts. Kant called these acts "transcendental" because, though never themselves experienced, they have to be presupposed to account for the existence of those empirical unities that are experienced, namely, "self" and "object." They have to be presupposed, that is, to account for the existence of experience as we know it. These synthetical acts depend on, and conform to, the categories.

There can be in us no modes of knowledge, no connection or unity of one mode of knowledge with another, without that unity of consciousness which precedes all data of intuitions, and by relation to which representation of objects is alone possible. This pure original unchangeable consciousness I shall name *transcendental apperception.* . . .

This transcendental unity of apperception forms out of all possible appearances, which can stand alongside one another in one experience, a connection of all these representations according to laws. For this unity of consciousness would be impossible if the mind in knowledge of the manifold could not become conscious of the identity of function whereby it synthetically combines it in one knowledge. The original and necessary consciousness of the identity of the self is thus at the same time a consciousness of an equally necessary unity of the synthesis of all appearances according to concepts, that is, according to rules, which not only make them necessarily reproducible but also in so doing determine an object for their intuition, that is, the concept of something wherein they are necessarily interconnected. . . .

The *a priori* conditions of a possible experience in general are at the same time conditions of the possibility of objects of experience. Now I maintain that the categories, above cited, are nothing but the conditions of thought in a possible experience, just as space and time are the conditions of intuition for that same experience. They are fundamental concepts by which we think objects in general for appearances, and have therefore *a priori* objective validity. This is exactly what we desired to prove. . . .

That the *laws* of appearances in nature must agree with the understanding and its *a priori* form, that is, with its faculty of *combining* the manifold in general, is no more surprising than that the appearances themselves must agree with the form of *a priori* sensible intuition. For just as appearances do not exist in themselves but only relatively to the subject in which, so far as it has senses, they inhere, so the laws do not exist in the appearances but only relatively to this same being, so far as it has understanding. Things in themselves would necessarily, apart from any understanding that knows them, conform to laws of their own. But appearances are only representations of things which are unknown as regards what they may be in themselves. As mere representations, they are subject to no law of connection save that which the connecting faculty prescribes. Now it is imagination that connects the manifold of sensible intuition; and imagination is dependent for the unity of its intellectual synthesis upon the understanding, and for the manifoldness of its apprehension upon sensibility. All possible perception is thus dependent upon synthesis of apprehension, and this empirical synthesis in turn upon transcendental synthesis, and therefore upon the categories. Consequently, all possible perceptions, and therefore everything that can come to empirical consciousness, that is, all appearances of nature, must, so far as their connection is concerned, be subject to the categories. Nature, considered merely as nature in general, is dependent upon these categories as the original ground of its necessary conformity to law (*natura formaliter spectata*). Pure understanding is not, however, in a position, through mere categories, to prescribe to appearances any *a priori* laws other than those which are involved in a *nature in general*, that is, in the conformity to law of all appearances in space and time. Special laws, as concerning those appearances which are empirically determined, cannot in their specific character be *derived* from the categories, although they are one and all subject to them. To obtain any knowledge whatsoever of these special laws, we must resort to experience; but it is the *a priori* laws that alone can instruct us in regard to experience in general, and as to what it is that can be known as an object of experience.[m]

A DISCUSSION OF KANT'S VIEW OF EXPERIENCE

This passage is undeniably difficult, partly because, like a juggler who has to keep a number of balls in the air at once, Kant found that the various concepts he was discussing—experience, self, and object—all involved one another and hence could not be discussed separately. But part of the difficulty also stems from the fact that—even after three hundred years—we are still so accustomed to thinking about the world in Cartesian and Lockian terms that it is hard for us to adjust to Kant's radically different way of looking at things.

Let us therefore examine a simple experience in terms of a traditional and then a Kantian type of analysis. Suppose that I hear a clock striking three. According to the traditional analysis, my experience is as follows: (1) The clock is an object out there, independent of me. That is, even if there were no "me" over here, the clock would still exist and still strike, unaffected in any way by my nonexistence. (2) I am over here, another independent object. If the clock did not exist I would still be myself, unaffected by its nonexistence—except, of course, that I would not now hear it strike. (3) But the clock does exist; it does strike. I hear it and then judge, "That is a clock striking three." This is the Cartesian and Lockian way of looking at things.

In contrast, Kant makes no metaphysical assumptions about independently existing minds and objects. Instead, he starts from the experience itself and asks, "What conditions make this experience possible?" In terms of the example, what must be the case for me to be able to have the particular experience of a clock striking three? In the first place, I must already have learned, at mother's knee or in school, that clocks strike and that one can tell time in this way. If I were a Zulu or a Bantu and told time by the sun, I might have had no prior acquaintance with clocks. In this event, when the clock strikes three I would not have the experience of hearing the clock strike three. Doubtless, I would hear noises, but I would not be able to judge, "That is a clock striking three." Accordingly, the first condition of my being able to have the experience that I do have is possession of a number of empirical concepts, that is, concepts learned in experience. Though nobody, presumably, would deny that I possess such concepts, the traditional analysis does not bring this out, since it does not focus on the conditions that make experience possible.

According to Kant, of course, a priori concepts as well as empirical concepts are necessary conditions for experience. Furthermore, when these a priori concepts are taken into account, a wholly different notion of the self and its objects emerges. The next stage in Kant's analysis was designed to bring out these points. According to this analysis, when I judge, "That is a clock striking three," I am assigning an objective order to the successive strikes and am attributing them to a clock as their cause. That is, though the strikes have an order and a date in my own experience (having occurred later and earlier than other experiences of mine), they also have a public order and a public date, which I attribute to them. This, indeed, is the way I distinguish them from a dream that I might have about a clock striking. "Dreamed" strikes have an order and a date in my experience, but in recognizing them as having been dreamed I do not assign them an objective order as well.

Hence it is fair to call these three strikes an object whose cause is the clock. Of course, they are only a very simple object, consisting of three auditory sense data. Nonetheless, they are an object—for an object is precisely some set of sense experiences to which a public order and a public date are assigned. Accordingly, Kant's question can be rephrased as follows: "What is necessary for there to be an experience of an object?" In the case of the object "three strikes of a clock," what is necessary in addition to such empirical concepts as "clock" and "strike"?

It is important to see, first, that even the simplest of simple experiences contains diversity. Yet to be *an* experience, this diversity must be collected, or put together into unity. According to Kant's thesis, this putting together involves the categories—that is, nothing less than the categories are necessary to make even the experience of three strikes possible.

So much for "object"; what of "self"? Like its objects, the self is a collection —but it is a collection of desires, memories, expectations, feelings, and attitudes rather than of sense data. Moreover, though the self *is* a collection, it is not *merely* a collection. For if the self unifies the various data (in this case, the strikes) by collecting them into an object (the experience of a clock striking three), what unifies the self into the object (collection) that the self is admitted to be? The self cannot be a mere collection, for a mere collection cannot collect itself.[9] In a word, what is true of the experience of objects is equally true of the experience of self: The experience of even the simplest of simple objects (three strikes) is possible only because of the syntheses that bind the experienced diversity into unity. But the self, too, is an object. Hence the syntheses in question underlie the self just as much as they underlie its objects.

Here, then, is a plurality of noises experienced as "three strikes of a clock." According to Kant's analysis, this experience can occur only under the following conditions. To begin with, I must apprehend all three experiences as being similar.[10] This does not mean that I must identify the noises explicitly as strikes. I may do this, of course; but it is not necessary that I do so in order to experience the strikes as three. It means simply that I must discriminate these noises from other, dissimilar noises. For instance, suppose a car happened to honk its horn between the first and second strikes; I do not count the horn noise in and thus get four. Furthermore, when I get to the second strike, it is necessary, in Kant's terminology, to "reproduce" the first strike.[11] By "reproduce" Kant did not mean consciously recall; he meant merely carry over. That is, I must carry the first strike forward after it is over and combine it with the second. Since the first

9 This point was put with devastating force by F. H. Bradley: "Mr. Bain collects that the mind is a collection. Has he ever thought who collects Mr. Bain?"—*Ethical Studies* (Oxford, 1927), p. 39, n. 1.
10 Kant called this the "synthesis of apprehension in imagination."
11 This is the "synthesis of reproduction in imagination."

strike is over and done, it is fair to say that in carrying it over to the second I "reproduce" it. If I could not do this, I would begin over again and never get beyond "one, . . . one, . . . one, . . ." Then, having collected this plurality (or "manifold," as Kant called it) into a unity, I must attribute it to the clock as its cause.[12] Otherwise I might be able to count three strikes, but I would not experience, as I do, three strikes *of* a clock. That is, it is not enough that I merely collect the plurality of noises under the empirical concept "strike." I must order them in accordance with an a priori rule—in this case, a rule that assigns the strikes specific locations in objective time. I must assign the strikes that I hear to a later time than the time that I assign to what is going on in the clock (clapper tapping bell), and this time must be *objectively* later, not merely later in my personal life. Finally, for the three strikes to be unified into one experience of three strikes of a clock, there must be a self that endures at least as long as the three strikes last. If I died and were reborn a different person between the first and second strikes, I would say "one," not "two," when the second strike occurred.

In insisting on the existence of a self that unifies experience, Kant did not mean that we are conscious of the puttings together involved in experiencing an object. It is not that I have to be self-conscious and say, "Now I am hearing the first strike of a clock; now I am hearing the second strike, and I am the same I that heard the first strike"; and so forth. Even if I were self-conscious about my experience, this would be simply *another* and more complicated experience the existence of which depended on prior, nonexperienced mental operations. These "puttings together" (or "transcendental syntheses," as Kant called them) are, in fact, even more obviously the conditions of such an involved, self-conscious experience than they are the conditions of the simple awareness of "three strikes."

As has been said, the three strikes of a clock are an object—doubtless a very rudimentary object as compared with a desk, St. Peter's in Rome, or Mount Everest, but still an object. What are put together in this instance are three identical, or nearly identical, noises. In the case of a desk, a much larger manifold of visual and tactile materials is involved; in the case of Mount Everest, a still vaster assemblage. But the principle is everywhere the same. They are all objects-for-a-self. They all involve a temporal succession of data, recognized, remembered, held together in a unifying experience, and assigned an objective order and date. Furthermore, my experience, taken in its entirety, is a whole in which the striking clock, the desk, St. Peter's, and Mount Everest all have temporal and spatial loci within a unified, one-dimensional time and a unified, three-dimensional space. That is, my experience, as a whole, is one object in the sense that it is a unified structure, or order, of sensory content. My experience is, in fact, a cosmos.

So far we have been considering the knowledge situation from the object

12 This is the "synthesis of recognition in concepts."

side (the strikes); the situation is the same when looked at from the point of view of the self. If the three strikes are, as has been said, an object, they are equally states of a self. And if the object is a synthesis of data of outer sense, the self is a synthesis of data of inner sense.[13] When we look for a self we never find more than various synthesized experiences. The self and its objects are not two distinct substances confronting each other in mutual independence; they are simply two aspects of a complex situation. Looked at from one point of view, experience is a self that knows a world of objects; looked at from the opposite point of view, it is a world of objects known by a self. There is just as much self as there is object and just as much object as there is self. Self and object are correlative concepts.

Instead of hypostatizing self and its objects as independent entities, Kant held that self and objects are both ordered elements in our experience. Experience, *to be experience,* must be ordered; this was Kant's point. This order presupposes the existence of certain synthesizing activities that are not themselves experienced. Without them, the order that is found in experience, and that is an empirical fact, would not be possible. This empirical self can become as much an object of experience as can a desk or Mount Everest. But the self as object is not the underlying synthetical activities. It as much presupposes those conditions as do the desk and the mountain; it is as much made possible by them as are the desk and the mountain. Experience is an ordered manifold, and "self" and "objects" are names for elements in this manifold. The key to the nature of knowledge, then, is order (or rule, or law); this is what makes experience—including the self and its objects—possible. Without order, there is no experience and hence no self and no objects.

DEDUCTION OF THE CATEGORIES

So far, Kant has shown (providing his argument is correct) that an order of *some* sort has to be presupposed as the condition of any experience, however rudimentary. Kant next undertook to show that the world as we actually experience it—a world of relatively stable objects—reflects precisely those patterns that he called categories and that he had derived from Aristotle's twelve types of judgment. To follow Kant through the detailed deduction of all twelve categories (the "Analytic of Principles") would require much more space than can be afforded here. Let us therefore examine his procedure by considering his account of the two most important categories, substance and causality.

Kant began his deduction of these two categories with some general remarks applicable to both:

> Experience is an empirical knowledge, that is, a knowledge which determines an object through perceptions. It is a synthesis of perceptions, not

---

13 Here we are considering what Kant called the empirical self. There is also, according to Kant, a transcendental self ("the transcendental unity of apperception"), which underlies and makes possible *both* the empirical self and the objects it experiences.

contained in perception but itself containing in one consciousness the synthetic unity of the manifold of perceptions. This synthetic unity constitutes the essential in any knowledge of *objects* of the senses, that is, in experience as distinguished from mere intuition of sensation of the senses. In experience, however, perceptions come together only in accidental order, so that no necessity determining their connection is or can be revealed in the perceptions themselves. For apprehension is only a placing together of the manifold of empirical intuition; and we can find in it no representation of any necessity which determines the appearances thus combined to have connected existence in space and time. But since experience is a knowledge of objects through perceptions, the relation [involved] in the existence of the manifold has to be represented in experience, not as it comes to be constructed in time but as it exists objectively in time. Since time, however, cannot itself be perceived, the determination of the existence of objects in time can take place only through their relation in time in general, and therefore only through concepts that connect them *a priori*. Since these always carry necessity with them, it follows that experience is only possible through a representation of necessary connection of perceptions.

The three modes of time are *duration, succession,* and *coexistence*.[14] There will, therefore, be three rules of all relations of appearances in time, and these rules will be prior to all experience, and indeed make it possible. By means of these rules the existence of every appearance can be determined in respect of the unity of all time.[n]

This argument starts, once again, from two basic distinctions. First, everyone constantly distinguishes between what is subjective (for example, dreamed strikes of a clock) and what is objective (actual strikes of a clock). Of course, I may on occasion be doubtful (Is that a dagger that I see before me? Am I awake or dreaming?). On occasion I may be mistaken. But everyone makes this fundamental distinction. Furthermore, it is not a distinction between what is inside experience and what is outside experience; it is a distinction *within* experience. Both the dreamed strikes and the actual strikes are segments of the flow of my experience; the mark of objectivity is the regularity and order of those segments to which I assign the status of objects.

Second, we all distinguish, within waking experience, between the order in which we happen to experience things and the order that those things have. For instance, we distinguish between the order in which we learn something and the order of the things we have learned: Many children study American history in school before they study ancient history; as a result, they hear about George Washington before they hear about Julius Caesar. But they do not, on this account, think that Washington lived before Caesar. Rather, they assign each to a single, public, temporal order that is independent of the subjective order in which they experienced it. Again, people may on occasion make mistakes, but

14 [Coexistence is the product of the third category of relation, or "Reciprocity" (see the table of categories, p. 35). It is necessary to pass over detailed discussion of the operation of this category—AUTHOR.]

the fact that mistakes are made itself validates the distinction in principle. And this distinction too is a fundamental one: Human experience would not be human experience without the notion of an order that is indifferent to the order of actual experience.

It follows that whatever is necessary for us to be able to make these distinctions must be the case, even though it may never be possible to verify this "whatever is necessary" directly in experience. To put this differently, the empirical criterion of meaning does not apply to itself. Hume had argued that we should accept nothing that cannot be verified (that is, encountered) in experience. Kant's reply to this, in effect, was that we nonetheless may—indeed must—accept whatever is necessary for us to have experience, even though that itself is never experienced.

THE CATEGORIES OF SUBSTANCE AND CAUSALITY

According to Hume (and Kant), we never experience substances and we never experience necessary connections; we experience only succession. How then do we get the "idea" of stable, enduring entities, objects related causally to other objects? Having looked in vain for objects, Hume concluded that we "feign" them. Kant concluded that they must be attributed to a priori concepts, namely, to relational structures, or patterns—not innate ideas such as Descartes thought God had implanted in us—in terms of which our minds organize our experiences. Specifically, what we bring to experience are the notions of permanence and regular sequence. These are the categories of substance and causality. As for substance,

> . . . our *apprehension* of the manifold of appearance is always successive, and is therefore always changing. Through it alone we can never determine whether this manifold, as object of experience, is coexistent or successive. For such determination we require an underlying ground which exists *at all times*, that is, something *abiding* and *permanent*, of which all change and coexistence are only so many ways (modes of time) in which the permanent exists. And simultaneity and succession being the only relations in time, it follows that only in the permanent are relations of time possible. In other words, the permanent is the *substratum* of the empirical representation of time itself; in it alone is any determination of time possible. . . . If we ascribe succession to time itself, we must think yet another time, in which the sequence would be possible. Only through the permanent does existence in different parts of the time-series acquire a magnitude which can be entitled duration. For in bare succession existence is always vanishing and recommencing, and never has the least magnitude. Without the permanent there is therefore no time-relation. Now time cannot be perceived in itself; the permanent in the appearances is therefore the substratum of all determination of time, and, as likewise follows, is also the condition of the possibility of all synthetic unity of perceptions, that is, of experience. All existence and all change in time have thus to be viewed as simply a mode of the existence

of that which remains and persists. In all appearances the permanent is the object itself, that is, substance as phenomenon; everything, on the other hand, which changes or can change belongs only to the way in which substance or substances exist, and therefore to their determinations. . . .

Permanence is thus a necessary condition under which alone appearances are determinable as things or objects in a possible experience.°

Thus Kant replaced the metaphysical relation of "inherence," which the rationalists venerated and the empiricists ridiculed, with an empirical and temporal relation—endurance through time. A substance is not a mysterious substratum that somehow owns, or has, various attributes. A substance is a complex pattern of sensory materials[15] that are experienced as permanent. And, of course, it is the *pattern* that is permanent, not the individual materials—these are constantly changing. In addition, since substance is one of the ways in which our minds organize our experiences, it follows that there are no transcendental, supersensible substances. The only substances are those stable, relatively permanent complexes that we encounter in experience. Finally, what is necessary is *not* that a particular empirical thing be a substance; what is necessary is simply that our minds order experience substantivally. To ascertain which particular segments, or aspects, of experience are substances and which are not is a purely empirical inquiry. And there is nothing final or definitive about the results of this inquiry. All particular judgments are provisional, and future investigation may well upset present indications about the specific nature of the relatively permanent parts of experience. All we can be sure of is that, however we judge a particular matter in detail, we shall continue to organize our experience substantivally.

This conception of substance is a good example of Kantian compromise. Kant was at one with the empiricists in denying any purely rational concept; he agreed with them that "substance-attribute" must be an observable relation. On the other hand, he held Hume to be mistaken in denying that the concept of substance has any objective validity at all. Substance-attribute is an empirically observable relation precisely because it is the product of a necessary function performed by the human mind in its task of regulating and ordering the world. Like the rationalists, Kant maintained that the necessity attributed to substance is real (not illusory, as the empiricists claimed). But, like the empiricists, he held that it is a mode of human experience (not an obscure force residing in allegedly independent substances-in-themselves, as the rationalists claimed).

Kant's treatment of the problem of causality parallels his treatment of the problem of substance. In his view, not only do we attribute permanance to objects; we also attribute causality to them. That is, we believe objects to be related to one another systematically according to a rule of succession. There is a rule that relates sensory materials to one another so that they are experienced

15 For a possible modification of this view, see the discussion of ambiguities in Kant's conception of the phenomenal object, pp. 48–49.

as a complex of sensory materials enduring together through time to form one object. In addition, there is a rule that relates each of these complexes to another complex so that the former is experienced as following the latter in a regular way—that is, one is experienced as the "effect" of the other.

The apprehension of the manifold of appearance is always successive. The representations of the parts follow upon one another. Whether they also follow one another in the object is a point which calls for further reflection. . . . For instance, the apprehension of the manifold in the appearance of a house which stands before me is successive. The question then arises, whether the manifold of the house is also in itself successive. This, however, is what no one will grant. . . . That which lies in the successive apprehension is here viewed as representation, while the appearance which is given to me, notwithstanding that it is nothing but the sum of these representations, is viewed as their object. . . . The object is *that* in the appearance which contains the condition of this necessary rule of apprehension.

Let us now proceed to our problem. . . . I also note, in an appearance which contains a happening (the preceding state of the perception we may entitle A, and the succeeding B) B can be apprehended only as following upon A; the perception A cannot follow upon B but only precede it. For instance, I see a ship move down stream. My perception of its lower position follows upon the perception of its position higher up in the stream, and it is impossible that in the apprehension of this appearance the ship should first be perceived lower down in the stream and afterwards higher up. The order in which the perceptions succeed one another in apprehension is in this instance determined, and to this order apprehension is bound down. In the previous example of a house my perceptions could begin with the apprehension of the roof and end with the basement, or could begin from below and end above; and I could similarly apprehend the manifold of the empirical intuition either from right to left or from left to right. In the series of these perceptions there was thus no determinate order specifying at what point I must begin in order to connect the manifold empirically. But in the perception of an event there is always a rule that makes the order in which the perceptions (in the apprehension of this appearance) follow upon one another a *necessary* order.

In this case, therefore, we must derive the *subjective succession* of apprehension from the *objective succession* of appearances. Otherwise the order of apprehension is entirely undetermined, and does not distinguish one appearance from another. . . . The objective succession will therefore consist in that order of the manifold of appearance according to which, *in conformity with a rule*, the apprehension of that which happens follows upon the apprehension of that which precedes. Thus only can I be justified in asserting, not merely of my apprehension, but of appearance itself, that a succession is to be met with in it. This is only another way of saying that I cannot arrange the apprehension otherwise than in this very succession. . . .

Let us suppose that there is nothing antecedent to an event, upon which it must follow according to rule. All succession of perception would then be only in the apprehension, that is, would be merely subjective. . . . We should then have only a play of representations, relating to no object. . . .

If, then, we experience that something happens, we in so doing always presuppose that something precedes it, on which it follows according to a rule. Otherwise I should not say of the object that it follows. For mere succession in my apprehension, if there be no rule determining the succession in relation to something that precedes, does not justify me in assuming any succession in the object.[p]

Kant's contention, in a word, is that if there were not (1) enduring complexes and (2) succession of these complexes according to a rule, we would not experience *objects*. But we do experience objects. Therefore there must be such rules, even though they can never be directly experienced as distinct elements in the manifold of sense.

Here, as with the concept of substance, Kant proposed a compromise between the empiricists' position and the rationalists' position. He agreed with the empiricists that there is no mysterious transfer of force, no exercise of power, in the causal relation. He agreed with them also that all particular causal judgments are based on observation of actual sequences and are provisional in character. But, according to Kant, although the empiricists were correct in maintaining that there is no necessary connection between particular matters of fact, they were mistaken in concluding that the principle of causality is false. To Kant, this was just the reverse of the mistake made by the rationalists, who concluded that because the principle of causality is necessarily true, the connections between particular events are necessary. According to Kant, the principle of causality is necessarily true, but the source of its necessity (as with substance) is in the structure of our minds.

THE PHENOMENAL OBJECT

We have now reached a point of major dispute in Kantian exegesis. What did Kant mean, in the transcendental deduction, by describing the object of representation as "something in general = x"?[16] There is general agreement about what Kant did not mean. He meant neither the metaphysical substratum of the Scholastics and the rationalists nor the mere lively-expectation-based-on-association of the empiricists. This is clear from his repeated criticisms of both positions. There is also general agreement that the x in the equation involves succession according to a rule. What distinguishes an object (or "thing") from a "mere blind play of representations, even less than a dream," is, as we have seen, the fact that when we experience an object, our representations succeed one another according to a rule, not according to a private fantasy in our own mind.

The parting of the ways in Kantian interpretation comes with the question,

16 See p. 37.

"What exactly are the elements, thus ordered, that succeed one another according to a rule?" The simplest interpretation is that by "representations" Kant meant the raw data of sense experience. According to this view, the desk you and I talk of seeing is not a public object "out there" in a public space. There are, in fact, two desks, or as many desks as there are viewers, for each viewer's sense data are his private subjective experiences. What is objective and public is simply the common order in which the various private sense data occur.

There seems to be no doubt that a great deal of the time Kant did think in terms of this relatively subjectivist point of view. There is also no doubt that he wanted to insist on more objectivity than this view permits. Kant was not particularly concerned by the fact that, according to the subjectivist view, an object is not at all what you and I uncritically suppose it to be. But he was concerned by the fact that, according to the subjectivist view, the object is not what Newtonian science supposes it to be—namely, objectively existing matter in motion.

As has been said, Kant wanted to show not merely that there is some order, or pattern, in experience (succession according to a rule) but that the rules according to which experience is ordered are those presupposed by Newtonian physics. Thus it is not surprising to find that the subjectivist view did not really satisfy him. In fact, he presents in the deduction, along with this view and by no means clearly distinguished from it, a much more complicated view in which the x involves not merely sense-data-according-to-a-rule but what Kant called a "phenomenal object." Because phenomenal objects (Newtonian matter in motion) are spatially and temporally organized, they are, like the sense data, modes of appearance.[17] But they are also supposed, by both common sense and natural science, to be the *causes* of the ordered sense data (which constitute the whole of appearance, according to the subjectivist view). The difficulty with this view is not merely that the phenomenal object complicates the picture and occupies an anomalous place between things-in-themselves and representations. The fundamental difficulty is that, according to Kantian principles, the phenomenal object itself must be a synthesis of representations. But if it is, it cannot be the cause of the representations in question. This would amount to supposing it to be the product of that of which it is the cause.[18]

SUMMARY

This discussion of the categories has brought us to a conclusion that parallels the conclusion drawn earlier about Kant's view of Euclidean geometry. As we

17 See pp. 31–32.
18 This difficulty has been put very effectively by T. D. Weldon in *Kant's Critique of Pure Reason* (Oxford, 1947), p. 25. According to the view in question, "it would appear that there must be perception to give material for synthesis before there can be perception caused by synthesized objects. In other words, something must happen before it happens, which is certainly rather peculiar."

have seen, Kant did not show that such-and-such a type of order (Euclidean for space, Newtonian for things) is a priori, but he did show that *some* order is necessary for there to be any experience at all. This conclusion will not be acceptable to those who insist (as Kant did) on the possibility of a rational knowledge of nature. The great tradition in the West has been strongly rationalistic; it will be a matter of concern to many people, therefore, that even Kant's modified, watered-down rationalism failed. On the other hand, those who accept the pragmatic point of view of modern science will hold that the full deduction was simply so much wasted motion and that it has only an antiquarian interest. The prevalent view today, indeed, is not merely that the Newtonian concepts are not a priori, but that *no* scientific concepts are ever more than provisional and hypothetical in character, and that their function is merely to provide principles for ordering experience.

But rejection of the second stage in Kant's argument (in which he tried to deduce the specific categories) does not mean that the first stage of the deduction (in which he formulated the new relation between the self and its objects) was inconsequential. In the first place, it enabled Kant to provide an intelligible basis for inductive inference and to show that only a dogmatic empiricism need end in scepticism. The root of the trouble was not empiricism; it was the assumption that only what is given in sensation is real. In Kant's view, the starting point of a true empiricism must be the empirical fact that men experience connections between matters of fact, for example, "objects." Since the connections are real, the conditions that make them possible must also be real, even though they are not themselves encountered, or verified, in experience.

Kant understood that it was fatal to assume that in the knowledge situation an independently existing self confronts an independently existing object. For one logical consequence of this assumption is that the self knows only its own states—but, indeed, it cannot know even these. Something is radically wrong with premises that lead to such a conclusion. Here again, according to Kant, the critical starting point must be the fact of experience. Self and its objects can be seen to grow out of, or to be formed in, experience. There must be self (in some sense) for there to be any experience at all; there must be experience for there to be any self at all. But self is not a content, not a thing. It is a form of unity. No wonder, if self is not a thing, that the empiricists could not find it, and that they became sceptical as they searched for it in vain. Having asked themselves the wrong questions, they naturally failed to get the right answers. By pointing out the right questions, Kant provided the basis for a philosophy of science that could be as radically empirical as it liked without contradicting itself the moment it opened its mouth.

In addition to rehabilitating empiricism, the deduction provided a devastating criticism of the pretensions of rationalism: "Concepts without percepts are empty." In Kant's view, the real function of all those concepts by means of which the rationalists had sought to explore and interpret a supersensuous metaphysical reality is to organize the manifold of sense into meaningful and stable patterns.

The concepts of substance, causality, and the rest are meaningless except as synthetical relationships within the spatiotemporal manifold. The very arguments that validate these concepts *for* experience limit them *to* experience. The result of their misapplication beyond experience is "transcendental illusion."

It follows that the answer to Kant's third main question—"Are synthetical a priori judgments possible in metaphysics?"—is negative. This general conclusion is obvious once the nature of the deduction has been grasped. But because metaphysical thinking had such a grip on men's minds in his day, Kant devoted many pages to an exhaustive demonstration of the principal fallacies of rationalistic metaphysics.

Critique of Rationalistic Metaphysics

Kant proposed to show that in each of the three main areas of rationalistic speculation—self, being-in-general, and God—the rationalists were involved in an illegitimate attempt to apply the categories to things-in-themselves.

THE SELF

As regards the self, the subject of study in rationalistic psychology,

> . . . since the proposition "I think" (taken problematically) contains the form of each and every judgment of understanding and accompanies all categories as their vehicle, it is evident that the inferences from it admit only of a transcendental employment of the understanding. . . . We therefore propose to follow it, with a critical eye, through all the predicaments of pure psychology. . . .
>
> (1) In all judgments I am the *determining* subject of that relation which constitutes the judgment. That the "I," the "I" that thinks, can be regarded always as *subject*, and as something which does not belong to thought as a mere predicate, must be granted. It is an apodeictic and indeed *identical* proposition; but it does not mean that I, as *object*, am for myself a *self-subsistent* being or *substance*. . . .
>
> (2) That the "I" of apperception, and therefore the "I" in every act of thought, is *one*, and cannot be resolved into a plurality of subjects, and consequently signifies a logically simple subject, is something already contained in the very concept of thought. . . . But this does not mean that the thinking "I" is a simple *substance*. . . .
>
> The analysis, then, of the consciousness of myself in thought in general, yields nothing whatsoever towards the knowledge of myself as object. The logical exposition of thought in general has been mistaken for a metaphysical determination of the object. . . .
>
> The whole procedure of rational psychology is determined by a paralogism, which is exhibited in the following syllogism:

That which cannot be thought otherwise than as subject does not exist otherwise than as subject, and is therefore substance.

A thinking being, considered merely as such, cannot be thought otherwise than as subject.

Therefore it exists also only as subject, that is, as substance.

In the major premiss we speak of a being that can be thought in general, in every relation, and therefore also as it may be given in intuition. But in the minor premiss we speak of it only in so far as it regards itself, as subject, simply in relation to thought and the unity of consciousness, and not as likewise in relation to the intuition through which it is given as object to thought. Thus the conclusion is arrived at fallaciously.[q]

This fallacy, called "the fallacy of four terms," occurs, in an obvious way, in the following argument:

All Greeks live in the Balkan peninsula
Kant's argument is Greek to me

Therefore Kant's argument lives in the Balkan peninsula

Since the term "Greek" is used in different senses in the two premises, the argument has four terms, not three. There is only a verbal link between "Kant's argument" and "Balkan peninsula," and hence no conclusion can be drawn.

According to Kant, the rationalists' argument about the self depends on exactly the same sort of ambiguity: "'Thought' is taken in . . . two . . . totally different senses: in the major premiss, as relating to an object in general and therefore to an object as it may be given in intuition; in the minor premiss, only as it consists in relation to self-consciousness. In this latter sense, no object whatsoever is being thought; all that is being represented is simply the relation to self as subject (as the form of thought)."[r] To put this in a slightly different way, the rationalists' argument depends on an ambiguity in the term "self" (or "I"). For there are, according to Kant, two kinds of self: the empirical self and the transcendental self. The rationalists' argument confuses them in the same way that the argument in the example above confuses two different kinds of "Greek." That there are two different kinds of self follows from the basic thesis of the *Critique*—that transcendental conditions, which are not themselves experienced, must nevertheless be presupposed to underlie our experience of objects.

Now, the term "self" can be used to designate one type of entity encountered in experience—for example, the object that is just now sitting at the desk, reading about Mount Everest, and listening to the clock strike three. This is the empirical self; it is no more and no less an object than is any other thing in experience. The categories apply to it; indeed, they are the a priori conditions of experiencing it. But they apply to it with the same sort of purely empirical relevance with which they apply to "desk," "clock striking," or "Everest." The empirical self is just as much an object for scientific study—and in just the same sense—as is any other empirical object. Its behavior follows according to a rule; it no more exercises a mysterious metaphysical energy than does the desk.

On the other hand, there are the transcendental conditions, the synthetical operations, that accompany and make possible all this empirical experience. Because the rationalists did not clearly distinguish these conditions from the empirical self, they designated them by the term "self." Yet, as Kant believed he had demonstrated in the *Critique,* these transcendental syntheses are very different from the empirical self. They are not objects; rather, they are conditions of there being any objects at all—including the empirical self. They are forms, functions of unity. Since the categories apply only to a sensuous content, the notion that these operations are substances and causes is complete nonsense. Hence questions that can arise only in connection with synthesized data ("Is the self divisible or simple?" "Is it permanent or impermanent?") have no meaning when applied to the "I think." No wonder contradictions arise.

It is evident that this argument does two things at once: It demolishes the pretensions of the old rationalistic a priori psychology and lays the basis for a new and thoroughly empirical psychology. There is a third consequence that is even more important: It follows that we never have, and never can have, direct awareness (intuition) of the self. Of the self viewed as the transcendental conditions underlying experience we have no experience at all. This self lies wholly beyond experience. Of the empirical self we do have experience, but, like our experience of every other object, this experience is not direct. It is mediated by space, time, and the categories. During the nineteenth and twentieth centuries, a dispute arose among philosophers over whether or not to accept this conclusion of Kant's. Although some philosophers willingly adjusted to it, most sought to escape from it. For the culture of the past two centuries has been increasingly dominated by a profound feeling of alienation, a sense of being forever at a distance from that with which one longs, deeply and passionately, to be identified. This was one of the consequences to which Kantianism seemed to lead.

BEING-IN-GENERAL

Next, Kant turned his attention to being-in-general, the principal topic of inquiry in the traditional, rationalistic metaphysics. Kant considered four theses of rationalistic metaphysics and showed each of them to be contradicted by an antithesis. He argued that, since *both* thesis and antithesis can be proved, the attempt to know being-in-general is illegitimate and knowledge is limited to the ordered spatiotemporal manifold of experience. The four theses and their antitheses are as follows:

Thesis	*Antithesis*
(1) The world has a beginning in time, and is also limited as regards space.	(1) The world has no beginning, and no limits in space; it is infinite as regards both time and space.

	Thesis		*Antithesis*
(2)	Every composite substance in the world is made up of simple parts, and nothing anywhere exists save the simple or what is composed of the simple.	(2)	No composite thing in the world is made up of simple parts, and there nowhere exists in the world anything simple.
(3)	Causality in accordance with laws of nature is not the only causality from which the appearances of the world can one and all be derived. To explain these appearances it is necessary to assume that there is also another causality, that of freedom.	(3)	There is no freedom; everything in the world takes place solely in accordance with laws of nature.
(4)	There belongs to the world, either as its part or as its cause, a being that is absolutely necessary.	(4)	An absolutely necessary being nowhere exists in the world, nor does it exist outside the world as its cause.[s]

The position taken in the antitheses (reflecting the empirical-scientific point of view) has whatever backing is to be derived from sticking close to verifiable facts and "never [taking] leave of the natural order." On the other hand, the position taken in the theses gains powerful support from

> . . . a certain *practical interest* in which every right-thinking man, if he has understanding of what truly concerns him, heartily shares. That the world has a beginning, that my thinking self is of simple and therefore indestructible nature, that it is free in its voluntary actions and raised above the compulsion of nature, and finally that all order in the things constituting the world is due to a primordial being, from which everything derives its unity and purposive connection—these are so many foundation stones of morals and religion. The antithesis robs us of all these supports, or at least appears to do so. . . .
>
> If there is no primordial being distinct from the world, if the world is without beginning and therefore without an Author, if our will is not free, and the soul is divisible and perishable like matter, *moral* ideas and principles lose all validity, and share in the fate of the *transcendental* ideas which served as their theoretical support.[t]

But questions of fact are decided by consideration of facts. Since the questions raised in the theses and antitheses are factual questions (and both the rationalists and the empiricists would have considered them to be such), the empiricists' case is correct—at least in its criticism of the claims of the rationalists to have positive knowledge of first causes, free wills, and so on. The trouble with the empiricists, Kant thought, was that they proceeded to make positive claims as dogmatic in their own way as those of the rationalists.

If the empirical philosopher had no other purpose in propounding his antithesis than to subdue the rashness and presumption of . . . [the rationalist], his principle would be a maxim urging moderation in our pretensions, modesty in our assertions, and yet at the same time the greatest possible extension of our understanding, through the teacher fittingly assigned to us, namely, through experience. If such were our procedure, we should not be cut off from employing intellectual *presuppositions* and *faith* on behalf of our practical interest; only they could never be permitted to assume the title and dignity of science and rational insight. . . .

But when empiricism itself, as frequently happens, becomes dogmatic in its attitude towards ideas, and confidently denies whatever lies beyond the sphere of its intuitive knowledge, it betrays the same lack of modesty; and this is all the more reprehensible owing to the irreparable injury which is thereby caused to the practical interests of reason.[u]

According to Kant, then, it is just as much a mistake to say there is no first cause as to say there is a first cause. All four of the theses and antitheses concern the totality, the whole. But the whole is not, and cannot be, an *object* of experience (for all objects are inside experience). The categories, therefore, do not apply to it. Hence questions about the nature of the whole—for instance, what sort of cause the whole is—are literally nonsense. Cause, as we have seen, is a category; it is a concept that has application only within experience. As long as the empiricists stuck to this, they were on firm ground, for there is no first (or free) cause in experience. Similarly, we can be sure we shall never come to the end of experience. But to infer from these truths that the world as a whole is an infinite, meaningless mechanism is illegitimate—just as illegitimate as it is to argue that the world has, or is, a free cause.

Kant's discussion of first causes and necessary beings in itself casts doubt on the rationalists' claims that a science of God is possible. Kant, however, devoted a special section to a criticism of the traditional arguments for the existence of God.

GOD

According to Kant, there are "only three possible ways of proving the existence of God by means of speculative reason." These are the *ontological,* the *cosmological,* and the *physico-theological* proofs. Kant attempted to show that all these arguments are invalid, and that, accordingly, a science of God (that is, rationalistic theology) is as impossible as is a science of totality or of pure self.

The first alleged proof of the existence of God is the ontological argument.

In all ages men have spoken of an *absolutely necessary* being, and in so doing have endeavoured, not so much to understand whether and how a thing of this kind allows even of being thought, but rather to prove its existence. There is, of course, no difficulty in giving a verbal definition of the concept, namely, that it is something the non-existence of which is impossible. But this yields no insight into the conditions which make it necessary to regard the non-existence of a thing as absolutely unthinkable. . . .

All the alleged examples are, without exception, taken from *judgments*, not from *things* and their existence. But the unconditioned necessity of judgments is not the same as an absolute necessity of things. The absolute necessity of the judgment is only a conditioned necessity of the thing, or of the predicate in the judgment. The [mathematical] proposition does not declare that three angles are absolutely necessary, but that, under the condition that there is a triangle (that is, that a triangle is given), three angles will necessarily be found in it. . . .

If, in an identical proposition, I reject the predicate while retaining the subject, contradiction results; and I therefore say that the former belongs necessarily to the latter. But if we reject subject and predicate alike, there is no contradiction; for nothing is then left that can be contradicted. To posit a triangle, and yet to reject its three angles, is self-contradictory; but there is no contradiction in rejecting the triangle together with its three angles. The same holds true of the concept of an absolutely necessary being. If its existence is rejected, we reject the thing itself with all its predicates; and no question of contradiction can then arise. . . . "God is omnipotent" is a necessary judgment. The omnipotence cannot be rejected if we posit a Deity, that is, an infinite being; for the two concepts are identical. But if we say, "There is no God," neither the omnipotence nor any other of its predicates is given; they are one and all rejected together with the subject, and there is therefore not the least contradiction in such a judgment. . . .

If . . . we admit, as every reasonable person must, that all existential propositions are synthetic, how can we profess to maintain that the predicate of existence cannot be rejected without contradiction? This is a feature which is found only in analytic propositions, and is indeed precisely what constitutes their analytic character. . . .

"Being" is obviously not a real predicate; that is, it is not a concept of something which could be added to the concept of a thing. It is merely the positing of a thing, or of certain determinations, as existing in themselves. Logically, it is merely the copula of a judgment. The proposition, "God is omnipotent," contains two concepts, each of which has its object—God and omnipotence. The small word "is" adds no new predicate, but only serves to posit the predicate *in its relation* to the subject. If, now, we take the subject (God) with all its predicates (among which is omnipotence), and say "God is," or "There is a God," we attach no new predicate to the concept of God, but only posit the subject in itself with all its predicates. . . . A hundred real thalers do not contain the least coin more than a hundred possible thalers. For as the latter signify the concept, and the former the object and the positing of the object, should the former contain more than the latter, my concept would not, in that case, express the whole object, and would not therefore be an adequate concept of it. My financial position is, however, affected very differently by a hundred real thalers than it is by the mere concept of them . . . ; yet the conceived hundred thalers are not themselves in the least increased through thus acquiring existence outside my concept.

By whatever and by however many predicates we may think a thing—even if we completely determine it—we do not make the least addition to the thing when we further declare that this thing *is*. Otherwise, it would not be exactly the same thing that exists, but something more than we had thought in the concept; and we could not, therefore, say that the exact object of my concept exists. . . .

The attempt to establish the existence of a supreme being by means of the famous ontological argument of Descartes is therefore merely so much labour and effort lost; we can no more extend our stock of [theoretical] insight by mere ideas, than a merchant can better his position by adding a few noughts to his cash account.[v]

The second argument is the cosmological proof.

It runs thus: If anything exists, an absolutely necessary being must also exist. Now I, at least, exist. Therefore an absolutely necessary being exists. The minor premiss contains an experience, the major premiss the inference from there being any experience at all to the existence of the necessary. . . .

In order to lay a secure foundation for itself, this proof takes its stand on experience, and thereby makes profession of being distinct from the ontological proof, which puts its entire trust in pure *a priori* concepts. But the cosmological proof uses this experience only for a single step in the argument, namely, to conclude the existence of a necessary being. What properties this being may have, the empirical premiss cannot tell us. Reason therefore abandons experience altogether, and endeavours to discover from mere concepts what properties an absolutely necessary being must have. . . . Thus the so-called cosmological proof really owes any cogency which it may have to the ontological proof from mere concepts. . . .

[Moreover] in this cosmological argument there lies hidden a whole nest of dialectical assumptions, which the transcendental critique can easily detect and destroy. . . .

We find, for instance, (1) the transcendental principle whereby from the contingent we infer a cause. This principle is applicable only in the sensible world; outside that world it has no meaning whatsoever. . . . The principle of causality has no meaning and no criterion for its application save only in the sensible world. But in the cosmological proof it is precisely in order to enable us to advance beyond the sensible world that it is employed. (2) The inference to a first cause, from the impossibility of an infinite series of causes, given one after the other, in the sensible world. The principles of the employment of reason do not justify this conclusion even within the world of experience, still less beyond this world in a realm into which this series can never be extended.[w]

The third proof is the argument from design, which Hume had already submitted to a devastating criticism. Kant called this the "physico-theological" proof.

This proof always deserves to be mentioned with respect. It is the oldest, the clearest, and the best suited to ordinary human reason. . . .

The chief points . . . are as follows: (1) In the world we everywhere find clear signs of an order in accordance with a determinate purpose, carried out with great wisdom; and this in a universe which is indescribably varied in content and unlimited in extent. (2) . . . the diverse things could not of themselves have co-operated, by so great a combination of diverse means, to the fulfilment of determinate final purposes, had they not been chosen and designed for these purposes by an ordering rational principle in conformity with underlying ideas. (3) There exists, therefore, a sublime and wise cause (or more than one) . . . of the world. . . . (4) The unity of this cause may be inferred from the unity of the reciprocal relations existing between the parts of the world, as members of an artfully arranged structure—inferred with certainty in so far as our observation suffices for its verification, and beyond these limits with probability, in accordance with the principles of analogy. . . .

On this method of argument, the purposiveness and harmonious adaptation of so much in nature can suffice to prove the contingency of the form merely, not of the matter, that is, not of the substance in the world. To prove the latter we should have to demonstrate that the things in the world would not of themselves be capable of such order and harmony, in accordance with universal laws, if they were not *in their substance* the product of supreme wisdom. But to prove this we should require quite other grounds of proof than those which are derived from the analogy with human art. The utmost, therefore, that the argument can prove is an *architect* of the world who is always very much hampered by the adaptability of the material in which he works, not a *creator* of the world to whose idea everything is subject. This, however, is altogether inadequate to the lofty purpose which we have before our eyes, namely, the proof of an all-sufficient primordial being.[x]

Thus examination of typical metaphysical assertions about the self, about the universe as a whole, and about God, and of the arguments by which the rationalists sought to sustain them, confirmed for Kant the general conclusion he had reached by a consideration of the nature of the categories as ordering principles—namely, that knowledge is limited to the spatiotemporal realm that the categories order. It therefore seemed to Kant that a science of metaphysics, of a realm of being that transcends the spatiotemporal, is clearly impossible.

Regulative Use of Reason

Are we then to conclude, as the empiricists did, that the concepts of God, self, and totality are vain and chimerical illusions? If we do so, we fly in the face of those practical interests that Kant considered to be the foundations of morality and religion. Moreover, it would be difficult to see how men ever came to accept these concepts in the first place, or why such concepts have survived so long and despite all criticism.

Since Kant held that nothing in nature is "in vain," he believed that these concepts, too, have a use. As a matter of fact, in his critique of rationalistic metaphysics he did not attack the concepts themselves. He merely pointed out that the rationalists misused them. The rationalists went wrong, first, in supposing that self, God, and totality are *objects* like desk or Mount Everest, and, second, in trying to cognize them by means of the categories, which are appropriate only to the interpretation of objects. The question therefore is, "What constitutes a legitimate employment of such concepts as God, self, and totality?"

Whatever the use of these concepts proves to be, it must be within the limits of, or in connection with, experience. Now the function of most concepts is to organize experience. Suppose we are social anthropologists making a statistical survey of a certain community. We set up various classificatory systems—male, female, high-school graduate, college graduate, and so on—and proceed to interpret our data in terms of these concepts. Some concepts, however, instead of functioning in the direct classification of experience, serve as maxims that guide us in the business of classifying. Occam's razor[19] is an example; so is the maxim, just cited, that nothing in nature is in vain. Kant called this function the regulative use of concepts, since concepts thus employed "regulate" our use of concepts in ordinary ways.

> Everything that has its basis in the nature of our powers must be appropriate to, and consistent with their right employment—if only we can guard against a certain misunderstanding and so can discover the proper direction of these powers. We are entitled, therefore, to suppose that transcendental ideas . . . have an excellent, and indeed indispensably necessary, regulative employment, namely, that of directing the understanding towards a certain goal upon which the routes marked out by all its rules converge, as upon their point of intersection. This point is indeed a mere idea, a *focus imaginarius*, from which, since it lies quite outside the bounds of possible experience, the concepts of the understanding do not in reality proceed; none the less it serves to give to these concepts the greatest [possible] unity combined with the greatest [possible] extension. Hence arises the illusion that the lines have their source in a real object lying outside the field of empirically possible knowledge—just as objects reflected in a mirror are seen as behind it. . . .
>
> We may illustrate this by an instance of the employment of reason. . . . At the start we have to assume just as many different powers as there are different effects. For instance, in the human mind we have sensation, consciousness, imagination, memory, wit, power of discrimination, pleasure, desire, etc. Now there is a logical maxim which requires that we should reduce, so far as may be possible, this seeming diversity, by comparing these

---

19 William of Occam, a fourteenth-century Franciscan, formulated the maxim that entities should not be multiplied beyond necessity—that is, when we are presented with two hypotheses, both of which account for a given fact, we should give preference to the simpler of the two.

with one another and detecting their hidden identity. . . . Though logic is not capable of deciding whether a *fundamental power* actually exists, the idea of such a power is the problem involved in a systematic representation of the multiplicity of powers. The logical principle of reason calls upon us to bring about such unity as completely as possible. . . .

Chemists have sought, step by step, to reduce the different kinds of earths (the material of stones and even of metals) to three, and at last to two; but, not content with this, they are unable to banish the thought that behind these varieties there is but one genus, nay, that there may even be a common principle for the earths and the salts. . . .

The logical principle of genera, which postulates identity, is balanced by another principle, namely, that of *species*, which calls for manifoldness and diversity in things, notwithstanding their agreement as coming under the same genus, and which prescribes to the understanding that it attend to the diversity no less than to the identity. . . .

This law of specification cannot be derived from experience, which can never open to our view any such extensive prospects. Empirical specification soon comes to a stop in the distinction of the manifold, if it be not guided by the antecedent transcendental law of specification, which, as a principle of reason, leads us to seek always for further differences, and to suspect their existence even when the senses are unable to disclose them. . . .

Reason thus prepares the field for the understanding: (1) through a principle of the *homogeneity* of the manifold under higher genera; (2) through a principle of the *variety* of the homogeneous under lower species; and (3) in order to complete the systematic unity, a further law, that of the *affinity* of all concepts—a law which prescribes that we proceed from each species to every other by gradual increase in the diversity. These we may entitle the principles of *homogeneity, specification,* and *continuity* of forms. . . .

The first law . . . keeps us from resting satisfied with an excessive number of different original genera, and bids us pay due regard to homogeneity; the second, in turn, imposes a check upon this tendency towards unity, and insists that before we proceed to apply a universal concept to individuals we distinguish subspecies within it. The third law combines these two laws by prescribing that even amidst the utmost manifoldness we observe homogeneity in the gradual transition from one species to another, and thus recognise a relationship of the different branches, as all springing from the same stem.[y]

GOD, SELF, AND TOTALITY AS REGULATIVE CONCEPTS

Kant next applied the notion of the regulative use of concepts to the ideas of God, self, and totality. That is, he showed how these three ideas function as important regulative maxims in scientific inquiry:

There is a great difference between something being given to my reason as an *object absolutely*, or merely as an *object in the idea*. In the former case our concepts are employed to determine the object; in the latter case there is in fact only a schema for which no object, not even a hypothetical one, is directly given, and which only enables us to represent to ourselves other objects in an indirect manner, namely in their systematic unity, by means of their relation to this idea. Thus I say that the concept of a highest intelligence is a mere idea, that is to say, its objective reality is not to be taken as consisting in its referring directly to an object (for in that sense we should not be able to justify its objective validity). It is only a schema constructed in accordance with the conditions of the greatest possible unity of reason—the schema of the concept of a thing in general, which serves only to secure the greatest possible systematic unity in the empirical employment of our reason. . . . We declare, for instance, that the things of the world must be viewed *as if* they received their existence from a highest intelligence. The idea is thus really only a heuristic, not an ostensive concept. It does not show us how an object is constituted, but how, under its guidance, we should *seek* to determine the constitution and connection of the objects of experience. If, then, it can be shown that the three transcendental ideas (the psychological, the cosmological, and the theological), although they do not directly relate to, or determine, any object corresponding to them, none the less, as rules of the empirical employment of reason, lead us to systematic unity, under the presupposition of such an *object in the idea;* and that they thus contribute to the extension of empirical knowledge, without ever being in a position to run counter to it, we may conclude that it is a necessary maxim of reason to proceed always in accordance with such ideas. This, indeed, is the transcendental deduction of all ideas of speculative reason, not as *constitutive* principles for the extension of our knowledge to more objects than experience can give, but as *regulative* principles of the systematic unity of the manifold of empirical knowledge in general, whereby this empirical knowledge is more adequately secured within its own limits and more effectively improved than would be possible, in the absence of such ideas, through the employment merely of the principles of the understanding.

I shall endeavour to make this clearer. . . .

The first [regulative] idea is the "I" itself, viewed simply as thinking nature or soul . . . ; in a word, the idea of a simple self-subsisting intelligence. Yet [reason] has nothing in view save principles of systematic unity in the explanation of the appearances of the soul. It is endeavouring to represent all determinations as existing in a single subject, all powers, so far as possible, as derived from a single fundamental power, all change as belonging to the states of one and the same permanent being, and all *appearances* in space as completely different from the actions of *thought*. The simplicity and other properties of substance are intended to be only the schema of this regulative principle, and are not presupposed as being the actual ground of the properties of the soul. For these may rest on altogether different grounds, of which we can know nothing. . . .

The second regulative idea of merely speculative reason is the concept of the world in general. . . . The absolute totality of the series of . . . conditions . . . is an idea which can never be completely realised in the empirical employment of reason, but which yet serves as a rule that prescribes how we ought to proceed in dealing with such series, namely, that in explaining

appearances, whether in their regressive or in their ascending order, we ought
to treat the series *as if* it were in itself infinite, that is, *as if* it proceeded
in indefinitum. . . . All this shows that the cosmological ideas are nothing
but simply regulative principles, and are very far from positing, in the manner
of constitutive principles, an actual totality of such series. . . .

The third idea of pure reason, which contains a merely relative supposition
of a being that is the sole and sufficient cause of all cosmological series, is
the idea of *God*. We have not the slightest ground to assume in an absolute
manner (to suppose in itself) the object of this idea. . . . It becomes evident
that the idea of such a being, like all speculative ideas, seeks only to formulate
the command of reason, that all connection in the world be viewed in
accordance with the principles of a systematic unity—*as if* all such connection
had its source in one single all-embracing being, as the supreme and all-
sufficient cause. It is thus evident that reason has here no other purpose than
to prescribe its own formal rule for the extension of its empirical employment,
and not any extension *beyond all limits of empirical employment.*[z]

This conception of a regulative principle was one of the most suggestive
notions in Kant's philosophy. It enabled him, while sticking to his emphasis on
verification and empirical meaning, to do justice (as a Humian empiricist could
not) to those deep urgings to transcend experience, to seek a totality, and to
find a necessary being that are so persistent a part of the human constitution.
One of the strengths of Kant's position, and one of the marks of his greatness,
was his refusal to write off any of the really persistent questions. Nothing would
be easier than to work out a philosophy that solved these problems by shouting
"Nonsense!" at them. But the persistent questions have a way of returning to
plague those who ignore them.

The point here is not that Kant was able to give an account of God, self, and
totality that would seem correct to everyone but that instead of writing them
off as whimsical survivals of an age of superstition, he recognized that an account
of them had to be given. Obviously, people who like to think in anthropomorphic
or imagistic terms will not be satisfied with Kant's account. Kant's reply to them
would have to have been that if one lives at an imagistic level one is not likely
to be concerned about the metaphysical and philosophical paradoxes that hypo-
statization involves.[20] But the fact that one does not recognize difficulties does
not mean that difficulties do not exist. As long as these concepts are thought
of as constitutive of objects, the difficulties remain; if they are taken as regulative
maxims, the difficulties vanish. Those basic urgings directed toward totality and
transcendence may not have the kind of object that literal-minded people (and
rationalistic philosophers) think of—a nonempirical, supernatural object. Nevertheless, they *do* have an empirical object, not in the sense of being directed toward
some particular concrete thing, but in the sense of performing an integral function
in ordinary, empirical knowing. Far from being inconsistent with a scientific view
of the world, they in fact complement it.

20 For further discussion of this problem, see p. 329.

THINGS-IN-THEMSELVES

The concept of thing-in-itself, or "noumenon," as Kant also called it, is a further complication of his view.[21] As we have seen, in Kant's view, all experience is of a spatiotemporal manifold, and space and time are simply forms of the human mode of perception. They are the basic ways in which our minds perceive things. It seems to follow that things have a nature in their own right, though it also follows that we can never have the remotest idea of what such things are like. Some other type of mind, one not limited to knowledge based on sensuous awareness, might know things as they really are. But we, obviously, cannot.

That we are forever excluded from knowledge of noumena is clearly the conclusion to be drawn from Kant's epistemology. Part of the time Kant understood this. At such times he pointed out that noumena are "unknowable" and "problematic," that they are "merely limiting concepts":

> At the very outset, . . . an ambiguity . . . may occasion serious misapprehension. The understanding, when it entitles an object in a [certain] relation mere phenomenon, at the same time forms, apart from that relation, a representation of an *object in itself*, and so comes to represent itself as also being able to form *concepts* of such objects. And since the understanding yields no concepts additional to the categories, it also supposes that the object in itself must at least be *thought* through these pure concepts, and so is misled into treating the entirely *indeterminate* concept of an intelligible entity, namely, of a something in general outside our sensibility, as being a *determinate* concept of an entity that allows of being known in a certain [purely intelligible] manner by means of the understanding.
>
> If by "noumenon" we mean a thing so far as it is *not an object of our sensible intuition*, and so abstract from our mode of intuiting it, this is a noumenon in the *negative* sense of the term. But if we understand by it an *object* of a *non-sensible intuition*, we thereby presuppose a special mode of intuition, namely, the intellectual, which is not that which we possess, and of which we cannot comprehend even the possibility. This would be "noumenon" in the *positive* sense of the term. . . .
>
> Since, however, such a type of intuition, intellectual intuition, forms no part whatsoever of our faculty of knowledge, it follows that the employment of the categories can never extend further than to the objects of experience. Doubtless, indeed, there are intelligible entities corresponding to the sensible entities; there may also be intelligible entities to which our sensible faculty of intuition has no relation whatsoever; but our concepts of understanding, being mere forms of thought for our sensible intuition, could not in the least apply to them. That, therefore, which we entitle "noumenon" must be understood as being such only in a *negative* sense. . . .
>
> If the objective reality of a concept cannot be in any way known, while yet the concept contains no contradiction and also at the same time is

---

21 The question of the exact relation between noumena and things-in-themselves, and of whether Kant intended to identify them, has been much debated by Kantian scholars.

connected with other modes of knowledge that involve given concepts which it serves to limit, I entitle that concept problematic. The concept of a *noumenon*—that is, of a thing which is not to be thought as object of the senses but as a thing in itself, solely through a pure understanding—is not in any way contradictory. For we cannot assert of sensibility that it is the sole possible kind of intuition. Further, the concept of a noumenon is necessary, to prevent sensible intuition from being extended to things in themselves, and thus to limit the objective validity of sensible knowledge. The remaining things, to which it does not apply, are entitled noumena, in order to show that this knowledge cannot extend its domain over everything which the understanding thinks. But none the less we are unable to comprehend how such noumena can be possible, and the domain that lies out beyond the sphere of appearances is for us empty. That is to say, we have an understanding which *problematically* extends further, but we have no intuition, indeed not even the concept of a possible intuition, through which objects outside the field of sensibility can be given, and through which the understanding can be employed *assertorically* beyond that field. The concept of a noumenon is thus a merely *limiting concept,* the function of which is to curb the pretensions of sensibility; and it is therefore only of negative employment. At the same time it is no arbitrary invention; it is bound up with the limitation of sensibility, though it cannot affirm anything positive beyond the field of sensibility. . . .

If the concept of a noumenon be taken in a merely problematic sense, it is not only admissible, but as setting limits to sensibility is likewise indispensable.[a]

This interpretation of noumena is consistent with the basic theses of the *Critique.* From this point of view, the concept of noumenon (thing-in-itself) is simply another regulative idea—a *focus imaginarius* for each individual thing (desk, Mount Everest, "I"), just as the concept of totality is a *focus imaginarius* for the pursuit of scientific truth.

Unfortunately, side by side with this view of noumena as regulative principles there is another and much less critical[22] conception. The truth is that Kant often lapsed into thinking of noumena as objects that exercise a causal efficacy in the phenomenal world. This application of the categories of substance and causality is, of course, quite as illegitimate as any of the applications that Kant himself criticized in discussing rationalistic metaphysics. Like everyone else, Kant had begun from the traditional Cartesian substantival dualism; here is a vestigial remnant of that way of thought, from which he had not been wholly able to free himself. Noumenal self and noumenal object (taken as things, not as regulative, or "limiting," concepts) are the two substances of Cartesianism with the new critical conception of the "Analytic" suspended between them.

22 Since Kant called his book a *Critique,* it is convenient to use the term "criticism" (or "the critical philosophy") to refer to his views, especially to those features of his thought that were consistent with the innovative insights of his theory of knowledge.

Facts and Values

As we have seen, one of the two main objects of Kant's philosophy was to justify, in the face of Humian scepticism, the claims of science to have real knowledge of matters of fact. The other main object was to justify traditional religious and moral insights against the scientific view of the world as a purposeless mechanism. Kant believed he had accomplished these two seemingly antithetical aims by his account of the nature of knowledge. According to Kant's interpretation, knowledge is possible just because it consists in recognizing an order projected into a sensuous manifold by certain synthetical mental acts. Knowledge in the scientific sense is *guaranteed* by the fact that it is *limited* to the spatiotemporal manifold. It is necessary only to point out that God and the self are not spatiotemporal in order to see that the conclusions of science have absolutely no relevance, one way or the other, to the moral and religious life. This general formula is discussed in detail in the next chapter. But it is easy to see, even at this point, that it was much more promising than the Cartesian line of attack on this problem. Instead of drawing a distinction on substantival lines, with all the concomitant complications of interaction, parallelism, and so on, Kant drew a distinction between what is within and what is beyond the spatiotemporal manifold.

If the object of moral judgment (the locus to which praise and blame, for instance, are ascribed) is the supposedly substantival self of Cartesianism, then morality is indeed a vain and chimerical illusion, for the existence of such a self is inconsistent with the principles of physics. But if space and time, substance and causality, are forms that the mind introduces into experience, then the self about which moral judgments are made is not a substance and does not act causally in the spatiotemporal world.

In Kant's view, it is true that we cannot *know* such a self, for knowledge is limited to what is within the spatiotemporal manifold. But it also follows, precisely because knowledge is thus confined to the manifold, that we cannot know that such a self does *not* exist. Indeed, we cannot know anything, one way or the other, about such a noumenal self. Thus, if there are any other grounds for believing in its existence, we are warranted in so believing.

> What is the value of the metaphysics that is alleged to be thus purified by criticism and established once for all? On a cursory view of the present work it may seem that its results are merely *negative*, warning us that we must never venture with speculative reason beyond the limits of experience. Such is in fact its primary use. . . . So far . . . as our Critique limits speculative reason, it is indeed *negative*; but since it thereby removes an obstacle which stands in the way of the employment of practical reason, nay threatens to destroy it, it has in reality a *positive* and very important use. At least this is so, immediately we are convinced that there is an absolutely necessary *practical* employment of pure reason—the *moral*—in which it inevitably goes

beyond the limits of sensibility. Though [practical] reason, in thus proceeding, requires no assistance from speculative reason, it must yet be assured against its opposition, that reason may not be brought into conflict with itself. To deny that the service which the Critique renders is *positive* in character, would thus be like saying that the police are of no positive benefit, inasmuch as their main business is merely to prevent the violence of which citizens stand in mutual fear, in order that each may pursue his vocation in peace and security. That space and time are only forms of sensible intuition, and so only conditions of the existence of things as appearances; that, moreover, we have no concepts of understanding, and consequently no elements for the knowledge of things, save in so far as intuition can be given corresponding to these concepts; and that we can therefore have no knowledge of any object as thing in itself, but only in so far as it is an object of sensible intuition, that is, an appearance—all this is proved in the analytical part of the Critique. Thus it does indeed follow that all possible speculative knowledge of reason is limited to mere objects of *experience*. But our further contention must also be duly borne in mind, namely, that though we cannot *know* these objects as things in themselves, we must yet be in position at least to *think* them as things in themselves; otherwise we should be landed in the absurd conclusion that there can be appearance without anything that appears. . . .

The doctrine of morality and the doctrine of nature may each, therefore, make good its position. This, however, is only possible in so far as criticism has previously established our unavoidable ignorance of things in themselves, and has limited all that we can theoretically *know* to mere appearances.

[From what has already been said, it is evident that] even the *assumption*—as made on behalf of the necessary practical employment of my reason—of *God, freedom,* and *immortality* is not permissible unless at the same time speculative reason be deprived of its pretensions to transcendent insight. For in order to arrive at such insight it must make use of principles which, in fact, extend only to objects of possible experience, and which, if also applied to what cannot be an object of experience, always really change this into an appearance, thus rendering all *practical extension* of pure reason impossible. I have therefore found it necessary to deny *knowledge*, in order to make room for *faith*.[b]

There are two main points in this passage: (1) the distinction between "knowing" and "thinking" and (2) the concept of "faith." As regards the first point, at the place where he introduced this distinction, Kant inserted a footnote:

To *know* an object I must be able to prove its possibility, either from its actuality as attested by experience, or *a priori* by means of reason. But I can *think* whatever I please, provided only that I do not contradict myself, that is, provided my concept is a possible thought. This suffices for the possibility of the concept, even though I may not be able to answer for there being, in the sum of all possibilities, an object corresponding to it. But something more is required before I can ascribe to such a concept objective validity, that is, real possibility; the former possibility is merely logical. This something more need not, however, be sought in the theoretical sources of knowledge; it may lie in those that are practical.[c]

An example will show how this distinction is to be understood. I cannot think "round square," for in attempting to do so, I contradict myself. I can, however, think "square," for there is nothing contradictory about the idea of a four-angled figure. Similarly, I can think "chiliagon," for there is nothing contradictory about the idea of a thousand-angled figure. Thus the square and the chiliagon are both logical possibilities. But how do I ascertain whether they are more than mere logical possibilities? One way is by means of experience: I know that the square, at least, is more than a mere logical possibility because I encounter squares in experience. This is what Kant meant by grounding objectivity validity in "the theoretical sources of knowledge."

Kant next applied this line of thought to God, freedom, and immortality. If God, freedom, and immortality are noumena, they are logically possible (according to Kant) because one can think them: There is nothing contradictory in the idea of something that is unknowable because it lies outside all experience. But are God, freedom, and immortality objectively valid as well? Theoretical knowledge (for example, the kind of knowledge obtained in physics) can prove nothing about their objective validity, since such knowledge is limited to phenomena, that is, to occurrences within the spatiotemporal manifold. But there is another way of moving from logical possibility to objective validity, namely, by grounding the latter in the "practical" sources of knowledge. Unless God, freedom, and immortality are objectively real (not mere logical possibilities), the moral life is a vain and chimerical illusion. Thus our own strong feeling about the genuineness of our duties to others is the "practical" ground that warrants our belief in the objective validity of these concepts, just as—at a completely different level, of course—our strong feeling about the genuineness of our percept of a square warrants our belief in the objectivity validity of the concept of four-angled figure.

But what sort of objective validity do God, freedom, and immortality have? In the Western tradition, at least since the time of Aristotle, the objectivity validity ascribed to God has usually been that of a substance exercising causal efficacy in the world. As for the supposed objective validity of the self—in Western thought the self, too, has been conceived of as a substance acting causally on its environment, including its own body. But the whole argument of the *Critique* rules out this way of thinking about God, freedom, and immortality. The objective validity that the *Critique* has shown them to have cannot be substantival or causal, since these concepts are explicitly limited to phenomena.[23] Unfortunately, all language, including both commonsensical language and philosophical language, is a thing-language, a language descriptive of objects interacting causally with other objects. Hence it is difficult to find a way of talking about God, freedom, and immortality that does not suggest them to be things. Perhaps the best way of dealing with this problem is to think of them as values. Kant does not make this suggestion himself, but "value" seems to be a good term to

23 As has already been seen, and as will be seen again, Kant was by no means consistent in staying within this self-imposed restriction. See pp. 64 and 84–88.

represent his view, for values are not commonly regarded as interacting causally, and they are the objects of enjoyings or appreciatings, not of perceivings.

This brings us to the second main point in the passage under examination—the concept of faith. By "faith" Kant did not mean any subjective, private, or whimsical belief that an individual may choose to hold. His position was not at all like that of saying, "Since nobody can ever see the surface of Venus, nothing can prevent my believing that it is chromium-plated and steam-heated." In saying that he "denied knowledge," Kant meant that he was limiting the *area of applicability* of science—limiting it, that is, to the spatiotemporal realm. By "belief" he really meant *another* kind of experience, one just as well grounded and just as public and objective, in its way, as scientific knowledge is in its. He would have expressed his meaning better had he written, "I have found it necessary to limit scientific knowledge in order to make room for an appreciation of values." What Kant actually proposed was to replace the Cartesian dual-substance theory with a dualism of kinds of experience. There is an experience of things in space and time, which he called "knowledge"; there is also an experience or appreciation of values, which he called "faith." Nomenclature apart, this distinction was to have important consequences not just in the history of philosophy but in the whole development of culture in the nineteenth and twentieth centuries.

CHAPTER 3

Kant: Theory of Value

Ethical Theory

Most pre-Kantian moral theories (even those of Christian philosophers) were based on the concept of good. In contrast, Kant's was based on the primacy of right. The first question a Greek philosopher asked himself was, "What is the good?" The next question was, "How shall I attain it?" Since it was generally agreed that "happiness" was the good, there was no need to show people that they *ought* to aim at it. In fact, the only puzzle was why so much of the time people did not aim at it. Philosophers like Plato thought the answer was ignorance. Men acted wrongly not because their wills were bad but, quite simply, because they did not know what would make them happy.

For this reason, Greek ethics had a means-end form, a form that very deeply marked the thought of many Christian philosophers—for instance, St. Thomas. There can be no doubt, however, that Christianity, with its concept of an omnipotent Father who ought to be obeyed in all things, introduced a new emphasis into moral philosophy. Since, in the Christian view, God's commands are rules, the notion of right, or conformity to rule, became important. At the same time, Christian thinkers took up the Stoic emphasis on motivation. These two concepts came together in the notion not merely of punctilious conformity to rule but of conformity because the rule issues from the source it issues from. To conform to the rule because we fear punishment is of no account. And to do so because we hope to be rewarded for obedience, or because conformity is a means to happiness, is to "reduce" morality to the Greek type, though of course with a very different set of prescriptions about how to be happy. From the Christian point of view, then, the morally good motive is a very special—one might almost say a very peculiar—one. To act morally, a man must see that the act is right (that is, commanded) and must do it because he sees that it is right. Thus a Christian ethics is likely to focus on the concept of duty as the exclusive moral motive. A Christian ethics is also likely to emphasize sin, rather than ignorance, as the cause of wrongdoing. Since God's commands are clear, a man who fails to conform must have a perverse or stubborn will.

More than almost any other thinker, Kant identified himself with this emphasis on duty and attempted to give it philosophical formulation. He did not, of course, talk about divine commands—he was concerned with ethics, not theology. As a matter of fact, in a way that shows how much he was a man of the Enlightenment, he made reason, not God, the source of the moral law. Nevertheless, duty is the central concept of Kant's ethical theory. In Kant's view, only a good will is morally valuable; and a good will is simply one that (1) knows what its duty is (that is, knows what reason commands) and (2) does the dutiful act because it is dutiful.

> Nothing can possibly be conceived in the world, or even out of it, which can be called good, without qualification, except a Good Will. Intelligence, wit, judgment, and the other *talents* of the mind, however they may be named, or courage, resolution, perseverance, as qualities of temperament, are undoubtedly good and desirable in many respects; but these gifts of nature may also become extremely bad and mischievous if the will which is to make use of them, and which, therefore, constitutes what is called *character*, is not good. It is the same with the *gifts of fortune*. Power, riches, honour, even health, and the general well-being and contentment with one's condition which is called *happiness*, inspire pride, and often presumption, if there is not a good will to correct the influence of these on the mind, and with this also to rectify the whole principle of acting, and adapt it to its end. The sight of a being who is not adorned with a single feature of a pure and good will, enjoying unbroken prosperity, can never give pleasure to an impartial rational spectator. Thus a good will appears to constitute the indispensable condition even of being worthy of happiness. . . .

A good will is good not because of what it performs or effects, not by its aptness for the attainment of some proposed end, but simply by virtue of the volition, that is, it is good in itself, and considered by itself is to be esteemed much higher than all that can be brought about by it in favour of any inclination, nay, even of the sum-total of all inclinations. Even if it should happen that, owing to special disfavour of fortune, or the niggardly provision of a step-motherly nature, this will should wholly lack power to accomplish its purpose, if with its greatest efforts it should yet achieve nothing, and there should remain only the good will (not, to be sure, a mere wish, but the summoning of all means in our power), then, like a jewel, it would still shine by its own light, as a thing which has its whole value in itself. Its usefulness or fruitlessness can neither add to nor take away anything from this value.[a]

CONCEPT OF GOOD WILL

This notion of a will that is good in itself without regard to what it effects seemed "so strange" to Kant himself that he tried to bolster it up by a complicated argument. Starting from the familiar thesis that "nothing in nature is in vain," Kant argued that reason must, therefore, have *some* function. But this function cannot be the preservation of life or the acquisition of happiness, for both these functions could be better performed (as with insects) by instinct. It follows, according to Kant, that "our existence has a different and far nobler end, for which . . . reason is properly intended." This end can only be cultivation of a "will not merely good as a means to something else but good in itself."

Kant's argument is unlikely to appeal to anyone who is not already convinced on other grounds. And Kant's position will seem to most people unduly narrow. Although he did not argue (as some of his critics have supposed) that a good will is "the sole and complete good," he did maintain that it is "the supreme good and the condition of every other." Are we then to think of a good will as a necessary ingredient in other goods, as eggs are a necessary ingredient in cake? This appears to be a part of what Kant meant. But he also believed that the goodness of a good will can come into competition with other goods. For example, one of the hard facts of life is that we sometimes have to choose between keeping a promise, and thereby doing our duty, and securing a better job that will enable us to provide more adequately for our family. In Kant's view, whenever we face such an alternative we should always choose the good will rather than the other good, no matter what it may be. These two points of view are not inconsistent—we might, for instance, have to choose between scrambling our eggs and using them in a cake. But it seems unreasonable to insist that it is always better to scramble our eggs than to use them in a cake.

Kant's stand here, with its exclusive emphasis on the good will, inevitably raises the question, "What is the basis, or principle, of choice among different values?" The utilitarian solution to this problem, a solution that was popular in Kant's own day, provided an easy criterion: The goodness of every value lies in the pleasure it produces.[1] According to this view, the goodness of a good will resides in the amount of pleasure such a will produces—just as the goodness of a beautiful picture resides, presumably, in the amount of pleasure it produces. There is thus never any *moral* problem, strictly speaking, in choosing among the different acts open to us. There may be a problem about ascertaining which of the acts will be productive of the greater good, but once that is settled, we know what we ought to do.

In insisting that virtue is valuable in its own right and apart from what it accomplishes, Kant was doubtless reacting against this oversimplified view. But though many people would agree that a good will is good "apart from anything further," they might deny that it is the *only* moral value. Like the Utilitarians, Kant oversimplified the problem of choice, but in a reverse way. In Kant's view, choice in effect is never a problem, for a good will is always supreme.

This position is so extreme that some commentators have doubted that Kant actually held it. What Kant was trying to express, they argue, is that although there are all sorts of values, a good will is the unique moral value. In the scale of, say, economic values or esthetic values, a good will might not rate so high, but in the scale of moral value, it is *eo ipso* highest. Hence, whenever we choose as moral beings, we ought to choose a good will.

Sometimes, certainly, Kant came close to saying this, but such a view only transfers the problem to another level: choice between different scales. As esthetic men, one kind of choice is correct; as moral men, another kind of choice is correct. But which kind of choice is better? It will not do to say, "Which *ought* we to choose?" for this is already to adopt the moral point of view. Obviously, we *ought* to choose the moral choice. Are we then to admit that these different scales of value are incommensurate?

We can be sure that Kant would have repudiated such an irrational (or arational) conclusion. But to repudiate a conclusion is unfortunately not to provide a satisfactory alternative. To find such an alternative is obviously essential for those people who hold that values should consist in some kind of single, rational hierarchy, or system. This remains a very difficult problem.

NATURE OF DUTY: CONFORMITY TO LAW IN GENERAL

In any case, whether or not the good will is supreme, in order to understand Kant's position we have to ask what, according to Kant, its structure is. This is equivalent to asking, "What is the nature of duty?" for, as we have seen, Kant held the good will to be one that does its duty.

> *Duty is the necessity of acting from respect for the law.* . . . It is only what is connected with my will as a principle, by no means as an effect—what

---

1 Utilitarians differed, however, as to whether we are to take account of (1) our own pleasure only, (2) other people's pleasure only, or (3) the greatest total amount of pleasure regardless of how it is distributed.

does not subserve my inclination, but overpowers it, or at least in case of choice excludes it from its calculation—in other words, simply the law of itself, which can be an object of respect, and hence a command. Now an action done from duty must wholly exclude the influence of inclination, and with it every object of the will, so that nothing remains which can determine the will except objectively the *law*, and subjectively *pure respect* for this practical law, and consequently the maxim that I should follow this law even to the thwarting of all my inclinations.

Thus the moral worth of an action does not lie in the effect expected from it, nor in any principle of action which requires to borrow its motive from this expected effect. For all these effects—agreeableness of one's condition, and even the promotion of the happiness of others—could have been also brought about by other causes so that for this there would have been no need of the will of a rational being; whereas it is in this alone that the supreme and unconditional good can be found. The preeminent good which we call moral can therefore consist in nothing else than *the conception of law* in itself, *which certainly is only possible in a rational being*, in so far as this conception, and not the expected effect, determines the will. This is a good which is already present in the person who acts accordingly, and we have not to wait for it to appear first in the result.[b]

Here again Kant believed he was merely stating with precision what everyone believes as a matter of course.

Kant's first point is that, to satisfy the moral requirement, it is not enough that an act of a certain kind be done. I might, for instance, while intending to lie, happen to tell the truth through a slip of the tongue. From a moral point of view I would have told a lie.[2]

Kant's second point is that it is not enough that the act be intended. If I am moved to keep a promise by a sudden feeling of pity for a man whom I have promised to help, my act is still without moral value. In Kant's view, it must be done from a "principle" (or "maxim," or "imperative")—that is, I must have a regular, explicitly formulated, and carefully thought-out rule, and I must perform the act because I see that it is an instance of the rule. Suppose, for instance, that I am the owner of a filling station. I may have the rule "Honesty is the best policy." From this I may have concluded that a reputation for integrity is more valuable than the petty profits that would accrue from refusing to make refunds on faulty repair jobs. Now suppose that a customer asks for a refund. If I give it to him because I like the color of his tie, or because I happen to be in a good mood, I am not acting on principle. Only if I give it to him because I see that the repairs I made on his car were faulty, and that this case comes under my general rule, am I acting on principle.

Kant's third point is that it is not enough to act merely on principle. For an act to have *moral* worth, the principle must be of a particular kind. "Honesty is the best policy," as it happens, is not a principle of the requisite kind; it is

2 Compare Jesus' dictum about the man who commits adultery in his heart.

only a "conditional" principle. Duty, on the other hand, is universally (or, as Kant said, "categorically") binding.

There are two points to be considered here. (1) *Is* duty universally binding? Kant did not try to prove this, for he thought it obvious that whatever is a duty for one man is equally a duty for all other men. (2) *Are* maxims like "Honesty is the best policy" conditional? This seems to be so, for (supposing this were one's maxim) if anyone happened not to want to make a profit, there would be no reason to be honest. Furthermore, "Honesty is the best policy" might not be binding for every situation. It might be a satisfactory principle, for example, for a big business but not for a small one, for dealing with steady customers but not for dealing with tourists just "passing through," and so on. The fact is that it is a means-end type of principle, and no such principle yields a categorical rule unless the end is a universal end.

It seemed to Kant that happiness might be thought just this kind of end.

> There is *one* end . . . which we may with certainty assume that all [men] actually *have* by a natural necessity, and this is *happiness*. . . . [But] the imperative which refers to the choice of means to one's own happiness, *i.e.* the precept of prudence, is still always *hypothetical;* the action is not commanded absolutely, but only as means to another purpose. . . .
>
> The notion of happiness is so indefinite that although every man wishes to attain it, yet he never can say definitely and consistently what it is that he really wishes and wills. The reason of this is that all the elements which belong to the notion of happiness are altogether empirical, *i.e.* they must be borrowed from experience, and nevertheless the idea of happiness requires an absolute whole, a maximum of welfare in my present and all future circumstances. Now it is impossible that the most clear-sighted [man] should frame to himself a definite conception of what he really wills in this. . . . We cannot therefore act on any definite principles to secure happiness, but only on empirical counsels, *ex. gr.* of regimen, frugality, courtesy, reserve, &c., which experience teaches do, on the average, most promote well-being. Hence it follows that the imperatives of prudence do not, strictly speaking, command at all, that is, they cannot present actions objectively as practically *necessary;* that they are rather to be regarded as counsels (*consilia*) than precepts (*praecepta*) of reason.[c]

In Kant's view, that is, "happiness" is not a definite state of affairs, like graduating from college or getting a job. It is a regulative concept that performs the same function with respect to conduct[3] that "totality" performs with respect to theory. Though happiness is in a sense an end, it is not a specific, concrete end to aim at (as a student may plan his courses so as to graduate); rather, it is the ideal in terms of which our pursuit of all such specific, concrete ends is organized.

Assuming, then, that duty is universally binding, what kind of principle guides

3 See pp. 60–62.

us when we act from a sense of duty? What kind of principle operates, that is, when I tell the truth not because it is prudent (the best policy) to do so but because I recognize that it is my duty to do so? The only answer, according to Kant, is that the principle is the "conception of law in general." If I do x for the sake of y, I am acting on a conditional principle; on the other hand, unless I do x in accordance with *some* principle, I am acting merely on whim or impulse. The only possibility, therefore, is that the principle that moves me is just the *idea* of principle. That is, what moves me cannot be the idea of any particular maxim ("An apple a day keeps the doctor away," "A stitch in time saves nine"), for all particular maxims are conditioned on our wanting the end they produce ("health" or "saving"). What moves me must be the idea of law in general.

Since, as Kant pointed out, his argument has

> . . . deprived the will of every impulse which could arise to it from obedience to any [particular] law, there remains nothing but the universal conformity of its actions to law in general, which alone is to serve the will as a principle, *i.e.* I am never to act otherwise than *so that I could also will that my maxim should become a universal law.* Here, now, it is the simple conformity to law in general, without assuming any particular law applicable to certain actions, that serves the will as its principle, and must so serve it, if duty is not to be a vain delusion and a chimerical notion.[d]

DIFFICULTIES WITH THIS FORMULATION

Kant believed that he had obtained this conclusion by analyzing the ordinary, commonsense conception of duty as a universally binding requirement. Yet some people may take Kant's analysis as confirming their suspicion that there is something very queer about this whole idea of an absolutely binding duty. This idea of law in general, which the analysis discloses to be what is meant by a sense of duty, is certainly rather odd. Does any such idea as Kant described ever move men to act? And if it does, why is being moved by it supremely valuable?

This line of criticism has nothing to do with the question of whether a good will is good in itself or has only a utilitarian good. It is quite possible to hold that a good will is good in itself and to deny that acting from a sense of duty (as described by Kant) ever occurs or is valuable. One might hold, for instance, that certain *other* motives are what make the good will good.

This, of course, is just what Hume had argued. As a matter of fact, his analysis of the goodness of the good will was in effect a criticism in advance of Kant's conception. Thus, although Hume agreed with Kant that "a good will" is the unique object of moral value, he held its goodness to lie in its benevolence, not in its dutifulness. He did not deny that action from a sense of duty occurs. But he gave a completely different account of it; far from assigning it supreme value, he thought it had only derivative value. Hume's main criticism of the type of position later taken by Kant was that it involved a vicious circle. "No action," he pointed out, "can be virtuous, or morally good, unless there be in human nature some motive to produce it, distinct from the sense of its morality."e For suppose it is claimed that the virtue of telling the truth lies in telling it *because it is virtuous* to do so. Unless we insist that telling the truth is virtuous on some other ground (as Kant denied), we are forced to say that the virtue of telling the truth lies in the virtue of telling the truth. Telling the truth per se is not virtuous. What is virtuous is telling-the-truth-because-telling-the-truth-is-virtuous. But this in turn requires correction, and it is easy to see that we become involved in an infinite regress—the virtue of telling the truth lies in the virtue of telling the truth lies in the virtue of telling the truth lies in the virtue. . . . The only way to stop the regress is to admit that something other than the virtue of telling the truth is the ground for the virtue of telling the truth.

> I conclude [Hume wrote] that the first virtuous motive, which bestows a merit on any action, can never be a regard to the virtue of that action, but must be some other natural motive or principle. To suppose, that the mere regard to the virtue of the action, may be the first motive, which produc'd the action, and render'd it virtuous, is to reason in a circle. Before we can have such a regard, the action must be really virtuous; and this virtue must be deriv'd from some virtuous motive. And consequently the virtuous motive must be different from the regard to the virtue of the action. A virtuous motive is requisite to render an action virtuous. An action must be virtuous, before we can have a regard to its virtue. Some virtuous motive, therefore, must be antecedent to that regard.

Hume did not deny, of course, that men sometimes act from what can fairly be described as a sense of duty. But that they do so, he believed, was capable of explanation by the general psychological law of association. Just as I may come to like a certain melody on its own account, even though I originally liked it only because I heard it frequently in the company of someone close to me, so I may come to admire truth-telling on its own account, but actually only because it was originally associated with some other motive. Thus, in the course of time, men have developed all sorts of categorical imperatives ("Tell the truth," "Keep promises," "Repay debts"). A sense of our duty to perform these actions may be our current motive for performing them, just as Kant claimed. But this is possible only because some specific, concrete motive (like benevolence) originally moved us to perform them. The merit of the benevolence motive has simply been transferred by association to the dutiful act. Thus what Kant believed to be so unique about duty (the concept of law in general) is merely the sign that the original maxim has been sloughed off and forgotten.

There are many categorical imperatives for which it is easy to revive the forgotten maxim. Take the imperative "Stop at a red traffic light." This has become so imbedded in our behavior that if we were asked why we ought to do so, we are likely to reply, quite simply, "Because, of course, it is *red.*" As soon as we think about it, however, we see that underlying the imperative is a maxim of the form "Violations of red traffic signals are dangerous to life and limb," or "Violations are likely to incur fines." Thus the "categoricalness" of the imperative disappears. Hume contended that the same process that produced this apparently categorical imperative also produced all others (like "Tell the truth" or "Keep promises"). The only difference is that the latter, being even more deeply imbedded in our behavior, have a more compulsive (that is, categorical) tone.

This capacity of the human mind to form categorical imperatives is of immense practical importance. If men lacked this capacity, the act of deciding what to do would require so much thought that life would hopelessly bog down. If every time we saw a red traffic light we had to stop, think of the general maxim, and ask ourselves whether this case comes under the maxim, our journeys would take much longer and the accident rate at intersections would greatly increase. Hume would have said that Kant simply erected this very useful capacity into a transcendent moral principle.

If such a criticism is correct, Kant's first formulation of the categorical imperative—"Act only on that maxim whereby thou canst at the same time will that it should become a universal law"—is seriously defective. Moreover, it is clear (on grounds that have nothing to do with Hume's analysis) that this formula is not an adequate statement of the nature of obligation. In the first place, it is possible to generalize into universal rules all sorts of maxims that no one (and certainly not Kant) would hold to be obligatory. For instance, I could perfectly well hold that every purchaser of a new book should write his name on the flyleaf when he acquires it. Although there is nothing self-contradictory about this maxim, it is also morally neutral. We feel no obligation either to inscribe our names or to abstain from inscribing them.

Kant might have replied that if I act in accordance with this, or any other, particular maxim, I am still not acting morally, even though the maxim can be universalized. To act morally, I must obey "nothing but . . . law in general." That is, the moral motive is "simple conformity to law in general." If this means, as it would seem, that I must ignore the specific character of the rule and act simply from the notion of following a rule because it is a rule, the result will be to justify all sorts of acts that most people would call immoral. For instance, during World War II Hitler laid down the rule that all Jews should be exterminated. Kant's argument would not justify the acts of Germans who exterminated Jews because they were afraid of disobeying Hitler or because they hated Jews or because they hoped to acquire the property of the Jews. But it *would* justify the acts of any Germans who exterminated Jews for the sole reason that they had been ordered to do so.

Or, to return to the maxim, "Every purchaser of a new book should write his name on the flyleaf": According to the present interpretation of Kant's meaning, I act morally not when I inscribe my name from the motive of obeying this particular maxim, but when I inscribe my name from the motive of obeying law in general. Yet the result, as far as *action* is concerned, is the same. I still inscribe my name on the flyleaf of my new book, and this is not an act that anyone would describe as morally good or virtuous. This must be the consequence as long as moral theorists concentrate attention on our acting from a certain motive without regard to the results that our action produces. They will find themselves praising as morally valuable actions that common sense calls indifferent or even wrong.

These considerations show that universalization cannot be a positive criterion of duty. But neither is it a negative criterion: There are many actions that Kant condemned (and that many other people would condemn) whose maxims can be universalized. For example, in Kant's view, it is our duty not to commit suicide. Yet there is nothing self-contradictory about a prospective suicide's willing that everyone else commit suicide. In Kant's view, it is our duty to repay debts. Yet there is nothing logically inconsistent about the position of a defaulter who is ready for everyone to repudiate promises to pay. Universal repudiation would, of course, soon lead to a general abandonment of the credit system. But economic chaos is not a logical impossibility, and Kant's argument cannot be used to appeal to the defaulter unless we admit that the imperative to pay debts is not categorical but prudential.

Thus it cannot be correct to say, as Kant did, that the essence of morality consists in acting in accordance with a categorical imperative. Nevertheless, if the emphasis is put not on the need for logical consistency but on the need for generality, then Kant's point does seem to have moral significance: We all tend to make exceptions to general rules when our own interests are involved. Suppose we have an imperative to the effect that contracts ought to be fulfilled (it does not matter here that the imperative is prudential). Since we know that every violation of a rule tends to weaken it, we are likely to be very stern with prospective violators on the basis of their selfishness and shortsightedness. It is only too easy, however, when *we* are the prospective violators, to shift our ground and emphasize the fact that a single exception "hardly matters at all." Hence, if before we act we always ask ourselves, "Do I want this kind of act to become a general rule?" our answer would have to be in the negative, and we might therefore abstain from making an exception for ourselves. Thus the real point of Kant's formulation seems to be that in morality we are not to count our own "I" differently from the way we count the "I's" of other people.

ANOTHER ACCOUNT OF DUTY: REASON AN END IN ITSELF

So far in his account of duty Kant has described a dutiful, or morally good, act as one whose principle is a universal and categorical imperative. It happens, however, that Kant gave a second formulation of the imperative of duty—"So act as to treat humanity whether in thine own person or that of any other, in every case as an end withal, never as means only." Though Kant believed his two formulations to be equivalent, the second, it will be seen, was much more fruitful.

> Man and generally any rational being *exists* as an end in himself, *not merely as a means* to be arbitrarily used by this or that will, but in all his actions, whether they concern himself or other rational beings, must be always regarded at the same time as an end. All objects of the inclinations have only a conditional worth; for if the inclinations and the wants founded on them did not exist, then their object would be without value. But the inclinations themselves being sources of want are so far from having an absolute worth for which they should be desired, that, on the contrary, it must be the universal wish of every rational being to be wholly free from them. Thus the worth of any object which is *to be acquired* by our action is always conditional. . . . Rational beings . . . are called *persons*, because their very nature points them out as ends in themselves. . . . These, therefore, are not merely subjective ends whose existence has a worth *for us* as an effect of our action, but *objective ends*, that is things whose existence is an end in itself: an end moreover for which no other can be substituted, which they should subserve *merely* as means, for otherwise nothing whatever would possess *absolute worth;* but if all worth were conditioned and therefore contingent, then there would be no supreme practical principle of reason whatever.
>
> If then there is a supreme practical principle or, in respect of the human will, a categorical imperative, it must be one which, being drawn from the conception of that which is necessarily an end for everyone because it is *an end in itself*, constitutes an *objective* principle of will, and can therefore serve as a universal practical law. The foundation of this principle is: *rational nature exists as an end in itself.*[f]

This passage epitomizes the spirit of the Enlightenment—the point of view to which Locke, for instance, gave such notable expression and the view that was one of the driving forces in the American and French revolutions. According to this belief, a human being has an intrinsic value just because he is a human being and quite apart from whatever special advantages may accrue from birth, wealth, beauty, or station in life.

Whereas Locke for the most part emphasized the rights men own as men, Kant emphasized the duties they owe as men. Most of the acts traditionally regarded as duties can be thought of as deriving their obligatory character from one primary obligation—the duty to treat men as ends in themselves. The act of lying—whether private lying or that public lying called, alternatively, propaganda or advertising—is a good example. Even if we lie not for our own selfish advantage but for the good of those to whom we are lying, we do wrong. We suggest to them that they cannot understand the facts and judge for themselves. We treat them as children still under tutelage, not as men; and, intentionally or not, we deny them their just title and their true dignity as rational creatures.

Finally, in demeaning them, we demean ourselves. We have a station in life to maintain; we have our own responsibilities as men and as rational creatures that it would be shameful to repudiate. *Noblesse oblige*—not the nobility of birth, but the nobility of humanity. We have to live up to our end and destiny as men; to do otherwise would be to let the whole race down.

This point of view—at once proud and humble—is well illustrated by a remark Kant made just before his death. He was very old, very ill, very weak, senile, and almost helpless. Yet when his physician entered his room he struggled to his feet to greet him and refused to sit down again until the visitor had taken a chair. "The feeling for humanity," he explained, "has not yet left me." [g] Standing up in the presence of one's doctor, not because he is a doctor, but because he is a man may be a little thing—a small punctilio of manners. But it does not differ in principle from telling him the truth—because he is a man. Between manners and morals, in this view, there is no chasm. Conduct at any level at once expresses and flows from one's understanding of one's status as a man in company with other men. Everyone counts as one—this is the point at which Kant's two formulations come together: My duties to others are no different from my duties to myself, and my rights are identical with theirs.

It would seem that Kant was expressing more here than the attitude of his own century—that he put his finger on, and gave cogent expression to, one of the abiding values of the West. Today, we would doubtless allow (though Kant, of course, would not have agreed) that the code of morals and manners varies from age to age and from place to place. Rising to greet one's guests, for instance, is merely a conventional, outward symbol of the respect one feels. Saluting with a sword or rubbing noses would do just as well. It is the respect that is important, not the gesture by which it is communicated. Or take lying: To tell one's servant to say one is "not at home" to a visitor is morally wrong only in a society that interprets this phrase literally. But in a society that understands it as a polite convention for saying one is tired or busy, it is no more untruthful than saying that the sun rose this morning.

It is important to note, too, that Kant's second formulation escapes the paradox that the virtue of a dutiful act lies in doing it because it is virtuous. For this formulation has uncovered a bona fide end that is realized in morally good (virtuous, dutiful) conduct. This end is the worth, or value, of the human personality. Kant's point, which is surely sound, is that this is a different kind of end from, say, that which moves a man when he tells the truth because he is afraid of being found out and punished. There is no moral worth in telling the truth to escape punishment; there *is* moral worth in telling the truth because one sees that it is his "end and destiny" as a man to do so. Kant's statement that morally good action does not aim at an end is a confused, and confusing, way of expressing what he meant. Nevertheless, Kant's point is a valid one—the end aimed at in morally good action is different from the end aimed at in other acts, and the structure of its maxim is different. The maxim in morally good conduct does not, strictly speaking, have a means-end structure; it has a class-inclusion structure. When we act morally we do not tell the truth as one step in a process aimed at achieving a result beyond itself; we tell it because we see that truth-telling belongs to the class of acts that the *noblesse* of human personality requires of us.

A THIRD ACCOUNT OF DUTY: THE AUTONOMOUS WILL

Kant also gave a third formulation of the categorical imperative: Act in accordance with the principle that "the laws to which you are subject are those of your own giving, though at the same time they are universal." In one sense, everything in nature is subject to laws: the stone as it falls and the animal as it feeds. But a will that acts on principle is subject to laws in a different sense from the stone or the animal. For when men act on principle (for example, when they eat an apple because "An apple a day keeps the doctor away") they know what they are doing, and why. This is the mark of rational behavior. Furthermore, a will that is subject to laws in the sense that it is attached to each of its laws by an interest (for example, health) must be distinguished from a will that is itself a lawgiver. In the former case, the law is derived from the circumstances of the physical or social world (a certain kind of vitamin deficiency is compensated for by eating apples); in the latter case, the will itself gives the law. Hence the latter will can be described as autonomous and free.

> The practical necessity of acting on this principle, *i.e.*, duty, does not rest at all on feelings, impulses, or inclinations, but solely on the relation of rational beings to one another, a relation in which the will of a rational being must always be regarded as *legislative*, since otherwise it could not be conceived as *an end in itself*. Reason then refers every maxim of the will, regarding it as legislating universally, to every other will and also to every action towards oneself; and this not on account of any other practical motive or any future advantage, but from the idea of the *dignity* of a rational being, obeying no law but that which he himself also gives.
>
> Now, morality is the condition under which alone a rational being can be an end in himself, since by this alone it is possible that he should be a legislating member in the kingdom of ends. Thus morality, and humanity as capable of it, is that which alone has dignity.
>
> What then is it which justifies virtue or the morally good disposition, in making such lofty claims? It is nothing less than the privilege it secures to the rational being of participating in the giving of universal laws, by which it qualifies him to be a member of a possible kingdom of ends, a privilege to which he was already destined by his own nature as being an end in himself, and on that account legislating in the kingdom of ends; free as regards all laws of physical nature, and obeying those only which he himself gives, and by which his maxims can belong to a system of universal law, to which at the same time he submits himself. For nothing has any worth except what the law assigns it. . . . *Autonomy* then is the basis of the dignity of human and of every rational nature.

From what has just been said, it is easy to see how it happens that although the conception of duty implies subjection to the law, we yet ascribe a certain *dignity* and sublimity to the person who fulfils all his duties. There is not, indeed, any sublimity in him, so far as he is *subject* to the moral law; but inasmuch as in regard to that very law he is likewise a *legislator*, and on that account alone subject to it, he has sublimity. We have also shown above that neither fear nor inclination, but simply respect for the law, is the spring which can give actions a moral worth. Our own will, so far as we suppose it to act only under the condition that its maxims are potentially universal laws, this ideal will which is possible to us is the proper object of respect; and the dignity of humanity consists just in this capacity of being universally legislative, though with the condition that it is itself subject to this same legislation.

Autonomy of the will is that property of it by which it is a law to itself (independently of any property of the objects of volition). The principle of autonomy then is: Always so to choose that the same volition shall comprehend the maxims of our choice as a universal law. . . . That the principle of autonomy in question is the sole principle of morals can be readily shown by mere analysis of the conceptions of morality. For by this analysis we find that its principle must be a categorical imperative, and that what this commands is neither more nor less than this very autonomy.[h]

Here, again, Kant is emphasizing what was called, in the discussion of the second formulation, the structure of the maxim that moves us to morally good conduct. According to that formulation, in morally good conduct we are moved by respect for personality. This maxim has quite a different structure from that which moves us when we eat an apple by a desire for health; and it seems appropriate to describe this difference in structure by saying that the morally good maxim is autonomous. Respect for personality is respect for ourselves—not, of course, for our private selves, but for the humanity we share with other men. Hence in morally good action the will can be said to be *self*-legislative.

Bearing in mind this concept of self-legislation, or "autonomy," let us return to the first formulation of the imperative. As was pointed out, the major weakness of that formulation was that it seemed to lead to the absurdity of saying, for example, that we have a duty to put our name on the flyleaf of every new book we purchase. This seemed to follow because it seemed that we had to interpret Kant as holding that we act morally either (1) whenever we follow a maxim that can be universalized or (2) whenever we obey the "idea of law in general." In view of the third formulation, however, we can now interpret Kant as meaning that we act morally whenever our motive is respect for ourselves and for other men as persons, or "lawgivers." That is, we act morally, not when we act out of respect for the idea of law in general, but when we act out of respect for men as creatures capable of understanding laws (rules) and of acting on them.

It is obvious that Kant's third formulation makes the notion of a moral imperative more intelligible. But can it still be called categorical? In Kant's view, this question turns on whether we do indeed attribute to personality an absolute and overriding value. "Supposing that there were something *whose existence* has *in itself* an absolute worth, something which, being *an end in itself,* could be a source of definite laws, then in this and this alone would lie the source of a possible categorical imperative, i.e., a practical law." [i] In other words, even an imperative of the form "Do *x* for the sake of *y*" would be categorical providing *y* is an absolutely necessary end. In Kant's view, of course, the absolute worth of personality makes it such a necessary end.

Was Kant correct? Certainly, some people seem to agree with him. For instance, conscientious objectors who refuse to fight under any circumstances because "human life is sacred" are really taking the position, as Kant did, that personality is the supreme value. Similarly, those who oppose capital punishment not on grounds of policy but simply because "it is always wrong to take another's life" are taking this position. Many people, however, would disagree with this view. As regards conscientious objection, they believe that there are circumstances in which we ought to resist. For example, they would hold that, far from it having been our duty to submit to Nazi tyranny rather than kill a single German in World War II, it would have been positively wicked to have submitted. It is not that such people do not value personality; it is simply that they do not attribute an absolutely overriding value to it.

Kant, of course, would have wanted to prove these people mistaken, for he held the supreme value of personality to be absolutely necessary. His argument here depends on the notion of a noumenal self.[4] Now *if* everyone had a noumenal self, and if this self (not the self that is a phenomenal object in space and time, not even the synthetical operations that make this phenomenal self possible) were supremely valuable, then there would be a categorical imperative absolutely binding on all men whether they recognized it or not.

But is there such a self? And if so, is it supremely valuable? Kant offered no evidence to support these contentions. He thought it enough to show merely that such a self is "possible." His position (as with his reply to Hume on the problem of induction)[5] can be summed up as follows: (1) Everyone initially believes the self to have supreme value. (2) This value becomes suspect only because of a puzzlement about its possibility and efficacy. (3) As soon, therefore, as this puzzlement is cleared up the original belief is reinstated.

Unfortunately for Kant, the reply to Hume regarding induction and this argument about the self are not on the same footing. Whatever may be thought about the logic of his reply to Hume, it is not enough merely to show (as Kant proposed to do) that our belief in the self and its value is possible. To begin with, although "everyone" initially believes that induction is possible, it is certainly not the case, as we have just seen, that "everyone" believes that the self is supremely valuable. Kant might have replied that though they do not think

4 See p. 64.
5 See pp. 25–26.

it supremely valuable, they ought to. But this would be to argue in a circle. Kant had hoped to explain "ought" by reference to the value of personality; therefore he could not turn around and use obligation to justify that value. Furthermore, even those who agree with Kant that the self is supremely valuable may not attribute this value, as he did, to the noumenal self. It may well be the empirical self that the conscientious objector values. For it is *that* self, not a timeless noumenal entity, that the conscientious objector refuses to kill. In addition, it is impossible to deduce the value of personality either from the notion of a transcendent unity of apperception or from the notion of the self as a lawgiver. Hence if the "ought" in the sentence, "People ought to recognize the supreme value of the noumenal self" is intended in its *logical* rather than its *moral* sense, the conclusion does not follow. Furthermore, as we have seen, the very notion of a noumenal self—the self that is outside the space-time world but somehow acting causally in it—is inconsistent with the main thesis of the *Critique*, which limits causality to the space-time manifold. Finally, as we have also seen, it is doubtful whether a categorical imperative (in the sense of a universally applicable duty) is required for morality, or indeed even compatible with morality.

The Free Will

Perhaps the most vexing question in Kant's philosophy is the question of free will. Kant held (with many other philosophers) that "ought" implies "can." [6] He also held obligation to be the essence of morality. Hence it was of fundamental importance to him, unless morality was to be admitted a vain and chimerical illusion, to prove "can." The difficulty was that he also believed that everything that happens is infallibly determined by antecedent events in time. If a psychologist knew enough about me and about the "laws" of human nature, he would be able to predict my future behavior as certainly as an astronomer is able to predict a solar or a lunar eclipse. Kant, it is important to note, had absolutely no doubt about this natural necessity. In his view, if we *had* to choose between it and freedom, we would have to abandon the latter, even though it meant abandoning the whole moral view of the world. But how can we avoid choosing? Is it possible to reconcile human freedom and natural necessity?

NOUMENAL CAUSALITY

To resolve this dilemma Kant fell back (as in the problem about an absolutely necessary value inhering in personality) on a positive conception of noumena,

---

6 Compare, for instance, "we *ought* to conform . . . ; consequently we must *be able* to do so"—*Religion Within the Limits of Reason Alone*, translated by T. M. Greene and H. H. Hudson (Open Court, Chicago, 1934), Bk. II, §1B, p. 55.

in contrast to the merely regulative role assigned them in accordance with the general doctrine of the critical philosophy. Kant admitted that to attribute freedom and natural necessity to the very same self is to become involved in contradictions. But he held that there are two selves, the noumenal self and the empirical self. It is the noumenal self that freely chooses and hence is morally responsible, and it is the empirical self whose behavior is completely determined by antecedent events in time. Thus, according to Kant, the contradiction is removed.

> The notion of causality as *physical necessity*, in opposition to the same notion as *freedom*, concerns only the existence of things so far as it is *determinable in time*, and, consequently, as phenomena, in opposition to their causality as things in themselves. Now if we take the attributes of existence of things in time for attributes of things in themselves (which is the common view), then it is impossible to reconcile the necessity of the causal relation with freedom; they are contradictory. For from the former it follows that every event, and consequently every action that takes place at a certain point of time, is a necessary result of what existed in time preceding. Now as time past is no longer in my power, hence every action that I perform must be the necessary result of certain determining grounds *which are not in my power,* that is, at the moment in which I am acting I am never free. . . .
>
> Consequently, if we would save [freedom], no other way remains but to consider that the existence of a thing, so far as it is determinable in time, and therefore its causality, according to the law of physical necessity, belong to *appearance,* and to attribute *freedom to the same being as a thing in itself.* . . . But . . . when we try to explain their combination in one and the same action, great difficulties present themselves. . . .
>
> When I say of a man who commits a theft that, by the physical law of causality, this deed is a necessary result of the determining causes in preceding time, then it was impossible that it could not have happened; how then can the judgment, according to the moral law, make any change, and suppose that it could have been omitted, because the law says that it ought to have been omitted: that is, how can a man be called quite free at the same moment, and with respect to the same action in which he is subject to an inevitable physical necessity? Some try to evade this by saying that the causes that determine his causality are . . . ideas produced by our own faculties, whereby desires are evoked on occasion of circumstances, and hence actions are wrought according to our own pleasure. This is a wretched subterfuge. . . . It does not matter whether the principles which necessarily determine causality by a physical law reside *within* the subject or *without* him, . . . if, as is admitted by these men themselves, these determining ideas have the ground of their existence in time and in the *antecedent state,* and this again in an antecedent, &c. Then it matters not that these are internal; it matters not that they have a psychological and not a mechanical causality. . . . Psychological freedom (if we choose to apply this term to a merely internal chain of ideas in the mind) . . . involves physical necessity, and therefore leaves no room for *transcendental freedom,* which must be conceived as

independence on everything empirical. . . . Without this freedom . . . no moral law and no moral imputation are possible. . . .

Now, in order to remove in the supposed case the apparent contradiction between freedom and the mechanism of nature in one and the same action, we must remember . . . that the necessity of nature . . . appertains only to the attributes of the thing that is subject to time-conditions, consequently only to those of the acting subject as a phenomenon; that therefore in this respect the determining principles of every action of the same reside in what belongs to past time, and *is no longer in his power* (in which must be included his own past actions and the character that these may determine for him in his own eyes as a phenomenon). But the very same subject being on the other side conscious of himself as a thing in himself, considers his existence also *in so far as it is not subject to time-conditions*, and regards himself as only determinable by laws which he gives himself through reason; and in this his existence nothing is antecedent to the determination of his will, but every action, and in general every modification of his existence, varying according to his internal sense, even the whole series of his existence as a sensible being, is in the consciousness of his supersensible existence nothing but the result, and never to be regarded as the determining principle, of his causality as a *noumenon*. In this view now the rational being can justly say of every unlawful action that he performs, that he could very well have left it undone; although as appearance it is sufficiently determined in the past, and in this respect is absolutely necessary; for it, with all the past which determines it, belongs to the one single phenomenon of his character which he makes for himself, in consequence of which he imputes the causality of those appearances to himself as a cause independent on sensibility.[j]

This is an extremely difficult passage. Does Kant mean (1) that the particular act (the theft) could have been otherwise or (2) that the whole empirical character, including this act, could have been otherwise? It is hard to see how the former assertion could be considered compatible with the claim that the act was determined by antecedent events in time.[7] The latter assertion is initially more plausible, for it seems to be possible to say, given a man's weak character, both (1) that antecedent events in time (slum upbringing, drunken father, shiftless mother, and so forth) infallibly determined that he would develop into a thief and (2) that he is responsible because there was an initial free act (before birth?) in which he chose the kind of character that would fall victim to this environment. But the second assertion is really not helpful. For even if we can accept the notion of such an initial choice as meaningful, this act cannot be held to initiate a closed series. A man and his character are not isolated events; they are parts

---

7 But compare such an explicit statement as this: "Whatever his previous deportment may have been, whatever natural causes may have been influencing him . . . , his action is yet free and determined by none of these causes; hence it can and must always be judged as an *original* use of his will. . . . However evil a man has been up to the very moment of an impending free act (so that evil has actually become custom or second nature) it was not only his duty to have been better [in the past], it is *now* still his duty to better himself. To do so must be within his power"—*Religion Within the Limits of Reason Alone*, translated by T. M. Greene and H. H. Hudson (Open Court, Chicago, 1934), Bk. I, §4, p. 36.

of a causal nexus—parents' genes, health of mother, and so forth. Hence precisely the same problem raised against the notion of a particular free act (this theft) must be raised against the notion of a free series (this empirical character), for taken as a whole the series is as particular as the act.[k] It is thus a foregone conclusion that, as long as one insists on freedom as a real spontaneity intruding into the natural world, no solution is possible.

This seems so obvious that we may wonder why Kant did not recognize it himself. The main reason is simply that the critical point of view was such a radical departure from the orthodox, traditional way of viewing the world that Kant could not prevent himself from sliding back into that old way of thinking. This is particularly true with respect to the two important concepts, noumena and freedom.

As regards noumena, the critical point of view required that objects (things, substances) and causality be limited to the realm of experience; and part of the time, of course, Kant saw that this was so and insisted on it. Yet he repeatedly lapsed into thinking of noumena as objects, and of the noumenal self as causally efficacious. The simple truth is that use of a thing-language is so habitual that it is very difficult not to reify whatever one tries to think about—including noumena. Thus, running through the whole of Kant's philosophy is a serious ambiguity between what may be called a critical conception of noumena and a conventional conception. This ambiguity becomes entangled in Kant's doctrine of freedom in the following way: In certain parts of the *Critique*, when Kant is discussing free will, he is referring (as we have seen) to a spontaneous cause that effects changes in the course of events. This may be described as the conventional view of freedom, and it fits in with the conventional view of noumena. But in other parts of the *Critique*, when Kant is discussing freedom, he describes the kind of maxim that he believed to be morally good. That is, part of the time he considers freedom to mean acting from a certain motive— namely, respect for men as creatures who are capable of understanding laws. Viewed in *this* way, freedom has nothing to do with spontaneous causality: We are free whenever we act from this motive, regardless of the fact that a psychologist could predict that, under such-and-such circumstances, we would act from it. And this view of freedom fits in with the critical conception of noumena.

How did Kant come to think of freedom in this double, and highly ambiguous, sense? The answer is that when he was thinking in terms of the third formulation of the categorical imperative, he naturally referred to the morally good will as "self-legislative," or "autonomous." And since "autonomy" and "freedom" are, in one sense, synonymous, he was led to call the morally good act free. But of course freedom, especially when predicated of the will, has a second meaning— "being spontaneous." There are, then, two quite different senses in which it is permissible to call the will free: when one is talking about "autonomy"—the unique structure of the morally good maxim—and when one is making an assertion about the relation of that maxim to antecedent events (or rather, about its lack of relation to any antecedent events).

Taken in the second sense, freedom is obviously inconsistent with natural necessity. To say that an act is free in this sense is to assert that it could have been otherwise, and to say that it is determined is to assert that it could not have been otherwise. But taken in the first sense, freedom is not inconsistent with natural necessity: Here we are merely saying that *when* a maxim with such-and-such a structure occurs and a man acts on it, that man is free ("autonomous") and his conduct is morally valuable. To say that the maxim is autonomous (free) is not to make any assertion at all about the circumstances that produce the maxim in question. If we knew enough about the man's past we could doubtless predict that at a particular time he would act in a certain way and from a motive that has this "autonomous" structure.

Kant's solution to the "antinomy" of freedom and natural necessity seems to have consisted in sliding back and forth between freedom as "spontaneous causality" and freedom as "maxim with autonomous structure." In the following passage an attentive reader can catch the shifts as they occur and observe how the conclusion depends on them.

> The *will* is a kind of causality belonging to living beings in so far as they are rational, and *freedom* would be this property of such causality that it can be efficient, independently on foreign causes *determining* it; just as *physical necessity* is the property that the causality of all irrational beings has of being determined to activity by the influence of foreign causes.
>
> The preceding definition of freedom is *negative*, and therefore unfruitful for the discovery of its essence; but it leads to a *positive* conception which is so much the more full and fruitful. Since the conception of causality involves that of laws, according to which, by something that we call cause, something else, namely, the effect, must be produced; . . . hence, although freedom is not a property of the will depending on physical laws, yet it is not for that reason lawless; on the contrary, it must be a causality acting according to immutable laws, but of a peculiar kind; otherwise a free will would be an absurdity. Physical necessity is a heteronomy of the efficient causes, for every effect is possible only according to this law, that something else determines the efficient cause to exert its causality. What else then can freedom of the will be but autonomy, that is the property of the will to be a law to itself? But the proposition: The will is in every action a law to itself, only expresses the principle, to act on no other maxim than that which can also have as an object itself as a universal law. Now this is precisely the formula of the categorical imperative and is the principle of morality, so that a free will and a will subject to moral laws are one and the same.[1]

SUMMARY

We can see, then, that as a result of an ambiguity in the term "freedom" Kant came to think that he had reconciled natural necessity and spontaneous causality and thus had solved the problem over which, as he said, "centuries have labored in vain." Kant, of course, had done nothing of the kind. But he *had* done something much more important. By rigorously limiting knowledge

in the strict sense to the spatiotemporal manifold, he made room for an appreciation of ourselves as moral beings with individual rights and with obligations
to others. Freedom in what may be called the critical sense is thus entirely in
accord with the spirit of the general solution of the problem of pure reason.
It falls within the province of what Kant misleadingly called "faith"—for by
faith he meant, not an ungrounded belief in something that contradicts the
evidence of the sciences, but a sensitivity to, and appreciation of, values.

To put this differently, freedom in the critical sense conforms to the central
theme of Kant's whole philosophy, the theme that knowledge of objects and
appreciation of values (including the value of being a person) are simply modes
of experience too different ever to conflict. Accordingly, if *before* the appearance
of modern physics we had any reason to accept the traditional appreciation of
man as a focus of values, we have the same reason for doing so *after* the appearance of modern physics. As soon as we realize that physics is concerned exclusively with knowledge of objects, and that the traditional view only *seems* to be
making assertions about objects, we see that physics has nothing to say one way
or the other about the traditional view. Just as the motor that runs a phonograph
turntable has nothing to do with the esthetic quality of the symphony we hear
on it (though it may have a great deal to do with how well or how poorly we
hear it), so the state of our cortex has nothing to do with the genuineness of
the value we experience (though it may have a great deal to do with the fact
that we experience it). It is the business of science (and especially of physiological
psychology) to examine the conditions under which such experiences occur. It
might be possible, for instance, to show that only a cortex of such-and-such a
configuration is able to experience the feeling that Kant called "respect." But
this would not mean that the feeling is illusory, or that the animals who experience it are not at the same time members of a "kingdom of ends," a world
of mutual rights and obligations that is as real, in its own dimensions of reality,
as the cortex is in its.

Kant's fundamental thesis is that we are dealing with two kinds of reality and
hence with different criteria of meaning and truth. If we suppose that values are
real in the way that facts are real and try to assess them by the criteria proper
to facts, the values disappear. But the same thing would happen to facts if we
tried to assess them by the criteria proper to values. Of course, it is unlikely that
anyone today would make the second kind of mistake. But this, as a matter of
fact, is exactly what medieval philosophers did, and it explains why they never
developed a competent science. Then, when the new physics appeared on the
scene, men began to make the first kind of identification and to assess values by
the standards of facts. In both cases, the identification was made to seem plausible by that confused mode of thought in which it appeared that both values and
facts are substances, and that therefore the same criteria ought to apply. It was
Kant's analysis of substance in phenomenalistic terms, as a spatiotemporally
organized manifold, that cleared up the confusion and paved the way for the
rehabilitation of the valuational point of view.

This is an important insight. But to make a place for values is not to give an account of them; to show that the criteria of truth and meaning that obtain in the natural sciences do not apply in the field of value is not to show what criteria *do* apply there. It seems clear, even at this point, that Kant's treatment of the field of value was far less adequate than his parallel treatment (in the *Critique of Pure Reason*) of the field of fact. There can hardly be any question, for instance, that his account of moral values (the kinds of value realized in conduct) was seriously one-sided. Although he was not committed to the narrow rigorism (duty for duty's sake) popularly attributed to him, his concentration on "right" to the exclusion of "good" resulted in his neglecting whole ranges of value that are capable of being realized in conduct, and with which moral philosophy should therefore be concerned.

Religion

The limitations of Kant's view of values appear also in his treatment of religion. We have seen that, in Kant's view, the only use theoretical reason can make of the idea of God is as a means to regulate inquiry, not as a means to designate an object. But, according to Kant, the whole meaning of the idea of God is not exhausted in its regulative use. On the contrary, just as the conception of the self as a limit leaves a "place" open for a real self in some other, valuational, non-thing sense, so the conception of God as a limit leaves a place open for a real God in some other sense. But, what other sense? For what kind of God is there a place in the Kantian system? As we shall see, Kant vacillated between a more critical view, in which he held God to be a value, and a less critical view, in which he held God to be a force or power in a more traditional sense. Thus Kant's conception of God reflects the same ambivalence found in his conception of freedom.

A "PRACTICAL" PROOF OF GOD'S EXISTENCE

Kant began his proof by pointing out that it does not follow, just because the existence of God cannot be proved by theoretical reason, that *no* proof of His existence is possible. The traditional proofs, whose inadequacy he had exposed in the *Critique of Pure Reason,* all rested in one way or another on theoretical considerations (such as the allegation that it is logically necessary to think of a first cause). Kant, however, based his own proof on moral considerations, and in doing so he supposed it to be exempt from the fallacies to which the traditional proofs fell victim.

Such a proof requires, first, a distinction between the *supreme* good (virtue) and the *perfect* good (virtue and happiness).

> To need happiness, to deserve it, and yet at the same time not to participate in it, cannot be consistent with the perfect volition of a rational being. . . . The distribution of happiness in exact proportion to morality (which is the worth of the person, and his worthiness to be happy) constitutes the *summum bonum* of a possible world; hence this *summum bonum* expresses the whole, the perfect good, in which, however, virtue as the condition is always the supreme good. . . .[m]

The argument proceeds as follows: Nothing we know about the physical world suggests that "virtue is the efficient cause of happiness." Indeed, in the mechanistic universe disclosed by natural science the proposition is false. Even if it should prove to be the case that the state of mind we call virtuous is followed by the state of mind we call happiness, the connection would not be moral. Nevertheless, to promote the *summum bonum* is an obligation imposed on all men. And since "ought implies can," this *summum bonum* must be realizable. Some other (and moral) force must therefore be operative in the universe, a force that will at some future date bring about the distribution of happiness in accordance with virtue.

> The possibility of . . . the *summum bonum,* viz. Happiness proportioned to that morality . . . must lead to the supposition of the existence of a cause adequate to this effect; in other words, it must postulate the *existence of God,* as the necessary condition of the possibility of the *summum bonum* (an object of the will which is necessarily connected with the moral legislation of pure reason). We proceed to exhibit this connexion in a convincing manner.
>
> *Happiness* is the condition of a rational being in the world with whom *everything goes according to his wish and will;* it rests, therefore, on the harmony of physical nature with his whole end, and likewise with the essential determining principle of his will. . . . There is not the least ground, therefore, in the moral law for a necessary connexion between morality and proportionate happiness in a being that belongs to the world. . . . Nevertheless, in the practical problem of pure reason, *i.e.* the necessary pursuit of the *summum bonum,* such a connexion is postulated as necessary: we ought to endeavour to promote the *summum bonum,* which, therefore, must be possible. Accordingly, the existence of a cause of all nature, distinct from nature itself, and containing the principle of this connexion, namely, of the exact harmony of happiness with morality, is also *postulated.* . . . The *summum bonum* is possible in the world only on the supposition of a Supreme Being having a causality corresponding to moral character. Now a being that is capable of acting on the conception of laws is an *intelligence* (a rational being), and the causality of such a being according to this conception of laws is his *will;* therefore the supreme cause of nature, which must be presupposed as a condition of the *summum bonum* is a being which is the cause of nature by *intelligence* and *will,* consequently its author, that is God. . . . Now it was seen to be a duty for us to promote the *summum bonum;* consequently it is not merely allowable, but it is a necessity connected with duty as a requisite, that we should presuppose the possibility of this *summum bonum;*

and as this is possible only on condition of the existence of God, it inseparably connects the supposition of this with duty; that is, it is morally necessary to assume the existence of God.[n]

PROOF OF THE IMMORTALITY OF THE SOUL

Kant believed that his argument also proved the immortality of the soul, for the adjustment of happiness to virtue depends on the attainment of virtue.

> The *perfect accordance* of the [will] with the moral law [i.e., complete virtue] is . . . perfection of which no rational being . . . is capable at any moment of his existence. Since, nevertheless, it is required as practically necessary [i.e., it is a state that ought to exist], it can only be found in a *progress in infinitum* towards that perfect accordance. . . .
>
> Now, this endless progress is only possible on the supposition of an *endless* duration of the *existence* and personality of the same rational being. . . . The *summum bonum*, then, practically is only possible on the supposition of the immortality of the soul; consequently this immortality, being inseparably connected with the moral law, is a postulate of pure practical reason (by which I mean a *theoretical* proposition, not demonstrable as such, but which is an inseparable result of an unconditional *a priori practical* law).[o]

There are two main objections to these proofs. First, they contradict the point on which Kant insisted in his moral theory—namely, that virtue is its own reward. Kant cannot have it both ways: If it is our duty to aim at happiness-in-accordance-with-virtue, it is not our duty to aim solely at virtue—and the moral imperative is no longer categorical but hypothetical. Thus, in his account of the *summum bonum,* Kant equates "worth of the person" and "worthiness to be happy."[8] But this is a play on words. The "worth of personality" on which he insists in his discussion of morality is simply the unique value that attaches to reason (whether in ourselves or in others); it has nothing whatever to do with desert.

Second, even supposing it to be our duty to try to produce a state of affairs in which happiness is distributed in accordance with virtue, Kant's conclusion still does not follow. In order to see that it does not, let us deny the conclusion and see what happens. Does it follow that we have no duties at all? Quite the contrary, as Kant himself was the first to point out.

> This proof . . . does not say: it is as necessary to assume the Being of God as to recognise the validity of the moral law; and consequently he who cannot convince himself of the first, can judge himself free from the obligations of the second. No! there must in such case only be given up the *aiming at* the final purpose in the world, to be brought about by the pursuit of the second (viz. a happiness of rational beings in harmony with the pursuit of moral laws, regarded as the highest good). Every rational being would yet have

8 See p. 9.

to cognise himself as straitly bound by the precepts of morality, for its laws are formal and command unconditionally without respect to purposes (as the matter of volition). . . . To further [happiness] so far as is in our power . . . is commanded us by the moral law; be the issue of this endeavour what it may. The fulfilling of duty consists in the form of the earnest will, not in the intermediate causes of success.

Suppose then that partly through the weakness of all the speculative arguments so highly extolled, and partly through many irregularities in nature and the world of sense which come before him, a man is persuaded of the proposition, There is no God; he would nevertheless be contemptible in his own eyes if on that account he were to imagine the laws of duty as empty, invalid and inobligatory.[p]

This argument in effect denies the premise of the moral proof of God's existence, yet surely it is in conformity with Kant's basic position. Our duty (so far as we have any duty in this connection) is to help to bring about such-and-such a state of affairs (to do so in our own sphere, as it were). It is immaterial whether in this action we fail to make a perfect and complete distribution. And even if it were true that the existence of an obligation to do something depended on the possibility of successfully bringing about the state of affairs in question, God's existence would not help to make *my* obligation real. Indeed, insofar as Kant's moral proof of the existence of God proves anything at all, it proves not that God must exist as a power capable of producing such-and-such a state of affairs, but that *I* must be capable of producing it.

NATURE OF GOD

There is another difficulty connected with the nature of God. Kant's arguments (supposing them to be valid) prove the existence only of a very limited God—merely an agent who distributes happiness in accordance with merit. But Kant, of course, wished to attribute omniscience, omnipotence, and the other theologically important properties to this God:

> From the principle, thus determined, of the causality of the Original Being we must not think Him merely as Intelligence and as legislative for nature. . . . We shall think this Original Being as *all-knowing:* thus our inmost dispositions (which constitute the proper moral worth of the actions of rational beings of the world) will not be hid from Him. We shall think Him as *all-mighty;* thus He will be able to make the whole of nature accord with this highest purpose. We shall think Him as *all-good,* and at the same time as *just:* because these two properties (which when united constitute *Wisdom*) are the conditions of the causality of a supreme Cause of the world, as highest good, under moral laws. So also all the other transcendental properties, such as *Eternity, Omnipresence,* etc. which are presupposed in reference to such a final purpose, must be thought in Him.[q]

It cannot be said that this argument is convincing. The most it proves is that God is a moral being who has considerable power. But such a being is far from either the God of Christian theology or the God of Christian piety. How, for instance, are we to get from "a principle that distributes happiness in accordance with righteousness" to an "only begotten Son"? According to Kant, since we are not the authors of the former idea, it is

> . . . appropriate to say that this archetype has *come down* to us from heaven and has assumed our humanity. . . . This ideal . . . of moral perfection . . . we can represent to ourselves only as the idea of a person. . . . For man can frame to himself no concept of the degree and strength of a force like that of moral disposition except by picturing it as encompassed by obstacles, and yet, in the face of the fiercest onslaughts, victorious. . . .
>
> We need therefore no [actual] empirical example to make [this] idea . . . our archetype. . . . Moreover, if anyone, in order to acknowledge, for his imitation, a particular individual as such an example of conformity to that idea, demands . . . that this individual should have performed miracles or had them performed for him—he who demands this thereby confesses to his own moral *unbelief,* that is, to his lack of faith in virtue. . . .
>
> Now if it were indeed a fact that such a truly godly-minded man at some particular time had descended, as it were, from heaven to earth and had given men in his own person, through his teachings, his conduct, and his sufferings, as perfect an *example* of a man well-pleasing to God as one can expect to find in external experience (for be it remembered that the *archetype* of such a person is to be sought nowhere but in our own reason), and if he had, through all this, produced immeasurably great good upon earth by effecting a revolution in the human race—even then we should have no cause for supposing him other than a man naturally begotten. . . . This is not, to be sure, absolutely to deny that he might be a man supernaturally begotten. But to suppose this can in no way benefit us practically.[r]

The "as it were" that Kant has slipped in here is significant—it is a mark of how greatly his view fails to satisfy the requirements of the orthodox Christian, who holds that Christ literally descended—that this is a matter of fact, not a manner of speaking. Yet even the rarefied and abstracted God that Kant describes is more than the critical philosophy can really allow. For the attribution of any sort of supernatural agency clearly contradicts the central theses of the *Critique of Pure Reason:* Causality is limited, by the whole procedure of the deduction, to phenomena. But there is no need to discuss this in detail, since there is no essential difference between assigning spontaneous, noumenal causality to the self and assigning it to God.

It is not surprising, in view of these difficulties, that Kant himself was not content with this position. Toward the end of his life, a new view began to emerge in his writings, but he died before fully developing it. Although this view was more consistent with the critical philosophy, it was even further removed from Christian orthodoxy than was the view it was replacing. For the essence of this final view lay in interpreting God not as a causal agent but (like the moral self) as a value. According to this interpretation, God would seem to be the same sort of value we attribute to ourselves as persons, the supreme example of that reason we respect in ourselves. What distinguishes God from man is the difference between right and duty. When we appreciate this value in ourselves, we experience it under the form of a compulsion. To respect it is a duty that, often enough, we fail to live up to. When we think of this value in its own right, as a good to be realized (not as an obligation imposed on us), we call it "God."

IDENTIFICATION OF RELIGION AND MORALITY

As stated above, Kant's view may sound odd. Perhaps it will sound less odd if it is pointed out that Kant in effect made a religion of morality. As we have seen, the language he used in discussing his moral law was essentially religious in tone.[9] We respect the moral law as a supreme value, in comparison with which our own personal wants, desires, and demands are completely trivial and insignificant. Now respect is not far from worship. Indeed, it is probably as near to worship as the mind of the Enlightenment, filled with a sense of man's dignity as a rational being, could come. Respect combines the pride of the classical mind (its sense of the autonomy and value of reason) with the humility of the Christian mind (its sense of man's distance from the realization of his ideal). Insofar as we think of the reason within us as imposing certain acts on the persons we feel ourselves to be, we are thinking in *moral* terms. Insofar as we think of reason, not as it is in us or in connection with the acts it dictates to us, but simply as a supreme value in itself, we are thinking in *religious* terms.

In thus identifying religion and morality, Kant revived a view that not only was congenial to the classical mind but that anticipated a trend that appeared in the nineteenth century. In this view, much dropped out that had been important in the Christian tradition. In fact, it may be said that what dropped out was, historically speaking, the core of Christianity—its religiosity, its belief in a personal *and* transcendent God. All the adherents of Christian doctrine would agree that Christianity is certainly a *moral* religion; but most of them would also insist that it is a moral *religion*.

Mechanism and Teleology

The widespread belief that the universe is purposive—not merely a meaningless machine—must also be considered. Since, as has been pointed out, the idea of real causal efficacy is inconsistent with the critical position,[10] we must ask

9 See, for instance, pp. 70–71.
10 See p. 87.

whether there is any interpretation of purposiveness that is consistent with the main theses of the *Critique of Pure Reason*. Kant devoted the *Critique of Judgment* to this question. Although his reply cannot be explored in detail, its main outlines are easily given.

Kant began by analyzing the concept of purposiveness-without-purpose. This may sound like a paradox, but Kant was actually using the concept descriptively. Some works of art, he believed, are planned to look as if they were not planned. An example is the so-called English style of garden. During the seventeenth and much of the eighteenth centuries, the French style of garden, such as that fashioned by Le Notre at Versailles, was the mode. Plants were forced into unnatural geometrical patterns and masses. For instance, trees were planted in straight rows and trimmed to exactly the same height; lawns were designed to look not like grass but like green carpets. The intent was to make the spectator think how much time, effort, and money had gone into making nature look unnatural. During the eighteenth century, however, taste began to change, and the English style of landscape gardening came into favor. This type of garden was just as carefully studied as Le Notre's, but the effect was entirely different. Trees and plants were set out to look as if they had grown up where their seeds happened to fall. Paths wandered artlessly back and forth (instead of being cut through woods on a rigid pattern) and brought one out at a view that the landscape artist intended one to enjoy. The emphasis was on naturalness, but it was designed naturalness. Here, then, is an example of purposiveness-without-purpose.

Kant believed purposiveness-without-purpose to be the essential factor in all esthetic experience. But surely he was mistaken, for witness our enjoyment of the French style of landscape gardening. The most that can be said is that purposiveness-without-purpose is *one* of the factors involved in *some* types of beauty. In esthetics, as in the field of morality, Kant tried to generalize a local (geographically and temporally) preference into a universal explanation.

Kant's primary interest in purposiveness-without-purpose, however, lay not in esthetics but in its supposed relevance to the problems of teleology in the natural world. According to Kant, some natural objects, namely, those objects called "organisms," have the same sort of structure as art objects; they must, therefore, be cognized by means of the same sort of concept. Kant did not mean, of course, that an organism has exactly the *same* structure as an object of art; he meant simply that in both organisms and art objects a means-end relationship among parts, and between parts and their whole, exists. This is why their parts are called "organs." This is *empirically* quite a different kind of relationship from a mechanical one. And this difference is reflected in the kind of question we ask when we set out to understand an organism. When we study an organism we do not look *behind* to the antecedent events in time that determined the state of affairs that now exists; we look *ahead* to the end that the current state of affairs is serving. Thus we ask, "What is the function of such-and-such a gland?" And when we have found, for example, that the gland regulates the organism's size, we feel we understand it—it is explained. According to Kant, all this takes place at a purely empirical level. That is, we do not have to suppose that someone actually *designed* the gland with this purpose in mind.

Purposiveness in organisms is an "as if" concept. We say that a gland functions *as if* God (or someone else) had planned it that way. The concept of purposiveness is thus descriptive and methodological; it designates a characteristic and empirically verifiable relation among parts. Hence we can say that every organism exemplifies purposiveness (a structure of such-and-such a kind) without purpose (no supernatural intellect that actually planned it that way). Thus the organism is like the English style of garden (of course, the garden actually was planned, but it *claims* not to be). For in both the organism and the garden we are judging about an actually existent relationship of parts. Nature, it may be said, is what art tries to be.

There is a difference, it should be noted, between the concept of purposiveness as applied to organisms and the concept as applied to the world in general. In the latter case, "purposiveness" is simply a regulative maxim ("Nothing in nature is in vain") that leads us to act as if every occurrence, however whimsical it may seem to be, has a cause. But with respect to organisms, the concept of purposiveness is more than a merely regulative maxim. Organisms *may* be explicable in mechanistic terms, but not for minds constituted like ours. We inevitably introduce purposive concepts, like the concept of function, if we want to understand organisms. This does not mean, of course, that there is any either-or condition to the situation. "Purposiveness" and "mechanism" are not rival hypotheses about the causes of the objects in question. For, in Kant's view, causality is not a transference of power but a pattern of regularity—a lawfulness in the sequence of events in the manifold. Hence, to say that organisms may be explicable in mechanistic terms is to say merely that it may be possible to find a formula for the pattern of regularity that is deducible from the laws of motion. To say that organisms are explicable in purposive terms is to assert merely that as a matter of fact we use means-end concepts.

There is, then, no conflict between mechanism and purposiveness-without-purpose, for neither is an assertion about what "really" produces a given state of affairs.[11] They are simply alternative descriptions of the state of affairs in question. Thus, for instance, I might describe a certain picture by saying that the artist used such-and-such a palette, such-and-such kinds of brushes, such-and-such a technique of laying on paint, and so on. There is no conflict between this and saying that the picture is "a Crucifixion in the manner of Tintoretto." Note that in the latter statement I am not attributing the canvas to Tintoretto. I am simply giving an alternative description of the canvas, perfectly adequate for anyone acquainted with the manner of Tintoretto. I am not saying that Tintoretto was the painter who "really" produced this canvas; I am saying merely

11 The point is that the *Critique of Pure Reason* had ruled out questions about "real" causality (that is, noumenal efficacy).

that the canvas is *as if* Tintoretto had painted it. That is, had he painted it, he would have used a palette like this and a technique like this, and the outcome would have been much the same.

Though purposiveness-without-purpose is a methodological concept of some importance, it may not be clear at first sight what bearing it has on the moral and religious considerations that led Kant to introduce it. According to Kant, the argument shows (1) that questions about whether or not the world "really" has an intelligent author are based on a misunderstanding and cannot be answered one way or the other; (2) that, given minds constituted like ours, we must inevitably think of the world as if it had such an author—that is, as if it had meaning and purpose; and (3) that, far from contradicting the presuppositions of the natural sciences, this "as-if purposiveness" actually supplements them and makes a complete and harmonious world view possible.

This position is obviously a long way from the view of providence that the orthodox Christian understands. Kant's reply to this implied criticism would doubtless have been that the orthodox Christian does not really *understand* what he is demanding of philosophy, and that when one tries to come to grips with the orthodox Christian's idea, it collapses into confusion and anthropomorphism.

Summary

It should now be clear why Kant's theories have often been regarded as difficult. But, despite the great complications encountered in analyzing the details of the various deductions, the basic ideas of the Kantian philosophy are easily grasped. Kant undertook to make a new analysis of the nature of knowledge that would not only show its proper limitations (as the empiricists had undertaken to do) but that would also validate knowledge within its own proper field (as the empiricists had notoriously failed to do). The main feature of this new analysis was the due weight given both to the empirical factor (Galileo's "observe") *and* to the universal and necessary factor (Galileo's "demonstrate"), which none of Kant's predecessors had known how to combine effectively. The main reason for Kant's success in this respect was his grasp of the role of experiment—his recognition, that is, that the answers one gets depend on the questions one asks. The result of Kant's recognition of the mind's role as a "questioner" of nature was a wholly new conception of the nature of the self and its objects, a conception that has had important implications in almost every field of inquiry, from physics and psychology to ethics and art criticism.

The main points in this new view of the nature of self and its objects are: (1) Self and not-self are not metaphysically distinct "ultimates" but "constructs" within the field of experience. (2) Experience is a spatiotemporal manifold in which distinctions are made, including the distinction between self and not-self.

(3) The natural sciences are limited to describing and generalizing about this spatiotemporal manifold and the various "objects" distinguished within it, including self (the science of psychology) and not-self (physics, chemistry, and so on). (4) Experience—the spatiotemporal manifold—is dependent on "transcendental" conditions. Because they are "transcendental," these conditions are not *in* experience (in the sense that red and blue, hot and cold, sweet and sour, are in experience). Hence, despite Hume's failure to find them, there is no evidence for denying their existence. Hume was simply looking for the wrong things in the wrong place. (5) Though these transcendental conditions are not *in* experience and hence cannot be objects of scientific cognition, we know *that* they exist, for they are the necessary conditions of experience. We can argue from what *is* known in experience to what must be true for there to be this knowledge in experience. (6) These transcendental conditions, which are nothing but the basic types of "questions" the mind asks of nature, validate the sciences in their own field and at the same time limit them to this field. (7) Since "God, freedom, and immortality" fall outside this field, the sciences can say nothing one way or the other about them. (8) It follows that God and the free immortal self are neither substantival nor causally efficacious, for substance and causality are concepts relevant only within the experiential field. (9) Nevertheless, God and the free immortal self are real, for their reality is guaranteed by the facts of moral experience.

These, then, are the main points that Kant undertook to establish. It is certainly true, as has already been noted, that he did not prove all he wanted to prove or all he thought he had proved. But the questions a philosopher asks are no less important than the answers he finds for them. The ways in which Kant framed his questions have become, for better or for worse, a part of the fabric of modern culture. Every great philosopher leaves his mark on the subsequent development of thought, not only by his theories, but by the way he formulates his problems. This was true of Plato and Aristotle; ever since their time philosophers have wrestled with the problems they defined. In the remaining chapters of this book we shall see that this was also true of Kant. It is a measure of his stature as a philosopher.

CHAPTER 4

Reactions Against Kantianism: Hegel and Schopenhauer

As we have seen, the Age of Reason was sustained by three basic assumptions: (1) that there is a rational order of eternal truths, (2) that man has a mind capable of understanding these truths, and (3) that he has a will capable of acting in accordance with them. According to the men of the Age of Reason, every science —not only physics and chemistry, but economics, politics, and ethics as well— begins from propositions whose truth is immediately recognizable. The business of each science is to formulate all the theorems that can be derived from its special set of principles; the business of rational men everywhere is to apply this whole body of truths in the ordinary affairs of daily life. "We hold these truths to be self-evident . . . ," said the founding fathers. "Let us sit down in a cool hour," added Bishop Butler, and find ways to apply the truths we all recognize to be the problems of practical life.[1]

1 Butler, who died in 1752, naturally did not have the founding fathers' self-evident truths specifically in mind.

During the nineteenth century all three of these basic propositions were attacked from a variety of points of view, and before long there came to be widespread scepticism about them—about the existence of such eternal truths; about the power of the human intellect to know them, even if they did exist; and about the capacity of the will to find a "cool hour," or to act rationally and in accordance with its long-range interests, even supposing that these interests could be discovered.

Taken as a whole, then, nineteenth-century philosophy can be characterized as a series of attempts to deal with the problems created by the collapse of the world view of the Age of Reason. Of the many solutions proposed, none came to dominate Western culture. Indeed, one of the chief characteristics of the nineteenth and twentieth centuries, as compared with earlier ages, is the diversity of world views.

The philosophers who followed Kant found his position an unsatisfactory form of fence-sitting, and most of them climbed down from the fence to one side or the other. As we have seen, Kant believed that there are things-in-themselves, but he denied that we can ever know them. Depending on their underlying values, post-Kantian philosophers either maintained that we do after all have access to things-in-themselves or denied that there are things-in-themselves and limited reality to the space-time manifold and to what Kant called the empirical self. In general, these philosophers also concluded that reason plays either a much larger or a much smaller role—both in cognition and in the moral life—than Kant had allowed. Yet none of these philosophers was untouched by Kant: Those who reaffirmed that knowledge of a transempirical reality is possible did not return to a pre-Kantian type of rationalism; those who limited reality to the space-time manifold did not return directly to Hume.

Why did post-Kantian philosophers accept Kant's distinctions rather than simply revert to earlier theories? In the first place, Kant's influence was too powerful. Everyone had to take account of his views; in fact, for a long time to come everyone thought not only in his terms but also largely in his vocabulary. Even those philosophers who reached conclusions very remote from Kant's were nevertheless Kantian in the sense that they started out from a basically Kantian orientation and merely found reasons for developing his thought in a different direction and with a different emphasis. In the second place, the whole mood of Western culture had changed since Kant's time—indeed, it had been changing even while Kant wrote. These changes in values and outlook greatly affected the course of philosophical speculation.

Romanticism

The new complex of attitudes can be brought under the rubric of "Romanticism." But this is only another of those broad terms (like "Renaissance" and "Reformation") that trap the unwary. For people tend to think that such terms name simple, self-identical entities—that there is a distinct little nugget of "Romanticism," for example, that attaches itself to poems, pictures, and manners during a certain well-defined period. Romanticism is a very complex phenomenon; hence no more than one aspect of it can be considered here, and that only very inadequately. Indeed, it will be necessary to limit discussion to Romanticism as a reaction against the mood of the Enlightenment—in particular, against its conception of knowledge.

Certainly, the spirit of the Enlightenment was open to criticism. Some people were annoyed by its irreligion; others by its complacency; others again by what they felt to be its narrowness and artificiality; and still others by its conviction that by stressing order, rule, and measure, both in the universe at large and in man in particular, everything can be neatly pigeonholed and labeled. To such minds, the universe seemed bigger, richer, more varied and exciting, and more of a unity than the thinkers of the Age of Reason had allowed.

HOSTILITY TO REASON

The focus of the Romantic attack was naturally against "reason," which the Romantics evaluated as "a false secondary power by which we multiply distinctions." To the Romantic mind, the distinctions that reason makes are artificial, imposed, and man-made; they divide, and in dividing destroy, the living whole of reality—"We murder to dissect." How, then, are we to get in touch with the real? By divesting ourselves, insofar as we can, of the whole apparatus of learning and scholarship and by becoming like children or simple, uneducated men; by attending to nature rather than to the works of man; by becoming passive and letting nature work upon us; by contemplation and communion, rather than by ratiocination and scientific method.

When Wordsworth was asked by a friend why he "wasted" his time in dreamy reverie and in contemplation of nature, he replied,

> Nor less I deem that there are Powers
> Which of themselves our minds impress;
> That we can feed this mind of ours
> In a wise passiveness.[a]

Inviting his sister to join him in a walk in the woods on a lovely spring day, he pointed out,

> One moment now may give us more
> Than years of toiling reason:
> Our minds shall drink at every pore
> The spirit of the season. . . .
> And bring no book: for this one day
> We'll give to idleness.[b]

And in *The Tables Turned:*

> Books! 'tis a dull and endless strife:
> Come, hear the woodland linnet,
> How sweet his music! on my life,
> There's more of wisdom in it. . . .
>
> One impulse from a vernal wood
> May teach you more of man,
> Of moral evil and of good,
> Than all the sages can. . . .
>
> Enough of Science and of Art;
> Close up those barren leaves;
> Come forth, and bring with you a heart
> That watches and receives.

Keats, too, expressed this feeling:

> O thou whose only book has been the light
> Of supreme darkness, which thou feddest on
> Night after night, when Phoebus was away!
> To thee the Spring shall be a triple morn.
> O fret not after knowledge. I have none,
> And yet my song comes native with the warmth.
> O fret not after knowledge! I have none,
> And yet the evening listens. He who saddens
> At thought of idleness cannot be idle,
> And he's awake who thinks himself asleep.[c]

The notion that only a difference of degree, rather than a difference of kind, exists between mind-awake and mind-asleep, and that, on the whole, our truest insights into the nature of reality come during the latter rather than the former state, is characteristic of Romanticism.

> Our life is twofold: Sleep hath its own world,
> A boundary between the things misnamed
> Death and existence: Sleep hath its own world,
> And a wide realm of wild reality,
> And dreams in their development have breath,
> And tears, and tortures, and the touch of joy;
> They leave a weight upon our waking thoughts,
> They take a weight from off our waking toils,
> They do divide our being; they become
> A portion of ourselves as of our time. . . .
> They make us what we were not—what they will,
> And shake us with the vision that's gone by,
> The dread of vanish'd shadows—Are they so?

> Is not the past all shadow? What are they?
> Creations of the mind?—The mind can make
> Substance, and people planets of its own
> With beings brighter than have been, and give
> A breath to forms which can outlive all flesh.[d]

And just as we are nearer to the truth about the universe when we dream than when we are awake, so we are nearer to it as children than as adults:

> Dear Child! dear Girl! that walkest with me here,
> If thou appear untouched by solemn thought,
> Thy nature is not therefore less divine:
> Thou liest in Abraham's bosom all the year;
> And worship'st at the Temple's inner shrine,
> God being with thee when we know it not.[e]

And as infants we are even nearer:

> Thou, whose exterior semblance doth belie
>   Thy soul's immensity:
> Thou best Philosopher. . . .
>   Mighty Prophet! Seer blest!
>   On whom those truths do rest,
> Which we are toiling all our lives to find . . . ,
> Thou little Child, yet glorious in the might
> Of heaven-born freedom on thy being's height. . . .
> Trailing clouds of glory do we come
>   From God who is our home:
> Heaven lies about us in our infancy!
> Shades of the prison-house begin to close
>   Upon the growing Boy
> But He beholds the light, and whence it flows,
>   He sees it in his joy;
> The Youth, who daily farther from the east
>   Must travel, still is Nature's Priest,
>   And by the vision splendid
>   Is on his way attended;
> At length the Man perceives it die away,
> And fade into the light of common day.[f]

The logical terminus of this line of thought is that animals, even more than humankind, are the best philosophers:

> Poor little Foal of an oppressed Race!
> I love the languid patience of thy face . . .
> Do prophetic Fears anticipate,
> Meek child of Misery! thy future fate? . . .

Or is thy sad heart thrill'd with filial pain
To see thy wretched Mother's shorten'd chain? . . .
Poor Ass! thy master should have learnt to show
Pity—best taught by fellowship of woe! . . .
Innocent Foal . . .
I hail thee Brother—spite of the fool's scorn! . . .
Yea! and more musically sweet to me
Thy dissonant harsh bray of joy would be,
Than warbled melodies that soothe to rest
The aching of pale Fashion's vacant breast!ᵍ

CONCEPTION OF REALITY

What, then, is the reality disclosed in "the drowsy numbness" of intoxication, in the innocence of childhood, "on the viewless wings of poesy," in silent communion with nature, or in the rapt contemplation of a beautiful work of art? Naturally what each poet found was colored by his individual temperament, but among the Romantics there was considerable unanimity. They were impressed by the largeness of reality, an immensity that baffled the methods of science and that made the whole human enterprise, on which the preceding age had set such store, petty and trivial.

A presence that disturbs me with the joy
Of elevated thoughts; a sense sublime
Of something far more deeply interfused,
Whose dwelling is the light of setting suns,
And the round ocean and the living air,
And the blue sky, and in the mind of man:
A motion and a spirit, that impels
All thinking things, all objects of all thought,
And rolls through all things.ʰ

If the gentler aspects of nature moved Wordsworth, the more turbulent touched Shelley's muse: "the wild West wind, destroyer and preserver," the dizzy ravines and wild waterfalls "where woods and winds contend," and the whole tremendous spectacle of the Alps.

The everlasting universe of things
Flows through the mind, and rolls its rapid waves,
Now dark—now glittering—now reflecting gloom—
Now lending splendour, where from secret springs
The source of human thought its tribute brings
Of waters. . . .
Some say that gleams of a remoter world
Visit the soul in sleep,—that death is slumber,
And that its shapes the busy thoughts outnumber

Of those who wake and live.—I look on high;
Has some unknown omnipotence unfurled
The veil of life and death? or do I lie
In dream, and does the mightier world of sleep
Spread far around and inaccessibly
Its circles? . . .
The wilderness has a mysterious tongue
Which teaches awful doubt, or faith so mild,
So solemn, so serene, that man may be,
But for such faith with nature reconciled;
Thou hast a voice, great Mountain, to repeal
Large codes of fraud and woe; not understood
By all, but which the wise, and great, and good
Interpret, or make felt, or deeply feel.[i]

There was, then, an ambivalence in the Romantic mood. On the one hand, the Romantics believed that their finiteness as men separated them from the immensity of the real:

Roll on, thou deep and dark blue Ocean, roll!
Ten thousand fleets sweep over thee in vain;
Man marks the earth with ruin, his control
Stops with the shore; upon the watery plain
The wrecks are all thy deed, nor doth remain
A shadow of man's ravage, save his own,
When, for a moment, like a drop of rain,
He sinks into thy depths with bubbling groan,
Without a grave, unknell'd, uncoffin'd, and unknown.

On the other hand, they felt an affinity with this great, sublime, and transcendent immensity:

And I have loved thee, Ocean! and my joy
Of youthful sports was on thy breast to be
Borne like thy bubbles, onward. From a boy
I wanton'd with thy breakers—they to me
Were a delight; and if the freshening sea
Made them a terror—'twas a pleasing fear,
For I was as it were a child of thee,
And trusted to thy billows far and near,
And laid my hand upon thy mane—as I do here.[j]

Thus the Romantics rejected two of the cardinal theses of the Enlightenment. The Enlightenment thinkers had perceived man as unique—as different from all the rest of nature because he alone possesses reason. Because the Romantics downgraded reason, they were disposed to think of man as a part of nature, as dependent on nature not only for bodily sustenance but also for his highest thoughts and noblest aspirations:

> The anchor of my purest thoughts, the nurse,
> The guide, the guardian of my heart, and soul
> Of all my moral being.[k]

In addition, because the Romantics disliked sharp distinctions of any kind, they rejected the Enlightenment view of the universe as made up of a large number of separate entities (selves, things) and viewed the universe as one continuous living and dynamic being. For example, in Goethe's *Faust* the Earth Spirit exclaims,

> In the floods of life, in the storm of work,
> In ebb and flow,
> In warp and weft,
> Cradle and grave,
> An eternal sea,
> A changing patchwork,
> A glowing life,
> At the whirring loom of Time I weave
> The living clothes of the Deity.[l]

REACTION TO KANTIANISM

The Romantic mind, as sketched here, would obviously have been both attracted to and repelled by Kantianism. The Romantics believed that Kant was correct in recognizing the limitations of rational knowledge and in pointing out the existence of a vast realm of true reality behind the phenomenal world. But no sooner had Kant opened up these vistas of immensity than he slammed the door in men's faces, maintaining that we can know nothing about that real world—only *that* it exists. To the Romantics, this was intolerable. From their point of view, Kantianism, by showing the radical incompetence of science—its inability to reach any knowledge of things-in-themselves—merely prepared the way for the development of a new metaphysics. Kant's position, in fact, depended on a delicate—one might almost say precarious—balance of antithetical forces; it could be maintained only by a mind sensitive to all these forces and at the same time capable of exercising great self-restraint with respect to its own preferences. Though Kant was unable to maintain this balance consistently, for him balance was at least an ideal. For the Romantics, in contrast, balance was an ideal no longer. The Romantic mind valued unity far more than balance, and identity and commitment far more than any neutral and objective weighing of evidence.

The two philosophers to be considered next—Hegel and Schopenhauer—were deeply influenced by this Romantic mood. Both were persuaded that reality is immense and complex—too complex to be exhaustively explained by the neat conceptual schemes of eighteenth-century rationalism. Both were strongly responsive to the movement and change that the Romantic poets emphasized. Hence for both of them Kant was still too much of an eighteenth-century rationalist. They appreciated the fact that he had conceded the existence of a realm of wide reality beyond the space-time manifold (the world to which he had confined Newtonian physics). But they reacted strongly against the sharp distinction that he had drawn between phenomena and noumena and rejected Kant's agnosticism in this respect. But here Hegel and Schopenhauer themselves parted company.

There are two logically possible arguments open to those who, in opposition to Kant, claim that the mind has access to noumena.[2] On the one hand, it is possible to argue that the "ideas of pure reason" are not merely regulative (as Kant had claimed[3]) but, like the categories, constitutive; and that, furthermore, they are constitutive of things as they are, not of things as they appear. On the other hand, it is possible to agree with Kant that the intellect is limited to things as they appear, and to maintain that the world of things as they really are is nevertheless accessible to us in intuition.

Hegel is the outstanding representative of the first type of criticism; Schopenhauer's philosophy illustrates the second type. Both these views are discussed in some detail below, for each reflects a movement of thought that exerted a powerful influence in many directions throughout the nineteenth century and even into our own day.

Hegel

G. W. F. Hegel, born in 1770, was the son of a minor official in Stuttgart in southern Germany. Though his family was poor, he managed to get a university education. He served for a number of years as a private tutor and later as a newspaper editor and as the principal of a school. Hegel was slow in securing a professorship, chiefly because he published very little until he was thirty-seven. Eventually, however, he was appointed to a chair at Heidelberg and, a year later, to one at Berlin. As he grew older, Hegel became conservative: He prized order above freedom and became deeply suspicious of "reform." Hegel found the

2 Of course, it is also possible to reject noumena and to maintain that reality is limited to the space-time manifold. See pp. 160–62.

3 According to Kant, it will be recalled, substance, causality, and the other categories are constitutive of, and limited to, the spatiotemporal manifold—that is, they provide an a priori order for experience. Concepts like God, self, and totality, on the other hand, are methodological aids. Rather than defining objects, they "regulate" our empirical inquiries. See pp. 58–62.

atmosphere of the kingdom of Prussia congenial, possibly because he received the official approval and support of the state. Once established in Berlin, his fame spread and something approaching a Hegelian cult developed.

Hegel is one of the most difficult of philosophers to study, partly, but by no means merely, because of the intrinsic difficulty of his theories. He wrote in an almost deliberately obfuscating manner and was able to complete only bits and pieces of the vast "system" that he envisioned. Hegel considered *The Phenomenology of the Spirit* (published in 1807) to be no more than a preface to the system he proposed—yet *The Phenomenology* is over seven hundred fifty pages in length and has a preface of its own of sixty-five pages. In 1817 he published an outline of the whole system, the *Encyclopaedia of the Philosophical Sciences*, which went through several revisions during his lifetime. The rest of his publications consist of the *Logic* (in two versions), the only completed part of the system, and the notes from his lectures on various subjects—philosophy of history, philosophy of art, history of philosophy—that were recorded by students and published after his death. It is not surprising that there is no agreement regarding the nature of Hegel's views. The discussion presented below relies chiefly on *The Phenomenology* and aims at bringing out only the main features of this great work.

Hegel's View of Reason

A good starting point for this discussion is Hegel's belief that the universe is rational. This, of course, is a conviction he shared with many other philosophers, in particular, the thinkers of the Age of Reason. But, as will be seen, Hegel's view of the nature of reason, and thus of the rationality of the universe, differed in important respects from theirs. However, on one point at least he did agree with them. According to Hegel, to say that the universe is rational is to say that no matter how far apart men may start out, given patience and good will, they can reach agreement regarding the truth. Indeed, to seek agreement is one aspect of being human. Those who refuse to do so "trample the roots of humanity underfoot": "The nature of humanity is to impel men to agree with one another, and its very existence lies simply in the explicit realization of a community of conscious life. What is anti-human, the condition of mere animals, consists in keeping within the sphere of feeling pure and simple, and in being able to communicate only by way of feeling-states."[m]

Hegel's point may be illustrated by a trivial example: Suppose that Mr. A looks at a colored patch and calls it red. Mr. B, looking at the patch, replies, "Oh, no; that's blue." So far A and B are in contradiction—a situation in which men too often find themselves. Perhaps A and B continue to insist dogmatically on their original assertions; but, if they are willing to "return upon and reconsider"[n] the colored patch that they have observed, they may agree that the color is royal purple—a bluish red or (if one prefers) a reddish blue. Thus A and B may come to see that they were in contradiction only because each was emphasizing one shade in the color and ignoring the other—each, while affirming his part of the truth, denied the part of the truth that the other was affirming.

A more complex example is that of the dispute over United States policy in Southeast Asia. Some people hold that the aim of United States policy is to protect weak states from subversion by Communist aggression; others maintain that this policy is a vicious neocolonial conspiracy. Those who accept Hegel's view that the universe is rational would have to hold that here too there is a formula, however difficult it may prove to work it out, that reconciles the conflicting interpretations of United States policy. Now, it is a truism that United States policy looks different from different points of view. A Vietnamese villager whose home has been destroyed by American bombers will look at the situation differently from an American marine who has been wounded by a guerrilla sniper. It is also a truism that some perspectives are more limited than others: Presumably, the military staff in Saigon has a more complete view of the course of the war than does the wounded marine. But it is not immediately evident that, as Hegel claims, *all* partial perspectives can be harmonized into a simple all-inclusive perspective.

Yet this is Hegel's claim: (1) Every particular assertion (for example, "This color is red") is only *partially* true, because it is always made from a limited point of view. (2) Every particular assertion *is* nevertheless partially true (the color really is red, when seen under certain lighting conditions or in juxtaposition with that other color). (3) Because every particular assertion ("The color is red") is only partially true, it tends to generate a compensatory assertion ("The color is blue"). (4) These conflicting assertions are reconcilable in a more inclusive assertion ("The color is royal purple"). (5) This more inclusive assertion in turn proves to be partial and thus requires correction by a still more adequate formulation.

MINDS AND THEIR OBJECTS

So far Hegel probably sounds like many another philosopher—like Plato, for instance. Plato, too, distinguished between what the world looks like to "common sense" and what it really is for "critical reason," and Plato also held that there is a "profound and fruitful process" by which one rises from the former level to the latter.[o] But whereas Plato believed that the truth consists in eternal and unchanging forms that lie outside the mind illumined by them, Hegel accepted Kant's "Copernican" revolution, his replacement of the notion of mind and its objects as completely independent entities with the radically different notion of mind and its objects as functionally related and as emerging together in experience. Indeed, Hegel carried this insight much farther than Kant had done:

In my view—a view which the developed exposition of the system itself can alone justify—everything depends on grasping and expressing the ultimate truth not as Substance but as Subject as well.

. . . .

In general, in virtue of the principle that . . . substance is implicitly and in itself subject, all content makes its reflection into itself in its own special way. The subsistence or substance of anything that exists is its self-identity; for its want of identity, or oneness with itself, would be its dissolution. But self-identity is pure abstraction; and this is just thinking. When I say Quality, I state simple determinateness; by means of its quality one existence is distinguished from another or is an "existence"; it is for itself, something on its own account, or subsists with itself because of its simple characteristic. But by doing so it is essentially Thought.

Here we find contained the principle that Being is Thought. . . .

Owing to the nature which being thus has, and so far as what is has this nature from the point of view of knowledge, this thinking is not an activity which treats the content as something alien and external; it is not reflection into self away from the content. . . . Rather, since knowledge sees the content go back into its own proper inner nature, the activity of knowledge is absorbed in that content—for it (the activity) is the immanent self of the content—and is also at the same time returned into itself, for this activity is pure self-identity in otherness. In this way the knowing activity is the artful device which, while seeming to refrain from activity, looks on and watches how specific determinateness with its concrete life, just where it believes it is working out its own self-preservation and its own private interest, is, in point of fact, doing the very opposite, is doing what brings about its own dissolution and makes itself a moment in the whole.[p]

Hegel's point in the first sentence is simply that he intends to replace the old metaphysics, which took it for granted that substance was the prime metaphysical concept, with a new metaphysics based on the notion of thought, or of consciousness. For philosophers adhering to the old metaphysics there had been a question about whether only one substance exists or several; and in the latter case, how such substances are related. But there had been general agreement about what a substance is: It is a self-identical and enduring entity that does not itself change but that possesses changing properties, or attributes. It is independent—it is that which stands alone. It is self-subsistent. And so on. Thus, when Descartes discovered his self in the course of methodological doubt, he assumed it to be "a thing which thinks." Hegel's position, in contrast, is much more psychologically acute and much less bound by prior metaphysical commitments. For surely, when we introspect we do not find a thing-self, as Hume had pointed out. But neither do we find only impressions and ideas, as Hume had claimed. What we do find is not easy to describe—the obscurities of the quoted passage testify to this. The difficulty results in part from the fact that Hegel is largely breaking new ground; but it also results from the fact that the only language available to him (and for that matter to us) is so saturated with substantival thinking that one inevitably falls into paradox when using it to talk about what is not a substance but an activity.

THE NATURE OF EXPERIENCE

Perhaps it will be helpful to rephrase Hegel's view of thought in language slightly different from his. Let us start with ordinary, everyday experience. What I find in experience is, first of all, "things"—desks, tables, chairs. Sometimes I am also aware of myself, but even when I am not I know perfectly well that the experience I am having is mine. Now, what I have called "things" Hegel calls "content." And to say that I experience content as mine is to say that I experience it as not-me. It is, as Hegel points out in the passage just quoted, experienced as "other," as over there, as what one is not. Furthermore, I do not experience self in the same sense that I experience "other." To be aware of self is not to be aware of *another* bit of content; it is to be aware of whatever content I happen to be aware of as other. Self-awareness is simply awareness of the object as more sharply distinguished than it once was, as more emphatically not *me* but other-than-me.

An example may be helpful. At the theater I may be "wholly absorbed" in *Hamlet*. Nevertheless, I do not sheerly identify with Hamlet; I "know," even if I am not consciously aware of it, that the Hamlet I see is not a prince of Denmark, but an actor, and that I am in my seat watching him out there on the stage. Hegel's point is that there must be this basic distinction for there to *be* experience at all. There is no experience without some awareness, however faint, that it *is* experience. To understand this point clearly, let us consider another Hegelian distinction, the distinction between an object as it is "in itself" and the object as it is "for" someone, say, for an observer. For example, I may distinguish between my desk as it is in itself and my desk as it is for me, that is, as an object of my experience. But this distinction is not made by the desk as well as by me; it can be made only by conscious beings, by minds. Indeed, the making of this distinction is precisely what "being conscious," or "having a mind," consists in.

Hence, if we accept Hegel's "ultimate truth" that consciousness, not substance, is the prime metaphysical concept, we give a very different account of reality from that given by the traditional metaphysics, which had been dominated by the concept of substance. In the Hegelian view, the notions of independence and unchanging self-subsistence disappear: The mind is not independent, because it can never get away from its other (or content). And if it were to free itself from its other, it would dissolve—for its "being" consists in experiencing content. Nor is the mind unchanging; on the contrary, it is changing all the time—developing, expanding, correcting, and revising itself and its experience.

Although it is possible to speak of the "self-identity" of the mind, or consciousness, this self-identity is very different from the self-identity that traditional metaphysics attributed to substance. The self-identity of substance is the sheer, unbroken self-identity of continuous being. The self-identity of consciousness is awareness of the other in a special, and enlightened, way. And the self-identity of consciousness, unlike the self-identity of substance, is a matter of degree, ranging all the way from the "bare" self-consciousness of the infant, who is marginally aware of, say, becoming warm (and hence of not being *identical* with warmth), to the more complex self-consciousness of a sophisticated and intro-spective adult. At every level, therefore, self-consciousness (self-identity) is the reciprocal, or reflection, of the degree of structure, order, complexity, and variety of the "other." The self of the baby is minimal, because its experience is ele-mentary; the self of the adult is richer, because its experience is more complex. A man who has seen *Hamlet* has a richer self than he had before he saw *Hamlet*, for he is now the-man-who-has-seen-*Hamlet*, that is, the man who has "absorbed" the play, who has compared himself with, and distinguished himself from, the protagonist.

J. Alfred Prufrock learns something about himself by comparing himself with, and distinguishing himself from, Hamlet:

> No! I am not Prince Hamlet, nor was meant to be;
> Am an attendant lord, one that will do
> To swell a progress, start a scene or two,
> Advise the prince; no doubt, an easy tool. . . .

Considered from Hegel's point of view, Prufrock is more of a self after he makes this discovery than before he makes it. He becomes more of a self as the objects from which he distinguishes himself become more various and richly diverse, and as the distinctions that he draws become more subtle and refined.

To summarize: Self and object are not distinct, unchanging entities that face each other across a metaphysical and epistemological chasm; self and object are structures that arise within experience. There is no object without self, and there is no self without object. This doctrine should be familiar, for it is the doctrine of Kant. It is also Kantian to "demote" substance, as Hegel did, from its meta-physical primacy. For Kant had already pointed out that reality does not consist in substances; on the contrary, substance is simply one of the twelve categories by means of which the human mind organizes its experiences.

THE EVOLUTION OF MIND

Kant not only maintained that there are but twelve structuring categories; he also took it for granted that all twelve categories are used by all minds every-where—by the infant as well as the adult, by the caveman as well as the eight-eenth-century *philosophe*. Although Hegel recognized that Kant had taken an immensely important step in shifting the philosophical focus from substance to subject, he held that Kant had not made effective use of this shift, that Kant's use of the concept of subject was vitiated by a culture-bound and time-bound (ahistorical) approach.[4] This "correction" of Kant's doctrine was possible because, in the quarter century between the publication of the *Critique of Pure Reason* and *The Phenomenology,* the notion of time change—that is, of evolution in the broadest sense—had entered, and was already deeply affecting, the European climate of opinion. Kant's conception of mind was largely static; Hegel's was developmental. Moreover, Hegel took account not only of the evolution of the individual mind from infancy to adulthood but also of the evolution of the mind from earliest times down to his own day. Indeed, he thought that these two evolutionary developments were parallel: Ontogeny recapitulates phylogeny. Hence, whereas Kant's metaphysical deduction of the twelve categories was a relatively simple procedure (Kant took them over at one fell swoop from Aristotle's logic[5]), Hegel's exposition of the changing and unfolding types, or levels, of consciousness occupies the whole of *The Phenomenology* and is (or at least purports to be) an empirical inquiry, rather than a strictly logical one.

The differences between Kant and Hegel in this respect are reflected in the contrasting metaphors they employ. A favorite Kantian metaphor is that of a judge in court. According to Kant, the mind is like a judge, who is not involved in the dispute being heard before him; the mind attends to the evidence presented to it and renders a verdict between the rival claims; it decides for one and against the other. Hegel's typical metaphor, in contrast, is that of a bud developing into a blossom:

> The bud disappears when the blossom breaks through, and we might say that the former is refuted by the latter; in the same way when the fruit comes, the blossom may be explained to be a false form of the plant's existence, for the fruit appears as its true nature in place of the blossom. These stages are not merely differentiated; they supplant one another as being incompatible with one another. But the ceaseless activity of their own inherent nature makes them at the same time moments[6] of an organic unity, where they not merely do not contradict one another, but where one is as necessary as the other; and this equal necessity of all moments constitutes alone and thereby the life of the whole.[r]

In Hegel's view, mind is not a judge disinterestedly contemplating a realm of already existent objects; it is an inner force creating and shaping the outer, observable forms. Specifically, at the level of both the individual and the race, mind creates the various esthetic, social, and political forms that, taken together, constitute a given culture at a particular time. This is what he means, in the passage just quoted, by calling mind "the life of the whole."

---

4 Though Hegel did not use these terms himself, the fact that his criticism of Kant can easily be stated in these terms is an example of Hegel's influence on twentieth-century thought.

5 See p. 35.

6 ["Moment" is a bad translation, since it suggests a very short time interval; Hegel's meaning would be rendered more clearly by a term like "aspect," or "feature," or even "part"— AUTHOR.]

Thus Hegel applied the general doctrine that contradictions are only apparent (because they result from taking a limited view of a complex object) to the notion of there being developmental stages through which consciousness passes. In the evolutionary process nothing is lost. As we have seen, the two conflicting assertions "That color is blue" and "That color is red" are not denied by the assertion "That color is royal purple"; they are incorporated in it as one-sided versions of it. Similarly, each successively higher level of consciousness (whether in the individual or in the race) incorporates all earlier, more elementary levels. Thus Hegel concluded that the higher the level of consciousness, the richer and more "concrete" the content of that consciousness. Accordingly, he rejected both the traditional rationalism and all forms of intuitionism.

CRITICISM OF THE TRADITIONAL RATIONALISM

The traditional rationalism, or *raisonnement,* as Hegel termed it, reflects a level of consciousness at which concepts are assumed to function like the pigeon-holes into which the postman tosses each day's accumulation of letters and packages. *Raisonnement* holds that science consists in classifying; science dumps everything, willy-nilly, into one or another of its pigeonholes. *Raisonnement,* that is, ignores the nuances that make each thing an individual. "If we say 'all animals,'" Hegel sarcastically observed, "that does not pass for zoology." [s] Indeed, it is barely the beginning of zoology. Animal species differ structurally; it is the business of zoology to discover the differences and similarities of structure. Furthermore, individual members of each species—as well as the species themselves—differ from one another. Accordingly, not only do we oversimplify (and thereby falsify) when we lump all species—giraffe, whale, gibbon—together in the single pigeonhole "animal"; we also oversimplify when we ignore individual differences among gibbons. Thus the weakness of *raisonnement* is its "formalism." It "adopts a negative attitude towards the content apprehended." [t] At this level of thought, instead of accommodating ourselves to differences in the content before us, we seek to force this content into conformity with our own more or less arbitrarily chosen concepts. A study of nature that relies on abstract universals

> . . . has no right to the name of science. For we see it there reduced to a lifeless schema, to nothing better than a mere shadow, and scientific organization to a synoptic table. This formalism . . . thinks it has comprehended and expressed the nature and life of a given form when it proclaims a determination of the schema to be its predicate. The predicate may be subjectivity or objectivity, or again magnetism, electricity, and so on, contraction or expansion, East or West, and such like. . . .
>
> The instrument for producing this monotonous formalism is no more difficult to handle than the palette of a painter, on which lie only two colours, say, red and green, the former for colouring the surface when we want a historical piece, the latter when we want a bit of landscape. . . . What results

from the use of this method . . . is . . . like a skeleton with tickets stuck all over it, or like the rows of boxes kept shut and labeled in a grocer's stall; and [it] is as intelligible as either the one or the other. It has lost hold of the living nature of concrete fact; just as in the former case we have merely dry bones with flesh and blood all gone, and in the latter, there is shut away in those boxes something equally lifeless too. We have already remarked that the final outcome of this style of thinking is, at the same time, to paint entirely in one kind of colour; for it turns with contempt from the distinctions in the schematic table, looks on them as belonging to the activity of mere reflection, and lets them drop out of sight in the void of the Absolute, and there reinstates pure identity, pure formless whiteness. Such uniformity of colouring in the schema with its lifeless determinations, this absolute identity, and the transition from one to the other—these are the one as well as the other, the expression of inert lifeless understanding, and equally an external process of knowledge.[u]

CRITICISM OF INTUITIONISM

So much for the traditional rationalism, with its abstract universals. Hegel was equally critical of intuitionism, which, in its pursuit of the immediacy of feeling, ignores the inevitably mediate character of experience. In this respect Hegel's view differed markedly from the typical Romantic attitude, as expressed, for instance, in *Faust*. When Gretchen asks Faust whether he believes in God, Faust replies,

> Who can name him? . . .
> Then call it what you will—
> Happiness! Heart! Love! God!
> I have no name for it!
> Feeling is all;
> Name is mere sound and reek
> Clouding Heaven's light.[v]

From Hegel's point of view, this reply of Faust's represents a level of consciousness that seeks to "run together" what *raisonnement* "has divided asunder." Rightly seeing the emptiness of abstract concepts, this mind mistakenly wants to abandon concepts altogether and to give itself up to sheer immediacy. Thus it corrects *raisonnement*, but it does so at the cost of an equal oversimplification. It wants to

> . . . restore the *feeling* of existence. What it wants from philosophy is not so much insight as edification. The beautiful, the holy, the eternal, religion, love—these are the bait required to awaken the desire to bite: not the notion, but ecstasy, not the march of cold necessity in the subject-matter, but ferment and enthusiasm—these are to be the ways by which the wealth of the concrete substance is to be stored and increasingly extended. . . .

The man who only seeks edification, who wants to envelop in mist the manifold diversity of his earthly existence and thought, and craves after the vague enjoyment of this vague and indeterminate Divinity . . . will easily find for himself the means to procure something he can rave over and puff himself up withal. But philosophy must beware of wishing to be edifying.

Still less must this kind of contentment, which holds science in contempt, take upon itself to claim that raving obscurantism of this sort is something higher than science. These apocalyptic utterances pretend to occupy the very centre and the deepest depths; they look askance at all definiteness and preciseness of meaning.

. . . .

To consider any specific fact as it is in the Absolute, consists here [that is, at this level of consciousness] in nothing else than saying about it that, while it is now doubtless spoken of as something specific, yet in the Absolute, in the abstract identity A = A, there is no such thing at all, for everything is there all one. To pit this single assertion, that "in the Absolute all is one," against the organized whole of determinate and complete knowledge, or of knowledge which at least aims at and demands complete development—to give out its Absolute as the night in which, as we say, all cows are black—that is the very *naïveté* of emptiness of knowledge.[w]

Thus, although intuitionism starts from an exactly opposite set of assumptions from those of rationalism, it ends in a formalism of its own, because it too neglects the concreteness, richness, and variety of actual experience.

Hegel's View of Scientific Knowledge

Hegel contrasted these two deficient modes of cognition—traditional rationalism and intuitionism—with a higher level of consciousness that, in accordance with the Hegelian pattern, incorporates them while transcending them. Although Hegel called this higher level "science," it must not be confused with the quantitative mathematical knowledge aimed at in the physical sciences. Rather, it is that "organized whole of determinate and complete knowledge" referred to at the end of the passage just quoted. Because scientific knowledge is conceptual and mediate it differs from the inarticulate feelings of intuitionism. And it differs from *raisonnement* because its concepts, being concrete instead of abstract, are adequate to the real diversity and richness of experience.

Hegel's term for the concrete universal of true science is *Begriff*, which translators formerly rendered in English as "notion" and which they now tend to translate as "concept." The former translation is somewhat inept, but it has the advantage of reminding us that Hegel's *Begriff* differs from an ordinary concept. A *Begriff*, in fact, is a concept that, instead of being imposed from outside, is generated within the content and therefore adequately reflects its uniqueness. Here the metaphor of bud-blossom-fruit is relevant. That is, Hegel's thought is dominated by the idea of life, of an energy that is self-generative and that expresses itself in successively unfolding forms. If we can imagine for a moment that a plant is conscious, we can certainly think of it as becoming increasingly self-conscious as it grows and advances from bud to flower to fruit; and we may think of the fruit as the plant's concept ("notion") of itself, that is, as the plant's understanding of itself as consisting in a succession of forms that have culminated in this fruit. Such a concept of what it is to be a fruit is obviously very different from the externally imposed concept of fruit that a botanist might employ. For the *notion* of fruit is not merely the abstract concept of fruit; it also includes the feeling of being fruit. On the other hand, the notion is conceptual and is hence not "mere" feeling. At the level of the notion feeling becomes "determinate" knowledge; the feeling of being fruit is transcended, but included, in the fruit's articulate self-knowledge of itself as the fulfillment of bud and flower.

> Science can become an organic system only by the inherent life of the notion. In science the determinateness, which was [at the level of *raisonnement*] taken from the schema and stuck on to existing facts in external fashion, is the self-directing inner soul of the concrete content. The movement of what is partly consists in becoming another to itself, and thus developing explicitly into its own immanent content; partly, again, it takes this evolved content, this existence it assumes, back into itself, i.e., makes *itself* into a moment,[7] and reduces itself to simple determinateness. In the first stage of the process negativity lies in the function of distinguishing and establishing existence; in this latter return into self, negativity consists in the bringing about of determinate simplicity. It is in this way that the content shows its specific characteristic not to be received from something else, and stuck on externally; the content gives itself this determinate characteristic, appoints itself of its own initiative to the rank of a moment and to a place in the whole. . . .
>
> Instead of making its way into the inherent content of the matter in hand, understanding[8] always . . . assumes a position above the particular existence about which it is speaking. . . . True scientific knowledge, on the contrary, demands abandonment to the very life of the object, or, which means the same thing, claims to have before it the inner necessity controlling the object, and to express this only. Steeping itself in its object, . . . being sunk into the material in hand, and following the course that such material takes, true knowledge returns back into itself, yet not before the content in its fullness is taken into itself, is reduced to . . . the level of being one aspect of an existing entity, and passes over into its higher truth. By this process the whole as such, surveying its entire content, itself emerges out of the wealth wherein its process of reflection seemed to be lost.[x]

---

7 [See note 6, p. 114—AUTHOR.]
8 [This is another term for the level of consciousness that Hegel called *raisonnement*. It derives from the Kantian distinction between *Verstand* (understanding) and *Vernunft* (reason)—AUTHOR.]

CONSEQUENCES OF THIS VIEW

Several important consequences follow. (1) It is impossible to get at the truth by examining the situation as of some (any) particular time. The only way to get at the truth is by an historical, or genetic, approach in which the evolution up to a particular stage is shown to be the "necessary" outcome of a series of conflicts and discrepancies, and their successive corrections. Thus we do not understand any stage in the life of a plant—say, the flower stage—unless we realize that this stage supersedes (but at the same time incorporates) an earlier bud stage.

(2) "Negation" is not to be feared. It is, in fact, the sign that the formulation so far achieved is one-sided and inadequate; hence it supplies the power that makes possible the advance of mind to higher levels. For instance, if no one says, "Oh no, that color is blue," I am likely to rest contentedly in my initial belief that the color is simply and sheerly red. But if someone contradicts me by calling the color blue, I am moved to advance to a more concrete concept— royal purple. This is what Hegel means, in the passage just quoted, by saying that "negativity consists in the bringing about of determinate simplicity." At the level of science each item is located in a context of related items. Concrete universals ("notions") are more adequate than abstract universals because the context in terms of which a particular item is located is more highly structured and hence more precise. For instance, a mind that is capable of distinguishing only between red and not-red is less capable of locating the exact nuance of this particular color than is a mind that can also distinguish old rose, magenta, royal purple, Prussian blue, and so on. And it is negation that leads the mind from the simple contradiction between red and not-red to these more refined color distinctions. Thus a man's attitude toward contradiction is a mark of what level of consciousness he has attained.

(3) Just as the seemingly "fixed and stable existence" of any object in our experience "carries the process of its own dissolution within itself," so the seemingly fixed and stable self-identity of any particular self—say, mine—carries its own dissolution within it. In the case of the self, too, there is a "process of dissolution" that refines and distinguishes—renders the self "determinate"—by means of negation and mediation. For example, at some point it may occur to me that I am like Hamlet in being indecisive. But then I think, "No, I am not a prince; I am only an attendant lord. Well, I am not *just* an attendant lord, for I *know* that I am one, whereas the typical attendant lord does not think of himself in this way."

But it is a mistake to use language that suggests that there are two separate processes of mediation, one by means of which the objects that I encounter within experience become more determinate and a second by means of which the self that I encounter there becomes more determinate. On the contrary, there is a single process. To distinguish a color as a relatively determinate royal purple rather than as merely an indeterminate red is at the same time, and in the same process, to become more determinate myself. I am now a self that is capable, as I once was not, of discriminating among reds and of distinguishing royal purple. Similarly, to render indecision more determinate by distinguishing a noble, Hamlet-like indecision from merely ordinary, run-of-the-mill indecision is at the same time to become more determinate myself, for I now perceive my own indecision more clearly. As we have seen,[9] in Hegel's view self and its objects are reciprocally related structures that emerge together in experience. A particular self—say, mine, at the level of consciousness that I have now reached—is as determinate as that self's objects are; and a self's objects are as determinate as that self is.

Common sense and philosophical realism, of course, describe the situation very differently. For instance, if I change my assessment of a man's character after I come to know him better, in the view of common sense and realistic philosophy I am contrasting an initial impression of mine with the facts that I have discovered about the man's character. In Hegel's view, this is a loose way of speaking. The correct comparison is not between what is in my experience (my initial impression) and what is outside my experience (the facts of the man's "true" character); the comparison is *within* my experience. My initial impression is not metaphysically different *in kind* from "knowing him better." "Knowing him better" is simply a later, and presumably more reliable, version of my "initial impression." It too is subject to correction as I get to know the man still better.

But we should not conclude that Hegel was a relativist. In his view, all the different types of mentality, all the different levels of consciousness, fall into a single objective order, or hierarchy. And all the different versions are ultimately incorporated and transcended in something that is not a version but the whole itself:

> The truth is the whole. The whole, however, is merely the essential nature reaching its completeness through the process of its own development. Of the Absolute it must be said that it is essentially a result, that only at the end is it what it is in very truth; and just in that consists its nature, which is to be actual, subject, or self-becoming, self-development.
> . . . .
> That the truth is only realized in the form of system, that substance is essentially subject, is expressed in the idea which represents the Absolute as Spirit (*Geist*)—the grandest conception of all. . . . Spirit is alone Reality. It is the inner being of the world, that which essentially is, and is *per se;* it assumes objective, determinate form, and enters into relations with itself— it is externality (otherness), and exists for self; yet, in this determination,

---

9 See p. 112. Note that this discussion of Hegel's theory is an application of his own doctrine of the transformation (incorporation and transcendence) of earlier stages in later stages. We began our study of Hegel with a preliminary account of his view of self-consciousness. We then passed on to a consideration of the role that negativity and mediation play in the development of the self and its objects. As a result, the initial version of Hegel's view of self-consciousness has been transformed (incorporated and transcended) in the present, relatively more determinate version.

and in its otherness, it is still one with itself—it is self-contained and self-complete, in itself and for itself at once.[y]

Thus, in Hegel's view, the old dualistic distinction between the self and its objects—which Kant had abandoned at the level of phenomena but which he had retained at the level of noumena, is transformed (incorporated but transcended) in a new monism, the monism of Spirit. But what is Spirit? Our best clue to what it is, is our own experience. And the best analogy is the bud-blossom-fruit sequence. Spirit is a living process; it is propelled by the energy of negation and mediation, in which both selves and their objects are continuously emerging, undergoing development, and being replaced by higher forms of themselves.

> The living substance is that being which is truly subject, or, what is the same thing, is truly realized and actual (*wirklich*) solely in the process of positing itself, or in mediating with its own self its transitions from one state or position, to the opposite. . . . True reality is merely this process of reinstating self-identity, of reflecting into its own self in and from its other. . . . It is the process of its own becoming, the circle which presupposes its end as its purpose, and has its end for its beginning; it becomes concrete and actual only by being carried out, and by the end it involves.[z]

SUMMARY OF THE DOCTRINE OF *THE PHENOMENOLOGY*

This long analysis of the doctrine of *The Phenomenology* is summarized below in a passage from its Introduction, in which many of the themes discussed so far are touched on. Since this Introduction, like everything else Hegel wrote, is difficult to read, a brief synopsis may be helpful. The Introduction begins with an attack on the presuppositions of "criticism," an attack not only on the specific assumptions of Kant in his *Critique* but on the presuppositions of any philosopher who holds (as Locke, for instance, did) that before we try to philosophize we must investigate the powers and limits of the mind. Hegel notes that, since such a philosopher uses the mind in his critical inquiries, he assumes the point at issue: The mind must be at least adequate enough to undertake criticism. But Hegel himself escapes this contradiction by asserting that the criteria for evaluating our judgments emerge in experience and that they are constantly being revised in the course of further experience. This "emerging and being revised" is, of course, nothing but the process of mediation that we have already encountered. To launch the mind on this project is to enter the pathway that leads to science. And science is not simply the knowledge that will be found at the end of the pathway; it is the process in its entirety, in which all earlier stages are included and transformed. Science, indeed, is the completely determinate, *total* system of knowledge. Furthermore, because it is the whole, it is not just knowledge about reality (that is, not a "version of" it); it is that reality itself. In the Absolute, in other words, the distinction between knowledge and reality is transcended.

It is natural to suppose that, before philosophy enters upon its subject proper—namely, the actual knowledge of what truly is—it is necessary to come first to an understanding concerning knowledge, which is looked upon as the instrument by which to take possession of the Absolute, or as the means through which to get a sight of it. . . .

For if knowledge is the instrument by which to get possession of absolute Reality, the suggestion immediately occurs that the application of an instrument to anything does *not* leave it as it is for itself, but rather entails . . . a moulding and alteration of it. Or again, if knowledge is . . . a kind of passive medium through which the light of the truth reaches us, then, here too, we do not receive it as it is in itself, but as it is through and in this medium. In either case we employ a means which immediately brings about the very opposite of its own end; or, rather, the absurdity lies in making use of any means at all. It seems indeed open to us to find in the knowledge of the way in which the *instrument* operates, a remedy for this parlous state; for thereby it becomes possible to remove from the result the part which, in our idea of the Absolute received through that instrument, belongs to the instrument, and thus to get the truth in its purity. But this improvement would, as a matter of fact, only bring us back to the point where we were before. . . . If the Absolute were only to be brought on the whole nearer to us by this agency, without any change being wrought in it, like a bird caught by a lime stick, it would certainly scorn a trick of that sort if it were not in its very nature, and did it not wish to be, beside us from the start. . . . Or, again, if the examination of knowledge, which we represent as a medium, makes us acquainted with the law of its refraction, it is likewise useless to eliminate this refraction from the result. For knowledge is not the divergence of the ray, but the ray itself by which the truth comes in contact with us; and if this be removed, the bare direction or the empty place would alone be indicated.

· ·

[A] critical examination into the reality of knowing does not seem able to be effected without some presupposition which is laid down as an ultimate criterion. For an examination consists in applying an accepted standard, and, on the final agreement or disagreement wherewith of what is tested, deciding whether the latter is right or wrong; and the standard in general, and so science, were this the criterion, is thereby accepted as the essence or inherently real (*Ansich*). But, here, where science first appears on the scene, neither science nor any sort of standard has justified itself as the essence or ultimate reality; and without this no examination seems able to be instituted.

This contradiction and the removal of it will become more definite if, to begin with, we call to mind the abstract determinations of knowledge and of truth as they are found in consciousness. Consciousness, we find, *distinguishes* from itself something, to which at the same time it *relates* itself; or, to use the current expression, there is something *for* consciousness; and the determinate form of this process of relating, or of there being something for a consciousness, is knowledge. But from this being for another we distinguish being in itself or *per se;* what is related to knowledge is likewise distinguished from it, and posited as also existing outside this relation; the aspect of being *per se* or in itself is called Truth. . . .

If now our inquiry deals with the truth of knowledge, it appears that we are inquiring what knowledge is in itself. But in this inquiry knowledge is *our* object, it is *for us;* and the essential nature (*Ansich*) of knowledge, were this to come to light, would be rather its being *for us;* what we should assert to be its essence would rather be, not the truth of knowledge, but only our knowledge of it. The essence or the criterion would lie in us; and that which was to be compared with this standard, and on which a decision was to be passed as a result of this comparison, would not necessarily have to recognize that criterion.

But the nature of the object which we are examining surmounts this separation, or semblance of separation, and presupposition. Consciousness furnishes its own criterion in itself, and the inquiry will thereby be a comparison of itself with its own self; for the distinction, just made, falls inside itself. . . . The essential fact . . . to be borne in mind throughout the whole inquiry is that both these moments, notion and object, "being for another" and "being in itself," themselves fall within that knowledge which we are examining. . . .

The object, it is true, appears only to be in such wise for consciousness as consciousness knows it. Consciousness does not seem able to get, so to say, behind it as it is, not for consciousness, but in itself, and consequently seems also unable to test knowledge by it. But just because consciousness has, in general, knowledge of an object, there is already present the distinction that the inherent nature, what the object is in itself, is one thing to consciousness, while knowledge, or the being of the object *for* consciousness, is another moment. Upon this distinction, which is present as a fact, the examination turns. Should both, when thus compared, not correspond, consciousness seems bound to alter its knowledge, in order to make it fit the object. But in the alteration of the knowledge, the object itself also, in point of fact, is altered; for the knowledge which existed was essentially a knowledge of the object; with change in the knowledge, the object also becomes different, since it belongs essentially to this knowledge. Hence consciousness comes to find that what formerly to it was the essence is not what is *per se*, or what was *per se* was only *per se for consciousness*. Since, then, in the case of its object consciousness finds its knowledge not corresponding with this object, the object likewise fails to hold out; or the standard for examining is altered when that, whose criterion this standard was to be, does not hold its ground in the course of the examination; and the examination is not only an examination of knowledge, but also of the criterion used in the process.

This dialectic process which consciousness executes on itself—on its knowledge as well as on its object—in the sense that out of it the new and true object arises, is precisely what is termed Experience. . . .

In this treatment of the course of experience, there is an element in virtue of which it does not seem to be in agreement with what is ordinarily understood by experience. The transition from the first object and the knowledge of it to the other object, in regard to which we say we have had experience, was so stated that the knowledge of the first object, the existence *for consciousness* of the first *ens per se*, is itself to be the second object. But it usually seems that we learn by experience the untruth of our first notion by appealing to some other object which we may happen to find casually and externally; so that, in general, what we have is merely the bare and simple apprehension of what is in and for itself. On the view above given, however, the new object is seen to have come about by a transformation or conversion of consciousness itself. This way of looking at the matter is *our* doing, what *we* contribute; by its means the series of experiences through which consciousness passes is lifted into a scientifically constituted sequence. . . . Since what at first appears as object is reduced, when it passes into consciousness, to what knowledge takes it to be, and the implicit nature, the real in itself, becomes what this entity *per se* is *for consciousness;* this latter is the new object, whereupon there appears also a new mode or embodiment of consciousness, of which the essence is something other than that of the preceding mode. It is this circumstance which carries forward the whole succession of the modes or attitudes of consciousness in their own necessity. . . .

In virtue of that necessity this pathway to science is itself *eo ipso* science, and is, moreover, as regards its content, Science of the Experience of Consciousness. . . .

In pressing forward to its true form of existence, consciousness will come to a point at which it lays aside its semblance of being hampered with what is foreign to it, with what is only for it and exists as an other; it will reach a position where appearance becomes identified with essence, where, in consequence, its exposition coincides with just this very point, this very stage of the science proper of mind. And, finally, when it grasps this its own essence, it will connote the nature of absolute knowledge itself.[a]

The System as a Whole: The Triadic Pattern

This, then, is Hegel's intention: "To bring philosophy nearer to the form of science—that goal where it can lay aside the name of *love* of knowledge and be actual *knowledge*—that is what I have set before me."[b] He proposed to bring consciousness up to a level at which the various bits and pieces of information that men have gleaned over the millenia are displayed in their true, systematic, determinate, and necessary relationships. Hegel, of course, regarded *The Phenomenology* as merely the preface to this awesome undertaking, as no more than a prospectus. The "toil" of working out the detail was left to a series of works that were to follow it in due course.

This undertaking was, needless to say, a failure. In the first place, Hegel never completed it. In the second place, the parts he finished certainly fall far short of displaying the necessary and determinate relations that Hegel held science to consist in. For these reasons the system is both less interesting and less important than his more programmatic work, *The Phenomenology*, and Hegel's detailed working-out of his vision has had far less influence on the history of philosophy and of culture than the vision itself. Nevertheless, in order to gain a balanced view of Hegel's philosophy, we must at least sample the system. And sample it is all we can do: Fragmentary though it is, it is too vast to be dealt with adequately in anything less than a long book.

As Hegel points out in *The Phenomenology*, thought advances toward truth by negation. Every assertion ("That color is red") is negated by some other assertion ("No, it is blue"), and these two are then reconciled in a third assertion ("Rather, it is royal purple"). Naturally, the thought that is working out the system also moves in this way; hence the system itself will consist of "triads," all of which will be "collected," ultimately, into an immense, all-inclusive "triad"—Idea-Nature-Spirit.

Further, each of the main subdivisions is composed of "subtriads," each of which displays the same pattern of "triplicity." And these subtriads are themselves systematically related, for each of the syntheses that reconciles two "conflicting" assertions is itself negated by a subsequent assertion, and the new conflict is then reconciled at a higher level. Finally, this triadic movement is not simply linear. It is not merely that an individual synthesis becomes the basis for a new advance; rather, a whole *group* of triads is negated by another group, and this conflict is then reconciled by a third group. Since the synthesis in turn becomes the basis for a new advance, the process results in syntheses of groups of groups of concepts. Taken as a whole, then, the system is an elaborate structure composed of triads, subtriads, and sub-subtriads, all related to one another "dialectically"—that is, each higher level reconciles (incorporates and transcends) discrepancies that are discovered at the next lower level.

A diagram may help:

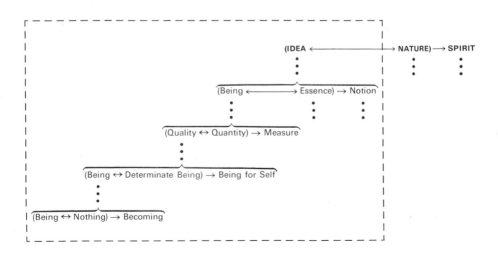

The box indicates the part of the whole "system" that is covered in the *Logic*.[10] A double arrow represents a conflict between two concepts; a single arrow indicates the concept that reconciles the two concepts within the parentheses. A dotted line represents an advance to a higher level, at which point the conflict breaks out again, requiring a new reconciliation. The diagram, of course, shows only a very small segment of the total system; even within the *Logic* the subtriads under Essence and Notion are omitted, and none of the subtriads in the domains of Nature and Spirit is indicated. But the diagram is not intended to be a synopsis; it is designed merely to give a clue as to how the system as a whole "works."

THE *LOGIC*

Let us now look more closely at a few representative segments, beginning with the *Logic*. The main triad of the *Logic* (represented in the diagram at the fourth level from the bottom) is Being-Essence-Notion. Each of these concepts is itself the synthesis of a subordinate triad. Being, for instance, is the synthesis of Quality-Quantity-Measure; Quality, the synthesis of a more subordinate triad, Being-Determinate Being-Being for Self; and Being, the synthesis of a still more subordinate triad, Being-Nothing-Becoming.[11]

BASIC TRIAD: BEING-NOTHING-BECOMING

An examination of the basic triad, Being-Nothing-Becoming, will illustrate the nature of the triadic movement. Let us start with Hegel's own account of this movement.

> Pure BEING makes the beginning: because it is on one hand pure thought, and on the other immediacy itself, simple and indeterminate; and the first beginning cannot be mediated by anything, or be further determined. . . .
>
> When thinking is to begin, we have nothing but thought in its merest indeterminateness: for we cannot determine unless there is both one and another; and in the beginning there is yet no other. The indeterminate, as we here have it, is the blank we begin with, not a featurelessness reached

---

10 The *Logic* was the only portion of the system that Hegel was able to publish in detail. There are two versions: the *Science of Logic* (1813–16) and the shorter *Encyclopaedia of the Philosophical Sciences* (1817).

11 It should be noted that Hegel used the term "Being" to designate the theses of three different triads. Since the "Being" that is the thesis of the first triad is not the same as the "Being" that is the thesis of the final triad, some philosophers accuse Hegel either of deliberate obfuscation or of extreme carelessness. But of course Hegel held that, though the concepts are different, they are *also* the same. Each time "Being" appears in a triad it has gained an "enriched" and deepened meaning as a result of the various qualifications, conditions, and significations that have been added to it on the way.

by abstraction, not the elimination of all character, but the original feature-lessness which precedes all definite character and is the very first of all. And this we call Being. It is not to be felt, or perceived by sense, or pictured in imagination: it is only and merely thought, and as such it forms the beginning. Essence also is indeterminate, but in another sense: it has tra-versed the process of mediation and contains implicit the determination it has absorbed. . . .

But this mere Being, as it is mere abstraction, is therefore the absolutely negative: which, in a similarly immediate aspect, is just NOTHING. . . .

Nothing, if it be thus immediate and equal to itself, is also conversely the same as Being is. The truth of Being and of Nothing is accordingly the unity of the two: and this unity is BECOMING.

The proposition that Being and Nothing is the same seems so paradoxical to the imagination or understanding, that it is perhaps taken for a joke. And indeed it is one of the hardest things thought expects itself to do: for Being and Nothing exhibit the fundamental contrast in all its immediacy,—that is, without the one term being invested with any attribute which would involve its connexion with the other. This attribute however, as the above paragraph points out, is implicit in them—the attribute which is just the same in both. . . . It is as correct however to say that Being and Nothing are altogether different, as to assert their unity. The one is *not* what the other is. But since the distinction has not at this point assumed definite shape (Being and Nothing are still the immediate), it is, in the way that they have it, something unutterable, which we merely *mean*. . . .

It may perhaps be said that nobody can form a notion of the unity of Being and Nought. . . . To say that we have no such conception can only mean, that in none of these images do we recognise the notion in question, and that we are not aware that they exemplify it. The readiest example of it is Becoming. Every one has a mental idea of Becoming, and will even allow that it is *one* idea: he will further allow that, when it is analysed, it involves the attribute of Being, and also what is the very reverse of Being, viz. Nothing: and that these two attributes lie undivided in the one idea: so that Becoming is the unity of Being and Nothing. . . .

It remains to note that such phrases as 'Being and Nothing are the same,' or 'The unity of Being and Nothing'—like all other such unities, that of subject and object, and others—give rise to reasonable objection. They misrepresent the facts, by giving an exclusive prominence to the unity, and leaving the difference which undoubtedly exists in it (because it is Being and Nothing, for example, the unity of which is declared) without any express mention or notice. It accordingly seems as if the diversity had been unduly put out of court and neglected. The fact is, no speculative principle can be correctly expressed by any such propositional form, for the unity has to be conceived *in* the diversity, which is all the while present and explicit. 'To become' is the true expression for the resultant of 'To be' and 'Not to be'; it is the unity of the two; but not only is it the unity, it is also inherent unrest,—the unity, which is no mere reference-to-self and therefore without movement, but which, through the diversity of Being and Nothing that is in it, is at war within itself.[c]

Being, according to Hegel, is the most primitive and least determinate, that is, vaguest, of all concepts. When we say merely that something "is," we are asserting the bare minimum that can be said if anything is said at all. We are not saying that the subject being judged about is a substance—or a quality, or a self, or an object, or a cause, or an effect; we are saying merely that it is. Contrariwise, when we make any assertion whatever, however complex or refined, we are also implicitly asserting that the subject being judged about "is." This is why the system, which is to progress continuously from the abstract and indeterminate to the determinate and concrete, begins with "Being."

But as soon as the first concept of the system is formulated, conflict breaks out: The minimum that is asserted when "isness" is claimed is so minimal that it amounts to nothing. Nothing has been said about the item in question. Thus Being "passes over" into its opposite—Nothing. On the basis of traditional Aristotelian logic, we would have to remain at this point, plunged in contradiction until the dispute could be adjudicated by an outside observer, who would decide whether it is correct to assert "Being" or whether it is correct to assert "Nothing." But, as was brought out in the discussion of *The Phenomenology*,[12] Hegel held that no finite assertion is sheerly true or sheerly false. Every assertion contains *some* truth, for unless the person making the assertion is "anti-human," he has detected something that is the case—however one-sided, fragmentary, and partial his perception of it may be. Hence, according to Hegel, what is called for is not a legal verdict that decides *between* conflicting assertions; what is called for is a formula, or concept, that reconciles the assertions by expressing what is true in both without also asserting what is false and one-sided in each. Thus, in the present case, Being and Nothing are reconciled by means of the concept "Becoming."

Becoming reconciles Being and Nothing by incorporating them. Being passes into Nothing: What is this but the concept of decease? Nothing passes into Being: What is this but the concept of origination? Taken together, this double passage yields the concept of Becoming. Notice that Being and Nothing are included in Becoming. They are held in suspension in the concept, not "devoured" by it. A being that merely is, does not become; a nothing that merely is not, does not become. Becoming is both an is and an is-not.

This is the model for all scientific thinking—according to Hegel's view of science. The system (which, taken in its entirety, *is* science) is the continuously expanding and increasingly determinate body of knowledge that results from resolving conflicts into ever larger wholes that incorporate and transcend them. It is impossible to trace this development in detail, as Hegel worked it out in his *Logic*. But we can at least consider the main triad, in which the whole nature of Thought (taken by Hegel as a subjective process occurring in individual minds) is supposedly brought together and synthesized.

12 See p. 110.

MAIN TRIAD: BEING-ESSENCE-NOTION

The same functional relationship obtains among Being-Essence-Notion as among Being-Nothing-Becoming. Let us now try to see how Essence conflicts with Being, and how Notion is the larger whole that includes both. Each of these main concepts, like each of its subconcepts, represents a level of consciousness; it is a way of looking at, or judging about, the world. That is, each is a "category" under which and in terms of which experience is organized. The main category of Being represents what may be called the naïve, or immediate, way of looking at the world. It consists in taking things at their face value, at what they claim to be. (This is true, of course, of all the subconcepts under the main concept Being. All these subconcepts give expression to the impression the world makes on the naïve observer—that things are, that they originate, that they pass away, and so forth.) In contrast to this view of the world is a more critical and sophisticated attitude that recognizes that things are not just what they claim to be. This way of thinking distinguishes, for instance, between substance and accident, between a thing and its properties, between matter and form. All these distinctions are subconcepts under the main concept Essence; each involves distinguishing between what a thing "really" is ("in itself") and what it appears to be ("for" some mind). Essence is that which, though not directly present to us, is mediated by what is directly present. Thus, if Being is immediate, Essence is mediate. And Notion is the synthesis in which these opposites are at once retained and transcended. The nature of this relationship may be indicated by calling Notion *self*-mediate.

The following comparison may be helpful: A high-school graduate who expects to be admitted to a college on the basis of his own estimate of his abilities and without having submitted (in triplicate) birth certificate, health certificate, transcript of record, and numerous other documents, is very naïve. He is operating at the level of Being. A dean of admissions who believes in the infallibility of the Scholastic Aptitude Test, and who never admits a candidate who falls below the minimum score set by his institution, is operating at the level of Essence. He distinguishes between appearance (the candidate's claims) and reality (the test scores), but he fails to see that the test scores themselves must be tested. To operate at the level of Notion would be (in terms of the analogy) to use the tests while recognizing that they are instruments, not absolutes—to use them, that is, but to check them against what the candidate says about himself, against the impression he makes in an interview, and so on.

In a word, at the level of Essence various sceptical doubts arise—for example, "Can we know the really real?" "Are we in contact only with appearance?" —that never occur to a mind thinking at the level of Being. At the level of Notion all these doubts are resolved, because we see that the distinctions on which they are based are made by Thought itself and are only distinctions within Thought.

At the level of Notion we do not, however, lapse back into the naïve confidence we had at the level of Being. We experience at this level neither dogmatic, uncritical certainty nor dogmatic, uncritical doubt. Rather, we feel a sceptical kind of confidence. If the tests are not infallible, they are at least reasonably reliable. Let us therefore use them; they are on the average better than an impressionistic gamble. But let us also be constantly alert to improve them as we use them.

As another example, compare (1) the freedom of arbitrariness ("Do what you will"), (2) the will restrained by rules and laws, and (3) the will that chooses the rules it follows—that does what it wills but wills to be lawful. The latter, which Kant called the self-legislative will, corresponds to Hegel's self-mediate Notion.

The concept of Notion[13] is derived in the following way. One of the subcategories of Essence is cause-and-effect. According to Hegel, we start out by thinking of an effect as different from its cause, but we soon see that the effect is in a sense identical with its cause, though at the same time different from it. That is, the concept of cause-and-effect "collapses" into the concept of reciprocity.

As an example, consider the relation between philosophical theory and the general culture. We operate at the level of *raisonnement* if we believe that we have to choose, for instance, between saying either (1) that a change in the general culture (such as the emergence of the Romantic style) caused a change in philosophical theory (such as the abandonment of Kant's sharp distinction between phenomena and noumena) or (2) that this change in philosophical theory caused the change in taste. Hegel denied that we are ever confronted with such a simple choice. He held that it is true (but one-sided) to say that philosophical changes cause changes in the general culture, and that it is also true (but equally one-sided) to say that changes in the general culture bring about changes in philosophical theory. He held, in short, that in such a situation A is the cause of B *and* B is the cause of A. This is the concept of reciprocity—a category that includes, while it transcends, the lower category of cause-and-effect.

Reciprocity "passes over" into Notion in the following way:

> We must not let the two sides [A is the cause of B; B is the cause of A] rest in their state of mere given facts, but recognise them . . . for factors of a third and higher, which is the notion and nothing else. To make, for example, the manners of the Spartans the cause of their constitution and their constitution conversely the cause of their manners, may no doubt be in a way correct. But, as we have comprehended neither the manners nor the constitution of the nation, the result of such reflections can never be final or satisfactory. The satisfactory point will be reached only when these two, as well as all other, special aspects of Spartan life and Spartan history are seen to be founded in this notion.[d]

13 See p. 117.

Just as all the subcategories of Essence show the character of mediation and all the subcategories of Being the character of immediacy, so all the subcategories of Notion show the character of self-mediation. It is impossible, however, to follow through the whole dialectical movement as worked out by Hegel. We must be content with the fact that it terminates in the category "Absolute Idea," which incorporates (while it transcends) *all* the distinctions and subcategories included in the *Logic*. It is therefore obviously the "richest" and most determinate of all categories and thus contrasts most markedly with the initial category of Being, the most barren and least determinate category. By the same token, Absolute Idea is the most self-mediate of all categories. In fact, since it includes all the others, it is the only category that is fully *self*-mediate. All the others are mediated by a category in some sense other than themselves.

FINAL TRIAD: IDEA-NATURE-SPIRIT

We have now reached the end of the *Logic* (admittedly by a series of gigantic jumps, which inevitably give a distorted impression of the terrain traversed). But from the point of view of the Hegelian system, logic taken as a whole is only the basis for a final, all-inclusive triad, Idea-Nature-Spirit. This final triad repeats on a more massive scale the movement that is supposed to be effected in the first, most elementary synthesis. Just as Nothing and Being are at once the same and different, and Becoming is their synthesis, so Idea passes over into Nature and Nature into Idea, and Spirit is *their* synthesis.

Let us see if Hegel's meaning can be made at all clear. So far discussion has centered on concepts and categories, and it has been tacitly assumed that these are the "ideas" of a mind thinking about an objective, independent world. Taken as Idea, thought has an other, an object; this other is Nature. At this stage, thought and its other are opposed and in contradiction. This, Hegel believed, is the contrast with which, ever since Descartes, philosophy had been confronted—the contrast between knowing subject and object known. In Hegel's view, this contradiction exists only at a rather low level of consciousness. Just as the dean of admissions can advance to a level of thought at which he becomes properly critical of test scores, so philosophers can arrive at a level of thought at which thought and its object are identical (and at the same time different). Idea and Nature are transcended, but not lost, in Spirit. Spirit, in a word, is Thought in the full sense; it is thought knowing itself not merely as thought, but as thought-of-object.

This elucidation may itself require elucidation. Let us consider it in less Hegelian terms. How, we may ask, is it possible to hold (as Hegel did) that thought *is* its object? Is there any difference more obvious or more fundamental than the difference between my idea about a particular thing (say, *Hamlet*) and the thing (*Hamlet*) about which I am thinking? Here am I reflecting on *Hamlet*, and I am thinking about an "object." But what *is* my present object except my (and, of course, other people's) earlier thoughts about (or "versions of")

Hamlet? I am thinking, for instance, about my "impressions" of the play when I last saw it or read it. And at every stage this process repeats itself: It is always a part of myself that I am engaged in thinking about.

This may suggest that Hegel was a "subjective idealist" of the kind Berkeley ought logically to have been. It would seem, that is, that in Hegel's view the world is *my* idea. But this overlooks the doctrine of *The Phenomenology*—namely, that "I" am transcended as well as "my object." [14] Or, to put this into the terminology of the *Logic*, the question of whether other knowers really exist or whether they are only ideas of mine is but a sceptical doubt that occurs at the level of Essence. Just as the distinction between knower and known is transcended in the Absolute, so the distinction between this knower and that one, between me and thee, is transcended.

Why did Hegel claim that reality is of the nature of thought? Because he believed that reality—the all-inclusive whole—*is* that dialectical movement into opposition and transcendence that we have been examining. And this dialectical movement is fairly called "thought," because (according to Hegel) it is precisely what is occurring in men when they think. My thought, *qua* mine, is simply one phase in this larger movement. In fact, nature as *my* object and Nature as the totality of otherness are both simply that "passage into opposition" that characterizes Thought. And just as I transcend my object in knowing it, so Thought transcends its object (in which I am of course included). This transcendence (the synthesis of Idea and Nature) is Spirit.

Thus Nature, the second main section of the Hegelian system, is the otherness of Idea. What natural science offers us is merely one version of reality. What it holds to be ultimate fact—the externality, objectivity, and factuality of the world it investigates—is merely one phase, or level, in the life of consciousness. This interpretation of nature gave Hegel a novel solution to the old problem of the place of values in a world of fact. Descartes had attempted to solve this problem by a substantival dualism; Kant by a cognitive dualism. As a thoroughgoing monist, Hegel could not have allowed that any form of dualism is ultimate. Since there is only one world, facts and values are the same—yet, of course, they are also different. The perspective from which the world seems to consist in facts-spread-out-in-space-and-time is a rather limited sort of perspective; that from which the world seems to be values-organized-teleologically includes the "lower" one while transcending it. But it, too, is only one perspective. It is important to understand that these perspectives, or versions, are not just *different;* they are related to each other dialectically.[15] Since the scientific perspective is included in the valuational perspective, it cannot possibly be superior to it. The latter does not deny the limited truth contained in the former; it illumines it and makes us understand it better, just as a second or third reading of *Hamlet*

14 See pp. 113–15.
15 See p. 110. "Science" is an ambiguous term in Hegel's vocabulary. Generally speaking, when he criticizes science as inadequate, he is referring to the natural science of his own day; when he looks forward to "true" science, he is equating science with philosophical knowledge.

makes us understand the play better. Hence, instead of our having to make a place for value in a world of fact, facts have to find a place for themselves in a world that is more truly understood in terms of purposes and values. Hegel thus believed that philosophers are quite justified in criticizing and correcting the basic concepts of science, for (in his view) philosophy represents a higher level of consciousness than science.

As has been said, Hegel's attempt to put science in its place was not very successful. Unfortunately, this failure has brought his whole view into unnecessary disrepute—unnecessary because it is possible to distinguish between (1) the detailed relationships Hegel supposed himself to be deriving by means of his dialectic and (2) the underlying thesis about the nature of thought and its objects. The latter point may prove to need correction, but it is not necessarily involved in the collapse of the triads that constitute Hegel's "philosophy of nature."

Let us pass on from Nature to Spirit. Spirit (which, as we have seen, is the synthesis of the main triad of the whole system) is itself divided into a subtriad, and this in turn is divided into series of subtriads in accordance with the now familiar Hegelian method. It is impossible to pursue all the ramifications of these triadic developments, but the broad outlines of Spirit may be indicated. According to Hegel, at the level of Spirit we are studying mind—not the abstraction of a concrete thought thinking an other (Logic) nor the opposite abstraction of the other that is being thought about (Nature), but the synthesis of both.

First, in a group of categories called "Subjective Spirit," Hegel considered the inner aspects of concrete mind—a field that today would be called psychology. He held that these categories, taken together, are all deficient and one-sided because they are too "immediate." Accordingly, they are negated by another set of categories—those of Objective Spirit. These in turn overcompensate for the immediacy of Subjective Spirit by an equally one-sided emphasis on mediacy. That is, the categories of Objective Spirit are also concerned with mind, but they are concerned not with mind as it looks to itself on the inside (introspection) but, and exclusively, with mind as it is in its external relations to other minds. In a word, these categories are concerned with what today would be called sociology, ethics, and politics.

The conflict between Subjective Spirit and Objective Spirit is resolved in a new synthesis—Absolute Spirit. The subcategories of this new group are concerned with the highest levels and manifestations of mind—art, religion, and philosophy. In philosophy, especially, we are supposed to have reached a level of consciousness in which knowledge is absolutely articulate and determinate. This is the self-knowledge of a self that has passed out of the finitude in which it is limited by, and contrasted with, an other; but it is not the empty self-knowledge of Aristotle's god, who knows no other and no diversity. To grasp what Hegel means, put Aristotle's god into the world, or rather, let him *be* the world, and let him know himself in all this diversity and totality. His knowledge would then be as complete as that of a transcendent god, and his nature would be as various and complex as that of an immanent god.

This absolute self-knowledge, to which the final triads of the Hegelian system are devoted, is perhaps too esoteric a doctrine for us. Let us return to the somewhat "lower" ground of the categories of Objective Spirit and briefly examine Hegel's social and political theory.

Social Philosophy

In Hegel's view, social philosophy is a purely theoretical undertaking. It is the systematic exposition, that is, the triadic derivation, of the various concepts relevant to this field. Hegel sought to show that such concepts as property, contract, right, police, marriage and the family, and the state form triads, each of which consists in a stage of immediacy followed by a stage of mediacy and a synthesis of the two in a third stage of self-mediation. Since "freedom" is the last category deduced in Subjective Spirit, it becomes the lowest of the present movement. Thus, according to Hegel's system, social philosophy is concerned throughout with human freedom. Each new triad of this section reveals a progressively determinate, and hence more adequate, conception of freedom.

In the first stage of the progression freedom is conceived of in the character of immediacy. This, according to Hegel, is the concept of personality, and at this level the moral problem appears merely as the problem of maintaining certain abstract rights conceived of as belonging to us as persons. Though the general imperative of right can be stated positively ("Be a person and respect others as persons"), Hegel held its negative form to be more fundamental— "Do not infringe personality and what personality entails." At this level, that is, the distinction between persons and things-that-are-not-persons is regarded as fundamental. The former are ends, just as we are. The latter are not ends and hence can be treated as means. Whatever destiny and soul they may acquire is derived from the fact that someone "puts his will into them" and thereby makes them his. Over whatever things a person has appropriated in this way he has an "absolute right"—at this level and subject to the reservation that all such abstract rights are modified at a higher level of thought. Property relations at the level of abstract right are governed by contract, to which (accordingly) Hegel devoted another section of Objective Spirit. This leads to a definition of "wrong" as the violation of contract.

All these concepts are relatively immediate and are negated by a new set of concepts that are relatively mediate. Thus the distinction between persons and things, which seems so important at the level of immediacy, is true as far as it goes; but it is an oversimplification and must be corrected (made more determinate) by distinguishing between inner and outer. So far, that is, we have been considering a level of consciousness that conceives of personality in a simple, uncomplicated way—moral goodness consists in keeping contracts (as between persons); moral badness in violating them. Hegel then proceeded to the negative stage, in which personality is seen to be not simple but complex, and not merely complex but often divided. At this stage will is seen to issue not merely in acts that are lawful or unlawful, but in *motivated* acts. And when we take motives into account we see that acts may be morally bad and legal, or morally good and illegal. Here we reach the level of Morality, in distinction from the lower level of Abstract Right.

In Hegel's view, it is wrongdoing that brings forcefully to our attention the difference between inner and outer. We would not feel an act to be *wrong* if we did not identify ourselves with the law we are breaking. But we also obviously identify ourselves with the breaking of it; otherwise we would not break it. Hence the self, which originally presented a solid front to the world, must admit itself divided. It finds in itself two loyalties—a loyalty to a lower and more immediate end and a loyalty to a higher and less immediate end. When this happens, we have advanced to the "moral standpoint."

The synthesis of Morality and Abstract Right is what Hegel called the Ethical Life. Although Hegel's reasoning here is obscure he seems to be arguing (1) that the notion of right is negated by the notion of good, (2) that these apparently opposing principles have to be brought into harmony in any really adequate account of the moral life, and (3) that the way to do this is to see that our finite, individual will and its private good are transcended in the larger will and larger good of the society of which we are organs. At any rate, this synthesis has brought us from a level of consciousness at which thought about conduct is limited to individuals and their relations to other individuals (for example, contract) to a level at which individuals are seen to be only parts, and at which their true good, and the truly moral (that is, "ethical") life, consists in sharing loyally and fully in the good of the whole.

Political Theory

At this point in the development of the system we pass from ethical theory to political theory. That is, Ethical Life, the synthesis we have just examined, consists in a series of triads that once again traverse the movement from immediacy through mediacy to self-mediation; but this time the concepts involved are concepts in what today would be called political theory. Hegel begins with the Family, finds its negation to be Civil Society, and finally achieves another synthesis, the State. In order to indicate how Hegel conceived of and handled the problems of society, a part of his account of the Family, which (it will be noted) consists in its turn of a subtriad, is quoted below.

> The family, as the immediate substantiality of mind, is specifically charac-
> terized by love, which is mind's feeling of its own unity. Hence in a family,

one's frame of mind is to have self-consciousness of one's individuality within this unity as the absolute essence of oneself, with the result that one is in it not as an independent person but as a member.
. . . .
The family is completed in these three phases:

(a) *Marriage*, the form assumed by the concept of the family in its immediate phase;

(b) *Family Property and Capital* (the external embodiment of the concept) and attention to these;

(c) *The Education of Children and the Dissolution of the Family.*

Marriage, as the immediate type of ethical relationship, contains first, the moment of physical life; and since marriage is a *substantial* tie, the life involved in it is life in its totality, i.e. as the actuality of the race and its life-process. But, secondly, in self-consciousness the natural sexual union—a union purely inward or implicit and for that very reason *existent* as purely external—is changed into a union on the level of mind, into self-conscious love.

On the subjective side, marriage may have a more obvious source in the particular inclination of the two persons who are entering upon the marriage tie, or in the foresight and contrivance of the parents, and so forth. But its objective source lies in the free consent of the persons, especially in their consent to make themselves one person, to renounce their natural and individual personality to this unity of one with the other. From this point of view, their union is a self-restriction, but in fact it is their liberation, because in it they attain their substantive self-consciousness.

The ethical aspect of marriage consists in the parties' consciousness of this unity as their substantive aim, and so in their love, trust and common sharing of their entire existence as individuals. When the parties are in this frame of mind and their union is actual, their physical passion sinks to the level of a physical moment, destined to vanish in its very satisfaction. On the other hand, the spiritual bond of union secures its rights as the substance of marriage and thus rises, inherently indissoluble, to a plane above the contingency of passion and the transience of particular caprice.
. . . .
In essence marriage is monogamy because it is personality—immediate exclusive individuality—which enters into this tie and surrenders itself to it; and hence the tie's truth and inwardness (i.e. the subjective form of its substantiality) proceeds only from the mutual, whole-hearted, surrender of this personality.

Further, marriage results from the free surrender by both sexes of their personality—a personality in every possible way unique in each of the parties. Consequently, it ought not to be entered by two people identical in stock who are already acquainted and perfectly known to one another; for individuals in the same circle of relationship have no special personality of their own in contrast with that of others in the same circle. On the contrary, the parties should be drawn from separate families and their personalities should be different in origin. Since the very conception of marriage is that it is a l freely undertaken ethical transaction, not a tie directly grounded in the physical organism and its desires, it follows that the marriage of blood-relations runs counter to this conception and so also to genuine natural feeling.[e]

As the thesis of a triad, the Family is "immediate," in contrast to the mediateness of Civil Society. In calling the family immediate, Hegel apparently had in mind the fact that it lacks the formal, organizational structure of a larger group like a trade union or a town meeting. In addition, the Family is dependent on the larger groups of which it is a part. This dependence (and incompleteness) is the basis for Hegel's passage to Civil Society, the Family's "other." Here, in the concept of Civil Society, we have arrived at the level of thought that characterized eighteenth-century political theorizing: Every citizen is a distinct, individual entity who enters into a compact with other individuals for benefits he expects to gain thereby. Instead of one good (the family's), there are a plurality of goods (those of all the citizens). Instead of natural and unconscious relations, there is an explicit and formal organization. But these relations are conceived, at the level of Civil Society, to be merely external links that bring together a number of men, each of whom is a complete and autonomous individual.

What Hegel called a Civil Society most people would simply call a state. But Hegel reserved the latter term for the superior type of organization that synthesizes (incorporates and transcends) both those intimate (immediate) relations that are found in the family and those abstract mediate relations that are found in Civil Society. Thus the State completes the triad. Naturally, the transition to the State is not abrupt.

Civil Society anticipates in primitive form the kind of organization and relationships that are fully articulated only in the State. For instance, consider what happens when citizens become interested in organizations like the Red Cross or the League of Women Voters. When, as people say, they have put enough of themselves into the organization, they identify themselves with its fortunes and find in its successes satisfaction that has nothing to do with private gain or profit. Thus, even in Civil Society, even in the "externality of the will," organizations develop in which this externality is absorbed—organizations in which individuals find their good in that of the larger whole of which they feel a part. In this way, we reach the State, which is the supreme type of social order.

It might be supposed that the logic of Hegel's dialectic would have led him to sweep past the State to incorporate it in a still larger society, of which states themselves would be organs, and which would include, eventually, the whole human race. Why, then, did Hegel stop with the State? Hegel could have replied that he was not writing prophesy; he was developing a system based on the situation as it existed in his own time, and the national territorial state was the largest political unit then in existence. But this answer is not satisfactory. To begin with, in the 1820's there were no "states" in Hegel's special sense of the term. Indeed, if he had confined himself to description based on the political situation as it existed in his day he would have had to limit himself to civil societies. However, Hegel was not really doing descriptive political science. Because he found the Prussia of his day congenial, he tended to idealize it, and idealizing it meant (he believed) identifying it with the State. Finally, if Hegel was going to import ideals into what purported to be a systematic exposition of the actual, there were better ideals to introduce. The national territorial unit was an inadequate type of political organization. Every such unit was then, and still is, limited in just the same way as the Family (though to a lesser degree). It would seem that, just as men have to go outside their families to find their true good, so they have to go outside the State. Economic and political developments since Hegel's death have doubtless made this fact more obvious than it was in his day. Nevertheless, his own dialectic as well as the plain facts of life at that time should have shown him that he could not stop with the State. Indeed, Dante had argued more than four centuries earlier that there must be a single human society, because—to put his case in Hegelian terms—security could not tolerate an "other."

Hegel did not merely contend that the State is complete; he also argued that it is the "true" individual. The State, that is, is not merely a collection of independent individuals; its members are related to it as organs are related to the organism of which they are parts. Just as the stomach's significance lies in the contribution it makes to the life of the body, and just as husband and wife lose their personal identities in their marriage,[16] so the citizens of a Civil Society lose their independence in the unity of the State. Hegel did not hold merely that some citizens do, as a matter of fact, identify with the State, just as some individuals identify themselves with their family; he also held that they *ought* to do so, and that if they do not they should be forced to do so, for their own good.

This brings us to the question of consent, which is a central problem for political theories that take the concepts of individual freedom and *laissez faire* seriously—that is, for political theories at the level of *raisonnement*. This question can best be approached via a late eighteenth-century criticism that anticipated much of Hegel's view (without, of course, the apparatus of the system).

Rousseau (1712–78) was temperamentally out of tune with the Enlightenment, the age during which he lived. He held that as long as sovereignty rests in a *plurality* of distinct wills it is necessary either to wait for unanimity (in which case the state will break down through inability to act) or to permit the majority to compel the minority. But does not the latter alternative destroy the moral basis of the state? Rousseau thought that it did, and to get around this difficulty he formulated the doctrine of what he called the "general will."

The "general will" is to be contrasted with the "will of all," or the merely coincidental agreement of a group of individualists. A group of wills is general

16 See p. 136. The State differs from the Family in that, whereas the latter's unity is a spontaneous and unconscious development, the former's is the result of deliberate and self-conscious legislation.

when each individual will aims at the common good. It is possible, of course, that the general will and the will of all might result in the same action, for it might just happen that each individualist sees that the way to obtain his private end is to agree to the action in question. But Rousseau held that agreement is much more likely to occur when everyone is trying to decide whether or not a proposed action (for example, an increase in the income tax) is for the good of all, rather than when everyone is trying to decide whether such an action is to his own advantage.

And quite apart from this practical advantage, Rousseau maintained that the general will, unlike the will of all, is a true consensus. It is what everyone really wants—the minority as well as the majority. Hence, even though the minority has to go along with the majority, it is not being compelled to do so. Hence, finally, the moral basis of the state is not destroyed. Suppose ten per cent of the voters think that lowering the tax exemption will increase the revenue and thereby promote the common good, while ninety per cent think that raising the surtax will promote the common good. Obviously, on democratic principles, the surtax will be raised; but those who lost (who voted against raising the surtax) and those who won all want, and get, exactly the same thing. For they do not differ about the *end;* they differ only about the *means.* And since they all get the end they want (promotion of the common good) they are all free, and no one is compelled. There are obviously many difficulties with this view. For one thing, it assumes that what the majority thinks is for the common good always really is for the common good—a view that is optimistic to say the least.

Hegel's theory is hardly more than a reformulation of the general-will doctrine in his own terminology, a reformulation designed to answer this and other objections. When the relations among citizens come to be self-mediate (instead of merely immediate or merely mediate), the result is the sort of political organization that Hegel called the State. It is also what Rousseau called the general will. This follows because at the level of the State the citizens, who formerly perceived themselves as separate and autonomous individuals, have come to see that they are but the organs of the one true individual, the State. Accordingly, what the State wills is also willed by them, as its organs; there is no problem of consent, for there is no compulsion. What appears to be compulsion (what *is* compulsion at lower levels of political organization) is only the process of inducing a man to choose what he really wants, in distinction from what he mistakenly believes he wants. Compulsion is exercised only against his finite, transitory will, which, truly *understood,* is absorbed, and transcended, in the State's will. The citizen is not being forced against his will, because his real will is what the State wants for him. But why is what the State wants what he really wants? Because what the State wants is his true good. And why is what the State wants his true good? Because he is a part of, an organ of, this larger organism. Its good is his—and not merely in the sense that the individual's good is his family's, for here the transcendence, or absorption, is only partial. The father has goods of his own, not identical with those of his son. In the State the absorption of the citizen is complete; nothing survives that is good for him in isolation.

Of course, this is at best only an ideal, for in no actual state, in Hegel's day or in ours, has such complete absorption and transcendence of individual wills been achieved. (Totalitarian regimes, of course, have gone a long way toward repressing dissent and individual differences, but this is not what Hegel had in mind.) The problem is that the larger the political unit, and the more economic, social, and cultural diversity included in it, the less likely that individual differences will be transcended. Realizing this, Rousseau argued in favor of very small communities on the model of the Greek city-state. But Hegel thought in terms of large, "modern" political units; and, as was pointed out earlier, he ought to have thought in terms of still larger ones. Hence the doctrine of the general will, whatever its theoretical value, does not seem particularly relevant to the actual conditions of modern political life.

Evaluation of Hegel's Philosophy

The history of commentary on Hegel's philosophy is itself an illustration of Hegelian dialectic. It has developed by a process that can fairly be called negation. During most of the nineteenth century commentators were chiefly impressed by Hegel's system, which seemed to answer a deep need in nineteenth-century society. As the world was becoming more and more complex, as more and more diversity in belief and in behavior came to light, it was obvious that the old absolutes were being exploded—not only the absolute proposed by the Church but that put forward by the eighteenth-century philosophers. To many people Hegel's system seemed to offer a new and viable absolute; that is, it seemed to claim that a complete account of the universe is possible, an account in which all the diversity is included but in which it is transcended in a final unity.[17] For such people the *Logic*, the only completed part of the system, was Hegel's most important work.

More recently, however, the system has been de-emphasized, and *The Phenomenology* is now considered the core of Hegel's theory. Today critics are inclined to think of the system as merely a sort of classificatory scheme by means of which Hegel provisionally arranged the various topics on which he chose to lecture.[18] From this point of view, the system has hardly more metaphysical significance than does a professor's decision about how to arrange the books in his library.

---

17 This claim to provide certainty and totality also explains to a large extent the appeal of other systems launched in the nineteenth century—Marxism, for instance, and Haeckel's "monistic cosmology." See pp. 184–86 and 199–200.

18 See Walter Kaufmann, *Hegel* (Doubleday, New York, 1965), pp. 225–53.

Evidence to support both these interpretations can be found in Hegel's work. On the one hand, Hegel certainly knew that the system he was working out was the result of his own thought, that is, a thought process occurring in a particular, individual mind. And he knew that he occupied a particular locus in space and time—the universe, Hegel was aware, existed before he was born and would continue to exist after he died. Social, political, and cultural developments would occur in the future, the nature of which he explicitly disclaimed the ability or the desire to predict. Hegel left it to later philosophers to systematize these developments, just as he himself was systematizing knowledge as of the 1820's.

On the other hand, Hegel repeatedly equated his system with scientific knowledge, which he defined as necessary and completely determinate. He did not deny, of course, that the system had emerged at a particular point in time; but he felt that its emergence in this form and at this time was itself a "moment" (phase) in a cosmic system.

> Our epoch is a birth-time, and a period of transition. The spirit of man has broken with the old order of things hitherto prevailing, and with old ways of thinking. . . . it is here as in the case of the birth of a child; after a long period of nutrition in silence, the continuity of the graduate growth in size, of quantitative change, is suddenly cut short by the first breath drawn—there is a break in the process, a qualitative change—and the child is born. In like manner the spirit of the time, growing slowly and quietly ripe for the new form it is to assume, disintegrates one fragment after another of the structure of its previous world. . . . This gradual crumbling to pieces . . . is interrupted by the sunrise, which, in a flash and at a single stroke, brings to view the form and structure of the new world.[f]

Viewed in this way, the system that Hegel worked out is much more than a convenient classificatory scheme. This system (with a small "s") reflects the articulations of the System (with a capital "S") that generated it. And the System, taken as a whole, is a cosmic process in which Mind generates its other, Nature, and then reabsorbs it. For instance, in the Introduction to the *Logic* Hegel states that this work is "the account of God as he is in his eternal essence before the creation of nature and any finite spirit." Here Hegel sounds like Plotinus, for whom the universe was a sequence of emanations issuing from, and returning to, the Absolute. Thus Hegel's own thought, as he was thinking out the system, was the Absolute thinking in him; he is a part of the process he describes.

Hegel's concept of the *Weltgeist*—a term that is variously translated as "world spirit" or "universal mind"—fits in with this interpretation of his philosophy. Hegel seems to have held that individual minds, insofar as they succeed in thinking scientifically, are incorporated in the universal mind. That is, as individual minds come to think scientifically, they undergo a development that exactly recapitulates the development of the universal mind. In so doing, they become "moments" in this mind.

> The task of conducting the individual mind from its unscientific standpoint to that of science had to be undertaken in its general sense; we had to contemplate the formative development of the universal individual, of self-conscious spirit. As to the relation between these two [the particular and general individual], every moment as it gains concrete form and its own proper shape and appearance, finds a place in the life of the universal individual. The particular individual is incomplete mind. . . .[g]

Thus evidence to support both interpretations of Hegel's position can be found. But which is the "true" Hegel? Readers of Hegel will know the answer to this question: Both interpretations are correct with regard to what they assert; both are false with regard to what they deny. Each negates the other precisely because each is a limited and one-sided truth. What is required, then, is a more determinate version of Hegel's position, one that incorporates (while transcending) these two interpretations. And this more adequate interpretation will eventually need to be incorporated in a still more adequate interpretation. And so on.

But how do we know that more and more determinate interpretations are possible? Perhaps Hegel simply and flatly contradicted himself. This question can be generalized as follows: In Hegel's view, all conflicts and discrepancies are amenable to harmonization—but what is the evidence that reality is through-and-through rational, in the Hegelian sense of "rational"? What is the guarantee that all those partial "versions of" can eventually be reconciled in something that is no longer a version of reality but is reality itself? Hegel would doubtless have replied with another question: What exactly are you asking for when you demand a "guarantee" that the universe is rational? Reason can guarantee specific truths, but what sort of guarantee can be given for reason other than the evidence it provides for specific truths? This is what Hegel's remark, quoted earlier, about "anti-human" means.[19] Men must have faith in the rationality of the universe; to lack this faith is not to be a man. Thus the business of philosophy is not to offer guarantees of men's deepest convictions; rather, it is to systematize and clarify these beliefs.

Very well. We may agree that it is not the business of philosophy to prove that the universe is rational; however, it is the business of philosophy to examine what "being rational" entails. Unfortunately, Hegel never made this clear. Although he constantly asserted that rationality involves necessity, he never gave a formal account of what (in his view) necessity is, and the parts of the system that he worked out in detail suggest that his idea of necessity was unfortunately very "indeterminate."

Hegel's system purports to make sense of the actual situation (the state of knowledge as of the 1820's) by showing that all accumulated data about history, anthropology, physics, and psychology—all the bits and pieces of theory and

---

19 See p. 109.

of fact—are systematically interrelated and in harmony. But in "demonstrating" this harmony, Hegel played fast and loose with the actual facts. Indeed, instead of making sense of the actual by uncovering the systematic interrelations among data, the system became a covert criterion by which Hegel decided what is "really" actual and eliminated what did not fit. As we have seen, Hegel tended to gloss over the actual facts about the Prussian state of 1820 and to interpret it in the light of his ideal of what the "State" ought to be. A similar confusion can be seen in his discussion of the Family. Hegel took it for granted that marriage is (that is, "ought to be") monogamous. But he never showed—indeed, he never could have shown—monogamy to be necessary.[20] If Hegel had been a professor in Salt Lake City in the 1870's, instead of in Berlin in the 1820's, he would doubtless have held that polygamy is "necessary."

This criticism of Hegel is not intended to suggest that it was a mistake for him to aim at systematizing knowledge of, for instance, sociology. Quite the contrary. A sociology that is drowned in data is not much better off than one lost in the clouds. But such a system should grow out of an empirical study of actual behavior and should derive its concepts from that study. This, of course, is exactly what Hegel repeatedly stated in *The Phenomenology*.[21] Thought, he pointed out, should not start with a ready-made set of abstract ideas. For this reason Hegel had nothing but contempt for *raisonnement*. The level of "notion" is more adequate than that of *raisonnement* precisely because it reflects the concrete life of the actual object of thought. All this is admirable, of course. But as the system was worked out in detail, it became a Procrustean bed into which the empirical materials were forced. This is true even though in Hegel's day psychology and sociology hardly existed as empirical sciences and there were precious few data to systematize.

Since Hegel's death, as data have accumulated at an exponential rate and as the difficulty of systematizing them has enormously increased, the artificiality of Hegel's specific system has become more obvious. Hegel, it must be allowed, gravely underestimated the problem of synthesis. Despite his frequent reference to the richness and variety of the actual, he was a monist at heart. This preference for monism over pluralism is also reflected in his failure to take account of the diversity of wills that exist in any large-scale political organization. Just as it may be that the only way to achieve unanimity in the state is by repression, so it may be that the only way to achieve an overall, all-inclusive scientific system is by an arbitrary forcing of the data into the theory. These were costs that Hegel would have regarded as too high to pay, but a persistent ambiguity in his terminology saved him from seeing and having to face this difficult choice.

This ambiguity appears in his use of the term *wirklich*, which Hegel repeatedly equated with the rational. *Wirklich* can be translated as "actual," in which

20 It might be possible to show that a statistically significant correlation holds between monogamy and certain parent-child relations that Hegel considered desirable. But this is quite another thing, of course.
21 See p. 115.

event the assertion that it is the rational is palpably false. Much of what is actual, far from being rational, is arbitrary—as Hegel well knew. However, *wirklich* can also be translated as "real." In this event the assertion is a tautology. The question of what kind of relation exists between the rational-real and the actual thus remains to be dealt with; but because Hegel shifted between this and the other meaning of *wirklich*, it seemed to him that he had answered it satisfactorily.

There are, then, serious difficulties with the Hegelian system, and these difficulties persist whether we interpret it as a simple classificatory system or as a cosmic drama. Let us therefore return to what was called, earlier, the "vision" of *The Phenomenology*. *The Phenomenology* was prophetic in that it set out what were to become central themes of twentieth-century culture. First, it brought into prominence the concept of mediation, with all that it implies about the inevitable distance between knower and known, between the self and its objects, including the self itself. This concept fits in with one of the major concerns of our time, as reflected in Dostoevsky's description of underground man—the impossibility of attaining complete self-knowledge, the alienation of the individual both from himself and from his society.

Second, *The Phenomenology* put forward the view that there are a variety of types of consciousness, each of which is reflected in a different version of reality. It is true that most people today would be sceptical of Hegel's claim that all this variety constitutes a hierarchy culminating in a special type of consciousness that, far from being merely another version, is itself truth and reality. But Hegel's recognition that each type of consciousness is reflected in the social, political, and economic institutions—as well as in the philosophy, science, art, and religion—of a given epoch, has influenced men's thinking in profound ways and may be said to be one of the marks that distinguishes us and our time from every other. To mention examples that range from the momentous to the trivial: It laid the basis for the intellectual revolutions launched by Marx and Freud; it also made possible the division of this history of philosophy into a series of volumes organized around the notion of distinctive types of "minds."

Schopenhauer

Arthur Schopenhauer (1788–1860) was born in Danzig, into a family of wealthy merchants—persons of culture and of an emotional instability that he seems to have inherited, or at least absorbed. The family business for which he was destined bored him, and he soon abandoned it for a literary career. Schopenhauer was vain and snobbish ("Common people certainly look like men; I have never seen any creatures that resembled men so closely"); he was also a brilliant conversationalist, a gourmet, and a man of sensitive taste in music and the other arts. Though he never married, he was attractive to women and had a number of amorous adventures in the fashion of the times. "I have taught what sainthood is," he declared with complacency, "but I myself am no saint."

The World as Idea

Schopenhauer's chief work, *The World as Will and Idea*, was published in 1818, when he was thirty. The title reflects his dual theory that the world is both idea and will. The world inevitably appears to us, given the sort of sensory makeup with which we are endowed, as idea; but in its essence, as we learn through intuition, it is will.

As regards appearance, in Schopenhauer's view what I experience in perception (and in all the modes of knowledge based on, or derived from, perception) is nothing but a series of changes produced in my body. An object out there (for instance, the sun) causes a change in my eye. The brightness that I experience is not "out there" in the sun; it is here, in my eye. Why, then, do I attribute what is an effect here in me (brightness) to the cause out there (sun)? The explanation, according to Schopenhauer, is that in perception two processes occur: By an ordinary causal process the object "out there" causes a change in a sense organ; then, by a curious kind of reverse process, this effect is referred back to its cause. Perception is thus a double process, from object to sense organ and from sense organ back to object. Since the second process is normally unconscious, I mistake the effect for its cause. What I am aware of when I say, "I see the sun," is a brightness-in-the-eye, but because of the unconscious reversing that refers the effect back to its cause, I believe myself to be aware of the sun (the cause of the brightness-in-the-eye).

And, of course, my eye, insofar as it is an object of perception, is as much an effect as is the sun itself. Hence Schopenhauer's view may be described as follows: An unknown x out there (sun as it really is) produces a change in an unknown y (my body as it really is), and this change is experienced as "bright, hot." Schopenhauer's position is thus much more complex than Berkeley's, which it otherwise resembles. Whereas Berkeley had dispensed with the unknown x and y and had held the whole process of perception to be merely a succession of sense data ("ideas"), Schopenhauer held that beneath the sense data are real entities the nature and relations of which are quite different from those reported by the sense data, and which are known in a totally different way.[22]

From this account of perception, Schopenhauer concluded (1) that in knowledge based on perception we never discover what things really are and (2) that we nevertheless know that such objects exist, for they are the causes of what

22 See p. 148.

we perceive. Thus perception cannot possibly give me any information about what the sun is in itself. It yields information regarding only the sorts of effects that the sun has on sense organs like mine.

This reverse passage from effect to cause is what Schopenhauer called "understanding," or knowledge. Although there are great differences in the degree of acuteness with which men make this passage, it is basically the same process, he believed, in stupid men and in clever ones. Stupidity, indeed, is simply a deficiency in the capacity to make the correct passage from effect to cause. A stupid man sees a movement on a dark night, and instead of referring it to its proper cause (a branch blowing in the wind), he refers it to a ghost walking. There is no difference in kind, Schopenhauer held, between such "thinking" and the thought of a man like Newton. The latter's thought process, like that of the former, is an immediate, unconscious passage from effect ("apple lands on head") to cause ("gravity"). Of course, in a great scientific discovery the passage is incomparably more acute, but it is "just like perception, an operation of the understanding, an immediate intuition, and as such is the work of an instant, an *aperçu*, a flash of insight."

It also follows that there is no difference in kind between the human and the animal intellect. In animals the passage is simply less acute than it is in even a stupid human intellect. Schopenhauer believed that animals are incapable of reasoning, and that this latter faculty does distinguish men from them. But this distinction is nothing to man's credit, for reason is very much a secondary power and more of a liability than an asset.

The essential characteristic of reason is that it is conceptual—it "serves to take up the objective connections which are immediately known by the understanding [and] makes them permanent for thought." [h] After Newton saw the nature of gravity in a single flash of direct insight, he was able to write it down in conceptual form—in words and in mathematical formulas. Reason thus has some use, Schopenhauer rather grudgingly admitted. It makes communication possible, and by enabling us to store up experience (by recording it) it makes long-range, planned activities possible. Without it, the complex economic and social relationships of modern civilization would be impossible. But these gains, Schopenhauer held, are more than offset by the damage that reasoning does. For with reason, "doubt, error, care, and sorrow" enter into human life.

As to the "error" that reason is supposed to introduce, Schopenhauer held that conceptual thinking falsifies the uniqueness and continuity of reality. The concept "green," for instance, is a pigeonhole into which we toss higgledy-piggledy a large number of items, each of which is a distinct shade, a unique tone. The concept "blue" is handled in an equally arbitrary way. We believe not only that all the various shades of blue are identically blue, but that blue is never green and that green is never blue. This is the second mistake reason makes. Not only does it identify things that are really different; it sharply separates things that are in varying degrees similar. Or, putting both mistakes together, it may be said that reason tries to impose distinctions in kind on a reality that is a continuum of differences in degree. This is the trouble with the classification of colors into "green" and "blue." Colors actually form a continuum of tones, and between two colors, one of which we call blue and the other green, there may be no more difference than between two other colors, both of which we call green.

Schopenhauer's position is thus a radical kind of nominalism: There is no common property that is named by a term like "blue." Carried to its logical conclusion, this means that the type of communication modern science holds as ideal—that is, communication by means of mathematical concepts—is hopelessly inadequate. It is doubtless useful in constructing buildings, bombs, and bridges, and in other activities in which rough approximations can be tolerated. In Schopenhauer's view, the fact that a building thirty stories high requires foundations of such-and-such a size is a useful but basically trivial thing to know. This kind of knowledge tells us nothing about the texture of the material of which the building is constructed, its color, its feel, or its beauty—all these things must be experienced directly in perception.

Reason, Schopenhauer held, is as practically incompetent and as morally bad as it is cognitively inadequate. In the field of practice, concepts throw our aim off. Thinking too precisely on an event, weighing the pros and cons, we lose our power of decision and fumble when we come to act. Thus the general who tries to plan a campaign in advance (that is, to act conceptually) will be at a disadvantage, as will the man who tries to apply the "science of mechanics" to the game of billiards. Similarly, in manners and in social intercourse, "all that is attractive, gracious, charming in behavior, all affectionateness and friendliness, must not proceed from concepts for if it does 'we feel intention and are put out of tune.'" [1] The same is true for virtue and holiness; they proceed not from reflection but from character. All that reasoning does in the moral sphere is to make lying and dissimulation possible.

As will be seen, Schopenhauer's position is closely related to Wordsworth's ("We murder to dissect") and to the general Romantic emphasis on feeling, immediacy, and intuition. Schopenhauer attacked everything that the Enlightenment held to be valuable and true. The very form of his argument—its lack of logical organization, its exaggeration, and its passion—is typically Romantic.

The World as Will

This brings us to the second point in Schopenhauer's theory—the fact that the world is will. So far we have seen merely that perception does not give us knowledge of the real world and that science is at an even further remove from reality: Science, as the conceptualization of perception, falsifies the latter's immediacy. Fortunately, however, man is not limited to perception and the sciences. He has an intuition of the inner nature of reality (of the unknown x's and y's that are the causes of perception), and this intuition discloses their inner nature to be will. Schopenhauer's starting point was the self—the central focus, in one way or another, of modern philosophy from Descartes to Kant. As we have seen, perception yields only appearance—not the sun as it really is but the sun as it affects my body, and my body is simply another perceptual object. But though we *perceive* ourselves as bodies, existing in various spatiotemporal relations with other bodies (for example, the sun), we *intuit* ourselves as will, and this self-knowledge becomes the basis for a further exploration of the world in intuition. Not only are we "really" will, but, according to Schopenhauer, the whole world is will: All those "things" that cause sensations in our bodies, and whose nature is forever hidden from perception and the sciences, are really in their inner nature "will," like ourselves. The passage in which Schopenhauer expounded this central thesis of his philosophy will serve to illustrate his method:

> The meaning for which we seek . . . would never be found if the investigator himself were nothing more than the pure knowing subject (a winged cherub without a body). But . . . his knowledge, which is the necessary supporter of the whole world as idea, is yet always given through the medium of a body. . . . His body is, for the pure knowing subject, an idea like every other idea, an object among objects. [Nevertheless he also experiences] its movements and actions . . . in an entirely different way. . . . The answer to the riddle is given to the subject of knowledge who appears as an individual, and the answer is *will*. This and this alone gives him the key to his own existence, reveals to him the significance, shows him the inner mechanism of his being, of his action, of his movements. The body is given in two entirely different ways to the subject of knowledge. . . . It is given as an idea in intelligent perception. . . . And it is also given in quite a different way as that which is immediately known to every one, and is signified by the word *will*. . . . The act of will and the movement of the body are not two different things objectively known, which the bond of causality unites; . . . they are one and the same, but they are given in entirely different ways,—immediately, and again in perception. . . . The action of the body is nothing but the act of the will objectified, *i.e.*, passed into perception. . . . The whole body is nothing but objectified will, *i.e.*, will become idea.[j]

This view is not without grave difficulties. According to Schopenhauer, body and will are the same thing experienced in different ways. Hunger, for instance, is "objectified" as teeth, throat, and bowels. But how can Schopenhauer "know" that the perceptual experience of body and the intuitive experience of will are experiences of the same thing (the self) and not experiences of two different things (body, will)? An example will point up the problem. When we put on distorting spectacles, we believe we are experiencing the same landscape that we experience without the spectacles. But there is a well-defined operation (taking off and putting on the glasses) by which we get from one experience to the other. Without such an operation we could never know that there was a correspondence. This is just what Schopenhauer's theory lacks: There is no well-defined operation that "connects" perception and intuition—they are completely different modes of experience.

Further, even if we could know that will and body are the same, what grounds are there for saying that the experience we call "will" is more real than the experience we call "body"? The spectacles are "distorting" because our experience when we wear them fails to agree with other people's experience. But perception as such can be called "distorting" only on the basis of a preference for one kind of experience over another. Here, then, Schopenhauer reveals a typical Romantic preference for the inner, the unmediated, the continuous, and the dynamic.

Passing over the hidden value-judgment on which rests the contention that I am "really" will, let us consider the next part of Schopenhauer's thesis, namely, that everything else is also "really" will. Schopenhauer sought to prove this thesis by an argument from analogy—indeed, this would seem to be the only possible form of proof. But such an argument is weak at best and becomes progressively weaker as the points of similarity become fewer. Thus I may say other men are surely will, because they are so much like me; and the same may be said, perhaps, for animals. But what about such inanimate objects as plants, trees, stones, the iron ore or coal buried deep in the earth, and the sun and the planets? Schopenhauer realized that this is not a proof in the ordinary sense. It is not an appeal to empirical evidence, as in the sciences. Rather, it is an appeal to an insight that Schopenhauer believed all men share, if only obscurely. Thus the truth that the world is will is proved by "raising" it from the level of immediate consciousness to the level of abstract knowledge.

When we read a poem we sometimes feel, "That is just what I have been trying to say!" We think that we and the poet have experienced the same sentiment, but that whereas our experience of it was vague, his was clear. It would seem that Schopenhauer intuited something—the fact that the world is will—and gave an account of this intuition that he believed all other men would come to accept as an adequate version of their own intuitions. When they read *The World as Will and Idea* they will say (he believed), "This is what I have all along obscurely felt about the world!"

It follows that anyone in whom *The World as Will and Idea* does not evoke this sense of recognition stands outside the whole affair. Perhaps this sounds like radical subjectivity, but we must remember that Schopenhauer thought everyone *would* recognize a community of feeling, and that this feeling was an insight into a real and objective state of affairs. In his affirmation of a public reality he agreed with the rationalists and stood against any sort of solipsism or scepticism. But here, of course, his kinship with rationalism ended. He was not interested, as the rationalists were, in a detailed, systematic knowledge of reality. Indeed, in his view, systematic knowledge is quite impossible: There is nothing to know about reality except that it is will—it has no articulate structure like

Spinoza's substance or Thomas' God. It is just blind struggle. But even if there were something to know about it, from Schopenhauer's point of view knowledge of it would be inconsequential. Conduct, not theory, certifies the truth;[23] theories about conduct are *ex post facto,* and their variety merely indicates the range of verbalisms by which different men rationalize what happens. What matters is not what we know but how we feel and what we do. A Romantic philosophy does not interest itself in epistemology or in metaphysics as formal, systematic disciplines. It is characteristic, therefore, that in Schopenhauer's philosophy the former was replaced by an examination of art, and the latter by a study of the religious attitude.

The Nature of Art

According to Schopenhauer, art has two functions. First, esthetic experience yields a more adequate vision of the world as it really is than does science. Second, the peculiar nature of the esthetic object often allows us to adopt toward this vision the kind of attitude that Schopenhauer regarded as moral. Hence esthetics has both a cognitive and an ethical function and leads eventually into religion.

THE COGNITIVE FUNCTION OF ART

In order to understand what Schopenhauer regarded as the cognitive function of art, let us look briefly at his account of architecture and sculpture. In both arts we experience the play of light and shadows on surfaces. This, Schopenhauer thought, gives us a truer insight into the nature of light than does the physical theory of light. The equations that the physicist uses give us merely a summary— and an artificial one at that—of the *perception* of light. But when we look at light *esthetically* (and one of the functions of any art object is to put us into the esthetic attitude), we grasp its inner nature. Of course, we cannot *say* what it is (that is, we cannot say it conceptually); but we *know* what it is. The statue (or the building) in its plastic handling of light "says" (non-conceptually) what light is; and if it is a fine work of art it will give an esthetically sensitive observer a complete knowledge of the nature of light. In Schopenhauer's view, there is only one reason for translating this complete knowledge into concepts. Though we lose almost all in the translation, the small particles of meaning that we catch in our crude conceptual net may prove to have pragmatic value.

Architecture also enables us to know gravity. In our esthetic appreciation of the vaulting of a Gothic cathedral, for instance, we come to know the inner nature of gravity. In contrast, Newton's inverse-square law gives us only the outer husks of meaning.

23 See pp. 156–57.

But what is the relation between light and gravity on the one hand and will on the other? Do we experience will when we experience gravity and light esthetically? If so, why do we call them "light" and "gravity," instead of "will"? Schopenhauer replied that will "manifests" itself at various levels and in various degrees of adequacy. Gravity and light are both very low, or unconscious, levels of manifestation. In gravity, for instance, there is a tension of opposites—the buttresses push against the vaulting, the vaulting bears down on the walls, and so on. In the progression from inanimate objects to plants, to animals, and finally to man successively higher manifestations of will occur. This holds, of course, only when we look at the objects in question esthetically—a scientific perception of man is no more revealing of the nature of will than is a scientific perception of gravity. But an esthetic experience of man is far more revealing of the nature of will than is an esthetic experience of gravity. For man really is a more complete expression of will than gravity, and if we can only adopt an esthetic attitude toward man, we shall see that this is the case.

This is what a painting (if it is a work of art) does. If we look at a man, most of us remain at the level of perception; if we look at a *portrait* of a man, we *may* remain at the level of perception, but we may also rise, with the painter's assistance, to an esthetic contemplation of man's inner nature as will. The difference between the artist and the ordinary man lies in the former's capacity to move into the esthetic attitude on his own, by looking at some natural object; most of us, on the other hand, depend on the "lead" the artist gives by the way he organizes the pigments on his canvas. The same is true of the poet. Few people have ever been put into the esthetic attitude by looking at a young ass. But Coleridge apparently was. Accordingly, his verses may put a sensitive reader into a similar attitude.

THE ESTHETIC ATTITUDE

So far the cognitive function of art has been under consideration. The moral function of art results directly from the nature of the esthetic attitude. We can best understand this nature by contrasting it with our usual practical attitude. Because we are, of course, "really" will, the will in us projects itself into every aspect of our phenomenal life—it drives us into activity. This is true even of the cognitive attitude, which, Schopenhauer believed, is anything but the calm, dispassionate contemplation that the rationalists supposed it to be. "Knowledge is completely subject to the will. . . . Only through [its] relations [to his body] is the object *interesting* to the individual, *i.e.*, related to the will. Therefore the knowledge which is subject to the will knows nothing further of objects than their relations." [k] This is most obviously true at the level of perception, for we attend only to what interests us or to what we hope to make use of. But it is equally true of science, for science, as has been said, is merely the systematization of perceptually experienced relationships. Hence the sciences are all equally rooted in, and geared to, the demands of the will.

It must be remembered that (according to Schopenhauer) will, though it may be conscious at the human level of manifestation, is essentially blind, and its struggles are pointless. Since it is not going anywhere in particular, it never gets anywhere. It merely desires, without knowing what it wants or why. Hence its satisfactions are ephemeral. A reflection of this general frustration appears in our fluctuation between unsatisfied craving and ennui. Until we attain what we want, we are unhappy; as soon as we possess it, we are bored. Our restless will has passed on to some other desire. Like Faust, we are always seeking, and never finding, the moment to which we can say, "Stay, thou art so fair!"

Obviously, the best thing that could happen to us would be somehow to break free from this fruitless, meaningless servitude to the will, so that we no longer desire at all. As Byron wrote,

> My blood is all meridian; were it not,
>   I had not left my clime, nor should I be,
> In spite of tortures ne'er to be forgot,
>   A slave again of love,—at least of thee.
>
> 'Tis vain to struggle—let me perish young—
>   Live as I lived, and love as I have loved;
> To dust if I return, from dust I sprung,
>   And then, at least, my heart can ne'er be moved.[1]

Doubtless the only final rest from will is in death, as Byron shortly found at Missolonghi. But meanwhile, Schopenhauer believed, a temporary surcease is possible in esthetic contemplation. The function of the esthetic object is, as we have seen, to throw us into the esthetic attitude, and what distinguishes this attitude from all others is precisely that it is *not* practical. In it we are not getting and spending and otherwise laying waste our powers. We are not identifying, classifying, organizing, pigeonholing, and systematizing for the sake of one or the other of our will's fleeting desires. On the contrary, as long as we are submerged in the object's beauty, these pressures relax their grip and we are free.

> If, raised by the power of the mind, a man relinquishes the common way of looking at things, gives up tracing . . . their relations to each other, the final goal of which is always a relation to his own will; if he thus ceases to consider the where, the when, the why, and the whither of things, and looks simply and solely at the *what;* if, further, he does not allow abstract thought, the concepts of the reason, to take possession of his consciousness, but, instead of all this, . . . lets his whole consciousness be filled with the quiet contemplation of the natural object actually present, whether a landscape, a tree, a mountain, a building, or whatever it may be; inasmuch as he *loses* himself in this object (to use a pregnant German idiom), *i.e.*, forgets even his individuality, his will, and only continues to exist as the pure subject, the clear mirror of the object, so that it is as if the object alone were there, without any one to perceive it, . . . then . . . he who is sunk in this perception is no longer

individual, for in such perception the individual has lost himself; but he is *pure,* will-less, painless, timeless *subject of knowledge.*[m]

This is virtually identical with the attitude expressed by Keats in his *Ode on a Grecian Urn:*

> Thou still unravish'd bride of quietness,
>   Thou foster-child of silence and slow time,
> Sylvan historian, who canst thus express
>   A flowery tale more sweetly than our rhyme:
> What leaf-fring'd legend haunts about thy shape
>   Of deities or mortals, or of both,
>   In Tempe or the dales of Arcady?
>   What men or gods are these? What maidens loth?
> What mad pursuit? What struggle to escape?
>   What pipes and timbrels? What wild ecstasy?
>
> Heard melodies are sweet, but those unheard
>   Are sweeter; therefore, ye soft pipes, play on;
> Not to the sensual ear, but, more endear'd,
>   Pipe to the spirit ditties of no tone:
> Fair youth, beneath the trees, thou canst not leave
>   Thy song, nor ever can those trees be bare;
>   Bold Lover, never, never canst thou kiss,
> Though winning near the goal—yet, do not grieve;
>   She cannot fade, though thou hast not thy bliss,
>   For ever wilt thou love, and she be fair! . . .
>
> O Attic shape! Fair attitude! with brede
>   Of marble men and maidens overwrought,
> With forest branches and the trodden weed;
>   Thou, silent form, dost tease us out of thought
> As doth eternity: Cold Pastoral!
>   When old age shall this generation waste,
>   Thou shalt remain, in midst of other woe
> Than ours, a friend to man, to whom thou say'st,
>   "Beauty is truth, truth beauty,"—that is all
>   Ye know on earth, and all ye need to know.

The function of art, then, is to "tease us out of thought" and to project us into a realm where pursuit is frozen and desire is stilled. Unfortunately, this relief is only temporary;[24] the pressure exerted by the will is strong, and we soon relapse into the senseless round of passion and frustration.

---

24 Schopenhauer's view excludes a good many objects commonly regarded as works of art. Paintings of the nude body and of fruits and flowers, if they arouse desire, only intensify the practical attitude. The same is true for paintings of subjects that fill us with loathing. Of course, the artist is not always responsible. Do what he may, vulgar people may misread the work of art. This is another limitation on the moral function of art: It is confined to a cultivated elite.

It might be thought that the logical solution would be suicide. But this is not true, according to Schopenhauer. To commit suicide is not to defeat the will; it is to allow the will to triumph over us. The notion that suicide is the way out of our misery is based on the illusion that this phenomenal self of ours, and its phenomenal life, is real. But life (objects in space and time and in causal relations with their environment) is merely the *appearance* of will; all the events of an individual life, including its beginning and its end, are merely incidents in this phenomenal flow. Hence, in killing ourselves we do not kill will; we merely eliminate one little segment of appearance.

> Will is the thing-in-itself, the inner content, the essence of the world. Life, the visible world, the phenomenon, is only the mirror of the will. . . . It is true we see the individual come into being and pass away; but the individual is only phenomenal. . . . Birth and death belong merely to the phenomenon of will, this to life. . . . The form of this phenomenon is time, space, and causality, and by means of these individuation, which carries with it that the individual must come into being and pass away. But this no more affects the will to live, of whose manifestation the individual is, as it were, only a particular example or specimen, than the death of an individual injures the whole of nature. . . . The man who has comprehended and retained this point of view may well console himself, when contemplating his own death and that of his friends, by turning his eyes to the immortal life of Nature, which he himself is. . . .
>
> Above all things, we must distinctly recognise that the form of the phenomenon of will, the form of life or reality, is really only the *present*, not the future nor the past. The latter are only in the conception, exist only in the connection of knowledge. . . . Our own past, the most recent part of it, and even yesterday, is now no more than an empty dream of the fancy, and such is the past of all those millions [who lived in thousands of years that are past]. What was? What is? The will, of which life is the mirror, and knowledge free from will, which beholds it clearly in that mirror. . . .
>
> Therefore, if a man fears death as his annihilation, it is just as if he were to think that the sun cries out at evening, "Woe is me! for I go down into eternal night." . . . Life is assured to the will to live; the form of life is an endless present, no matter how the individuals, the phenomena of the Idea, arise and pass away in time, like fleeting dreams. Thus even already suicide appears to us as a vain and therefore a foolish action.[n]

But the realization that life is appearance and that the multiplicity of selves, and their private interests, is illusion points the way to a solution. Knowledge that the objects of desire are illusion, that the distinctions and honors we prize, the goals we aim at, the self on which we insist, are illusions, acts as a quieter of the will, in the same way that art does, but permanently. In this kind of knowledge, indeed, "the will suppresses itself." This, and not suicide, is the real denial of the will.

Moral Theory

This marks the transition from esthetics to ethics. Schopenhauer related the various types of conduct—from the undiluted egoism of Hobbes' "war of all against all" to the sainthood of the Christian and Hindu religions—to the successive degrees of man's realization of the truth about the world. The first advance from Hobbesian egoism occurs when a man comes to see that his is not the only will in the world and that other men are, like himself, foci of desire. At this stage pure egoism is replaced by fellow-feeling and a sense of justice and equality. The just man still asserts his own will, but unlike the egoist he does not deny the rights of others to assert their wills. In other words, this is the level of the *laissez-faire* philosophy of the Enlightenment.

The next step is the realization that all these foci of desire are manifestations of one underlying will—that is, that differences between us are only phenomenal and that we are all basically one. This stage, Schopenhauer believed, was reached by the ancient Hindus. In their religion the identity of all the real was asserted. "This thou art," the Hindu was taught to say, as all the beings in the world, living and lifeless, passed successively before him. Doubtless the Hindus expressed this truth—"the fruit of the highest human knowledge and wisdom"—in a mythological language, but "never has a myth entered, and never will one enter, more closely into the philosophical truth which is attainable to so few than this primitive doctrine of the noblest and most ancient nation." How inferior, then, is the Christian religion! How ridiculous to seek to convert the Hindus! "In India our religions will never take root. The ancient wisdom of the human race will not be displaced by what happened in Galilee. On the contrary, Indian philosophy streams back to Europe, and will produce a fundamental change in our knowledge and thought."⁰

Here, where sympathy and pity replace justice, we attain to sainthood and renunciation. At this level, when a man

> . . . no longer makes the egotistical distinction between his person and that of others, but takes as much interest in the sufferings of other individuals as in his own, and therefore is not only benevolent in the highest degree, but even ready to sacrifice his own individuality whenever such a sacrifice will save a number of other persons, then it clearly follows that such a man, who recognises in all beings his own inmost and true self, must also regard the infinite suffering of all suffering beings as his own, and take on himself the pain of the whole world. . . . Knowledge of the whole, of the nature of the thing-in-itself which has been described, becomes a *quieter* of all and every volition. The will now turns away from life; it now shudders at the pleasures in which it recognises the assertion of life. Man now attains to the state of voluntary renunciation, resignation, true indifference, and perfect will-lessness. . . .
>
> The phenomenon by which this change is marked, is the transition from virtue to asceticism. . . . There arises within him a horror of the nature of

which his own phenomenal existence is an expression, the will to live, the
kernel and inner nature of that world which is recognised as full of misery.
He therefore disowns this nature which appears in him, and is already
expressed through his body, and his action gives the lie to his phenomenal
existence, and appears in open contradiction to it. . . . His body, healthy
and strong, expresses through the genitals, the sexual impulse; but he denies
the will and gives the lie to the body; he desires no sensual gratification under
any condition. Voluntary and complete chastity is the first step in asceticism
or the denial of the will to live. . . . Nature, always true and naïve, declares
that if this maxim became universal, the human race would die out; and I
think I may assume, in accordance with what was said . . . about the connection of all manifestations of will, that with its highest manifestation, the
weaker reflection of it would also pass away, as the twilight vanishes along
with the full light. With the entire abolition of knowledge, the rest of the
world would of itself vanish into nothing; for without a subject there is no
object.ᴾ

It is not easy to see the difference between individual suicide and the race
suicide that Schopenhauer recommended. Nor is there any reason to suppose
that the great universal will that Schopenhauer hypothecated, with all its grades
of manifestation, would vanish if man himself disappeared. But it serves no
purpose to press Schopenhauer's position too closely, since, in his own view, he
was communicating an insight that transcends conceptual analysis. And he was
aware, of course, that this insight has affinities not only with the Vedas but with
Christian mysticism.

What I have here described with feeble tongue and only in general terms,
is no philosophical fable, invented by myself, and only of to-day; no, it was
the enviable life of so many saints and beautiful souls among Christians, and
still more among Hindus and Buddhists, and also among the believers of other
religions. However different were the dogmas impressed on their reason, the
same inward, direct, intuitive knowledge, from which alone all virtue and
holiness proceed, expressed itself in precisely the same way in the conduct
of life. For here also the great distinction between intuitive and abstract
knowledge shows itself. . . . There is a wide gulf between the two, which
can only be crossed by the aid of philosophy, as regards the knowledge of
the nature of the world. Intuitively or *in concreto*, every man is really
conscious of all philosophical truths, but to bring them to abstract knowledge,
to reflection, is the work of philosophy, which neither ought nor is able to
do more than this.

Thus it may be that the inner nature of holiness, self-renunciation, mortifi-
cation of our own will, asceticism, is here for the first time expressed abstractly, and free from all mythical elements, as *denial of the will to live,*
appearing after the complete knowledge of its own nature has become a
quieter of all volition. On the other hand, it has been known directly and
realised in practice by saints and ascetics, who had all the same inward
knowledge, though they used very different language with regard to it,

according to the dogmas which their reason had accepted, and in consequence of which an Indian, a Christian, or a Lama saint must each give a very different account of his conduct, which is, however, of no importance as regards the fact. A saint may be full of the absurdest superstition, or, on the contrary, he may be a philosopher, it is all the same. His conduct alone certifies that he is a saint, for, in a moral regard, it proceeds from knowledge of the world and its nature, which is not abstractly but intuitively and directly apprehended, and is only expressed by him in any dogma of the satisfaction of his reason. . . . To repeat the whole nature of the world abstractly, universally, and distinctly in concepts, and thus to store up, as it were, a reflected image of it in permanent concepts always at the command of the reason; this and nothing else is philosophy.q

The Paradoxical Role of Philosophy

Thus, according to Schopenhauer, philosophy is a bridge between intuition (which is true, but unfortunately incommunicable) and abstract conceptual knowledge (which is communicable, but false). But, in his own account as well as in his own usage, philosophy is conceptual and abstract. How, then, is it distinguished from that abstract conceptual knowledge that Schopenhauer depreciated? And, if "conduct alone certifies sainthood," why go beyond the mystic's intuitive state? Salvation comes not through communicating the truth that we feel, but through living the life that this feeling causes us to live.

In any case, of course, we *cannot* communicate successfully. Hence, if we are to choose among communications, why prefer the philosophical to the mythological? There seems every reason to argue, on Schopenhauer's own premises, that the latter is less false and less inadequate than the former.

Apparently, however, Schopenhauer was correct in pointing out that the philosophical enterprise *begins* from experiences (or, in his terminology, intuitions) that seem important to the philosopher. He was also correct in noting that linguistic conventions often disguise experiential similarities and that it is the task of philosophical analysis to articulate these experiences into a system of abstract concepts. This, as a matter of fact, is just what most philosophers have attempted to do. Thus, to give but one example, Augustine sought to give a rational account of those experiences of sin, frustration, and hope that climaxed in the voice that spoke to him from the sunlight in a garden at Milan. Philosophy is necessarily rationalistic in the sense that it attempts to find some logical structure into which the experiences can be incorporated.

Here we reach the central paradox of Schopenhauer's position. His view of the nature of the real that intuition is supposed to know made a *rational* account of experience impossible. Schopenhauer, of course, happened to be interested less in giving an account of experience than in *feeling* and in getting into a right relation with the reality he felt. In this sense, he and all the other Romantics have a far stronger affinity with the mystical mind than with the strictly philosophical or theological mind. From the point of view of the historian of philosophy, however, Schopenhauer's views are important, for his dislike of system, his distrust of reason, his exaltation of feeling, and his emphasis on practice are all expressive of what proved to be one of the major themes of the nineteenth century.

Hegel and Schopenhauer

In this discussion of Hegel and Schopenhauer the differences between the two philosophers have been emphasized. That there are differences is obvious; in fact, in some respects their views are antithetical. Thus, whereas Hegel claimed that reason is a valid instrument for the cognition of reality, Schopenhauer limited reason to the phenomenal world. In other respects, however, their views are curiously parallel. For example, neither was willing to accept Kant's exclusion of the possibility of metaphysical knowledge: Both wanted to know ultimate reality. Further, Hegel and Schopenhauer were in much closer agreement about the nature of this ultimate reality than might appear at first sight. Both held that it is continuous rather than discrete, and that its nature transcends the capacity of "ordinary" logic. They differed, indeed, chiefly because Hegel believed he had discovered a new logic capable of dealing with this continuous real. It is interesting to note that before he hit upon this new logic, Hegel himself passed through a phase in which he believed thought to be basically inadequate to its object. Thus in an early note in *The Phenomenology* he remarked, "Philosophy must end in religion, because philosophy is thought, and thought always involves finitude and opposition, e.g., the oppositions of subject and object, and of the mind that thinks to matter that does not think. Its business, therefore, is to show the finitude of all that is finite, and through reason to demand its complement or completion in the infinite." [r]

Because Schopenhauer did not conceive of any logic except the "either-or" Aristotelian logic, and because he believed that it was incompetent, he wound up with intuitionism. What enabled Hegel to remain a rationalist was his belief that the principle of identity-in-difference makes possible the reconciliation of opposites in a higher synthesis.

But though Hegel remained a rationalist, his rationalism was very different from the rationalism of the Enlightenment. Hegel was far from unresponsive to the mood of the times, as expressed in the poetry of Goethe, Shelley, Wordsworth, and Byron. Like the Romantics, he had a strong sense of the unity of things. Like them, he believed that the "finite" is incomplete and partial and that it gains its significance from a "larger-than" that is experienced in, while it constantly transcends, the here and now. Thus, just as Schopenhauer held that in intuition we come to see the unity of being ("This thou art"), so Hegel held that all individual thoughts and thinkers are contained in an absolute thought. This is a radical shift from the Enlightenment's insistence on the distinctness and separateness of things. Every individual person, it held, is complete in himself and valuable in his own right; every individual science is an independent system derived from its own set of first principles. Hence, where the Enlightenment had advocated *laissez faire* in politics and economics, both Schopenhauer and Hegel regarded this as merely a rather low level in the development of moral and political ideals.

Schopenhauer, of course, made a direct attack on rationalism, but Hegel's surrender of finite reason (which was what the Enlightenment had understood by reason) in favor of an absolute reason (of which the Enlightenment did not even dream) was equally a sign of the uneasiness that marked the new century, of an awareness that all was not well in the best of all possible worlds. It is true, of course, that Hegel believed he was refurbishing the rationalistic ideal, but (as some of his followers were to point out) a transcendent thought is unknowable by finite means; an absolute reason is, from our human point of view, suprarational. Hence Hegelianism was deeply influenced by Romanticism. As much as Schopenhauer's intuitionism, it was a quest for a new kind of certainty.

CHAPTER 5

Science,
Scientism, and
Social Philosophy

The Heritage of Kant

Most of the nineteenth-century philosophers considered in this chapter began, like Hegel and Schopenhauer, from an essentially Kantian position. But because their interests and outlook were very different—not only from Kant's but also from Hegel's and from Schopenhauer's—they came up with very different conclusions. Unlike Hegel, these thinkers were for the most part either indifferent or even hostile to the idea of system. Unlike Schopenhauer, they felt no urge to penetrate to a transcendent reality beyond this world. Temperamentally they were secularists—it was in this world, not in the next, they held, that man lived and moved and had his being. Thus these philosophers fixed their attention on what Kant had called the spatiotemporal manifold; they differed from Kant, however, in rigorously limiting reality to this manifold. They emphasized the Kantian thesis that the manifold consists in events that are completely amenable to scientific treatment, but they ignored Kant's argument that this characteristic of the manifold is made possible only by means of "transcendental syntheses." Thus they can be called "phenomenalists," for they rejected the notion of noumena (things-in-themselves) and identified reality with what Kant had called phenomena.

Accordingly, these philosophers were far more antimetaphysical than Kant had been. Although Kant had denied that any knowledge of metaphysical entities is possible, he had nevertheless held that the inclination to pursue metaphysical inquiries is a "natural disposition" of great significance in human life. The secularistic bias of these post-Kantian thinkers led them to write metaphysics off as a massive delusion. They naturally included religion in this assessment— though some of them were quite prepared to use the religious aspirations of the masses as an instrument of power politics. Indeed, because they took their phenomenalism very seriously, these thinkers tended to treat all ideas—not merely religious ones—as ideology; that is, they held that the important question to ask about ideas is not whether they are true or false but how they affect conduct and policy. These philosophers also maintained that all the ideas entertained by any group of people at a given time are elements in their world view and can be predicted from other features of the group's culture. One of the consequences of this position is the general derogation of theory, for in this view theories—including philosophical speculation—become mere ideology. The obvious implications of this position for these thinkers' own theories were either ignored or dealt with only very inadequately by them.

These new trends in philosophy can be said to have followed more or less directly from these philosophers' limited but genuinely Kantian starting point. Other elements in their views, however, were quite different from Kant's. For example, all these philosophers were profoundly influenced by the great shift from an essentially static view of the universe, a view that had predominated in the eighteenth century, to a conception of the universe as evolving through time. As was pointed out in the preceding chapter, this new emphasis affected Hegel's revision of Kant's doctrine, and it was to have an increasing impact on philosophy as the century advanced. One of the consequences of this shift, it will be seen, was a new interest in history and in philosophies of history.

Another way in which this group of nineteenth-century thinkers differed from Kant was in their attitude toward ethics. Kant had valued not what men actually achieve but the motive from which they act—that is, purity of will. The philosophers who followed Kant were much more practically oriented. They recognized that Europe faced major economic and social problems as a result of the failure of institutional structures to adjust to the immense changes that were occurring in men's values and expectations and in their ways of living. Hence all these philosophers were in some measure reformers, and some of them were revolutionaries. In a word, the focus of attention was shifting from the traditional problems of epistemology and ethics to social philosophy, with much less emphasis on the formal elaboration of theory than on the application of theory to concrete problems.

Finally, all these thinkers were convinced that scientific knowledge, which they conceived of in the broadest sense as an empirical method, could be brought to bear on the solution of grave social problems. These thinkers shared Condorcet's optimistic conviction that unlimited progress is possible, for they accepted Bacon's dicta that "knowledge is power" and that this power should be used for the "improvement of man's estate." But they differed greatly from Bacon in their conception of the kind of knowledge that results in power. Here their phenomenalism, their interest in development, and their conception of ideology came together. For all these thinkers, the view that ideas are ideology suggested that men's minds as well as their bodies, their thoughts as well as their actions, could be studied scientifically; the emphasis on development suggested that the old geometric model of explanation could be replaced by a new genetic model; the interest in social problems resulted in an application of science to the study of society. Thus the sciences of sociology and, somewhat later, psychology were born. The formulation of the theory of evolution naturally greatly accelerated all these tendencies. It not only gave additional support to the genetic model of explanation; it also seemed to show that man is a part of nature and is thus subject to its laws. Indeed, the new triumphs of biology led to a rather facile belief in science and its "iron laws," and to an assumption on the part of some thinkers that science provides simple, straightforward answers to all philosophical problems. This point of view, which may be described as "scientism," became increasingly dominant in the second half of the nineteenth century.

It will be useful, before turning to study these social philosophers themselves, to consider some of the political and economic changes that formed the social context of their thought and to which their views were a response.

Revolution and Reaction

When Hegel died in the late autumn of 1831, agitation over the Reform Bill, then before the British Parliament, was at its height. In order to understand why social philosophy increasingly preoccupied men of the new century a word must be said about the developments of which the Reform Bill was a part. The Enlightenment's strong sense of humanity and of the rights of man had been a driving force in the French Revolution, which began as an attempt to put into practice the theory that there are eternal, rational principles that all men can come to know and live by. The chaos of the Revolution itself and of the Napoleonic wars that followed put the movement for reform on ice for almost a quarter of a century. And in 1815, with the restoration of peace after Waterloo, the scene was complicated by new factors that had emerged during the interim.

For one thing, the excesses of the revolutionary mob had alarmed conservatives everywhere—especially the rulers of the European states. The conservatives' notion of peace was the restoration of the *status quo,* and their immediate reaction—the lesson they had learned during the eventful quarter century preceding—was to try to bottle up the forces that had released the Revolution and that in turn had been nourished by it. The result was the formation among the victorious powers (Britain excepted) of a Holy Alliance to repress any suggestion of liberalism.

Meanwhile, pressure for reform had been mounting among the masses. Before the French Revolution, agitation for reform had come largely from above: The *philosophes* had sought not so much to rouse the downtrodden peasant as to provide for him what these enlightened gentlemen deemed to be his due. As industry developed, partly because of the stimulus of the long period of war, an increasingly articulate urban proletariat emerged. This new group knew what it wanted and became unwilling to accept the leadership of its upper-class sponsors.

The application of the new science to production—the development of technology—had begun in a small way in England early in the eighteenth century. Machines were introduced to do the work of men's hands, and steam became the major source of industrial power. The factory replaced the home as the manufacturing center. Weaving, for instance, which had been farmed out to families in their cottages, was replaced by power-driven looms in the factory. As a consequence, the population of many small towns expanded at an enormous rate. For example, between 1800 and 1831, Leeds, Sheffield, and Birmingham more than doubled in population, and Manchester and Liverpool were not far behind. Landlords naturally got fantastic rentals for jerry-built houses. Houses without water or sewage facilities and built for £65–70 rented for £12 per annum; the owner's investment was thus returned in five years. These high rentals resulted in appalling overcrowding; families often occupied a single room, and in Manchester as late as 1845 twenty-seven cases were reported of as many as seven people trying to sleep in a single bed.

Work conditions corresponded. In 1840 the workday still averaged twelve to thirteen hours, excluding time for meals; and occasional holidays had to be made up. Children entered the factories when they were nine years old and were expected to do labor of the hardest kind. Nearly as many children as adults were employed in the mines—167,000 compared with 191,000. Pay was pathetically low, and owners managed to reduce their labor costs still further by such devices as "truck" (payment in commodities) and arbitrary fines for breakage and bad work.

It is not surprising that liberal-minded people were shocked by such conditions or that the laboring class itself began to agitate for "reform." The House of Commons was regarded—and rightly—as the key to the situation. In 1830 the Commons still represented the landowners, the men who had ruled old, agrarian England. The large, new towns were almost totally without representation, and in numerous "rotten boroughs" a mere handful of electors controlled a seat. The struggle over the redistribution of seats in the Commons reflected the larger conflict between the old, dominant class and the new classes that the Industrial Revolution was producing. The passage of the Reform Bill of 1832[1] was a great victory for the middle and lower classes. Although these classes did not become permanent allies, their success in this opening battle meant that the ensuing struggle would take place within the framework of due process, rather than, as on the Continent, in a series of civil disturbances. In continental Europe, repression instead of parliamentary compromise was the order of the day, and dissent had no outlet. Eventually, as in 1848, it welled up in outbreaks of open violence that called forth even more vigorous repression. The result was alternating moods of hope and despair, of hatred and fear, and these moods were reflected in the philosophical theories of the thinkers discussed below.

The Utilitarians

Jeremy Bentham, James Mill, and his son, John Stuart Mill, were the leaders of the Utilitarians, a group of thinkers who dominated British philosophy during most of the century. They were the inheritors of Hume's empiricism and of his psychological associationism, but their interests lay primarily in social theory rather than in epistemology.

"GREATEST HAPPINESS" PRINCIPLE

It was significant of the changing temper of the times and of the influence of Hume that, whereas Locke had sought to base his social philosophy on a number of "eternal verities," the Utilitarians rested theirs on one basic principle, and they believed this principle could be proved by empirical means. Bentham's[2] version of this principle was the starting point for all subsequent Utilitarian theorizing:

> The end and aim of a legislator should be the HAPPINESS of the people. In matters of legislation, GENERAL UTILITY should be his guiding principle. The science of legislation consists, therefore, in determining what makes for the good of the particular community whose interests are at stake, while its

---

1 The Reform Bill disenfranchised fifty-six rotten boroughs. By this and other means, a total of 146 seats were provided for distribution: London got ten; Liverpool, Manchester, Birmingham, and Newcastle, two each; and a large number of other towns, one each. The franchise was made uniform, but a fairly high property qualification was retained.

2 Jeremy Bentham (1748–1832) was the son of a well-to-do attorney. He studied law but never practiced it, for he was more interested in legal theory than in a career at the bar. He wrote extensively on legal and economic subjects and devoted much time to an elaborate scheme for prison reform.

art consists in contriving some means of realization. . . . To apply [this principle] with complete efficiency, that is, to make it the very foundation of a system of reasoning, three conditions must be fulfilled.

First, we must attach to the word *Utility* a clear and precise connotation. . . .

Second, we must assert the supreme and undivided sovereignty of this principle by rigorously discarding every other. . . . No exception to its applicability can, in any circumstances, be allowed.

Thirdly, we must discover some calculus or process of "moral arithmetic" by means of which we may arrive at uniform results.

Nature has placed mankind under the governance of two sovereign masters, *Pleasure* and *Pain.* To them . . . we refer all our decisions, every resolve that we make in life. The man who affects to have withdrawn himself from their despotic sway does not know what he is talking about. To seek pleasure and to shun pain is his sole aim, even at the moment when he is denying himself the greatest enjoyment or courting penalties the most severe. . . . To these two motives the *principle of utility* subjects everything. . . .

The *Principle of Utility,* accordingly, consists in taking as our starting-point, in every process of ordered reasoning, the calculus or comparative estimate of pains and pleasures, and in not allowing any other to intervene.

I am an adherent of the *Principle of Utility* when I measure my approval or disapproval of any act, public or private, by its tendency to produce pains and pleasures. . . . And it must always be understood that I use these words *Pain* and *Pleasure* in their ordinary signification, without having recourse to arbitrary definitions for the purpose of ruling out certain forms of pleasure. . . .

An adherent to the *Principle of Utility* holds virtue to be a good thing by reason only of the pleasures which result from the practice of it: he esteems vice to be a bad thing by reason only of the pains which follow in its train. Moral good is *good* only on account of its tendency to secure physical benefits: moral evil is *evil* only on account of its tendency to induce physical mischief. . . .

The diffusion of Pleasures and the avoidance of Pains are the only ends which a legislator should have in view. It behoves him, then, to acquire a just and precise appreciation of their respective values. Seeing that Pleasures and Pains are the *instruments* he has to work with, he ought to make a very careful study of their magnitude and strength, which, indeed, from another point of view, constitute their value.

Now, if we examine the *value* of a pleasure, considered by itself and in relation to a single individual, we shall find that it depends on four circumstances: (1) *Its Intensity;* (2) *its Duration;* (3) *its Certainty;* (4) *its Proximity.*

The value of a pain depends upon like considerations.

But, in dealing with Pains and Pleasures, it is not enough to assess their value as though they were, necessarily, isolated and independent. Pains and pleasures may have as *consequences* other pains and pleasures. If, therefore, we wish to estimate the *tendency* of any act from which pain or pleasure directly results, we must take into account two other circumstances: These are (5) *its Fecundity* or *Productiveness;* (6) *its Purity. A productive pleasure* is one which is likely to be followed by other pleasures of the same kind. A *productive pain* is one which is likely to be followed by other pains of the same kind. A *pure pleasure* is one which is not likely to produce pain. A *pure pain* is one which is not likely to produce pleasure.

When the calculation is to be made in relation to a number of individuals, yet another circumstance is to be taken into account—(7) *its Extent*. That is, the number of persons who are likely to be affected by this particular pleasure or pain, as the case may be.

Suppose we wish to take exact account of the value of a certain action. We must follow, in detail, the various operations which have just been indicated. These provide the elements of a moral calculus, and Legislation may thus become a mere matter of Arithmetic. The *evil*, or *pain*, inflicted is the expenditure; the *good*, or *pleasure*, engendered is the income.[a]

MILL'S APPLICATION OF THE PRINCIPLE

John Stuart Mill's[3] *Essay on Liberty* is a typical application of the greatest happiness principle. Instead of arguing, as an eighteenth-century rationalist might have done, that liberty is a self-evident right, he tried to show that the greatest good for the greatest number is promoted by allowing citizens to criticize their government, to worship as they please, to choose their own mode of life, and to think and to act as they choose.

> The object of this Essay is to assert one very simple principle, as entitled to govern absolutely the dealing of society with the individual in the way of compulsion and control. . . . That principle is, that the sole end for which mankind are warranted, individually or collectively, in interfering with the liberty of action of any of their number, is self-protection. . . . Over himself, over his own body and mind, the individual is sovereign. . . .
>
> It is proper to state that I forego any advantage which could be derived to my argument from the idea of abstract right, as a thing independent of utility. I regard utility as the ultimate appeal on all ethical questions; but it must be utility in the largest sense, grounded on the permanent interests of a man as a progressive being. . . . In all things which regard the external relations of the individual, he is *de jure* amenable to those whose interests are concerned, and, if need be, to society as their protector. . . .
>
> But there is a sphere of action in which society, as distinguished from the individual, has, if any, only an indirect interest; comprehending all that portion of a person's life and conduct which affects only himself. . . . This, then, is the appropriate region of human liberty. It comprises, first, the inward

3 J. S. Mill (1806–73) was educated on a plan worked out by his father and by Bentham. By the age of three he had begun learning Greek; by the time he was eight he had read Xenophon, Herodotus, and Plato. In 1822 he entered India House as a junior clerk and rose rapidly to head of the office, a position equivalent to that of a modern permanent undersecretary of a leading ministry. He wrote voluminously on logic, economics, parliamentary reform, and women's rights (he was one of the founders of the first women's suffrage society) and served briefly as a member of Parliament.

domain of consciousness; . . . liberty of thought and feeling; absolute freedom
of opinion and sentiment on all subjects; . . . liberty of tastes and pursuits;
of framing the plan of our life to suit our own character; of doing what we
like . . . without impediment from our fellow-creatures, so long as what we
do does not harm them, even though they should think our conduct foolish,
perverse, or wrong. . . .[b]

The difference between basing a defense of liberty on an abstract consideration of right (or on a Kantian categorical imperative) and basing it on a utilitarian
calculation of consequences comes out very clearly in Mill's argument in favor
of liberty of thought. Opponents of liberty will argue, Mill says, that they are
at least justified in repressing false opinions. Mill replies:

We can never be sure that the opinion we are endeavouring to stifle is
a false opinion; and if we were sure, stifling it would be an evil still.
First: the opinion which it is attempted to suppress by authority may
possibly be true. Those who desire to suppress it, of course deny its truth;
but they are not infallible. . . . To refuse a hearing to an opinion, because
they are sure that it is false, is to assume that *their* certainty is the same
as *absolute* certainty. . . . Ages are no more infallible than individuals; every
age having held many opinions which subsequent ages have deemed not only
false but absurd; and it is as certain that many opinions now general will
be rejected by future ages, as it is that many, once general, are rejected by
the present.
There is the greatest difference between presuming an opinion to be true,
because, with every opportunity for contesting it, it has not been refuted,
and assuming its truth for the purpose of not permitting its refutation.
Complete liberty of contradicting and disproving our opinion is the very
condition which justifies us in assuming its truth for purposes of action; and
on no other terms can a being with human faculties have any rational
assurance of being right.
Let us now pass to the second division of the argument, and dismissing
the supposition that any of the received opinions may be false, let us assume
them to be true, and examine into the worth of the manner in which
they are likely to be held, when their truth is not freely and openly can-
vassed. . . .
Both teachers and learners go to sleep at their post, as soon as there is
no enemy in the field. . . . There are many truths of which the full meaning
cannot be realised until personal experience has brought it home. But much
more of the meaning even of these would have been understood, and what
was understood would have been far more deeply impressed on the mind,
if the man had been accustomed to hear it argued *pro* and *con* by people
who did understand it. The fatal tendency of mankind to leave off thinking
about a thing when it is no longer doubtful, is the cause of half their errors.[c]

Mill realized that it was not enough to protect freedom of thought from
arbitrary and tyrannical governments. Even in parliamentary democracies liberty

is always in danger, both because of the tendency of the majority to pass laws that infringe the rights of minorities and also, indirectly but no less harmfully, because of the pressure of public opinion toward conformity. The truth is that though Mill certainly prized liberty, he prized "individuality" and "spiritual development" even more. In fact, liberty was valuable to Mill chiefly because he believed it to be the only social mode in which these ends could be realized: "Individuality is the same thing with development, and it is only the cultivation of individuality which produces, or can produce, well-developed human beings." [d]

It follows that Mill had no sympathy for the Hegelian notion of the state as the "true" individual, of which all the finite citizens are but organs. From Mill's point of view, to talk in this way is to put metaphysical jargon to work in the service of tyranny. Mill's assumption of the basic autonomy of the finite individual can be seen in the very way in which he poses the question, "What are the *limits* of justifiable restriction?"

But those who share Mill's antipathy to the Hegelian ideal of transcending finite individuality in that larger self, the state, must admit that the finite individual is not so completely self-subsistent as Mill held him to be. Consider Mill's contention that restraint is warranted only in the case of "actions where the interest of others is menaced." Given the interlocking and organic nature of society, is there any action that does not have an impact, large or small, on *some* circle of others?

Mill's discussion of "applications" of the utility principle to concrete policy issues reveals serious difficulties of this kind. For instance, to the question of whether the sale of poisons ought to be limited, Mill replies:

> It is one of the undisputed functions of government to take precautions against crime before it has been committed, as well as to detect and punish it afterwards. The preventive function of government, however, is far more liable to be abused, to the prejudice of liberty, than the punitory function. . . . If poisons were never bought or used for any purpose except the commission of murder it would be right to prohibit their manufacture and sale. They may, however, be wanted not only for innocent but for useful purposes, and restrictions cannot be imposed in the one case without operating in the other. . . . Such a precaution, for example, as that of labelling the drug with some word expressive of its dangerous character, may be enforced without violation of liberty: the buyer cannot wish not to know that the thing he possesses has poisonous qualities.[e]

Similar considerations led Mill to maintain that "fornication, for example, must be tolerated, and so must gambling; but should a person be free to be a pimp, or to keep a gambling house? . . . There are arguments on both sides."[f] The trouble is that there are *always* arguments on both sides. Would Mill have wanted to treat cigarettes as poisons, on the ground that inhalation of cigarette smoke is presumably conducive to lung cancer? What about smog? A strict application of the utility principle is likely to lead to more restrictions on liberty, not fewer. Alternatively, had Mill continued to insist on the maximum possible liberty, he would have found himself in the awkward position of advocating policies that, far from maximizing happiness and well-being, actually produce more social harm than good. In the conditions of modern life, an argument like Mill's, which begins by emphasizing the right of every individual to fashion his own destiny unrestrained by police or public opinion, is likely to end by defending the oppression of the individual by other (for example, economic) forces. Thus, in the course of the century since Mill wrote, *laissez-faire* individualism has become a conservative rather than a radical doctrine.

CRITICISM OF THE "GREATEST HAPPINESS" PRINCIPLE

Mill's *Essay on Liberty* illustrates the way in which the Utilitarians applied the greatest happiness principle to the solution of social problems. It can hardly be denied that this principle is more practicable than either the Enlightenment's belief in intuition of self-evident truths or Hegel's elaborate dialectic. Taken simply as a rule-of-thumb reminder that the social order exists for everyone and that what is relevant in the consideration of social change is the well-being of individual citizens rather than logical symmetry, the principle is very valuable. But its advocates demanded a great deal more of it; indeed, they regarded it as that final authority for which, as has been seen, the whole century was searching. That the principle was unfit for such an exalted role will be clear from a study of Bentham's formulation of it.

Bentham accepted Locke's view that everyone aims at his own pleasure and that the essence of social control consists in making certain that socially desirable acts are sufficiently "weighted" with pleasurable consequences to induce men to do them. But whereas Locke believed that the ultimate weighting of social acts is done by God (in the form of promises of heavenly bliss and threats of hellish tortures), Bentham assigned this function to a human legislator. This raised problems that Locke's theory did not have to face. For example, there is no reason to suppose that the legislator is exempt from the universal egoism that (in Bentham's view) causes everyone to seek his own private pleasure. Bentham never asked himself how it comes about that the legislator desires to promote the common good by a suitable arrangement of sanctions.

But, even if Bentham be allowed an altruistic legislator, his theory is still involved in serious difficulties, for the principle by which the legislator is supposed to operate is far from having the "clear and precise connotation" that Bentham attributed to it. To begin with, quantum of good and range of distribution are quite distinct variables in the Utilitarian equation. As between act A and act B, two possible acts open to us in a given case, A may produce the greatest quantum of good, but with a very narrow distribution; B may produce a lesser quantum, but with a much wider distribution. As Utilitarians, which should we choose? The greatest happiness principle does not tell us. "Greatest good" is thus an ambiguous term in its formula. It may mean either (1) largest quantum or (2) widest distribution.

Furthermore, the principle focuses on results, that is, on a future state of affairs. But the future is (1) uncertain (and the more remote, the more uncertain) and (2) indefinitely extensive. We cannot calculate the good and bad consequences of A and B for the *whole* future; if we were to try, we would never act. And there comes a point at which probabilities fade off into guesses. Where do we draw the line? The principle does not tell us. Nor could Bentham have replied that we should stop at the point at which consideration becomes "useless." Unless the greatest happiness principle is redefined, an appeal to it here is circular.

Finally, it seems clear that pleasures cannot be measured with accuracy and hence are not comparable. It is doubtless possible to say that the pleasure of contemplating one's favorite heroine on the movie screen is more intense than the pleasure of reading this account of Utilitarianism, but one cannot say that the former pleasure is twice (or ten times, or a hundred times) more pleasurable. Yet, if Bentham's greatest happiness principle is really to work (if intensity is to be weighed against, say, duration, purity, and extent), intensity must be capable of exact measurement.

The fact is, as Hume had pointed out, that pleasures differ qualitatively rather than quantitatively. Psychologically speaking, it is an oversimplification to talk about pleasure as if it were a qualitatively constant feeling that attaches itself in varying amounts to different activities. For surely the pleasure of eating lobster and the pleasure of eating oysters are not so much quantitatively different as qualitatively different. Hence measurement of the quantity of pleasures is not merely difficult; it is impossible.

UTILITARIAN MORAL THEORY

These criticisms have been confined to pointing out that the Utilitarians were mistaken in supposing that their principle provides a completely satisfactory decision-making instrument. But those who attribute an intrinsic value to motives will find still another deficiency in Utilitarianism: The theory can assign to motives no more than an extrinsic value. Many people, for instance, hold that although it is good to contribute to charities like the Community Chest, it is morally worthless or even contemptible to do so from a motive like publicity-seeking. It is only morally valuable to contribute from a motive like benevolence. Utilitarianism cannot account for this kind of distinction. The only possible utilitarian ground for valuing the benevolence motive above the publicity motive would be the propensity of the former to be more productive of charitable giving than the latter. That benevolence actually has this propensity is debatable; but even if it did, this fact does not seem to be the basis for our preference for it.

Another weakness of Bentham's version of Utilitarianism is its narrow conception of good. Here the question is not whether men always *do* aim at their own pleasure, but whether, if they did always aim at it, they would be leading as fully moral a life as possible. Mill saw the limitations of Bentham's position, and in his essay *Utilitarianism* he tried to correct it. The good, Mill held, cannot be defined simply as a quantity of pleasure, for some pleasures are superior to others. The morally sensitive Utilitarian must therefore aim at producing the greatest possible number of superior pleasures in as wide a distribution as possible. If men were given the choice between being a pig and being Socrates, who, Mill asked, would choose the former? No one, he thought. But since the pig wallowing innocently in his sty obviously has a greater quantum of pleasure than did Socrates brooding in an Athenian jail, the strict Benthamite would have to prefer piggery to philosophy. The fact that he would choose philosophy proves (Mill argued) that utility must take account of the fact that some pleasures (in this case, the pleasure of knowledge) are qualitatively preferable to others (the pleasure of a full stomach).

Mill, it will be seen, did not doubt that "pleasure" is quantifiable. He merely held that pleasures vary not only quantitatively (pleasure A is more intense or more durable than pleasure B) but morally (pleasure A is "higher" than pleasure B). But in thus improving on Bentham's position ethically, Mill introduced a second factor, moral superiority, without giving any criterion for comparison. Suppose pleasure A is more intense than pleasure B, but that B is "higher" than A. How are we to choose between them?

Here again Utilitarianism has run into a problem of incommensurate values. In his essay *On Liberty* Mill failed to face up to this difficulty because he mistakenly believed that maximization of utility leads to the same policy decisions as those reached by consideration of the value of freedom. But, as has been pointed out, liberty and utility are unfortunately often in conflict. It would appear, then, that self-consciousness and the "higher" kinds of knowledge, like liberty, may be incommensurate with the maximization of pleasure.

Let us examine Mill's proof that pleasure (as he understood it, and including the qualitative distinctions just noted) is the supreme end for man.

> Questions about ends are . . . questions what things are desirable. The utilitarian doctrine is, that happiness is desirable, and the only thing desirable, as an end; all other things being only desirable as means to that end. What ought to be required of this doctrine—what conditions is it requisite that the doctrine should fulfil—to make good its claim to be believed?
>
> The only proof capable of being given that an object is visible, is that people actually see it. The only proof that a sound is audible, is that people hear it: and so of the other sources of our experience. In like manner, I apprehend, the sole evidence it is possible to produce that anything is desirable, is that people do actually desire it. . . . This being a fact, we have not only all the proof which the case admits of, but all which it is possible to require, that happiness is a good: that each person's happiness is a good to that person, and the general happiness, therefore, a good to the aggregate of all persons.[g]

Even if we agree that pleasure is the only thing men do desire, does it follow that pleasure is the only thing men ought to desire? Surely not. Mill's confusion here results from his mistaken belief that "visible" and "desirable" are analogous concepts. Since "visible" means "capable of being seen," the fact that people actually see an object is certain proof that it is visible. But "desirable" does not mean "capable of being desired"; it means "worth desiring." And the fact that I desire something no more implies that it is worth desiring than does the fact that I see something prove that it is worth seeing. Doubtless Mill would never have fallen into this confusion of facts (what I do desire) with values (what I ought to desire) if he had not been dominated by the utilitarian ambition to fashion a "scientific" theory of value.

SUMMARY

Utilitarianism (especially in the form of Bentham's moral calculus) is in fact a good example of the deleterious effect that results from treating the natural sciences as the ideal of knowledge per se, and from trying to impose on value-judgments the same criteria that hold in science. The calculus appealed to the Utilitarians, not only because it was useful, but because it seemed to make a science of morality. It claimed, that is, to yield precise, measurable, and objectively valid results. But it is only a pseudoscience, for (as is clearly shown by Mill's correction of Bentham's position) nuances of judgments about taste and morals escape between its quantified categories.

But if, instead of examining Utilitarianism at the theoretical level, we consider it at the level of practice—that is, if we consider the impact it had on social legislation—its influence was great and, on the whole, benign. The Utilitarians were, indeed, not so much theorists as reformers; their theories were designed to be judged by their efficacy as instruments of reform as well as by criteria of logical consistency. In their pragmatism and empiricism, the Utilitarians were spokesmen for the coming age, and they were far in advance of, say, Hegel, who was almost an exact contemporary of Bentham. Yet in one respect Hegel was in advance of Bentham. For in his conception of dialectic Hegel caught a glimpse of the idea of process, one of the leading motifs of nineteenth-century thought. Bentham, in contrast, had virtually no sense of history—no sense, that is, of the slow growth and unfolding of institutions in the course of which they carry their past into their present.

When Bentham looked at existing institutions, he was filled with disgust. In his view, the common law was a hopeless hodgepodge, a confused jungle of precedents dating back to remote antiquity. Let us then do away with all this rubbish, he argued, and provide judges with a single, complete, simple, and above all convenient code of laws. And let us do the same for every other department of life. Everything must be reorganized and put on a rational basis. This rather naïve belief in the possibility of a neat package, this notion that the universe is basically simple and that the mind can fathom its simplicities and use the knowledge of them as a model for conduct, shows how close the Benthamites were to the Age of Reason. It is this duality of view—this Janus-like posture in which they faced both toward the past and toward the future—that makes the Utilitarians so interesting to historians of culture.

Comte

Like the Utilitarians, Comte[4] saw that the development of science had given man great powers to improve his lot and to create a satisfactory environment for himself. He also saw, as they did, that science had created vast social problems that had not existed in earlier and simpler times. Like the Utilitarians, he noted the disparity between the high level of knowledge of physical nature and the almost total lack of application of the new methods to the study of man. Like the Utilitarians, he thought the solution was to create a science of man and to utilize it to solve all the menacing social problems that had followed in the wake of the Industrial Revolution. To develop and to apply such a science seemed to Comte a relatively easy task; he would have been amazed had he known that men are still calling upon science to solve the problems that science helped to create.

THE ADMINISTRATIVE POINT OF VIEW

One reason why Comte was optimistic about the development of a scientific sociology was that, like the Utilitarians, he shared the Enlightenment's sense of human rationality and of the orderliness of the universe. But he had lost the Enlightenment's conviction that all (or, at least, most) men are rational and capable of acting on the basis of a long-range, intelligent analysis. He thought that in most men emotion is dominant and that only a few men—an elite—are capable of sitting down in a cool hour and using scientific method to ascertain *the* answers. Hence his is the administrative point of view *par excellence:* Although the social world looks like a mighty maze to the layman, to the administrator it falls into a relatively simple pattern. The whole problem, therefore, is to enable the administrator to put his scientific knowledge to work in improving the condition of society.

But how is the administrator to induce citizens to adopt his programs? Given the inferior intellects of the majority of citizens, Comte did not think it practicable to rely on each individual's recognition that conformity is, in the long run, most likely to promote his own self-interest. Rather, Comte advocated a

4 Auguste Comte (1798–1857) was the son of a French tax collector. He suffered most of his life from poverty and ill health, to which was added an unhappy marriage. For the last nine years of his life, however, Comte was supported by a subsidy raised by public subscription.

highly organized and tightly controlled society of the kind that "economic planning" has made familiar in our time; within this framework, conformity would be assured by appeals to emotion and sentiment. Though this is a thorough rejection of *laissez faire*, there is less difference between Comte's position and that of the Benthamites than might be supposed. Bentham could believe in more *laissez* and less *faire* because, men being simple pleasure-machines, the administrator's job becomes simply one of adding and subtracting suitable units of pleasure. Comte had to argue for less *laissez* and more *faire* because he rejected this simple conception of motivation. Hence, instead of depending on citizens to make the pleasure-pain calculus that Bentham believed them capable of, Comte invented an elaborate religion, with a new calendar of saints, new festivals, and a new cult, designed to move men to adopt the socially acceptable conduct that the administrators wished them to follow.[5]

Thus Comte belongs to the Platonic tradition, both in the sense that he held there is a definite set of answers and in the sense that he believed only relatively few people capable of discerning and acting on them. But whereas Plato believed that these answers are eternal forms cognized by pure acts of reason, Comte held them to be empirical connections ascertainable by methods similar to those used in the natural sciences.

PRIMACY OF CONCEPT OF PROCESS

Another important element in Comte's philosophy is his emphasis on process. During the whole of the period from Hobbes and Descartes through Kant, philosophers had thought of cognition as the analysis of a static reality. This was true because all these thinkers—even the empiricists and the nominalists— were dominated by a belief in the geometric ideal and by the conviction that there is an eternal order of eternal truths.

In Hegel, however, the new point of view had begun to emerge. Hegel's whole dialectical method resulted from a belief that reality is dynamic, not static, and that it therefore requires an analysis different from anything that earlier thinkers had believed appropriate. But Hegel had also held that the real is rational. Comte abandoned this rationalistic dictum and concentrated his attention on the actual, dynamic social process, which he tried to make sense of by showing that it conforms to "law." This law was derived not from reflection

---

5 This calendar was divided into thirteen months, each named for a great man—for example, Homer, Aristotle, Charlemagne, Gutenberg, and Shakespeare. To every day in the year a "saint" was assigned. The saints were arranged systematically under their appropriate months—Fielding, Voltaire, Goethe, Molière, and Lope de Vega, for instance, were all assigned days in the month of Shakespeare. Comte also set out in detail the forms of worship, the symbols ("a woman of the age of thirty with her son in her arms"), and the banners (green and white) to be carried in processions. The intention was to rouse men's feelings for "humanity"—to make them aware of their unity and thus to counteract the selfish motives that normally lead to divisive action and conflicts of all kinds. Comte described all this in exhaustive detail in *The Catechism of the Positive Religion*.

on the nature of what a rational-real must be, but from a supposedly "scientific" and empirical study of the historical process itself. In other words, Comte attempted to apply to the study of man the empirical methods of the natural sciences.

THE LAW OF THREE STAGES

Comte's major generalization about human history was formulated in what he called the "law of three stages." According to this law, every branch of knowledge evolves through three distinct phases. In the first stage, or *theological* phase, causal explanation is based on the idea of volition. This level was reached in physics when, for instance, thunder and lightning were attributed to Zeus's desire to frighten lesser gods and men. The second stage, or *metaphysical* phase, marks a distinct advance. Crude anthropomorphism is replaced by causal explanation based on abstract concepts. This was the level reached in physics when causes were "taken to be abstract forces, veritable entities (that is, personified abstractions) inherent in all beings"—when, that is, men believed that entelechies and vital forces caused stones to seek the center of the earth and acorns to grow up into oaks. The third and final stage, or *scientific* phase, is reached when the attempt to explain is abandoned for the attempt to describe. This stage was reached in physics when Galileo said it was his "purpose merely to investigate . . . some of the properties of accelerated motion, whatever the cause of this acceleration may be."

Note that Comte has radically transformed Kant's account of metaphysics. He agreed with Kant, of course, that metaphysical knowledge is impossible; he also agreed that metaphysics is a "natural disposition." But he denied that this disposition has the intrinsic value that Kant attributed to it. Metaphysical thinking, according to Comte, occurs only at an immature stage in the development of the human mind, and it is destined to die out. The fact that Comte treated metaphysics entirely in an historical context and refused to evaluate it except as relative to that context is typical of the new emphasis on historicity, relativism, and development. Note also that Comte's third stage reflects the phenomenalistic outlook that was coming to the fore. At the third stage men finally understand the world as it really is. That is, according to Comte, reality is identical with Kant's spatiotemporal manifold. Explanation is impossible, because there is nothing to explain; there are only temporal relations of coexistence and succession. The sole business of science is to formulate generalizations regarding the relations actually observed to exist among events.

Is the law of three stages really a law? It is certainly not itself an instance of third-phase thinking (as Comte supposed it to be). That the physical sciences have passed, roughly speaking, through a developmental sequence of the kind Comte described seems to be the case. But this is very scanty evidence on which to formulate a universal historical law. It is, rather, as if Newton had concluded from a few observations of apples in his orchard that gravity is a universal law.

Here it can be seen, even more plainly than with the Utilitarians, that the attempt to take over the criteria and techniques of the physical sciences is likely to result, at the level of social study, in pseudoscience.

It should also be noted that Comte confusedly identified facts and values. Because he held that the scientific level of explanation is the latest reached (a statement of fact), he assumed that it is the best (a statement of value). The assumption, commonly made by thinkers who emphasize process and development, that "later equals better" corresponds to the old rationalistic assumption that "more real equals better."

It was easy for Comte to make this assumption, since, like the Utilitarians, he was interested less in theory—whether theory of knowledge or theory of value—than in practice. Using natural science as his model, he proposed to advance the study of society to the scientific level of thought, which natural science had already reached. In its theological stage, sociology had explained social events by reference to the will of God, and it had justified political authority by divine-right doctrines. In its metaphysical stage (in which, Comte believed, it had bogged down), it explained social events in terms of fictitious abstractions like "state of nature" and "social contract." But positivism, as Comte called his view,[6] would be a real science of society—a social physics, as it were. This scientific sociology would be divided into two main branches: social statics, concerned with describing the laws of order, and social dynamics, concerned with describing the laws of progress.

Comte believed that men had only to look around them to see the need of developing this new social physics, the instrument by which administrators and bureaucrats would bring order out of chaos. To Comte, the chaos—moral, social, political, and intellectual—of the nineteenth century had resulted from the fact that, although the ideas that formerly ordered society had been destroyed, social physics was not yet sufficiently developed to supply new ideas. The old military-feudal social organization, which was simply a reflection of the theological level of thinking, had been outmoded since the sixteenth century. Science had destroyed the theological spirit, while industry had destroyed the feudal-military spirit. To Comte, the view that survived was hopelessly retrograde—holders of this view wished to revert to a type of social organization that was wholly incompatible with the industrialized and urbanized society they also wished to retain. Here, of course, Comte was referring to the type of reactionary politics that had animated the Holy Alliance and that was still stubbornly opposing change both at home and abroad.

ATTACK ON LIBERALISM AND DEMOCRACY

But Comte had equally little use for the liberal opinion that was also at large in the world, busily urging reform. For Comte, liberalism was merely a reflection

---

6 This should not be confused with Logical Positivism, a movement that developed about one hundred years later, partly in an attempt to carry out Russell's program of philosophical reform. See pp. 205 and 348.

of the second, or metaphysical, level of thought, and its insistence on democracy, liberty, equality, and fraternity made it very dangerous. It was true, he thought, that this "metaphysical polity" had been useful in demolishing the old feudal-military polity and in exploding the myth of divine right by insisting on the "rights of man." But it was totally incapable of formulating any positive conceptions to take the place of those it had destroyed. Every so-called liberal principle was in fact only a "dogma" created by trying to erect a particular criticism of the theological level of thought into a positive doctrine. An example is the "dogma of the sovereignty of the people." Because it "condemns all subordination of inferiors to superiors," it results in anarchy if retained as a positive doctrine. Another example is the "dogma of liberty of conscience." This is

> . . . the mere abstract expression (such as is common in metaphysics) of the temporary state of unbounded liberty in which the human mind was left by the decay of the theological philosophy, and which must last till the social advent of the positive philosophy. . . .
>
> Indispensable and salutary as it has been, this dogma . . . constitutes an obstacle to reorganization. . . . We ignore the deepest necessities of human reason when we would protract that scepticism which is produced by the passage from one mode of belief to another, and which is, in our need of fixed points of conviction, a kind of morbid perturbation which cannot be prolonged beyond the corresponding crisis without serious danger. To be always examining and never deciding would be regarded as something like madness in private conduct. . . . There are very few persons who consider themselves fit to sit in judgment on the astronomical, physical, and chemical ideas which are destined to enter into social circulation; and everybody is willing that those ideas should direct corresponding operations. . . . Can it be supposed that the most important and the most delicate conceptions, and those which by their complexity are accessible to only a small number of highly-prepared understandings, are to be abandoned to the arbitrary and variable decisions of the least competent minds? [h]

It was therefore natural that Comte would be critical of British (and American) parliamentary democracy. The features that some people regard as the strengths of this type of organization—its endless debate and compromise, its dislike of having to make a clean-cut decision, its preference for dealing with specific grievances instead of committing itself to grand principles or large programs—all these infuriated Comte's administrative mind. How much one sympathizes with his criticisms will depend, not so much on whether one thinks that Comte himself supplied "the" answers, as on what one holds to be the chance of developing a true science of society. Obviously, as the conditions of modern life have grown more complex, the need for expert knowledge has increased. The incompetence of ordinary citizens and of their ordinary, elected representatives to resolve the complicated economic and social problems that face modern societies is too notorious to require illustration. On the other hand, it is notoriously dangerous to turn political power over to experts. In the first place, a pseudo-science that is held to be infallible (and that thus becomes doctrinaire) could be disastrous, even though its proponents had the best intentions in the world. In the second place, even granting that a true social science is possible, one must ask whether the superior knowledge of the social scientist is accompanied by a higher order of morality that makes it safe to trust him with the power that knowledge brings. There is little in the history of the century that has elapsed since Comte's death to give us much confidence on either of these scores; there is much to make us realize that the dual problem of acquiring expert knowledge and applying it effectively is one of the critical questions for modern man.

Marx

In many respects Marx's[7] philosophical position is similar to those of the other thinkers whose views are examined in this chapter. Like them, he was deeply concerned about social problems and believed that "science" could guide the continued progress of man by supplying the correct answers to all social questions. Like them, too, he had a phenomenalistic outlook. For Marx, reality was coextensive with Kant's spatiotemporal manifold: There is no transcendent realm beyond the world encountered in experience. Theology and metaphysics, which claim to provide information about such a transcendent world, are only ideologies, by-products of social forces and thus without cognitive reference. In these respects Marx belongs, like the Benthamites and the positivists, to that empirical and scientific tradition that combined Condorcet's optimistic belief in the inevitability of "progress" with the belief that human nature as well as the physical universe conforms to simple "laws" that can be discovered by science.

On the other hand, Marx was much more deeply influenced by Hegel than was any of these other thinkers. Like Hegel, he was a systematizer in the grand manner, and he too held that the key to system is dialectic. And, like Hegel, Marx was responsive to the notion of development, a notion that was becoming a major element in the nineteenth-century climate of opinion, with a concomitant focusing of attention on the philosophy of history. Finally, for Marx as well as for Hegel, "alienation" was a central concept.

ALIENATION

The notion of alienation appears in Hegel's thought as the negative phase of the dialectic—the phase of "otherness," of opposition, of conflict, of media-

7 Karl Marx (1818–83) was born in Trier, in the Rhineland, of well-to-do Jewish parents who became Christians when Marx was a child. He was a student at the University of Berlin shortly after Hegel's death, while the latter's influence was still strong. Marx's radical opinions made an academic career impossible; he was tried for treason for his part in the abortive German revolution of 1848–49, and, though acquitted, he was exiled. He spent the remainder of his life in England, where he supported himself by acting as a correspondent for various newspapers, among them, the New York *Tribune*.

tion. By uncovering a discrepancy, it is the driving force for progress and advance to a higher level—it is the Nothing that negates Being at the very start of the Hegelian system. At a later level it is Civil Society, which replaces the "immediacy" of the Family. More generally, and in terms of the admission-procedures analogy discussed earlier,[8] it is the phase of reliance on "objective" tests and formal procedures, which results from having come to distrust the policy of accepting students on the basis of the immediate impression they make in a face-to-face interview. Hegel not only thought of this phase of alienation, of criticism and negativity, as the impetus to advance; he also believed that alienation is finally overcome in a synthesis that includes it while transcending it. For instance, Civil Society is transcended in the State (a political organization modeled on the Prussian monarchy of Hegel's day), which supposedly incorporates the best features both of the Family and of Civil Society. This generally optimistic attitude places Hegel, however much he differed from the Enlightenment thinkers in other respects, in the mainstream of eighteenth-century rationalism.

The Enlightenment philosophers had simply not experienced alienation as a problem, for they had found the world they lived in to be basically congenial. Increasingly, however, in the course of the nineteenth century alienation came to be regarded as an inevitable part of the human condition. It is not surprising that, as the nineteenth century advanced, man came to feel more and more alone and a stranger in the world. Urbanization, with the anonymity it entails; the rootlessness of modern life; mass production, with its separation of the producer from the product and from any sense of fulfillment he might experience; and above all, perhaps, an increasingly secularistic attitude that seemed to leave no place for God or for gods—all these factors contributed to man's feeling of alienation.

The Romantic poets, who wanted to be at one with nature, often felt estranged from it: It seemed to them that the universe had been depersonalized, deanimated, and demythologized by a mechanistic science. This mood was expressed by Keats:

> There was an awful rainbow once in heaven:
> We know her woof, her texture; she is given
> In the dull catalogue of common things.
> Philosophy will clip an Angel's wings,
> Conquer all mysteries by rule and line,
> Empty the haunted air, and gnomed mine—
> Unweave a rainbow. . . .[i]

This sense that man is alone in an indifferent or even hostile universe, this sense of being estranged not only from nature but from other men and even from oneself, deepened as the century advanced. Dostoevsky's underground man is

8 See p. 129.

a powerful example of this sense of alienation. The thinkers discussed in the next chapter typify the way in which this mood profoundly altered the tonality of philosophical theory. For Kierkegaard and later nineteenth-century thinkers, alienation was an inevitable feature of the human condition, from which man is redeemed, if at all, only by grace.

Hegel and Marx, however, were transitional figures in this respect: Although they experienced alienation as a serious problem, they held it to be only a phase in the unfolding of human history; it could and would be overcome. Though both interpreted alienation in historical terms, Hegel thought of it primarily cognitively—as a stage in the development of the spirit toward increasingly full and articulated self-consciousness. Marx interpreted it in socioeconomic and psychological terms. The alienation that concerned him was the estrangement of the worker in an industrial and capitalistic society, an estrangement both from himself and from his fellow men:

> From political economy itself we have shown that the worker sinks to the level of a commodity, and to a most miserable commodity; that the misery of the worker increases with the power and volume of his production; that the necessary result of competition is the accumulation of capital in a few hands, and thus a restoration of monopoly in a more terrible form; and finally that the distinction between capitalist and landlord, and between agricultural labourer and industrial worker, must disappear, and the whole of society divide into the two classes of property owners and *propertyless* workers.
>
> Thus we have now to grasp the real connexion between this whole system of alienation—private property, acquisitiveness, the separation of labour, capital and land, exchange and competition, value and the devaluation of man, monopoly and competition—and the system of *money*.
>
> We shall begin from a *contemporary* economic fact. The worker becomes poorer the more wealth he produces and the more his production increases in power and extent. The worker becomes an ever cheaper commodity the more goods he creates. The *devaluation* of the human world increases in direct relation with the *increase in value* of the world of things. Labour does not only create goods; it also produces itself and the worker as a *commodity*, and indeed in the same proportion as it produces goods.
>
> This fact simply implies that the object produced by labour, its product, now stands opposed to it as an *alien being*, as a *power independent* of the producer. The product of labour is labour which has been embodied in an object and turned into a physical thing; this product is an objectification of labour. . . . The performance of work [is] a *vitiation* of the worker, objectification [is] a loss and *servitude to the object*, and appropriation [is] *alienation*.
>
> So much does the performance of work appear as vitiation that the worker is vitiated to the point of starvation. So much does objectification appear as loss of the object that the worker is deprived of the most essential things not only of life but also of work. . . . So much does the appropriation of the object appear as alienation that the more objects the worker produces the fewer he can possess and the more he falls under the domination of his product, of capital.

All of these consequences follow from the fact that the worker is related to the *product of his labour* as to an *alien* object. . . . The more the worker expends himself in work the more powerful becomes the world of objects which he creates in face of himself, the poorer he becomes in his inner life, and the less he belongs to himself. . . . The worker puts his life into the object, and his life then belongs no longer to himself but to the object. The greater his activity, therefore, the less he possesses. What is embodied in the product of his labour is no longer his own. The greater this product is, therefore, the more he is diminished. The *alienation* of the worker in his product means not only that his labour becomes an object, assumes an *external* existence, but that it exists independently, *outside himself*, and alien to him, and that it stands opposed to him as an autonomous power. The life which he has given to the object sets itself against him as an alien and hostile force.

What constitutes the alienation of labour? First, that the work is *external* to the worker, that it is not part of his nature; and that, consequently, he does not fulfil himself in his work, but denies himself, has a feeling of misery rather than well-being, does not develop freely his mental and physical energies but is physically exhausted and mentally debased. . . . Finally, the external character of work for the worker is shown by the fact that it is not his own work but work for someone else, that in work he does not belong to himself but to another person.[j]

SURPLUS VALUE AND THE EXPLOITATION OF THE WORKERS

The clue to understanding the causes of alienation was the discovery of *surplus value*. Locke had worked out a defense of property based on the distinction between what exists simply in the state of nature (for example, trees growing in a forest) and what man has "removed" from that state by "mixing his labor with it" (trees chopped down and cut into logs). According to Locke, I am justified in appropriating for my own use, to dispose of as I will, whatever I have mixed my labor with. Locke, of course, had in mind very simple societies (for example, nut and berry gatherers); Marx realized that the argument had a very different effect when applied to a society in which many men contribute their labor to machines that a few men own. Under such an economic system, the workers do not retain the surplus value that is produced when they mix their labor with the raw materials of nature; on the contrary, the surplus value accrues to the owners of the machines. As it was stated by Marx's friend and collaborator, Friedrich Engels,[9]

. . . the appropriation of unpaid labor is the basis of the capitalist mode of production, and of the exploitation of the worker that occurs under it; even

9 Engels (1820–95), Marx's collaborator for forty years, was born in Prussia but lived most of his later life in England. According to his own modest assessment, he "had a certain independent share in laying the foundations of the theory, and, more particularly in its elaboration. But the greater part of its leading basic principles . . . belong to Marx. What I contributed . . . Marx could very well have done without me. What Marx accomplished, I would not have achieved"—*Ludwig Feuerbach and the End of Classical German Philosophy* (Feuer 224).

> if the capitalist buys the labor power of his laborer at its full value as a commodity on the market he yet extracts more value from it than he paid for, and in the ultimate analysis this surplus value forms those sums of value from which are heaped up the constantly increasing masses of capital in the hands of the possessing classes.[k]

The concept of surplus value thus raises a difficult economic question. Fortunately, it is not necessary to evaluate this question in order to understand the main steps in Marx's and Engels' argument: As a result of the industrialization of Europe a fundamental incompatibility had developed between the modes of production on the one hand and the modes of appropriation on the other:

> In the medieval stage of evolution of the production of commodities, the question as to the owner of the product of labor could not arise. The individual producer, as a rule, had, from raw materials belonging to himself . . . , produced it with his own tools. . . . It belonged wholly to him, as a matter of course. His property in the product was, therefore, based *upon his own labor*. . . .
>
> Then came the concentration of the means of production and of the producers in large workshops and manufactories, their transformation into actual socialized means of production and socialized producers. But the socialized producers and means of production and their products were still treated, after this change, just as they had been before, i.e., as the means of production and the products of individuals. Hitherto the owner of the instruments of labor had himself appropriated the product, because, as a rule, it was his own product. . . . Now the owner of the instruments of labor always appropriated to himself the product, although it was no longer *his* product, but exclusively the product of the *labor of others*. . . .
>
> This contradiction, which gives to the new mode of production its capitalistic character, *contains the germ of the whole of the social antagonisms of today*. . . .
>
> *The contradiction between socialized production and capitalistic appropriation manifested itself as the antagonism of proletariat and bourgeoisie.*[l]

There is thus a grave disparity between the means of production, which have long since been socialized, and property, which remains in private hands and which resists socialization. To remove this disparity, property must be socialized. In a word, since capitalism is responsible for the alienation of the worker (by expropriating his product and by objectifying his relation to it), capitalism must be destroyed. The solution of existing problems "can only consist in the practical recognition of the social nature of the modern force of production, and therefore in the harmonizing of the modes of production, appropriation, and exchange with the socialized character of the means of production. And this can only come about by society openly and directly taking possession of the productive forces. . . ."[m]

What will life be like when this happens? Marx makes it seem idyllic:

> In communist society, where nobody has one exclusive sphere of activity but each can become accomplished in any branch he wishes, society regulates the general production and thus makes it possible for me to do one thing today and another tomorrow, to hunt in the morning, fish in the afternoon, rear cattle in the evening, criticize after dinner, just as I have a mind, without ever becoming hunter, fisherman, shepherd or critic.[n]

This is certainly a utopian outlook, and Marx did not for long believe that it would be possible to escape division of labor in industrial societies merely by changing the modes of appropriation. The main and persistent note, however, is freedom—specifically, the freedom to become a person, a full human being. In a Communist society every man will not only have an existence that is "fully sufficient materially"; he will also have "an existence guaranteeing the free development and exercise" of his "physical and mental faculties."

Communist freedom, then, is the opposite of alienation and objectification. Instead of being treated by other men as an object, and instead of perceiving himself as an object, a mere thing, every man becomes a center of life, creating himself by and through his free choices.

> The extraneous objective forces that have hitherto governed history pass under the control of man himself. Only from that time will man himself, more and more consciously, make his own history—only from that time will the social causes set in movement by him have, in the main and in a constantly growing measure, the results intended by him. It is the ascent of man from the kingdom of necessity to the kingdom of freedom.[o]

The high value that Marx attributes here to human personality is of course common to many thinkers—for instance, to the philosophers of the Enlightenment and to Mill and the Utilitarians. But the language in which this value is stated and the particular quality and flavor given it are different. Marx emphasizes subjectivity, freedom, and self-consciousness; he stresses *making* a life by one's own choices, as distinct from merely *being* a thing. These emphases stem directly from Hegel's theory and ultimately from Kant's contrast between inner and outer experience and from his conception of the self as the synthesizer, the "transcendental unity" whose activity makes experience possible. This conception of "subjectivity" as the goal toward which individuals and societies should aim, despite all the circumstances that increasingly produce "objectivity," was to become one of the central structural and organizing ideas of the nineteenth century, and it was to be adopted by thinkers who in other respects were hostile to Marx and to Marxism.

In discussing their theories of the alienation and exploitation of the worker, Marx and Engels alternate between playing the role of propagandists and playing the role of scientists. In their role as propagandists they urge the workers to unite, and they denounce the crimes of the capitalists: The existing regime must be overthrown, and the purpose of their writings is to mobilize the forces necessary to accomplish this. In their role as scientists they do not incite; rather, they describe and generalize. From this point of view it is not necessary to mobilize the workers: The overthrow of capitalism will not be "brought about"; it will inevitably occur, as a result of economic forces, laws that individuals are powerless to control.

THEORY OF SOCIAL CAUSATION

The propagandistic and scientific points of view are obviously not easy to reconcile. Let us begin discussion of them with Marx's and Engels' theories of social causation and historical determinism. These theories have had perhaps even greater influence than their economic doctrines and deserve examination on their own merits, independent of the concept of surplus value. One of the simplest statements of this theory is contained in the *Manifesto of the Communist Party*, which Marx and Engels wrote in 1847 in anticipation of the revolutionary movement that broke out the following year. The fundamental thesis of the *Manifesto* is stated in the opening sentence: "The history of all hitherto existing society is the history of class struggles." This is expanded by Engels (in a preface written in 1888, after Marx's death) into the assertion

> ... that in every historical epoch, the prevailing mode of economic production and exchange, and the social organization necessarily following from it, form the basis upon which is built up, and from which alone can be explained, the political and intellectual history of that epoch; that consequently the whole history of mankind . . . has been a history of class struggles, contests between exploiting and exploited, ruling and oppressed classes; that the history of these class struggles forms a series of evolutions in which a stage has [now] been reached where the exploited and oppressed class—the proletariat—cannot attain its emancipation from the sway of the exploiting and ruling class—the bourgeoisie—without at the same time, and once and for all, emancipating society at large from all exploitation, oppression, class distinctions and class struggles.

What evidence did Marx and Engels adduce to support the thesis that the whole history of European society is but the reflection of "a series of revolutions in the modes of production and exchange"? Although they considered chiefly political factors, they held that alterations in esthetic and literary taste, in philosophical theory, and indeed in every department of life reflect these same underlying economic changes.

> Does it require deep intuition to comprehend that man's ideas, views, and conceptions, in one word, man's consciousness, changes with every change in the conditions of his material existence, in his social relations, and in his social life?
> What else does the history of ideas prove than that intellectual production changes in character in proportion as material production is changed? The ruling ideas of each age have ever been the ideas of its ruling class.[p]

Thus the feudal nobility, whose power rested on the prevailing type of economic organization, created a culture—artistic, architectural, literary, and philosophical—that was the expression of the feudal social structure. And this society, together with its various cultural idiosyncrasies, collapsed when the modes of production and exchange that had made possible the dominance of a military aristocracy were replaced by modes of production and exchange that were incompatible with feudal property relations. The social organization of the Middle Ages had therefore to give way to a new type of social structure. The first steps in this development occurred with the discovery and colonization of America and the expansion of trade into the Indian and Chinese markets. The guild system of manufacture was unable to supply these growing markets and was eventually replaced by a new organization of production (by division of labor in a single workshop) that was, relatively speaking, much more competent. And this in turn was revolutionized by the invention of machinery and the application of steam power. The result of all these economic changes was the emergence of a new dominant class. The burghers, who in feudal times had been oppressed in a manner indistinguishable from serfs, came to be first an "armed and self-governing" class in their free cities, then a "counterpoise" to the old nobility on the side of the new national monarchies, and finally the ruling class in the modern type of constitutional government.

This shift in the focus of power did not, however, abolish oppression and exploitation; it merely created a more efficient form of exploitation: "For exploitation, veiled by religious and political illusions [there has been] substituted naked, shameless, direct and brutal exploitation."

According to Marx, this bourgeois class proceeded to create a new (and very inferior) culture in its own image. Both moral and esthetic standards were determined by monetary considerations, and much touted political values like "freedom" and "individuality" merely reflected the absence of restriction and control that permitted the bourgeoisie to exploit the workers. These "fine, brave words" meant only a free market in which the capitalist hoped to buy labor cheaply and to sell goods dearly. Freedom and *laissez faire* meant freedom for the capitalist to exploit the worker.

But, according to Marx, this bourgeois class and its institutions are doomed by the very dialectic that enabled them to overthrow feudalism. Just as the feudal nobility was unable to control the economic forces it called up, so the bourgeoisie is confronted with the fact that the property relations underlying bourgeois society are incompatible with modern conditions of production. "The bourgeoisie is unfit . . . to rule because it is incompetent to assure an existence to its slave within his slavery, because it cannot help letting him sink into such a state that it has to feed him, instead of being fed by him. Society can no longer live under this bourgeoisie, in other words, its existence is no longer compatible with society."[q]

Because it is based on private ownership and private profits, bourgeois economy falls inevitably into periodic crises of "overproduction." The desire to make high profits reduces wages and hence cuts down the purchasing power of the public and creates surpluses. These crises are resolved only by opening up new markets or by more thoroughly exploiting old ones. But the new markets eventually become new centers of production themselves, and there is a limit to the absorption of goods by old markets. Thus an era of ever increasing stress develops.

Meanwhile, and again quite inevitably, the bourgeoisie has created the social class that will soon seize the opportunity presented by these recurring crises. For the conditions of modern production have first called into existence the proletariat and then collected it in urban centers where it gains strength and knowledge from this concentration in great masses. What is a proletarian? From the point of view of the capitalist owner, he is merely a soulless appendage to the machine. But the proletarians are gradually becoming aware of themselves and of their destiny. They are coming to realize that the old sanctions of law, morality, and religion, which formerly reconciled them to their lot, are "merely so many bourgeois prejudices behind which lurk just as many bourgeois interests." They are coming to realize the truth of dialectical materialism—namely, that the present conditions of ownership are not "eternally right" but merely a particular stage in social history; that every dominant class has always gained the upper hand by securing the "conditions of appropriation"; and that they can rise only by following the example of their present masters and "destroying the whole superincumbent strata of official society."

But the triumph of the proletariat will not merely bring about the rise of one more new class to repeat in its turn the old story of exploitation and oppression. On the contrary, as soon as the dictatorship of the proletariat has accomplished its purpose and destroyed the last vestiges of the old capitalistic society, the class type of society will disappear. Political power will also disappear, for political power is merely the organization of one class for the suppression of others.

Obviously, this new classless society will develop a culture radically different from anything yet known. For however much earlier societies have differed from one another, they have all had one common feature—class structure.

> No wonder, then, that the social consciousness of past ages, despite all the multiplicity and variety it displays, moves within certain common forms, or general ideas, which cannot completely vanish except with the total disappearance of class antagonisms.
>
> The Communist revolution is the most radical rupture with traditional property relations; no wonder that its development involves the most radical rupture with traditional ideas.[r]

PHILOSOPHY OF HISTORY

Before Marx's day and, as a matter of fact, for a long time afterwards, history was conceived of chiefly in political terms, as the product of decisions made by kings and statesmen to sign a treaty or not to sign it, to go to war or to remain at peace. Marx at once enlarged the scope of history and altered its scale by reducing the great personalities to a very minor role as compared with the economic forces that operated in the society that these men and their biographers supposed them to be guiding. How sympathetic this view is to what has been called the Romantic mood should be obvious. To Marx, Schopenhauer's real will was doubtless a merely anthropomorphic concept. But Marx and Schopenhauer were at least in agreement that the behavior of such individuals is determined by larger-than-individual, and less-than-rational, forces, and that the accounts that the individuals themselves offer of their behavior are inaccurate rationalizations of these underlying and impersonal causes.

There is little doubt that men's conduct is less rational and less enlightened than eighteenth-century thinkers had supposed, and it is important for historians and sociologists to take cognizance of this fact and to seek the nonrational factors that enter into the determination of conduct. But are economic causes more fundamental than other causes? If, for instance, economic factors determine esthetic taste, then esthetic taste (preference for silk over cotton, and so on) determines economic trends. The truth seems to be that a culture constitutes a very complex, interlocking set of relationships that can hardly be surveyed all at once. Hence one must adopt, every time one looks at a given culture, some point of view. From each of these points of view one set of relations necessarily occupies the foreground, and the other sets recede into the background. Because his interest in social reform and his sympathy for the plight of the alienated workers made economic conditions particularly important to Marx, economic relations remained consistently in the foreground of his thought; then, because he noted their prominence without noting the reason for it, he developed a theory of social causation to explain the supposed fact. It is as if a physician interested in the history of medicine first assumed that medical developments were always the basic factors in cultural movement and then tried to work out a medical dialectic to show why.

This serious oversimplification in his view of social causation was hidden from Marx by the ambiguity of his language—especially, the lack of precision in the key terms "production" and "exchange." In different contexts they have different meanings. Sometimes they refer in the most narrow way to purely technological changes—development of the wheel, application of steam, and so forth; sometimes they broaden to include "ideas" and "ideals." The broader meanings are more adequate to the complexity of the facts; the narrower meanings satisfy demands for an elegantly simple and "scientific" formula. Because he failed to notice the shifts from one meaning to another, Marx believed he had found a simple formula adequate to the facts.

That Marx's philosophy of history owes much to Hegel is obvious. It differs from Hegel's, of course, in the all-important fact that the spiritual dialectic (development of consciousness) has been replaced by a materialistic dialectic (changes in modes of production and exchange). The main difference, however, is one of tone. Hegel's favorite metaphor was the unfolding of bud into blossom into flower. According to Hegel, "world historical" figures, like Napoleon, may effect revolutionary changes, but the modal type of change, as it were, is gradual and natural, almost easy. In Marx's view, the modal type of change is revolutionary. Change is not a synthesis in which lower forms are incorporated and transcended in a higher form. Change involves the destruction of one class by another. In his belief that violence and conflict are fundamental realities Marx is far closer to Schopenhauer and to later thinkers like Nietzsche and the survival-of-the-fittest philosophers than he is to the Enlightenment and its rationalist descendants.

One major consequence of shifting to a materialistic dialectic is a transformation in the status of ideas and theories. For Hegel, ideas were the generating causes of all other changes. It was the recognition of some discrepancy or contradiction that led men to move on to a more inclusive and more comprehensive view of themselves and of the world. For Marx, ideas and theories were not causes but epiphenomena, passive by-products of the economic forces that are the real determinants of change. From this ideological way of thinking about theory, it is fair to say that theory has never quite recovered.

Marx's view of religion is a good introduction to his conception of the ideological character of thought in general.

> *Man makes religion;* religion does not make man. Religion is indeed man's self-consciousness and self-awareness so long as he has not found himself or has lost himself again. But *man* is not an abstract being, squatting outside the world. Man is *the human world,* the state, society. This state, this society, produce religion which is an *inverted world consciousness,* because they are an *inverted world.* . . .
>
> *Religious* suffering is at the same time an *expression* of real suffering and a *protest* against real suffering. Religion is the sigh of the oppressed creature, the sentiment of a heartless world, and the soul of soulless conditions. It is the *opium* of the people.
>
> The abolition of religion as the *illusory* happiness of men, is a demand for their *real* happiness. The call to abandon their illusions about their condition is a *call to abandon a condition which requires illusions.* The criticism of religion is, therefore, *the embryonic criticism of this vale of tears* of which religion is the halo.
>
> Criticism has plucked the imaginary flowers from the chain, not in order that men shall bear the chain without . . . consolation but so that he shall cast off the chain and pluck the living flower. The criticism of religion disillusions man so that he will think, act and fashion his reality as a man who has lost his illusions and regained his reason; so that he will revolve about himself as his own true sun. Religion is only the illusory sun about which man revolves so long as he does not revolve about himself. . . .
>
> Luther . . . shattered the faith in authority by restoring the authority of faith. He transformed the priests into laymen by turning laymen into priests. He liberated man from external religiosity by making religiosity the innermost

essence of man. He liberated the body from its chains because he fettered the heart with chains.

But if Protestantism was not the solution it did at least pose the problem correctly. It was no longer a question, thereafter, of the layman's struggle against the priest outside himself, but of his struggle against his *own internal priest*, against his own *priestly nature*.[s]

Thus, though religions claim to be making assertions, for instance, about God, the language of religion is not cognitive; it is only expressive. Religions do not report what is true of the world; they express our inner feelings, tensions, and anxieties. Specifically, they express our despair at "the alienation of man from himself and from nature." Furthermore, religions express this despair in forms that exactly correspond to the other institutions of a culture at any given time. For instance, the objectification and alienation that infect economic and social institutions are reflected in religious beliefs and practices. "Objectification is the practice of alienation. Just as man, so long as he is engrossed in religion, can only objectify his essence by an *alien* and fantastic being; so under the sway of egoistic need, he can only affirm himself and produce objects in practice by subordinating his products and his own activity to the domination of an alien entity, . . . namely money."[t] It follows that the different religions of men living in different places and in different ages "are nothing more than *stages in the development of the human mind*—snake skins which have been cast off by history, and *man* is the snake who clothed himself in them. . . ."[u]

What is true of religion is true of philosophy, and of theory in general. Changes in political theory, or in the legal system, for instance, "are not explained by the so-called general progress of the human mind." They express and reflect "the material conditions of life."

> The mode of production in material life determines the general character of the social, political and spiritual processes of life. It is not the consciousness of men that determines their existence, but, on the contrary, their social existence determines their consciousness. . . . With [any] change of the economic foundation the entire immense superstructure is more or less rapidly transformed. In considering such transformations the distinction should always be made between the material transformation of the economic conditions of production, which can be determined with the precision of natural science, and the legal, political, religious, aesthetic, or philosophic—in short, ideological forms in which men become conscious of this conflict and fight it out.[v]

Thus in the eighteenth century a philosophical theory had emerged that was appropriate for that age. According to this theory,

> . . . superstition, injustice, privilege, oppression were to be superseded by eternal truth, eternal Right, equality based on Nature and the inalienable rights of man.

> We know today that this kingdom of reason was nothing more than the
> idealized kingdom of the bourgeoisie; that this eternal Right found its realiza-
> tion in bourgeois justice; that this equality reduced itself to bourgeois equality
> before the law; that bourgeois property was proclaimed as one of the essential
> rights of man. . . . The great thinkers of the eighteenth century could, no
> more than their predecessors, go beyond the limits imposed upon them by
> their epoch.[w]

But what about the great thinkers of the nineteenth century? Did Marx believe
that he had succeeded in going beyond the limits imposed by *his* epoch? It is
impossible to find in his writings an unambiguous answer. Part of the time—or
perhaps it is fairer to say, "all of the time with a part of his mind"—Marx holds
that his theory is an exception. It is somehow (but how, exactly?) immune to
the cultural relativism that infects all other theories. It is no mere ideology; it
is *true*. For instance, the conflict between what religion claims to be and what
Marx says it is not merely an ideological dispute reflecting the differing class
interests of the contestants. It is a conflict between false claims and scientifically
proven assertions: "It is the *task of history*, therefore, once the *other-world of
truth* has vanished, to establish the *truth of this world*. The immediate *task of
philosophy*, which is in the service of history, is to unmask human self-alienation
in its *secular form* now that it has been unmasked in its *sacred form*."[x]

On the other hand, in the same work Marx suggests that his theory will
undermine religion, not because it is true and religion is false, but because it
is a more powerful ideology.

> Material force can only be overthrown by material force; but theory itself
> becomes a material force when it has seized the masses. Theory is capable
> of seizing the masses when it demonstrates *ad hominem*, and it demonstrates
> *ad hominem*, as soon as it becomes radical. To be radical is to grasp things
> by the root. But for man the root is man himself. What proves beyond doubt
> the radicalism of German theory, and thus its practical energy, is that it begins
> from the resolute *positive* abolition of religion.[y]

The fact is that Marx alternated between two quite different epistemological
positions. One is a kind of scientific realism. According to this view, the truth
is defined in terms of correspondence between ideas (or theories) and facts, and
the empirical method of the natural sciences is the best—indeed, the only really
reliable—method for discovering and checking these correspondences. The other
position is radically pragmatic. From its point of view, the truth is what works,
and the test of the truth of a particular theory about society or about history
is whether it achieves the desired overthrow of capitalism.

In the following passage, for instance, the correspondence theory is rejected
on the grounds that it is open to a sceptical attack that the pragmatic test
survives:

Our agnostic admits that all our knowledge is based upon the information imparted to us by our senses. But, he adds, how do we know that our senses give us correct representations of the objects we perceive through them? . . . Now, this line of reasoning seems undoubtedly hard to meet by mere argumentation. But before there was argumentation, there was action. *Im Anfang war die Tat.*[10] And human action had solved the difficulty long before human ingenuity invented it. The proof of the pudding is in the eating. From the moment we turn to our own use these objects, according to the qualities we perceive in them, we put to an infallible test the correctness or otherwise of our sense perceptions. If these perceptions have been wrong, then our estimate of the use to which an object can be turned must also be wrong, and our attempt must fail.[z]

In the *Theses on Feuerbach* Marx's pragmatism is even more explicitly stated:

The chief defect of all hitherto existing materialism . . . is that the object, reality, sensuousness, is conceived only in the form of the *object* or *contemplation*, but not as *human sensuous activity, practice,* not subjectively. . . .

The question whether objective truth can be attributed to human thinking is not a question of theory but is a practical question. In practice man must prove the truth, i.e., the reality and power, the "this-sidedness" of his thinking. The dispute over the reality or non-reality of thinking which is isolated from practice is a purely scholastic question.

The materialist doctrine that men are products of circumstances and upbringing, and that, therefore, changed men are products of other circumstances and changed upbringings, forgets that circumstances are changed precisely by men, and that the educator must himself be educated. . . .

The coincidence of the changing of circumstances and of human activity can only be conceived and rationally understood as revolutionizing practice.

The philosophers have *interpreted* the world, in various ways; the point, however, is to *change* it.[a]

This attack on what Dewey later called spectator theories of knowledge[11] not only undermines epistemological theories of the classical type, whether idealistic or realistic; it also undermines Marx's own claim to have formulated the "correct" version of materialism. From the pragmatic point of view stated in the *Theses,* dialectical materialism is only another form of scientism, a rather naïve version of the traditional metaphysics that differs from it only in relying on an allegedly scientific method instead of on perception or reason. Thus in the *Theses* Marx is far more revolutionary—in an intellectual sense—than in his economic theory, for he is attacking a fundamental belief in Western thought, the notion that the objects of human experience are separate entities "out there," that they are complete in themselves and independent of us and our activity.

10 [A quotation from Goethe's *Faust:* "In the beginning was the deed"—AUTHOR.]
11 See pp. 294–95.

Yet here, at his most revolutionary, Marx is developing but one phase of the Kantian heritage, for it was Kant who, more than anyone else, broke down the sharp dualistic distinction between mind and its objects that earlier theory had imposed.

Evolution

As has been frequently pointed out, in the nineteenth century the concept of development was in the air. Darwin[12] felt this interest and focused it on a specific biological problem; in doing so he collected an immense amount of concrete evidence and thus "proved" (doubtless only in a limited area, but this was overlooked by adherents and opponents alike) what had earlier been only a philosophical hypothesis. This gave great impetus to the use of the concept of development as a general methodological tool.

The view that Darwin attacked—that the various species of animals are direct creations of the Deity and are thus eternal and unchanging—was of hoary antiquity, buttressed both by a formidable array of theological arguments and by several important philosophical concepts, such as the doctrines of universals, of essences, and of teleology. Criticism of this view, unlike most intrascientific arguments, therefore touched a great number of very sensitive spots in lay opinion.

ARTIFICIAL SELECTION

Darwin's main thesis, moreover, was so simple that almost anyone could understand it. He pointed out what every animal breeder already knew, that it is possible to select and perpetuate certain strains in domestic animals by breeding to whatever individual differences the owner chooses.

Suppose an owner of collies fancies dogs with longer and narrower skulls. He need only eliminate from every litter the puppies with short, broad skulls and breed those with long, narrow skulls. Since the characteristics of parents tend to be inherited, in each new generation the desired characteristics will appear more frequently. Moreover, as long as the process of elimination is continued, standards of selection will rise; the narrow skulls of one generation

---

12 Charles Darwin (1809–82) was the son of a well-to-do country doctor and the grandson of Erasmus Darwin and Josiah Wedgwood. After an abortive start toward a medical career, he decided rather unenthusiastically on the church. Before he had progressed very far, he had an opportunity to go on a scientific expedition in Southern waters. Darwin spent five years on this cruise aboard H.M.S. *Beagle* and returned in 1838 an enthusiastic student of natural history. For more than twenty years he slowly worked at his theory of evolution and accumulated evidence to support it. It was only at his friends' insistence that he brought himself to publish it in 1859.

will get narrower and more "aristocratic" in the next. If this characteristic catches the public eye, an economic factor enters the picture, for breeders will not raise dogs they cannot sell. If the public fancies narrow-skulled collies, there is no point in wasting feed on broad-skulled ones. Hence a new variant of the collie may emerge, and if several features (long coat, bushy tail) are jointly selected in this way, a new "species" will soon appear. "Who will believe that animals closely resembling the Italian greyhound, the bloodhound, the bull-dog, pug-dog, or Blenheim spaniel, etc.—so unlike all wild Canidae—ever existed freely in a state of nature?" [b] Though this canine diversity is in part the product of crossing "a few aboriginal species," it results in the main from the selection of certain characteristics from "an immense amount of inherited variation."

NATURAL SELECTION

Though in Darwin's time man's capacity to select and thus produce new variants and species was common knowledge among breeders of domestic animals, no one had ever thought about it in just this connection. Yet, if this process occurs in the case of domestic animals, why may it not occur in the case of wild animals?

> Altogether at least a score of pigeons might be chosen which, if shown to an ornithologist, and he were told they were wild birds, would certainly be ranked by him as well-defined species. Moreover, I do not believe that any ornithologist would place the English carrier, the short-faced tumbler, the runt, the barb, pouter, and fantail in the same genus. . . .
> Great as are the differences between the breeds of the pigeons, I am fully convinced that . . . all are descended from the rock-pigeon (*Columba livia*).[13c]

May there not then be a principle of *natural* selection that operates exactly like the breeder's conscious plan, to perpetuate certain characteristics and to eliminate others? Darwin believed he could show there is such a principle.

The first point to note, according to Darwin, is that there is a "universal struggle for existence."

> We behold the face of nature bright with gladness, we often see super-abundance of food; we do not see or we forget that the birds which are idly singing round us mostly live on insects or seeds, and are thus constantly destroying life; or we forget how largely these songsters, or their eggs, or their nestlings, are destroyed by birds and beasts of prey; we do not always bear in mind, that, though food may be now superabundant, it is not so at all seasons of each recurring year.

13 [The sentences quoted are followed by several pages of supporting evidence, themselves but a brief abstract of the material Darwin had at hand; he constantly remarked on the "limitations of space," which compelled him to report his data at what he felt was "insufficient length"— AUTHOR.]

> A struggle for existence inevitably follows from the high rate at which all organic beings tend to increase.[14] . . . As more individuals are produced than can possibly survive, there must in every case be a struggle for existence, either one individual with another of the same species, or with the individuals of distinct species, or with the physical conditions of life. It is the doctrine of Malthus[15] applied with manifold force to the whole animal and vegetable kingdom; for in this case there can be no artificial increase of food, and no prudential restraint from marriage.[d]

Obviously, in this kind of competition, any individual difference that makes one member of a species (or one species) even slightly fitter to survive will tend to be perpetuated. This individual will live a little longer and will thus have more offspring, and these offspring will tend to inherit the characteristic in question. Individual members of the species who lack this property will tend to die sooner and so have fewer offspring. Therefore, in the course of time, a variant of the species will emerge characterized by the property that was originally an individual difference in an occasional member of the species. When enough variants are produced in this way a new species in effect evolves. The struggle for survival is thus a principle of natural selection that operates in precisely the same way as deliberate human selection operates in the breeding of domestic animals.

> In order to make it clear how, as I believe, natural selection acts, I must beg permission to give one or two imaginary illustrations. Let us take the case of a wolf, which preys on various animals, securing some by craft, some by strength, some by fleetness; and let us suppose that the fleetest prey, a deer for instance, had from any change in the country increased in numbers, or that other prey had decreased in numbers, during that season of the year when the wolf was hardest pressed for food. Under such circumstances the swiftest and slimmest wolves have the best chance of surviving, and so be

14 [Darwin noted that the elephant is the slowest breeder of all known animals; yet if every elephant born lived out its normal life span and produced an average number of offspring, there would be alive, after a period of seven hundred forty to seven hundred fifty years, nearly 19,000,000 elephants descended from the first pair. T. H. Morgan, in *The Scientific Basis of Evolution* (Norton, New York, 1932), p. 121, gives even more impressive figures of fecundity: "It is said that a salmon may produce 28,361,000 eggs . . . ; the queen bee may lay in three years 5,000,000 eggs. The American oyster produces from 15,000,000 to 114,000,000 eggs at each spawning and may spawn four or five times a year. . . . According to Punnett, a rotifer (Hydatina) lays about thirty eggs measuring 0.01 cm. At the end of a year, after sixty-five generations (if all lived), the total mass of material produced would make a sphere larger than the confines of 'the known universe'"—AUTHOR.]

15 [Malthus (1766–1834) was the author of an *Essay on Population* (1798), in which he argued that, but for war, pestilence, and famine, human population would increase at a much greater rate than means of subsistence. This gave Darwin the hint he needed: "In October 1838, I happened to read for amusement Malthus on Population, and being well prepared to appreciate the struggle for existence which everywhere goes on, from long continued observation of the habits of plants and animals, it at once struck me that under these circumstances favourable variations would tend to be preserved and unfavourable ones to be destroyed. The result of this would be a new species. Here then I had a theory by which to work"—AUTHOR.]

preserved or selected, provided always that they retained strength to master their prey at this or some other period of the year, when they were compelled to prey on other animals. I can see no more reason to doubt that this would be the result, than that man should be able to improve the fleetness of his greyhounds by careful and methodical selection, or by the kind of unconscious selection which results from each man trying to keep the best dogs without any thought of modifying the breed. I may add that, according to Mr. Pierce, there are two varieties of the wolf inhabiting the Catskill Mountains, in the United States, one with a light greyhound-like form, which pursues deer, and the other more bulky, with shorter legs, which more frequently attacks the shepherd's flocks.[e]

THE TREE OF LIFE

It is quite impossible in a few extracts to give any idea of the voluminous and impressive evidence, drawn from all manner of sources, including experimental studies of his own, with which Darwin supported his hypothesis. We shall have to content ourselves with Darwin's description of the Tree of Life, the image that sums up his whole theory. According to Darwin, the species do not constitute separate classes frozen in eternal independence and connected only in the will of the deity who created them. Rather, they are comparable to a great tree:

> The green and budding twigs may represent existing species; and those produced during former years may represent the long succession of extinct species. At each period of growth all the growing twigs have tried to branch out on all sides, and to overtop and kill the surrounding twigs and branches, in the same manner as species and groups of species have at all times overmastered other species in the great battle for life. The limbs divided into great branches, and these into lesser and lesser branches, were themselves once, when the tree was young, budding twigs; and this connection of the former and present buds by ramifying branches may well represent the classification of all extinct and living species in groups subordinate to groups. Of the many twigs which flourished when the tree was a mere bush, only two or three, now grown into great branches, yet survive and bear the other branches; so with the species which lived during long-past geological periods, very few now have living and modified descendants. From the first growth of the tree, many a limb and branch has decayed and dropped off; and these fallen branches of various sizes may represent those whole orders, families and genera which have now no living representatives, and which are known to us only in a fossil state. As we here and there see a thin, straggling branch springing from a fork low down on a tree, and which by some chance has been favored and is still alive on its summit, so we occasionally see an animal like the Ornithorhynchus or Lepidosiren, which in some small degree connects by its affinities two large branches of life, and which has apparently been saved from fatal competition by having inhabited a protected station. As buds give rise by growth to fresh buds, and these, if vigorous, branch out and overtop on all sides many a feebler branch, so by generation I believe

it has been with the great Tree of Life, which fills with its dead and broken branches the crust of the earth, and covers the surface with its ever-branching and beautiful ramifications.[f]

This metaphor became, in effect, the guide for the next generation of natural scientists. They were natural historians who sought in the "record of the rocks" those "missing links" that would reveal, as it were, the structure of the Tree of Life, whose surface of leaves and buds is all that we actually see. This work has now been largely done, and the attention of the biological sciences has turned chiefly to the study of those "variations" whose causes Darwin himself did not explain but simply assumed to be the basis on which the process of natural selection operates. The focus of interest has therefore shifted from paleontology to genetics, from the study of fossils to experimental work in laboratories. It has been shown, for instance, that Darwin was wrong in supposing that variations are always slight and that evolution consequently proceeds very slowly by the accumulation of many small differences. And "natural selection," on which Darwin concentrated his attention as the active principle involved, has lost its central importance. It is now held that many structures either are not adaptive or are adaptive only at the end of a process of development, the earlier stages of which had no selective advantage. From this view the doctrine of "natural selection" reduces merely to the truism that whatever new types emerge must be able to survive. What now interests biologists is the mode of origin of the new types.

DARWIN'S INFLUENCE

Though no one today is a Darwinian in the strict sense, Darwin's theory made an immense contribution to the biological sciences. By pointing to the importance of variation, Darwin indicated the crucial area for further study, and, by offering an account in terms of a purely objective, nonteleological concept, he showed that biology could be as much of a science as physics. Far more important than the details of Darwin's explanation of the origin of species was the fact that he thought species had an empirical, rather than divine, origin—an origin of which it is possible to give a scientific account. Darwin's image of the Tree of Life inspired biologists to see their subject as a *unified* field of study, and his example gave them the courage to think about it as a *neutral* field of study, untrammeled by extrascientific conceptions.[16]

16 In *Science and Christian Tradition*, Thomas Huxley (who was known as "Darwin's bulldog") described the vexations scientists experienced: "I had set out on a journey, with no other purpose than that of exploring a certain province of natural knowledge which it was my right and duty to pursue; and yet I found that, whatever route I took, before long I came to a tall and formidable-looking fence. Confident as I might be in the existence of an ancient and indefeasible right of way, before me stood the thorny barrier with its comminatory notice board—'No thoroughfare—By order, Moses.' There seemed no way over; nor did the prospect of creeping round, as I saw some do, attract me. True there was no longer any cause to fear the spring guns and man-traps set by the former lords of the manor; but one is apt to get very dirty going on all-fours. The only alternatives were to give up my journey—which I was not minded to do—or to break the fence down and go through it."

Important as Darwinism has been in biology, its impact in other fields, where Darwin himself did not dream of applying it, has been even more consequential. This history of philosophy is an example of that wider influence, for it is based on the assumption that modern men cannot understand themselves unless they know something of their past. Such a notion would hardly have occurred to the thinkers of the Enlightenment, and it certainly would not have seemed to them a truism, as it does to us today. This, of course, is not merely a matter of "taking an interest" in history, in the narrow sense of the human past; it is, rather, a basic methodological orientation. The fact is that it has now become natural to explain things—all sorts of things—genetically. Men no longer think of things simply as occurring at a specific point in time. They think of things, rather, as enduring through time and they want to know how they develop *through* time.[17] Darwinism was certainly not the exclusive cause of this change in point of view. As a matter of fact, it was in some respects a reflection of changes that were already under way. But its success in dealing with its own specific problem and the influence it had on the course of the biological and social sciences and of philosophy were powerful factors in the further development of this new climate of opinion.

Darwinism made its first immediate impact on the public, however, in connection with the old controversy between science and religion, and it brought this controversy to a new intensity. The very aspects of the theory of natural selection that stimulated the biological scientists were deeply offensive to the conventional religious mind. Actually, there was nothing in the view—as Darwin tried to point out[18]—that was incompatible with the religious outlook. The new physics had raised a much more serious and fundamental problem than had the theory of natural selection. But evolution brought the problem home as an abstract science could never do. After stating his conclusion, "I believe that animals are descended from at most only four or five progenitors, and plants from an equal or lesser number," Darwin went on to say that "argument from analogy" would lead him "one step further"—to the conclusion that "all the organic beings which have ever lived on this earth may be descended from some one primordial form." If this be true, "much light will be thrown on the origin of man and his history."[g]

---

17 "To regard all things in their historical setting appears, indeed, to be an instructive [sic] procedure of the modern mind. We do it without thinking, because we can scarcely think at all without doing it. The modern climate of opinion is such that we cannot seemingly understand our world unless we regard it as a going concern. . . . What is peculiar to the modern mind is the disposition and the determination to regard ideas and concepts, the truth of things as well as the things themselves, as changing entities. . . . Historical-mindedness is so much a preconception of modern thought that we can identify a particular thing only by pointing to the various things it successively was before it became that particular thing it will presently cease to be"—C. Becker, *The Heavenly City of the Eighteenth-Century Philosophers* (Yale University Press, 1932), p. 19.

18 "I see no good reason why the views given in this volume should shock the religious feelings of any one." And he was glad to add in subsequent editions that "a celebrated author and divine" had assured him that it is "just as noble a conception of the Deity to believe He created a few original forms capable of self-development . . . , as to believe that He required a fresh act of creation" for each separate species—*Origin of Species*, p. 496.

The reaction was instantaneous and violent. A meeting of the British Association in June 1860 was almost broken up by a discussion of the new book. Samuel Wilberforce, Bishop of Oxford, attacked it bitterly, ridiculing Darwin's "proofs" and describing the theory as a mere "hypothesis raised most unphilosophically to the dignity of a causal." Unfortunately for Wilberforce, he was not content to attack the theory; he then turned to Huxley, who was sitting near him, and inquired sarcastically whether it was through his grandfather or his grandmother that he claimed descent from a monkey. This gave Huxley, who was a clever debater, the opening he needed: He would much rather, Huxley replied, have a monkey for an ancestor than a man who, like Wilberforce, "prostituted the gifts of culture and of eloquence to the service of prejudice and falsehood." Ladies fainted, the audience burst into protest or applause, and over it all an Admiral of the Royal Navy waved a Bible, affirming its inspired and literal truth and denouncing his old friend Darwin and all his works.[h]

While bishops ranted and scientists in retaliation elevated Darwinism to the level of dogma,[19] the theory began slowly and certainly to operate upon men's minds. Attention, at least of laymen, focused on one or the other of two main points. One was the conviction that the outcome of this struggle is "progress"— bigger, better, newer forms. This was the leading impression that the theory had made on Darwin himself: "There is grandeur in this view . . . that, while this planet has gone cycling on according to the fixed law of gravity, from so simple a beginning endless forms most beautiful and most wonderful have been, and are being evolved." [i] And of course this point of view comports with the aspects of nineteenth-century thought that have been the theme of this chapter—its emphasis on the idea of development, its belief in the value of a scientific approach to the study of man and his problems, and its generally empirical and optimistic outlook.

The other main point in Darwinism on which lay opinion focused was the discovery that nature is a struggle for survival, a savage competition in which the weak and the helpless go to the wall. This aspect of Darwinism powerfully reinforced the contrasting strain in nineteenth-century thought—hostility to science on the grounds that it is responsible not only for the secularization of life (through its mechanistic world view) but also for the alienation of the industrial workers (through its mass-production technology). Some of the thinkers who represent this counter-revolution, or resistance movement, against the predominantly scientific culture of the nineteenth century are examined in the next chapter. This chapter will be brought to a close by considering a few thinkers who are representative of the former, more positive, response to Darwinism.

19 As Samuel Butler (who had no love of bishops) caustically noted, "Science is being daily more and more personified and anthropomorphized into a god. By and by they will say that science took our nature upon him, and sent down his only begotten son, Charles Darwin, or Huxley, into the world so that those who believe in him, etc.; and they will burn people for saying that science, after all, is only an expression for our ignorance of our own ignorance."

Scientific Philosophy

The philosophers of science who were the immediate heirs of evolutionary theory fall into two main groups: those who were old-fashioned metaphysicians (without, however, recognizing it) and those who were openly and admittedly positivists. Thus, once again, but with still another twist, philosophical development moved within a fundamentally Kantian context. Kant had distinguished between phenomena (the spatiotemporal manifold) and noumena (things-in-themselves), and he had held that, although our knowledge is limited to the former, we can nevertheless be confident that things-in-themselves exist. None of the philosophers of science believed in a noumenal realm beyond the spatiotemporal manifold; in this sense they were all phenomenalists. But some of them identified the spatiotemporal manifold with ultimate reality (which Kant, of course, had never done), and they went on to identify current scientific theories with ultimate truth (despite all the growing evidence that science itself has a history). This point of view may be called scientism. Though certainly rather naïve, it was widely accepted, and among its adherents were both materialists and vitalists.

MATERIALISM

Representative of the materialist thesis was the view of Ernst Haeckel.[20] Haeckel believed that science had indubitably proved that "the universe, or the cosmos, is eternal, infinite, and illimitable, [and that] its substance, with its two attributes (matter and energy), fills infinite space, and is in eternal motion. . . . This motion runs on through infinite time as an unbroken development" in the course of which "countless organic forms" gradually emerge. "Our mother-earth is a mere speck in the sunbeam in the illimitable universe, [and] man himself is but a tiny grain of protoplasm in the perishable framework of organic nature."[j]

There is no problem, Haeckel held, about the "origins of life" or about the nature of "sensation and rational thought." Everything can be explained in terms of the evolutionary development (in accordance with the "laws of the conservation of matter and the conservation of energy") of material substance. Haeckel called his philosophy "monism" to emphasize his denial of the various nonmaterial substances—minds, souls, and so on—of traditional philosophy.

> Monistic cosmology proved . . . that there is no personal God; comparative and genetic psychology showed that there cannot be an immortal soul; and monistic physiology proved the futility of the assumption of "free will." Finally, the science of evolution made it clear that the same eternal iron laws that rule in the inorganic world are valid too in the organic and moral world.[k]

20 Ernst Haeckel (1834–1919) was a biologist who taught at the University of Jena. He was one of the earliest German adherents of Darwinism.

This conclusion is very sweeping—and it is as dogmatic as any religion. But the crucial question for any materialistic monism is whether life can in fact be explained in mechanistic terms, by means of the "law of the evolution of substance," as Haeckel held. Long before Haeckel, Hobbes had held that it can be; Descartes had excluded only man—and not man's body but merely man's soul—from his otherwise universal mechanism. For such early modern philosophers, however, the question had been entirely theoretical; no one had regarded himself as being in a position to offer such an explanation in detail. But toward the end of the nineteenth century advances in biology made it seem likely that a complete explanation was actually possible. Many scientists came to believe that "ultimately life can be unequivocally explained in physico-chemical terms."[1]

In Jacques Loeb's[21] work on animal tropisms this point of view was explicitly asserted:

> That in the case of our inner life a physico-chemical explanation is not beyond the realm of possibility is proved by the fact that it is already possible for us to explain cases of simple manifestations of animal instinct and will on a physico-chemical basis; namely, the phenomena . . . of animal tropisms. As the most simple example we may mention [that] the tendency of certain animals to fly or creep to the light . . . might be explained by the . . . law of Bunsen and Roscoe, which explains the photochemical effects in inanimate nature. This law states that within wide limits the photochemical effect equals the product of the intensity of light into the duration of illumination. . . .
>
> The positively heliotropic animals—i.e., the animals which go instinctively to a source of light—have in their eyes (and occasionally also in their skin) photosensitive substances which undergo chemical alterations by light. The products formed in this process influence the contraction of the muscles. . . . If the animal is illuminated on one side only, the mass of photochemical reaction products formed on that side in the unit of time is greater than on the opposite side. Consequently the development of energy in the symmetrical muscles on both sides of the body becomes unequal. . . . [Therefore] the animal is automatically forced to turn toward one side [until] the symmetrical spots of its surface are struck by the light at the same angle. . . . Consequently the velocity of reaction of the photochemical processes on both sides of the animal become equal. There is no more reason for the animal to deviate from the motion in a straight line and the positively heliotropic animal will move in this line to the source of light. . . . Heliotropic animals are therefore in reality photometric machines.[m]

And what earlier philosophers had believed to be man's "free will"—his capacity for planning, and for appreciating values and choosing the best among them—has a similar source: "We eat, drink, and reproduce not because mankind has reached an agreement that this is desirable, but because, machine-like, we are compelled to do so."[n]

---

21 Jacques Loeb (1859–1924) was born in Germany. He studied medicine, worked at the zoological institute in Naples, and taught physiology before coming to the United States in 1891. He subsequently taught at the universities of Chicago and California.

VITALISM

Such mechanistic solutions to life's "riddles" were attacked by another school of metaphysician-scientists called vitalists. These thinkers held life to be *sui generis* and inexplicable in terms of physical or chemical laws. Characteristically, they did not use metaphysical and theological arguments to attack mechanism. For the vitalists, mechanism was poor philosophy because it was poor biology.

Representative of this version of scientism was the view of Hans Driesch.[22] According to Driesch, "the processes of life" have an "unanalysable autonomy"; they are not "the result of a special constellation of factors known already" in physics and chemistry. An organism differs from a machine because it operates as a whole, as an individual; hence it cannot be explained mechanistically. "Analytical experimental embryology" shows, for instance, that

> . . . there are many kinds of embryonic organs or even animals which, if by an operation deprived of part of their cells, behave in the following way: of whatever material you deprive these organs or animals, the remainder, unless it is very small, will always develop in the normal manner, though, so to speak, in miniature. That is to say: there will develop out of the part of the embryonic organ or animal left by the operation, as might be expected, not a part of the organization *but the whole*, only on a smaller scale. I have proposed the name of *harmonious-equipotential systems* for organs or animals of this type. . . .[o]

Driesch may well be correct in maintaining that "mechanical causality is *not* sufficient for an explanation of what happens" in this sort of situation. But the notion of "individualising causality," or "entelechy," that he puts forward as an alternative is also far from sufficient: "Entelechy . . . is itself neither 'an energy' nor 'a material substance' of any special kind: such an assumption would lead to absurdities. Entelechy is an agent *sui generis*, non-material and non-spatial, but acting 'into' space, so to speak; an agent, however, that belongs to nature."[p]

Thus, if (as Driesch points out) Loeb fell prey to the "materialistic dogmatism of his time" by stating "a very important *problem* in the form of a fact,"[q] Driesch himself was committed to an exactly opposite dogmatism. Indeed, the metaphysical tendency of both these thinkers, as well as of Haeckel, is obvious. Not only did they generalize too hastily from insufficient data—Loeb from his tropisms, Driesch from his harmonious-equipotential systems, Haeckel from his "two great laws." They were also philosophically naïve in assuming that what science reveals is the truth about ultimate reality. There is a question, as the second group of scientific philosophers were to show, about the status of scientific truth. If the dispute over mechanism and vitalism as rival explanations of behavior is now

---

22 Hans Driesch (1867–1941) began his career as a biologist and worked for a time at the zoological institute in Naples. In 1909 he went to Heidelberg to teach philosophy.

largely a dead issue, it is because more careful study of the methodology of science shows that neither "mechanism" nor "vitalism" has a very clear meaning and that "explanation" is itself subject to varying explanations.

POSITIVISM

Under the rubric of "positivism" may be grouped a number of thinkers who, in contrast to the disguised metaphysicians just considered, accepted the self-denying clause by which Kant had limited knowledge to phenomena. But they differed from Kant in rejecting the possibility of synthetical a priori knowledge and in being uninterested in making a place for faith, a task that Kant, of course, had regarded as the whole purpose of limiting knowledge to phenomena. Indeed, these thinkers combined Hume's mitigated scepticism with Kant's phenomenalism.

Comte can be considered a founder of this new point of view insofar as he insisted that the function of science is not to show why things happen but to generalize about how they happen—to provide, that is, an instrument of control rather than a knowledge of ultimate reality. Later positivist thinkers, of whom Ernst Mach[23] and Karl Pearson[24] are examples, carried forward and applied more systematically the empiricism and pragmatism that were implicit in Comte's point of view.

Mach's main contention was that metaphysics is no more justified in science than it is in philosophy. Why reject God, soul, and free will on the grounds that they are unobservable and then introduce equally unknowable elements—entelechies or, for that matter, atoms—as new ultimates? The ultimate reals of both the materialists and the vitalists are only "mental artifices."[r] Reality, that is, consists neither in "minds" nor in "atoms." It consists in experiences—in colors, sounds, tastes, and other data of sensation. But are these data mental or physical? In themselves they are neither, according to Mach. In themselves experiences are "neutral." But no experience is isolated; each stands in relation to other experiences, and it is the context of an experience that determines whether we are to regard it as "mental" or "physical." Thus, in itself, a particular experience of red is neutral. If the context in which we are experiencing red includes, say, "light," we regard it as physical. If, on the other hand, the context includes "optic nerve," we regard it as mental. That is all. The various sciences deal with the same experiences in different contexts: In the former context, for instance, red is a part of the subject matter of physics; in the latter, it is a part of the subject matter of physiology.

What, then, is a science? It is merely an instrument that men use for summarizing and communicating about the various relations among their experiences.

---

23 Ernst Mach (1838–1916) was an Austrian. He taught mathematics and physics at the universities of Prague and Vienna.
24 Karl Pearson (1857–1936) studied mathematics at Cambridge. Later he became interested in law and eugenics. He taught mathematics and eugenics at the University of London.

My fundamental conception [is] the nature of science as Economy of Thought. . . .

It is the object of science to replace, or *save*, experiences, by the reproduction and anticipation of facts in thought. . . .

In the reproduction of facts in thought, we never reproduce the facts in full, but only that side of them which is important to us, moved to this directly or indirectly by a practical interest. Our reproductions are invariably abstractions. Here again is an economical tendency.

Nature is composed of sensations as its elements. Primitive man, however, first picks out certain compounds of these elements—those namely that are relatively permanent and of greater importance to him. The first and oldest words are names of "things." . . . No inalterable thing exists. The thing is an abstraction, the name a symbol, for a compound of elements from whose changes we abstract. The reason we assign a single word to a whole compound is that we need to suggest all the constituent sensations at once. . . . Sensations are not signs of things; but, on the contrary, a thing is a thought-symbol for a compound sensation of relative fixedness. Properly speaking the world is not composed of "things" as its elements, but of colors, tones, pressures, spaces, times, in short what we ordinarily call individual sensations.[s]

Everywhere we look for regularities among our sensations. We do so for the following reasons. First, the practical needs of everyday living—the "struggle to satisfy our wants"—require us to be able to anticipate the behavior of nature. Second, we want to communicate with our fellow men, and we cannot do so unless we discover regularities: "That only can be . . . conceptually represented which is uniform and conformable to law; for description presupposes the employment of names by which to designate its elements; and names can acquire meanings only when applied to elements that constantly reappear."[t] Third, experience of regularity is the basis of all explanation. The "uncommon" is always "perplexing and astonishing." When, however, as a result of repetition things become familiar, "we are no longer surprised, there is nothing new or strange to us in the phenomena, we feel at home with them . . . , they are *explained*."

It behooves us, therefore, to search out, in "the infinite variety of nature," those "simple elements" that "are the same, and that amid all multiplicity are ever present." In this undertaking there is no fundamental difference in kind between prescientific and scientific thinking. Scientific thinking is merely more "economical" in satisfying the basic requirements just enumerated. Thus, "water" is a prescientific word that fixes an enduring element amid change; "H_2O" is a more exact, and hence more economical, symbol. That is, the "sensations" designated by "H_2O" are more "comprehensive, compact, and consistent" than those designated by "water."

It follows that neither "water" nor "H_2O" names a real entity (as do, for instance, "cold" and "wet"); both are only "mental artifices." Further, scientific concepts evolve as much as does the world they describe. Science does not reveal "eternal iron laws," as Haeckel supposed. It gives us flexible instrumentalities for organizing and controlling our experience.

It follows, finally, that scientific concepts can be understood only in their historical setting.

> The history of the development of mechanics is quite indispensable to a full comprehension of the science in its present condition. . . .
>
> An *instinctive*, irreflective knowledge of the processes of nature will doubtless always precede the scientific, conscious apprehension, or *investigation*, of phenomena. The former is the outcome of the relation in which the processes of nature stand to the satisfaction of our wants. The acquisition of the most elementary truth does not devolve upon the individual alone: it is pre-effected in the development of the race. . . . [But] the experiments that man heedlessly and instinctively makes in his struggle to satisfy his wants, are just as thoughtlessly and unconsciously applied . . . , and as a rule will never supply an impetus to further thought. . . .
>
> [While] there is, therefore, no result of science which in point of principle could not have been arrived at wholly without methods, . . . as a matter of fact, within the short span of a human life and with man's limited powers of memory, any stock of knowledge worthy of the name is unattainable except by the *greatest* mental economy. Science itself, therefore, may be regarded as a minimal problem, consisting of the completest possible presentment of facts with the *least possible expenditure of thought.*[u]

These ideas were further developed by Pearson in *The Grammar of Science*. Scientific concepts, he held, are merely "conceptual shorthand by aid of which [we] can briefly describe and resume phenomena."

> Atom and molecule are intellectual conceptions by aid of which physicists classify phenomena and formulate the relationships between their sequences. From a certain standpoint, therefore, these conceptions of the physicist are *supersensuous*, that is, they do not . . . represent direct sense-impressions; but the reader must be careful not to confuse this kind of supersensuousness with that of the metaphysician. . . . [The physicist's supersensuousness is a] construct of his own imagination, just so far useful as it describes his experience, and certain to be replaced by a wider concept as his insight expands. . . . On the other hand, the metaphysician asserts an existence for the supersensuous which is unconditioned . . . and has a real existence apart from the imagination of men.[v]

From this "phenomenalistic," or positivistic, point of view, the whole dispute between the materialists and the vitalists became largely verbal:

> Mechanics does not differ, as so often has been asserted, from biology or any other branch of science in its essential principles. The laws of motion no more account than the laws of cell-development for the routine of perception; both solely attempt to describe as completely and simply as possible the repeated sequences of our sense perceptions. . . . The difference between

the two branches of science is rather quantitative than qualitative; that is, the descriptions of mechanics are simpler and more general than those of biology. . . . It is not a question of reducing the universe to a "dead mechanism," but of measuring the amount of probability that one description of change of a highly generalised and simple kind will ultimately be recognised as capable of replacing another description of a more specialised and complex character. . . . Regarded from this standpoint the laws of mechanics are seen to be essentially an intellectual product, and it appears absolutely unreasonable to contrast the mechanical with the intellectual when once these words are defined in an accurate manner.[w]

Thus the problem of the "origin of life," which Driesch and Loeb had believed themselves to be solving, turns out according to a positivistic analysis to be only a pseudo-problem. The metaphysician who asks about the "source" of life, and who seeks as an answer anything more than relations among sequences of sensations, "may call it *Matter*, or *God*, or *Will*, or *Mind-stuff*, but to do so serves no useful purpose. . . . I can as little accept or deny his assertion as he forsooth can demonstrate anything about his shadowy thing-in-itself."[x]

The only "intelligible definition which can be given of the word *knowledge*" limits it to experience, to the "careful and accurate classification of facts and observation of their correlation and sequence." In a word, "there is no sphere of inquiry which lies outside the legitimate field of science." "The metaphysician is a poet, often a very great one, but unfortunately he is not known to be a poet, because he strives to clothe his poetry in the language of reason, and hence it follows that he is liable to be a dangerous member of the community."[y]

But if metaphysics, which has been regarded traditionally as the core of philosophy, is ruled out, what is the business of philosophy? The philosopher can no longer build systems or criticize the concepts of science in the Hegelian manner. He can only accept the results of modern physics; "it is the language in which these results are stated that he believes needs reconsideration." Though much reduced, philosophy still has an important function. Its business is the kind of task to which *The Grammar of Science* was devoted: the analysis and definition of the various concepts employed by the scientists in their special fields—concepts like matter, force, cause, and external world.

Logical Positivism, a movement that originated in Vienna between World War I and World War II, was the lineal descendant of Machian positivism. Perhaps its chief distinguishing mark was its reformulation of Locke's and Hume's empirical criterion of meaning. According to this reformulation, the method of verifying a proposition is the meaning of that proposition. Hence propositions that cannot be verified are meaningless, and metaphysics is disposed of at one stroke.

Mach's influence on the Viennese Circle was direct, but many philosophers who are not themselves Logical Positivists would agree with Mach and Pearson that the main business of philosophy "consists in criticizing and clarifying notions which are apt to be regarded as fundamental and accepted uncritically."[z]

Summary

Some twentieth-century writers look back on the nineteenth century, whether with scorn or with nostalgia, as a period of superb self-confidence, immutable belief, and rocklike stability. Actually, it was a century of tension and change, and of upheavals so great that even today we are struggling to adjust to them. The Industrial Revolution brought a massive shift of population to the towns, and although it created the long-range possibility of a vast improvement in man's lot, it actually produced distress, poverty, and disease—problems that we have not yet eradicated. Another and more gradual result of the Industrial Revolution was the economic unification of the world. In the course of the century Western industrial culture spread over large parts of the world, and everywhere the activities of formerly separate communities became closely meshed and interdependent. But, as society became economically more unified, other forces were working in a contrary direction. Among these was the sentiment of nationalism, the emergence of which was undoubtedly facilitated by another great nineteenth-century development—the awakening of the masses. For, although the old upper classes had been essentially cosmopolitan in outlook, with a common cultural heritage and a common ideal, the masses were rooted in the soil and in local traditions and found it natural to connect their claims to economic and political independence with a claim to national sovereignty. The new articulateness of the masses everywhere brought a broadening of the franchise, but, despite the optimism of some political theorists, it cannot be said that this development automatically solved the old problems of political control with which Plato and Aristotle had wrestled. Indeed, the new conditions of life in the nineteenth century and the development of techniques for the manipulation of public opinion made these problems even more acute.

Philosophical thinking naturally reflected all these complex currents and crosscurrents. However much they may have disagreed in other respects, all the philosophers whose views have been examined in this chapter were persuaded that reality is dynamic. But though they abandoned the Enlightenment's belief in immutable truths and inalienable rights, they held that there are "iron laws" of development that can be ascertained by applying scientific method to the study of man. Thus metaphysics was in effect replaced by philosophy of history. Comte's law of three stages, Marx's dialectical materialism, and Darwin's theory of "survival of the fittest" are examples of this development. Toward the end of the century, however, men began to suspect that all such formulas were as dogmatic in their own way as the much-scorned rationalism had been in its. Accordingly, a tendency was discernible for philosophers to conceive of their subject pragmatically and instrumentally, either as a critique of method and a means of clarifying linguistic confusion or—and here the influence of one of the major motifs of the century can be seen—as an instrument for the solution of pressing social and political problems.

CHAPTER 6

Kierkegaard and Nietzsche

However much Mill and Marx and the other philosophers discussed in the preceding chapter may have differed among themselves, they nevertheless shared certain basic assumptions. They all believed that an objective knowledge of man is attainable by applying the methods of empirical science to the study of social and psychological processes. They were all rationalists—in the broad sense that they attributed most of men's mistakes to ignorance, which is remediable, and not to sin, which Christian teaching considers "original." And they were optimists and meliorists in that they looked forward to a steady improvement in man's estate.

Though for many years this ethos remained dominant in Europe and America, a countermovement, hardly noticed at first, was also under way. The representatives of this countermovement, reflected in Dostoevsky's attack on "2 + 2" (science) and on the "Crystal Palace" (technology), rejected all the assumptions of the dominant ethos. They were as hostile to science as a cognitive enterprise as they were suspicious of the application of scientific method to the solution of economic and political problems; they were, indeed, indifferent to social welfare. All of this they wrote off contemptuously as mere "objectivity." The focus of their attention was on what they called "subjectivity." In this one respect they were a part of the mainstream of Western thought, for interest in the self had been a characteristic of philosophy since Descartes. And not only of philosophy: Since the time of the Renaissance, the culture in all its aspects had been marked by an increasing attention to the subjective flow of experience. But whereas most philosophers—Kant and Hegel, for instance—had thought of the self chiefly as a knower, the philosophers of the countermovement thought of the self as a decider and chooser; they held that we become truly a self not in the neutral contemplation of a truth but in the passionate commitment to a deed.

Kierkegaard and Nietzsche are representative of this countermovement. Both were born out of their time, when social and cultural conditions evoked neither sympathy nor understanding for their opinions. For many decades Kierkegaard was hardly known outside his native Denmark, and Nietzsche was easily written off as insane. But World War I—and, to a greater extent, World War II—drew men's attention forcefully to facts about human nature that earlier generations had ignored. The revelation of Nazi efforts to exterminate the Jews, the American atom-bomb attacks on Japanese cities, the insanities of the Cold War, the callous injustice done to Negroes, the repeated failure to resolve conflicts by peaceful means—all these suggested that man is indeed as "spiteful" as Dostoevsky had declared him to be.

In these circumstances the dominant philosophy of reasonableness and progress began to appear naïve. Almost two millenia earlier Augustine had gazed into the mirror of self-knowledge and had found himself to be ulcerous, sinful, and corrupt. During the centuries of the Enlightenment this view had been regarded not as a profound insight into human nature but as a distorted perception of a neurotic mind. But when, in the early twentieth century, men again experienced alienation and estrangement from their fellows and from the natural world, they began to regard Augustine as an unusually honest and perceptive psychologist. Even those men who were not by any means Christians came to share his—and Paul's—conviction that the human will is deeply divided and at odds with itself.

Thus, in the aftermath of World War II, the times seemed increasingly out of joint and men felt increasingly incapable of setting things right. At this point they began to take seriously thinkers like Kierkegaard and Nietzsche, philosophers who had condemned the culture that produced such alienation and estrangement, and who emphasized inwardness, rejected optimism, and taught that becoming a complete self is more important than improving one's relation with one's environment.

Kierkegaard

The bare facts of Kierkegaard's life are easily summarized. He was born in 1813. His mother had been a servant, and his father had grown up as a poverty-stricken peasant in Jutland before he settled in Copenhagen and made his fortune. Kierkegaard was a rather frail but clever boy; as a youth he lived a frivolous social life of which his father disapproved. As a result they became estranged, but just before his father's death in 1838 they were reconciled. In 1840 Kierkegaard became engaged to Regine Olsen, but the next year he broke off the engagement. Thereafter he wrote voluminously on a variety of subjects, and under a variety of complicated pseudonyms. In 1848, after experiencing a momentous conversion, he launched an attack on the Danish State Church, which seemed to him to be in a deplorable condition. While engaged in this controversy he died suddenly in 1855.

So much for externals. The facts about Kierkegaard's inner life are more interesting, and also more difficult to fathom. But it is important to ascertain them, for they stand in the closest possible relation to the development of his philosophy. That this should be the case is itself revelatory of the leading characteristic of that philosophy—its "existentialism" in fact.

Kierkegaard's Starting Point: What Am I To Do?

What I really lack is to be clear in my mind *what I am to do*, not what I am to know, except in so far as a certain understanding must precede every action. The thing is to understand myself, to see what God really wishes *me* to do; the thing is to find a truth which is true *for me*, to find *the idea for which I can live and die.* What would be the use of discovering so-called objective truth, of working through all the systems of philosophy and of being able if required, to review them all and show up the inconsistencies within each system;—what good would it do me to be able to develop a theory of the state and combine all the details into a single whole, and so construct a world in which I did not live, but only held up to the view of others;—what good would it do me to be able to explain the meaning of Christianity if it had *no* deeper significance *for me and for my life;*—what good would it do me if truth stood before me, cold and naked, not caring whether I recognised her or not, and producing in me a shudder of fear rather than a trusting devotion? I certainly do not deny that I still recognise an *imperative of understanding* and that through it one can work upon men, *but it must be taken up into my life,* and *that is* what I now recognise as the most important thing. That is what my soul longs after, as the African desert thirsts for water. That is what I lack, and that is why I am left standing like a man who has rented a house and gathered all the furniture and household things together, but has not yet found the beloved with whom to share the joys and sorrows of his life.[a]

Aristotle had believed that philosophy starts with wonder—with a kind of dispassionate curiosity about nature and about man; and most philosophers of the Western world have seemingly agreed with him. This is certainly true of Thomas, and even of Augustine, for though the latter was passionately concerned with getting into a right relation with God, he was also deeply interested in understanding what the fact of sin and the possibility of redemption tell us about the nature of God and man. Kierkegaard, however, was not a philosopher in the Aristotelian sense. For him, the philosophical enterprise was exhausted in a single, all-important question: What was he to do in order to find "peace and significance"? Or, to rephrase the question in the more psychological language Kierkegaard sometimes used: How was he to find a way of integrating his life, of giving it a "focus and a center," so that it would no longer be "a chance assemblage" of meaningless details? Kierkegaard's philosophy, then, was an intensely personal one that grew directly out of his deeply felt life-experiences. He left a detailed, if ambiguous and characteristically "indirect," record of some of these experiences—in particular, his relationship with his father and his relationship with Regine Olsen.

KIERKEGAARD AND HIS FATHER

Kierkegaard's father was an old man when Kierkegaard was born; he was a successful businessman who had risen from peasantry by a combination of good luck and hard work. He was deeply religious in a stern Protestant way, and he brought up his children to fear and venerate the Lord. The son also feared, loved, and deeply respected his father. As a child, even as a young man, Kierkegaard believed that his father led an exemplary Christian life. It was a terrible shock, then, to discover that this pious, God-fearing old man had lived in sin with his children's mother (who had been a servant in his house) before he married her. And even more shocking, to find out that his father had once cursed God in despair. "How terrible about the man who once as a little boy, while herding sheep on the heaths of Jutland, suffering greatly, in hunger and in want, stood upon a hill and cursed God—and the man was unable to forget it even when he was eighty-two years old."[b]

Kierkegaard's reaction to these discoveries is reflected at several points in his *Journals:*

> I still remember the impression it made upon me when some years ago [this entry was made in 1837, when Kierkegaard was twenty-four] . . . father said very solemnly: "there are offenses which one can only fight against with God's continual help." I hurried down to my room and looked at myself in the glass . . . —or when father said, as he often did, that it would be a good

thing to have "a venerable confessor to whom one could open one's heart." [c]

Then it was [1835] that the great earthquake occurred, the terrible revolution which suddenly forced upon me a new and infallible law of interpretation of all the facts. Then I suspected that my father's great age was not a divine blessing but rather a curse; that the outstanding intellectual gifts of our family were only given to us in order that we should rend each other to pieces. . . . There must be a guilt upon the whole family, the punishment of God must be on it. . . . [d]

I could perhaps reproduce the tragedy of my childhood . . . in a novel called "the mysterious family." It would begin on a completely idyllic, patriarchal note so that no one suspected anything until suddenly the word sounded which translated everything into terror. [e]

Thus the contrast between surface appearance and inner reality was dramatically called to the young man's attention. Furthermore, he experienced this contrast in his own life. He lived a gay and social life and was regarded by those who knew him as clever but rather superficial. Within was deep despair:

I have just returned from a party of which I was the life and soul; wit poured from my lips, everyone laughed and admired me—but I went away —and the dash should be as long as the earth's orbit _____

_____ and wanted to shoot myself. [f]

The *Journals* are full of references to "melancholy," which Kierkegaard was determined to hide from the world:

I feel so dull and so completely without joy, my soul is so empty and void that I cannot even conceive what could satisfy it—oh, not even the blessedness of heaven. [g]

It is terrible when I think, even for a single moment, over the dark background which, from the very earliest time, was part of my life. The dread[1] with which my father filled my soul, his own frightful melancholy, and all the things in this connection which I do not even note down. I felt a dread of Christianity and yet felt myself so strongly drawn towards it. [h]

An old man, himself prodigiously melancholy (wherefore I shall not write down) had a son in his old age upon whom the whole of that melancholy descended in inheritance—but at the same time he had such an elasticity of mind that he was able to conceal it. [i]

From a child I was under the sway of a prodigious melancholy, the depth of which finds its only adequate measure in the equally prodigious dexterity I possessed of hiding it under an apparent gaity and *joie de vivre*. [j]

1 [In another entry in the *Journals* (pp. 79–80) Kierkegaard defines dread as precisely this kind of ambivalence: "Dread is a desire for what one fears, a sympathetic antipathy; dread is an alien power which takes hold of the individual, and yet one cannot extricate oneself from it, does not wish to, because one is afraid, but what one fears attracts one. Dread renders the individual powerless." It is, he thought, the principal element in original sin—AUTHOR.]

But Kierkegaard had not only to hide his melancholy from the world; like his father, he had committed a secret sin:

> In his early youth a man once let himself be carried away while in a state of intoxication, and visited a prostitute. The whole thing is forgotten. Now he wants to marry. Then comes dread. The possibility of his being a father, that somewhere in the world there might be living a creature owing its existence to him, tortures him day and night. He cannot confide in anyone, he has not even any absolute assurance of the fact. —It must therefore have occurred with a prostitute, in the wild recklessness of youth; had it been a little love affair or a real seduction one could not imagine his being ignorant, but it is precisely his ignorance which is the disturbing element in his torture. On the other hand his doubt could only really appear when he falls in love, precisely because of the thoughtlessness of the whole affair.[2][k]

KIERKEGAARD AND REGINE OLSEN

This brings us to the second life-experience that profoundly affected the development of Kierkegaard's philosophy. In 1837 he met Regine Olsen, who had just turned fourteen. For him it was love at first sight. They became engaged in 1840, but about a year later, despite Regine's protests, he broke off the engagement. When he had first proposed to her he had "warned her against myself, against my melancholy."[1] Yet he had not told her *all*, and since he could not bring himself to do so, he felt that their relationship was false (in a terminology that later became fashionable, he felt himself to be in "bad faith").

> If I had not been a penitent, . . . had not been melancholy, my union with her would have made me happier than I had ever dreamed of being. But in so far as I was what, alas, I was, I had to say that I could be happier in my unhappiness without her than with her. . . .
>
> There was a divine protest, that is how I understood it. The wedding. I had to hide such a tremendous amount from her, had to base the whole thing upon something untrue.[m]
>
> Had I not honoured her above myself, as my future wife, had I not been prouder of her honour than of mine, then I should have remained silent and have fulfilled her desire and mine, and have been married to her—there are so many marriages that conceal their little tale. That I did not want; in that way she would have become my concubine; I would rather have murdered her. —But if I had had to explain myself then I would have had to initiate her into terrible things, my relation to my father, his melancholy, the eternal darkness that broods deep within, my going astray, pleasures and excesses which in the eyes of God are not perhaps so terrible, for it was dread that drove me to excess, and where was I to look for something to hold on to when I knew, or suspected that the one man I revered for his power and strength had wavered.[n]

2 [Like so many of Kierkegaard's self-revelations, this was recorded as if it were the sketch of a plot for a novel. But there is little doubt that it had a real-life basis—AUTHOR.]

After he had sacrificed Regine, he apparently hoped that God would give her back to him—as Yahweh had returned Isaac to Abraham after Abraham had prepared himself to sacrifice Isaac for Yahweh.[3] He was greatly chagrined when Regine promptly married the suitor whom Kierkegaard had replaced, but later he concluded that this was for the best: Love for Regine was incompatible with love for God; he had to choose between them.

> She has not, after all, the first place in my life. No, no, humanly speaking certainly—and how willing would I not prove it, she has and shall have the first place in my life—but God has the first place. My engagement to her and the break are really my relation to God, they are, if I may say so, divinely speaking, my engagement with God.[o]

The inner struggle over what he should do, the terribly difficult decision, and the bitterly disappointing and humiliating aftermath produced a crisis:

> I was so deeply shaken that I understood perfectly well that I could not possibly succeed in striking the comforting and secure *via media* in which most people pass their lives: I had either to cast myself into perdition and sensuality, or to choose the religious absolutely as the only thing—either the world in a measure that would be dreadful, or the cloister. That it was the second I would and must choose was at bottom already determined . . . ; I had become thoroughly aware how impossible it would be for me to be religious only up to a certain point.[p]

By "cloister" Kierkegaard of course did not mean literally a monastic life. He meant a life that, though perhaps outwardly indistinguishable from that of other men, was wholly dedicated to God, a life in which he was to devote himself to the task of becoming a Christian and, at the same time, of bringing to the attention of others what is involved in becoming a Christian. It is in the light of this double task that his huge literary and philosophical production should be read.

Existence and Reality

Perhaps the most philosophical item in this production is the *Concluding Unscientific Postscript*. Its highly personal and "expressive" style reveals Kierkegaard's conception of the nature and function of philosophy. The purpose of philosophy is not to instruct, but to "edify," that is, to improve us by changing us. The point of view is passionate, not neutral; practical, not speculative; subjective, not objective; inner, not outer; existential, not systematic. And the

3 See pp. 225–26.

point of departure is the self—not the self in general but the particular, existing self of Søren Kierkegaard.

> It is impossible to exist without passion, unless we understand the word "exist" in the loose sense of a so-called existence. Every Greek thinker was therefore essentially a passionate thinker. I have often reflected how one might bring a man into a state of passion. I have thought in this connection that if I could get him seated on a horse and the horse made to take fright and gallop wildly, or better still, for the sake of bringing the passion out, if I could take a man who wanted to arrive at a certain place as quickly as possible, and hence already had some passion, and could set him astride a horse that can scarcely walk—and yet this is what existence is like if one is to become consciously aware of it. Or if a driver were otherwise not especially inclined toward passion, if someone hitched a team of horses to a wagon for him, one of them a Pegasus and the other a worn-out jade, and told him to drive—I think one might succeed. And it is just this that it means to exist, if one is to become conscious of it. Eternity is the winged horse, infinitely fast, and time is a worn-out jade; the existing individual is the driver. That is to say, he is such a driver when his mode of existence is not an existence loosely so called; for then he is no driver, but a drunken peasant who lies asleep in the wagon and lets the horses take care of themselves. To be sure, he also drives and is a driver; and so there are perhaps many who—also exist.q

Two important points are brought out in this passage. First, existence is a qualitative matter: It is true that there is something that people *call* existence—living the life of daily routine, conforming to social norms that others have established for them. But real existence differs qualitatively from what T. S. Eliot called "a little life of dried tubers." Truly to exist is to struggle, to strain, to encounter opposition, to experience passion; it is to make decisions, not to drift with the tide. Second, existence and selfhood are identical; to exist in what has just been called the "real" sense is to *become*, not merely to be, a self. Hence, though Kierkegaard did not draw this conclusion explicitly, things that are not selves do not have an independent status; they "are" only insofar as they are "for" selves.

Ironically, despite all the contempt he had for Hegel's philosophy, Kierkegaard's views are in many ways similar to Hegel's.[4] For instance, according to Kierkegaard the self is not a preexisting, fully formed thing that can be discovered by looking in the right direction, as the continent of North America was once discovered by sailing in the right direction; it is not something "shut in a box with a spring-lock."r To put this insight in Hegelian terms, the self is not substance but subject. But whereas Hegel's subject-self was primarily a self-conscious knower, Kierkegaard's was primarily a doer; and whereas Hegel

4 See pp. 110–13.

had held that things exist "for" minds, as objects of knowledge, Kierkegaard believed that things exist "for" agents, as objects encountered and mastered.

Furthermore, Hegel had certainly included passion in his theory. Nothing great, he said, is accomplished without passion: It is passion that moves those world-historical individuals (for instance, Julius Caesar and Napoleon) who destroy an outmoded society and create a new social order.[5] In some respects—in their energy and their passion—Hegel's world-historical figures are very close to Kierkegaard's "true" selves; but though Kierkegaard held that creativity involves the destruction of old social norms, he by no means identified creativity with the fashioning of new ones. And there are other differences of emphasis that made it easy for Kierkegaard—who was a passionate advocate, not a neutral judge—to regard Hegel as the very model of the abstract thinker. Above all, whatever Hegel might *say* about passion and subjectivity, he was certainly neither passionate nor subjective in his attitude toward them. In calling attention to the difference between saying and doing (or, rather, between saying and being), Kierkegaard scored effectively—and by no means merely against Hegel.

> The difficulty that inheres in existence, with which the existing individual is confronted, is one that never really comes to expression in the language of abstract thought, much less receives an explanation. . . . Abstract thought . . . ignores the concrete and the temporal, the existential process, the predicament of the existing individual arising from his being a synthesis of the temporal and the eternal situated in existence. . . .
>
> One must therefore be very careful in dealing with a philosopher of the Hegelian school, and, above all, to make certain of the identity of the being with whom one has the honor to discourse. Is he a human being, an existing human being? Is he himself *sub specie aeterni*, even when he sleeps, eats, blows his nose, or whatever else a human being does? Is he himself the pure "I am I"? . . . Does he in fact exist? And if he does, is he then not in process of becoming? And if he is in process of becoming, does he not face the future? And does he ever face the future by way of action? And if he never does, will he not forgive an ethical individuality for saying in passion and with dramatic truth, that he is an ass? But if he ever acts *sensu eminenti*, does he not in that case face the future with infinite passion? Is there not then for him an either-or? Is it not the case that eternity is for an existing individual not eternity, but the future, and that eternity is eternity only for the Eternal, who is not in process of becoming? . . .
>
> All logical thinking employs the language of abstraction, and is *sub specie aeterni*. To think existence logically is thus to ignore the difficulty, the difficulty, that is, of thinking the eternal as in process or becoming. But this difficulty is unavoidable, since the thinker himself is in process of becoming. It is easier to indulge in abstract thought than it is to exist, unless we understand by this latter term what is loosely called existing, in analogy with what is loosely called being a subject. Here we have again an example of the fact that the simplest tasks are the most difficult. Existing is ordinarily

5 See p. 188.

regarded as no very complex matter, much less an art, since we all exist; but abstract thinking takes rank as an accomplishment. But really to exist, so as to interpenetrate one's existence with consciousness, at one and the same time eternal and as if far removed from existence, and yet also present in existence and in the process of becoming: that is truly difficult. . . .[s]

THE AGONY OF DECISION

Here, then, are two contrasting notions of what it is to exist. One of these notions equates existing with thinking: Descartes' "I think, therefore I am" is typical of the point of view of abstract philosophy. The other view equates existing with the "predicament" of decision, with the suffering of a man who wants desperately to do right but who lacks the information he feels he needs for making a choice. These two notions of existence may be contrasted in the following way. One is characteristic of an observer who contemplates the agony of decision from the neutral vantage point of a thinker, who dispassionately "takes note of" the blood, sweat, and tears from outside. The other notion is characteristic of a participant, who shares in and directly experiences the agony of decision—he bleeds, sweats, and weeps with the decider.

Kierkegaard regarded the external and detached point of view as easy (anyone can be a "subject," if this means only to think) and also superficial. It wholly misses the inner reality of what it is to be human. Of course, when Kierkegaard equated existence with the agony of being in a predicament, he was really describing his own life-experience, which was characterized by conflict and division. He both loved and feared his father, both admired and condemned him. He both hoped to marry Regine and wished to reject her. Thus, Kierkegaard's approach to philosophy was in a sense empirical. Indeed, he can be said to have been more rigorously empirical than so-called empiricists like Locke or Hume: His conception of the self was rooted in the deepest, most direct life-experience; their conception was actually derived from metaphysical and logical considerations. Further, whereas most empiricists were interested in formulating generalizations (for instance, the "laws" of association) about the nature of the self, Kierkegaard was an empiricist only in order to shed light on the predicament of every man who is honest with himself and who takes decision seriously.

And, of course, Kierkegaard did not merely want men to take decision seriously. He wanted, first, to relate the predicament of decision to his religious beliefs and, second, to persuade others of what he himself had become persuaded— that the only "cure" for the agony was to become a Christian. Kierkegaard solved the first problem, and laid the basis for solving the second, by interweaving a number of closely related themes—the contrasts between infinity and finitude, eternity and time, movement and stasis, possibility and actuality.

> Existence . . . is a difficult category to deal with; for if I think it, I abrogate it, and then I do not think it. It might therefore seem to be the proper thing to say that there is something which cannot be thought, namely, existence.

But the difficulty persists, in that existence itself combines thinking with existing, in so far as the thinker exists. . . .

It is on this point about existence, and the demand which the ethical makes upon each existing individual, that one must insist when an abstract philosophy and a pure thought assume to explain everything by explaining away what is decisive. It is necessary only to have the courage to be human, and to refuse to be terrified or tricked into becoming a phantom merely to save embarrassment. . . .

In so far as existence consists in movement there must be something which can give continuity to the movement and hold it together, for otherwise there is no movement. Just as the assertion that everything is true means that nothing is true, so the assertion that everything is in motion means that there is no motion as its measure and its end. . . . Now while pure thought either abrogates motion altogether, or meaninglessly imports it into logic, the difficulty facing an existing individual is now to give his existence the continuity without which everything simply vanishes. An abstract continuity is no continuity, and the very existence of the existing individual is sufficient to prevent his continuity from having essential stability; while passion gives him a momentary continuity, a continuity which at one and the same time is a restraining influence and a moving impulse. The goal of movement for an existing individual is to arrive at a decision, and to renew it.

Existence constitutes the highest interest of the existing individual, and his interest in his existence constitutes his reality. What reality is, cannot be expressed in the language of abstraction . . . Abstract thought can get hold of reality only by nullifying it. . . .

All knowledge about reality is possibility. The only reality to which an existing individual may have a relation that is more than cognitive, is his own reality, the fact that he exists; this reality constitutes his absolute interest. Abstract thought requires him to become disinterested in order to acquire knowledge; the ethical demand is that he become infinitely interested in existing.

The only reality that exists for an existing individual is his own ethical reality. To every other reality he stands in a cognitive relation; but true knowledge consists in translating the real into the possible.

The real subject is not the cognitive subject, since in knowing he moves in the sphere of the possible; the real subject is the ethically existing subject. . . .[t]

These, then, are the reasons why the self is divided and in conflict. To begin with, though we men live in time, we have an idea of eternity. Time—change through time, getting older, not having time for everything—is an omnipresent and painful feature of life-experience. Life would be easy indeed if we were merely animals. We would, of course, actually live out our lives in time—present, past, and future; but we would not be conscious of ourselves as temporal beings. However, since we are men and not animals, we know that we are going to die, that at some point time will stop for us. To live in time is to be limited with respect to what one can do. To be conscious is to be aware of this limitation;

it is to know that there are many options and that, when we choose one, all the others are excluded. Though we presumably gain something by choosing this option, we certainly lose something as well—we lose all the others. The trouble is that we can never be sure, it would seem, that what we have gained exceeds what we have lost. Hence the agony of decision.

THE CURE FOR THE AGONY

If these are the causes of agony, what is the cure? According to Kierkegaard, it is to become passionately committed to one of the options. It is a psychological fact that, to the extent that we commit ourselves utterly and passionately to one option (from the psychological point of view, it does not matter which one), we no longer care about the others. At this moment the agony of decision obviously disappears. Passion alone may be satisfactory psychologically, but it is hardly satisfactory ethically. It is possible, for instance, in a moment of passionate anger to strike out impulsively and kill a man. This is why Kierkegaard emphasized commitment as well as passion. His point was that the act to which one becomes passionately committed must be deliberately chosen. Or, as stated in the passage above, "Really to exist is to interpenetrate one's existence with consciousness. . . . Existence itself combines thinking with existence." Unfortunately, most men probably alternate between being conscious and being passionate. Like Hamlet, they find that consciousness makes them cowards—it makes them cautious, careful, and hesitant. And caution, care, and hesitation are incompatible with passion.

Yet, although the state in which an "interpenetration" of consciousness and passion occurs is perhaps rare, it is not a psychological impossibility. Would it then be the cure for which Kierkegaard was looking? No; there is one additional, and all-important, requirement. To understand what this is, contrast Kierkegaard's position with that of a psychiatrist who wishes to help a patient agonizing over decision. If the psychiatrist adopted Kierkegaard's psychological theory, he would aim at getting his patient to interpenetrate consciousness with passion. If the patient's agony were thereby alleviated, he would be satisfied; his job would be done. For Kierkegaard, this was not enough; he was not a psychiatrist but a Christian advocate. He was interested not in mental health but in salvation. Hence he could not be satisfied with any passionate commitment that happened to alleviate suffering; it had to be a passionate commitment to the Christian God. His contention was that only this commitment would alleviate the agony, and his reasoning seems to have been that a complete cure requires a complete commitment, that is, an "infinite" commitment. But only a commitment to an infinite person can be infinite. Hence only a religious—and, specifically, a Christian—commitment is really a solution to man's existential problem.

This move from a psychological to a religious resolution of despair was fundamental for Kierkegaard, who was, above all else, a Christian thinker. If it is doubtful that his discussion would convince anyone not already convinced on other grounds, it is also true that, unlike most other philosophers, Kierkegaard held that no discussion ever convinces on logical grounds. It may, however, edify; that is, it may move men to change their ways. If it does, that is enough; it is, indeed, everything. It is necessary to bear this point of view in mind as the discussion develops.

The Nature of Choice

Since Kierkegaard's starting point was the existential fact that men are faced with an either-or, we must understand the nature of choice. There is a fundamental difference—which everyone can experience within himself—between choosing and merely wishing or wanting. This distinction must not be confused with the difference between bringing about some external change and failing to bring it about. Choosing is inner; it is not at all dependent on successfully producing a change in the state of affairs. It is distinguished from mere wishing or wanting in that it is an act of will; that is, it involves a commitment, a movement, of the personality.

> The real action is not the external act, but an internal decision in which the individual puts an end to the mere possibility and identifies himself with the content of his thought in order to exist in it. . . .
> When I think of something good that I intend to do, is this identical with having done it? By no means. But neither is it the external that constitutes the criterion of action; for the human being who does not own a penny can be as charitable as one who gives away a kingdom. When the Levite journeyed along the road traversed by the unfortunate man who, between Jericho and Jerusalem, had fallen among thieves, it may well have occurred to him while he was still some distance away, how beautiful a deed it is to help a sufferer in his distress. He may perhaps even have thought, by way of anticipation, that a good deed of this sort has its reward in itself; and perhaps he rode more slowly because of his absorption in this thought. But as he came nearer the place where the victim was, the difficulties began to heap themselves up before his mind—and he rode past. Now he doubtless began to make haste, in order to get away quickly from the thought of the insecurity of the road, from the thought of the possible presence of the robbers near by, from the thought of how readily the victim might be led to confuse him with the robbers who had left him there to die. He failed to act. But now suppose that he was seized by remorse, that he turned quickly about, fearing neither the robbers nor other difficulties, but fearing only lest he arrive too late. Let us suppose that he did arrive too late, the good Samaritan having already managed to get the sufferer into the shelter of the inn. Had he not then acted? Certainly he had acted, and that in spite of the fact that he had no opportunity to act in the external sense. . . .[u]

In his emphasis on inner motivation rather than on overt action Kierkegaard was close to Kant; and both philosophers, of course, were echoing the Christian thesis that "it is what comes out of a man that pollutes him. For it is from inside, from men's hearts, that designs of evil come." [v] But Kierkegaard's interpretation of inwardness differs from Kant's in a way that reflects the great movement that culminated, before the end of the nineteenth century, in abandonment of the Enlightenment's emphasis on rationality and autonomy. Kant had distinguished between what he called heteronomy and freedom of the will. Man is free when he acts autonomously, that is, when he acts from respect for a law he has imposed on himself.[6] From Kierkegaard's point of view a self-imposed law is no law, for the essence of law is compulsion. To act from self-respect is not (as Kant had thought) to achieve the highest morality; it is to fall into the sin of pride.

> Kant held that man was his own law (autonomy), *i.e.* bound himself under the law which he gave himself. In a deeper sense that means to say: lawlessness or experimentation. It is no harder than the thwacks which Sancho Panza applied to his own bottom. . . . There [must be] some third and compelling factor, which is not the individual himself. . . .
>
> Not only is the law which I give myself . . . not a law; but there is a law which is given to me by one higher than I. And not only that; but that lawgiver takes the liberty of joining in at the same time in the character of educator and applies the compulsion.
>
> Now if during the whole of his life a man never acts in so decisive a way that the educator can get a hold on him: well, then the man is certainly allowed to live on complacently in a state of illusion, imagination, experimentation—but that also connotes: the greatest lack of grace.[w]

THE ETHICAL LIFE CONTRASTED WITH THE ESTHETIC

Whereas Kant had distinguished two kinds of choice, heteronomy and autonomy, Kierkegaard distinguished three. He called these three ways of choosing, or attitudes toward choice, the esthetic, the ethical, and the religious. In the esthetic life choice is not taken seriously. At this level a man may take the view that "it doesn't matter what I choose; it will all turn out equally well"—or, alternatively, "equally badly." Thus, the esthetic life is either happy-go-lucky or cynical. The ethical life, in contrast, is serious. At this level men live, not by whim or impulse, but by an ethical code. Choice becomes problematic and serious since ethical men must decide how their code applies to the various concrete situations in which they find themselves. From this point of view, the particular code that they live by is less important than the fact that they have chosen to live by a code—if, indeed, they have *chosen* their code instead of merely drifting into it as a part of their inheritance from the culture in which they grew up.

6 See pp. 81–82.

> It is not so much a question of choosing the right as of the energy, the earnestness, the pathos with which one chooses. Thereby the personality announces its inner infinity, and thereby, in turn, the personality is consolidated. . . .
>
> My either/or does not in the first instance denote the choice between good and evil; it denotes the choice whereby one chooses good *and* evil/or excludes them. Here the question is under what determinants one would contemplate the whole of existence and would himself live. That the man who chooses good and evil chooses good is indeed true, but this becomes evident only afterwards; for the aesthetical is not the evil but neutrality. . . . It is, therefore, not so much a question of choosing between willing the good *or* the evil, as of choosing to will, but by this in turn the good and the evil are posited. . . . Here you see again how important it is that a choice be made, and that the crucial thing is not deliberation but the baptism of the will which lifts up the choice into the ethical.[x]

If this passage sounds like Kant, it is because Kierkegaard has not yet reached the religious level in his discussion, and because Kant, in Kierkegaard's view, never remotely reached it. Thus, though both philosophers emphasized the primacy of motive (and moral seriousness, as distinct from a merely esthetic life), they differed profoundly about what this motive is. Kant believed that the morally good motive consisted in treating men as ends in themselves, not merely as means.[7] In this respect his view exemplified the Enlightenment's belief in self-respect and its high regard for human nature. But Kierkegaard held that this view turned everything upside down. Man is finite, God is infinite; man is a sinner, God is merciful. It is essential for each man to recognize these relations and to act on them—to give himself to God utterly and completely. Further, whereas Kant believed that it is possible to work out rationally how we ought to act (the categorical imperative is universal and demonstrable, since its denial involves a contradiction), Kierkegaard believed that nothing can be proved and that a leap of faith is necessary. And this leap is necessary not merely in the sense that it is something we have to put up with in our state of ignorance, in the way I might say that it is necessary to walk because I do not have the money for a taxi. Rather, the leap of faith is necessary in the sense that it makes religion "religion." Indeed, it is just that passionate commitment that has already been described at the psychological level.[8]

THE RELIGIOUS LIFE CONTRASTED WITH THE ETHICAL

Socrates' decision to believe in immortality when there was, and could be, no proof of immortality is an example of such a commitment and is thus religious in nature.

7 See pp. 79–80.
8 See pp. 214–15.

When one man investigates objectively the problem of immortality, and another embraces an uncertainty with the passion of the infinite: where is there most truth, and who has the greater certainty? The one has entered upon a never-ending approximation, for the certainty of immortality lies precisely in the subjectivity of the individual; the other is immortal, and fights for his immortality by struggling with the uncertainty. Let us consider Socrates. Nowadays everyone dabbles in a few proofs; some have several such proofs, others fewer. But Socrates! He puts the question objectively in a problematic manner: *if* there is an immortality. He must therefore be accounted a doubter in comparison with one of our modern thinkers with the three proofs?[9] By no means. On this "if" he risks his entire life, he has the courage to meet death, and he has with the passion of the infinite so determined the pattern of his life that it must be found acceptable—*if* there is an immortality. Is any better proof capable of being given for the immortality of the soul? But those who have the three proofs do not at all determine their lives in conformity therewith; if there is an immortality it must feel disgust over their manner of life: can any better refutation be given of these three proofs? The bit of uncertainty that Socrates had, helped him because he himself contributed the passion of the infinite; the three proofs that the others have do not profit them at all, because they are dead to spirit and enthusiasm. . . . The Socratic ignorance, which Socrates held fast with the entire passion of his inwardness, was thus an expression for the principle that the eternal truth is related to an existing individual, and that this truth must therefore be a paradox for him as long as he exists. . . .[y]

Though Socrates' passionate commitment to an immortality that he knew could not be proved shows him to have been religious "in the highest sense in which this was possible within paganism,"[z] there is an enormous difference between his religion and Christianity. For though there is no objective evidence for personal immortality, belief in immortality is not absurd. In contrast, the Christian belief in a God who became man and suffered on the cross for sinners is literally absurd. The Christian's commitment is, then, far more difficult than was Socrates'. Nevertheless, "carefully used," Socrates' story can be "adapted to the problem of becoming a Christian."[a] For the Socratic affirmation of immortality "is an analogue to faith; only that the inwardness of faith, corresponding as it does, not to the repulsion of the Socratic ignorance, but to the repulsion exerted by the absurd, is infinitely more profound."[b]

Thus the difference between the ethical stage and the religious stage is not the difference between two kinds of acts, for the same act may be done from a merely ethical motive (or indeed from an esthetic motive) as from a religious motive. Nor is it merely the difference between calculation and commitment, for a man may be passionately serious at the ethical stage. The difference, rather, is that between commitment to, say, a cause or code and commitment to God.

9 [Kierkegaard is referring to the three "classic" proofs of the existence of God, which Kant had criticized. See pp. 55–58—AUTHOR.]

Only when we make the latter commitment does our life acquire the focus and center for which we have been longing; this is because, as has been said, an infinite commitment is necessary, and it can be made only to an infinite person.

As long as a person lives by what Kant called the principle of autonomy he is in despair. He can be, as Kant himself was, passionately serious about duty. Indeed, in a sense, the more serious a person is, the more he is in despair, because he realizes that as long as he relies on his own judgment, he can never be sure what he is doing is right. It is not enough for someone to say to himself that he has done the best he can; the only exit from self-destructive doubt is for him to see that, if he relies on himself, he is *never* right. Then he is ready, in despair, to throw himself on God.

> No earnest doubt, no really deep concern, is put to rest by the saying that one does what one can. If a man is sometimes in the right, sometimes in the wrong, to a certain degree in the right, to a certain degree in the wrong, who, then, is to decide this except man; but in deciding it may he not be to a certain degree in the right, to a certain degree in the wrong? . . . Must doubt then prevail, constantly discovering new difficulties . . . ? We have, then, only the choice of being nothing before God, or the eternal torture of beginning over again every instant, but without being able to begin. For if we are to be able to determine definitely whether at the present instant we are in the right, this question must be definitely determined with a view to the preceding instant and then further and further back. . . .
>
> How might a man be able to depict his relationship to God by a more or a less, or by an approximate definition? . . . Only by an infinite relationship to God [can] doubt be calmed, only by an infinitely free relationship to God [can] anxiety be transformed into joy. [A man] is in an infinite relationship to God when he recognizes that God is always in the right, in an infinitely free relationship to God when he recognizes that he himself is always in the wrong. In this way, therefore, doubt is checked, for the movement of doubt consists precisely in the fact that at one instant he might be in the right, at another in the wrong, to a certain degree in the right, to a certain degree in the wrong. . . . So whenever doubt would . . . teach him that he suffers too much, that he is tried beyond his powers, he thereupon forgets the finite in the infinite thought that he is always in the wrong. Whenever the affliction of doubt would make him sad, he thereupon raises himself above the finite into the infinite; for the thought that he is always in the wrong is the wing whereby he soars above finitude, it is the longing wherewith he seeks God, it is the love wherein he finds God.[c]

In contrast to the despair of doubt is the assurance of faith. This assurance is compatible with uncertainty; indeed, what distinguishes faith from other states of mind is the tension between assurance and objective uncertainty. This brings us back to Kierkegaard's earlier distinction between the thinker and the existing individual. Truth for the thinker is an objective state of affairs that is capable of being formulated more and more precisely by an approximation process. Truth for the existing individual is that to which he is passionately committed. Thus for the existing individual, as distinct from the abstract thinker, truth and faith are the same. Both truth and faith involve

> . . . the tension of the subjective inwardness. Here is such a definition of truth: *An objective uncertainty held fast in an appropriation-process of the most passionate inwardness is the truth*, the highest truth attainable for an *existing* individual. . . . Thus the subject merely has, objectively, the uncertainty; but it is this which precisely increases the tension of that infinite passion which constitutes his inwardness. The truth is precisely the venture which chooses an objective uncertainty with the passion of the infinite. I contemplate the order of nature in the hope of finding God, and I see omnipotence and wisdom; but I also see much else that disturbs my mind and excites anxiety. The sum of all this is an objective uncertainty. But it is for this very reason that the inwardness becomes as intense as it is, for it embraces this objective uncertainty with the entire passion of the infinite. In the case of a mathematic proposition the objectivity is given, but for this reason the truth of such a proposition is an indifferent truth [that is, the sort of truth that is contemplated by a thinker].
>
> But the above definition of truth is an equivalent expression for faith. Without risk there is no faith. Faith is precisely the contradiction between the infinite passion of the individual's inwardness and the objective uncertainty. If I am capable of grasping God objectively, I do not believe, but precisely because I cannot do this I must believe. If I wish to preserve myself in faith I must constantly be intent upon holding fast to the objective uncertainty, so as to remain out upon the deep, over seventy thousand fathoms of water, still preserving my faith.[d]

Thus, as we have seen, the cure for doubt, the cure for the agonizing suspicion that despite all our efforts we *may* have chosen wrongly, is to realize that if we rely on our own efforts we *always* choose wrongly. We should, then, give up trying and put ourselves completely and unreservedly in God's hand. We must have faith that what we are doing has been chosen for us by God. A person who acts in this spirit is released from distress; he is "saved."

But, someone may ask, cannot such a person be mistaken? Of course, as long as he is persuaded that God has chosen for him, he will be spared all anxiety. But is he really saved, or does he only *think* he is saved? One answer to this question—and perhaps in the end the only answer—is that by raising this doubt one has adopted an abstract point of view. The questioner has become a "thinker". He is no longer an existing individual; he has taken himself out of the religious sphere. To reenter it he must once again enclose his doubt within the passionate commitment of faith.

This answer is admittedly a paradox. It is best to postpone further consideration of it until one of Kierkegaard's most characteristic notions—the teleological suspension of the ethical—has been examined, for this concept provides still another account of the all-important contrast between the ethical and the religious stages.

The Teleological Suspension of the Ethical

According to Kierkegaard, just as Socrates may be considered the paradigm of pagan religion, so Abraham can be taken as an exemplar of Christian attitudes. For both Socrates and Abraham truth was subjective; it involved a total commitment of their lives to something they knew could not be proved. But whereas Socrates' passion was directed toward an idea, Abraham's was directed toward a person, a God who commands absolute obedience and who will educate men[10] if they only act in a sufficiently decisive way.

This point about Abraham can best be understood by contrasting him with a tragic hero like Brutus. Both men disobeyed the universal moral requirement that fathers should succour, support, and defend the lives of their children. Brutus ordered his son killed when he was found to be conspiring against the Roman republic. This was a tragic decision, but it remained within the sphere of the ethical, for his decision was in accordance with a universal moral requirement—the duty of a political leader to preserve the state. In fact, this duty is an even higher expression of the ethical than is the universal moral requirement that parents love their children more than they love themselves.

> With Abraham the situation was different. By his act he overstepped the ethical entirely and possessed a higher *telos* outside of it, in relation to which he suspended the former. For I should very much like to know how one would bring Abraham's act into relation with the universal, and whether it is possible to discover any connection whatever between what Abraham did and the universal . . . except the fact that he transgressed it. It was not for the sake of saving a people, not to maintain the idea of the state, that Abraham did this. . . . Abraham's whole action stands in no relation to the universal, is a purely private undertaking. . . .
>
> Here is evident the necessity of a new category if one would understand Abraham. Such a relationship to the deity paganism did not know. The tragic hero does not enter into any private relationship with the deity, but for him the ethical is the divine, hence the paradox implied in his situation can be mediated in the universal.
>
> Therefore, though Abraham arouses my admiration, he at the same time appalls me. . . . The tragic hero gives up the certain for the still more certain, and the eye of the beholder rests upon him confidently. But he who gives up the universal in order to grasp something still higher which is not the universal—what is he doing? Is it possible that this can be anything else but a temptation (*Anfechtung*)? And if . . . the individual was mistaken—what can save him? He suffers all the pain of the tragic hero, he brings to naught his joy in the world, he renounces everything . . . and perhaps at the same instant debars himself from the sublime joy which to him was so precious that he would purchase it at any price. Him the beholder cannot understand nor let his eye rest confidently upon him. Perhaps it is not possible to do what the believer proposes, since it is indeed unthinkable. Or if it could be

10 See p. 220.

done, but if the individual had misunderstood the deity—what can save him? . . .

But now when the ethical is thus teleologically suspended, how does the individual exist in whom it is suspended? . . . How then did Abraham exist? He believed. This is the paradox which keeps him upon the sheer edge and which he cannot make clear to any other man, for the paradox is that he as the individual puts himself in an absolute relation to the absolute . . . .[e]

When Kierkegaard wrote this account of Abraham, he was thinking of his own situation. Just as Abraham had had to choose between God and Isaac, so, it seemed to Kierkegaard, he had had to choose between God and Regine. Now, it may be that on occasion religion demands this kind of choice; certainly individuals who have violated an existing moral code have sometimes justified their actions in this way. But the very drama of a decision like Abraham's, suggesting as it does that religion appertains only to exceptional circumstances, distorts the point Kierkegaard wanted to make: Actually, he wanted to bring together "the absoluteness of the religious and the particularities of life."[f] That is, he thought it important to show that it is possible for the ordinary man to be religious in even the most ordinary of circumstances.

The example Kierkegaard chose to illustrate this thesis was deliberately as trivial as possible. It was the question of how to choose to go on an outing to the Deer Park, a favorite expedition for the citizens of Copenhagen in Kierkegaard's day. He set out to show that it is not necessary to choose between God and the outing: One can become "so religious that he is able before God to resolve to take an outing in the Deer Park,"[g] just as Abraham was able before God to resolve to slay Isaac. Once again, the critical issue for religion is not what one does but the spirit in which one acts (the intense inwardness of one's commitment to that act).

What is necessary—whether a person is trying to decide to kill his son or whether he is only trying to decide to go to the Deer Park—is to recognize that he cannot reach certainty by an approximation process. Equally as many doubts can arise about whether he should make the excursion, and if so, when he should set out and at what hour he should return, as can arise about whether it is really God who is telling him to kill his son. Doubtless from the point of view of a utilitarian calculation of results in *this* world, the latter decision is much more difficult because so much more depends on it. But, in Kierkegaard's view, utilitarian results are trivial as compared with the need for getting in a right relation with God. Getting in a right relation with God consists in bringing one's will into loving obedience. This is no more difficult in the case of the Deer Park decision than in the case of Abraham's decision, for—and this is the whole point—the individual can *never* achieve this for himself. In every case, therefore, he must have faith that God has brought his will into obedience, for this is no more problematic in one case than in any other.

The religious individual is unable to bring the God-idea together with such accidental finitude as . . . taking a pleasure outing in the Deer Park. He feels the pain of this. . . . The difficulty is first and foremost to attain to a compre-hension of his inability, and so to annul the illusion, since he should always bear in mind that he can do nothing of himself—this difficulty [the religious man] has conquered, and now there remains the second difficulty: with God to be able to do it.[h]

Abraham, or any man in his position, could never be certain he is obeying God; indeed, the more he knows (as a thinker, as a result of an approximation process), the more uncertain he must become. Since he cannot exclude the possibility that he is moved by unconscious jealousy, by a reverse Oedipal complex, he experiences agony as he presses the knife to his son's throat. The uncertainty holds also for the citizen of Copenhagen who is trying to decide whether to take an outing in the Deer Park. And the same is true for Kierkegaard himself: The more he thought about it, the less certain he was that he had really abandoned Regine for God's sake and not for his own sake—because he was ashamed to confess his earlier delinquencies, or because he was afraid of a sexual relationship, or simply because he was bored by the girl. In all three cases—in all cases whatever—the religious requirement is the same. One must be fully aware of the objective uncertainty and one must embrace this uncertainty with "the entire passion of the infinite." Thus religion does not consist simply in obeying God (an objective state of affairs), for one can never *know* that one is obeying God, and if one could know, one's faith would disappear. Rather, religion consists in having faith that one is obeying God.

Was Kierkegaard a Christian?

Holding such views as these, was Kierkegaard a Christian? He certainly wanted to be; he certainly thought he was. Indeed, in emphasizing inwardness he believed himself to be returning to the "true" Christianity. But, given his subjective view of truth, in what sense can any conception of Christianity be objectively truer than any other?

It is easy, of course, to understand why Kierkegaard emphasized inwardness. He saw that it had been relatively easy to be a Christian when Christianity consisted of but a small persecuted sect. In those days one knew whether or not one was a Christian, for it took a conscious decision, an act of will, a real commitment, to be a Christian. In nineteenth-century Europe, however, where "everyone" was a Christian, in a sense no one was. Someone who is born into a Christian family and is brought up as Christian finds himself going to Church on Sundays and performing the rites as a matter of routine, or possibly because he feels the service is "beautiful." This person calls himself a Christian without deciding to be one, or even thinking about what being a Christian means. It was natural, then, for Kierkegaard to insist on passion and commitment as the heart of inwardness.

But it may be that he went too far in the direction of subjectivity—farther than he himself intended to go. "If only the mode of this relationship is in the truth, the individual is in the truth even if he should happen to be thus related to what is not true." [i] When truth is defined as passionate inwardness, it seems to follow that the belief of a Hindu that Vishnu is God, the belief of a Mohammedan that Allah is God, the belief of a Nuer that *kwoth* is God—even the belief of an atheist that there is no God—are all true, providing only that in each of these beliefs an objective uncertainty is embraced with passionate intensity. "The objective accent falls on *what* is said, the subjective accent on *how* it is said." [j] This seems unequivocal: Though the beliefs differ with respect to content, the objective aspect is unimportant from the religious point of view; what is important from that point of view is the attitude adopted toward the content, and the same attitude can be adopted toward beliefs of very different contents. It would appear that religion has collapsed into feeling and that "God" is simply the name that Kierkegaard gave to the mental state in which he had come to feel a passionate commitment.

An analogous problem arises as soon as one tries to distinguish between true and false suspensions of the ethical. Kierkegaard wanted to hold that Abraham was truly a paradigm of Christian faith; he also wanted to hold that Magister Adler was deluded.[11] But if truth is subjective, Adler could have been false only if he were a deliberate liar. If Adler really experienced a passionate inwardness, his affirmation was as truly religious, in Kierkegaard's own account of religion, as was Abraham's. Indeed, it is possible that Adler was the only paradigm, for conceivably Abraham was lying.

Of course, Kierkegaard might have replied that he did not care about the lack of evidence on the basis of which it would be possible to infer that Abraham was true and Adler false: He did not want evidence; he had made a leap of faith for Abraham and against Adler. But then Adler could equally well have said (and believed) that *he* had made a leap of faith for himself and against Kierkegaard. It would seem, then, that Kierkegaard became involved in a kind of Protagoreanism in which every man is the measure of his own religiosity. Though Kierkegaard insisted that the believer's leap of faith "puts him in an absolute relation to the absolute," the only available criterion for judging whether he has in fact achieved this relation is his own private feeling. Thus Kierkegaard's absolutism turns out, on scrutiny, to be a radical relativism.

Kierkegaard attempted to extricate himself from this extreme position by defining God objectively as the being who has such-and-such properties—for instance, He commands, He educates. But can this account be brought into harmony with the other account in which God is defined subjectively as the being who (regardless of what objective properties he may have or lack) evokes such-and-such attitudes on the part of the believer? This would be possible if there

---

11 A. P. Adler (1812–69) was a Danish clergyman who, midway in a quiet and conventional career, suddenly announced that he had had a special revelation and proceeded to publish what God had told him.

were only one thing to which men can commit themselves absolutely, and if this thing were the being who possesses the properties of commanding, educating, and so on. But to take this line of defense is to rest one's case on an empirical, and therefore at best only probable, fact about human psychology.[12]

It is possible, of course, to avoid facing up to this consequence by shifting so swiftly between the subjective and the objective points of view that one does not see what is going on. This escape route is often taken by modern theologians who have been influenced by existentialism but who have also wanted to remain "orthodox." Though Kierkegaard himself sometimes used these tactics, he was not, as has already been pointed out, sufficiently interested in evidence, logic, or argument to feel the need of an escape route. Even if he could have been convinced that logic was against him and that the infinite person he called "God" might just possibly be Allah—or that Adler, not Abraham, might be the paradigmatic Christian—Kierkegaard would have replied that this is just one more objective uncertainty (which he had not thought of himself) that his leap of faith must embrace.

Subjective, Not Objective, Truth

Kierkegaard's distinction between subjective and objective truth deserves more detailed examination, for it plays an important role in defining his own view of religion and is highly interesting as a sign of the direction in which Western culture was moving. As we have seen, this distinction was important to Kierkegaard because he held faith to be the essence of religion. But since he also held faith to be incompatible with objective evidence, it was necessary for him to show that all the so-called proofs of Christianity are incompetent. Here again Kierkegaard may resemble Kant, who had undertaken to demonstrate that the three traditional proofs of the existence of God are invalid. But whereas Kant had criticized the proofs on logical grounds, Kierkegaard sought only to show that the mental state, or attitude, in which one is seeking to prove something is irreconcilable with religion.

12 In a parallel way, when Kierkegaard was attacking Adler, he cited a number of objective characteristics that supposedly distinguish true revelations from spurious ones. It appears that "a real *extraordinarius*" is silent; Adler talked and wrote a lot. Furthermore, Adler burned the theological treatise that he had been writing when he had his great experience; had he been an *extraordinarius* he would have kept it by him at least for a while. And so on. Poor Kierkegaard! it must have been evident to him that all these considerations were wholly irrelevant. Inferences from behavior to mental states are at best only probable. But even passing over the hazards of diagnosing delusional fantasy, insofar as Kierkegaard succeeded in making a case against Adler's claims, he did so only by converting questions about religious inwardness into questions about mental states. This "reduction" of religion to empirical psychology was a cost that Kierkegaard was certainly unwilling to pay. Kierkegaard's criticism of Adler is contained in *On Authority and Revelation*, translated by W. Lowrie with an introduction by F. Sontag (Harper & Row, New York, 1966). See, for instance, pp. 52 ff.

It was as a preliminary step in this undertaking that Kierkegaard distinguished between objective and subjective truth. The point of view of the seeker of objective truth is reflected in Kant's favorite image of the disinterested judge, who, because he is not a party to the case, listens to plaintiff and defendant and weighs their evidence impartially and dispassionately. For the most part, philosophers have accepted this ideal of impartiality and have merely disagreed about whether it is actually attainable or whether men can only approximate to it. Most philosophers, therefore, have regarded words like "impartial," "disinterested," and "dispassionate" as highly honorific. For Kierkegaard, however, they were pejorative. In his view, objective truth, like "system," is an impossible ideal. There is no such thing as an impartial observer, for all truth is in varying degrees interested. "Impartiality" is itself an interest, and, as it happens, an unfortunate one. In the first place, pursuit of impartiality, which is doomed to failure anyway, is a distraction insofar as it draws our energies away from what ought to be our sole concern—finding our center, becoming a Christian. In the second place, pursuit of impartiality is a form of escapism. Constructing systems, weighing evidence, attempting to reach an objective truth, are all subtle ways in which men seek to avoid the anguish of decision.

If Kierkegaard had been concerned with theory of knowledge, his notion of a truth that is always interested would have brought him into sympathetic relation with one important aspect of Marxism[13] and might even have made him anticipate pragmatism.[14] However, because his interests were so exclusively moral and religious, and because his bias in favor of inwardness was so strong, he failed to develop this idea. Instead, he was content to show that neither method of seeking objective truth—neither historical scholarship nor philosophical speculation—is a possible way to Christianity.

THE HISTORICAL POINT OF VIEW

Given Kierkegaard's demand for certainty, it was easy for him to show the inadequacy of historical research. Central to the Christians' claims are a number of historical assertions—that Jesus lived, that he was crucified, and so on. If we examine these claims objectively, that is, in the same way we would investigate the claim that Caesar was bald or that Cicero was the editor of Lucretius' poem, we see that, like all assertions about the past, they can be no more than merely probable.

> When one raises the historical question of the truth of Christianity, or of what is and is not Christian truth, the Scriptures at once present themselves as documents of decisive significance. The historical inquiry therefore first concentrates upon the Bible. . . . [But] even with the most stupendous learning and persistence in research, and even if all the brains of all the critics were

13 See pp. 190–91.
14 See pp. 299–300.

concentrated in one, it would still be impossible to obtain anything more than an approximation; and an approximation is essentially incommensurable with an infinite personal interest in an eternal happiness.

[But let us] assume that the critics have succeeded in proving about the Bible everything that any learned theologian in his happiest moment has ever wished to prove about the Bible. These books and no others belong to the canon; they are authentic; they are integral; their authors are trust-worthy—one may well say, that it is as if every letter were inspired. . . .

Well, then, everything being assumed in order with respect to the Scrip-tures—what follows? Has anyone who previously did not have faith been brought a single step nearer to its acquisition? No, not a single step. Faith does not result simply from a scientific inquiry; it does not come directly at all. On the contrary, in this objectivity one tends to lose that infinite personal interestedness in passion which is the condition of faith.

· ·

When the question is treated in an objective manner it becomes impossible for the subject to face the decision with passion, least of all with an infinitely interested passion. It is a self-contradiction and therefore comical, to be infinitely interested in that which in its maximum still always remains an approximation. If in spite of this, passion is nevertheless imported, we get fanaticism. . . . The fault is not in the infinitely interested passion, but in the fact that its object has become an approximation-object. . . .[k]

THE SPECULATIVE POINT OF VIEW

Having thus demolished the historical, or scientific, version of objectivity, Kierkegaard next directed his attack against the speculative version. By specu-lation Kierkegaard meant any interpretation of religion based on a very general set of metaphysical concepts, which thereby render it "intelligible." Kierkegaard was thinking primarily of Hegel's attempt to bring Christianity within the structure of his triadic system; but any philosophical theology—for instance, Aristotle's definition of God in terms of the basic metaphysical distinctions between form and matter, actuality and potentiality—represents the sort of procedure Kierkegaard found offensive. To try to make religious feeling "under-standable" is to distort it by destroying its passionate inwardness. For any such undertaking Kierkegaard had even more contempt, if that be possible, than for historical scholarship. History at least restricts itself to the concrete and particu-lar; philosophical theology is not only "objective" but abstract as well.

> The speculative philosopher . . . proposes to contemplate Christianity from the philosophical standpoint . . . for the sake of interpenetrating it with his speculative thought; aye, with his genuinely speculative thought. But suppose this whole proceeding were a chimera, a sheer impossibility; suppose that Christianity is subjectivity, an inner transformation, an actualization of inwardness, and that only two kinds of people can know anything about it: those who with an infinite passionate interest in an eternal happiness

base their happiness upon their believing relationship to Christianity, and those who with an opposite passion, but in passion, reject it—the happy and the unhappy lovers. Suppose that an objective indifference can therefore learn nothing at all. Only the like is understood by the like. . . .

Now if Christianity is essentially something objective, it is necessary for the observer to be objective. But if Christianity is essentially subjectivity, it is a mistake for the observer to be objective. In every case where the object of knowledge is the very inwardness of the subjectivity of the individual, it is necessary for the knower to be in a corresponding condition.[1]

Kierkegaard's attack on the abstraction of "speculative philosophy"—his reminder that it is individual men who speculate and that their speculations are inevitably affected by their beliefs, by their "passions"—is very salutary. In general, he is effective as long as he is criticizing one extreme position, but many people will think that he himself adopted the opposite, and equally mistaken, extreme. They will say that pure subjectivity is no more adequate than pure objectivity.

This criticism of Kierkegaard's position can be put in Kantian and in Hegelian terms. Kant drew a distinction between what he called percepts and concepts— between a direct, experiential element in cognition and an abstract, structural, and relational element.[15] Hegel developed this relatively simple distinction into the more subtle notion of there being a movement of thought from "immediacy" through "mediation" to "self-mediation"—from the immediacy and directness of feeling, through externalization and criticism, to a renewal of immediacy on a higher level of sophisticated understanding.[16] With respect to the quality of experience, Kierkegaard's subjectivity and Hegel's immediacy are about equivalent; but Kierkegaard would have lumped together Hegel's mediation and self-mediation. From Kierkegaard's point of view, the latter is as defective as the former because it too involves objectivity. In short, he would have held that thought can never become self-transcendent (its object always remains an other for it). As evidence of this, Kierkegaard would undoubtedly have cited the fact that Hegel himself, despite all the claims he made, never got beyond the level of *raisonnement*.

There is force to this criticism. Hegel certainly tended, in his own thought about thinking, to slip rather easily from the notion of degrees of adequacy (degrees of self-mediation) to the notion of complete adequacy (a self-mediation that is absolute). He sometimes wrote as if this ideal could actually be achieved; indeed, at times he wrote as if he thought that he had achieved it, and that his version of the system was the System itself. Kierkegaard's reminder that thought's object remains an other is a useful corrective to Hegel's tendency to suppose that *his* thought had somehow managed to incorporate the other in complete transcendence. Nevertheless, much can be said for Hegel's underlying

15 See pp. 33–34.
16 See pp. 119–20.

thesis that cognition involves not only an element of immediacy but also an element of conscious reflection and evaluation. To put this in Kantian terms, since percepts without concepts are blind and concepts without percepts are empty, all adequate thought involves a blend, or mix, of both elements.

Kant and Hegel would have agreed with Kierkegaard that consciousness involves externality, a kind of detachment from direct experience. And they would also have allowed that in this process of externalization something is lost—immediacy. But they would have argued that something is gained, which is even more valuable than what is lost—comparison, evaluation, interpretation, understanding, the setting of the moment of immediacy in a comparative context of earlier than, different from, similar to, and better than.

Kierkegaard would not have been responsive to this line of reasoning, for as a "line of reasoning" it had all the characteristics of objectivity that he hated. He also hated balance and compromise—attitudes that are associated with objectivity. Thus, if asked to weigh evidence that he had exaggerated the role of the direct, experiential element in cognition, he would have declined to do so, replying that he had direct experience of the preferred status of direct experience as compared with the weighing-of-evidence approach. If asked to consider whether he had not overemphasized the passionate element in cognition, he would have replied passionately that it is impossible to put too much emphasis on the passionate element. And he might well have added that to ask him to adopt a balanced, objective stance toward his thesis that imbalance and subjectivity are desirable was to invite him to fall into contradiction. Kierkegaard might have granted that the stance he adopted closed the issue in advance in his favor, but he could have added that Kant and Hegel, for their part, had done no better. They had closed the issue in their favor by the stance *they* had adopted—for they had adopted a judicious, balanced position toward a balanced blend of direct experience and abstract, conceptual knowledge.

Here, then, we are confronted with a major parting of the ways, one that reflects very deep temperamental differences. Despite the slippages just referred to, Hegel was essentially a gradualist: In his view, self-mediation was not an all-or-none affair but a matter of degree. On the whole, therefore, he was fairly reconciled to the notion of an "adequate" that was always becoming "more adequate," but that never actually became "completely" adequate. Kierkegaard was temperamentally impatient: Not to have all was as bad as to have none. He demanded certainty, finality, completeness; approximation was wholly inacceptable to him.

Kierkegaard had similar views regarding alienation. Alienation, considered in its social sense, is a concept closely related to mediation, considered as an element in cognition. Marx was greatly concerned about the existence of alienation in nineteenth-century culture, but he believed that this alienation could be, and would be, overcome in the course of time by the overthrow of capitalism. Moreover, he thought he could help this process along. His attitude was therefore not at all dissimilar to that of Hegel, who contemplated the history of thought in much the same way as Marx contemplated the history of class struggle. Basically, both were optimists. Kierkegaard was far more profoundly alienated, both in the intellectual sense and in the social sense, than was either Hegel or Marx. The division he experienced within himself was so intolerable that a philosophical theory offering no more than gradual improvement seemed utterly irrelevant. He was persuaded—again by direct personal experience—that no rational, scientific, or economic procedure could heal the break within the self and between the self and its world; only a leap of faith could accomplish that. And God—this was his faith—had helped him, Søren Kierkegaard, to make the leap that had brought his life into "focus" and given it a "center."

Kierkegaard and ''The Age''

Kierkegaard expressed his experience of division and conflict in the religious language of sin and guilt. To many people today this language is foreign; they have not made, nor can they make, his leap of faith. Nonetheless, Kierkegaard speaks meaningfully to these "atheistic" (or perhaps "agnostic") existentialists because they too experience division, alienation, and loneliness and because they share his conviction that men are far less rational and far less capable of ordering and directing their affairs than they like to believe. Since these attitudes and beliefs increasingly characterize our own times, what Kierkegaard said about his own age seems even truer of the second half of the twentieth century:

> Our age reminds one vividly of the dissolution of the Greek city-state: everything goes on as usual, and yet there is no longer anyone who believes in it.
>
> Passion is the real thing. . . . And the age in which we live is wretched, because it is without passion.
>
> People must have lived ever so much more simply in the days when they believed that God made his will known in dreams. . . . Think of life in big cities and the manner of life: no wonder people attribute their dreams to devils and demons. —Moreover the poor opinion in which dreams are held nowadays is also connected with the intellectualism which really only values the conscious, while in simpler ages people piously believed that the unconscious life in man was the more important as well as the profounder.
>
> Have you seen a boat aground in the mud, it is almost impossible to float it again because it is impossible to punt, no punt-pole can touch bottom so that one can push against it. And so the whole generation is stuck in the mud banks of reason. . . .
>
> Mankind *en masse* gives itself up to evil, . . . nowadays it happens *en masse*. That is why people flock together, in order that natural and animal hysteria should get hold of them, in order to feel themselves stimulated, inflamed and *ausser sich*.

> Just as desert travellers combine into great caravans from fear of robbers and wild beasts, so the individuals of the contemporary generation are fearful of existence, because it is God-forsaken; only in great masses do they dare to live, and they cluster together *en masse* in order to feel that they amount to something.[m]

Wherever and whenever men evaluate their age and their culture in this way, Kierkegaard will be read—despite his exaggeration, his one-sidedness, and his radical subjectivity. Indeed, he will be read *because* of these qualities; they are central to this view of man.

Nietzsche

Friedrich Nietzsche was born in 1844 in Prussian Saxony. His family background was Lutheran, clerical, and royalist; his father and both his grandfathers were pastors, and he was named for the reigning king of Prussia. Nietzsche's father died when he was a child, and he was brought up in a house filled with women—his mother, grandmother, two maiden aunts, and a sister. He was educated at the universities of Bonn and Leipzig; at twenty-five (an unprecedentedly early age), even before he had taken his degree, he was appointed to a professorship of classical philology at the University of Basel. Although he had become a Swiss citizen, when the Franco-Prussian War broke out in 1870 Nietzsche volunteered and served briefly as a medical orderly in the Prussian Army. Ill health caused him to withdraw from active duty and, in 1879, to retire from teaching. However, despite terrible migraine headaches, severe stomach upsets, insomnia, and very bad eyesight, he continued to write and publish. He lived a solitary life in near poverty and spent his winters in boarding houses in Italy and his summers in Switzerland. Early in 1889 he became hopelessly insane, probably as a result of a syphilitic infection (which must have been contracted very early, for he lived a very ascetic life). He died in 1900.

Nietzsche's life spanned almost exactly the second half of the nineteenth century. When he was born, Hegel had been dead only thirteen years; Mill was thirty-eight years old; and Kierkegaard was thirty-one. Nietzsche himself was four when the *Manifesto of the Communist Party* was published and fifteen when *The Origin of Species* appeared. In the year he died both Bergson and Dewey were already forty-one and Russell was twenty-eight. During this period the optimistic mood of the Enlightenment was ending and the democratization, industrialization, and urbanization of Europe, which had initially been greeted with enthusiasm, were seen to be having unpredicted consequences—the commercialization, vulgarization, and impersonalization of life.

In many respects, Nietzsche's attitudes were similar to Kierkegaard's. He too was deeply alienated from the contemporary culture and internally divided.

Hence, though he was more interested than Kierkegaard in the traditional problems of philosophy—for instance, theory of knowledge and esthetics—most of his writings bore directly or indirectly on the existential problem of a man who finds himself alone in a world that is irrational, purposeless, and ultimately meaningless. What stance should he adopt toward such a world? How can he find "a center and a focus" for his life? Nietzsche was as passionately concerned with this problem as Kierkegaard had been, but temperamentally he was more robust. He had nothing but contempt for Kierkegaard's leap of faith. In contrast, he found fulfillment precisely in the hardness and courage with which he faced up to the terrible truths he had discovered.

Which of these highly personal solutions appeals to the reader—if, indeed, either does—depends less on the evidence presented by the two philosophers than on the reader's own temperament and outlook. As a matter of fact, neither Kierkegaard nor Nietzsche offered any evidence in the strict sense; they agreed that a way of life is not subject to proof, and their writings were designed to draw the reader's attention to painful "truths" that he would prefer to ignore. Furthermore, since both believed that most readers have developed ingenious techniques for avoiding unpleasant facts, neither expected to make many converts. Neither addressed himself to the "masses," who they believed had been dehumanized by the conditions of life; but both these lonely men reached out with longing for the exceptional individual here and there who might understand the nature of selfhood and join in the quest for it.

Cognition an Interpretive Process

Although Nietzsche was almost as hostile to the idea of "system" as was Kierkegaard, it is nonetheless possible to find the elements of an epistemological theory scattered in his writings. A convenient starting point for discussing this theory is Nietzsche's own experience as a classical philologist—an experience dominated by the distinction between an original text and its various interpretations.

The printed version of a play by Sophocles or of a dialogue by Plato that is available to readers today is a reconstruction; it is the product of collating several surviving manuscript "sources." But these manuscripts themselves are only versions—and late ones at that, probably medieval copies of copies of copies, and so on—of the long-lost original, which (presumably) Sophocles or Plato had dictated to his own copyist. Beginning with the first copy, errors and mistakes have crept in; pages have been lost; paragraphs have been transposed. Each successive copyist, faced with something in the version before him that did not make sense, had to interpret it as best he could, and his interpretation was transmitted to later copyists. Although nineteenth- and twentieth-century philologists have more versions to work with and employ more scholarly techniques, basically their procedures do not differ from those of earlier copyists—they provide us only with more interpretations. And none of these can possibly be "final" or "definitive," for each reflects the "subjectivity" of the scholar making it—his temperament and outlook, his philological skills (and also his limitations), and his knowledge of classical history (and also his ignorance).

In a word, Nietzsche was impressed by the distinction between an inaccessible "original" and a plurality of "versions," or interpretations, of it. He then applied this model to the knowledge situation generally. In perception and thought, he held, we do not contemplate objects "out there," objects that are complete in themselves and independent of us. We are *active*, not passively receptive. Perceiving and thinking are acts of interpretation, in which our desires, memories, and passions affect in greater or less degree the outcome—the object that we perceive or think about.

> "Disinterested contemplation" . . . is a rank absurdity. . . . Let us, from now on, be on our guard against the hallowed philosophers' myth of a "pure, will-less, painless, timeless knower"; let us beware of the tentacles of such contradictory notions as "pure reason," "absolute knowledge," "absolute intelligence." All these concepts presuppose an eye such as no living creature can imagine, an eye required to have no direction, to abrogate its active and interpretative powers—precisely those powers that alone make of seeing, seeing *something*. All seeing is essentially perspective, and so is all knowing.
>
> Whoever has pursued the history of any single science finds in its development a clue for the understanding of the most ancient and common processes of all "knowing and cognizing." There as here, the premature hypotheses, the fictitious creations, the good stupid will to "believe," the lack of suspiciousness and patience, are developed first. Our senses learn late, and never wholly, to be subtle, faithful and cautious organs of cognition. It feels more comfortable to our eyes to reproduce upon a given stimulus an image already produced than to retain what is different and new in a given impression; the latter process requires more energy, more "morality." To hear something new is painful and difficult for the ear; we hear new music poorly. When we hear a foreign language we try unconsciously to reform the sounds into words that sound more familiar and home-like. Thus, for example, the Germans fixed up for themselves the word *Armbrust* (arm-breast) when they heard *arcubalista* (cross-bow). Everything new finds even our senses hostile and unwilling, and more than unwilling. The passions like fear, love, and hatred (including the passive passions like laziness) *rule* the "simplest" processes of our sense activity. As little as a modern reader reads the individual words (not to mention syllables) on a page, but out of every twenty words takes perhaps five at random and "guesses" the presumable sense that goes with these five, so little do we see a tree exactly and completely as to its leaves, branches, colors, and forms. It is so much easier to imagine an approximation of a tree. . . . We invent the largest part of the thing experienced and can hardly be compelled *not* to observe some process with

the eyes of an "inventor." All of this wants to say that we are basically and from time immemorial *accustomed to lying.* Or, to say it more virtuously and slyly, hence pleasantly: we are much greater artists than we know. —In the course of an animated conversation I often see the face of my partner, depending on the thought he has uttered or that I think I have evoked, so significantly and subtly defined that the degree of significance surpasses by far my visual capabilities. The subtlety of the play of muscles and the expression of the eyes that I "saw" *must* have been fictitiously created by me.[n]

Nietzsche's starting point, like the starting point of so many nineteenth-century philosophers, was Kantian. Kant had maintained that the objects we encounter in experience are actually constructs, products of a "transcendental synthesis." Kant, it is true, had limited the contribution of mind to a minimum. He held that it consisted in twelve "categories" that are universal and necessary features of all human minds. Hegel, as has been seen, greatly expanded the role of mind in experience and argued that this role has a history in that it varies with the level of mental and cultural development. That Nietzsche put even more emphasis on construction and interpretation than did Hegel is not only in accordance with his experience as a philologist; it also reflects a focus of attention on the individual person and his individual needs and problems that has already been encountered in Kierkegaard and that was becoming increasingly prominent in nineteenth-century thought.

It is indeed possible to hold that Nietzsche's insight into the nature of the cognitive process is itself an instance of his general thesis about cognition: It was his interest in subjectivity that caused him to interpret cognition as an interpretive process. Thus Nietzsche attended to features of perceptual experience that Kant and Hegel did not notice but that they might have observed had these features interested them, such as the phenomenon of overlooking a typographical error in a sentence because the reader knows so well what the word "really" is—as, for instance, the erroneous spelling of the second word in this sentence. Another example is the phenomenon of hearing one's own name when it is mentioned across the room at a noisy party, even though one is not listening for it and can discriminate nothing else in the din. Here one's interest in oneself brings this part of the perceptual field into focus without conscious intent.

The Role of Language

That men's interests and expectations—what is sometimes called their perceptual set—influence their perceptions is now a commonplace. But Nietzsche was one of the first philosophers to observe this phenomenon and to see its relevance to theory of knowledge. He viewed it as derivative in part from what he called "laziness"—the tendency, once we have achieved a concept or hypothesis, to persist in using it to interpret our experiences, even though it may no longer apply when circumstances change. This kind of inertia, Nietzsche saw, increases as soon as the concept is formulated linguistically. To cast an interpretation into language is to rigidify it; it then becomes a Procrustean bed that our experience of the world is forced to fit. According to Nietzsche, many of the concepts that have seemed to be of fundamental importance in philosophy are nothing but linguistic traps of this kind—for instance, the concept of substance, conceived of either as an enduring encapsulated object that "has" properties or as an enduring encapsulated self that "has" various faculties and powers.

As regards the notion of object,

> . . . there is no set of maxims more important for an historian than this: that the actual causes of a thing's origin and its eventual uses, the manner of its incorporation into a system of purposes, are worlds apart; that everything that exists, no matter what its origin, is periodically reinterpreted by those in power in terms of fresh intentions; that all processes in the organic world are processes of outstripping and overcoming, and that, in turn, all outstripping and overcoming means reinterpretation, rearrangment, in the course of which the earlier meaning and purpose are necessarily either obscured or lost. No matter how well we understand the utility of a certain physiological organ (or of a legal institution, a custom, a political convention, an artistic genre, a cultic trait) we do not thereby understand anything of its origin. I realize that this truth must distress the traditionalist. . . . But . . . the whole history of a thing, an organ, a custom, [is] a continuous *chain* of reinterpretations and rearrangements, which need not be causally connected among themselves, which may simply follow one another. The "evolution" of a thing, a custom, an organ is not its *progressus* towards a goal, let alone the most logical and shortest *progressus*, requiring the least energy and expenditure. Rather it is a sequence of more or less profound, more or less independent processes of appropriation, including the resistances used in each instance, the attempted transformations for purposes of defense or reaction, as well as the results of successful counterattacks. While forms are fluid, their "meaning" is even more so.°

In terms of the analogy of a long-lost classical text and its interpretations, Nietzsche's thesis is that since the original text is inaccessible, since it cannot enter into our calculations and reflections when we try to ascertain the meaning of Sophocles' play or of Plato's dialogue, and since all we ever do is compare one interpretation with others, we might as well abandon the "myth" that there was once an original. Similarly, the supposedly independently existing object with enduring properties of its own is also a myth. An uninterpreted original is never available; there are only the varied "meanings" that the object has had at different times for different people.

Or, to substitute "perspective"—another favorite term of Nietzsche's—for "interpretation," the history of mankind is the history of a succession of perspectives from which different social groups have viewed the universe. Each perspective shapes the social institutions, art, religion, and literature of that group. Questions about what is good, what is beautiful, and what is true are meaningless in the abstract; they are answerable only when a time has been specified, and the answers are to be ascertained by empirical inquiries, by investigations undertaken by anthropologists and psychologists into the basic drives that animate the dominant members of the group at that particular time. Further, changes in the culture—for instance, a shift from one "truth" or from one "good" to another—are explicable in terms of "appropriations and resistances" that occur at the level of values, and values in their turn are but reflections of the basic drives of the group.

Nietzsche's discussion of interpretation can be set in an interpretive context of its own. Considered from an historical point of view, which is the way Nietzsche recommended looking at things, it is easy to see that his view of history and culture is a typical nineteenth-century phenomenon. It stems from the Kantian distinction between things-in-themselves and appearances. And it is clear, further, that Nietzsche in effect duplicated Hegel's rejection of the unknown and unknowable things-in-themselves (that is, the inaccessible "original" play or dialogue). The result is that what Kant called "appearance" becomes reality and that this reality is viewed as a product—the phenomenology of spirit.

In this respect, Nietzsche was a Hegelian. But, according to Hegel, spirit expresses itself in an essentially rational manner: Successive stages in the development of spirit follow one another in a systematic way as "contradictions" emerge. Accordingly, in Hegel's view, the idea of progress or of teleology is applicable to the history of culture. In Nietzsche's view, however, there may not even be causal relations among the stages; indeed, the so-called stages are stages in name only, and the idea of purpose or teleology is only an idea—just another interpretation that reflects the underlying values of Hegel and other scholars and philosophers.

Spirit was perceived by Nietzsche chiefly in terms of will and volition, rather than in terms of thought. The life of the spirit was a struggle between the desire to appropriate and the desire to resist appropriation—note his use of such terms as "counterattack," "outstrip," and "overcome." In this respect—in de-emphasizing the logicality of the course of historical change—Nietzsche was closer to Marx and to Darwin than he was to Hegel, for both Marx and Darwin saw the world process as a struggle. According to the one it was for class supremacy; according to the other, for material survival. Nevertheless, like Hegel, they regarded successive stages of this struggle as constituting a development; if it did not have a *telos*, it had a pattern. Hence in their view the outcome of the struggle was sufficiently predictable for a science of culture to be possible. This Nietzsche denied.

Nietzsche's discussion of the way language encapsulates objects can be applied to the self. Just as, if we are not careful, we slip into thinking of an object as having a nature of its own that exists independently of us and our interpretations, so we easily slip into the fallacy of thinking of the self (our own self, for instance) as existing "completely, laid out as if in an illuminated glass case."[p] In both cases language is to blame:

> A quantum of strength is equivalent to a quantum of urge, will, activity, and it is only the snare of language (of the arch-fallacies of reason petrified in language), presenting all activity as conditioned by an agent—the "subject"—that blinds us to this fact. For, just as popular superstition divorces the lightning from its brilliance, viewing the latter as an activity whose subject is the lightning, so does popular morality divorce strength from its manifestations, as though there were behind the strong a neutral agent, free to manifest its strength or contain it. But no such agent exists; there is no "being" behind the doing, acting, becoming; the "doer" has simply been added to the deed by the imagination—the doing is everything. The common man actually doubles the doing by making the lightning flash; he states the same event once as cause and then again as effect. The natural scientists are no better when they say that "energy *moves*," "energy *causes*." For all its detachment and freedom from emotion, our science is still the dupe of linguistic habits; it has never yet got rid of those changelings called "subjects." The atom is one such changeling, another is the Kantian "thing-in-itself."[q]

Nietzsche's point here is that everything that anyone might ever say about the self can be expressed by verbs (doing, acting, becoming); we introduce the complexity of a subject that acts and becomes only because it happens that a declarative sentence takes a noun as its grammatical subject.

> A thought comes when "it" will and not when "I" will. It is thus a *falsification* of the evidence to say that the subject "I" conditions the predicate "think." *It* is thought, to be sure, but that this "it" should be that old famous "I" is, to put it mildly, only a supposition, an assertion. Above all it is not an "immediate certainty." In the end even "it is thought" says too much. Even this "it" contains an *interpretation* of the process and does not belong to the process itself. Our conclusion is here formulated out of our grammatical custom: "Thinking is an activity; every activity presumes something which is active, hence. . . ."[r]

The Psychological Bases of Thought

In some respects these comments can be viewed as but another attack in the long series of criticisms—begun by the British Empiricists and continued by Kant, Hegel, and Kierkegaard—of the Cartesian concept of substance. Nietzsche's attack, however, was far more drastic than any of the others. Whereas Kant and Hegel had held the philosophical enterprise as a whole to be the most significant of human activities (though they had, of course, criticized specific philosophical practices), and whereas Kierkegaard had merely declared it to be idle and distracting, Nietzsche regarded it as thoroughly phony. Philosophers think that they aim at Truth (with a capital "T"), but their theories are only elaborate attempts to justify the beliefs that they hold on instinctive (and hence unthinking) grounds. Philosophers are in fact like lawyers, who are hired to "make a case" for their clients. They differ from lawyers only in being too simpleminded to recognize what they are doing; they are lawyers who are taken in by their own statements to the jury:

> After keeping an eye on and reading between the lines of the philosophers for a long time, I find that I must tell myself the following: the largest part of conscious thinking must be considered an instinctual activity, even in the case of philosophical thinking. . . . Most of the conscious thinking of a philosopher is secretly guided by his instincts and forced along certain lines. Even behind logic and its apparent sovereignty of development stand value judgments, or, to speak more plainly, physiological demands for preserving a certain type of life. Such as for example, that the definite is worth more than the indefinite, that appearance is less valuable than "the truth." . . .
>
> What tempts us to look at all philosophers half suspiciously and half mockingly is not so much that we recognize again and again how innocent they are, how often and how easily they make mistakes and lose their way, in short their childishness and childlike-ness—but rather that they are not sufficiently candid, though they make a great virtuous noisy to-do as soon as the problem of truthfulness is even remotely touched upon. Every one of them pretends that he has discovered and reached his opinions through the self-development of cold, pure, divinely untroubled dialectic (in distinction to the mystics of every rank who, more honest and fatuous, talk about "inspiration"), whereas, at bottom, a pre-conceived dogma, a notion, an "institution," or mostly a heart's desire, made abstract and refined, is defended by them with arguments sought after the fact. They are all of them lawyers (though wanting to be called anything but that). . . .
>
> Gradually I have come to realize what every great philosophy up to now has been: the personal confession of its originator, a type of involuntary and unaware memoirs. . . .[s]

And what is true of philosophy is also true of science. "Physics, too, is only an interpretation of the universe, an arrangement of it (to suit us, if I may be so bold!), rather than a clarification."[t] As examples Nietzsche chose "causality" and "natural law," which all the sciences uncritically assume to be fundamental concepts:

> One should make use of "cause" and "effect" only as pure *concepts*, i.e., as conventional fictions for the purpose of designation and mutual understanding, *not* for explanation. In "being-as-such" there are no "causal connections" or "necessities" or "psychological lack of freedom"; effect there does *not* follow upon a cause; there *is* no "law" which rules phenomena. It is *we*, we alone, who have dreamed up the causes, the one-thing-after-

anothers, the one-thing-reciprocating-anothers, the relativity, the constraint, the numbers, the laws, the freedom, the "reason why," the purpose. And when we mix up this world of symbols with the world of things as though the symbols existed "in themselves," then we are merely doing once more what we have always done: we are creating myths. . . .

One will forgive, I hope, an old philologist who cannot desist from the malice of pointing his finger at poor interpretation. But really, that "conformity of nature unto law" of which you physicists talk so proudly as if . . . , that lawfulness is the result only of your *explication de texte*, of your bad philology! It is not a fact, not a "text" at all, but only a naive, humanitarian arrangement and misinterpretation that you use for truckling to the democratic instincts of the modern soul. "Everywhere equality before the law—and nature is no better off than we are"—surely a fine *arrière-pensée*. . . . This is explication, not text, and someone might come along who, with opposite intention and interpretive skill, might read out of the same nature and the same phenomena quite another thing: a tyrannical, inconsiderate, relentless enforcement of claims to power. . . . Let us admit that this, too, would be only an interpretation—and you will be eager enough to make this objection! Well, all the better![u]

Consciousness a Disease

Indeed, *all* thinking, not merely the thinking of professional philosophers and scientists, must be regarded as an aberration. Thought is a product of consciousness, and consciousness is an evolutionary blind alley.

> In some remote corner of the universe, poured out and glittering in innumerable solar systems, there once was a star on which clever animals invented knowledge. That was the haughtiest and most mendacious minute of "world history"—yet only a minute. After nature had drawn a few breaths the star grew cold, and the clever animals had to die.
>
> One might invent such a fable and still not have illustrated sufficiently how wretched, how shadowy and flighty, how aimless and arbitrary, the human intellect appears in nature. There have been eternities when it did not exist; and when it is done for again, nothing will have happened. For this intellect has no further mission that would lead beyond human life. . . .
>
> The intellect, as a means for the preservation of the individual, unfolds its chief powers in simulation; for this is the means by which the weaker, less robust individuals preserve themselves, since they are denied the chance of waging the struggle for existence with horns or the fangs of beast of prey. In man this art of simulation reaches its peak: here deception, flattery, lying and cheating, talking behind the back, posing, living in borrowed splendor, being masked . . . [are] so much the rule and the law that almost nothing is more incomprehensible than how an honest and pure urge for truth could

make its appearance among men. They are deeply immersed in illusions and dream images; their eye glides only over the surface of things and sees "forms"; their feeling nowhere leads into truth, but contents itself with the reception of stimuli, playing, as it were, a game of blindman's buff on the backs of things. . . .

Let us give special consideration to the formation of concepts. Every word immediately becomes a concept, inasmuch as it is not intended to serve as a reminder of the unique and wholly individualized original experience to which it owes its birth, but must at the same time fit innumerable, more or less similar cases—which means, strictly speaking, never equal—in other words, a lot of unequal cases. Every concept originates through our equating what is unequal. No leaf ever wholly equals another, and the concept "leaf" is formed through an arbitrary abstraction from these individual differences, through forgetting the distinctions; and now it gives rise to the idea that in nature there might be something besides the leaves which would be "leaf"—some kind of original form after which all leaves have been woven, marked, copied, colored, curled, and painted, but by unskilled hands, so that no copy turned out to be a correct, reliable, and faithful image of the original form. We call a person "honest." Why did he act so honestly today? we ask. Our answer usually sounds like this: because of his honesty. Honesty! That is to say again: the leaf is the cause of the leaves. After all, we know nothing of an essence-like quality named "honesty"; we know only numerous individualized, and thus unequal actions, which we equate by omitting the unequal and by then calling them honest actions. In the end, we distill from them a *qualitas occulta* with the name of "honesty." . . .

What, then, is truth? A mobile army of metaphors, metonyms, and anthropomorphisms— . . . truths are illusions about which one has forgotten that this is what they are; metaphors which are worn out and without sensuous power; coins which have lost their pictures and now matter only as metal, no longer as coins. . . .[v]

This attack on Truth is far more radical than the criticism that has already been considered. According to the latter, cognition is a series of interpretations of a world that is inaccessible save through interpretations; nevertheless, the various interpretations can be compared among themselves with respect to their adequacy—just as one philologist's reconstruction of the *Bacchae* can be adjudged better than another's, even though the original text has disappeared. But from the point of view presented in the passage above all interpretations are equally inadequate just because they are interpretations. Better by far is the relationship in which the plants and the lower animals stand to the world, a relationship that is simple and direct because it does not involve interpretation at all.

Nietzsche was not troubled by the conflict between this romantic primitivism (as it may be called) and his perspective theory. Instead, he pointed out that consciousness not only brings "knowledge"—that is, interpretations—in its train; it also brings conscience. Lacking the capacity to reflect, animals are happily without the notion of an abstract good, just as they are without the concept of an abstract Truth to which, supposedly, their beliefs fail to correspond, and an abstract Reality from which, supposedly, the actual spaciotemporal world deviates. Accordingly, since they do not have the illusory notion of an "ideal" from which their behavior deviates, animals do not experience a sense of duty, sin, guilt, or bad conscience. Animal behavior is simply the spontaneous response of instinct to the external world; it is not mediated by consciousness and hence is without the complications that thought and deliberation inevitably introduce.

Why did consciousness and conscience evolve? Nietzsche's answer is that man became socialized, that socialization necessitated the repression of many of his most powerful instincts, and that repressed instincts then turned within. The result was that for the first time an interior psychic life developed—a mental world of thoughts, motives, hypotheses, dreams, illusions, and simulations.

> I take bad conscience to be a deep-seated malady to which man succumbed under the pressure of the most profound transformation he ever underwent—the one that made him once and for all a sociable and pacific creature. Just as happened in the case of those sea creatures who were forced to become land animals in order to survive, these semi-animals, happily adapted to the wilderness, to war, free roaming, and adventure, were forced to change their nature. Of a sudden they found all their instincts devalued, unhinged. They must walk on legs and carry themselves, where before the water had carried them: a terrible heaviness weighed upon them. They felt inapt for the simplest manipulations, for in this new, unknown world they could no longer count on the guidance of their unconscious drives. They were forced to think, deduce, calculate, weigh cause and effect—unhappy people, reduced to their weakest, most fallible organ, their consciousness! I doubt that there has ever been on earth such a feeling of misery, such a leaden discomfort. It was not that those old instincts had abruptly ceased making their demands; but now their satisfaction was rare and difficult. . . . All instincts that are not allowed free play turn inward. This is what I call man's interiorization; it alone provides the soil for the growth of what is later called man's *soul*. Man's interior world, originally meager and tenuous, was expanding in every dimension, in proportion as the outward discharge of his feelings was curtailed. The formidable bulwarks by means of which the polity protected itself against the ancient instincts of freedom (punishment was one of the strongest of these bulwarks) caused those wild, extravagant instincts to turn in upon man. Hostility, cruelty, the delight in persecution, raids, excitement, destruction all turned against their begetter. Lacking external enemies and resistances, and confined within an oppressive narrowness and regularity, man began rending, persecuting, terrifying himself, like a wild beast hurling itself against the bars of its cage. . . . Also the generator of the greatest and most disastrous of maladies, of which humanity has not to this day been cured: his sickness of himself, brought on by the violent severance from his animal past, by his sudden leap and fall into new layers and conditions of existence, by his declaration of war against the old instincts that had hitherto been the foundation of his power, his joy, and his awesomeness.

> Man, with his need for self-torture, his sublimated cruelty resulting from the cooping up of his animal nature within a polity, invented bad conscience in order to hurt himself, after the blocking of the more natural outlet of his cruelty.[w]

NIETZSCHE AND THE WAVE OF THE FUTURE

It is astounding to see the prodigality with which Nietzsche tossed off seminal ideas. Such notions as repression, sublimation, and the mythical element in science were enunciated in these scattered paragraphs and aphorisms (without being developed in detail, it is true) long before they were formulated by Freud, Jung, and the other psychoanalysts. Indeed, in the last paragraphs quoted, Nietzsche anticipated the main arguments of Freud's *Civilization and Its Discontents* by almost half a century.

Even more impressive perhaps than such specific insights are the two themes that dominate Nietzsche's whole discussion. The first of these is the derogation of consciousness as a mode of life and experience. Men came to feel that consciousness entailed externality and objectivity (or, in Hegel's terminology, "mediation") and hence the repression of freedom, spontaneity, and inwardness. This hostility to consciousness, which had been expressed very early in Dostoevsky's account of underground man, became increasingly prominent in the next century: Surrealism, Dadaism, sensitivity training, encounter groups, happenings in the theater, "mind-expanding" drugs, Zen, the antinovel, the new wave in the cinema, are all manifestations of the emphasis on immediacy and so of the Nietzschian attitude toward consciousness.[17]

The second main theme is the "expressiveness" of cultural phenomena. That all cultural phenomena are expressive of deep, often unconscious, elements in the psyche has become one of the most widely held articles of faith in contemporary society, influencing not only the art and literature but also the science and philosophy of our time. It has influenced, for example, the writing of this chapter on Kierkegaard and Nietzsche, and, quite specifically, the last sentence of the paragraph above, which asserts that surrealism, Zen, and other twentieth-century phenomena are "manifestations" of a particular attitude toward consciousness. In these respects, and in so many others, Nietzsche was a pioneer, truly one of those "creative" individuals whom he so much admired.

One paragraph quoted above—the discussion of the formation of concepts—requires more detailed examination. Nietzsche's insistence that concepts are inevitably distorting because they treat as "equal" things that are unequal echoes Schopenhauer and the Romantic poets (for instance, Wordsworth's castigation of reason as "that false secondary power by which we multiply distinctions"). But Nietzsche's line of attack was far more destructive than Schopenhauer's. Schopenhauer's argument would be convincing only to an extreme nominalist who held that every individual object is unique. Nietzsche agreed with Schopen-

17 About consciousness, as about many things, Nietzsche was of two minds. See pp. 249 and 259.

hauer that abstract universals falsify the facts of empirical diversity, but he then proceeded to undermine the case for conceptualism as much as for realism by uncovering the psychological source of our love of universals, concepts, and Platonic "forms." They are all products of "laziness." And not only of laziness. Platonism, like the Egyptian pyramids, is evidence of a hatred of becoming. Belief in abstract universals and eternal forms is a way of escaping from the real world of growth, decay, and death into the security of a changeless realm.

NIETZSCHE'S RELATIVISM

This psychologizing strategy is almost too powerful an instrument of destruction. The theory that all theories are expressions of underlying elements in the psyche is presumably an expression of underlying elements in the personality of Nietzsche. What Nietzsche says about consciousness as an evolutionary mistake is, on his own account, only an interpretation, not a text. Furthermore, this interpretation is a reflection of Nietzsche's values and attitudes—his alienation, his isolation, and his own tormented consciousness. It is clear, for instance, that Nietzsche greatly prized smoothness, rapidity, and sureness of response—perhaps because he himself was hesitant, shy, and introspective. "Happiness," he wrote in 1874, "lies in the swiftness of feeling and thinking: all the rest of the world is slow, gradual, and stupid. Whoever could feel the course of a light ray would be very happy, for it is very swift." [x] There is no reason, of course, why Nietzsche should not have found happiness in the swiftness of feeling, and no reason why he should not have derogated consciousness insofar as it impedes the swift flow of feeling. But why should another man, who prizes deliberation, reflection, and calculation and who is therefore led to make a different evaluation of consciousness, accept Nietzsche's conclusion that consciousness is an "ineluctable disaster"? [y] If all criteria are subjective, every man is the measure of his own conclusion regarding the value of consciousness.

Nietzsche might have attempted to extricate himself from such a radical conclusion by introducing an "objective" criterion. Indeed, on occasion he did exactly this. At one point, for instance, he suggested that interpretations can be assessed objectively as life-preserving or life-defeating. This suggestion, had he developed it, would have taken him in the direction that Bergson and Dewey were to go. But whatever one thinks of *their* use of this argument, Nietzsche's version of it was inadequate. First, using empirical evidence, one would conclude that consciousness is more life-preserving than instinct—the opposite conclusion from the one Nietzsche wanted to draw. Second, his psychological stance makes the very notion of empirical evidence suspect. The conclusion that consciousness is in fact destructive—if this indeed is the conclusion the evidence seems to call for—is itself an interpretation, not a text. One's assessment of the empirical evidence is in part a reflection of one's bias against (or in favor of) consciousness and hence adds no independent support to one's initial assessment of the value of consciousness.

Nietzsche was, of course, much too acute not to see that this objection could be raised against him. A sentence in which he referred to this possibility has already been quoted: "Let us admit that this, too, would be only an interpretation—and you will be eager to make this objection! Well, all the better." [18] This cavalier attitude will disturb philosophers who take truth seriously. But, for his part, Nietzsche did not take such philosophers seriously. He regarded them as old maids: respectable, dull, uninspiring, and full of petty jealousies. Nietzsche could afford to be cavalier because, like Kierkegaard, he distinguished two kinds of truth—objective and subjective. Objective truth is a fiction of the philosophers, a product of their insecurity and laziness. Subjective truth is any new interpretation launched by a creative individual. Every such truth, precisely because it is novel, must do battle for survival against old, entrenched interpretations that claim to be objectively true. In this struggle, the new interpretation may win or may lose; but even if it wins, victory is only temporary: Sooner or later it will be replaced by newer, more creative interpretations. Nietzsche would have been inconsistent had he claimed objective truth for his view, but he was content to claim only subjective truth for it. Because it was only an interpretation that he had placed in competition, it was "all the better" to have objections raised against him. To raise objections was to launch an attack; and only by meeting and surviving an attack could his view become true in the way in which he wanted it to be true.

The Will to Power

So much for comment on what may be called the ontological status of Nietzsche's interpretation. The central feature of that interpretation was Nietzsche's discovery of the will to power. This insight was, he felt, creative in the way in which subjective truth always is creative: It offered men a new perspective from which to view themselves and nature.

But what, exactly, is the will to power? To begin with, it is a cosmological principle. Let us, Nietzsche in effect said, replace the old billiard-ball model of the physical universe with one derived from our experience of life. The trouble with the billiard-ball model (apart from the fact that it involves the "lazy" fiction of encapsulated, enduring things) is that it commits us to dualism, for this model is inapplicable in biology, psychology, and sociology. It is worth experimenting, therefore, to see whether the notion of drive, which is common to these fields, may not also serve in physics; if it does, we will have a single, unified world view.

> Let us assume that nothing is "given" as real except our world of desires and passions, that we cannot step down or step up to any kind of "reality"

18 See p. 243.

except the reality of our drives. . . . Would we not be allowed to experiment with the question whether these "givens" are not *sufficient* for understanding the so-called mechanistic (or material) world? . . . To understand the material world as a *pre-form* of life? In the end this experimental question is not merely allowed; it is demanded by the conscience of *methodology*. Not to assume several types of causality until the experiment of getting along with a single one has been followed to its utmost conclusion: . . . this is the morality of methodology. . . . In the end, the question is whether we really acknowledge the will as *effective;* whether we believe in the causality of the will. If we do (and basically our faith in the causality of the will amounts to our belief in causality itself), we *must* experiment with taking will-causality as our only hypothesis. Will, of course, can only act on will, not on matter (on "nerves," for example). Enough said: we must risk the hypothesis that everywhere we recognize "effects" there is an effect of will upon will; that all mechanical happenings, insofar as they are activated by some energy, are will-power, will-effects. —Assuming, finally, that we succeeded in explaining our entire instinctual life as the development and ramification of one basic form of will (of the will to power, as I hold); assuming that one could trace back all the organic functions to this will to power, including the solution of the problem of generation and nutrition (they are one problem)—if this were done, we should be justified in defining *all* effective energy unequivocally as *will to power.*[z]

Characteristically, Nietzsche never worked out this insight in detail. But that it was not merely an idle fantasy is shown by Whitehead's "process" philosophy. His notion of prehension and Nietzsche's concept of power drive are similar, and the basic strategies of the two philosophers—their attempts to achieve a unified world view by replacing the billiard-ball model with a more organic one—are identical.[19]

Although the will to power remained for Nietzsche a mere undeveloped suggestion at the level of cosmology, he worked it out in considerable detail at the level of psychology. His aim here was to show that all the multiform drives that seemingly motivate men's acts are but variants of this one basic drive, the will to power. At the preconscious level the will to power expresses itself directly and immediately in the attempt of every organism to use, and thus to overcome, those that are less powerful than itself. "Life itself is essential assimilation, injury, violation of the foreign and the weaker, suppression, hardness, the forcing of one's own forms upon something else, ingestion and—at least in its mildest form—exploitation." [a]

At the human level, consciousness naturally adds complications, but these complications do not alter the basic nature of the drive. Consciousness introduces inhibitions ("bad conscience") in the instinctive exercise of power on the part of those who possess power and provides justifications, excuses, and alternative routes to power for those who lack power. In this way a variety of goods emerge,

19 See pp. 314–21.

but the only thing good in itself is power. All other goods, all values, and all virtues are expressions of, and hence relative to, the power positions of various individuals and groups. Thus there is one set of goods and virtues for the strong and another for the weak. The latter, which Nietzsche called "slave morality" or "herd morality," is essentially the morality that was taught by the Greek philosophers and the Christian theologians. It emphasizes justice, prudence, equality, consideration for others, respect for the law, and moderation—all of which are virtues of the weak and based, ultimately, on the resentment and rancor that the weak feel against the strong.

THE GENESIS OF SLAVE MORALITY

The slave revolt in morals begins by rancor turning creative and giving birth to values—the rancor of beings who, deprived of the direct outlet of action, compensate by an imaginary vengeance. All truly noble morality grows out of triumphant self-affirmation. Slave ethics, on the other hand, begins by saying *no* to an "outside," an "other," a non-self, and that *no* is its creative act. This reversal of direction of the evaluating look, this invariable looking outward instead of inward, is a fundamental feature of rancor. Slave ethics requires for its inception a sphere different from and hostile to its own. Physiologically speaking, it requires an outside stimulus in order to act at all; all its action is reaction. The opposite is true of aristocratic valuations: such values grow and act spontaneously, seeking out their contraries only in order to affirm themselves even more gratefully and delightedly. . . . The Greek aristocracy, for example . . . , did not have to construct their happiness factitiously by looking at their enemies, as all rancorous men are wont to do, and being fully active, energetic people they were incapable of divorcing happiness from action. . . .

All this stands in utter contrast to what is called happiness among the impotent and oppressed, who are full of bottled-up aggressions. Their happiness is purely passive and takes the form of drugged tranquility, . . . peace, . . . emotional slackness. Whereas the noble lives before his own conscience with confidence and frankness . . . , the rancorous person is neither truthful nor ingenuous nor honest and forthright with himself. His soul squints; his mind loves hide-outs, secret paths, and back doors. . . ; he is expert in silence, in long memory, in waiting, in provisional self-depreciation, and in self-humiliation.[b]

This resentful slave is in fact Dostoevsky's underground man. And the function of all religions and transcendent moralities (for example, Platonism) is to make life tolerable for such men by appeasing and reducing their feelings of resentment—"the black melancholy of the physiologically incapacitated." "To put it quite generally, the main object of all great religions has been to counteract a certain epidemic malaise due to unreleased tension"—the tension that is built up as a result of the interiorization of instinctual drives.[c] Nietzsche proceeded to outline the "main forms" in which the weak have waged their "battle against anxiety."

Since melancholy and depression are the products of the repression of natural drives, the first way to relieve depression is to try to "reduce the vital energy [of these drives] to its lowest point." This is why religion advocates asceticism:

> No love; no hate; equanimity; no retaliation; no acquisition of riches; no work; mendicancy; preferably no woman, or as little woman as possible; in intellectual matters, Pascal's maxim, "We must stultify ourselves." . . . The result . . . in physiological terms is hypnosis—the attempt to achieve for man something approximating the hibernation of certain animal species. . . .[d]

This technique has had considerable success. It is true that it has also had a number of unfortunate by-products, including "all kind of mental disorders." But since these by-products are explained by the sufferers themselves in quite different terms—"as a return to the ground of being, a deliverance from all illusion"—the technique is not impaired for those who use it. "Though it goes without saying that the subjects' own explanations of these phenomena have always been extravagantly false, we cannot fail to notice the sincere gratitude that makes them *want* to give explanations of this kind."[e]

A second "regimen for combatting depression" is mechanical activity:

> There is no doubt that such activity can appreciably alleviate man's suffering. Nowadays it is spoken of rather dishonestly as "the blessing of labor." It brings relief by turning the attention of the sufferer away from his suffering. Since he is constantly preoccupied with doing, there is little room left in his mind for suffering—the chamber of man's consciousness is pretty narrow, after all.[f]

A third prescription for relieving melancholy is "emotional debauch." Naturally, it is described by its priestly advocates "under the most sacred names," but "any strong emotion will do—rage, fear, lust, vengeance, hope, triumph, despair, cruelty—provided it has sudden release."[g]

To sum up, religion and transcendental ethics are instruments for preserving the unfit and for suborning the strong by duping them into accepting the small virtues of small people.

> [Religions] side with the defectives; . . . they confirm the rights of all those who suffer from life as though it were a disease; they would like to render invalid and impossible any other sentiment besides theirs. . . . They [have] preserved too much of what *should have perished*. . . . To turn upside down all valuations—*that* is what they had to do! To shatter the strong, to infect great hopes, to cast suspicion on the enjoyment of beauty, to break down everything autonomous, manly, victorious, dominating, all the instincts natural to the highest and best turned-out type of mankind, and bend it over

into uncertainty, distress of conscience, and self-destruction—to reverse every bit of love for the earth and things earthly and control of the earth into hatred of things earthly and of the earth: this was the self-assumed task of the church.[h]

The Decadence of Contemporary Culture

In every age the great majority of people are weak; slave morality therefore always tends to predominate. But Nietzsche believed that the nineteenth century was even more mediocre, flat, conventional, and cautious than earlier periods. So-called progress was producing the "factory-slave," who was no longer a person but a gear, and who was so debased that he thought his shame was a virtue. Nietzsche concentrated his attack on the new German *Reich*, which Bismarck had brought into being after Prussia's victory over France and which (it seemed to Nietzsche) represented in advanced form every vice of the times. His discussion of German universities, for instance, has an extraordinarily modern sound:

> For seventeen years I have never tired of calling attention to the *despiritualizing* influence of our current science-industry. The hard helotism[20] to which the tremendous range of the sciences condemns every scholar today is a main reason why those with a fuller, richer, *profounder* disposition no longer find a congenial education and congenial *educators*. There is nothing of which our culture suffers more than of the super-abundance of pretentious jobbers and fragments of humanity; our universities are, *against* their will, the real hothouses for this kind of withering of the instincts of the spirit. And the whole of Europe already has some idea of this—power politics deceives nobody. Germany is considered more and more as Europe's *flatland*.[i]

And, in a passage prophetic of the rise of totalitarian dictatorships in the twentieth century, Nietzsche points out that the circumstances that have turned most men into factory slaves also tend to produce a few strong types:

> The same new conditions which will, on the average, bring about an equalization and mediocritization of man, a useful, hardworking, adaptable herd-animal of many uses, are also disposed in the highest degree to the creation of exceptional men of most dangerous and fascinating quality. For while . . . the total impression that these future Europeans will make will probably be one of manifold, gossipy, willpower-poor and extremely employable workers who *need* a boss, a master who gives them commands, as they need their daily bread; while, in other words, the democratization of Europe will amount to the creation of a type prepared in the subtlest sense for

20 [Helots were the slaves of ancient Sparta—AUTHOR.]

slavery—the individual, meanwhile, the exceptional case, the *strong* man, will turn out to be stronger and richer than he has probably ever been, thanks to the lack of prejudice in his schooling, thanks to the enormous varied practice he can get in skills and disguises. . . . The democratization of Europe is at the same time an involuntary arrangement for the training of tyrants. . . .[j]

The Existential Problem

Some of the sociological, economic, and political causes of herd mentality have been mentioned above, but Nietzsche believed that the most fundamental cause is our horror at the "abyss" in man and nature. There have always been a few perceptive individuals who have known that man is "merciless, greedy, insatiable, murderous," that he hangs "upon the back of a tiger."[k] But for centuries most men have managed to repress this knowledge by the fiction that man is a unique species specially created by a beneficent God and that the universe in which He placed him is a neat and tidy teleological system. According to Nietzsche, science has finally exploded these rationalizations; the knowledge that they are myths is beginning to enter our consciousness, despite our desire not to hear. Our conventionality, our blandness, and our discretion are actually protective devices, designed to prevent us from recognizing the true nature of the world. We are determined to stay at the surface, to think safe thoughts and to live by safe values, because we are terrified to look beyond them and find that the world is purposeless and meaningless—simply brute fact.

These insights were expressed by Nietzsche in two phrases that have become famous as a summary of his view—"God is dead" and "Everything eternally recurs." To say that God is dead is to say that men no longer believe there is a cosmic order. What looks like an objective order is merely a projection into chaos of man's desperate human need to believe there is reason and purpose in the universe. From this point of view a universe in which there is a malevolent god who could be held responsible for our misfortunes would be better than a universe in which God is dead and everything that happens might just as well not have happened. This is the feeling expressed in Hardy's poem *Hap:*

> If but some vengeful god would call to me
> From up the sky, and laugh: "Thou suffering thing,
> Know that thy sorrow is my ecstasy,
> That thy love's loss is my hate's profiting!"
>
> Then would I bear it, clench myself, and die,
> Steeled by the sense of ire unmerited;
> Half eased in that a Powerfuller than I
> Had willed and meted me the tears I shed.

> But not so. How arrives it joy lies slain,
> And why unblooms the best hope ever sown?
> —Crass Causality obstructs the sun and rain,
> And dicing Time for gladness casts a moan. . . .
> These purblind Doomsters had as readily strown
> Blisses about my pilgrimage as pain.[1]

To say that everything eternally recurs is to say that everything that has ever happened happens again and again an infinite number of times. At first, there may seem to be a conflict between this statement and the assertion that God is dead (that there is no order). The assurance that everything happens again and again implies a kind of order after all. But these poetical expressions of Nietzsche's must not be taken too literally. Underlying both of them is the denial that there is anything in the universe that could provide a rationale for human struggles. Men make great sacrifices for causes in which they believe and to whose eventual triumph they are committed. But if God is dead, progress is an illusion. All our efforts, all our seeming achievements, become infinitely inconsequential as they eternally recur. This, according to Nietzsche, is the terrible truth that every man must sooner or later face. How he himself faced it is described in "The Vision of the Loneliest."

"THE VISION OF THE LONELIEST"

Not long ago I walked gloomily through the deadly pallor of dusk—gloomy and hard, with lips pressed together. Not only one sun had set for me. A path that ascended defiantly through stones, malicious, lonely, not cheered by herb or shrub—a mountain path crunched under the defiance of my foot. . . . Upward—defying the spirit that drew it downward toward the abyss, the spirit of gravity, my devil and archenemy. Upward—although he sat on me, half dwarf, half mole, lame, making lame, dripping lead into my ear, leaden thoughts into my brain. . . .

But there is something in me that I call courage; that has so far slain my every discouragement. This courage finally bade me stand still and speak: "Dwarf! It is you or I!"

For courage is the best slayer, courage which attacks. . . .

Courage also slays dizziness at the edge of abysses: and where does man not stand at the edge of abysses? Is not seeing always—seeing abysses?

Courage is the best slayer: courage slays even pity. But pity is the deepest abyss: as deeply as man sees into life, he also sees into suffering.

Courage, however, is the best slayer—courage which attacks: which slays even death itself, for it says, "Was *that* life? Well then! Once more!" . . .

Then something happened that made me lighter, for the dwarf jumped from my shoulder, being curious, and he crouched on a stone before me. But there was a gateway just where he had stopped.

"Behold this gateway, dwarf!" I continued. "It has two faces. Two paths meet here; no one has yet followed either to its end. This long lane stretches back for an eternity. And the long lane out there, that is another eternity. They contradict each other, these paths; they offend each other face to face; and it is here at this gateway that they come together. The name of the gateway is inscribed above: 'Moment.' . . .

"Behold," I continued, "this moment! From this gateway, Moment, a long eternal lane leads *backward:* behind us lies an eternity. Must not whatever *can* walk have walked on this lane before? Must not whatever *can* happen have happened, have been done, have passed by before? And if everything has been there before—what do you think, dwarf, of this moment? Must not this gateway too have been there before? And are not all things knotted together so firmly that this moment draws after it *all* that is to come? Therefore—itself too? For whatever *can* walk—in this long lane out *there,* too, it *must* walk once more.

"And this slow spider, which crawls in the moonlight, and this moonlight itself, and I and you in the gateway, whispering together, whispering of eternal things—must not all of us have been there before? And return and walk in that other lane, out there, before us, in this long dreadful lane,—must we not eternally return?"

Thus I spoke, more and more softly; for I was afraid of my own thoughts and the thoughts behind my thoughts. . . .

Where was the dwarf gone now? And the gateway? And the spider? And all the whispering? Was I dreaming, then? Was I waking up?

Among wild cliffs, I stood suddenly alone, bleak, in the bleakest moonlight. But *there lay a man.* . . . A young shepherd I saw, writhing, gagging, in spasms, his face distorted, and a heavy black snake hung out of his mouth. Had I ever seen so much nausea and pale dread on one face? He seemed to have been asleep when the snake crawled into his throat, and there bit itself fast. My hand tore at the snake and tore in vain; it did not tear the snake out of his throat. Then it cried out of me: "Bite! Bite its head off! Bite!" Thus it cried out of me—my dread, my hatred, my nausea, my pity, all that is good and wicked in me cried out of me with a single cry.

The shepherd . . . bit as my cry counseled him; he bit with a good bite. Far away he spewed the head of the snake—and he jumped up. No longer shepherd, no longer human—one changed, radiant, *laughing!* Never yet on earth has a human being laughed as he laughed! O my brothers, I heard a laughter that was no human laughter; and now a thirst gnaws at me, a longing that never grows still. My longing for this laughter gnaws at me; oh, how do I bear to go on living! And how could I bear to die now![m]

It is instructive to compare this vision of the loneliest with Plato's myth of the cave. In the *Republic* Plato pictured men as chained deep in a cave, contemplating flickering shadows that they mistakenly hold to be real objects. Nietzsche—and Kierkegaard, too, of course—would have agreed with this view of man; indeed, they would have said that nineteenth-century Europeans were chained in an even deeper and darker cave than Plato's Greeks. Furthermore, according to Plato's myth, here and there an exceptional man manages to free himself from his chains and begins the long and difficult climb out of the cave.

Again, Kierkegaard and Nietzsche would have agreed that there is an ascent, and that this ascent is difficult and rare. Finally, according to Plato, the climbers eventually reach the mouth of the cave and find themselves in a world that is beautiful and good and that is illumined by the splendid light of the sun. Here Kierkegaard and Nietzsche part company with Plato. Of course, Kierkegaard held that there is a world outside the cave, and that this world is beautiful and good. But he wholly rejected Plato's view that men can find their way to this world by their own, unaided "natural" powers. Escape is possible, he held, only by a leap of faith—by the climber's passionate commitment to the sun outside that he has never seen and for whose existence he has, as yet, no evidence.

According to Nietzsche, Plato and Kierkegaard were deluding themselves: There is no world outside the cave. Both Plato's conviction that the existence of such a world can be established by rational means and Kierkegaard's admitted leap of faith are refuges of "slaves" who, having become fainthearted, weary, and dizzy from looking into the abyss, have given up the climb. Where does the climb lead? Nowhere. There is only the climber and his knowledge that, however far and long he climbs, he is doomed to repeat the same ascent endlessly. Why climb at all then? Because it is our nature to do so. The only question is how well we climb and how we cope with our knowledge that the climb is meaningless. A man who is strong enough to accept this "truth" and to laugh—a man who can bite the snake and spew it forth—is strong indeed. He is, in fact, no mere man but a master, a superman, an overman.

Overman

Nietzsche's overman, it is clear, is not a future evolutionary product that will someday emerge and "lord it over" man, as man now lords it over the species from which he has evolved. Overmen in fact are just those rare individuals (those "windfalls") who become masters by mastering themselves and their passions, their powers, and their weaknesses. They feel nausea as they contemplate the nature of existence, for they are human; but they are not "all too human," because they are strong enough to overcome their nausea. They are those exceptional individuals who pass through pessimism to affirmation. An overman, wherever and whenever he appears, is simply

> . . . the truly exuberant, alive and world-affirming man who does not merely resign himself to and learn to get along with all that was and is, but who wants everything *as it was and is* back again, back forever and ever, insatiably calling *da capo*, not only to himself but to the whole spectacle and perform-ance, and not only to the performance but basically to that which necessitates and needs the performance because it forever and ever necessitates and needs itself![n]

Among the overmen whom Nietzsche specifically mentioned are Alcibiades, Alexander the Great, Julius Caesar, Cesare Borgia, and Napoleon. Their chief characteristics, apart from will power, were hardness, courage, and creativity. To be creative, if one is a politician, is to take existing institutions and shape them to new uses: For instance, Alexander destroyed the Greek city-state and Caesar destroyed the Roman republic in order to create great empires. To be creative is necessarily to be "hard," "beyond good and evil," indifferent to existing traditions, institutions, and values, and courageous enough to operate without norms because one is creating new ones. Thus the overman "suspends the ethical" (in Kierkegaard's terminology), but he does so out of the strength of his self-affirmation, not out of a weakness disguised as affirmation of a transcendent being.

Most of the overmen whom Nietzsche mentioned by name were politicians and generals whose creativity often expressed itself in the conquest of alien peoples or the subjugation of their fellow citizens. It would appear, however, that the creativity Nietzsche most admired was that of the artist; and everything that he says about the hardness, ruthlessness, and destructiveness of his overmen applies to Leonardo and Michelangelo as well as to Alexander and Caesar.

ARTISTIC CREATIVITY

The nature of artistic creativity was a theme that recurred in Nietzsche's writing from the start. His first book, *The Birth of Tragedy,* was a pioneering work on the psychology of the artist and on the Greek psyche. According to Nietzsche, the Greeks were not, as men of the Enlightenment had thought, a people of balance and moderation. On the contrary, they were unusually passionate and violent. Anyone who looks closely at Homeric and pre-Homeric man will see the "abyss of a terrifying savagery of hatred and the lust to annihilate." The Greek dramatists—Aeschylus and Sophocles, for instance—were fully aware of the abyss, but they were strong enough to look into it and still create works of art. The calm of mind achieved in their dramas should not deceive us:

> The luminous images of the Sophoclean heroes—those Apollonian masks—are the necessary productions of a deep look into the horror of nature; luminous spots, as it were, designed to cure an eye hurt by the ghastly night. Only in this way can we form an adequate notion of the seriousness of Greek "serenity"; whereas we find that serenity generally misinterpreted nowadays as a condition of undisturbed complacence.°

The balance of a great work of art is not static but dynamic. Like the balancing act of a tightrope walker, it reflects a continuous tension, an overcoming of opposing forces. The Greeks realized that artistic achievement is *won:* It is the outcome of a struggle against intractable materials and a competition for supremacy against other artists. This is why the *agon,* or contest, was so important in Greek life. The institution of ostracism, the educational practices of the Sophists, the musical theories of Pindar and Simonides, the dialogue form in which Plato wrote—all of these were expressions of the Greek preference for competition. "The Greek knows the artist *only as engaged in a personal fight*,"[p] and it is the omnipresence of competition in Greek society that brought about the superiority of Greek culture.

Nietzsche held that artistic creativity, like all creativity, is an expression of power; it is the overcoming of passion. Without passion, without frenzy, there would be no creativity.

> If there is to be art, if there is to be any aesthetic doing and seeing, one physiological condition is indispensable: frenzy. Frenzy must first have enhanced the excitability of the whole machine; else there is no art. All kinds of frenzy, however diversely conditioned, have the strength to accomplish this: above all, the frenzy of sexual excitement, this most ancient and original form of frenzy. Also the frenzy that follows all great cravings, all strong affects; the frenzy of feasts, contests, feats of daring, victory, all extreme movement; the frenzy of cruelty; the frenzy in destruction; the frenzy under certain meteorological influences, as for example the frenzy of spring; or under the influence of narcotics; and finally the frenzy of will, the frenzy of an overcharged and swollen will. What is essential in such frenzy is the feeling of increased strength and fullness. Out of this feeling one lends to things, one *forces* them to accept from us, one violates them. . . . A man in this state transforms things until they mirror his power—until they are reflections of his perfection. This *having to* transform into perfection is—art.[q]

Or, as Zarathustra put it more succinctly, "One must still have chaos in oneself to be able to give birth to a dancing star."[r] Thus frenzy is the precondition of creativity, but it is only the precondition. There must be the achievement, the projection, of order and pattern. That which is given order and pattern is the work of art, whether this be a painting, a symphony, a new state, or a dancing star.

Nietzsche's view of creativity can be rephrased in terms of the concept of sublimation—one of those seminal ideas in which Nietzsche anticipated Freud.[21] The will to power can, and on occasion does, express itself simply in hitting out in all directions, in a wild, unrestrained thrashing about. But this is animal; there is nothing human about it. What makes man human is the ability to contain and direct his will to power. Such self-discipline is not a sign of weakness, as is knuckling under to someone else's ideas and orders. Indeed, to be able to exercise self-restraint for the sake of an ideal of order that a person has himself chosen is the highest possible expression of the will to power. What the noblest of all overmen overcome is themselves, not others.

From the fact that Nietzsche made "self-overcoming" the fundamental aspect of artistic creativity it follows that in his view the greatest work of art a

21 See p. 246.

man can create is himself. Goethe is an example of this latter, and best, type of overman, for of all the works of art Goethe created, the finest was Goethe himself.

> *Goethe*—not a German event, but a European one; a magnificent attempt to overcome the eighteenth century by a return to nature, by an *ascent* to the naturalness of the Renaissance—a kind of self-overcoming on the part of that century. He bore its strongest instincts within himself: the sensibility, the idolatry of nature, the anti-historic, the idealistic, the unreal and revolutionary (the latter being merely a form of the unreal). He sought help from history, natural science, antiquity, and also Spinoza, but, above all, from practical activity; he surrounded himself with limited horizons; he did not retire from life but put himself into the midst of it; he was not fainthearted but took as much as possible upon himself, over himself, into himself. What he wanted was *totality;* he fought the mutual extraneousness of reason, sense, feeling, and will (preached with the most abhorrent scholasticism by *Kant,* the antipode of Goethe); he disciplined himself to wholeness, he *created* himself.[s]

Nietzsche the admirer of overman evaluated consciousness very differently from Nietzsche the romantic primitivist. When the latter strain was dominant in Nietzsche's thought, consciousness seemed to him to have been an evolutionary mistake.[22] As an admirer of overman, however, he believed that it is precisely consciousness that makes it possible for the strong man to be strong. If, for instance, a man was, like the animals and plants, unconscious (even if he was only partially conscious, as ordinary men are), he would not know that God is dead. He would never experience cosmic loneliness, and there would be nothing to overcome. Nor, obviously, would it be possible for him to be a creator—to conceive of an ideal of order and to impose discipline on himself—without the fullest kind of consciousness and self-awareness. From the one point of view Nietzsche dreaded the snake of consciousness. This is the point of view that he shared with Dostoevsky and that is echoed in much of twentieth-century culture. From the other point of view Nietzsche welcomed the snake, for its bite is the peculiar mark and badge of overman.

It may seem that the aspect of Nietzsche's thought that emphasizes the superiority of the intellect and the nobility of the ideal of self-realization does no more than express, with the fervor of personal discovery, ideas that have been familiar at least since Aristotle. That there are similarities with Aristotle's philosophy is obvious, but there are also differences. It is easy to maintain one's balance when one walks on the ground; it is an achievement to do so on a tightrope. Aristotle's ethics focused on the beauty of balance achieved; Nietzsche's focused on the overcoming of difficulties. Nietzsche may well have been right in maintaining that the Greeks themselves did not achieve balance easily, but it is also probably true (as Nietzsche himself would certainly have maintained) that balance was much harder to achieve in the nineteenth century. In his

22 See pp. 249–50.

interpretation of the ideal of self-realization he thus reflected the age in which he lived. In a world in which every man is alone, confronted with an alien and hostile environment, and aware of the ultimate meaninglessness and futility of his life, the achievement of balance is rare indeed and must be continuously renewed.

It is suggestive, too, of the differences between Greek and modern culture that whereas for Aristotle the citizen was the model for self-realization, for Nietzsche the artist was the paradigm. In former times men believed that God created the universal cosmos out of chaos. In a world in which the myth of the creator god has been exploded, the artist is the most godlike of beings, for in the work of art he creates a miniature cosmos from the chaos within him. Perhaps it is a thought such as this, first enunciated by Nietzsche, that explains the preoccupation of modern writers (Joyce, Mann, Hesse, and Eliot, to name a few) with the artist and his creativity.

Interpretations of Nietzsche's Interpretation

Nietzsche held that men can never get back to the "original text"; they are confined to interpretations that reflect their biases and preconceptions. This at least is the interpretation of Nietzsche presented in this chapter. But few philosophers have been the subject of more varied interpretations. For instance, though most of his writing was strongly anti-anti-Semitic, Nietzsche sometimes sounded like those he criticized.[23] It is not surprising, therefore, that he has been regarded as an anti-Semite. He has also been called a precursor of the Nazis; he was certainly claimed by them as one of their own. It is not difficult to see why: He too praised war and warriors, hardness and cruelty; he too loathed such bourgeois virtues as respect for the "sanctity" of promises and contracts. If he praised Leonardo and Goethe, he also praised Alcibiades and Cesare Borgia, who were overmen only in the magnitude of their self-affirmation and destructiveness.

What would Nietzsche have thought of Hitler? It is impossible to say—except that, like most people, he would probably have made different assessments at different times, depending on his own mood and also, of course, on the stage in Hitler's career. And like many people, but unlike most philosophers, Nietzsche would have written down and published all these assessments just as they occurred to him, without making an effort to reach an overall, balanced appraisal. This approach characterized Nietzsche's writing generally. Far from being systematic, he was, like Kierkegaard, positively antisystematic: For Nietzsche, to aim at consistency was a sign of weakness. Thus in discussing creativity, if he sometimes

23 For instance, "It was the Jew who . . . dared to invert the aristocratic value equations good/noble/powerful/beautiful/happy/favored-of-the-gods and . . . who started the slave revolt in morals . . ."—*Genealogy of Morals*, pp. 167–68.

emphasized the "dancing star" that is finally achieved, he also on occasion emphasized the initial chaos, frenzy, and destruction. Similarly, though much of his enthusiastic talk about war and warriors was undoubtedly metaphorical, some of it appears to have been literal praise of war and the destruction it entails.

But Nietzsche was not inconsistent merely as a result of carelessness and indifference. He was quite deliberately ambiguous. To be misunderstood by the many was the risk he ran in order to be understood by the few. "Every deep thinker fears being understood more than he fears being misunderstood." [t] Nietzsche meant that he did not want to pass along nuggets of meaning unchanged to his readers; he wanted, rather, to induce them to be creative by finding new meanings for themselves in his writings. This is why he so often wrote in aphorisms. They were designed to shock, to challenge convictions and prejudices. "An aphorism that has been honestly struck cannot be deciphered simply by reading it off; this is only the beginning of the work of interpretation. . . ." [u]

But Nietzsche also desperately wanted to be understood in the ordinary sense of "being understood"—that is, he wanted to establish a real communion with his readers. At one and the same time, then, he wanted his writings to be both a text and also only a starting point for other men's interpretations. This paradox reflects the basic division in Nietzsche's personality and in his view of man: On the one hand, man is a creature capable of transcending himself and becoming an overman. On the other hand, he is a mere evolutionary quirk, an oddity. From this point of view, the whole conception of the overman is only a rationalization— a rationalization that, try as we may, we men never quite manage to believe in. Hence, if men cannot learn to laugh at themselves, their only alternative is to weep. This is Nietzsche's central "message." It is significant of the great change that has occurred in contemporary culture that what was once regarded as a madman's ravings is now more and more widely regarded as a realistic assessment of the human condition.

CHAPTER 7

Three Philosophies of Process: Bergson, Dewey, and Whitehead

The three philosophers whose views are examined in this chapter differ markedly from those studied in the preceding chapter in their outlook on life as well as in their conception of philosophy. Kierkegaard and Nietzsche were representative of what was described in that chapter as the countermovement against the world view that was predominant in their day. Though Bergson, Dewey, and Whitehead belonged to a later generation, and though they were in their own ways innovators, their break with the past was less radical than that of Kierkegaard and Nietzsche, for all three were members of the philosophical establishment. These philosophers (especially Dewey) were critics of the *status quo*, but they were not alienated from it; temperamentally each of them was well adapted (too well adapted, critics might say) to his social environment. They believed in the possibility of progress, which they thought could be promoted by intelligent action on men's part. They were reformers, not rebels.

Further, though each of these philosophers presumably had to face his own existential problem, this problem did not fill his whole mental and emotional horizon. These philosophers regarded existence as essentially a matter to be dealt with in private; philosophy, as they conceived of it, was concerned with public problems. In this respect, they were inheritors and continuators of the tradition of philosophizing in the grand manner; they believed that the business of philosophers was to tackle the classical questions about the nature of reality, of knowledge, and of value, and to produce well-rounded, articulated treatises on metaphysics, ethics, art, religion, and similar topics. This belief was true of Bergson and Dewey, both of whom attacked what they thought were the exaggerated claims of "reason," but it was especially true of Whitehead, whose philosophy of organism is the latest in a series of vast philosophical syntheses that began with Aristotle and continued with Thomas and Hegel.

Finally, Bergson, Dewey, and Whitehead shared an interest in process. The two developments in nineteenth-century philosophy that most deeply influenced all three of these thinkers were the notion of a dynamic, changing reality, and the prestige accorded to the natural sciences. These two trends came together, as has been seen, in the concept of evolution; and in a very real sense the three thinkers discussed in this chapter were all philosophers of evolution. They recognized that thought, as well as its objects, evolves, that ideas have a history relevant to their present status, and that philosophical theories are outgrowths of culture rather than eternal truths discovered by disembodied spirits.

Despite these basic similarities, the three philosophers differed greatly in the ways in which they responded to other leading ideas in nineteenth- and early twentieth-century culture. Bergson and Whitehead represented the metaphysical interest that survived Kant's "criticism" and continued to dominate much of nineteenth-century thought. Dewey, on the other hand, represented the empirical, antimetaphysical trend that, since Hume, has been an increasingly powerful influence on Western thought.

Bergson's metaphysical position grew directly out of the materialism versus vitalism controversy examined in Chapter 5.[1] It was an attempt to use scientific findings to sustain an essentially antiscientific conception of reality. His metaphysics was "Romantic" in its emphasis on dynamism and continuity, in its denial of the capacity of reason to know the inner nature of reality, and in its assertion that reality can nonetheless be known—in intuition. In all these respects, Bergson was close to Schopenhauer, but because he took the theory of evolution seriously as a doctrine of progress, he had none of Schopenhauer's exaggerated pessimism.

If Bergson was close to Schopenhauer, Whitehead was in many ways close to Hegel. Whitehead reaffirmed the capacity of reason to know reality, and he sought to establish a new categoreal scheme of metaphysically valid concepts. But whereas Hegel had derived his categoreal scheme by reflecting on the meaning of an alleged identity-in-difference, Whitehead attempted to generalize

1 See pp. 199–202.

the concepts underlying modern physics. Hence (and this is symptomatic of the change in nineteenth-century thought) Whitehead claimed to be empirical and scientific in a way Hegel had scorned.

Dewey, in contrast, was sceptical of both the possibility and the desirability of building philosophical systems; like Nietzsche, he regarded the system-building urge as a reflection of man's sense of insecurity. But, unlike Nietzsche, Dewey believed that philosophy has a useful function to perform—provided that it is modeled on the natural sciences and is content with probability, instead of aiming at absolute certainty. His emphasis on the instrumental and pragmatic character of knowledge was closely related to his deep interest in social problems. More so than either Bergson or Whitehead, Dewey represented the great drive for social reform that had developed in the nineteenth century.

Each of these philosophers was thus the continuator of trends and attitudes that have their roots deep in the Western past. But each was also an original thinker of stature; each enjoyed a great vogue among his contemporaries precisely because he had something to say that was significant to them. A study of their work will show once again to what extent the life of the mind is continuous, open-ended, and diverse.

Bergson

Bergson's[2] starting point was an attack on conceptual knowledge very similar to Schopenhauer's; it too was rooted in the conviction that concepts falsify a continuous real by dividing it. And, like Schopenhauer, Bergson believed that there is a superior kind of knowledge, which he called intuition, by means of which men have direct and immediate access to the nature of reality.

> [There are] two profoundly different ways of knowing a thing. The first implies that we move round the object; the second that we enter into it. The first depends on the point of view at which we are placed and on the symbols by which we express ourselves. The second neither depends on a point of view nor relies on any symbol. The first kind of knowledge may be said to stop at the *relative;* the second, in those cases where it is possible, to attain the *absolute.*
>
> Consider, for example, the movement of an object in space. My perception of the motion will vary with the point of view, moving or stationary, from which I observe it. My expression of it will vary with the system of axes,

2 Henri Bergson was born in France in 1859 and lived and taught there all his life. When, after the fall of France in 1940, the Vichy government introduced anti-Semitic measures based on the Nazi model, it was proposed, because of Bergson's international reputation, that he be exempted from them. He refused to be treated differently, resigned his various honors, and, although at that time an enfeebled old man who had to be supported while standing in line, registered with the other Jews. He died a few days later, in January, 1941.

or points of reference, to which I relate it; that is, with the symbols by which I translate it. For this double reason I call such motion *relative:* in the one case, as in the other, I am placed outside the object itself. But when I speak of an *absolute* movement, I am attributing to the moving object an interior and, so to speak, states of mind; I also imply that I am in sympathy with those states, and that I insert myself in them by an effort of imagination. . . . I shall no longer grasp the movement from without, remaining where I am, but from where it is, from within, as it is in itself. I shall possess an absolute.

Consider, again, a character whose adventures are related to me in a novel. The author may multiply the traits of his hero's character, may make him speak and act as much as he pleases, but all this can never be equivalent to the simple and indivisible feeling which I should experience if I were able for an instant to identify myself with the person of the hero himself. . . . Description, history, and analysis leave me here in the relative. Coincidence with the person himself would alone give me the absolute.

. . . .

It follows from this that an absolute could only be given in an *intuition,* whilst everything else falls within the province of *analysis.* By intuition is meant the kind of *intellectual sympathy* by which one places oneself within an object in order to coincide with what is unique in it and consequently inexpressible. Analysis, on the contrary, is the operation which reduces the object to elements already known, that is, to elements common both to it and other objects. To analyze, therefore, is to express a thing as a function of something other than itself. All analysis is thus a translation, a development into symbols, a representation taken from successive points of view. . . . In its eternally unsatisfied desire to embrace the object around which it is compelled to turn, analysis multiplies without end the number of its points of view . . . , and ceaselessly varies its symbols that it may perfect the always imperfect translation. It goes on, therefore, to infinity. But intuition, if intuition is possible, is a simple act. . . .

There is one reality, at least, which we all seize from within, by intuition and not by simple analysis. It is our own personality in its flowing through time—our self which endures. . . . [This inner life] is a continuous flux which is not comparable to any flux I have ever seen. There is a succession of states . . . so profoundly animated with a common life that I [cannot say] where any one of them finishe[s] or where another commence[s]. In reality no one of them begins or ends, but all extend into each other. . . .

The inner life is all this at once: variety of qualities, continuity of progress, and unity of direction. It cannot be represented by . . . *concepts,* that is by abstract, general, or simple ideas. . . . Concepts . . . have the disadvantage of being in reality symbols substituted for the object they symbolize. . . . Just in so far as abstract ideas can render service to analysis, that is, to the scientific study of the object in its relations to other objects, so far are they incapable of replacing intuition, that is, the metaphysical investigation of what is essential and unique in the object. . . . Concepts, laid side by side, never actually give us more than an artificial reconstruction of the object. . . . Besides the illusion [that they give us the object instead of only its shadow] there is also a very serious danger. For the concept . . . can only symbolize a particular property by making it common to an infinity of things. It therefore always more or less deforms the property by the extension it gives to it. . . .[a]

Limitations of Conceptual Knowledge

Kierkegaard would have felt considerable sympathy with much of this discussion. For instance, the distinction Bergson draws in this passage between reading about a character in a novel and *being* that character is close to Kierkegaard's distinction between objective and subjective truth. Both thinkers derogated whatever is indirect, impartial, and neutral. Furthermore, like Kierkegaard, Bergson believed that the prime example of intuitive knowledge is the self—and not the abstract and impersonal self of traditional philosophy, but the individual self of the intuitive knower. However, though Bergson believed that intuitive knowledge starts with the self, he did not think it stopped there. Whereas Kierkegaard was interested exclusively in his own existential problems and in how subjective knowledge could illumine them, Bergson was interested in what philosophy has traditionally been concerned with—the nature of reality. Hence, unlike Kierkegaard, he developed a metaphysics.

> Metaphysics . . . is only truly itself when it goes beyond the concept, or at least when it frees itself from rigid and ready-made concepts in order to create a kind very different from those we habitually use; I mean supple, mobile, and almost fluid representations, always ready to mould themselves on the fleeting forms of intuition. . . .
>
> Concepts . . . generally go together in couples and represent two contraries. There is hardly any concrete reality which cannot be observed from two opposing standpoints, which cannot consequently be subsumed under two antagonistic concepts [for example, the self is both a unity and a multiplicity]. Hence a thesis and an antithesis which we endeavor in vain to reconcile logically, for the very simple reason that it is impossible, with concepts and observations taken from outside points of view, to make a thing. But from the object, seized by intuition, we pass easily in many cases to the two contrary concepts; and as in that way thesis and antithesis can be seen to spring from reality, we grasp at the same time how it is that the two are opposed and how they are reconciled.[b]

The last few sentences obviously refer to Hegel's account of thought as a triadic movement from thesis to antithesis to synthesis.[3] Bergson believed that Hegel was correct in aiming at unity, in not being content with plurality and diversity. But he thought Hegel was mistaken in holding that the same cognitive

3 See pp. 124–26.

process that develops the contradictions can also resolve them. To reconcile thesis and antithesis a radically different kind of cognitive process is needed—intuition.

Hegel had already dealt with this argument—at least to his own satisfaction. Intuition is a lower, not a higher, level of cognition. To appeal to it is to return to the level of immediacy instead of rising to the level of self-mediation. In a word, Hegel took his stand on Kant's dictum that concepts without percepts are empty and percepts without concepts are blind. Intuitions are percepts without concepts—they are "the night in which all cows are black." Experience without the structure and organization that concepts supply is merely an undifferentiated "Aha!" The feeling may be powerful, moving, and exciting, but it does not *know* what it is or what it means.

Bergson was certainly not alone in rejecting this basically Kantian thesis. One of the central tenets of the Romantic movement was the belief that conceptual knowledge is distorting. But it is one thing for a Romantic poet to reject conceptual knowledge, or even for an existential thinker like Kierkegaard to do so, for the former is concerned chiefly to "express" his feelings and the latter focuses primarily on his own personal problem. It is another thing for a metaphysician to attack conceptual knowledge, for he is committed to describing reality in general terms. To use a conceptual mode of discourse to argue that conceptual discourse is intrinsically distorting and inadequate is paradoxical. If reality is "unique," as Bergson claimed, this truth about it cannot be uttered. If reality is "inexpressible" by conceptual means, it is surely more appropriate to express its nature poetically than to expound a metaphysical and epistemological theory about its inexpressibility.

It is interesting in this connection to note that Bergson's writing is highly metaphorical. Though his reliance on metaphor is doubtless consistent with his derogation of analysis, Bergson did not recognize the limitations this imposed. It seemed to him that his metaphors functioned as a part of a reasoned argument—at least until they were challenged, at which point they became metaphors that were not to be taken literally. In his writings he gives the impression of having tried to make the best of both worlds. On the one hand, the reader is made to feel that what is presented is a connected *theory*, not a poetic or mystic vision. On the other hand, as soon as the reader accepts it as a theory and looks for evidence, he is reminded that evidence is only a fiction created by intellect in its own image.

The Nature of Reality

But if we pass over this fundamental difficulty, the next question is, "What does intuition disclose the real to be?" The clue, as has already been seen, is the intuition each man has—or is presumably capable of having—of his own nature.

We are, then, to look within. What we find when we do so Bergson variously called "duration," "mobility," and "life." It is an experience of change—not of states that change or of things with changing properties, but of change itself. It is an experience in which past infiltrates present through and through. This experience of duration, Bergson admitted, is very difficult to achieve. At best it is only momentary; furthermore, it is wholly private and incommunicable ("inexpressible" conceptually). Yet it is all the philosopher has to go on when he sets out to construct a metaphysics.

INTUITION OF THE SELF AS DURATION

I find, first of all, that I pass from state to state. I am warm or cold, I am merry or sad, I work or I do nothing, I look at what is around me or I think of something else. . . . I change, then, without ceasing. But this is not saying enough. Change is far more radical than we are at first inclined to suppose.

For I speak of each of my states as if it formed a block and were a separate whole. . . . Of each state, taken separately, I am apt to think that it remains the same during all the time that it prevails. Nevertheless, a slight effort of attention would reveal to me that there is no feeling, no idea, no volition which is not undergoing change every moment: if a mental state ceased to vary, its duration would cease to flow. Let us take the most stable of internal states, the visual perception of a motionless external object. The object may remain the same, I may look at it from the same side, at the same angle, in the same light; nevertheless the vision I now have of it differs from that which I had just had, even if only because the one is an instant older than the other. My memory is there, which conveys something of the past into the present. My mental state, as it advances on the road of time, is continually swelling with the duration which it accumulates: it goes on increasing— rolling upon itself, as a snowball on the snow. . . .

Duration is the continuous progress of the past which gnaws into the future and which swells as it advances. And as the past grows without ceasing, so also there is no limit to its preservation. . . . In its entirety, probably, it follows us at every instant; all that we have felt, thought and willed from our earliest infancy is there, leaning over the present which is about to join it, pressing against the portals of consciousness that would fain leave it outside. The cerebral mechanism is arranged just so as to drive back into the unconscious almost the whole of this past, and to admit beyond the threshold only that which can cast light on the present situation or further the action now being prepared—in short, only that which can give *useful* work. At the most, a few superfluous recollections may succeed in smuggling themselves through the half-open door. These memories, messengers from the unconscious, remind us of what we are dragging behind us unawares. . . . Doubtless we think with only a small part of our past, but it is with our entire past, including the original bent of our soul, that we desire, will and act.[c]

To take knowledge of the self as the starting point for construction of a metaphysical theory has been a characteristic of philosophy since Descartes; and it is of course typical of post-Kantian views of the self to hold that self is activity and not a static, encapsulated substance. This view was as true of Hegel and Schopenhauer as it was of Kierkegaard and Nietzsche. There is thus nothing new in Bergson's basic thesis; it differs, however, in important ways from earlier versions, chiefly because it was deeply influenced by Bergson's understanding of the theory of evolution. What impressed Bergson about this theory was not the struggle for survival but the emergence of new forms of life; what caught his imagination was the vision of a great energy pouring itself forth in endless fecundity, instead of being confined to a few eternal archetypes. It was this cosmic vision that he transferred—in miniature, as it were—to the life-experience of the individual: The self that is revealed in intuition, he maintained, is the continuous unfolding of new experiences that include and incorporate the past while moving steadily into the future.

In emphasizing the self as a continuous flow, Bergson differed sharply from psychologists of the then-dominant associationist school, who tended to think of the psychic life as consisting of a number of discrete blocks, or units, externally related to one another. He also differed from Kierkegaard and Nietzsche. They too rejected atomism in psychology and defined the self in terms of activity. But whereas Bergson viewed this activity as the continuous and relatively smooth unfolding of new experience, they viewed it as choosing and deciding. This divergence reflects the difference between an interest in the self that is primarily psychological and descriptive and one that is primarily concerned with existential problems. These differing views of the nature of the psychic life thus confirm Nietzsche's contention that our varied interpretations of the "original text" reveal our differing underlying values.

REALITY AS DURATION

But even if the self is correctly intuited to be duration, how does the philosopher who has intuited this truth get outside himself to a public reality? How can he know that the world is constituted of this same duration that he finds in himself? This is the problem Schopenhauer confronted and failed to solve when he maintained that the world is "really" will.[4] But in Bergson's case the problem is complicated by his claim that duration not only flows but is also creative and efficacious—that it is the underlying cause of the various visible and empirical transformations that are studied in the sciences. The following passage shows the inadequacy of the evidence by which Bergson moved from duration as a psychological characteristic of the self to duration as the metaphysical principle that explains all evolutionary change.

> But if metaphysics is to proceed by intuition, if intuition has the mobility of duration as its object, and if duration is of a psychical nature, shall we not be confining the philosopher to the exclusive contemplation of himself? . . . To talk in this way would be . . . to misconceive the singular nature

4 See p. 149.

of duration, and at the same time the essentially active, I might almost say violent, character of metaphysical intuition. It would be failing to see that the method we speak of alone permits us to go beyond idealism, as well as realism, to affirm the existence of objects inferior and superior (though in a certain sense interior) to us, to make them coexist together without difficulty, and to dissipate gradually the obscurities that analysis accumulates round these great problems. . . .

[Let us] place ourselves, by an effort of intuition, in the concrete flow of duration. . . . Strictly, there might well be no other duration than our own, as, for example, there might be no other color in the world but orange. But just as a consciousness based on color, which sympathized internally with orange, instead of perceiving it externally, would feel itself held between red and yellow, would even perhaps suspect beyond this last color a complete spectrum into which the continuity from red to yellow might expand naturally, so the intuition of our duration, far from leaving us suspended in the void as pure analysis would do, brings us into contact with a whole continuity of durations which we must try to follow, whether downwards or upwards; in both cases we can extend ourselves indefinitely by an increasingly violent effort, in both cases we transcend ourselves. In the first we advance towards a more and more attenuated duration, the pulsations of which, being rapider than ours, and dividing our simple sensation, dilute its quality into quantity; at the limit would be pure homogeneity, that pure *repetition* by which we define materiality. Advancing in the other direction, we approach a duration which *strains*, contracts, and intensifies itself more and more; at the limit would be eternity. No longer conceptual eternity, which is an eternity of death, but an eternity of life. A living, and therefore still moving eternity in which our own particular duration would be included as the vibrations are in light; an eternity which would be the concentration of all duration, as materiality is its dispersion. Between these two extreme limits intuition moves, and this movement is the very essence of metaphysics.[d]

Let us examine the difficulties with this view. The assertion that species evolve is an empirical hypothesis, subject to verification or disverification by biological and anatomical evidence. The assertion that duration is the force underlying all this evolutionary development is not an empirical hypothesis but a bald metaphysical statement, for there can be no evidence for or against it. Moreover, the assertion is highly ambiguous: Bergson became trapped in the old puzzle about the relation between reality and appearance—between the process (experienced in intuition) and the things processing (the material and bodily structures experienced in sense perception and studied in science). At times, as in the passage just quoted, Bergson wrote as if "matter" were one phase ("attenuated") of intuition; this suggests that Bergson's view was a form of monism. At other times, he assumed that matter is what the living force experienced in intuition works on. This suggests that matter has an independent existence of sorts and that Bergsonianism was a kind of dualism:

We may compare the process by which nature constructs an eye to the simple act by which we raise the hand. . . . Let us now imagine that . . . the hand has to pass through iron filings which are compressed and offer resistance to it in proportion as it goes forward. At a certain moment the hand will have exhausted its effort, and, at this very moment, the filings will be massed and coördinated in a certain definite form, to wit, that of the hand that is stopped and of a part of the arm. Now, suppose that the hand and arm are invisible. Lookers-on will seek the reason of the arrangement in the filings themselves and in forces within the mass. Some will account for the position of each filing by the action exerted upon it by the neighboring filings: these are the mechanists. Others will prefer to think that a plan of the whole has presided over the detail of these elementary actions: they are the finalists. But the truth is that there has been merely one indivisible act, that of the hand passing through the filings. . . .

The greater the effort of the hand, the farther it will go into the filings. But at whatever point it stops, instantaneously and automatically the filings coördinate and find their equilibrium. So with vision and its organ. According as the undivided act constituting vision advances more or less, the materiality of the organ is made of a more or less considerable number of mutually coördinated elements, but the order is necessarily complete and perfect.[e]

It is probably not possible to reconcile these different points of view. On the one hand Bergson spoke of "external resistances" to the living force; on the other, of "the materiality which it has had to assume."[f] Bergson wrote as if the evolutionary development he described was an objective fact. But the intellect that knows materiality has had a life history and has itself evolved. Hence the species and all their empirical unfoldings are merely appearances to intellects at a particular stage of their development. But this does not explain what is developing, and we are thrown back on our intuition of duration as the only real.

The Evolution of Intellect

Though this is a fundamental difficulty, it may nonetheless be useful to give a brief summary of Bergson's account of the course of evolution. The life force is "limited"; it "remains inadequate to the work it would fain produce" and operates on an "inert matter." As a result, evolutionary movement is not simple: "The resistance of inert matter was the obstacle that had first to be overcome. Life seems to have succeeded in this by dint of humility, by making itself very small and very insinuating, bending to physical and chemical forces . . . , [entering] into the habits of inert matter." In this way Bergson sought to account, in terms of his metaphysical scheme, for the fact that the evolutionary process began not from fully developed organisms but from "tiny masses of scarcely differentiated protoplasm." Despite their simplicity, these forms nevertheless possessed a "tremendous internal push." [g]

These most primitive forms cannot, properly speaking, be called either plants or animals, but they were more plantlike than animal-like. The first divergence occurred when differences in "alimentation" emerged. Plants derive their food directly from air, water, and soil; animals cannot assimilate their food unless it has already been transformed into organic substances by plants. This means that animals must be able to move about.

> Between mobility and consciousness there is an obvious relationship. No doubt, the consciousness of the higher organisms seems bound up with certain cerebral arrangements . . . , but . . . it would be as absurd to refuse consciousness to an animal because it has no brain as to declare it incapable of nourishing itself because it has no stomach. . . . [Even] the humblest organism is conscious in proportion to its power to move *freely*.[h]

Another divergence occurred when some animals "renounced" the protection of an "armor-plated sheath" and relied instead on "an agility that enabled them to escape their enemies, and also to assume the offensive, to choose the place and the moment of encounter. . . . It was to the animal's interest to make itself more mobile." [i] This naturally called for a correspondingly more complex nervous system. And the greater mobility resulted, also naturally, in higher forms of consciousness.

The next divergence was the most important of all. It marked the different ways in which the nervous system developed to meet the needs of the new mobility. In one line of development, it was "distributed amongst a varying— sometimes a considerable number—of appendages, each of which has its special function." In the main line of development, it was "concentrated in two pairs of members only, and these organs perform functions which depend much less strictly on their form." [j]

Bergson was not interested in the actual evolution of the nervous system; nor did he know anything about these matters at first hand. All this descriptive detail was only a springboard to what *did* interest him—the "two powers immanent in life and originally intermingled," which (he was persuaded) have produced, respectively, the two types of nervous systems just described. These powers, Bergson held, are "instinct" and "intelligence." But what, exactly, do these terms name? The two types of nervous systems are observable facts, as are the specific behaviors associated with each. Unless "instinct" and "intelligence" are simply names for these behaviors, they do not name empirical facts. How, then, do these terms function in Bergson's writings? Bearing in mind Nietzsche's analysis of the meaning of "cause," [5] we may suspect that instinct and intelligence are "fictions" ("myths" was another term Nietzsche used) in which "the personality betrays itself"—that is, these concepts enabled Bergson to express his

5 See pp. 242–43.

preference for unmediated experience and his dislike of an objective, conceptual approach.

But as soon as he started talking about "powers" in distinction from nervous systems Bergson shifted from empirically grounded concepts to speculation. Because he did not notice this drift, however, he was able to assume that the metaphysical generalizations he was developing did not differ in kind from the scientific generalizations he had taken over from the biologists and anatomists. The former, he thought, were merely of much greater scope and hence more important. Accordingly, he proceeded to use the contrasting ideas of instinct and intelligence as if they were scientific concepts.

Instinct, as it has developed in insects like ants and bees, makes use of "organized tools," that is, tools that are a part of the insect's body and that are each designed to perform a specific function necessary for the insect's survival. There is thus a wonderful certainty, precision, and inevitability about an insect's knowledge.

Intelligence, on the other hand, which has reached its highest development in man, operates by means of "unorganized tools." "Considered in what seems to be its original feature, [intelligence] is the faculty of manufacturing artificial objects, especially tools to make tools, and of indefinitely varying the manufacture." Thus, whereas the insect has a limited repertoire of actions, which it performs with great success, man has a much greater range of activities, but these are less certain and less effortless. "The advantages and drawbacks of these two modes of activity" are precisely complementary; indeed, they "balance so well" that "at the outset . . . it is hard to foretell which of the two will secure to the living being the greater empire over nature." [k]

INTELLECT AND ACTION

Consciousness occurs in its most complete form in intelligent animals, because intelligence presents the animal with options. Alternatives exist—the animal can use this tool or that one. The insect, on the other hand, does not have to worry about choices—its bodily organs are either adapted or not adapted to the situation. Consciousness in the full sense is always connected with "hesitation and choice":

> Consciousness is the light that plays around the zone of possible actions or potential activity which surrounds the action really performed by the living being. It signifies hesitation or choice. Where many equally possible actions are indicated without there being any real action (as in a deliberation that has not come to an end), consciousness is intense. Where the action performed is the only action possible (as in activity of the somnambulistic or more generally automatic kind), consciousness is reduced to nothing. . . . From this point of view, *the consciousness of a living being may be defined as an arithmetical difference between potential and real activity. It measures the interval between representation and action.*[l]

In a word, consciousness has a purely *practical* role. "Postulate action, and the very form of the intellect can be deduced from it." Because it is the function of intelligence (in contrast to instinct) to construct tools, intelligence must be especially competent to deal with matter.

> *Intelligence, as it leaves the hands of nature, has for its chief object the unorganized solid. . . .*
> The intellect is never quite at its ease, never entirely at home, except when it is working upon inert matter. [But] what is the most general property of the material world? It is extended: it presents to us objects external to other objects, and, in these objects, parts external to parts.[m]

In a word, the prime function of intellect is to arrange and rearrange bits of solid matter in various spatial relations.

Now, because men live in communities they must communicate with one another.[6] This requires language, and it is natural that language and the concepts employed in it should reflect the prime characteristic of intellect just described.

> Intelligence, even when it no longer operates upon its own object [that is, the unorganized solid], follows habits it has contracted in that operation. . . . Concepts, in fact, are outside each other, like objects in space; and they have the same stability as such objects, on which they have been modeled.[n]

It follows that "intellect is characterized by a natural inability to comprehend life"—that life and motion "escape it altogether."[o] Thus examination of evolutionary development has "confirmed"—at least in Bergson's view—the thesis of the *Introduction to Metaphysics;* by tracing the natural history of intellect, Bergson believed he had explained why conceptual thinking has those disabilities pointed out earlier. Because intellect is tied down to the useful, to the manipulation of solids, it never can comprehend the true, inner meaning of anything. If men had to depend on it, they would remain forever in outer darkness.

> The normal work of the intellect is far from being disinterested. We do not aim generally at knowledge for the sake of knowledge, but in order to take sides, to draw profit—in short, to satisfy an interest. . . . To try to fit a concept on an object is simply to ask what we can do with the object, and what it can do for us. To label an object with a certain concept is to mark in precise terms the kind of action or attitude the object should suggest to us. . . . But to carry this *modus operandi* into philosophy, . . . to use in order to obtain a disinterested knowledge of an object (that this time we desire to grasp as it is in itself) a manner of knowing inspired by a determinate interest, . . . is to go against the end we have chosen. . . . Either there is no philosophy possible, and all knowledge of things is practical knowledge

---

6 Insects also live in societies, of course. But since instinct has already produced the cooperation required for communal living, it is not necessary that language evolve among them.

aimed at the profit to be drawn from them, or else philosophy consists in placing oneself within the object itself by an effort of intuition.[p]

Bergson's attitude toward consciousness is thus different from Kierkegaard's and Nietzsche's. Whereas they derogated consciousness completely, Bergson held it to be useful at the level of action in the empirical world; it is seriously inadequate only when we mistakenly believe that it gives information about the inner nature of the things we encounter in our interactions with our environment. Given his presuppositions about evolution, Bergson was bound to assume that consciousness is useful: Because it has survived, it must have some survival value. Doubtless this less critical evaluation of consciousness also reflects a temperament very different from Kierkegaard's and Nietzsche's. Whereas they are deeply alienated, Bergson was generally sunny and optimistic. In his view the universe is basically good, and despite its infinite variety it is unified, for it is the expression of a single life force.

These fundamental attitudes are also revealed in Bergson's insistence that, though intellect and instinct are divergent evolutionary paths, they are not completely sundered. "Everywhere we find them mingled; it is the proportion that differs. [Hence] there is no intelligence in which some traces of instinct are not to be discovered, . . . no instinct that is not surrounded with a fringe of intelligence." But instinct *is* sympathy; in contrast to intellect, which, as we have seen, "guides us into matter," instinct is "turned towards life" and thus gives us "the key to vital operations." It might be thought to follow that insects, in whom instinct predominates, are better metaphysicians than men and have a fuller understanding of duration. But this is not so. Though instinct is the *basic* element in intuition, it is not the only element. Intuition involves not just sympathy but "disinterested sympathy"; and to become disinterested, intelligence is required. Accordingly, intuition may be defined as "instinct that has become disinterested, self-conscious, capable of reflecting upon its object and of enlarging it indefinitely." Hence it turns out that men are better metaphysicians than the hymenoptera.[q]

Bergson has traced the evolutionary development as far as man, the highest stage yet reached. It is quite impossible, he thought, to predict what form duration will take in the future, or when it will make another evolutionary leap. Although it is possible, *after* an event occurs, to show why it came to be what it is, one can never say in advance what it is going to be.

The Two Sources of Morality and Religion

As has often been remarked, a metaphysical scheme provides an overarching set of concepts that gives the various domains of experience a unified interpretation. This function of metaphysics can be plainly seen in Bergson's account of morality and religion. Just as he used his basic distinction between the creative force and the "deposits" on which this force works to describe and evaluate two different kinds of cognitive processes, so he used this distinction to describe and evaluate two different kinds of morality and two different kinds of religion. The creative force results in a "dynamic" religion and an "open" morality; the external forms result in a "static" religion and a "closed" morality. The former is a religion and morality of love and freedom; the latter is one of obligation and law. Once again, however, these two sources are divergent rather than sheerly distinct. Elements of both can be found in contemporary morals and religions.

CLOSED MORALITY AND STATIC RELIGION

According to Bergson, the whole apparatus of human obligations, ranging from moral duties like keeping promises to social customs like kissing, has its origin in those social pressures by which societies hold themselves together. Societies can survive only by organization, discipline, and division of labor. On the whole, social cohesion is provided for more adequately in insect societies than in human societies. The systems of laws, duties, and customs that operate in human societies are the rather inadequate reflections of the drives that operate instinctively in insects. Of course, human laws are more flexible and more diverse, precisely because the activities of men are more varied; but flexibility and variety are necessarily accompanied by a weakening of the drives for cohesion and by a strengthening of egocentric impulses. It follows from this view that philosophers like Kant, who try to derive obligation from "reason," are talking nonsense. As a matter of fact, to the extent that reason and intelligence cause the individual to think of himself as distinct from the community of which he is really an organ, they are disruptive of morality and order and must be counteracted by other forces. It is true that they have a positive (though subordinate) function in that they help to determine what particular, concrete forms the underlying impulse toward social cohesion will take. But the ultimate sanction, the ultimate "categorical imperative," is always this social impulse.

> The work done by intelligence in weighing reasons, comparing maxims, going back to first principles, was to introduce more logical consistency into a line of conduct subordinated by its very nature to the claims of society; but this social claim was the real root of obligation. . . .
>
> [In civilized societies] social demands have . . . been co-ordinated with each other and subordinated to principles. But . . . the essence of obligation is a different thing from a requirement of reason. This is all we have tried to suggest so far. Our description would, we think, correspond more and more to reality as one came to deal with less developed communities and more rudimentary stages of consciousness. . . . Conceive obligation as weighing on the will like a habit, each obligation dragging behind it the accumulated mass of the others, and utilising thus for the pressure it is exerting the weight of the whole: here you have the totality of obligation for a simple, elementary,

moral conscience. That is the essential: that is what obligation could, if necessary, be reduced to, even in those cases where it attains its highest complexity.

This shows when and in what sense (how slightly Kantian!) obligation in its elementary state takes the form of a "categorical imperative." We should find it very difficult to discover examples of such an imperative in everyday life. . . . So let us imagine an ant who is stirred by a gleam of reflexion and thereupon judges she has been wrong to work unremittingly for others. Her inclination to laziness would indeed endure but a few moments, just as long as the ray of intelligence. In the last of these moments, when instinct regaining the mastery would drag her back by sheer force to her task, intelligence at the point of relapsing into instinct would say, as its parting word: "You must because you must." This "must because you must" would only be the momentary feeling of awareness of a tug which the ant experiences—the tug which the string, momentarily relaxed, exerts as it drags her back. . . . In a word, an absolutely categorical imperative is instinctive or somnambulistic, enacted as such in a normal state, represented as such if reflexion is roused long enough to take form, not long enough to seek for reasons. But, then, is it not evident that, in a reasonable being, an imperative will tend to become categorical in proportion as the activity brought into play, although intelligent, will tend to become instinctive? But an activity which, starting as intelligent, progresses towards an imitation of instinct is exactly what we call, in man, a habit. And the most powerful habit, the habit whose strength is made up of the accumulated force of all the elementary social habits, is necessarily the one which best imitates instinct. Is it then surprising that, in the short moment which separates obligation merely experienced as a living force from obligation fully realized and justified by all sorts of reasons, obligation should indeed take the form of the categorical imperative: "you must because you must"? [r]

There is, then, no *reason* for being moral—the basis for morality is merely a blind "you must because you must." And this imperative can never be "proved" by argument or "justified" by logic; it simply expresses the elementary urge to self-preservation by which societies, like all other organisms, protect themselves from the "dissolvent power of intelligence."

This type of morality is accompanied by static religion, which functions to "reinforce and sustain the claims of society." By means of its myth-making power, static religion counteracts the dangerous inhibitions against effective, forceful action that intelligence creates by making known to us "the inevitability of death." [s]

OPEN MORALITY AND DYNAMIC RELIGION

Open morality and dynamic religion have a wholly different source. In this case, the impulse is not social pressure but the sense of life and movement that rare individuals possess. Here is still another modulation of the Hegelian theme of the great man, the creative individual who breaks down old forms and fashions new ones. It is interesting to see this theme appearing again and again in nineteenth-century thought and to see also how the paradigm of the great man—whether it is Jesus, Socrates, Alcibiades, Napoleon, or Goethe—varies from one philosopher to another depending on that thinker's own creative individuality.

For Bergson, the model of the great man was not an artist or a warrior but a moral and religious leader like Jesus or Buddha. The saints of all the religions of the world are, as it were, orifices through which wells up the life force itself. A saint thus has an enormous drive and energy—he is able to "move mountains," to inspire whole generations of lesser men to higher and nobler conceptions of morality. Such a saint is, in fact, just one of those creative leaps that the life force periodically makes and that is productive of a genuine novelty, like the leap by which animals developed out of plants. At such times the sense of obligation to some closed society is replaced by a morality of aspiration and love rooted in a feeling of our common unity.

> The great moral figures that have made their mark on history join hands across the centuries, above our human cities; they unite into a divine city which they bid us enter. We may not hear their voices distinctly, the call has none the less gone forth, and something answers from the depth of our soul. . . . It is these men who draw us towards an ideal society, while we yield to the pressure of the real one.[t]

After making such a leap into a saintly personality, the life force relaxes for a time; the great leader passes on and mankind relapses into static religion and closed social morality. But although most men are unable to live up to the ideals of the great personality who has departed from their midst, they remember his teachings and try to emulate them in their feeble way. Hence all actual moralities and religions are a blend of elements from these two sources. Thus, for instance, "justice [social morality] finds itself continually broadened by pity; 'charity' assumes more and more the shape of justice"[u]; and so on.

Mysticism, Asceticism, and a Universal Society

According to Bergson, man was designed "for very small societies. . . . Yet nature, which ordained small societies, left them with an opening for expansion." This opening is the capacity for "the mystic life," which appears whenever "the fringe of intuition surrounding [man's] intelligence is capable of expanding sufficiently to envelop its object," and which points in the direction of a truly democratic, free, and peaceful society that incorporates all mankind. Is this merely an ideal? Or can it be hoped that the deeply rooted instincts pulling men down into closed societies may be finally eradicated? It is possible, Bergson believed, that they may be. For centuries men have made a cult of comfort and luxury, but it is possible that they may be approaching a new period of asceticism and mysticism. There are two reasons, at any rate, to believe this may come about. First, there is a "possible link" between mysticism and industrialism. Second, a "law of twofold frenzy" seems to operate. As regards the role of industrialism, Bergson believed that mystic intuition is liable to relapse into ecstatic contemplation unless the mystic has a sense of power. Industrialism and the "advent of the machine" may give the mystic this necessary "faith in action." Hence, "instead of turning inwards and closing, the soul [can] open wide its gates to a universal love." [v] As regards the "law of twofold frenzy," Bergson held that periods of asceticism and of luxury seem not only to alternate but to produce each other by their own excesses. In medieval times, the "ascetic ideal" led to such "exaggerations" that men finally revolted against it. Thus, since "one frenzy brings on a counter-frenzy," "there is nothing improbable in the return to a simpler life." [w] And this simple life may be productive of a new "mystic genius," who

> . . . will draw after him a humanity already vastly grown in body, and whose soul he has transfigured. He will yearn to make of it a new species, or rather deliver it from the necessity of being a species; for every species means a collective halt. . . . Let once the summons of the hero come, we shall not all follow it, but we shall all feel that we ought to, and we shall see the path before us, which will become a highway if we pass along it. . . . It is always the stop which requires explanation, and not the movement. [x]

Bergson and the Spirit of the Age

Nothing shows more strikingly Bergson's temperamental difference from Kierkegaard and Nietzsche than these points about industrialism and the return to a simpler and better life. Kierkegaard and Nietzsche had been deeply suspicious of the Enlightenment's idea of progress; Bergson was still committed to it, though not to the Enlightenment's belief in "reason." Whereas both Kierkegaard and Nietzsche had given up the masses and concentrated whatever hopes they had on a few rare individuals, and whereas Nietzsche had held that industrialism was producing a race of factory-slaves and preparing the way for the rise of totalitarian dictatorships, Bergson believed that mankind might be on the verge of making a new creative advance.[7] Further, whereas Kierkegaard and Nietzsche were completely sceptical (though for different reasons) regarding the findings of science, Bergson believed that his views were as "scientific" as Darwin's hypothesis about natural selection. Finally, Bergson was deeply committed to

---

7 Nietzsche made his grimly prophetic observations in the 1880's; Bergson's optimistic views were published only a year before Hitler became the German chancellor.

metaphysical inquiry, whereas Kierkegaard was indifferent to it and Nietzsche regarded it as phony.

Bergson, then, represented older, more traditional modes of thought that stem directly from the eighteenth century and ultimately from a tradition going back beyond the Renaissance to Plato and Aristotle. Yet, despite his differences from Kierkegaard and Nietzsche, he shared several fundamental attitudes with them that show him to have been deeply affected by the antirationalistic "counter-movement" in which they participated. Bergson thought that his discussions of instinct and intelligence were scientific, but they were actually highly speculative. Bergson was, in fact, as hostile to the positivism that characterizes the actual procedures of working scientists as any Romantic poet had been. "It is one thing," he said, "to recognize that outer circumstances [like natural selection] are forces evolution must reckon with, another to claim that they were the directing causes." And in another place he remarked that, although scientific theories of evolution are true in a "limited way," they take "a partial view." [y]

This commitment to metaphysical entities, which a Comtian empiricist would have regarded as redundant or worse, was thus all-important for Bergson. There is nothing unusual, of course, in demands for answers to the "why" questions; attempts to link these answers into a systematic world view have recurred in the history of the Western mind since Plato's day. What was unusual about Bergson's position (and very suggestive of the new climate of opinion) was his denial that answers to the "why" questions could be found within any of the traditional frames of reference—within either a rational or even a teleological order. Instead, he sought and found the answers in the life force, a process as irrational and purposeless as Schopenhauer's blind "will."

Like Goethe's Faust, Bergson wanted to probe deep below the surface to uncover those forces that bind the world together and that are the creative sources of all changes—forces of whose existence he was convinced on meta-physical grounds, not as a result of empirical observation. Like Faust, he was not content to be told *how* things evolve and change; he wanted to know *why* they do so. And, like Faust, he believed that it was possible to reach this deeper level of reality and of explanation in—but only in—intuition. As a result, Bergson's metaphysics took a nontraditional form. Explanation in terms of a systematic conceptual structure ("matter-form," "dialectic," or whatever) was replaced by a referral of all problems, all issues, and all questions to the same unintelligible source.

Further, Bergson's very quest for the nature of reality was undermined from the start by his attack on conceptual knowledge and his recognition that intelligence is always "interested." The fact that Bergson did not see and face up to the paradox that Nietzsche was delighted to accept[8] suggests the central tension in his position, as indeed in so much of the thought of our age. An antirationalistic metaphysics like Bergson's, in contrast both to the assured rationalism of the traditional metaphysics and to the confident antimetaphysical

8 See p. 248.

attitudes of positivism and pragmatism, is like the uneasy mixture of love and hatred that some men experience for their wives or mothers. It is one thing to throw out the "why" questions as phony; it is another thing to complain because intelligence cannot answer them. To complain that intelligence is inadequate suggests that it *ought* to be adequate; one then should look around for something better, or at least for a substitute. But once one begins the pursuit of substitutes there is no telling in what "leap of faith" or other "absolute" one is going to end.[9] However much the views of Kierkegaard and Nietzsche differ from those of Bergson, which reflect a more unified and confident personality, one is conscious of a very deep affinity among them. For all three philosophers gave expression to the deep irrationalism, or at least the antirationalism, that seems increasingly to characterize contemporary culture.

Dewey

It is sometimes said that the movement variously called pragmatism, instrumentalism, and radical empiricism is an expression of "Americanism." It is true that most of the leading pragmatists have been Americans, and that pragmatism has had a wider impact in this country than in others.[10] But actually much more than merely local influence went into the development of pragmatism. Hume's empirical analysis, Kant's phenomena (but not his noumena), Hegel's phenomenology and his soft-pedaling of "spirit," the social orientation of the Utilitarians, the positivism of Comte, and Bergson's activism—these and other lines of thought influenced Dewey.[11]

Dewey's version of pragmatism had both a negative thesis and a positive thesis. It was both an all-out attack on traditional philosophy and a vigorous "reconstruction" of philosophy on a new basis. The negative thesis can be stated in terms of the comment Dewey would have been disposed to make on Bergson.

9 It is interesting in this connection to note that Bergson himself ultimately turned to Catholicism. After the publication of *The Two Sources* (1932) his thoughts turned more and more to religious matters, and by 1937 he had reached the point where only the violent anti-Semitism of the age (which made him loath to give the appearance of abandoning his religious group) prevented his conversion and baptism. He asked, however, that a Catholic priest be permitted to pray at his funeral, and this was authorized. In view of the fact that his principal works had long been on the *Index*, and of the attack on conceptualism and dogmatism that was fundamental to his whole position, it might be supposed that his formal, official conversion would have occasioned some difficulties. But this is merely another episode in the old problem of reconciling mysticism and orthodoxy, in which the Church has had a rich experience.

10 Charles Saunders Peirce (1839–1914) was the founder of the movement and William James (1842–1910) was its prophet. But Peirce was so unhappy about the dilution that pragmatism underwent in the course of James's popularization of it that, in 1905, he "announced the birth of the word 'pragmaticism,' which is ugly enough to be safe from kidnappers." He was right; it was. No one today uses that term.

11 John Dewey (1859–1952) was born in Vermont and grew up there. He was educated at Johns Hopkins and taught at the universities of Michigan and Chicago. In 1904 he went to Columbia, where he continued to teach until his retirement.

As has been seen, Bergson maintained that "the normal work of the intellect is far from being disinterested"; it follows, he held, that "either there is no philosophy possible, and all knowledge is practical, or else philosophy consists in intuition." [12] Bergson, of course, opted for the second alternative; Dewey, for the first. Because Dewey affirmed that all knowledge is "practical" and denied that intuition is knowledge, he concluded that "philosophy"—both in the traditional sense and in Bergson's sense—is impossible. Thus Dewey used the insight that intellect is "interested" in a negative way to destroy the old metaphysics. But he also used this insight in a positive way to rehabilitate empiricism by emphasizing the active, experimental, purposive elements in cognition.

In Dewey's view, intelligence cannot attain to eternal truths; but, rightly understood and rightly applied, it is capable of dealing effectively with pressing social and political problems. Whereas Bergson had been interested in the esthetic enjoyment of "duration" as he experienced it in intuition, and whereas Kierkegaard and Nietzsche had been preoccupied with their personal existential problems, Dewey focused on the actual world and on what "interested" thought can do in it. He was concerned with men's "traffic with nature," which he wanted to make "freer and more secure." Thus his motives were similar to those of the social philosophers whose views have been examined in Chapter 5, and he shared their generally optimistic outlook about men's capacity to act intelligently. But to this undertaking he brought a much more sophisticated grasp of the nature of intelligence; indeed, it is characteristic of his concept of intelligence that he preferred the term "inquiry," which reflected his view that mind is directive and active, not merely an observer and recorder of information. In this respect he shared Kant's and, to a greater extent, Hegel's belief that experience is a product in which mind plays a decisive role. Kant and Hegel, however, emphasized construction of a world to be known; Dewey emphasized the construction of a world to be lived in and acted on.

Concept of Human Nature

The center of interest in Dewey's thought was man and his practical problems. And since man is not only an active animal but a social one, Dewey's starting point was social psychology. Three factors in this connection require examination: habit, impulse, and intelligence.

HABIT

A habit is a "mechanism" for dealing with certain recurrent "classes of stimuli, standing predilections and aversions." But a habit is not necessarily a mere automatic mechanism, like the machine that prints, folds, conveys, and does everything but read, newspapers. It is necessary to distinguish between "two kinds of habit, intelligent and routine." And "the higher the form of life the more complex, sure and flexible" the habit. Furthermore, habits involve a functional relation between organism and environment, "in which the environment has its say as surely as the [organism]." A habit is a *function* between organism and environment by means of which life is furthered and maintained. It is possible, therefore, to look at habits as *arts*. "They involve skill of sensory and motor organs, cunning or craft, and objective materials. They assimilate objective energies, and eventuate in command of environment." z

IMPULSE

Habits are, of course, learned. What is original is impulse; habits are simply the shapings and canalizings of impulses. It is a mistake, according to Dewey, to suppose that any impulse has a specific character in itself. Impulses are indefinitely plastic and malleable. They acquire their meanings from the interaction of the organism with a "matured social medium." Under the influence of environment, that is, they develop into those relatively precise and specialized functions that Dewey called habits.

> In the case of the young it is patent that impulses are highly flexible starting points for activities which are diversified according to the ways in which they are used. Any impulse may become organized into almost any disposition according to the way it interacts with surroundings. Fear may become abject cowardice, prudent caution, reverence for superiors or respect for equals; an agency for credulous swallowing of absurd superstitions or for wary scepticism. . . . The actual outcome depends upon how the impulse of fear is interwoven with other impulses. This depends in turn upon the outlets and inhibitions supplied by the social environment.
>
> The traditional psychology of instincts obscures recognition of this fact. It sets up a hard-and-fast preordained class under which specific acts are subsumed, so that their own quality and originality are lost from view. This is why the novelist and dramatist are so much more illuminating as well as more interesting commentators on conduct than the schematizing psychologist. . . .
>
> In the career of any impulse activity there are speaking generally three possibilities. It may find a surging, explosive discharge—blind, unintelligent. It may be sublimated—that is, become a factor coordinated intelligently with others in a continuing course of action. Thus a gust of anger may, because of its dynamic incorporation into disposition, be converted into an abiding conviction of social injustice to be remedied, and furnish the dynamic to carry the conviction into execution. . . . Such an outcome represents the normal or desirable functioning of impulse; in which, to use our previous language, the impulse operates as a pivot, or reorganization of habit. Or again a released impulsive activity may be neither immediately expressed in isolated spas-

modic action, nor indirectly employed in an enduring interest. It may be "suppressed."

Suppression is not annihilation. "Psychic" energy is no more capable of being abolished than the forms we recognize as physical. If it is neither exploded nor converted, it is turned inwards, to lead a surreptitious, subterranean life. . . . A suppressed activity is the cause of all kinds of intellectual and moral pathology.[a]

INTELLIGENCE

Properly understood, intelligence is merely an unusually flexible and finely adjusted habit that functions to improve the organism's relation to its environment. Specifically, it is a habit that intervenes when other, more routine habits fail to perform efficiently. Man is not a passive, inert spectator of a neutral world. He is an organism plunged into an environment that infiltrates at every point his own nature. Habits are the functions by which men normally make the necessary adjustments. But since the environment is immensely complex and anything but static, these habitual adjustments constantly require modification. Their modification is the work of intelligence.

> *The function of reflective thought is to transform a situation in which there is experienced obscurity, doubt, conflict, disturbance of some sort, into a situation that is clear, coherent, settled, harmonious. . . .*

When a situation arises containing a difficulty or perplexity, the person who finds himself in it may take one of a number of courses. He may dodge it, dropping the activity that brought it about, turning to something else. He may indulge in a flight of fancy, imagining himself powerful or wealthy, or in some other way in possession of the means that would enable him to deal with the difficulty. Or, finally, he may face the situation. In this case, he begins to reflect.

The moment he begins to reflect, he begins of necessity to observe in order to take stock of conditions. . . . Some of the conditions are obstacles and others are aids, resources. No matter whether these conditions come to him by direct perception or by memory, they form the "*facts* of the case." They are the things that are *there*, that have to be reckoned with. . . . Until the habit of thinking is well formed, facing the situation to discover the facts requires an effort. For the mind tends to dislike what is unpleasant and so to sheer off from an adequate notice of that which is especially annoying.

Along with noting the conditions that constitute the facts to be dealt with, suggestions arise of possible courses of action. . . . [These lead] to new observations and recollections and to a reconsideration of observations already made in order to test the worth of the suggested way out. . . . The newly noted facts may (and in any complex situation surely will) cause new suggestions to spring up. . . . This continuous interaction of the facts disclosed by observation and of the suggested proposals of solution and the suggested methods of dealing with conditions goes on till some suggested solution meets all the conditions of the case and does not run counter to any discoverable feature of it. . . .

We shall illustrate what has been said by a simple case. Suppose you are walking where there is no regular path. As long as everything goes smoothly, you do not have to think about your walking; your already formed habit takes care of it. Suddenly you find a ditch in your way. You think you will jump it (supposition, plan); but to make sure, you survey it with your eyes (observation), and you find that it is pretty wide and that the bank on the other side is slippery (facts, data). You then wonder if the ditch may not be narrower somewhere else (idea), and you look up and down the stream (observation) to see how matters stand (test of idea by observation). You do not find any good place and so are thrown back upon forming a new plan. As you are casting about, you discover a log (fact again). You ask yourself whether you could not haul that to the ditch and get it across the ditch to use as a bridge (idea again). You judge that idea is worth trying, and so you get the log and manage to put it in place and walk across (test and confirmation by overt action). . . .

The two limits of every unit of thinking are a perplexed, troubled, or confused situation at the beginning and a cleared-up, unified, resolved situation at the close. . . .

In between, as states of thinking, are (1) *suggestions*, in which the mind leaps forward to a possible solution; (2) an intellectualization of the difficulty or perplexity that has been *felt* (directly experienced) into a *problem* to be solved, a question for which the answer must be sought; (3) the use of one suggestion after another as a leading idea, or *hypothesis*, to initiate and guide observation and other operations in collection of factual material; (4) the mental elaboration of the idea or supposition as an idea or supposition (*reasoning*, in the sense in which reasoning is a part, not the whole, of inference); and (5) testing the hypothesis by overt or imaginative action. . . .[b]

Theory of Education

As has been said, all habits, including the habit called thinking, are learned. Unfortunately, most of them are learned unsystematically, with little care or forethought on the part of those who do the teaching. As a matter of fact, few people think of their behavior to others as being a form of teaching; fewer still understand the functional relationships, just described, that exist among habits, impulses, and intelligence. Even at the conscious, planned level, educational practice is often based on a mistaken conception of human nature. Is it surprising, therefore, that so many bad habits, so many maladjustments, and so many inefficient ways of functioning exist?

Very early in life sets of mind are formed without attentive thought, and these sets persist and control the mature mind. The child learns to avoid the shock of unpleasant disagreement, to find the easy way out, to appear to conform to customs which are wholly mysterious to him in order to get his own way—that is to display some natural impulse without exciting the unfavorable notice of those in authority. Adults distrust the intelligence which a child has while making upon him demands for a kind of conduct that requires a high order of intelligence, if it is to be intelligent at all. The inconsistency is reconciled by instilling in him "moral" habits which have a maximum of emotional empressment and adamantine hold with a minimum of understanding. These habitudes . . . govern conscious later thought. They are usually deepest and most unget-at-able just where critical thought is most needed—in morals, religion and politics. These "infantilisms" account for the mass of irrationalities that prevail among men of otherwise rational tastes. . . . To list them would perhaps oust one from "respectable" society. . . .

When we face this fact in its general significance, we confront one of the ominous aspects of the history of man. We realize how little the progress of man has been the product of intelligent guidance, how largely it has been a by-product of accidental upheavals.[c]

Accordingly, one of Dewey's primary interests was education—both in the narrow sense of curriculum reform and teacher training, and in the more extended sense of the whole adjustment of the individual to his social and physical environment, including problems of sociology, politics, and international relations. In this respect Dewey belonged to the mainstream of social thought, along with the Utilitarians and the Comtians. But he tackled the problem of improving man's traffic with nature in a radically different way. For one thing, he was far more aware than these earlier philosophers had been of the functional, organic relationships that exist between men and their environment. Further, although their view was relatively empirical, their conception of knowledge was what Dewey called the "spectator-type" of knowledge.[13] Differences about the nature of knowledge profoundly affect ideas of how knowledge should be put to work in the interests of reform. Thus Dewey agreed with Comte that the key to solving social problems lay in the application of the methods of natural science to those problems. And he was, if anything, even more optimistic than Comte had been about the possible fruits of such a social science. But his understanding of the nature of scientific method (and hence his conception of sociology) was more radically empirical than Comte's. Although Comte had reached the point of seeing that so-called natural laws are merely generalized descriptions of what happens, he held that it is possible to formulate general descriptions that are completely (and therefore permanently) adequate. He believed this to be possible because he took Newtonian physics as his model for social science. Just as the "law" of gravity is applicable to the universe at all times, so, Comte thought, the laws of sociology are applicable to human societies at all times. Hence he believed that once these laws are correctly formulated, they can be applied in a more or less mechanical manner.

13 See p. 290.

Dewey rejected the idea of law even in this descriptive sense. He held that there are no final, or completely adequate, descriptions; there are merely more and more adequate instrumentalities for dealing with always changing and growing human situations. From this point of view there would be no danger of a doctrinaire application of oversimplified formulas to the solution of social problems. On the contrary, every application would be tentative, experimental, and hypothetical, capable of being adjusted in light of the new data that the preliminary solution generates.

Democracy

Dewey's assertion that there are no answers that are *the* answers had another important result. It led to his belief that social science is not the prerogative of a special elite who is to design the good life *for* the masses. In Dewey's view, the good life is a matter of mutual makings. And precisely because human nature and human impulses are indefinitely malleable, it is possible to bring all citizens up to ever higher levels of sensitive and responsible conduct. The problem of constructing the good life, therefore, is not the old Platonic problem of selection but the Christian problem of opportunity. Thus Dewey's conception of human nature was the basis for a fundamentally democratic political and social order rather than a humanely motivated authoritarianism. It might be said, indeed, that Dewey was trying to reinterpret, in a more empirical and practical spirit, the ideas of the founding fathers, which they had stated in the spirit of the rationalism of the Enlightenment.

> The political and governmental phase of democracy is a means, the best means so far found, for realizing ends that lie in the wide domain of human relationships and the development of human personality. . . . The keynote of democracy as a way of life may be expressed, it seems to me, as the necessity for the participation of every mature human being in formation of the values that regulate the living of men together: which is necessary from the standpoint of both the general social welfare and the full development of human beings as individuals. . . .
>
> The development of political democracy came about through substitution of the method of mutual consultation and voluntary agreement for the method of subordination of the many to the few enforced from above. . . . When [coercion] is habitual and embodied in social institutions, it seems the normal and natural state of affairs. The mass usually become unaware that they have a claim to a development of their own powers. Their experience is so restricted that they are not conscious of restriction. It is part of the democratic conception that they as individuals are not the only sufferers, but that the whole social body is deprived of the potential resources that should be at its service. . . .

The foundation of democracy is faith in the capacities of human nature; faith in human intelligence and in the power of pooled and coöperative experience. It is not belief that these things are complete but that if given a show they will grow and be able to generate progressively the knowledge and wisdom needed to guide collective action. Every autocratic and authoritarian scheme of social action rests on a belief that the needed intelligence is confined to a superior few, who because of inherent natural gifts are endowed with the ability and the right to control the conduct of others. . . .

While what we call intelligence may be distributed in unequal amounts, it is the democratic faith that it is sufficiently general so that each individual has something to contribute, and the value of each contribution can be assessed only as it enters into the final pooled intelligence constituted by the contributions of all. . . .

I have emphasized . . . the importance of the effective release of intelligence . . . because democracy is so often and so naturally associated in our minds with freedom of *action*, forgetting the importance of freed intelligence which is necessary to direct and to warrant freedom of action. Unless freedom of individual action has intelligence and informed conviction back of it, its manifestation is almost sure to result in confusion and disorder. The democratic idea of freedom is not the right of each individual to *do* as he pleases, even if it be qualified by adding "provided he does not interfere with the same freedom on the part of others." . . . The basic freedom is that of freedom of *mind* and of whatever degree of freedom of action and experience is necessary to produce freedom of intelligence.[d]

Attitude Toward Metaphysics

Dewey thus had little interest in the traditional view of philosophical inquiry. In Dewey's view philosophical thinking, like all thinking, is "interested thinking." The problems metaphysics is concerned with are real problems, but the metaphysical solutions are fictitious and downright harmful. However much traditional philosophers differ among themselves, all of them—rationalists, empiricists, and intuitionists alike—believe they are exploring the nature of "reality." This whole enterprise, Dewey held, results from a maladjustment to environment. Men have a fundamental urge to seek security. The pursuit of security is the real problem to which traditional philosophy provides only a pseudo-solution. Instead of looking for security in the control of environment by scientific means, along the lines Dewey suggested, traditional philosophers flee to a dream world of their own creation, a never-never land of "absolutes" and "eternal verities." According to Dewey, philosophers of this type are unable to face up to the fact that security never is, and never can be, perfect—that even science never gives us *the* answers, and that life accordingly is a growing, living adventure. The traditional philosophers are simply men who are too weak to accept the world as it is, and their theories are nothing but a projection of their inner uneasiness, a flight from reality.

METAPHYSICS A QUEST FOR CERTAINTY

Exaltation of pure intellect and its activity above practical affairs is fundamentally connected with the quest for a certainty which shall be absolute and unshakeable. . . .

Practical activity deals with individualized and unique situations which are never exactly duplicable and about which, accordingly, no complete assurance is possible. All activity, moreover, involves change. The intellect, however, according to the traditional doctrine, may grasp universal Being, and Being which is universal is fixed and immutable. . . . Man's distrust of himself has caused him to desire to get beyond and above himself; in pure knowledge he has thought he could attain this self-transcendence.

. . . .

Primitive [man] had none of the elaborate arts of protection and use which we now enjoy and no confidence in his own powers when they were reinforced by appliances of art. He lived under conditions in which he was extraordinarily exposed to peril. . . . Men faced the forces of nature in a state of nakedness which was more than physical. . . .

In such an atmosphere primitive religion was born and fostered. Rather this atmosphere *was* the religious disposition. . . .

The two dominant conceptions, cultural categories one might call them, which grew and flourished under such circumstances were those of the holy and the fortunate, with their opposites, the profane and the unlucky. . . . To secure the favor of the holy [was] to be on the road to success. . . . Because of its surcharge of power, ambivalent in quality, the holy has to be approached . . . with . . . rites of purification, humiliation, fasting and prayer.

. . . .

Prosaic beliefs about verifiable facts, beliefs backed up by evidence of the senses and by useful fruits, had little glamour and prestige compared with the vogue of objects of rite and ceremony. . . . Herein is the source of the fundamental dualism of human attention and regard. The distinction between the two attitudes of everyday control and dependence on something superior was finally generalized . . . in the conception of two distinct realms. The inferior was that in which man could foresee and in which he had instruments and arts by which he might expect a reasonable degree of control. The superior was that of occurrences so uncontrollable that they testified to the presence and operation of powers beyond the scope of everyday and mundane things.

The philosophical tradition regarding knowledge and practice, the immaterial or spiritual and the material . . . had for its background [this] state of culture. . . . Philosophy inherited the realm with which religion had been concerned.

. . . .

If one looks at the foundations of the philosophies of Plato and Aristotle as an anthropologist looks at his material, that is, as cultural subject-matter, it is clear that these philosophies were systematizations in rational form of the content of Greek religious and artistic beliefs. The systematization involved a purification. Logic provided the patterns to which ultimately real objects had to conform, while physical science was possible in the degree in which the natural world, even in its mutabilities, exhibited exemplification of ultimate immutable rational objects. Thus, along with the elimination of myths and grosser superstitions, there were set up the ideals of science and of a life of reason. Ends which could justify themselves to reason were to take the place of custom as the guide of conduct. These two ideals form a permanent contribution to western civilization.

But . . . they [also] brought with them the . . . notion, which has ruled philosophy ever since the time of the Greeks, that the office of knowledge is to uncover the antecedently real, rather than, as is the case with our practical judgments, to gain the kind of understanding which is necessary to deal with problems as they arise.

It thus diverted thought from inquiring into the purposes which experience of actual conditions suggest and from concrete means of their actualization. It translated into a rational form the doctrine of escape from the vicissitudes of existence by means of measures which do not demand an active coping with conditions. For deliverance by means of rites and cults, it substituted deliverance through reason.

. . . .

Although this Greek formulation was made long ago and much of it is now strange in its specific terms, . . . the main tradition of western culture has retained intact this framework of ideas. . . .

There is involved in these doctrines a whole system of philosophical conclusions. The first and foremost is that . . . what is known, what is true for cognition, is what is real in being. The objects of knowledge form the standards of measures of the reality of all other objects of experience. Are the objects of the affections, of desire, effort, choice, that is to say everything to which we attach value, real? Yes, if they can be warranted by knowledge; . . . as objects of desire and purpose they have no sure place in Being until they are approached and validated through knowledge. The idea is so familiar that we overlook the unexpressed premise upon which it rests, namely that only the completely fixed and unchanging can be real. The quest for certitude has determined our basic metaphysics.

Secondly, the theory of knowledge has its basic premises fixed by the same doctrine.

. . . .

The theory of knowing is modeled after what was supposed to take place in the act of vision. The object refracts light to the eye and is seen; it makes a difference to the eye and to the person having an optical apparatus, but none to the thing seen. . . . A spectator theory of knowledge is the inevitable outcome. There have been theories which hold that mental activity intervenes, but they have retained the old premise. They have therefore concluded that it is impossible to know reality. . . . It would be hard to find a more thoroughgoing confirmation than this conclusion provides of the complete hold possessed by the belief that the object of knowledge is a reality fixed and complete in itself. . . .

All of these notions about certainty and the fixed, about the nature of the real world, about the nature of the mind and its organs of knowing, . . . flow—such is my basic thesis—from the separation (set up in the interest of the quest for absolute certainty) between theory and practice, knowledge and actions.[e]

NIETZSCHE AND DEWEY CONTRASTED

Dewey's anthropological and psychological analysis of metaphysics is obviously very similar to Nietzsche's. Both philosophers agreed that the objects of metaphysical thinking are "fictions" that function to allay the insecurity men feel in the presence of change, decay, and death. But they differed sharply in their attitudes toward this discovery about the basic insecurity in human nature, as is shown not only by what they said but by the very styles in which they wrote. Nietzsche's writing was metaphorical, contentious, and highly personal. He shared the underlying insecurity that other men experienced but differed from them in choosing to face it rather than flee from it. He felt, as they did, that man is hanging precariously on the edge of an abyss; his reponse was to affirm life despite its terror. In contrast, Dewey's exposition of the roots of metaphysics was calm, detailed, and scholarly. Since he did not experience an abyss within himself, since he did not feel divided and alienated, he was not *personally* involved in the discovery that most men experience deep insecurity. Rather, he looked at the situation from the outside, as a physician or psychiatrist might. He believed that the cure for insecurity was not (as Nietzsche had held) to bite the snake that had bitten one—to Dewey, this was a truly desperate remedy. The cure was to become involved in the day-to-day task of improving man's estate. Hence, though Dewey too affirmed life, he did not feel this affirmation to be particularly difficult or heroic. Furthermore, the life that he affirmed did not involve a quantum jump to a level "beyond good and evil": It consisted in a gradual, even "prosaic," advance to more intelligent practice.

The Nature of Reality: "Experience"

Despite his "reduction" of metaphysics to the quest for certainty, and despite his belief that many of the traditional metaphysical problems are pseudo-problems, Dewey realized that instrumentalism could not escape dealing, at least in its own way, with some of the questions of "first philosophy." Here his position was much stronger than that of the earlier pragmatists, who were inclined to dispose of metaphysics by declaring that any metaphysics was true provided that it "worked."

Thus though Dewey did not ask, in the traditional way, "What is the real?" "What are the ultimate values?" he nevertheless recognized that he had to ask and to answer equivalent questions. So far it has been said that Dewey emphasized that men live in, and must adjust to, their social and physical environment. But what is this environment, and how are men to evaluate the values that their interested activity is constantly realizing in it?

One answer to the first question is "experience"; another is "nature." But what are experience and nature, and how are they related? To begin with, like the Kantians and the Hegelians, Dewey regarded reality as a whole within which distinctions are made and meanings develop. Our experience and the nature of which it is the experience—subject and object, knower and known—"are not enemies or alien." "Experience is *of* as well as *in* nature. . . . [It] reaches down into nature; it has depth. It also has breadth and to an indefinitely elastic extent. It stretches. That stretch constitutes inference."[f]

EVENTS AND OBJECTS

In ordinary everyday experience of objects, Dewey held that "events" (or "existences") are distinguished from meanings. An event is an "ongoing"; its *"intrinsic* nature is revealed in experience as the immediately felt qualities of things." And events are not just the ingredients of ordinary experience. Science, too, thinks in terms of events. "The tendency of modern science [is] to substitute qualitative events, marked by certain similar properties and by recurrences, for the older notion of fixed substances."[g] The concept of event may thus be said to have had the same pivotal importance and unifying function in Dewey's theory that substance had in the Cartesian metaphysics. This is an indication of the extent to which, as has already been suggested, process was becoming a fundamental modern idea.

"Event" seems a far more satisfactory metaphysical principle than "substance." Since a substance is by definition an independent, enclosed, and complete entity, any attempt to interpret reality substantively runs into hopeless dilemmas. For instance, is there one substance or are there several? Either answer is unsatisfactory. If there is but one substance, it is impossible to account for the experienced diversity. If there are many substances, it seems impossible that they can be related in any significant way. In contrast, the concept of event allows for the flexibility, multiple-relatedness, and change of state that Nietzsche's "will to power" as a cosmological principle was intended to achieve. Yet it does this without the danger of anthropomorphism that is inherent in that notion.

So much for event. According to Dewey, an object (whether a "gross, macroscopic" object of ordinary experience or a "refined, derived" object of scientific experience) can be defined as an "event with meaning." Consider any of the things ordinarily called objects: "Tables, the milky way, chairs, stars, cats, dogs, electrons, ghosts, centaurs, historic epochs"—these are all events with meanings. Take, for instance, the event that a writer would call "a piece of paper." This is but one meaning of the event in question; it merely happens to be foremost in the writer's mind because he is concerned about something to write on. This same event

> . . . has as many other explicit meanings as it has important consequences recognised in the various connective interactions into which it enters. Since possibilities of conjunction are endless, and since the consequences of any of them may at some time be significant, its potential meanings are endless. It signifies something to start a fire with; something like snow; made of wood-pulp; manufactured for profit; property in the legal sense; a definite

combination illustrative of certain principles of chemical science; an article the invention of which has made a tremendous difference in human history, and so on indefinitely. There is no conceivable universe of discourse in which the thing may not figure, having in each its own characteristic meaning. And if we say that after all it is "paper" which has all these different meanings, we are at bottom but asserting that . . . paper is its ordinary meaning for human intercourse.[h]

"ESSENCE" A PSEUDO-PROBLEM

Dewey believed that the fact that an event can have many meanings provides a way of disposing of the traditional philosophical concern with "essence," which can now be seen to be a pseudo-problem. There is nothing unique, special, or privileged about essence; it is merely "a pronounced instance of meaning," hypostatized by our pursuit of certainty into an alleged eternal entity. "To be partial, and to assign *a* meaning to a thing as *the* meaning is but to evince human subjection to bias. . . . The very essence of a thing is identified with those consummatory consequences which the thing has when conditions are felicitous."[i] There is no more reason to say that the essence of an existent is "white surface for writing" than to say that its essence is "wood-pulp." Any such claim merely reflects the predominant interest that the definer happens to have in the existent in question.

This way of thinking also frees philosophy from the dualism of appearance and reality—another pseudo-problem. For instance, Galileo and the other early physicists held that the paper is "really" matter in motion and only "appears" to be a continuous, white surface. According to Dewey, they were simply giving preferred ontological status to one of two equally real meanings, which happened to be rooted in different frames of reference. Similarly, a modern physicist might maintain that the paper is "really" electrons, but this merely reflects his preference for the electron frame of reference, possibly because of its practical significance or possibly because of its greater elegance.

STATUS OF UNIVERSALS

Universals, then, are not things but instruments; they are, specifically, the instruments by means of which problems are solved and meanings built up. The universal "piece of paper" is an instrument for solving the problem of taking notes at a lecture. The universal "wood-pulp" is an instrument for solving the problem of producing more paper. The universal "electron" is an instrument for solving the problem of relating many different existents by means of a single, generalized description. There is thus no intrinsic difference between ordinary commonsense thinking, as described by Dewey above, and scientific thinking. It is true that in their pursuit of certainty philosophers and philosophically minded scientists sometimes suppose that they are exploring a realm of mathematico-material entities; but as a matter of fact "the history of the development of the physical sciences is [only] the story of the enlarging possession by mankind of more efficacious instrumentalities for dealing with the conditions of life and action."ʲ

DEFECTS OF TRADITIONAL RATIONALISM AND EMPIRICISM

One of the test cases for Dewey's whole analysis is the nature and status of mathematical thinking. Is it, as the rationalists have always insisted, knowledge of an independent and intelligible order of eternal truths? Or are mathematical concepts simply instruments for implementing action, whose uniqueness lies in their very high degree of precision?

> Does the doctrine of the operational and experimentally empirical nature of conceptions break down when applied to "pure" mathematical objects? The key to the answer is to be found in a distinction between operations overtly performed (or imagined to be performed) and operations *symbolically* executed. . . .
>
> For long ages, symbols were . . . employed incidentally and for some fairly immediate end. . . . They carried all sorts of irrelevant associations that hampered their efficacy. . . . The loose and restricted character of popular thinking has its origin in these facts; its progress is encumbered by the vague and vacillating nature of ordinary words. Thus the second great step forward was made when special symbols were devised that were emancipated from the load of irrelevancy carried by words developed for social rather than for intellectual purposes. . . . Instead of being adapted to local and directly present situations, they were framed in detachment from direct overt use and *with respect to one another*. One has only to look at mathematical symbols to note that the operations they designate are others of the same kind as themselves, that is, symbolic not actual. . . .
>
> Abstraction from use in special and direct situations . . . is a process, however, which is subject to interpretation by a fallacy. Independence from any specified application is readily taken to be equivalent to independence from application as such. . . . This fallacy . . . played its part in the generation of a *priori* rationalism. It is the origin of that idolatrous attitude toward universals so often recurring in the history of thought. Those who handle ideas through symbols as if they were things . . . are ready victims to thinking of these objects as if they had no sort of reference to things, to existence.
>
> In fact, the distinction is one between operations to be actually performed and possible operations as such, as merely possible. Shift of reflection to development of possible operations in their logical relations *to one another* opens up opportunities for operations that would never be directly suggested. But its origin and eventual meaning lie in acts that deal with concrete situations. As to origin in overt operations there can be no doubt. Operations of keeping tally and scoring are found in both work and games. . . . These acts are the originals of number and of all developments of number. . . . If we generalize what happens in such instances, we see that the indispensable need is that of *adjusting things as means, as resources, to other things as ends.*

The origin of counting and measuring is in economy and efficiency of such adjustments. . . .

The failure of empiricism to account for mathematical ideas is due to its failure to connect them with acts performed. In accord with its sensationalistic character, traditional empiricism sought their origin in sensory impressions, or at most in supposed abstraction from properties antecedently characterizing physical things. Experimental empiricism has none of the difficulties of Hume and Mill in explaining the origin of mathematical truths. . . .

Once the idea of possible operations, indicated by symbols and performed *only* by means of symbols, is discovered, the road is opened to operations of ever increasing definiteness and comprehensiveness. Any group of symbolic operations suggests further operations that may be performed. *Technical* symbols [e.g., "H_2O"] are framed with precisely this end in view. . . . They are selected with a view to designating unambiguously one mode of interaction and one only. . . .

Mathematical conceptions [e.g., "3"], by means of symbols of operations that are irrespective of actual performance, carry abstraction much further. . . . [Each such symbol] designates an operative relation applic*able* to anything whatsoever, though not actually applied to any specified object. . . . The difficulties and paradoxes which have been found to attend the logic of number disappear when instead of their being treated as either essences or as properties of things in existence, they are viewed as designations of potential operations. Mathematical space is not a kind of space distinct from so-called physical and empirical space, but is a name given to operations ideally or formally possible with respect to things having spacious qualities: it is not a mode of Being, but a way of thinking things so that connections among them are liberated from fixity in experience and implication from one to another is made possible.[k]

Though Dewey believed that "traditional rationalism" has misread the nature of thought more seriously than has "traditional empiricism," he did not spare the latter. Dewey conceded that it has one great advantage in that it at least deals with the actual; but he held that it makes two serious mistakes. The first is that is conceives of the actual as a static world. The ideas of traditional empiricism are "dead" because "their value and function are essentially retrospective," not forward-looking. Like rationalism, traditional empiricism fails to see that all ideas and meanings are instruments for dealing with concrete problems. A good example of this is empiricism's attempt to derive mathematical ideas by "comparing particular objects" instead of recognizing their practical and operational origins.

In order to understand the second mistake Dewey attributed to the traditional empiricists, it is necessary to consider Dewey's criticism of "traditional nominalism." He held that it does not understand that meanings are shared, that "language is specifically a mode of interaction of at least two beings, a speaker and a hearer; it presupposes an organized group to which these creatures belong."[1] When A requests B to bring him something, the stimulus activating B is not the sounds uttered by A. It is, rather, B's "anticipatory share in the consummation of a transaction in which both participate. The heart of language is . . . the establishment of cooperation in an activity in which there are partners, and in which the activity of each is modified and regulated by partnership." In Dewey's view, such facts as these reveal the defect of traditional nominalism: It fails to see that a word is "a mode of social action" and supposes it to be the "expression of a ready-made, exclusively individual, mental state. . . . Nominalism ignores organization and thus makes nonsense of meanings."[m]

DEFECTS OF IDEALISM

If these are the weaknesses of traditional rationalism and traditional empiricism, what about "idealism"?[14] The trouble with idealism, Dewey held, is, first, that it tries to do away with the existent. It tries to resolve existents into "combinations of meanings." But "to cause existences in their particularity to disappear into combinations of universals is at least an extreme measure." For his part, therefore, he preferred to "stick to the common-sense belief that universals, relations, meanings, are of and about existences, not their exhaustive ingredients."[n]

Dewey's criticism can be stated in another way. In his opinion idealism assumes that thought is more real than anything else and hence concludes that thought's products have a superior ontological status as compared with the feelings and the "gross macroscopic" objects that thought articulates. For example, Hegel set out a doctrine of degrees of reality—"Being" is barely real; "Absolute Spirit" is most real of all, and so on. But in Dewey's view this metaphysical interpretation of thought's function is simply another aspect of philosophy's quest for certainty. Far from having such an exalted mission, thought simply serves as "an intermediary between some empirical objects and others." Hence thought's products are no more real than thought's starting points, just as the sculptor's figure is no more real (though it may be more beautiful or more useful) than the clay from which it is fashioned.

Thought's products are more useful than thought's starting points—that is why we think! But they have utility precisely because they can be referred back to the empirical needs that generated the thought. Idealism, just because it regards the "refined products" as more real, is "arbitrary and aloof" and "occupies a realm of its own without contact with the things of ordinary experience."

> A first-rate test of the value of any philosophy which is offered us [is]: Does it end in conclusions which, when they are referred back to ordinary life-experiences and their predicaments, render them more significant, more luminous to us, and make our dealings with them more fruitful? Or does it

14 By this Dewey meant, of course, views of the Hegelian type.

terminate in rendering the things of ordinary experience more opaque than they were before, and in depriving them of having in "reality" even the significance they had previously seemed to have? . . . It is the fact . . . that so many philosophies terminate in conclusions that make it necessary to disparage and condemn primary experience, leading those who hold them to measure the sublimity of their "realities" as philosophically defined by remoteness from the concerns of daily life, which leads cultivated common-sense to look askance at philosophy.[o]

This sense of the actual and the active, which Descartes had faintly felt and which had made him unwilling to be a simon-pure rationalist, was thus one of the cornerstones of Dewey's position. This is why he rejected Hegel's idealism as cloudy and unreal and insisted on the "irreducibility" of events. This is why he rejected Kant's compromise formula, according to which thought orders a sensuous manifold: In Dewey's view, the sensuous manifold is not sufficiently eventful. Although it doubtless saves meanings from dissolving into meanings of meanings of meanings, and so on, and thus performs a necessary *cognitive* function, it is hardly more than a limit. It is certainly not full-blooded, warm, and palpable. It fails to satisfy that aspect of reality that William James called its stubborn and irreducible factuality.

PUZZLES ABOUT RELATION OF THOUGHT TO EXPERIENCE

But what exactly *is* an existent? One can feel it or (as with Bergson) intuit it. But how is it to be incorporated in a philosophical theory except on thought's terms? Thought, as Dewey of cours saw, has a special status, and this special status is what theories like Kant's and Hegel's attempted to recognize—the fact that, as Dewey put it, "any experienced subject-matter whatever may *become* an object of reflection and cognitive inspection." Even the actual, even the intuited, *insofar as it is known,* has been taken up and included in the "all-inclusiveness of cognitive experience." Must Dewey not admit with Hegel that only thought and its articulations are real? Or at least agree with Kant that the notion of an other-than-thought is simply the concept of a limit? On the contrary. According to Dewey,

> . . . the emphasis [in the sentence just quoted] is upon "become"; the cognitive never *is* all-inclusive: that is, when the material of a prior non-cognitive experience is the object of knowledge, it and the act of knowing are themselves included within a new and wider noncognitive experience—and *this* situation can never be transcended. It is only when the temporal character of experienced things is forgotten that the idea of the total "transcendence" of knowledge is asserted.[p]

But this view is hardly an improvement over Kant's. Insofar as the noncognitive experience is *in* thought, it is articulated *by* thought (that is, it becomes an object, an existent with meaning); insofar as it is *out of* thought, it is not known (that is, it reduces to a pure existent). And though perhaps otherwise experienced, it is incapable of being included in a philosophical theory.

This difficulty can be stated in another way. According to Dewey, objects are existents with meanings. But what are they *in themselves*, when not articulated by thought? Thought is a "late comer" in the evolutionary process. Moreover, it "occurs only under highly specialized conditions, such as are found in a highly organized creature which in turn requires a specialized environment." [q] If it be admitted that galaxies, solar systems, and our own planet had an immensely long development before consciousness ever appeared, what kind of existence did they have during all those millennia? If they were not objects with meaning, what were they? This puzzle recalls Kant's difficulty with the status of phenomenal objects.[15] Phenomenal objects (planets, solar systems, galaxies) are needed to approximate to anything like common sense and to escape a radically subjective view of experience. But how, according to Dewey's view of meaning, can there be phenomenal objects?

PUZZLES ABOUT NATURE OF TRUTH

Much the same sort of problem arises in connection with the nature of truth. It is clear that any view that, like Dewey's or Hegel's, denies the ultimacy of the distinction between experience and nature will have to abandon, or at least radically revise, the commonsense notion that truth consists in the correspondence of ideas with external facts. For it is no longer possible to say, with common sense, that the judgment "There is a centaur in my office" is true if it agrees with the facts and false if it does not. In Dewey's view, what common sense calls the "facts" (office, centaur) are not pure existents but objects—existents with meaning. Truth, it would seem, lies in the expansion of meanings. Or to put it another way, truth consists in the degree to which one meaning coheres with others.

But now another difficulty arises. If truth is a matter of the coherence of a judgment with other judgments, rather than of the correspondence of judgments with "external" facts, what is the difference between a judgment about centaurs and a judgment about horses? Is a judgment about horses "truer" than a judgment about centaurs merely because, as it happens, the former coheres with the very large body of judgments called the science of zoology, whereas the latter coheres only with the much smaller body of judgments called Greek mythology? Is the difference between the reality of a horse and the fictionality of a centaur merely a difference in degree of meaning-expansion? Dewey wanted, of course, to eliminate the possibility that his doctrine of experience would collapse into a version of "idealism."

15 See pp. 48–49.

The proposition that the perception of a horse is objectively valid and that of a centaur fanciful and mythical does not denote that one is a meaning of natural events and the other is not. It denotes that they are meanings referable to *different* natural events, and that confused and harmful consequences result from attributing them to the same events. . . .

Genuinely to believe the centaur-meaning is to assert that events characterized by it interact in certain ways with other now unperceived events. Since belief that centaur has the same kind of objective meaning as has horse denotes expectation of like efficacies and consequences, the difference of validity between them is extrinsic. It is capable of being revealed only by the results of acting upon them. The awareness of centaur-meaning is fanciful not simply because part of its conditions lie within the organism; part of the conditions of *any* perception, valid as well as invalid, scientific as well as esthetic, lie within the organism. Nor is it fanciful, simply because it is supposed not to have adequate existential antecedents. Natural conditions, physiological, physical and social, may be specified in one case as in the other. But since the conditions in the two cases are different, consequences are bound to be different. Knowing, believing, involves something additive and extrinsic to having a meaning.

No knowledge is ever merely immediate. The proposition that the perception of a horse is valid and that a centaur is fanciful or hallucinatory, does not denote that there are two modes of awareness, differing intrinsically from each other. It denotes something . . . with respect to consequences, namely, that action upon the respective meanings will bring to light (to apparency or awareness) such different kinds of consequences that we should use the two meanings in very different ways.[r]

Since Dewey refused to follow Hegel in identifying truth and reality—though he agreed with him that truth is a matter of degree—he had to find a place somehow for the difference (which is a difference in *kind*) between the actual and the nonactual.

This he did by shifting the focus of the problem of truth from the coherence of meanings with other meanings, in the purely cognitive sense, to the coherence of meanings with events, in the sense of behavioral consequences. Accordingly, he was able to hold that there is a difference (of kind, not merely of degree) between the real and the fictional. The difference between "horse" and "centaur" is thus not merely a difference in their meaning-expansion coefficients. There is also a difference in the way the meanings operate. According to Dewey, "this is the meaning of truth: processes of change so directed that they achieve an intended consummation." Consider any scientific hypothesis or theory. What makes it true? The fact that it "modifies old beliefs," that it converts "actual immediate objects into *better*, into more secure and significant, objects."[s]

This definition of truth indicates where Dewey's interest lay—in social problems, and hence in truths and solutions that work. And this was not just a matter of a preference for one kind of philosophy over another. From his point of view, interest in truth in the traditional sense is merely a reflection of that quest for absolutes by which men seek to compensate for their sense of insecurity. But in what sense are Dewey's philosophical preferences better than those of more traditional philosophers? Certainly, in the sense that they are more useful they are better, for this is the whole point of such preferences. But by the same logic traditional philosophers might claim that their view of truth is better in terms of *their* preferences. And is there not a sense in which one can ask whether it is *true* that such-and-such a view or solution is more useful than another—a sense, that is, in which "true" is not equivalent to "useful"?

The problem of escaping truth in the traditional sense parallels the problem, just discussed, of avoiding "the all-inclusiveness of cognitive experience," for truth (in the traditional sense) is a property of "cognitive experience." It would seem, then, that Dewey did not solve, except by shelving it, the problem of how the empirical and the rational elements in knowledge are related. If he seemed to many of his contemporaries to have done so, it was because they, too, were prepared to shelve it.[16]

The Nature of Value

Dewey's view of philosophical discussions about value parallels his view of philosophical discussions about metaphysics: Though there are questions about value that have genuine importance, most of the questions that have been traditionally discussed by philosophers are only pseudo-problems.

> Modern science, modern industry and politics, have presented us with an immense amount of material foreign to, often inconsistent with, the most prized intellectual and moral heritage of the western world. This is the cause of our modern intellectual perplexities and confusions. It sets the especial problem for philosophy to-day and for many days to come. Every significant philosophy is an attempt to deal with it. . . .
>
> I believe that the method of empirical naturalism presented in this volume provides the way, and the only way—although of course no two thinkers will travel it in just the same fashion—by which one can freely accept the standpoint and conclusions of modern science: the way by which we can be genuinely naturalistic and yet maintain cherished values, provided they are critically clarified and reinforced. The naturalistic method, when it is consistently followed, destroys many things once cherished; but it destroys them by revealing their inconsistency with the nature of things—a flaw that always attended them and deprived them of efficacy for aught save emotional consolation. But its main purport is not destructive; empirical naturalism is rather a winnowing fan. Only chaff goes, though perhaps the chaff had once

---

16 For the kind of reply Dewey might have made to this criticism, see pp. 305–06.

been treasured. An empirical method which remains true to nature does not "save"; it is not an insurance device nor a mechanical antiseptic. But it inspires the mind with courage and vitality to create new ideals and values in the face of the perplexities of a new world.[t]

VALUES ARE FACTS FOUND IN EXPERIENCE

Thus, according to Dewey, men discover values in nature just as they discover any other facts. "Experience actually presents esthetic and moral traits. . . . When found, their ideal qualities are as relevant to the philosophic theory of nature as are the traits found by physical inquiry." Such traits as poignancy, beauty, humor, annoyance, consolation, and splendor are as real as are colors, sounds, qualities of contact, taste, and smell. They all stand on "the same level"; indeed, in a way the former are prior: "Things are objects to be treated, used, acted upon and with, enjoyed and endured, even more than things to be known. They are things *had* before they are things cognized."[u]

This doctrine is obviously connected to Dewey's denial of the all-inclusiveness of thought and his assertion of the reality of the actual. What is relevant here is its bearing on his theory of value. So far facts have been defined as ongoings, or events. But events are not only ongoings. They have beginnings and proceed to "endings," to "consummations." "The presence of uncertain and precarious factors" makes these ends "unstable and evanescent," but because they are ends and hence fulfillments, "there is a tendency to perpetuate them, render them stable, and repeat them." The intervening stages in a process toward an end come to be thought of as means; when they are brought under control they become "tools, techniques, mechanisms." Hence, far from being the foes of values, facts are the means for realizing them; they are also the criteria for "differentiating genuine aims from merely emotional and fantastic ideals."[v]

VALUE A PRACTICAL, NOT A METAPHYSICAL PROBLEM

Thus, according to Dewey, the problem of value is not a metaphysical problem about the "status" of value or about the rank of values in some eternal hierarchy. These problems seemed real to the traditional philosophers because in their quest for certainty they first erected a "realm of values" and then proceeded to locate especially precious things in this realm. As soon as they did this, the problem of the "two worlds" naturally arose: How is this realm of absolute values related to the spatiotemporal world of actual decision-making? "Is the world of value that of ultimate and transcendent Being from which the world of existence is a derivative or a fall? Or is it but a manifestation of human subjectivity, a factor somehow miraculously supervening upon an order complete and closed in physical structure?"[w]

Some philosophers adopt the first alternative: From this point of view values are the only realities, and attention becomes focused on questions about the order in which the precious things supposedly exist in the special realm of values, instead of on questions about current practice. Other philosophers adopt the second alternative: Then only "facts" are real; values become subjective preferences and there is no basis for intelligent choice among current practices. Happily, a choice between these two alternatives "is arbitrary because the problem is arbitrary."

But if the problem of values is not a metaphysical question, what is it? According to Dewey, it is just the practical, social, and human problem of intelligent choice, and philosophy is nothing but the study of the methods of making intelligent choices.

> The important consideration and concern is not a theory of values but a theory of criticism; a method of discriminating among goods on the basis of the conditions of their appearance, and of their consequences. . . .
>
> Either . . . the difference between genuine, valid, good and a counterfeit, specious good is unreal, or it is a difference consequent upon reflection, or criticism, and the significant point is that this difference is equivalent to that made by discovery of relationships, of conditions and consequences. With this conclusion are bound up two other propositions: Of immediate values as such, values which occur and which are possessed and enjoyed, there is no theory at all; they just occur, are enjoyed, possessed; and that is all. The moment we begin to discourse about these values, to define and generalize, to make distinctions in kinds, we are passing beyond value-objects themselves; we are entering, even if only blindly, upon an inquiry into causal antecedents and causative consequents, with a view to appraising the "real," that is the eventual, goodness of the thing in question. . . .
>
> The other proposition is that philosophy is and can be nothing but this critical operation and function become aware of itself and its implications, pursued deliberately and systematically. It starts from actual situations of belief, conduct and appreciative perception which are characterized by immediate qualities of good and bad, and from the modes of critical judgment current at any given time in all the regions of value; these are its data, its subject-matter. . . . [Its] function is to regulate the further appreciation of goods and bads; to give greater freedom and security in those acts of direct selection, appropriation, identification and of rejection, elimination, destruction which enstate and which exclude objects of belief, conduct and contemplation. . . .[x]

Dewey's approach to values was, then, empirical and antimetaphysical. What would Dewey have had to say about Kierkegaard's existentialist approach, which was also antimetaphysical? He would certainly have agreed that finding "a focus and a center" for one's life is a genuine problem, but he would have considered it an empirical problem—no different *in kind* from the problem of deciding how to vote in the next election or how to spend a summer vacation. Fortunately, some men can solve their existential problem by immersing themselves in action—for instance, in social reform and other "good causes." Clearly Kierkegaard was not of this type. His writings reveal that his situation was desperate, as he himself recognized. But in Dewey's view Kierkegaard misunderstood the nature of the help that he needed: He should have sought not God's help but that of a competent psychiatrist. The solution to the existential problem, like that of any other problem, requires intelligence, not a leap of faith.

COMMENT ON THIS VIEW OF VALUE

We may agree with Dewey that values are facts, in the sense that enjoyings stand on just as firm a footing as any other aspects of our experience. We may also agree with Dewey that intelligence is the faculty of choice and that one of the criteria for evaluating intelligence is its success in forging instruments for resolving choice situations. Obviously, as the Utilitarians had pointed out, knowledge of the causal context of our various options is relevant to intelligent choice.

For instance, to make an intelligent choice between going to a movie and staying home to study, a student would need to know the probable effects in *this* situation, at *this* time of the academic year, with his work in *this* stage of preparation, and so on, of going to a movie. He must not only have a method that enables him to predict the probable effects of the various alternatives open to him; he must also have one that provides him with a way of choosing intelligently between two rival enjoyings. This can be done only on the basis of a preference for some other good to which one or the other of these enjoyings is a means.

All of this, of course, was said long ago by Aristotle, and all of it was well said and useful. But though Aristotle was interested in the problems of intelligent choice, he was also interested in the metaphysical implications of the practical situation just described. The fact that men have to choose among values and can do so only on the basis of other values to which they are means led Aristotle to conclude that values form precisely that kind of hierarchy, or pyramid, whose existence Dewey denied.

The argument against Dewey runs roughly as follows. A person cannot choose intelligently between two rival enjoyments unless he has a basis for saying that one is better than the other. But Dewey's view allows for no such basis. How, in his view, can a person distinguish between what seems to be good now (because it is an enjoying) and what is *really* good? How is he to distinguish between what is desired and what is desirable? between what is enjoyed and what is enjoyable (that is, worthy to be enjoyed)? Must there not be some criterion other than more (subsequent, later) enjoyings? Not all traditional philosophers based this criterion for choice, as Aristotle did, on a hierarchy of goods leading up to a supreme good-in-itself: Kant, for instance, derived it from a categorical imperative. But they all believed that some nonempirical standard was required. Dewey's naturalism, his critics maintained, committed him to a "fatal" relativism.

Dewey, of course, rejected this conclusion. It is possible, he thought, to maintain "a distinction between likings and that which is worth liking, between the desired and the desirable, between the is and the ought," [y] without reference to any transcendental, or absolute, standards. The basis for making this distinction, he held, is exactly the same sort of operation as that by which we interrogate and establish "belief-judgments" about external events. No one proposes to use transcendental criteria to test a scientific hypothesis; everyone agrees that such belief-judgments are validated by means of empirical criteria. This is equally true, Dewey held, for belief-judgments about desirings, enjoyings, and (generally) values. Indeed, Dewey proposed to turn the tables on his critics by arguing that any appeal to standards that "descend from the blue," far from being the only basis for intelligent and reasonable choice, actually makes intelligent choice impossible.

Operational thinking needs to be applied to the judgment of values just as it has now finally been applied in conceptions of physical objects. Experimental empiricism in the field of ideas of good and bad is demanded to meet the conditions of the present situation.

The scientific revolution came about when material of direct and uncontrolled experience was taken as problematic; as supplying material to be transformed by reflective operations into known objects. The contrast between experienced and known objects was found to be a temporal one; namely, one between empirical subject-matters which were had or "given" prior to the acts of experimental variation and redisposition and those which succeeded these acts and issued from them. The notion of an act whether of sense or thought which supplied a valid measure of thought in immediate knowledge was discredited. Consequences of operations became the important thing. . . .

Analogy suggests that we regard our direct and original experience of things liked and enjoyed as only *possibilities* of values to be achieved; that enjoyment becomes a value when we discover the relations upon which its presence depends. Such a causal and operational definition gives only a conception of a value, not a value itself. But the utilization of the conception in action results in an object having secure and significant value.

The formal statement may be given concrete content by pointing to the difference between the enjoyed and the enjoyable, the desired and the desirable, the satis*fying* and the satis*factory*. To say that something is enjoyed is to make a statement about a fact, something already in existence; it is not to judge the value of that fact. There is no difference between such a proposition and one which says that something is sweet or sour, red or black. It is just correct or incorrect and that is the end of the matter. But to call an object a value is to assert that it satisfies or fulfills certain conditions. Function and status in meeting conditions is a different matter from bare existence. The fact that something is desired only raises the *question* of its desirability; it does not settle it. Only a child in the degree of his immaturity thinks to settle the question of desirability by reiterated proclamation: "I want it, I want it, I want it." . . . Take for example the difference between the ideas of "satisfying" and "satisfactory." To say that something satisfies is to report something as an isolated finality. To assert that it is satis*factory* is to define it in its connections and interactions. The fact that it pleases or is immediately congenial poses a problem to judgment. How shall the satisfaction be rated? Is it a value or is it not? Is it something to be prized and cherished, *to be* enjoyed? Not stern moralists alone but everyday experience informs us that finding satisfaction in a thing may be a warning, a summons to be on the lookout for consequences. To declare something satis*factory* is to assert that it meets specifiable conditions. It is, in effect, a judgment that the thing "will do." It involves a prediction; it contemplates a future in which the thing will continue to serve. . . . It denotes an attitude *to be* taken, that of striving to perpetuate and to make secure.[z]

Thus, according to Dewey, the situation with respect to values is exactly the same as the situation with respect to physical objects. In our perceptual field there are all sorts of sensory experiences. Do we accept all of them at their face value? We do not; or at least if we begin by doing so, we are soon forced to become a bit more careful. For example, in my perceptual field at this moment there is a rowboat, with an oar bent in the water. Is the oar really bent? I run my hand along it to find out. Is this a dagger that I see before me? I reach out and try to touch it. These are commonsense procedures for distinguishing between the seemingly true and the really true, between initial impressions of physical objects and the objects themselves. Such procedures have been greatly refined by the methods of scientific investigation and by the introduction of instruments like telescopes, microscopes, and thermometers; and all these procedures and instruments are capable of continuous refinement and improvement. A "fact" is simply an initial experience that has survived the tests available at any given time. For instance, a witness' initial impression may be that the man he now sees in the police lineup is the same man he saw leaving the scene of a crime; but fingerprints or tests of blood type may correct this impression and "establish" the fact that he is not the same man.

Now, as Dewey argued, values are not intrinsically different from other facts: There are initial enjoyings, just as there are initial impressions of the characteristics of physical objects. Insofar as and as long as the initial enjoyings are enjoyed, they are good. But experience shows that some of these initial enjoyings, like some initial sense experiences, are deceptive. Thus a bit of scepticism and a disposition to test enjoyings before we commit ourselves to them soon emerges. Just as the initial sense experiences that survive the tests of subsequent experience become "facts," so initial enjoyments that survive the tests of experience become values.

Although Dewey admitted—indeed, insisted—that no belief-judgment (whether about physical objects or about values) can ever be absolutely true, he maintained that many such judgments are "reasonable." For instance, it is reasonable to conclude that the man in the police lineup is not the man who was seen leaving the crime, if chemical tests show that the blood types are different. This is the reasonable conclusion to draw, even though the possibility cannot be excluded that further experimentation by chemists may someday throw doubt on the validity of currently accepted blood tests. To ask for more than this, to expect that men can ever be absolutely certain about a matter of fact such as the identity of the man in the lineup, is unreasonable. It is as unreasonable (quite literally) as it is for a child to demand to be in the front seat and in the back seat of the family car at the same time. In Dewey's view, the notion that a belief-judgment can be absolutely true is a fiction, a product of human insecurity. We live in a world that will always be insecure, because it is living and changing. But by intelligent action we can make it progressively less insecure; we can make it into a world that "will do."

Similarly, as regards the problem of what is "good," we can never be absolutely sure that something we now assess as "desirable" will continue to be desirable. It may change, or we may change. Nonetheless, knowledge that a particular object or experience is desirable—that is, that it has survived the best available tests—"will do." This knowledge is a reasonably reliable rule for guiding conduct, and it is far better and far more reliable than a rule derived in any other way—say, a rule that tells us to obey strange voices that speak to us from the air, even though these voices order us to sacrifice our child.

Is Dewey's answer to the charge of relativism adequate? To begin with, it should be noted that Dewey did not deny that his view was relativistic; he claimed that relativism need not be "fatal" and that a relativism that makes available continuously improving criteria for choice is *not* fatal. Indeed, to ask for more than this—to look for an absolutely valid criterion—would probably be fatal, in the sense that such a demand would lead to poorer rather than better decisions in concrete situations.

Dewey recognized, of course, that this reply would not be acceptable to those who, like Kierkegaard, long for certainty. But then, in Dewey's estimation, such people are seriously disturbed. He did not expect his theory to satisfy neurotics, and he would not have regarded their rejection of it as relevant. He asked only that his theory be tried, that it be tested. That is, he applied to his own theory his general thesis about the nature of truth. He had defined truth as "processes of change so directed that they achieve an intended consummation"; the test of any theory, accordingly, is whether application of it leads to more enlightened and more effective practice in the domain of experience covered by the theory. The theory of empirical naturalism in the domain of decision-making has not yet been tried. Dewey held that in ethics men are at the level they were in physics before the appearance of Galileo and the other early modern scientists. It was dogmatic to reject out of hand, as many people did in the seventeenth century, the proposal to apply empirical methods to the study of physical nature. It is equally dogmatic to reject out of hand, and prior to testing, the proposal to apply empirical methods to the problems of choice.

What the method of intelligence, thoughtful valuation will accomplish, if once it be tried, is for the result of trial to determine. Since it is relative to the intersection in existence of hazard and rule, of contingency and order, faith in a wholesale and final triumph is fantastic. But some procedure has to be tried; for life is itself a sequence of trials. Carelessness and routine, Olympian aloofness, secluded contemplation are themselves choices. To claim that intelligence is a better method than its alternatives, authority, imitation, caprice and ignorance, prejudice and passion, is hardly an excessive claim. These procedures have been tried and have worked their will. The result is not such as to make it clear that the method of intelligence, the use of science in criticizing and recreating the casual goods of nature into intentional and conclusive goods of art, the union of knowledge and values in production, is not worth trying.[a]

To many readers this passage will sound badly dated. Dewey assumed that to a very great extent a consensus exists among men that "the positive concrete goods of science, art, and social companionship" *are* good, and further, that it is better for these goods to be widely, rather than narrowly, distributed. In this respect he shared the optimism of the Utilitarians and their eighteenth-century predecessors. Like them, he thought that the main problem of ethics was that of implementing agreed-on values, not that of reaching an agreement about values. The methods of empirical science are more obviously applicable to the former problem than to the latter.

In the years since Dewey wrote, people have become increasingly doubtful about whether the consensus Dewey described exists. World War II and its aftermath suggest that Dewey's view of human nature may be naïve. Men, it seems, are less socially conscious than they are selfish, aggressive, sadistic, and irrational and far from being guided by a consideration of the consequences of their actions, they often deliberately choose to destroy themselves. The traditional theological way of describing these weaknesses in human nature is to attribute them to "original sin"; people who find this terminology old-fashioned are likely to talk about the "absurdity" of man's existence in an indifferent universe. Dewey's world view allowed neither for original sin nor for absurdity. He claimed to be able to "differentiate genuine aims from merely fantastic ideals" on the basis of future empirical consequences. The trouble is that a man who believes all Jews ought to be exterminated is as unlikely to be won over by a consideration of the deleterious consequences of this belief as a man who believes the world is flat is unlikely to be shaken by the accumulation of empirical evidence to the contrary. Dewey recognized this, of course; but he evidently did not consider the possibility that large numbers of men, for one reason or another, are deeply committed to such "fantastic ideals."

Dewey's theory of value is workable only on the assumption that fanaticism, neurosis, and the "death wish" are minority phenomena. If the more pessimistic estimate of human nature proves to be correct, Dewey's theory may turn out to be untrue by its own criterion of truth.

Whitehead

The basic orientation of Whitehead's[17] mind was quite different from that of Dewey's. He had, for instance, a nostalgia for the past and a sense of tradition that Dewey lacked. Reminiscing about Sandwich, a town in the south of England near which he grew up, Whitehead remarked that the sleepy sixteenth- and seventeenth-century town he had known as a boy was no more. "In the last half century it has been revived by a golf-course, one of the best in England. I feel a sense of profanation amidst the relics of the Romans, of the Saxons, of Augustine, the medieval monks, and the ships of the Tudors and the Stuarts."[b] It seems unlikely that Dewey would have cared much if Burlington, Vermont, had suffered this fate, or that he would have found golf "a cheap ending to the story."

Whitehead, however, did not live solely in the past; nor was he uninterested in contemporary social problems. On the contrary, he had a very lively interest in such problems and wrote with power and insight on such subjects as education. Nevertheless, for Whitehead, philosophy was primarily a cognitive enterprise, and his primary interest was metaphysical. In a sense both he and Dewey wanted their theories to perform a social function. They wanted to make men's lives richer and more significant by helping them to understand their experience. But whereas Dewey thought of this task primarily in terms of solving a variety of fairly immediate, concrete problems, Whitehead thought of it in terms of a long-range and systematic interpretation of the whole range of experience. Because he was a systematizer, his point of view was less "modern" than Dewey's; on the other hand, he belongs to the great tradition that has always regarded the role of philosophy as more a matter of understanding the world than of changing it.

If Dewey represented the empirical spirit of the modern mind, modified, as has been seen, by his sense of man's functional and active relation to the data of experience, Whitehead can be fairly said to have represented the rationalist tradition. But his relation to this tradition must be stated with care. To begin with, like every other philosopher of the last century, he took process very seriously. This serves to distinguish him from the rationalists of the Enlightenment, but not from Hegel. The chief differences between Whitehead and Hegel are, first, that Whitehead drew his conceptual scheme from the physical sciences instead of from "pure" logic and, second, that there is no Whiteheadian "dialectic." In addition, Whitehead was quite clear that his conceptual scheme was not the final answer, whereas Hegel sometimes slipped into thinking of his in this way. Whitehead's thought about his own thinking was open-ended like Dewey's rather than dogmatic, as the traditional rationalism tended to be.

17 Alfred North Whitehead (1861–1947) was born in England and educated at Trinity College, Cambridge. After teaching mathematics there for some years, he moved to London, where he continued teaching and writing on scientific subjects. In 1924, at an age when most men would be thinking of retiring, he became a professor at Harvard and subsequently published most of his work on purely philosophical subjects.

The Function of Philosophy

Philosophy, Whitehead held, is simply the search for the pattern in the universe. In one sense men always have the pattern in their grasp; in another sense it forever eludes them. Philosophy works with feeble instruments, but it perfects these instruments as it goes. It is an "attempt to express the infinity of the universe in terms of the limitations of language." [c] It is the enemy of half-truths, dogmatic generalizations, watertight compartmentalizations, and doctrinaire solutions. It knows that "all general truths condition each other; and the limits of their application cannot be adequately defined apart from their correlation by yet wider generalities." [d] To perform this never-ending work of criticism and revision, to move forward to ever less inadequate formulations of the underlying pattern, is the task of philosophy.

> Philosophy is an attitude of mind towards doctrines ignorantly entertained. By the phrase "ignorantly entertained" I mean that the full meaning of the doctrine in respect to the infinitude of circumstances to which it is relevant, is not understood. . . .
>
> The use of philosophy is to maintain an active novelty of fundamental ideas illuminating the social system. It reverses the slow descent of accepted thought towards the inactive commonplace. If you like to phrase it so, philosophy is mystical. For mysticism is direct insight into depths as yet unspoken. But the purpose of philosophy is to rationalize mysticism: not by explaining it away, but by the introduction of novel verbal characterizations, rationally coördinated.
>
> Philosophy is akin to poetry, and both of them seek to express that ultimate good sense which we term civilization. In each case there is reference to form beyond the direct meanings of words. Poetry allies itself to metre, philosophy to mathematic pattern. [e]

FAITH IN A PATTERN

Whitehead thus believed that "the ultimate natures of things lie together in a harmony which excludes mere arbitrariness." [f] Since "we are finite beings," the *complete* grasp of this pattern "in its totality is denied us." [g] It follows that belief in an order of nature, belief that "at the basis of things we shall not find mere arbitrary mystery," is, in the final analysis, an "act of faith." But Whitehead's faith was not remotely like Kierkegaard's leap of faith. Whitehead's was a faith in the continuity of things—a faith that the patterns already discovered are the basis for patterns yet to be found. Kierkegaard's faith involved a quantum jump, a complete break with the evidence. Whitehead's was a faith in an objective truth, in a cosmological principle. Kierkegaard's faith claimed only subjective truth; although for Kierkegaard it "made all the difference," the difference it made was entirely in his own life. Finally, and most important, Whitehead's was a faith that men's minds and the universe are interfused in harmony; Kierkegaard's faith presupposed that an abyss separates them.

Guided by his faith in the ultimate rationality of the universe, philosophy is "to seek the forms in the facts" [h] and to display these forms in their systematic interconnections. Since Whitehead believed that the pattern thus revealed has affinities with the pattern found in mathematics, it is important to understand what he conceived the nature of mathematics to be. The following passage should be contrasted with Dewey's account of mathematics, which has already been examined.[18]

> The science of Pure Mathematics, in its modern developments, may claim to be the most original creation of the human spirit. . . . [Its] originality consists in the fact that in mathematical science connections between things are exhibited which, apart from the agency of human reason, are extremely unobvious. . . .
>
> The point of mathematics is that in it we have always got rid of the particular instance, and even of any particular sorts of entities. . . . All you assert is, that reason insists on the admission that, if any entities whatever have any relations which satisfy such-and-such purely abstract conditions, then they must have other relations which satisfy other purely abstract conditions.
>
> In the pure mathematics of geometrical relationships, we say that, if *any* group [of] entities enjoy *any* relationships among its members satisfying *this* set of abstract geometrical conditions, then such-and-such additional abstract conditions must also hold for such relationships. But when we come to physical space, we say that some definitely observed group of physical entities enjoys some definitely observed relationships among its members which do satisfy this above-mentioned set of abstract geometrical conditions. We thence conclude that the additional relationships which we concluded to hold in *any* such case, must therefore hold in *this particular* case. . . .
>
> Pure mathematics . . . is a resolute attempt to go the whole way in the direction of complete analysis, so as to separate the elements of mere matter of fact from the purely abstract conditions which they exemplify. . . .
>
> The exercise of logical reason is always concerned with these absolutely general conditions. In its broadest sense, the discovery of mathematics is the discovery that the totality of these general abstract conditions, which are concurrently applicable to the relationships among the entities of any one concrete occasion, are themselves inter-connected in the manner of a pattern with a key to it. . . .
>
> The key to the patterns means this fact:—that from a select set of those general conditions, exemplified in any one and the same occasion, a pattern involving an infinite variety of other such conditions, also exemplified in the same occasion, can be developed by the pure exercise of abstract logic. Any such select set is called the set of postulates, or premises, from which the reasoning proceeds. . . .
>
> The complete pattern of general conditions, thus exemplified, is determined by any one of many select sets of these conditions. These key sets are sets of equivalent postulates. This reasonable harmony of being, which is required

18 See pp. 294–95.

for the unity of a complex occasion, together with the completeness of the realisation (in that occasion) of all that is involved in its logical harmony, is the primary article of metaphysical doctrine. It means that for things to be together involves that they are reasonably together. This means that thought can penetrate into every occasion of fact, so that by comprehending its key conditions, the whole complex of its pattern of conditions lies open before it. It comes to this:—provided we know something which is perfectly general about the elements in any occasion, we can then know an indefinite number of other equally general concepts which must also be exemplified in that same occasion.[i]

It is clear from this passage that Whitehead belonged to the Platonic tradition. He would not have denied, of course, that mathematics can have a purely calculative role of the kind that nominalists assign to it; he would have agreed that from this point of view it is "a way of avoiding reasoning." But it is, he believed, *also* an insight into real connections. Whitehead held, as Descartes did, that it is necessary to distinguish between (1) the movement of thought or inference in our own minds, (2) the eternal objects thought about, whose real connections are revealed when we think truly, and (3) the possible exemplification of these connections in the physical world. One of the tasks of the "philosophy of organism" (as Whitehead called his view) is to put these three factors back into organic unity instead of leaving them separate as Descartes had been obliged to do. But the point to understand here is simply that in Whitehead's view mathematical reasoning is more than a mere computation of the agreements and disagreements of names; it traverses an objectively real pattern. This pattern is something men *find* (they "seek the forms in the facts"), not a subjective order that they impose on experience.

But what is the source of the concepts that constitute this pattern, or categoreal scheme—that is, what are those highest and pervasive concepts that apply to all experience whatever and thus "never fail of exemplification"? It was once thought that such highest forms had a "peculiar certainty and initial clarity," that they could therefore easily be recognized as self-evident axioms, and that, once they had been ascertained, the task of philosophy was "to erect upon those premises a deductive system of thought." Unfortunately, according to Whitehead, there are no intrinsically clear and certain starting points. Theorems derived in one system can become postulates in another, and "the verification of a rationalistic scheme is to be sought in its general success," that is, in the way in which a deductive structure is developed. Until such a structure emerges, "every premise . . . is under suspicion."[j]

INCLUSIVENESS THE CRITERION

Since there are no self-evident axioms, it is necessary (Whitehead held) to make a start with the concepts that seem to form a satisfactory pattern for some less inclusive region of experience (such as physics). The next step is to try to show that this set of concepts is also adequate for the interpretation of other regions of experience. Eventually the concepts may prove to be the categoreal scheme that is being sought. All claimants to categoreal status must be challenged to show their relevance to *all* the facts.

> Speculative Philosophy is the endeavour to frame a coherent, logical, necessary system of general ideas in terms of which every element of our experience can be interpreted. By this notion of "interpretation" I mean that everything of which we are conscious, as enjoyed, perceived, willed, or thought, shall have the character of a particular instance of the general scheme. . . .
>
> "Coherence," as here employed, means that the fundamental ideas, in terms of which the scheme is developed, presuppose each other so that in isolation they are meaningless. . . .
>
> The term "logical" has its ordinary meaning, including "logical" consistency, or lack of contradiction. . . . It will be observed that logical notions must themselves find their places in the scheme of philosophic notions.
>
> It will also be noticed that this ideal of speculative philosophy has its rational side and its empirical side. The rational side is expressed by the terms "coherent" and "logical." The empirical side is expressed by the terms "applicable" and "adequate." [k]

THE ROLE OF IMAGINATION

But though the verification of a proposed categoreal scheme is straightforwardly empirical, the initial formulation of the scheme is not. It is more like poetic insight than like generalization from the enumeration of instances. This is the case because of the very great generality of the concepts contained in a categoreal scheme. Normally, science and common sense alike proceed by the method of difference: The range of a generalization is specified by noting the cases for which it does not hold. But metaphysical principles, precisely because they are categoreal, hold universally.

> We habitually observe by the method of difference. Sometimes we see an elephant, and sometimes we do not. The result is that an elephant, when present, is noticed. . . .
>
> The metaphysical first principles can never fail of exemplification. We can never catch the actual world taking a holiday from their sway. Thus, for the discovery of metaphysics, the method of pinning down thought to the strict systematization of detailed discrimination, already effected by antecedent observation, breaks down. This collapse of the method of rigid empiricism is not confined to metaphysics. It occurs whenever we seek the larger generalities. In natural science this rigid method is the Baconian method of induction, a method which, if consistently pursued, would have left science where it found it. What Bacon omitted was the play of a free imagination, controlled by the requirements of coherence and logic. The true method of

discovery is like the flight of an aeroplane. It starts from the ground of particular observation; it makes a flight in the thin air of imaginative generalization; and it again lands for renewed observation rendered acute by rational interpretation. The reason for the success of this method of imaginative rationalization is that, when the method of difference fails, factors which are constantly present may yet be observed under the influence of imaginative thought. Such thought supplies the differences which the direct observation lacks. It can even play with inconsistency; and can thus throw light on the consistent, and persistent, elements in experience by comparison with what in imagination is inconsistent with them. . . . The success of the imaginative experiment is always to be tested by the applicability of its results beyond the restricted locus from which it originated. . . . The partially successful philosophic generalization will, if derived from physics, find applications in fields of experience beyond physics. It will enlighten observation in those remote fields, so that general principles can be discerned as in process of illustration, which in the absence of the imaginative generalization are obscured by their persistent exemplification. . . .

There may be rival schemes, inconsistent among themselves; each with its own merits and its own failures. It will then be the purpose of research to conciliate the differences. Metaphysical categories are not dogmatic statements of the obvious; they are tentative formulations of the ultimate generalities.

If we consider any scheme of philosophic categories as one complex assertion, and apply to it the logician's alternative, true or false, the answer must be that the scheme is false. . . .

The scheme is true with unformulated qualifications, exceptions, limitations, and new interpretations in terms of more general notions. . . . [It] is a matrix from which true propositions applicable to particular circumstances can be derived. We can at present only trust our trained instincts as to the discrimination of the circumstances in respect to which the scheme is valid. . . .

Rationalism is an adventure in the clarification of thought, progressive and never final. But it is an adventure in which even partial success has importance.[1]

This notion of imaginative rationalization, with the related ideas of adventure, poetic vision, and instinct, is one of the major clues to understanding Whitehead's conception of philosophy and his constant emphasis on growth and openness.

THE UTILITY OF METAPHYSICS

The chief criticisms of such an attempt at speculative philosophy, Whitehead believed, will be (1) that it is impossible and (2) that even if it is possible it is useless. It is a sign of the marked empiricism and pragmatism of one aspect of contemporary culture that Whitehead felt he had to defend himself on the second, as well as on the first, of these scores. As regards the claim that speculative philosophy is impossible, Whitehead believed that "all constructive thought is dominated by some such scheme, unacknowledged but no less influential in guiding the imagination." Thus philosophy has an important role to perform in making "such schemes explicit and thereby capable of criticism and improvement."[m]

Obviously, this is also a reply to the charge that speculative philosophy is useless. If it is true that constructive thought is always guided by some underlying metaphysical scheme, any improvement of the scheme by means of philosophical criticism should result in an improved empirical understanding of the world about us.

> The main objection . . . is that we ought to describe detailed matter of fact, and elicit the laws with a generality strictly limited to the systematization of these described details. General interpretation, it is held, has no bearing upon this procedure; and thus any system of general interpretation, be it true or false, remains intrinsically barren. Unfortunately for this objection, there are no brute, self-contained matters of fact, capable of being understood apart from interpretation as an element in a system. Whenever we attempt to express the matter of immediate experience, we find that its understanding leads us beyond itself, to its contemporaries, to its past, to its future, and to the universals in terms of which its definiteness is exhibited. . . . When thought comes upon the scene, it finds the interpretations as matters of practice. Philosophy does not initiate interpretations. Its search for a rationalistic scheme is the search for more adequate criticism, and for more adequate justification, of the interpretations which we perforce employ. . . .
>
> The useful function of philosophy is to promote the most general systematization of civilized thought. There is a constant reaction between specialism and common sense. It is the part of the special sciences to modify common sense. Philosophy is the welding of imagination and common sense into a restraint upon specialists, and also into an enlargement of their imaginations.[n]

Criticism of the Dominant Philosophical Scheme

According to Whitehead, then, all thought has as its underlying presupposition some categoreal scheme. These categoreal schemes are often largely unconscious and chaotic; yet each one shapes the actual concepts, hypotheses, and theories by means of which the scientists—as well as the ordinary men—of any age seek to understand themselves and the world they live in.

Stated in this general way, Whitehead's assertion is clearly an echo of Hegel's contention that what men experience is in part a product of the mind's activity, and that the mind's role in this production has a history. But in one respect Whitehead was perhaps closer to Nietzsche than to any of the other nineteenth-century philosophers who held this kind of view. He agreed with Nietzsche that the categoreal scheme underlying modern thought was the product in large measure of seventeenth-century physics; he agreed, too, that although this scheme had worked reasonably well for a long time in the field of physics, its application to other fields—psychology, ethics, and theory of knowledge, for instance—was never even remotely adequate. Further, Whitehead pointed out that relativity theory and quantum physics (which Nietzsche, of course, had not known) demonstrated that the dominant categoreal scheme was no longer adequate even in its own sphere.

But although Nietzsche and Whitehead agreed that the dominant categoreal scheme had collapsed, Nietzsche was content merely to suggest a new one in a cursory and sketchy fashion. Whitehead, for his part, regarded this collapse as an occasion for the exercise of those constructive functions that he assigned to speculative philosophy. These radically different attitudes toward the role of speculative philosophy reflect, once again, two persistently different personality types that have appeared again and again in Western culture. Nietzsche was too deeply concerned with his existential problem—with the need to affirm life despite its horrors—to be seriously interested in cosmology. Moreover, he believed that all categoreal schemes—including, of course, any that he himself might put forward—were mechanisms designed to protect philosophers from insecurity, and he held that it was more noble and "masterly" to face insecurity boldly than to invent a categoreal defense against it. In contrast, Whitehead's faith in a pattern led him to believe that categoreal schemes are not merely products of insecurity; they are also expressions of the human passion to understand. In his view, since the schemes can come to correspond more and more adequately to the "facts" of the cosmological pattern, this passion is reasonable: It is capable of progressive, though never complete, satisfaction. But not only did Whitehead believe that the application of intelligence can result in improved categoreal schemes; he also had surplus energy to expend on that improvement because he was not deeply immersed in an existential problem of his own.

Whitehead's philosophy of organism thus falls into two parts. First, he undertook to demonstrate the incompetence of the existing categoreal scheme. Second, he sought to develop a new scheme that would avoid the difficulties of the existing one.

THE NOTION OF SIMPLE LOCATION

Whitehead believed that the root idea, and the source of much of the trouble, in the dominant categoreal scheme was the notion of "simple location."

> One . . . assumption [underlying] the whole philosophy of nature during the modern period . . . is embodied in the conception which is supposed to express the most concrete aspect of nature. The Ionian philosophers asked, What is nature made of? The answer is couched in terms of stuff, or matter, or material—the particular name chosen is indifferent—which has the property of simple location in space and time, or, if you adopt the more modern

ideas, in space-time. What I mean by matter, or material, is anything which has this property of *simple location*. . . .

The characteristic common both to space and time is that material can be said to be *here* in space and *here* in time, or *here* in space-time, in a perfectly definite sense which does not require for its explanation any reference to other regions of space-time. Curiously enough this character of simple location holds whether we look on a region of space-time as determined absolutely or relatively. . . .

This fact that the material is indifferent to the division of time leads to the conclusion that the lapse of time is an accident, rather than of the essence, of the material. The material is fully itself in any sub-period however short. . . .

The answer, therefore, which the seventeenth century gave to the ancient question of the Ionian thinkers, "What is the world made of?" was that the world is a succession of instantaneous configurations of matter—or of material, if you wish to include stuff more subtle than ordinary matter, the ether for example.

We cannot wonder that science rested content with this assumption as to the fundamental elements of nature. . . . This is the famous mechanistic theory of nature, which has reigned supreme ever since the seventeenth century. It is the orthodox creed of physical science. Furthermore, the creed justified itself by the pragmatic test. It worked. . . . But the difficulties of this theory of materialistic mechanism very soon became apparent. The history of thought in the eighteenth and nineteenth centuries is governed by the fact that the world had got hold of a general idea which it could neither live with nor live without.°

THE PROBLEM OF INDUCTION

In Whitehead's view, the first thing wrong with the dominant scheme is that developments in physics in the twentieth century (such as discoveries about the properties of electrons) have made interpretation in terms of simple location hopelessly complex and even contradictory. Men used to think that it would someday be possible to give a mechanical explanation of all natural phenomena— this was the "ideal" of science. But "what is the sense of talking about a mechanical explanation when you do not know what you mean by mechanics?"ᵖ

But apart from such difficulties posed by twentieth-century discoveries, the dominant scheme is ill-equipped even for dealing with the kind of world it supposes itself to be facing. "It is obvious," for instance, "that the concept of simple location is going to make great difficulties for induction." For the assumption that there is no inherent connection between heres and theres or between nows and thens means that inference from what happened at one instantaneous configuration of matter to what may happen at another is quite impossible.

The governing principle underlying [the orthodox] scheme is that extension, namely extension in time or extension in space, expresses disconnection. This principle issues in the assumptions that causal action between entities separated in time or in space is impossible and that extension in space and unity of being are inconsistent. . . . This governing principle has to be limited in respect to extension in time. The same material exists at different times. This concession introduces the many perplexities centering round the notion of change. . . .

The ultimate fact embracing all nature is (in this traditional point of view) a distribution of material throughout all space at a durationless instant of time, and another such ultimate fact will be another distribution of the same material throughout the same space at another durationless instant of time. The difficulties of this extreme statement are evident and were pointed out even in classical times when the concept first took shape. . . .

We must therefore in the ultimate fact, beyond which science ceases to analyse, include the notion of a state of change. But a state of change at a durationless instant is a very difficult conception. It is impossible to define velocity without some reference to the past and the future. Thus change is essentially the importation of the past and of the future into the immediate fact embodied in the durationless present instant.

This conclusion is destructive of the fundamental assumption that the ultimate facts for science are to be found at durationless instants of time. . . .

In biology the concept of an organism cannot be expressed in terms of a material distribution at an instant. The essence of an organism is that it is one thing which functions and is spread through space. Now functioning takes time. Thus a biological organism is a unity with the spatio-temporal extension which is of the essence of its being. This biological conception is obviously incompatible with the traditional ideas. This argument does not in any way depend on the assumption that biological phenomena belong to a different category to other physical phenomena. The essential point of the criticism on traditional concepts which has occupied us so far is that the concept of unities, functioning and with spatio-temporal extensions, cannot be extruded from physical concepts.[q]

Of course, as Whitehead pointed out, such "theoretical difficulties . . . have never worried practical scientists."[r] Scientists are content to operate pragmatically; they do not worry about the fact that their tacit assumption of arbitrariness and disconnectedness undermines the rationale of their procedure. For they have quietly gone on *believing* in the rationality of the universe even while *saying* that it is irrational. "It does not matter what men say in words, so long as their activities are controlled by settled instincts. . . . Since the time of Hume, the fashionable scientific philosophy has been such as to deny the rationality of science. . . . But scientific faith has risen to the occasion, and has tacitly removed the philosophic mountain."[s]

Nevertheless, however pragmatically minded practicing scientists may be, no one can enjoy operating from contradictory premises. If it is the notion of simple location that is responsible for "this strange contradiction in scientific thought," the sensible procedure is to abandon the concept in question.

THE "BIFURCATION OF NATURE"

Another difficulty with the concept of simple location is connected with the theory of perception. The minds that observe nature are supposed to be different sorts of things from the nature they observe. This notion of "bifurcation of nature," which is another by-product of the assumption of simple location, is hopelessly contradictory. According to this view, the ordinary objects of sense perception (for example, the castle seen at a distance, the planet in the sky) are unreal. They are actually only material particles that cause changes in the observer via his sense organs and cortex. But

> . . . the difficulty to be faced is just this. We may not lightly abandon the castle [and] the planet, . . . and hope to retain the eye, its retina, and the brain. Such a philosophy is too simple-minded—or at least might be thought so, except for its wide diffusion.
>
> Suppose we make a clean sweep. Science then becomes a formula for calculating mental "phenomena" or "impressions." But where is science? In books? But the castle and the planet took their libraries with them.
>
> No, science is in the minds of men. But men sleep and forget, and at their best in any one moment of insight entertain but scanty thoughts. Science therefore is nothing but a confident expectation that relevant thoughts will occasionally occur. . . . Yet this won't do; for this succession is only known by recollection, and recollection is subject to the same criticism as that applied . . . to the castle [and] the planet. . . . In their departure "you" also have accompanied them; and I am left solitary in the character of a void of experience without significance.[t]

CONFLICTS WITH ESTHETIC AND MORAL VIEWS OF THE WORLD

Even apart from such epistemological puzzles, the dominant view of the world is "quite unbelievable." According to Whitehead, ordinary, everyday experience—including even the ordinary, everyday experience of those physicists and philosophers who affirm the "truth" of the dominant categoreal scheme—is not experience of temporally and spatially discrete entities that are wholly without sensuous differentiations. Everyone's experience includes continuity, endurance, value, and sensuous detail. But according to the dominant scheme, nature is "a dull affair, soundless, scentless, colourless; merely the hurrying of material endlessly, meaninglessly." From this point of view it is we, not the rose, who should get the credit for its scent; we, not the nightingale, the credit for its song. "The poets are entirely mistaken. They should address their lyrics to themselves, and should turn them into odes of self-congratulation on the excellency of the human mind."[u]

But Whitehead held the poets to be right in refusing to believe this scientific dogma about the unreality of secondary qualities. Moreover, by insisting on the endurance and interpenetration of things, poets "bear witness that nature cannot be divorced from its aesthetic values; and that these values arise from the cumulation, in some sense, of the brooding presence of the whole on to its various parts." [v]

In addition to conflicting with the esthetic view, the old scientific scheme is incompatible with the moral and religious view of the world. The problem of free will is an example. According to the scientific scheme,

> . . . each molecule blindly runs. The human body is a collection of molecules. Therefore, the human body blindly runs. . . .
>
> There are then two possible theories as to the mind. You can either deny that it can supply for itself any experiences other than those provided for it by the body, or you can admit them.
>
> If you refuse to admit the additional experiences, then all individual moral responsibility is swept away. If you do admit them, then a human being may be responsible for the state of his mind though he has no responsibility for the actions of his body. . . .
>
> The question as to the metaphysical status of molecules does not come in. The statement that they are mere formulae has no bearing on the argument. For presumably the formulae mean something. If they mean nothing, the whole mechanical doctrine is likewise without meaning, and the question drops. But if the formulae mean anything, the argument applies to exactly what they do mean. The traditional way of evading the difficulty—other than the simple way of ignoring it—is to have recourse to some form of what is now termed "vitalism." This doctrine is really a compromise. It allows a free run to mechanism throughout the whole of inanimate nature, and holds that the mechanism is partially mitigated within living bodies. I feel that this theory is an unsatisfactory compromise. The gap between living and dead matter is too vague and problematical to bear the weight of such an arbitrary assumption, which involves an essential dualism somewhere. [w]

Whitehead's position can be summarized by saying that the metaphysical scheme based on simple location, which modern science inherited from the seventeenth century and which it is still trying to apply, is far too narrow to serve as a satisfactory categoreal scheme; it is even too narrow for science itself. What is required is "an alternative cosmological doctrine, which shall be wide enough to include what is fundamental both for science and for its critics." [x] Such a scheme will first replace the concept of simple location by concepts more adequate to the new developments in physics and then try to show that these new concepts are also more adequate for interpreting esthetic, moral, and religious experience.

Whitehead's New Categoreal Scheme

The new categoreal scheme that Whitehead constructed is not only the center of his own philosophy; it also represents the last of the great efforts of speculative philosophy. Unfortunately, it is as difficult and obscure as anything in modern philosophy.[19] The concepts that form the core of Whitehead's view are those of event (or occasion), prehension, eternal object, and organism.

EVENTS

According to Whitehead, the notion of a thing as existing at a particular here and enduring through a succession of instantaneous nows must be replaced by the concept of event. Here again the pervasive influence of the idea of process can be seen. Like Dewey, Whitehead held that the concept of event involves the notions of beginning, ongoing, and consummation. But the measure of Whitehead's greater metaphysical interest is the more thorough analysis to which he subjected these ideas.

A Whiteheadian event is "the ultimate unit of natural occurrence." The simplest example is any act of perception. I say that from the top of this hill I see a castle across the valley, or that I see a planet in the sky. Thinking in terms of the old scheme of simple location, I regard myself as wholly "here" and the castle and the planet as wholly "there," with all the ensuing difficulties that have been pointed out. But let me abandon the notion of simple location. Then the things "grasped into a realized unity" here and now are not the castle and the planet simply in themselves; they are the castle and the planet from the point in space and time of my here and now. And there are innumerable other points from which other aspects of castle and planet are grasped and with which they are united in similar ways. What, indeed, are *the* castle and *the* planet except the endless variety of standpoints (including, if they were conscious, their "own" standpoints) from which, and into which, they are perceived? And what is this "here and now" from which I am perceiving? The phrase used above was that "from the top of this hill" I saw the castle. But hill is "too wide for our peculiar *locus standi*." What I am conscious of is merely the relation of my "bodily events to the simultaneous events throughout the rest of the universe." [y] Hence an event is the interpenetrating of all the infinitely various aspects of the universe at some particular standpoint.

PREHENSIONS

Applied to events at the level of human perceivings, Whitehead's conception is most interesting and ingenious, but difficulties arise as soon as we try to pass from the level of human perception (which leaves us in "idealism") to the "realism" Whitehead wanted to maintain. According to him, these graspings into

---

19 Whitehead's most systematic treatment of his proposed scheme is contained in *Process and Reality*, in which the "category of the ultimate" ("creativity," "many," "one"), eight "categories of existence," twenty-seven "categories of explanation," and nine "categorical obligations" are defined and elaborated. For the most part, however, the present account will follow the somewhat simpler, but sufficiently abstruse version given in *Science and the Modern World*.

unity are not merely ways by which the human mind synthesizes its materials; they are objective occurrences going on all over the universe at all sorts of levels below the level of conscious comprehension. Most unifyings take place, that is, without consciousness of the fact of unification. This is why Whitehead talked about "prehendings" instead of "perceivings." He intended, on analogy with "apprehension," that the term "prehension" suggest the unifying function of perception and consciousness, but without definitely implying the perception and consciousness. In this way, he believed he had obtained a concept that would serve equally well for interpreting such diverse phenomena as an electron and my view of the castle. "Prehension" and "event" are categoreal concepts precisely because (Whitehead believed) they hold good for—that is, are exemplified in—the whole of nature.

Unfortunately, one cannot escape the feeling that categoreal interpretation is secured by a verbal trick. Is the electron a prehension into unity in the sense in which my view of the castle is? If so, how do we know that it is? The terminological relationship between "prehension" and "apprehension" suggests somewhat facilely an objective relationship about whose existence not everyone will be persuaded. But is it in fact possible to have any clear idea at all, verbal relationship apart, of a prehension that is not an *apprehension*? Thus the *effect* of categorality is achieved, but the cost is ambiguity.

Applications of the Categoreal Scheme

So much for two of the main elements in the scheme itself. The next step is to see how they are applied. This examination should make the concept more intelligible and perhaps clear up some of the ambiguity. To begin with, how does the concept of event fit in with developments in quantum physics?

> One of the most hopeful lines of explanation [in quantum physics] is to assume that an electron does not continuously traverse its path in space. The alternative notion as to its mode of existence is that it appears at a series of discrete positions in space which it occupies for successive durations of time. It is as though an automobile, moving at the average rate of thirty miles an hour along a road, did not traverse the road continuously; but appeared successively at the successive milestones, remaining for two minutes at each milestone. . . .
>
> But now a problem is handed over to the philosophers. This discontinuous existence in space, thus assigned to electrons, is very unlike the continuous existence of material entities which we habitually assume as obvious. The electron seems to be borrowing the character which some people have assigned to the Mahatmas of Tibet. . . .
>
> There is no difficulty in explaining the paradox, if we consent to apply to the apparently steady undifferentiated endurance of matter the same

principles as those now accepted for sound and light. A steadily sounding note is explained as the outcome of vibrations in the air: a steady colour is explained as the outcome of vibrations in ether. If we explain the steady endurance of matter on the same principle, we shall conceive each primordial element as a vibratory ebb and flow of an underlying energy, or activity. . . . Accordingly there will be a definite period associated with each element; and within that period the stream-system will sway from one stationary maximum to another stationary maximum. . . . This system, forming the primordial element, is nothing at any instant. It requires its whole period in which to manifest itself. . . .

Accordingly, in asking where the primordial element is, we must settle on its average position at the centre of each period. If we divide time into smaller elements, the vibratory system as one electronic entity has no existence. The path in space of such a vibratory entity—where the entity is *constituted by* the vibrations—must be represented by a series of detached positions in space, analogously to the automobile which is found at successive milestones and at nowhere between. . . .

[This] hypothesis of essentially vibratory existence is the most hopeful way of explaining the paradox of the discontinuous orbit.

In the second place, a new problem is now placed before philosophers and physicists, if we entertain the hypothesis that the ultimate elements of matter are in their essence vibratory. By this I mean that apart from being a periodic system, such an element would have no existence. With this hypothesis we have to ask, what are the ingredients which form the vibratory organism. We have already got rid of the matter with its appearance of undifferentiated endurance. . . . The field is now open for the introduction of some new doctrine of organism which may take the place of the materialism with which, since the seventeenth century, science has saddled philosophy.[z]

What is here called an organism is simply an event—that is, a coming into being of a prehensive unity, whose present includes its past and looks ahead into its future. The organism's life has a structure, or pattern, that arises from the particular way it prehends into unity all the manifold aspects of nature that it includes. Its endurance through time is simply the successive prehension of past patterns along with present aspects.

For example, a molecule is a pattern exhibited in an event of one minute, and of any second of that minute. It is obvious that such an enduring pattern may be of more, or of less, importance. It may express some slight fact connecting the underlying activities thus individualised; or it may express some very close connection. . . . [In the latter case] there is then an enduring object with a certain unity for itself and for the rest of nature. Let us use the term physical endurance to express endurance of this type. Then physical endurance is the process of continuously inheriting a certain identity of character transmitted throughout a historical route of events. This character belongs to the whole route, and to every event of the route. This is the exact property of material. If it has existed for ten minutes, it has existed during every minute of the ten minutes, and during every second of every minute. Only if you take *material* to be fundamental, this property of endurance is an arbitrary fact at the base of the order of nature; but if you take *organism* to be fundamental, this property is the result of evolution. . . .

Endurance is the repetition of the pattern in successive events. Thus endurance requires a succession of durations, each exhibiting the pattern.[a]

In contrast to the very simple, material points that the old scheme took as its ultimate reals, events are thus very complex affairs. What physics studies is only a part of the total complex. Of the manifold aspects of nature prehended into an event, physics is concerned only with "their effects on patterns and on locomotion [insofar as they] are expressible in spatio-temporal terms. . . . An electron for us is merely the pattern of its aspects in its environment, so far as those aspects are relevant to the electromagnetic field." In other words, White-head replaced the old notion that "happenings of nature are to be explained in terms of the locomotion of material" with the notion of two radically different kinds of locomotion—the "vibratory locomotion of a given pattern as a whole" and the "vibratory change of pattern."[b]

Thus physics is simply an abstraction from the full nature of an organism, that is, from all the other aspects that are relevant in other ways to other fields. Hence there is no fundamental difference between, for instance, physics and biology. "Science is taking on a new aspect which is neither purely physical, nor purely biological. It is becoming the study of organisms. Biology is the study of the larger organisms; whereas physics is the study of the smaller organisms."[c] Nor is there any difference, ultimately, between the relatively simple organisms studied in physics and biology and those much larger and richer organisms called men. Beginning with the simplest event, or prehension into unity, we can advance into more and more complex organic structures, as a given structure at one level is prehended into a higher structure at another level.

In this way, eventually, the level of ordinary everyday experience is reached, from which (as has just been seen) physics is an abstraction. One of the troubles with the dominant metaphysical scheme was precisely its failure to see that it was dealing with an abstraction. Since, according to that scheme, the abstract, simply located material particles were "real," it was necessary to relegate the concrete, sensuous world to "appearance." Whitehead called this the Fallacy of Misplaced Concreteness, the mistake of treating an abstraction as if it were a concrete fact. One of the advantages claimed by Whitehead for his philosophy of organism was that it enables us to escape this particular fallacy. Once philosophers understand that they are dealing with prehendings into unity, they will no longer feel that scientific objects and everyday objects are in competition as rival claimants to an exclusive reality. On the contrary, they will see that a so-called scientific object—electron, molecule, and so on—is simply a selection from the full diversity of aspects that are being prehended into unity here and now. Hence the poetic-esthetic view of the world, as well as the everyday view, is rehabilitated. Indeed, Whitehead believed that what the poets express in their imaginative language is precisely that interpenetration of aspects and prehension into unity that he himself was describing in abstract and philosophical prose.

Whitehead's Account of Value

One of the most fundamental aspects of everyday, as well as of poetic and religious, experience is the experience of value. Whitehead believed that one main advantage of his philosophy of organism was its ability to make a place for value in a world of fact. In order to deal with this question it is necessary to describe an aspect of prehension into unity that has so far been omitted from the discussion. What is it that is prehended? Up to now the answer has been simply "aspects of nature." It is time to examine this matter more precisely. Some organisms obviously prehend other organisms, but what about those simpler organisms that are the prehensions prehended by more complex organisms? Eventually, we have to face the question, "Of what are the simplest events the prehension?" Whitehead's answer was "eternal objects"—but what is an eternal object?

ETERNAL OBJECTS

An eternal object is "any entity whose conceptual recognition does not involve a necessary reference to any definite actual entities of the temporal world." [d] Some entities—a fire engine, for example—are obviously cognized in spatiotemporal relations to other events: the garage in which it is housed, the men who operate it, the citizens who pay for it, and so forth. The color "fire-engine red" has a different status. It "ingresses" into many particular, actual occasions, including the fire engine. But its nature is what it is, indifferent to any of the occasions into which it ingresses. As has been seen, events change and endure; eternal objects are the eternal elements that become the ingredients of various transitory events.

> Enduring things are thus the outcome of a temporal process; whereas eternal things are the elements required for the very being of the process. . . .
> Every scheme for the analysis of nature has to face these two facts, *change* and *endurance*. There is yet a third fact to be placed by it, *eternality*, I will call it. The mountain endures. But when after ages it has been worn away, it has gone. If a replica arises, it is yet a new mountain. A colour is eternal. It haunts time like a spirit. It comes and it goes. But where it comes, it is the same colour. It neither survives nor does it live. It appears when it is wanted. The mountain has to time and space a different relation from that which colour has. . . .

In any occasion of cognition, that which is known is an actual occasion of experience, as diversified by reference to a realm of entities which transcend that immediate occasion in that they have analogous or different connections with other occasions of experience. For example a definite shade of red may, in the immediate occasion, be implicated with the shape of sphericity in some definite way. But that shade of red, and that spherical shape, exhibit themselves as transcending that occasion, in that either of them has other relationships to other occasions. Also, apart from the actual occurrence of the same things in other occasions, every actual occasion is set within a realm of alternative interconnected entities. This realm is disclosed by all the untrue propositions which can be predicated significantly of that occasion. . . . It is the foundation of the metaphysical position which I am maintaining that the understanding of actuality requires a reference to ideality. The two realms are intrinsically inherent in the total metaphysical situation. The truth that some proposition respecting an actual occasion is untrue may express the vital truth as to the aesthetic achievement. . . . An event is decisive in proportion to the importance (for it) of its untrue propositions: their relevance to the event cannot be dissociated from what the event is in itself by way of achievement. These transcendent entities . . . are thus, in their nature, . . . comprehensible without reference to some one particular occasion of experience. . . . But to transcend an actual occasion does not mean being disconnected from it. On the contrary, I hold that each eternal object has its own proper connection with each such occasion.[e]

POSSIBILITY, LIMITATION, AND VALUE

The realm of eternal objects is the realm of possibility; the realm of events is the realm of actuality. Since there are always possibilities not realized in the complex of interlocking events, a principle of selection is necessary. Prehending unities, that is, are not merely passive contemplators of "aspects of nature"; they are at the same time includings and excludings of eternal objects. Every realized, actual occasion is a limitation. This is the basis for Whitehead's conception of value.

The element of value, of being valuable, of having value, of being an end in itself, of being something which is for its own sake, must not be omitted in any account of an event as the most concrete actual something. "Value" is the word I use for the intrinsic reality of an event. . . . But there is no such thing as mere value. Value is the outcome of limitation. The definite finite entity is the selected mode which is the shaping of attainment; apart from such shaping into individual matter of fact there is no attainment. The mere fusion of all that there is would be the nonentity of indefiniteness. . . . That which endures is limited, obstructive, intolerant, infecting its environment with its own aspects. But it is not self-sufficient. The aspects of all things enter into its very nature. It is only itself as drawing together into its own limitation the larger whole in which it finds itself. Conversely it is only itself by lending its aspects to this same environment in which it finds itself. The problem of evolution is the development of enduring harmonies of enduring shapes of value, which merge into higher attainments of things beyond themselves. Aesthetic attainment is interwoven in the texture of realisation. The endurance of an entity represents the attainment of a limited aesthetic success, though if we look beyond it to its external effects, it may represent an aesthetic failure.[f]

An organism, then, is a "unit of emergent value, a real fusion of the characters of eternal objects, emerging for its own sake." This, once again, is easier to understand if we think of it at the human level (for example, the esthetic process going on in the mind of the artist—what emerges is a work of art, a "fusion" of selected eternal objects) than if we try to think of it as a universal ontological principle. But the latter is the way we must think of it if we want to follow Whitehead. Thus an electron is just as much a unit of emergent value (and for the same reason) as is Michelangelo's "David" or Socrates' decision to sit in prison instead of fleeing to Megara.

GOD THE ULTIMATE PRINCIPLE OF CHOICE

The realm of possibility, of eternal objects, is not a hodgepodge of diverse entities. The eternal objects are arranged in orders and hierarchies. If some are selected, others must be excluded—as a child soon enough finds out when he is first confronted with the hard fact of alternatives. And ultimately, of course, these are not merely matters of private choice. There is a metaphysical principle at work, and this is God.

> We require God as the Principle of Concretion. This position can be substantiated only by the discussion of the general implication of the course of actual occasions—that is to say, of the process of realisation.
>
> We conceive actuality as in essential relation to an unfathomable possibility. Eternal objects inform actual occasions with hierarchic patterns, included and excluded in every variety of discrimination. Another view of the same truth is that every actual occasion is a limitation imposed on possibility, and that by virtue of this limitation the particular value of that shaped togetherness of things emerges. . . .
>
> Consider an occasion α:—we have to enumerate how other actual occasions are in α, in the sense that their relationships with α are constitutive of the essence of α. What α is in itself, is that it is a unit of realised experience; accordingly we ask how other occasions are in the experience which is α. . . .
>
> There is also in α . . . the "abrupt" realisation of finite eternal objects. . . . This abrupt synthesis of eternal objects in each occasion . . . is how the actual includes what (in one sense) is not-being as a positive factor in its own achievement. It is the source of error, of truth, of art, of ethics, and of religion. By it, fact is confronted with alternatives. . . .
>
> Restriction is the price of value. There cannot be value without antecedent standards of value, to discriminate the acceptance or rejection of what is

before the envisaging mode of activity. Thus there is an antecedent limitation among values, introducing contraries, grades, and oppositions. . . .

[Eventually there must be] a ground for limitation . . . for which no reason can be given: for all reason flows from it. God is the ultimate limitation, and His existence is the ultimate irrationality. For no reason can be given for just that limitation which it stands in His nature to impose. God is not concrete, but He is the ground for concrete actuality. No reason can be given for the nature of God, because that nature is the ground of rationality. . . .

We have come to the limit of rationality. . . . What further can be known about God must be sought in the region of particular experiences, and therefore rests on an empirical basis. In respect to the interpretation of these experiences, mankind have differed profoundly. He has been named respectively, Jehovah, Allah, Brahma, Father in Heaven, Order of Heaven, First Cause, Supreme Being, Chance. Each name corresponds to a system of thought derived from the experiences of those who have used it.[g]

COMMENT ON WHITEHEAD'S ACCOUNT OF VALUE

It will be noted that Whitehead's theory of value depends on the doctrine of eternal objects, and it should be clear that eternal objects are nothing but Platonic forms. But if this is true, why not call them "universals" and be done with it? Whitehead answered, "I prefer to use the term 'eternal objects', in order to disengage myself from presuppositions which cling to the former term [universals] owing to its prolonged philosophical history."[h] It is certainly easy to sympathize with a philosopher's desire to escape the difficulties clustering around the problem of universals. But can one "disengage" merely by using a different term? It is difficult to see how Whitehead's "prehensions" and "events" resolve the old difficulties about participation, or indeed why Whitehead's theory of knowledge requires eternal objects at all. Though it is impossible to go into this matter here, it should be noted that any difficulties with Whitehead's eternal objects will "infect" his account of value.

Even apart from this consideration, his theory of value is in trouble. For one thing, it is not clear whether value is a structure or a feeling, that is, whether value resides in the limitation—the structure achieved—or in the fact that in this structure the aim of some feeling happens to be realized. In the latter case, that is, if a structure is valuable insofar as it facilitates the achievement of some feeling's aim, Whitehead's values are indistinguishable from Dewey's enjoyings; and it is not at all evident that Whitehead would have found congenial the relativistic and empirical naturalism that Dewey openly espoused.[20] On the other hand, if feelings are valuable only insofar as they are realized in certain structures, objectivity is attained. But what does it mean to say that such-and-such a structure is valuable in itself, apart from any interest or need that is thereby satisfied? It would seem that if ontological significance is attributed to values by defining

20 See pp. 301–03.

them in terms of structure, they lose just those characteristics that, in most men's view, make them valuable. Whitehead's predominant metaphysical interest naturally inclined him to put the emphasis on structure rather than on feeling:

> All value is the gift of finitude which is the necessary condition for activity. Also activity means the origination of patterns of assemblage. . . .
> Thus the infusion of pattern into natural occurrences, and the stability of such patterns, and the modification of such patterns, is the necessary condition for the realization of the Good.[i]

And again:

> Value is in its nature timeless and immortal. Its essence is not rooted in any passing circumstance. The immediacy of some mortal circumstance is only valuable because it shares in the immortality of some value.[j]

Of course, no sooner had Whitehead erected this dualism of a "world of value" and a "world of fact" than he tried to break it down. Either "considered by itself is an abstraction"; they "require each other, and together constitute the concrete universe. . . . The value inherent in the Universe has an essential independence of any moment of time; and yet it loses its meaning apart from its necessary reference to the World of passing fact. Value refers to Fact, and Fact refers to Value."

Religion

Obviously Whitehead was confronted with Plato's old problem—the question of the relation between the forms and the particulars that supposedly "participate" in them. Reformulation of this puzzle in terms of the ingression of eternal objects into events hardly clears the matter up. Nevertheless, let us assume for the sake of argument that God somehow performs the metaphysical role that Whitehead assigned to Him as the principle of concretion—that He effects the transition between the eternal and the actual. Then the metaphysical scheme satisfies the demands of logic, but does it satisfy the requirements of feeling? Is the principle of concretion "available for religious purposes"? This depends in part on what one means by religion. According to Whitehead,

> . . . religion is the vision of something which stands beyond, behind, and within, the passing flux of immediate things; something which is real, and yet waiting to be realised; something which is a remote possibility, and yet the greatest of present facts; something that gives meaning to all that passes, and yet eludes apprehension; something whose possession is the final good, and yet is beyond all reach; something which is the ultimate ideal, and the hopeless quest. . . .

> The fact of the religious vision, and its history of persistent expansion, is our one ground for optimism. Apart from it, human life is a flash of occasional enjoyments lighting up a mass of pain and misery, a bagatelle of transient experience.[k]

Eloquent as this passage is, it misses both the personality and the providence, as well as the theological precision, that some people require in religion. On the whole, it would seem that Whitehead was correct in remarking that "it may be doubted whether any properly general metaphysics can ever, without the illicit introduction of other considerations, get much further than Aristotle," who certainly did not get "very far towards the production of a God available for religious purposes."[l] Although Whitehead put forward a more available God in *Process and Reality*, it was one that seems to have been reached by "the illicit introduction of other considerations." But Whitehead was not the first philosopher to find it difficult to reconcile religious demands with the requirements for philosophical consistency.[21]

Perhaps enough has been said to suggest that there are difficulties with Whitehead's categoreal scheme. But Whitehead would not have expected it to be otherwise. The whole point of his position was that philosophical thinking, like all other thinking, is open-ended. "A clash of doctrines is not a disaster—it is an opportunity. . . . The clash is a sign that there are wider truths and finer perspectives within which a reconciliation . . . will be found."[m] Although Whitehead would not, therefore, have regarded deficiency as per se an objection to his view, he surely hoped that his categoreal scheme would be more "coherent" than it seems to be. His emphasis was always (and rightly) on inclusiveness. Yet inclusiveness is just where the scheme is weakest: He wanted his concept of God to be available for religious purposes as well as necessary for metaphysical purposes; he wanted his concept of event to be relevant to everyday experience as well as to quantum physics; and so on. The fact that these concepts are not so inclusive as Whitehead believed them to be was hidden from him by the ambiguity of such terms as "prehension," which allowed him to think that he had hit on a generic relationship that transcended "apprehension" while including it.

But such criticisms as these are in some respects beside the point. Philosophers who admire Whitehead and who are impressed by the boldness of his categoreal scheme will rightly regard his majestic vision of a single explanatory system for the universe as being of central importance; criticism of this or that detail will seem to them trivial. On the other hand, philosophers who are indifferent or hostile to metaphysics will say that it is a waste of time to attack specific points in Whitehead's categoreal scheme; the whole enterprise, they will hold, is mistaken from start to finish.

Here again, clearly, we have reached a fundamental parting of the ways in

21 See pp. 62 and 93–95.

philosophy. An antimetaphysical spirit is probably dominant in contemporary philosophy, at least in the United States and Britain. The remark just made, and so often repeated in this *History*, that we have now reached a "parting of the ways," surely reflects this spirit: If there are fundamental partings of the way, the pursuit of an all-inclusive, systematic metaphysical scheme is certainly illusory. But *are* there fundamental partings of the way in philosophy? Though this seems to be a straightforward empirical question, it involves deep metaphysical issues. Thus, as Dewey discovered, even the most determined of antimetaphysicians is likely to find himself doing metaphysics in the course of demonstrating that it is not "do-able." For this reason, although metaphysics has been "killed off" many times in the history of Western thought, it has always revived. Metaphysicians need not be distressed by these swings. Indeed if, like Whitehead, they take process seriously, they will expect them and seek to explain them by means of a meta-metaphysical scheme.

CHAPTER 8

The Analytical Tradition: Russell and Wittgenstein

The three philosophies discussed in the preceding chapter were worked out, for the most part, in the early decades of this century. By the beginning of World War II they had been to a large extent superseded by two new movements that came increasingly to dominate philosophical thought. One of these movements may be called analytical philosophy and the other phenomenology. Though these movements were new, each had roots in the past; it is fair therefore to speak of the analytical and the phenomenological "traditions." Two representatives of the former are examined in this chapter; two representatives of the latter, in the next chapter.

The roots of the analytical tradition can be traced far back into the past—to Hume, and beyond Hume to Hobbes. Although this tradition is too loose and fluid for any general description to hold for all the philosophers considered a part of it,[1] it is nonetheless possible to list certain basic attitudes, certain more

---

1 They have, in fact, only a family resemblance. See pp. 362–65.

or less implicit assumptions about the nature of the world and about the nature of philosophical inquiry that characterize the analytical tradition—at least up to Wittgenstein.[2]

One characteristic is a commitment to atomicity, that is, to the belief that the universe consists of a very large number of independent, encapsulated entities. Analytical philosophers have conceived of these entities in various ways—as material particles, as sense data, as impressions, as "facts." But common to all the philosophers of this tradition is the conviction that the ultimate entities of which the universe is composed are only externally related—that they are, in Hume's language, "loose and separate."

From this basic assumption follows the importance of analysis for these philosophers: The primary task of philosophy, they held, is the analysis of complex entities into the simple entities of which they are composed. Because the simple entities *are* simple, they are directly understandable whenever they are encountered. Accordingly, complex entities are completely explained as soon as their analysis into simples has been correctly carried out. Philosophers of the analytical tradition thus put a very high valuation on "clarity," which they conceived of as a very sharply focused kind of experience. It seemed to philosophers of this persuasion that much of our experience is an experience of rather amorphous, vaguely bounded conglomerates. Clarity is achieved when an experience of such a conglomerate is replaced by an understanding of the set of unambiguous simples of which it is composed, each of which (in the language of Bishop Butler) "is itself and not another thing."

The analytical philosophers' interest in clarity led them to be greatly concerned about language. In their view most of our language is seriously inadequate, for everyday language suggests that the universe consists of untidy conglomerates like dogs and cats and apples and oranges, instead of such neat, encapsulated atomistic entities as sweetness, redness, and sphericality. Accordingly, these philosophers were convinced that before philosophical inquiry can begin everyday language must be refined and purified. For want of this preliminary work, they believed, many philosophers have ended in blind alleys and confusions; but if this work is carefully performed, most philosophical questions can be rather easily answered. This attitude was expressed, for instance, by Hobbes:

> Seeing that truth consists in the right ordering of names in our affirmations, a man that seeks precise truth had need to remember what every name he uses stands for and to place it accordingly, or else he will find himself entangled in words as a bird in lime twigs, the more he struggles the more belimed. . . . By this it appears how necessary it is for any man that aspires to true knowledge to examine the definitions of former authors, and either to correct them where they are negligently set down or to make them himself. For the errors of definitions multiply themselves according as the reckoning proceeds, and lead men into absurdities. . . .[a]

2 Post-Wittgensteinian developments in the analytical tradition do not come within the purview of this volume.

And Locke:

> It is ambition enough to be employed as an under-labourer in clearing the
> ground a little, and removing some of the rubbish that lies in the way to
> knowledge. . . . Vague and insignificant forms of speech, and abuse of lan-
> guage, have . . . long passed for mysteries of science; and hard or misapplied
> words, with little or no meaning, have [been] mistaken for deep learning.
> . . . They are but the covers of ignorance, [and] hindrance of true knowledge.[b]

And Berkeley:

> We need only to draw the curtain of words, to behold the fairest tree of
> knowledge, whose fruit is excellent, and within the reach of our hand.[c]

And also G. E. Moore, who formulated an influential contemporary version of
the analytical tradition:

> It appears to me that in Ethics, as in all other philosophical studies, the
> difficulties and disagreements, of which its history is full, are mainly due to
> a very simple cause: namely to the attempt to answer questions, without first
> discovering precisely *what* question it is which you desire to answer. . . . The
> work of analysis and distinction is often very difficult. . . . But I am inclined
> to think that in many cases a resolute attempt would be sufficient to ensure
> success; so that, if only this attempt were made, many of the most glaring
> difficulties and disagreements in philosophy would disappear.[d]

It is this interest in language, this conviction that philosophical problems are
best approached by a tough-minded, critical examination of linguistic usage, that
chiefly distinguishes contemporary philosophers of the analytical persuasion from
other post-Kantians. Once Kant's distinction between phenomena and noumena
had been drawn, the basic choice for philosophers was either to reaffirm that
some sort of knowledge of noumena is possible or to confine their attention to
phenomena.[3] Like many other nineteenth- and twentieth-century thinkers, the
analytical philosophers unhesitatingly rejected the former alternative: Unknowable things-in-themselves seemed to them to be useless and redundant. But whereas
one group of post-Kantians focused on the part of Kant's doctrine that conceived
of the relations among phenomena as being the products, at least in part, of
synthesizing activities of the mind, philosophers of the analytical tradition
concentrated on the language in which men talk about these phenomena. Thus,
whereas the Hegelians, the Marxists, and the Nietzschians were led increasingly
in the direction of social psychology, anthropology, and cultural history, philosophers of the analytical tradition were led in the direction of logic and mathematics. Indeed, it was new developments in these fields toward the end of the
nineteenth century that provided these philosophers with a more powerful
instrument of linguistic analysis and thus gave early twentieth-century versions
of analytical philosophy their characteristic form.

3 See p. 101.

As long as logic had been dominated by the Aristotelian conviction that all propositions are reducible to the subject-predicate form, it was easy to assume that words are the names of objects and that they mean the objects that they name. This assumption about naming (evident in the passage just quoted from Hobbes) and the assumption about atomicity reinforce each other. Since words are clearly atomistic units, it seemed evident that corresponding to the words there must be self-enclosed, encapsulated entities named by them. These assumptions occasioned a number of paradoxes that preoccupied analytical philosophers at the beginning of this century, and the emergence of relational logics seemed to them to make the resolution of these paradoxes possible.[4] But this new start was made within the framework of the analytical-linguistic tradition; that is, it was taken for granted that complexes could be, and should be, analyzed into simples and that the proper method of attack was to uncover the "true meaning" of the language that we ordinarily use loosely and ambiguously. The only difference was that the new, relational logic was to be the instrument of this analysis.

In what other ways can the analytical tradition be characterized and at the same time distinguished from other nineteenth- and twentieth-century philosophical movements? The analytical philosophers—Mill and Russell, for instance—doubtless had existential problems, as all men presumably do. But like Dewey, Whitehead, and Bergson, and unlike Kierkegaard and Nietzsche, they kept these problems under reasonably adequate control and out of their philosophical writings. For them philosophy was primarily a cognitive enterprise, not a moral one. Again, like Dewey, Whitehead, and Bergson, they were interested in science—but less in biology than in physics. Differences in temperament also marked off the analytical philosophers from other thinkers who were sympathetic to the scientific point of view. For example, even though Whitehead started as a physicist and even though he joined with Russell in pioneering very important studies of logic, he and Russell subsequently moved in very different directions. Whitehead used the concepts of physics as a "categoreal scheme" for a new metaphysics of the traditional type; Russell employed the concepts of logic as the basis for clearing up puzzles about "meaning" occasioned by people's slipshod use of language.

In addition, philosophers of the analytical tradition were almost untouched by the idea of process; certainly, they were not in the least moved by the vision of creative fecundity and the emergence of new forms of life that so stirred Bergson and Whitehead. One reason for this is undoubtedly the analytical commitment to atomicity: The ultimate simples by definition do not undergo internal change; they are whatever they are. Therefore, though they endure through time they do not, in the strict sense of the word, have a history. New forms of life occur, but their "emergence" is merely the arrangement of the changeless simples in different combinations.

Further, the philosophers of the analytical tradition have tended not to be

4 See pp. 336–42.

deeply interested in social reform. There are exceptions of course—Bentham, Mill, Comte, and Russell.[5] But Russell the reformer and Russell the philosopher were much more sharply distinguished (and not merely as far as writing goes) than were, say, Dewey the reformer and Dewey the philosopher. Dewey was essentially a social philosopher—his "reconstruction of philosophy" was part and parcel of his whole program of social reform; Russell was a philosopher who happened also to be a critic of the social and political status quo. But the reforming zeal of most philosophers of the analytical tradition has been largely focused on philosophy itself—not in the interest of improving men's "traffic with nature" but simply in the interest of obtaining "clarity."

Finally, whereas Nietzsche, Bergson, and Dewey attacked the concept of truth and replaced it—each, of course, in his own way—with the concept of interpretation, the philosophers of the analytical tradition wholly rejected this procedure as "psychologizing." They wanted, not to abandon the notion of truth, but to refine it. In doing so, they certainly exposed many old "truths": Their assault on traditional metaphysics, traditional ethics, and traditional theology was every bit as radical as was that of the pragmatists. But the spirit of their attack was quite different: False or mistaken assertions about the nature of reality were to be replaced by true ones, attained by means of rigorous analysis. Here again the ideal of clarity is relevant. According to the analytical tradition, things are what they are; the philosopher's task is merely to get clear in his own mind about their nature.

The two representatives of this long tradition examined in this chapter are Russell and Wittgenstein. Russell worked out both a method of inquiry and also a metaphysical sketch of the nature of the entities to be inquired about that constituted a complete program for analytical philosophy—a program that the logical positivists attempted to carry out in detail. Wittgenstein, who at first accepted this program (at least in its broad outlines), eventually came to question much of it. In doing so, he not only moved the analytical tradition in a radically new direction but also had a decisive influence on contemporary philosophers who are not at all a part of this tradition.

Russell

Like Whitehead, Russell[6] is an example of the recurrent tendency, ever since Pythagoras and Plato, for philosophy and mathematics to be closely linked:

5 See pp. 164–78 and 351–52.
6 Bertrand A. W. Russell (b. 1872) was brought up in the home of his grandfather, who was a son of the Duke of Bedford and who had been prime minister under Queen Victoria. Russell was educated at Trinity College, Cambridge, where he subsequently taught for some years. In 1931 he succeeded to the peerage, on the death of his elder brother, as third Earl of Russell. In 1950 he was awarded the Nobel Prize for literature. His support of unpopular opinions

> I came to philosophy through mathematics, or rather through the wish to find some reason to believe in the truth of mathematics. From early youth, I had an ardent desire to believe that there can be such a thing as knowledge, combined with a great difficulty in accepting much that passes as knowledge. It seemed clear that the best chance of finding indubitable truth would be in pure mathematics.[e]

But, as has already been pointed out, Russell and Whitehead are also examples of the way in which temperament and outlook can affect a man's conception of mathematics, and through it his philosophy. Thus, although Russell and Whitehead collaborated on the revolutionary treatise *Principia Mathematica* (1910–13), Whitehead concluded in Platonic fashion that the truths of mathematics imply an eternal pattern in the universe, whereas Russell decided that mathematics is a much more powerful instrument than ordinary grammar for analyzing the meaning of propositions.

Mathematics and Logic

Before turning to Russell's application of mathematics to philosophical analysis, it is necessary to say a word about developments in mathematics and in logic during the latter part of the nineteenth century. Though philosophers had continued to talk about logic as the "organon of thought," ever since Galileo's day science had abandoned logic and adopted mathematics as *its* organon. Physics, that is, did not deduce its conclusions syllogistically; it derived them mathematically. And though almost all philosophers agreed that logic and mathematics were somehow connected, no one had thought through what this relation was; they were held to be different sciences. Mathematics was thought to be the science of quantity, or magnitude. Arithmetic, for instance, was the science of number; geometry was the science of spatial magnitudes. Logic, on the other hand, was regarded as the science of the laws of thought.

The first step toward the merging of mathematics and logic was taken when, as a result of the discovery of non-Euclidean geometries, mathematicians gradually came to realize that geometry was not the science of space—at least not of space conceived of in the Newtonian fashion as an independently existing, three-dimensional box in which events occur. The second step was taken when it was shown (to quote the language in which Russell was later to describe this development) that "all traditional pure mathematics, including analytical geom-

---

often brought him the antagonism of authorities. Russell was imprisoned during World War I for pacificism and for support of conscientious objectors. In 1940 he was forbidden to teach at City College in New York on the grounds that his views on morals were likely to corrupt innocent young minds. In the 1950's and 1960's he became increasingly preoccupied with the dangers of thermonuclear war and participated in various disarmament demonstrations, for which at the age of 90 he was again, but only briefly, imprisoned.

etry, may be regarded as consisting wholly of propositions about the natural numbers."[f] That is, the propositions of geometry can be derived from the properties of numbers. The next step was taken when it was shown that "the entire theory of the natural numbers could be derived from three primitive ideas and five primitive propositions in addition to those of pure logic. These three ideas and five propositions thus became, as it were, hostages for the whole of traditional pure mathematics. If they could be defined and proved in terms of others, so could all pure mathematics." This was precisely what was done. The three primitive ideas (0, number, successor) were shown to be definable in terms of *class*, *belonging to a class*, and *similarity*—all of which are purely logical notions.[g]

DEFINITION OF NUMBER

Many philosophers, when attempting to define number, are really setting to work to define plurality, which is quite a different thing. *Number* is what is characteristic of numbers, as *man* is what is characteristic of men. A plurality is not an instance of number, but of some particular number. A trio of men, for example, is an instance of the number 3, and the number 3 is an instance of number; but the trio is not an instance of number. . . .

Number is a way of bringing together certain collections, namely, those that have a given number of terms. We can suppose all couples to be in one bundle, all trios in another, and so on. In this way we obtain various bundles of collections, each bundle consisting of all the collections that have a certain number of terms. Each bundle is a class whose members are collections, *i.e.* classes; thus each is a class of classes. . . .

Two classes are said to be "similar" when there is a one-one relation which correlates the terms of the one class each with one term of the other class. . . .

We may thus use the notion of "similarity" to decide when two collections are to belong to the same bundle. . . . We want to make one bundle containing the class that has no members: this will be for the number 0. Then we want a bundle of all the classes that have one member: this will be for the number 1 . . . and so on. Given any collection, we can define the bundle it is to belong to as being the class of all those collections that are "similar" to it. . . .

So far we have not suggested anything in the slightest degree paradoxical. But when we come to the actual definition of numbers we cannot avoid what must at first sight seem a paradox, though this impression will soon wear off. We naturally think that the class of couples (for example) is something different from the number 2. But there is no doubt about the class of couples: it is indubitable and not difficult to define, whereas the number 2, in any other sense, is a metaphysical entity . . . which must always remain elusive. Accordingly we set up the following definition:—

The number of a class is the class of all those classes that are similar to it. . . .

At the expense of a little oddity, this definition secures definiteness and indubitableness; and it is not difficult to prove that numbers so defined have all the properties that we expect numbers to have.[h]

A good deal of the work described in this passage had been done before Russell and Whitehead began their investigations, but they were the first to see its full significance—to see, that is, that the reduction of the three "hostages" to logical conceptions had shown that mathematics was a branch of logic. To show this in detail was what Russell and Whitehead undertook to do in *Principia Mathematica:* "Starting with premisses . . . universally admitted to belong to logic," they arrived "by deduction at results which as obviously belong to mathematics." Accordingly, it became impossible to draw a line between mathematics and logic.[i]

It is fair to say that *Principia Mathematica* was one of the most important books of the twentieth century. The kinds of relations dealt with in mathematics (greater than, equal to, and so on) are quite different from the attribution of a predicate to a subject. The newly discovered identity of logic and mathematics therefore resulted in a great expansion of the kinds of relations studied in logic. Syllogism came to be regarded, not as the whole of logic, but as one (and a relatively minor) subdivision of logic. At the same time the formal character of logic came to be emphasized. Aristotle and other logicians had, of course, distinguished between truth and validity, between the assertion that a proposition is true and the assertion that the proposition implies, or is implied by, another proposition. But until the development of mathematical logic the full significance of this distinction had not been grasped. According to Russell, logic is concerned exclusively with validity, and what determines validity is not the content of the propositions (not what is judged about) but their form.

MODERN AND TRADITIONAL LOGIC

In every proposition and in every inference there is, besides the particular subject-matter concerned, a certain *form,* a way in which the constituents of the proposition or inference are put together. . . . Take (say) the series of propositions, "Socrates drank the hemlock," "Coleridge drank the hemlock," "Coleridge drank opium," "Coleridge ate opium." The form remains unchanged throughout this series, but all the constituents are altered. Thus form is not another constituent, but is the way the constituents are put together. It is forms, in this sense, that are the proper object of philosophical logic. . . .

But the forms of propositions giving rise to inferences are not the simplest forms: they are always hypothetical, stating that if one proposition is true, then so is another. Before considering inference, therefore, logic must consider those simpler forms which inference presupposes. Here the traditional logic failed completely: it believed that there was only one form of simple proposition (*i.e.* of proposition not stating a relation between two or more other propositions), namely, the form which ascribes a predicate to a subject. . . . Grammar favours this form, but philosophically it is so far from universal that it is not even very common. If we say "this thing is bigger than that," we are not assigning a mere quality of "this," but a relation of "this" and "that." We might express the same fact by saying "that thing is smaller than this," where grammatically the subject is changed. Thus propositions stating that two things have a certain relation have a different form from subject-predicate propositions, and the failure to perceive this difference or to allow for it has been the source of many errors in traditional metaphysics. . . .

Modern logic . . . has the effect of enlarging our abstract imagination, and providing an infinite number of possible hypotheses to be applied in the analysis of any complex fact. In this respect it is the exact opposite of the logic practised by the classical tradition. In that logic, hypotheses which seem *prima facie* possible are professedly proved impossible, and it is decreed in advance that reality must have a certain special character. In modern logic, on the contrary, while the *prima facie* hypotheses as a rule remain admissible, others, which only [modern] logic would have suggested, are added to our stock, and are very often found to be indispensable if a right analysis of the facts is to be obtained. The old logic put thought in fetters, while the new logic gives it wings. It has, in my opinion, introduced the same kind of advance into philosophy as Galileo introduced into physics, making it possible at last to see what kinds of problems may be capable of solution, and what kinds must be abandoned as beyond human powers.[j]

THEORY OF DESCRIPTIONS

Let us examine one or two examples of Russell's use of this new relational logic. What are we judging about when we judge, for instance, "The present king of France does not exist"? Initially we might be inclined to say that we are judging about the king of France, as we would say that we are judging about the king of Sweden in "The present king of Sweden lives in Stockholm." But this cannot be correct, for there *is* no present king of France. Nevertheless, it would seem that there must be *something* that is being judged about. Accordingly, some philosophers have introduced what they call a realm of "subsisting entities," which is supposed to include nonexistents and contradictions—for example, "gold mountain" and "round square." But, as Russell pointed out, this does not solve the puzzle, for how is the distinction between subsistence and existence to be defined? And, even if it could be defined with precision, the distinction "does not help us. . . . [For] 'the present king of France does not subsist' is just as true as 'the present king of France does not exist.' "

Russell proposed to do away with any alleged need for subsistent entities by showing that philosophers have been "misled by grammar." [k] Judgments of the type in question only *seem* to be about an object; actually, there is no real constituent corresponding to phrases like "the king of France," "the gold mountain," and "the author of *Waverley*." These phrases are simply linguistic devices ("descriptions") mistakenly believed to be the names of specific entities. In one respect Russell's position was not unlike Nietzsche's conclusion about such notions as "cause." [7] But whereas Nietzsche had approached the study of language under

7 See pp. 242–43.

the assumption that its vocabulary is affected by the unconscious needs of those who speak the language, Russell ignored motives and addressed himself to a study of the propositional forms that language takes. Because he approached the matter from this frame of reference, Russell's analysis was not only different from Nietzsche's but far more rigorous and complete.

Consider the phrase "the author of *Waverley.*" Analysis shows that it means "the value of x for which 'x wrote *Waverley*' is true." Thus, in a sentence like "The author of *Waverley* was Scotch," the phrase "the author of *Waverley*" disappears and is replaced by a propositional function that obviously does not designate a specific entity. Hence the puzzle about what specific entity can possibly be designated by "the present king of France" or "the gold mountain" is cleared up. These and similar phrases are not the names of specific entities; they are propositional functions.

Russell's analysis will be clearer if what he called a definite description ("the so-and-so") is contrasted with an indefinite description ("a so-and-so"). The proposition "I met a man" would be true if I met Plato or if I met Socrates, and so on. But when I say, "I met a man," I am not saying that I met Plato or that I met Socrates. The proposition "I met a man" does not contain as a constituent any particular man, for the phrase "a man" is not the name of any particular man, as "Plato" is the name of a particular man. Similarly, the phrase "the author of *Waverley*" is not the name of a particular man (Scott); it only *seems* to be because it is a definite, instead of an indefinite, description.

> No one could suppose that "a man" was a definite object, which could be defined by itself. . . . Whatever there is in the world is definite: if it is a man it is one definite man and not any other. Thus there cannot be such an entity as "a man" to be found in the world, as opposed to specific man. And accordingly it is natural that we do not define "a man" itself, but only the propositions in which it occurs.
>
> In the case of "the so-and-so" this is equally true, though at first sight less obvious. We may demonstrate that this must be the case, by a consideration of the difference between a *name* and a *definite description*. . . .
>
> Propositions about "the so-and-so" always imply the corresponding propositions about "a so-and-so," with the addendum that there is not more than one so-and-so. . . . The proposition "the author of *Waverley* was Scotch," for example, involves:
>
> (1) "x wrote *Waverley*" is not always false;
> (2) "if x and y wrote *Waverley*, x and y are identical" is always true;
> (3) "if x wrote *Waverley*, x was Scotch" is always true. These three propositions, translated into ordinary language, state:
> (1) at least one person wrote *Waverley;*
> (2) at most one person wrote *Waverley;*
> (3) whoever wrote *Waverley* was Scotch.[1]

It is clear that the grammatical simplicity of a sentence like "The author of *Waverley* was Scotch" hides a real complexity, which is only revealed by a careful analysis. And in the course of this analysis "the author of *Waverley*" disappears. It does not name any real constituent of the proposition in which it occurs—no more than "gold mountain" and "present king of France" name any real constituents of the propositions in which *they* occur.

According to Russell, one of the advantages of this analysis is that it clears up puzzles about "existence" and "being" that have plagued metaphysics since its birth. Consider the sentence "The author of *Waverley* exists." Analysis shows that it means (1) at least one person wrote *Waverley* and (2) at most one person wrote *Waverley*. To say "Scott exists" is nonsense unless what we mean by "Scott" is "author of *Waverley*." Existence, that is, is a property of descriptions.

> An important consequence of the theory of descriptions is that it is mean-ingless to say "A exists" unless "A" is (or stands for) a phrase of the form "the so-and-so." If the so-and-so exists, and x is the so-and-so, to say "x exists" is nonsense. Existence, in the sense in which it is ascribed to single entities, is thus removed altogether from the list of fundamentals. The ontological argument and most of its refutations are found to depend upon bad gram-mar.[m]

THEORY OF TYPES

Another example of Russell's use of logical analysis is his solution of a number of paradoxes that had puzzled philosophers since the Greeks. There is, for instance, an ancient argument, attributed to Epimenides the Cretan, to the effect that all Cretans are liars. If all Cretans are liars and the speaker is a Cretan, the assertion that all Cretans are liars is a lie and hence false. The assertion contradicts itself. The same consideration applies to assertions like "All general-izations are false" (for this is a generalization and hence must be false), "All rules have exceptions" (for this is a rule and therefore has an exception, and what it asserts will not be true of its exception), and "There is no absolute truth" (for is it not absolutely true that there is no absolute truth?).

Russell dealt with paradoxes of this kind by pointing out that propositions fall into hierarchical types and that propositions of the form "All Cretans are liars" are not of the same type as the propositions they describe. Epimenides' assertion is about a class of propositions; his assertion is not a member of that class, because it is a proposition of a higher type.

This can be put somewhat differently by saying that "whatever involves *all* of a collection must not be one of the collection." It is necessary, that is, to distinguish (as in Russell's account of number) between classes, classes of classes, classes of classes of classes, and so on. A class composed of individuals belongs to a different logical type from a class composed of classes of individuals. Socrates and Plato, for instance, are philosophers and hence members of the class "philosopher," but the class "philosopher" is not itself a philosopher. "This is plain common sense, but unfortunately almost all philosophy consists in an attempt to forget it."[n]

One of the results of this kind of logical analysis is the tendency to treat all questions about meaning as if they could be decided by logic. Thus for Russell logic became not only the test of validity (which it had always been) but also the test of meaning. To put this differently, whatever is meaningful can be, and should be, stated in a form that is prescribed by logic. This was the beginning of a movement to develop an ideal, absolutely clear language to replace the muddled and ambiguous language by means of which men ordinarily try to communicate with one another.

Criticism the Primary Business of Philosophy

Since in Russell's view much of what has traditionally passed for profound philosophical speculation has resulted from logical confusions, it is not surprising that Russell believed that the primary business of modern philosophy is criticism. Yet Russell also held that there is a limited place for construction in philosophy.

> The business of philosophy, as I conceive it, is essentially that of logical analysis, followed by logical synthesis. . . . Philosophy should be comprehensive, and should be bold in suggesting hypotheses as to the universe which science is not yet in a position to confirm or confute. But these should always be presented *as* hypotheses, not (as is too often done) as immutable certainties like the dogmas of religion. Although, moreover, comprehensive construction is part of the business of philosophy, I do not believe it is the most important part. The most important part, to my mind, consists in criticizing and clarifying notions which are apt to be regarded as fundamental and accepted uncritically. As instances I might mention: mind, matter, consciousness, knowledge, experience, causality, will, time. I believe all these notions to be inexact and approximate, essentially infected with vagueness, incapable of forming part of any exact science.[o]

Philosophy must base itself on the sciences, the only field in which, as yet, any knowledge has been achieved. And it must base itself on the methods, not the results, of science:

> There are two different ways in which a philosophy may seek to base itself upon science. It may emphasise the most general *results* of science, and seek to give even greater generality and unity to these results. Or it may study the *methods* of science, and seek to apply these methods, with the necessary adaptations, to its own peculiar province. Much philosophy inspired by science has gone astray through preoccupation with the *results* momentarily supposed to have been achieved. It is not results, but *methods*, that can be transferred with profit from the sphere of the special sciences to the sphere of philosophy. . . .

Philosophy involves a criticism of scientific knowledge, not from a point of view ultimately different from that of science, but from a point of view less concerned with details and more concerned with the harmony of the whole body of special sciences.

The special sciences have all grown up by the use of notions derived from common sense, such as things and their qualities, space, time, and causation. Science itself has shown that none of these common-sense notions will quite serve for the explanation of the world; but it is hardly the province of any special science to undertake the necessary reconstruction of fundamentals. This must be the business of philosophy. . . . I believe that the philosophical errors in common-sense beliefs not only produce confusion in science, but also do harm in ethics and politics, in social institutions, and in the conduct of everyday life.[p]

This passage sounds very much like Dewey's attack on traditional philosophy, but though Dewey and Russell both recommended that philosophy adopt the methods of science, they perceived these methods quite differently. For Dewey the important element in scientific method was its experimentalism and its tentativeness. He was not only content with provisional and probable conclusions; he would have deeply distrusted conclusions of any other kind. Russell, in contrast, believed that the sciences yield, or can yield, the truth about things. Hence his criticisms of the traditional metaphysics consisted in arguing that its conclusions about the world were *false*—not, as with Dewey, that they were neither true nor false but merely fictions generated by men's quest for certainty.

CRITICISM OF TRADITIONAL METAPHYSICS

As has already been seen, in Russell's view the ascription of predicates to subjects is but one of many equally real logical relations. The old logic's restriction of "form" to this relation is but one example of the pernicious influence of ordinary language on philosophy. It is "doubtful" whether the subject-predicate logic "would have been invented by a people speaking a non-Aryan language," yet this subject-predicate logic gave rise to a substance-attribute metaphysics to which almost all earlier philosophers were quite unconsciously committed.

Almost any proposition can be put into a form in which it has a subject and a predicate, united by a copula. It is natural to infer that every fact has a corresponding form, and consists in the possession of a quality by a substance. This leads, of course, to monism, since the fact that there were several substances (if it were a fact) would not have the requisite form.[q]

Quite apart from thus fatally committing philosophers to monism, the subject-predicate logic forced them to deny the reality of space and time; it therefore "rendered them incapable of giving any account of the world of science and daily life." As we have seen, spatial relations (above, below) and temporal relations (before, after) cannot be reduced to subject-predicate relations. Hence philosophers who cling to the old logic must deny spatial and temperal relations.

> Asymmetrical relations are involved in all series—in space and time, greater and less, whole and part, and many others of the most important characteristics of the actual world. All these aspects, therefore, the logic which reduces anything to subjects and predicates is compelled to condemn as error and mere appearance. To those whose logic is not malicious, such a wholesale condemnation appears impossible.[r]

Leibniz and Spinoza were among those whose metaphysics was "shattered" by the discoveries of mathematical logic, but in Russell's view Hegel was the worst offender. Consider the crucial concept of identity-in-difference:

> Hegel's argument . . . depends throughout upon confusing the "is" of predication, as in "Socrates is mortal," with the "is" of identity, as in "Socrates is the philosopher who drank the hemlock." Owing to this confusion, he thinks that "Socrates" and "mortal" must be identical. Seeing that they are different, he does not infer, as others would, that there is a mistake somewhere, but that they exhibit "identity in difference." Again, Socrates is particular, "mortal" is universal. Therefore, he says, since Socrates is mortal, it follows that the particular is the universal—taking the "is" to be throughout expressive of identity. But to say "the particular is the universal" is self-contradictory. Again Hegel does not suspect a mistake, but proceeds to synthesise particular and universal in the individual, or concrete universal. This is an example of how, for want of care at the start, vast and imposing systems of philosophy are built upon stupid and trivial confusions, which, but for the almost incredible fact that they are unintentional, one would be tempted to characterise as puns.[s]

Though Russell's main attack was directed against rationalistic metaphysics and its claim "that by mere thinking . . . the whole of reality could be established with a certainty which no contrary observations could shake,"[t] this was merely because he regarded it as his most formidable and most plausible antagonist. He had no more use for rationalism's rivals—pragmatism and Bergsonianism.

CRITICISM OF PRAGMATISM

> As applied to the general hypotheses of science and religion, there is a great deal to be said for [pragmatism]. Given a careful definition of what is meant by "working," and a proviso that the cases concerned are those where we do not really know the truth, there is no need to quarrel with the doctrine in this region. . . .
>
> In practice, however, pragmatism has a more sinister side. The truth, it says, is what pays in the way of beliefs. Now a belief may be made to pay through the operation of the criminal law. In the seventeenth century,

Catholicism paid in Catholic countries and Protestantism in Protestant countries. Energetic people can manufacture "truth" by getting hold of the Government and persecuting opinions other than their own.[u]

In a word, Russell shared pragmatism's scepticism about whatever is not accessible to science, for example, rationalistic metaphysics and dogmatic theology. Like the pragmatists, he held that the "truth" of assertions in such fields is related to emotional and temperamental needs. But he was too much of a mathematician to be willing to apply pragmatism to mathematics and to science. He was unwilling to accept the kind of account of "experience" Dewey gave,[8] for he wanted to draw a sharp distinction between beliefs and facts. Beliefs, he held, are "vague and complex"; facts are just precisely whatever they are. Beliefs do depend on "human occurrences"; they are relative to cultural conditions; and so on. But facts are "only within our control to a certain very limited extent, as regards some of the minor circumstances on or near the surface of a certain planet." The pragmatists went wrong first by confusing beliefs with facts[9] and then by concentrating their attention on events at or near the earth's surface. Such events are doubtless of great practical importance to men, but a sound theory of knowledge cannot be based on them alone. Since many facts have no relevance to men and their needs, a sound theory of knowledge must admit that truth resides in correspondence rather than in "workability"—in the correspondence of men's beliefs to the facts of the case.

This is effective criticism, but as an examination of Russell's own view will show it is not easy to ascertain what the facts "in themselves" are or how beliefs can be known to correspond to them.

CRITICISM OF BERGSONIANISM

Despite its inadequacy as a theory of knowledge and its dangerous social implications, pragmatism "has certain important merits." But according to Russell there is nothing whatever to be said in favor of Bergsonianism:

A great part of Bergson's philosophy is merely traditional mysticism expressed in slightly novel language. The doctrine of interpenetration, according to which different things are not really separate, but are merely so conceived by the analytic intellect, is to be found in every mystic, eastern or western, from Parmenides to [the Hegelians]. . . .

In this part of his philosophy, apart from phraseology, Bergson has added nothing to Plotinus. The invention of the phraseology certainly shows great ability, but it is that of the company-promoter rather than the philosopher. . . .

Traditional mysticism has been contemplative, convinced of the unreality of time, and essentially a lazy man's philosophy. [Bergson's innovation was

8 See pp. 291–94 and 297–300.
9 From Russell's point of view, this was another trouble with the Hegelians.

that he] sought to adapt mysticism to those who believe in activity and "life," who believe in the reality of progress. . . .

[But] if one might venture to apply to Bergson's philosophy so vulgar a thing as logic, certain difficulties would appear in this [adaptation]. If the new elements which are added in later states of the world are not external to the old elements, there is no genuine novelty, creative evolution has created nothing, and we are back in the system of Plotinus. Of course Bergson's answer to this dilemma is that what happens is "growth" [that is, "duration"], in which everything changes and yet remains the same. This conception, however, is a mystery, which the profane cannot hope to fathom.[v]

Russell's "Synthesis"

As a critic Russell was very effective. But when we turn from "logical analysis" to "logical synthesis," we can only be disappointed at the meager results of Russell's "construction." Of course, it would be foolish to expect synthesis in the Hegelian or even the Whiteheadian sense; Russell deliberately chose "piece-meal, detailed, and verifiable results" in preference to "large untested generalities recommended only by a certain appeal to imagination." [w] Hence he always stated his views very tentatively and in "outline form." But even in outline form his views changed a great deal, almost from year to year, and he was never able to establish even the relatively little he had once thought possible.

In these circumstances it is best to concentrate on the central belief to which Russell clung through all of these changes of position—his conviction that reality consists of a plurality of entities, each of which is just what it is, independent of us and our beliefs about it and independent too of the relations in which it stands to the other real entities.

As regards Russell's pluralism, he quite rightly pointed out that the monism of philosophers like Hegel was the logical consequence of their acceptance of the traditional subject-predicate logic. But he did not see that his pluralistic version of reality was determined by his own relational logic. Thus, in Nietzsche's terminology, although Russell believed himself to be presenting us with the original text, he was in fact only putting forward one more interpretation, one that seemed "true" to him because it reflected his own temperamental biases. From this point of view, Russell's "realism" looks rather naïve.

However this may be, what exactly are the entities that, with their external relations, constitute the world? To this question Russell gave various answers at different stages in the development of his thought, because he was constantly attempting to reduce—in accordance with Occam's razor[10]—the number of different types of entities whose existence must be presupposed. Russell's rule was to replace "inferred entities" (that is, entities that are not directly experi-

10 See note 19, p. 59.

enced) with "logical constructions." This procedure resulted, on the one hand, in a limited number of types of directly experienced, real entities and, on the other hand, in a language (together with logical rules) for analyzing all other entities into some one of those that are directly experienced.

Unfortunately, Russell's list of types of real entities, and the corresponding list of inferred entities that can be eliminated from metaphysics, kept changing. For instance, in *The Analysis of Matter* Russell concluded that "from the standpoint of philosophy the distinction between physical and mental events is superficial and unreal." Reality consists, rather, in a "neutral stuff," and what is called "ego" and what is called "matter" are constructions out of it. The result is not only a simplification of metaphysics from a Cartesian dualism to a "neutral monism"; it is also an immense simplification of science.

> I incline—though with hesitation—to the view that there will ultimately be a science embracing both physics and psychology, though distinct from either as at present developed. The technique of physics was developed under the influence of a belief in the metaphysical reality of "matter" which now no longer exists. . . . The technique of psychology to some extent was developed under a belief in the metaphysical reality of the "mind." It seems possible that, when physics and psychology have both been completely freed from these lingering errors, they will both develop into one science dealing neither with mind nor with matter, but with events, which will not be labelled either "physical" or "mental." [x]

In other words, the real entities out of which minds and physical objects are to be constructed will not be "neutral stuff" but sense data.[11] This in effect was Hume's position, except that Hume had called the sense data "impressions" and had thereby given them a regrettably mentalistic interpretation. And because Hume had lacked the resources of the new relational logic to carry out the constructions, he had ended in scepticism. But though Russell had developed an instrument of logical analysis vastly superior to anything that had been available to Hume, he too failed to show that minds and physical objects are complex constructions made from sense data. Accordingly, the list of types of real entities was expanded—as is evident from the following passage, in which the distinction between real entities and logical constructions has been replaced by a distinction between "hard data" and "soft data."

HARD DATA AND SOFT DATA

> I mean by "hard" data those which resist the solvent influence of critical reflection, and by "soft" data those which, under the operation of this process, become to our minds more or less doubtful. The hardest of hard data are of two sorts: . . .

---

11 And "sensibilia," which are exactly like sense data except that they are not actually experienced by anyone.

The facts of sense (*i.e.* of *our own* sense-data) and the laws of logic. But even the severest scrutiny will allow some additions to this slender stock. Some facts of memory—especially of recent memory— . . . and some introspective facts are as certain as any facts of sense. . . . Spatial and temporal relations must sometimes be included, for example in the case of a swift motion falling wholly within the specious present. . . .

Certain common beliefs are undoubtedly excluded from hard data. Such is the belief . . . that sensible objects in general persist when we are not perceiving them. Such also is the belief in other people's minds. . . . Belief in what is reported by the testimony of others, including all that we learn from books, is of course involved in the doubt as to whether other people have minds at all. Thus the world from which our reconstruction is to begin is very fragmentary. The best we can say for it is that it is slightly more extensive than the world at which Descartes arrived by a similar process, since that world contained nothing except himself and his thoughts. . . .

The problem really is: Can the existence of anything other than our own hard data be inferred from the existence of those data? [y]

The metaphysical distinction between real entities and logical constructions (between hard and soft data) is entirely in harmony with the theory of meaning to which, as has been seen, Russell had been led by his logical studies. According to that theory, there is one sort of meaning that is *the* meaning of "meaning" and logic prescribes what this meaning is; all other claimants to meaningfulness are ruled out as "meaning*less*." Taken together, these doctrines led to a program for reconstruction in philosophy very different from Dewey's. According to this program it is necessary only (1) to anchor each ultimate unit of meaning to some hard datum and then (2) to construct complex descriptions of the world in accordance with the prescribed logical rules. The result should be a completely adequate description of everything that is. This kind of program is very appealing to those who yearn for simplicity and certainty. Hence Russell's own repeated failure to settle on the exact nature of the real entities (hard data) of which the universe is constituted did not deter other philosophers.

However, while the Logical Positivists were beginning to undertake this utopian program Russell himself was developing fundamental doubts about it—partly as a result of Wittgenstein's investigations[12] and partly because of some thoughts of his own. For instance, he was not able to solve the basic problem he had himself raised in the last sentence quoted in the passage above. Accordingly, he had to admit that philosophy cannot prove the existence of the world that physics believes in. It can only show that there *is* a problem, that there is reason to doubt what the plain man uncritically believes. This, surely, is a somewhat meager result.

If you say to a person untrained in philosophy, "How do you know I have two eyes?" he or she will reply, "What a silly question! I can see you have." It is not to be supposed that, when our inquiry is finished, we shall have

12 See pp. 370–75.

arrived at anything radically different from this unphilosophical position. What will have happened will be that . . . we shall find doubt more frequently justified than we supposed, and that even the most plausible premises will have shown themselves capable of yielding unplausible conclusions. The net result is to substitute articulate hesitation for inarticulate certainty. Whether this result has any value is a question which I shall not consider.[z]

The conclusion of Russell's analysis is to show that science is "at war with itself: when it most means to be objective, it finds itself plunged into subjectivity against its will. Naive realism leads to physics, and physics, if true, shows that naive realism is false. Therefore naive realism, if true, is false; therefore it is false."[a]

It seems to follow that Russell's account of the "business of philosophy" is mistaken. How can philosophy model itself on science if science is "at war with itself"? The fact is that Russell's methodological doubt was less like Descartes' than like Hume's. Whereas Descartes believed he had established the existence of a real world, Hume knew that he had not. But Hume had been reasonably content with his "mitigated" scepticism. Since Russell, in contrast, hoped that his logical analysis would take him beyond Hume and validate inferences from sense data to the world of physics, Russell was a disappointed Descartes.

Russell's two descriptions of the universe—as "neutral stuff" and as "hard data"—reflect unreconciled sides of his thought. To talk about neutral stuff is to *talk* an objective language, but there is no doubt that from beginning to end Russell's whole position was infected by a subjectivism from which he extricated himself only by an appeal to irrational belief.

> In ontology, I start by accepting the truth of physics. . . . Philosophers may say: What justification have you for accepting the truth of physics? I reply: merely a commonsense basis. . . .
> I believe (though without good grounds) in the world of physics as well as in the world of psychology. . . .
> If we are to hold that we know anything of the external world, we must accept the canons of scientific knowledge. Whether . . . an individual decides to accept or reject these canons, is a purely personal affair, not susceptible to argument.[b]

If Russell had been willing to adopt the point of view of pragmatism, he could have argued that, though these beliefs are logically unfounded, they are nevertheless instrumentally true. That is, it is socially advantageous to accept them and to guide one's conduct by them and disastrous to reject them. But instrumental truth was not enough for Russell. He always sought the "indubitable" and professed himself a rationalist, sharply critical of those who accept belief uncritically.

> It is undesirable to believe a proposition when there is no ground whatever for supposing it true. . . .
> I am in the habit of thinking of myself as a Rationalist. . . . Pragmatism

emphasizes the irrationality of opinion, and psycho-analysis emphasizes the irrationality of conduct. . . . I believe such an outlook to be very dangerous, and, in the long run, fatal to civilization. I shall, therefore, endeavour to show that the ideal of rationality remains unaffected by the ideas that have been thought fatal to it.[c]

There is irony in this. The cost of rejecting an instrumental truth while at the same time denying the possibility of rational argument for certain important beliefs is a radical subjectivism. Without realizing it, Russell simply accepted scientific beliefs (and *some* ethical and religious beliefs) because he preferred them and rejected many religious and ethical beliefs because he disliked them.

Ethics

In Russell's view, there is little to be said about ethics: "Ethics is traditionally a department of philosophy, and that is my reason for discussing it. I hardly think myself that it ought to be included in the domain of philosophy."[d] The reasons for this attitude are obvious: All our knowledge is limited to science, and

> . . . science has nothing to say about values. . . . Science can tell us much about the *means* of realizing our desires, but it cannot say that one desire is preferable to another. . . .
>
> When we assert that this or that has "value," we are giving expression to our own emotions, not to a fact which would still be true if our personal feelings were different. To make this clear, we must try to analyse the conception of the Good. . . .
>
> When a man says "this is good in itself," he *seems* to be making a statement, just as much as if he said "this is square" or "this is sweet." I believe this to be a mistake. I think that what the man really means is: "I wish everybody to desire this," or rather "Would that everybody desired this." If what he says is interpreted as a statement, it is merely an affirmation of his own personal wish; if, on the other hand, it is interpreted in a general way, it states nothing, but merely desires something. The wish, as an occurrence, is personal, but what it desires is universal. It is, I think, this curious interlocking of the particular and the universal which has caused so much confusion in ethics. . . .
>
> The consequences of this doctrine are considerable. In the first place, there can be no such thing as "sin" in any absolute sense; what one man calls "sin" another man call "virtue," and though they may dislike each other on account of this difference, neither can convict the other of intellectual error. . . .
>
> In the second place, it is impossible to uphold the way of speaking about values which is common among those who believe in Cosmic Purpose. . . . Our values have been evolved along with the rest of our constitution, and nothing as to any original purpose can be inferred from the fact that they are what they are.[e]

If Russell's analysis of the nature of ethical statements is correct, he was obviously right in holding that ethics is not a "department" of philosophy. It belongs in the field of propaganda, or (to use a more pleasant word) "persuasion," and results from the fact that men's various desires conflict. If all men agreed in their desires, there would be no ethics. Ethics is simply the art of inducing others to desire what we desire. (It is irrelevant here whether what we desire is something we believe to be good for ourselves alone or something we believe to be good for mankind; the point is that we are trying to bring others to desire whatever we desire.)

There are two chief ways of accomplishing this "unification" of desires: the "way of the legislator" and the "way of the preacher." The legislator persuades people to follow his way of thinking by promulgating a code of laws and of punishments and, generally, by instituting "a system of moral instruction." Insofar as he "makes men feel wicked if they pursue other purposes than his" he is successful. The preacher desires to produce the same result (to persuade others to desire what he desires), but since he "does not control the machinery of the State," he must use different means. His appeal is to the emotions (often disguised as an appeal to "evidence"); he knows how, by means of the "moving effect of rhythmical prose," to rouse feelings similar to his own in other men's minds.[f]

It is not easy to see much difference between this view and the views of the wicked pragmatists. The similarity may have been hidden from Russell by the fact that when he described his own values (desires) he forgot the subjectivity and relativism that he attributed to values generally. This can be put in terms of Dewey's distinction between desirings and desirables: Russell took it for granted that his own desiring (for other men's good) was desirable. Perhaps he was right. But surely this assumption is not self-evident, and his rejection of instrumentalism prevented him from adopting Dewey's proposed method for ascertaining whether a desiring is in fact a desirable.

RUSSELL'S VALUES

But passing over this point, it is evident that since Russell was not a legislator he was a preacher. What, then, were the ethical beliefs Russell desired men to accept? One belief has already been touched on: He wanted men to believe that "rationalism" is a good thing and that uncritical acceptance of conventional standards of value is a bad thing. It must be said that here and elsewhere Russell was an effective preacher. As a master of "rhythmical prose" he is persuasive. His strategy was to appeal both to egoism and to idealism, for in his view an intelligent pursuit of self-interest also produces the best results for society at large.

Consider, for instance, a little essay by Russell called *The Impact of Science on Society*. The thesis is that science, unwisely used, can intensify men's troubles by breeding war and tyranny. But wisely used, "it can diminish bad things, and it can increase good things." It can, for instance, "abolish poverty and excessive hours of labor." But in order for it to do so democracy must be maintained at home and birth control must be introduced among the prolific peoples of the East. For if population increases more rapidly than the means of producing goods and supplies, it will not be possible to abolish poverty, and the result will be ever increasing international tension.

Now, almost everyone agrees that the abolition of war and of poverty are good things. Why, then, has science not realized them for us? Because we do not desire these good things strongly enough. What "keeps evil in being" is the fact that "we have less desire for the welfare of our friends than for the punishment of our enemies." But though the passion of hate is very strong, it is capable of being changed.[13] What is needed to dissipate hatred and "generate" goodness is a "very simple and old-fashioned thing. . . . It is love, Christian love, or compassion. If you feel this, you have a motive for existence, a guide in action, a reason for courage, an imperative necessity for intellectual honesty. If you feel this, you have all that anybody should need in the way of religion."[g]

Religion

It is necessary, Russell held, to distinguish between "personal religion as a way of feeling" and the formal, historical religions. Each of the formal religions "has three aspects: (1) a church, (2) a creed, and (3) a code of personal morals"; and each has "three central doctrines—God, immortality, and freedom." The doctrines of formal religion can be neither proved nor, in the strict sense, disproved. On the whole, formal religion has had a pernicious influence, insofar as it has persistently tried to limit the freedom of inquiry that is the essence of science. Writing in 1935, Russell seemed to believe that science had for some years been almost continuously victorious in its warfare with formal religion, "but the rise of new religions in Russia and Germany, equipped with new means of missionary activity provided by science, has again put the issue in doubt."[h]

In contrast to formal religion, personal religion is valuable;[14] far from being in conflict with science, it is inspired by science. For the essence of personal religion is not merely compassion; it is also humility. By revealing the "vastness of the universe," science inspires men with "a new form of humility to replace that which atheism has rendered obsolete." This feeling of what can fairly be described as sublimity was always very strong in Russell. It accounts for the attraction Hegelianism had for him as a young man: In Hegel's conception of the absolute as "one single harmonious system . . . there is undeniably something sublime, something to which we could wish to yield assent." As an expression

---

13 Of course, the essay in which all of this was described was itself an effort to change passion—to cause the reader to desire what Russell desired.

14 Russell often wrote as if it were valuable in some other sense than merely as something desired by him and by other men.

of his own "feeling about the universe and about human passions," Russell quoted Leopardi's poem *The Infinite:*

> And then I call to mind eternity,
> And the ages that are dead, and this that now
> Is living, and the noise of it. And so
> In this immensity my thought sinks drowned:
> And sweet it seems to shipwreck in this sea.[i]

Yet Russell would not, or could not, yield assent; evidence was lacking. "When the arguments . . . are carefully examined," they are all seen to involve "confusion and many unwarrantable assumptions." The result of his insisting on "indubitableness" was therefore a romantic, almost melodramatic, conception of man's relation to the cosmos.

> Brief and powerless is Man's life; on him and all his race the slow, sure doom falls pitiless and dark. Blind to good and evil, reckless of destruction, omnipotent matter rolls on its relentless way; for Man, condemned to-day to lose his dearest, to-morrow himself to pass through the gate of darkness, it remains only to cherish, ere yet the blow falls, the lofty thoughts that ennoble his little day; disdaining the coward terrors of the slave of Fate, to worship at the shrine that his own hands have built; undismayed by the empire of chance, to preserve a mind free from the wanton tyranny that rules his outward life; proudly defiant of the irresistible forces that tolerate, for a moment, his knowledge and his condemnation, to sustain alone, a weary but unyielding Atlas, the world that his own ideals have fashioned despite the trampling march of unconscious power.[j]

It is not clear why it is appropriate for man to react in this way to "the world which Science presents for our belief," or on what grounds, if anyone were to react differently, it would be possible for Russell to "convict him of intellectual error." Indeed, it would seem, on Russell's own premises, that *all* reactions of whatever kind must be as "devoid of meaning" as the universe itself is supposed to be. Human reactions are included in the universe. Like it, therefore, they are merely phases of "Nature's secular hurryings through the abysses of space."

To understand the curious ambivalence in Russell's position—an ambivalence that is shared by many people today—it is necessary to see that, like Kierkegaard and Nietzsche, Russell experienced existential anguish, but that unlike them he was also a rationalist, a logician, and a social critic and reformer. To bring out still another aspect of Russell's complex personality, he was in many respects a Humian. But Hume would never have written about "a free man's worship." He had no sense of the sublime and the transcendent that Russell *felt* so strongly but to which he was unwilling to commit himself fully. Hume was content in his scepticism; Russell was unhappy in his. Whether this made Russell a better philosopher than he would otherwise have been is perhaps an open question, but there is no doubt that it made him an antimetaphysician in spite of himself.

Wittgenstein

Wittgenstein's[15] impact on contemporary thought—not merely on philosophy—has been great. In the first place, he criticized a set of assumptions, or attitudes, that had been widely held by philosophers of very different schools. Usually these philosophers were themselves unaware of the extent to which these attitudes and assumptions affected their thought. In the second place, he put forward an alternative view about the function of language and about the nature of meaning that seemed to revolutionize most of the classical problems of philosophy, such as the mind-body problem that had obsessed philosophers ever since Descartes.

Finally, and above all, Wittgenstein developed a conception of the nature of philosophy that differed in a dramatic way from most philosophers' conception of what it is to "do" philosophy. Prior to Wittgenstein, most philosophers had regarded philosophy as the pursuit of truth. Wittgenstein regarded it as a kind of therapy. According to his view, philosophy as it is usually practiced is a form—or perhaps better, a symptom—of mental illness. Instead of solving his problems the philosopher only exacerbates them by his theorizing. Philosophy, as Wittgenstein practiced it, was designed not to solve problems but to *dis*solve them. His aim, he said, was "to show the fly the way out of the fly-bottle."[k] Or, as he had written in the *Tractatus*, a reader will fully understand Wittgenstein's views only "when he has climbed out through them, on them, over them. (He must so to speak throw away the ladder, after he has climbed up on it.)"[l] Or, to put it differently again, anyone who has fully understood the nature of the "ladder" that Wittgenstein offered him no longer needs the ladder; he has escaped from philosophy. Thus, according to Wittgenstein, philosophy is a strange sort of enterprise: To the extent that it is successful, it simply disappears. From this point of view, his *Philosophical Investigations* was less radically different from the *Tractatus* than might be supposed. Though the methods of therapy proposed in the two works were different, the notion of philosophy as therapy remained central.

15 Ludwig Wittgenstein (1889–1951) was born in Vienna into a wealthy and cultivated family. After studying engineering in Austria, he went in 1911 to Manchester to continue his studies and to do research in the design of airplane propellers and engines. Soon his interests shifted to mathematics and logic, and he moved to Cambridge, where he was a pupil of Russell's. While serving in the Austrian army during World War I, he finished his *Tractatus Logico-Philosophicus*. Though at the time he thought he had solved all philosophical problems, he gradually came to question many of the doctrines of the *Tractatus*. Accordingly, after teaching school in Austria for a few years, he returned to Cambridge in 1929 and resumed the study and teaching of philosophy. He had given away the fortune he had inherited from his father and lived in great simplicity. He published nothing but dictated notes to his pupils. These notes circulated widely in an unauthorized form and began to have a great influence in Britain and the United States. A corrected version appeared after his death under the title *Philosophical Investigations*. Because controversy rages over the exact place of the *Tractatus* in the development of Wittgenstein's thought, and because there is much more agreement about the *Investigations*, the discussion presented in this chapter will rely chiefly on the latter work.

Wittgenstein's view of philosophy as it is ordinarily practiced was obviously close to Dewey's conception of philosophical inquiry as being generated by a quest for certainty. His view was also similar in some respects to that of the positivists. But Wittgenstein did not think that the preoccupations of the traditional philosophers were merely silly. Rather, he believed that their perplexities arose from "deep inquietudes." In this respect Wittgenstein was very close to Nietzsche. Like Nietzsche, and unlike Dewey, Wittgenstein conducted his therapy by exposing the myths and fictions concealed within the standard philosophical vocabulary.[16] But Nietzsche's technique was amateurish compared with the subtlety and finesse of Wittgenstein's. Nietzsche had anticipated Freud in suggesting that the language men use often expresses their unconscious needs; this was insightful, but speculative. Wittgenstein's approach, in contrast, was empirical. He saw that when language is performing its everyday practical functions, it is too busy to get into trouble. But sometimes, unfortunately, language "goes on holiday." Whenever it idles in this way, philosophical problems arise. The cure is to put language back into gear, as it were, by showing it at work in various concrete contexts relevant to the particular "holiday" that language happens to be taking. In collecting these contexts—in "assembling reminders" that were relevant to each of the classical philosophical problems— Wittgenstein showed the greatest skill. His aim was to approach each problem "from different directions," to "criss-cross [the field] in every direction." The result was not "*a* philosophical method" but a number of different methods, each of which, "like different therapies," was suitable for treating a particular form of mental illness.[m]

By thus bringing together and comparing a large number of similar but slightly different cases, Wittgenstein displayed in a striking way the varied meanings that the same words have in different contexts and the many different uses to which they are put. Thus, though his conception of philosophy as therapy was indeed very different from Russell's and from the usual analytical conception, his conviction that the proper method of philosophical inquiry is rigorous linguistic analysis revealed his relationship to this tradition and won a hearing for his views from tough-minded philosophers who would have considered listening to Nietzsche a waste of time.

The Nature of Language

THE PICTURE THEORY

Philosophical Investigations begins with a quotation from Augustine in which a view of language is stated that Wittgenstein proposed to criticize:

16 See pp. 238–43.

> When they (my elders) named some object, and accordingly moved towards something, I saw this and I grasped that the thing was called by the sound they uttered when they meant to point it out. Their intention was shewn by their bodily movements. . . . Thus, as I heard words repeatedly used in their proper places in various sentences, I gradually learnt to understand what objects they signified; and after I had trained my mouth to form these signs, I used them to express my own desires.[n]

To illustrate the view he was opposing Wittgenstein might just as well have used the passage from Hobbes that was quoted at the beginning of this chapter.[17] Although Augustine and Hobbes differed about almost everything else—from the nature of God to the nature of the earth—they had much the same view of language. This is a good example of the way in which certain very general assumptions about meaning may underlie theories of quite different types.

The particular assumptions common to Augustine and to Hobbes (and of course to many other philosophers) are as follows. First, it is taken for granted that objects are perceived quite independently of language. Note that Augustine first saw the object and then "grasped that the thing was called by the sound." That is, he believed that before a child learns the word "chair," he sees a chair just as fully and completely as he sees the chair after he has learned its name. Language in no way affects what we experience; it affects only our ability to communicate to others what we have experienced. Second, it is assumed that individual words name objects. Every word thus has its own individual meaning that, once attached to it, stays with it. Not to use the word to name the object is to misuse the word; it is to equivocate, or simply to lie. Third, it is assumed that the object the word names is its meaning. (In some variations of this theory, a distinction is drawn between the object named by the word and the mental image of that object called up in the mind of the hearer; the meaning of the word is then identified with the image rather than with the object. But even in this case meaning is regarded as determinate, specific, and fixed.) Fourth, it is held that sentences are combinations of such names and that the relations between the words in a sentence correspond to (that is, mirror) the relations among the parts of the complex fact described in the sentence in question. And it is only because of this correspondence, or mirroring, that sentences are meaningful and true.

If one thinks of such sentences as "The book is on the desk" or "Snoopy is lying on his doghouse," this theory has a certain plausibility; indeed, Wittgenstein himself had put forward a theory of this general type in his *Tractatus*. In framing this theory, he had been influenced by a report of a legal suit arising out of an automobile accident; in this suit dolls and miniature cars were used to represent the real people and automobiles involved in the accident. It seemed to Wittgenstein at the time he wrote the *Tractatus* that sentences represent facts in much the same way as the arrangement of dolls and miniature cars represented

17 See p. 332.

facts—or in the way in which the spatial relations pictured in a portrait (for example, nose between eyes and mouth) correspond to the spatial relations among the features of the sitter's face. Thus he pictured language to himself as a kind of picture of reality.

But by the time he wrote *Philosophical Investigations* he had decided that this picture of language as a picture of reality was mistaken. The picture was inadequate not merely because it failed to correspond to reality (for if failure to conform to reality were the only problem, a more faithful picture could doubtless be designed that would correspond to the facts), but because the concept of language as being a picture of the facts was at best appropriate only for a very small part of the whole domain of language and meanings.

WITTGENSTEIN'S CRITICISM OF THE PICTURE THEORY

Wittgenstein did not deny that in some circumstances some words represent ("name", "signify") objects; nouns like "chair," "table," and "bread" often do, as do proper names. Nor did Wittgenstein deny that we learn the meanings of some words in the way Augustine described, that is, by having other people point to the objects whose names they want us to learn. But Wittgenstein insisted that by no means all words function in this way; nor do we always learn the meanings of words by ostensive definition (by pointing). We learn them this way, for instance, when we are adding to our vocabulary in a language with which we are already familiar, but not (according to Wittgenstein) when we are learning a new language.

> Augustine, we might say, does describe a system of communication; only not everything that we call language is this system. And one has to say this in many cases where the question arises "Is this an appropriate description or not?" The answer is: "Yes, it is appropriate, but only for this narrowly circumscribed region, not for the whole of what you were claiming to describe."
>
> It is as if someone were to say: "A game consists in moving objects about on a surface according to certain rules . . ." —and we replied: You seem to be thinking of board games, but there are others. You can make your definition correct by expressly restricting it to those games.°

Wittgenstein observed that the tendency of people, including philosophers, to overgeneralize is unfortunately all too evident; Nietzsche had attributed this proclivity to man's sense of insecurity.[18] Whatever the psychological roots of the tendency, people are prone to conclude from a few cases that are striking in some way (or that are perhaps just the first cases they have encountered) that the properties characterizing these cases also characterize the whole class. Thus, according to Wittgenstein, the overgeneralization that Augustine (and Hobbes

18 See pp. 253–54.

and many other philosophers) made about language and about meaning resulted from concentrating on nouns (which happen to be rather prominent in European languages). Because all words look more or less alike and because they sound more or less alike, Augustine (and Hobbes) assumed that all words mean in the same way that nouns mean. But if he had paid even the least attention to such words as "is," "not," "this," and "here"—let alone to the ways in which nouns themselves mean in many contexts—he would have come to realize the inadequacy of this theory of meaning.

Unfortunately, this overgeneralization "surrounds the working of language with a haze which makes clear vision impossible." How can this fog be dispersed? By considering a number of primitive languages—or, rather, a number of languages "in primitive kinds of application in which one can command a clear view of the aim and functioning of the words."[p]

Here is one such language:

> I send someone shopping. I give him a slip marked "five red apples." He takes the slip to the shopkeeper, who opens the drawer marked "apples"; then he looks up the word "red" in a table and finds a colour sample opposite it; then he says the series of cardinal numbers—I assume that he knows them by heart—up to the word "five" and for each number he takes an apple of the same colour as the sample out of the drawer.[q]

Here is another:

> Let us imagine a language which . . . is meant to serve for communication between a builder A and an assistant B. A is building with building stones: there are blocks, pillars, slabs, and beams. B has to pass the stones, and that in the order in which A needs them. For this purpose they use a language consisting of the words "block," "pillar," "slab," "beam." A calls them out; —B brings the stone which he has learnt to bring at such-and-such a call. —Conceive this as a complete primitive language . . . the *whole* language of A and B; even the whole language of a tribe. The children are brought up to perform *these* actions, to use *these* words as they do so, and to react in *this* way to the words of others.
>
> An important part of the training will consist in the teacher's pointing to the objects, directing the child's attention to them, and at the same time uttering a word; for instance, the word "slab" as he points to that shape. . . . This ostensive teaching of words can be said to establish an association between the word and the thing. But what does this mean? Well, it can mean various things; but one very likely thinks first of all that a picture of the object comes before the child's mind when it hears the word. But now, if this does happen—is it the purpose of the word? —Yes, it *can* be the purpose—I can imagine such a use of words (or series of sounds). (Uttering a word is like striking a note on the keyboard of the imagination.) But in the language [of the builder and his assistant] it is *not* the purpose of the words to evoke images. (It may, of course, be discovered that that helps to attain the actual purpose.)

But if the ostensive teaching has this effect, am I to say that it effects an understanding of the word? Don't you understand the call "Slab!" if you act upon it in such-and-such a way? —Doubtless the ostensive teaching helped to bring this about; but only together with a particular training. With different training the same ostensive teaching of these words would have effected a quite different understanding.

"I set the brake up by connecting up rod and lever." —Yes, given the whole rest of the mechanism. Only in conjunction with that is it a brake-lever, and separated from its support it is not even a lever; it may be anything, or nothing.[r]

Several important points are brought out in these examples. First, language arises in a particular social context—for instance, in an apple-buying context or in a building-construction context—and reflects that social context. Second, any system of signs is a language insofar as it facilitates the purpose implicit in the social context in which this system of signs is being used. Thus the color sample is as much a sign in the apple-buying language as the word "red" is in some other language. Furthermore, what looks like a word (for example, "Slab!") and what might be only a word in some languages, is a sentence in the builder's language. Third, if the language (whatever it looks like and however odd it may seem when compared with standard written English, as taught in schools) is effective in promoting the purpose for which the language has been introduced, then meaning is conveyed and understanding occurs. The critical point Wittgenstein is making here is that the test of meaningfulness is not whether a particular language conforms to some set of criteria that have been prescribed by logic[19] but, quite simply, whether it is successful in accomplishing whatever it set out to accomplish—buying five apples to bring home, getting the building materials to the building site in the right order, and so on.

Fourth, though the meaning of a word may occasionally be some image of the thing named by the word (one can think of social contexts in which the word "slab" might call up in the mind of the hearer the mental image of a slab), this sort of meaning, far from being standard, is exceptional. In the social context of the builder and his assistant, the word "Slab!" spoken by the builder probably does not conjure up the mental image of a slab in the mind of the assistant; nor was it intended by the builder to do so. Are we to infer from the fact that no image is conjured up in the assistant's mind that "Slab!" has no meaning for him, that he does not understand what is said to him? To draw this conclusion is to unduly and arbitrarily restrict the meaning of "meaning." It is evident that he has understood, that the word is meaningful to him without an image having occurred, because he brings the item of building material that the builder wanted him to bring.

Finally, and most important, if we want to understand what understanding consists in, we must watch the way language functions in each particular circum-

19 See p. 342.

stance in which it is actually used. We must look not to the meaning but to the use. In this aphorism Wittgenstein used "meaning" in the same sense as those philosophers who identify the meaning of a word either with the object named by the word or with the mental image of that object. It is in this limited sense of "meaning" that Wittgenstein says the meaning of a word must be ignored. However, Wittgenstein might just as well have expanded the meaning of "meaning" and said that there is no one standard meaning that is *the* meaning of a given word, but that each word or other sign has as many meanings as it has uses, and that these are countless.

> Think of the tools in a tool-box: there is a hammer, pliers, a saw, a screw-driver, a rule, a glue-pot, glue, nails and screws. —The functions of words are as diverse as the functions of these objects. (And in both cases there are similarities.)
>
> Of course, what confuses us is the uniform appearance of words when we hear them spoken or meet them in script and print. For their *application* is not presented to us so clearly. Especially not, when we are doing philosophy!
>
> It is like looking into the cabin of a locomotive. We see handles all looking more or less alike. (Naturally, since they are all supposed to be handled.) But one is the handle of a crank which can be moved continuously (it regulates the opening of a valve); another is the handle of a switch, which has only two effective positions, it is either off or on; a third is the handle of a brake-lever, the harder one pulls on it, the harder it brakes; a fourth, the handle of a pump: it has an effect only so long as it is moved to and fro.
>
> When we say: "Every word in language signifies something" we have so far said *nothing whatever;* unless we have explained *exactly what* distinction we wish to make. . . .
>
> Imagine someone's saying: "*All* tools serve to modify something. Thus the hammer modifies the position of the nail, the saw the shape of the board, and so on." —And what is modified by the rule, the glue-pot, the nails? —"Our knowledge of a thing's length, the temperature of the glue, and the solidity of the box." —Would anything be gained by this assimilation of expressions?
>
> The word "to signify" is perhaps used in the most straightforward way when the object signified is marked with the sign. Suppose that the tools A uses in building bear certain marks. When A shews his assistant such a mark, he brings the tool that has that mark on it.
>
> It is in this and more or less similar ways that a name means and is given to a thing. —It will often prove useful in philosophy to say to ourselves: naming something is like attaching a label to a thing.
>
> What about the colour samples that A shews to B: are they part of the *language?* Well, it is as you please. They do not belong among the words; yet when I say to someone: "Pronounce the word 'the'," you will count the second "the" as part of the sentence. Yet it has a role just like that of a colour sample [in the apple-buying language]; that is, it is a sample of what the other is meant to say.

It is most natural, and causes least confusion, to reckon the samples among the instruments of the language. . . .

It will be possible to say: In [most languages] we have different *kinds of word*. . . . But how we group words into kinds will depend on the aim of the classification, —and on our own inclination.

Think of the different points of view from which one can classify tools or chess-men.

Do not be troubled by the fact that [some] languages . . . consist only of orders. If you want to say that this shews them to be incomplete, ask yourself whether our language is complete; —whether it was so before the symbolism of chemistry and the notation of the infinitesimal calculus were incorporated in it; for these are, so to speak, suburbs of our language. (And how many houses or streets does it take before a town begins to be a town?) Our language can be seen as an ancient city: a maze of little streets and squares, of old and new houses, and of houses with additions from various periods; and this surrounded by a multitude of new boroughs with straight regular streets and uniform houses.

It is easy to imagine a language consisting only of orders and reports in battle. —Or a language consisting only of questions and expressions for answering yes and no. And innumerable others. —And to imagine a language means to imagine a form of life. . . .

But how many kinds of sentence are there? Say assertion, question, and command? —There are *countless* kinds: countless different kinds of use of what we call "symbols," "words," "sentences." And this multiplicity is not something fixed, given once for all; but new types of language, new language-games, as we may say, come into existence, and others become obsolete and get forgotten. . . .

Here the term "language-*game*" is meant to bring into prominence the fact that the *speaking* of language is part of any activity, or of a form of life.

Review the multiplicity of language-games in the following examples, and in others:

    Giving orders, and obeying them—
    Describing the appearance of an object, or giving its measurements—
    Constructing an object from a description (a drawing)—
    Reporting an event—
    Speculating about an event—
    Forming and testing a hypothesis—
    Presenting the results of an experiment in tables and diagrams—
    Making up a story; and reading it—
    Play-acting—
    Singing catches—
    Guessing riddles—
    Making a joke; telling it—
    Solving a problem in practical arithmetic—
    Translating from one language into another—
    Asking, thanking, cursing, greeting, praying—

It is interesting to compare the multiplicity of the tools in language and of the ways in which they are used, the multiplicity of kinds of word and sentence, with what logicians have said about the structure of language. (Including the author of the *Tractatus Logico-Philosophicus*.) . . .

One thinks that learning language consists in giving names to objects. Viz., to human beings, to shapes, to colours, to pains, to moods, to numbers, etc. To repeat,—naming is something like attaching a label to a thing. One can say that this is preparatory to the use of a word. But *what* is it a preparation *for?*

"We name things and then we can talk about them: can refer to them in talk." —As if what we did next were given with the mere act of naming. As if there were only one thing called "talking about a thing." Whereas in fact we do the most various things with our sentences. Think of exclamations alone, with their completely different functions.

Water!
Away!
Ow!
Help!
Fine!
No!

Are you inclined still to call these words "names of objects"? . . .

Naming is so far not a move in the language-game—any more than putting a piece in its place on the board is a move in chess. We may say: *nothing* has so far been done, when a thing has been named. It has not even *got* a name except in the language-game.[s]

Why do philosophers describe Wittgenstein's views as revolutionary? After all, what he says in this passage seems no more than common sense. But that is precisely the point: To have introduced common sense into the esoteric domain of philosophy *was* revolutionary. It was the function of Wittgenstein's own version of philosophy to dissolve all those special, "philosophical" problems with which philosophy had traditionally been preoccupied and then, having dissolved them, to disappear. Let us then see how doing philosophy in Wittgenstein's way dissolves philosophical problems.

Universals and Family Resemblance

One question that philosophers have debated inconclusively since the time of Plato is the problem of universals. Plato's whole metaphysics, as well as his ethical and political philosophy, presupposed the existence of what he called forms. According to this view, in addition to such spatiotemporal entities as Dobbin, Bucephalus, Man o' War, and Swaps there is the form "horse." The form is the true reality; the individual flesh-and-blood horses encountered in this world gain what reality they possess by participating in the forms. Though few philosophers have accepted all the details of Plato's theory of forms, many, including White-head, have agreed that universals are real existents.

Wittgenstein's criticism of the picture theory of meaning both accounts for the persistence of this belief in real universals and provides a reasonable alternative. According to the picture theory, every word names an individual object: "Bucephalus" names the particular horse that was owned by Alexander the Great; "Swaps" the particular horse that is commemorated in bronze at Hollywood Park; and so on. But in addition to such words the English language contains the word "horse." What does "horse" name? To philosophers caught in the fly-bottle of the picture theory, the answer seemed obvious. Since every word names, un-ambiguously, a quite definite object, it seemed evident to philosophical realists that the word "horse" must name an entity of a very special kind, nonperceptible, nonspatial, and nontemporal. Whenever the word "horse" is used, this entity, the universal "horse," is always meant, just as whenever the word "Bucephalus" is mentioned, the physical object, Bucephalus, is always meant. The only differ-ence is that whenever the word "Bucephalus" is mentioned the object always meant is a particular, whereas when the word "horse" is mentioned the object always meant is a universal.

This theory of universals can be plainly seen in the following argument by St. Anselm, in which he believed he had established the existence of a supremely good and powerful being, that is, God.

> Since there are goods so innumerable, whose great diversity we experience by the bodily sense, and discern by our mental faculties, must we not believe that there is some one thing, through which all goods whatever are good? . . . For, whatsoever things are said to be *just*, when compared one with another, whether equally, or more, or less, cannot be understood as just, except through the quality of *justness*, which is not one thing in one instance, and another in another. . . .
>
> But, since the reasoning which we have observed is in no wise refutable, necessarily, again, all things, whether useful or honorable, if they are truly good, are good through the same being through which all goods exist. . . . But who can doubt this very being, through which all goods exist, to be a great good? . . .
>
> It follows, therefore, that all other goods are good through another being than that which they themselves are, and this being alone is good through itself. Hence, this alone is supremely good, which is alone good through itself. But that which is supremely good, is also supremely great. There is, therefore, some one being which is supremely good, and supremely great, that is, the highest of all existing beings.[t]

This argument, which seemed to its author (and to many another philosopher) "irrefutable," depends for its plausibility on the picture theory of meaning.

The picture theory is not only responsible for a belief in universals (and the accompanying belief that God, as the most universal of universals, necessarily exists); it is also responsible for similar accounts of the nature of numbers (the notion that "one," "two," "square root of minus one," and the like are the names of more nonspatial, nontemporal, nonperceptible entities), the nature of geometric objects, and the nature of such oddities as the present king of France, whose nonexistence happened to be affirmed.[20]

Russell was able to dispose of the nonexistent king of France by a piece of purely logical analysis. In the *Investigations* Wittgenstein disposed of universals simply by calling attention to the varied ways in which words like "horse" (or "just," or "good," or "two") are used in actual discourse. Every word is used in "countless" different ways, each of which constitutes a meaning of the word. No one meaning is intrinsically better, more meaningful, truer, or more really horselike than any other. These varied meanings do not have an identical entity (horseness) in common. Rather, Wittgenstein held, there are a number of similarities. None of the meanings is characterized by all these similarities, but every one of the meanings is characterized by some of them. It is as if they were all members of a human family, who are recognizable as members not because they all share an identical set of characteristics but because—red hair, roman noses, and full lips being characteristic of this family—some members have roman noses and full lips, others have full lips and red hair, and still others have red hair and roman noses. In the same way, the meanings of "horse" have a family resemblance—and this is all there is to a universal. The famous problem of universals is thus dissolved.[21]

Wittgenstein's own example for his argument was what Plato would have called the form "game," what some epistemological realists call a universal, and what others would call "essence" of games. Wittgenstein himself described it simply as the family resemblance among all the various uses (meanings) of the word "game."

> Someone might object against me: "You take the easy way out! You talk about all sorts of language-games, but have nowhere said what the essence of a language-game, and hence of language, is: what is common to all these activities, and what makes them into language or parts of language. . . ."
> And this is true. —Instead of producing something common to all that we call language, I am saying that these phenomena have no one thing in common which makes us use the same word for all, —but that they are *related*

20 See p. 339.
21 Philosophers of the nominalistic persuasion, who rightly found the notion of nontemporal, nonspatial, nonperceptible entities excessively odd were also trapped in the fly-bottle of the picture theory. Though they rejected universals as the entities named by such words as "horse," most of them nevertheless took it for granted that "horse" must name a quite specific object and that this selfsame, identical entity is meant each time the word "horse" is used. Accordingly, they decided that "horse" names an image. This (they reasoned) must be an abstract image, since it can include only what is common to Bucephalus, Dobbin, Swaps, and all other particular horses. Hence the color of the image named by "horse" cannot be gray or black or roan, for these are the colors of particular horses. But what sort of color would a nonparticular, abstract color be? Clearly, these nominalists were involved in almost as many puzzles and paradoxes as were the realists.

to one another in many different ways. And it is because of this relationship, or these relationships, that we call them all "language." I will try to explain this.

Consider for example the proceedings that we call "games." I mean board-games, card-games, ball-games, Olympic games, and so on. What is common to them all? —Don't say: "There *must* be something common, or they would not be called 'games'"—but *look and see* whether there is anything common to all. —For if you look at them you will not see something that is common to *all*, but similarities, relationships, and a whole series of them at that. To repeat: don't think, but look! —Look for example at board-games, with their multifarious relationships. Now pass to card-games; here you find many correspondences with the first group, but many common features drop out, and others appear. When we pass next to ball-games, much that is common is retained, but much is lost. —Are they all "amusing"? Compare chess with noughts and crosses. Or is there always winning and losing, or competition between players? Think of patience. . . . Look at the parts played by skill and luck; and at the difference between skill in chess and skill in tennis. . . . And we can go through the many, many other groups of games in the same way; can see how similarities crop up and disappear.

And the result of this examination is: we see a complicated network of similarities overlapping and criss-crossing: sometimes overall similarities, sometimes similarities of detail.

I can think of no better expression to characterize these similarities than "family resemblances"; for the various resemblances between members of a family: build, features, colour of eyes, gait, temperament, etc., etc., over-lap and criss-cross in the same way. —And I shall say: "games" form a family. . . .

One might say that the concept "game" is a concept with blurred edges. —"But is a blurred concept a concept at all?" —Is an indistinct photograph a picture of a person at all? Is it even always an advantage to replace an indistinct picture by a sharp one? Isn't the indistinct one often exactly what we need? . . .

When philosophers use a word—"knowledge," "being," "object," "I," "proposition," "name"—and try to grasp the *essence* of the thing, one must always ask oneself: is the word ever actually used in this way in the language-game which is its original home?—

What *we* do is to bring words back from their metaphysical to their everyday use.[u]

The result of bringing words back from their special metaphysical use to their everyday use is to dissolve the metaphysical problems associated with the meta-physical use. Thus the debate between the nominalists and the realists disappears as soon as it is realized that there is no problem at all about the status of universals in connection with any of the everyday uses of such words as "horse." The problem about the status of universals arises only within a very special language game. Yet—such is the irony of the situation—philosophers have supposed that their special philosophical use of "horse" is necessary to solve the problem of universals!

The Question of Precision

In his discussion of family resemblance Wittgenstein pointed out that some concepts have blurred edges and that others have sharp edges. Philosophers have usually preferred those concepts with sharp edges. If we take seriously Nietzsche's and Dewey's psychological analyses, the explanation for this preference is obvious—it is connected with the philosophical quest for certainty. If a concept has vague, fuzzy boundaries a person cannot be certain whether the particular object he is considering belongs inside or outside the concept. If, for instance, the definition of "game" is open and indeterminate, it may be debatable whether a particular activity is a game. Whenever philosophers find themselves in such a situation, they tend to sharpen the edges of the concept, to define it in such a way that it becomes absolutely clear that the activity in question either is or is not a game. This move reduces philosophical anxiety, but only at the cost of creating an artificial situation.

This artificiality is just what the Romantic poets were objecting to when (as with Wordsworth) they condemned "that false secondary power by which we multiply distinctions." And it is what Schopenhauer was criticizing in his mosaic metaphor.[22] It is instructive to compare Schopenhauer's approach with Wittgenstein's. Whereas his was metaphysical, Wittgenstein's was linguistic. Schopenhauer (and the Romantic poets) asked, "What is the real nature of things?" Their answer was, "Reality is continuous, and this is why clear-cut distinctions falsify." Wittgenstein, for his part, simply pointed out that in some language games sharp edges are appropriate and that in other games blurred edges are appropriate.

"BLURRED" VERSUS "SHARP" CONCEPTS

Since he happened to be arguing against the precisionists, Wittgenstein was chiefly concerned to show that we can get on very nicely with concepts whose edges are blurred—that is, we get along very nicely without knowing, or at least without being able to say, *exactly* what we mean. But this emphasis on the utility of blurred concepts was tactical; he did not mean that they are intrinsically better than sharply edged concepts, or that language games in which we cannot say what we know are somehow intrinsically better than those in which we can. As usual, he opposed the disposition to regard any one usage as "right," and he would have been as critical of the Romantics' disposition to say that reality *is* continuous as they were critical of their opponents' assumption that it consists in a number of discrete elements.

> I *can* give the concept "number" rigid limits . . . , but I can also use it
> so that the extension of concept is *not* closed by a frontier. And this is how

22 See pp. 146–47. According to von Wright, Wittgenstein said "he had read Schopenhauer's *Die Welt als Wille und Vorstellung* in his youth, and his first philosophy was a Schopenhaurian epistemological idealism"—in N. Malcolm, Biographical Sketch, *Ludwig Wittgenstein: A Memoir* (Oxford University Press, 1966), p. 5.

we do use the word "game." For how is the concept of a game bounded? What still counts as a game and what no longer goes? Can you give the boundary? No. You can *draw* one; for none has so far been drawn. (But that never troubled you before when you used the word "game.")

"But then the use of the word is unregulated, the 'game' we play with it is unregulated." —It is not everywhere circumscribed by rules; but no more are there any rules for how high one throws the ball in tennis, or how hard; yet tennis is a game for all that and has rules too.

How should we explain to someone what a game is? I imagine that we should describe *games* to him, and we might add: "This *and similar things* are called 'games'." And do we know any more about it ourselves? Is it only other people whom we cannot tell exactly what a game is? —But this is not ignorance. We do not know the boundaries because none have been drawn. To repeat, we can draw a boundary—for a special purpose. Does it take that to make the concept usable? Not at all! (Except for that special purpose.) No more than it took the definition: 1 pace = 75 cm. to make the measure of length "one pace" usable. And if you want to say "But still, before that it wasn't an exact measure," then I reply: very well, it was an inexact one. —Though you still owe me a definition of exactness. . . .

What does it mean to know what a game is? What does it mean, to know it and not be able to say it? Is this knowledge somehow equivalent to an unformulated definition? So that if it were formulated I should be able to recognize it as the expression of my knowledge? Isn't my knowledge, my concept of a game, completely expressed in the explanations that I could give? That is, in my describing examples of various kinds of game; shewing how all sorts of other games can be constructed on the analogy of these; saying that I should scarcely include this or this among games; and so on.

 If someone were to draw a sharp boundary I could not acknowledge it as the one that I too always wanted to draw, or had drawn in my mind. For I did not want to draw one at all. His concept can then be said to be not the same as mine, but akin to it. The kinship is that of two pictures, one of which consists of colour patches with vague contours, and the other of patches similarly shaped and distributed, but with clear contours. The kinship is just as undeniable as the difference. . . .

Compare *knowing* and *saying:*
   how many feet high Mont Blanc is—
   how the word "game" is used—
   how a clarinet sounds.
If you are surprised that one can know something and not be able to say it, you are perhaps thinking of a case like the first. Certainly not of one like the third.

Consider this example. If one says "Moses did not exist," this may mean various things. It may mean: the Israelites did not have a *single* leader when they withdrew from Egypt —— or: their leader was not called Moses —— or: there cannot have been anyone who accomplished all that the Bible relates of Moses —— or: etc., etc. —We may say, following Russell: the name "Moses" can be defined by means of various descriptions. . . .

But when I make a statement about Moses, —am I always ready to substitute some *one* of these descriptions for "Moses"? I shall perhaps say:

By "Moses" I understand the man who did what the Bible relates of Moses, or at any rate a good deal of it. But how much? Have I decided how much must be proved false for me to give up my proposition as false? Has the name Moses got a fixed and unequivocal use for me in all possible cases? —Is it not the case that I have, so to speak, a whole series of props in readiness, and am ready to lean on one if another should be taken from under me and vice versa?

And this can be expressed like this: I use the name "N" without a *fixed* meaning. (But that detracts as little from its usefulness, as it detracts from that of a table that it stands on four legs instead of three and so sometimes wobbles.)

Should it be said that I am using a word whose meaning I don't know, and so am talking nonsense? —Say what you choose, so long as it does not prevent you from seeing the facts. . . .ᵛ

DEFINITIONS AND RULES

A definition may be thought of as a rule, a rule for determining what circumstances are appropriate for the use of a word—for instance, for determining whether "horse" is the appropriate word to use when talking about that object over there in the field. Wittgenstein's point about definitions and concepts can therefore be restated in terms of rules. Here again the notion of game is relevant, for games are played according to rules. The rules of every game are subject to interpretation, and they change from time to time. Yet this does not make it impossible to play the game: We simply make up new rules as they are needed, to cover the doubtful cases, and proceed. Indeed, what sort of game would it be whose play was *absolutely* fixed by its rules?

> But what does a game look like that is everywhere bounded by rules? whose rules never let a doubt creep in, but stop up all the cracks where it might? —Can't we imagine a rule determining the application of a rule, and a doubt which it removes—and so on?
>
> But that is not to say that we are in doubt because it is possible for us to *imagine* a doubt. I can easily imagine someone always doubting before he opened his front door whether an abyss did not yawn behind it; and making sure about it before he went through the door (and he might on some occasion prove to be right)—but that does not make me doubt in the same case.ʷ

To draw another analogy, definitions and rules are like signposts. Although a signpost gives a person direction, it can still leave him in doubt. If it proves to be ambiguous, supplementary instructions can be added, but no matter how extensive these instructions are they cannot *guarantee* that no one ever loses the way. In any case, the pursuit of more and more precise signposts is not a philosophical matter but an empirical one.

This can be applied to such a problem as the meaning of "Moses." According to Wittgenstein, to seek an absolutely unambiguous meaning is a philosophical illness.

Suppose I give this explanation: "I take 'Moses' to mean the man, if there was such a man, who led the Israelites out of Egypt, whatever he was called then and whatever he may or may not have done besides." —But similar doubts to those about "Moses" are possible about the words of this explanation (what are you calling "Egypt," whom the "Israelites" etc.?). Nor would these questions come to an end when we got down to words like "red," "dark," "sweet." —"But then how does an explanation help me to understand, if after all it is not the final one? In that case the explanation is never completed; so I still don't understand what he means, and never shall!" —As though an explanation as it were hung in the air unless supported by another one. Whereas an explanation may indeed rest on another one that has been given, but none stands in need of another—unless *we* require it to prevent a misunderstanding. One might say: an explanation serves to remove or to avert a misunderstanding—one, that is, that would occur but for the explanation; not every one that I can imagine.

It may easily look as if every doubt merely *revealed* an existing gap in the foundations; so that secure understanding is only possible if we first doubt everything that *can* be doubted, and then remove all these doubts.

The sign-post is in order—if, under normal circumstances, it fulfills its purpose.

If I tell some one "Stand roughly here"—may not this explanation work perfectly? And cannot every other one fail too?

But isn't it an inexact explanation? —Yes; why shouldn't we call it "inexact"? Only let us understand what "inexact" means. For it does not mean "unusable." . . .

We understand what it means to set a pocket watch to the exact time or to regulate it to be exact. But what if it were asked: is this exactness ideal exactness, or how nearly does it approach the ideal? —Of course, we can speak of measurements of time in which there is a different, and as we should say a greater, exactness than in the measurement of time by a pocket watch; in which the words "to set the clock to the exact time" have a different, though related meaning. . . . Now, if I tell someone: "You should come to dinner more punctually; you know it begins at one o'clock exactly"—is there really no question of *exactness* here? because it is possible to say: "Think of the determination of time in the laboratory or the observatory; *there* you see what 'exactness' means"?

"Inexact" is really a reproach, and "exact" is praise. And that is to say that what is inexact attains its goal less perfectly than what is more exact. Thus the point here is what we call "the goal." Am I inexact when I do not give our distance from the sun to the nearest foot, or tell a joiner the width of a table to the nearest thousandth of an inch?

No *single* ideal of exactness has been laid down; we do not know what we should be supposed to imagine under this head. . . .[x]

Thus a definition—or a rule or a signpost—is "exact" if it is good enough for whatever purpose it has been introduced, and because purposes differ exactnesses too will differ. That is all there is to the question of precision. To ask for more is to become entangled in a whole nest of philosophical problems, all of which have their source in a quest for certainty. To realize this is to dissolve all these problems at one stroke.

Critique of Logical Atomism

At this point, Wittgenstein evidently had in mind the program that Russell had formulated and that the Logical Positivists were attempting to carry out—the project, that is, of analyzing all complex propositions into atomistic propositions about simple, elementary occurrences ("Red here now," "Dark here now," and the like), which could then be recombined according to the rules of a logically exact language. In a word, the quest for certainty and precision had led these philosophers to logical atomism as a metaphysical doctrine and to analysis as a methodology.

In criticizing logical atomism Wittgenstein was of course attacking a contemporary version of the underlying theses of the analytical tradition—the assumptions (1) that the universe consists in a number of elementary, encapsulated entities, each itself and not another thing; (2) that everything that is not a simple is a composite composed of several such simples; and (3) that when we are confronted with a composite we can come to understand it by analyzing it into its constituent simples.[23] To these basic assumptions proponents of the picture theory added the doctrine that the simple elements can only be named (pointed to by ostensive definition); they cannot be described, for description involves analysis.

Let us first consider Wittgenstein's comments on analysis, bearing in mind that in the *Tractatus* he had himself put forward a view very similar to Russell's.

LIMITATIONS OF THE METHOD OF ANALYSIS

Characteristically, Wittgenstein pointed out that "analysis" has a variety of meanings, each appropriate in its own context, that is, in the language game in which it occurs. The logical atomists (Wittgenstein included, in his earlier work) had simply taken one of these meanings as *the* meaning of "analysis." The same was true for "composite" and the other terms in the lexicon of logical atomism. When this is understood, Wittgenstein held, it no longer seems plausible to characterize analysis as the ideal philosophical method.

> But what are the simple constituent parts of which reality is composed?
> —What are the simple constituent parts of a chair? —The bits of wood of
> which it is made? or the molecules, or the atoms? —"Simple" means: not

23 See p. 332.

composite. And here the point is: in what sense "composite"? It makes no sense at all to speak absolutely of the "simple parts of a chair."

Again, Does my visual image of this tree, of this chair, consist of parts? And what are its simple constituent parts? Multi-colouredness is one kind of complexity; another is, for example, that of a broken outline composed of straight bits. And a curve can be said to be composed of an ascending and a descending segment.

If I tell someone without any further explanation: "What I see before me now is composite," he will have the right to ask: "What do you mean by 'composite'? For there are all sorts of things that that can mean!" —The question "Is what you see composite?" makes good sense if it is already established what kind of complexity—that is, which particular use of the word—is in question. If it had been laid down that the visual image of a tree was to be called "composite" if one saw not just a single trunk but also branches, then the question "Is the visual image of this tree simple or composite?" and the question "What are its simple component parts?" would have a clear sense—a clear use. And of course the answer to the second question is not "The branches" (that would be an answer to the grammatical question: "What are here called 'simple component parts'?") but rather a description of the individual branches. . . .

We use the word "composite" (and therefore the word "simple") in an enormous number of different and differently related ways. (Is the colour of a square on a chessboard simple, or does it consist of pure white and pure yellow? And is white simple, or does it consist of the colours of the rainbow? —Is this length of 2 cm. simple, or does it consist of two parts, each 1 cm. long? But why not of one bit 3 cm. long, and one bit 1 cm. long measured in the opposite direction?)

To the *philosophical* question: "Is the visual image of this tree composite, and what are its component parts?" the correct answer is: "That depends on what you understand by 'composite'." (And that is of course not an answer but a rejection of the question.) ʸ

Diversity of meaning apart, analysis seems an ideal method only to those who have allowed a particular requirement to slip into their notion of what they are aiming at in the communications they make to other people. This, according to Wittgenstein, is the requirement of simplicity. But is simplicity always preferable? Suppose I ask someone to bring the broom from the kitchen. He must understand me, because he fetches the broom. Would I have made things clearer (to him? to myself?) if I had said, "Bring me the broomstick and the brush that is fitted on it?" If I had said that would he not be likely to respond, "Do you want the broom? Why do you put it so oddly?" What would I have gained by the translation? The second sentence may be said to be a "further analysed form of the first one," in the sense that the requirement of greater simplicity has been met. But it achieves no more than the first sentence and it accomplishes its purpose only in a very roundabout way; in this sense, the second sentence is not simpler but more complex.

So much for "simplicity." What of "further analysed form"? It is possible to think of two languages, in one of which, (a), the names of composites (such names as "broom") occur, and in the other of which, (b), only the names of simples (well, of such *relative* simples as "broomstick" and "brush") occur. What is meant by saying that (b) is an "analysed form" of (a)?

> In what sense is an order in the second game an analysed form of an order in the first? Does the former lie concealed in the latter, and is it now brought out by analysis? .—. *empirical* DAT?·
>
> To say . . . that a sentence in (b) is an "analysed" form of one in (a) readily seduces us into thinking that the former is the more fundamental form; that it alone shews what is meant by the other, and so on. For example, we think: If you have only the unanalysed form you miss the analysis; but if you know the analysed form that gives you everything. —But can I not say that an aspect of the matter is lost on you in the *latter* case as well as the former? [z]

Possibly (b) is better for some purposes than (a), but is anyone going to argue that (b) is intrinsically superior to (a)? Everything depends on the context in which the language game is played, and in everyday contexts (such as asking someone to fetch a broom), (a) is preferable. It is much the same as in the case of the blurred and the sharply focused pictures. Something is gained when the picture is brought into focus, but something is lost.

IDEAL LANGUAGES

We come now to the question of ideal languages, or as Wittgenstein put it, the "subliming" of logic. It is often said that logic is a "normative science." It lays down the rules for correct—for valid—thinking. Once these rules are formulated it is possible to examine actual instances and accept or reject them, depending on how well they approximate to the logical norms. Everything that Wittgenstein said about definitions and signposts, and about the "open" character of the rules by which games are played, naturally applies to logic and to the notion of an ideal language. Thus logic is indeed a normative science, in the sense that we can compare and criticize actual instances of thinking and everyday uses of language (just as, for that matter, we can compare and criticize actual instances of chess-playing). But in Wittgenstein's view we do not need an absolutely definitive set of logical rules or an ideal language in order to make these comparisons (any more than we need an absolutely definitive set of rules about chess to criticize actual games of chess). Unfortunately, however, the phrase "normative sciences" suggests just such a set of rules.

> F. P. Ramsey once emphasized in conversation with me that logic was a "normative science." I do not know exactly what he had in mind, but it was doubtless closely related to what only dawned on me later: namely, that in philosophy we often *compare* the use of words with games and calculi which

have fixed rules, but cannot say that someone who is using language *must* be playing such a game. —But if you say that our languages only *approximate* to such calculi you are standing on the very brink of a misunderstanding. For then it may look as if what we were talking about were an *ideal* language. . . . Here the word "ideal" is liable to mislead, for it sounds as if these languages were better, more perfect, than our everyday language; and as if it took the logician to shew people at last what a correct sentence looked like. . . .[a]

In other words, the ideal of "exactness," which Wittgenstein had deflated insofar as it affected the notion of definition, has also infected men's thinking about logic. That ideal has led to a conception of logic as "something sublime," as something having "peculiar depth" and "universal significance."[b] It has also led to a corresponding derogation of actual, everyday thought and language. As a result we tend to focus attention on what does not help us solve our philosophical problems and to neglect what can dissolve them.

Let us consider the way in which the ideal of exactness has led to the subliming of logic.

Logic lay, it seemed, at the bottom of all the sciences. —For logical investigation explores the nature of all things. It seeks to see to the bottom of things and is not meant to concern itself whether what actually happens is this or that. —It takes its rise, not from an interest in the facts of nature, nor from a need to grasp causal connexions; but from an urge to understand the basis, or essence, of everything empirical. Not, however as if to this end we had to hunt out new facts; it is, rather, of the essence of our investigation that we do not seek to learn anything *new* by it. We want to *understand* something that is already in plain view. For *this* is what we seem in some sense not to understand. . . .

We feel as if we had to *penetrate* phenomena: our investigation, however, is directed not towards phenomena, but, as one might say, towards the *possibilities* of phenomena. . . .

[Thus] it may come to look as if there were something like a final analysis of our forms of language, and so a *single* completely resolved form of every expression. That is, as if our usual forms of expression were, essentially, unanalysed; as if there were something hidden in them that had to be brought to light. When this is done the expression is completely clarified and our problem solved.

It can also be put like this: we eliminate misunderstandings by making our expressions more exact; but now it may look as if we were moving toward a particular state, a state of complete exactness; and as if this were the real goal of our investigation. . . .

Thought is surrounded by a halo. —Its essence, logic, presents an order, in fact the a priori order of the world: that is, the order of *possibilities*, which must be common to both world and thought. But this order, it seems, must be *utterly simple*. It is *prior* to all experience, must run through all experience;

> no empirical cloudiness or uncertainty can be allowed to affect it. —It must rather be of the purest crystal. . . .
>
> We are under the illusion that what is peculiar, profound, essential, in our investigation, resides in its trying to grasp the incomparable essence of language. That is, the order existing between the concepts of proposition, word, proof, truth, experience, and so on. This order is a *super*-order be-tween—so to speak—*super*-concepts. Whereas, of course, if the words "lan-guage," "experience," "world," have a use, it must be as humble a one as that of the words "table," "lamp," "door." [c]

This placement of a halo around thought, this etherialization of logic into a superscience, results directly from the seemingly innocent assumption that "there can't be any vagueness in logic." [d] And where did we get this idea? Those crystal-clear rules of thought that logicians are forever polishing were not *discovered* by them as a result of any study of thought processes; they slipped unnoticed into the logicians' investigations at the outset as a requirement, a demand, that the logicians themselves imposed on their own investigations. Thus the assumption that there cannot be any vagueness in logic is but another reflection of the philosophical need for precision and exactness.

> The more narrowly we examine actual language, the sharper becomes the conflict between it and our requirement. (For crystalline purity of logic was, of course, not a *result of investigation:* it was a requirement.) The conflict becomes intolerable; the requirement is now in danger of becoming empty. —We have got on to slippery ice where there is no friction and so in a certain sense the conditions are ideal, but also, just because of that, we are unable to walk. We want to walk: so we need *friction.* Back to the rough ground!
>
> We see that what we call "sentence" and "language" have not the formal unity that I imagined, but are families of structures more or less related to one another. —But what becomes of logic now? Its rigour seems to be giving way here. —But in that case doesn't logic altogether disappear? —For how can it lose its rigour? Of course not by our bargaining any of its rigour out of it. —The *preconceived idea* of crystalline purity can only be removed by turning our whole examination round. (One might say: the axis of reference of our examination must be rotated, but about the fixed point of our real need.) [e]

Thus Wittgenstein proposed a radical reform of logic: The purpose of logic was no longer to attempt to *correct* everyday language but to *understand* how everyday language functions. In a word, he proposed as the model for logic what he was doing in the *Investigations,* not the sort of analysis Russell had done, or that he himself had done in the *Tractatus.* This is what he meant by the rotation of the axis. Wittgenstein's contention was that everyday language is good enough for everyday purposes. Implicit in this position is a survival-of-the-fittest notion: Everyday language would not have survived if it did not perform the functions for which it was introduced. In Wittgenstein's view we do not need a "sublimed" logic for everyday purposes. Nor do we need a sublimed logic to clear up the special philosophical problems that plague us. To dissolve *these* problems we need only to understand how everyday language actually functions, for it is our misunderstanding of how it functions that has created the problems.

> We must do away with all *explanation*, and description alone must take its place. And this description gets its light, that is to say its purpose—from the philosophical problems. These are, of course, not empirical problems; they are solved, rather, by looking into the workings of our language, and that in such a way as to make us realize these workings: *in despite of* an urge to misunderstand them. The problems are solved, not by giving new information, but by arranging what we have always known. Philosophy is a battle against the bewitchment of our intelligence by means of language.[f]

Examples of How Philosophical Problems Are Dissolved

THE MIND-BODY PROBLEM

The mind-body problem is another typical philosophical puzzle that Wittgenstein undertook to dissolve. It is, in fact, a whole nest of puzzles. For instance, when I will to move my finger and it moves, how does my mind bring about this movement of my body on command? What sorts of processes, or mental states, are intending, hoping, expecting, imagining? What, in general, is the nature of thought, and how is thought related to the brain state that "causes" it or (possibly) that is "correlated" with it? Since my experiences (my psychic life) are private to me and inaccessible to others, how can anyone else ever know what I am experiencing—for instance, what my pain is like? And how can I know this about others?

Descartes' dual-substance theory, which dominated philosophy during most of the early modern period, made these questions wholly unanswerable. If there are two completely independent sorts of substances—minds and bodies—how can they interact? How can an entity that is nonmaterial (mind) cause changes in an entity that is material and that moves only on contact (body)? How can a change in body cause a change in mental state? That is, how does it happen that such a psychic event as seeing a red color-patch occurs as a result of some change in the physical condition of the cortex, a change itself caused by light waves impinging on the retina and thus setting up a movement along the optic nerve?

Hume reported that, even after careful introspection, he could observe no mental states. This was correct, but it did not occur to him that mental states are not the sort of things that can be looked for. Had such a thought occurred to him, he might have been led to a new start. Instead, he argued that there are no mental states, which was merely to reach a sceptical conclusion. Kant too attacked the Cartesian formula; he argued that we should think of mind and body as functions, not as independently existing substances. This was a more fruitful approach, but Kant and his successors still thought in terms of the Cartesian question, "What sort of things, or processes, must mind and body *be*, for thoughts and acts of will to occur?" They simply gave a more sophisticated answer than did Descartes.

Wittgenstein regarded this whole approach as a blind alley. His own approach was, characteristically, linguistic. Instead of asking, "What is thinking? What is willing?" he asked, "How are words like 'thinking' and 'willing' actually used in everyday circumstances?" He held that, because we have misunderstood the nature of language, our thoughts about thinking are guided by misleading models. It is these models that have created the mind-body problem, and once we have managed to free ourselves from these models—by coming to understand the nature of language—the problem dissolves.

The root difficulty, according to Wittgenstein, is that we slip into supposing that thinking is some sort of special state (mental, psychic, or spiritual) that accompanies speech but is distinct from it and may occur independently (that is, in the absence of speech, when we think silently or "to ourselves"). The picture theory of meaning is responsible for our belief in mental states, as it is responsible for our belief in real universals, and for the same reason. Just as we suppose there is some specific entity named by "horse," which cannot be any of the particular horses named by "Bucephalus," "Dobbin," or "Swaps," so we suppose that there is some specific activity that always occurs whenever we correctly affirm that we are thinking.

> Because we cannot specify any *one* bodily action which we call pointing to the shape (as opposed, for example, to the colour), we say that a spiritual [mental, intellectual] activity corresponds to these words.
> Where our language suggests a body and there is none: there, we should like to say, is a *spirit*. . . .[g]

Once the notion occurs to us that there is something (a spiritual activity) named by "thinking" (and of course other things named by "intending," "hoping," and imagining"), we expect to be able to observe these processes. But realizing that they are very special and move very swiftly, we think we must catch them on the run, much as if we were astronomers who have to set up a telescope just so in order to see a meteor as it flashes past. To make these assumptions, Wittgenstein held, is to enter the path that leads to a Humian type of scepticism.

> Here it is easy to get into that dead-end in philosophy, where one believes that the difficulty of the task consists in this: our having to describe phenomena that are hard to get hold of, the present experience that slips quickly by, or something of the kind. Where we find ordinary language too crude, and it looks as if we were having to do not with the phenomena of every-day, but with ones that [as Augustine said] "easily elude us, and, in their coming to be and passing away, produce those others as an average effect." [h]

It might seem from such passages as these that Wittgenstein was a kind of crypto-behaviorist—that given the belief that "an 'inner process' stands in need of outward criteria" [i] the next logical step would be to deny that an inner process, which cannot be observed, ever occurs. But behaviorism is a metaphysical position. The behaviorist starts from the basic Cartesian dichotomy between mind and body, and because he eliminates mind he concludes that body alone is real. In contrast, Wittgenstein rejected the dichotomy and with it the metaphysical question of whether minds or bodies (or both) are real.

> "But you surely cannot deny that, for example, in remembering, an inner process takes place." —What gives the impression that we want to deny anything? . . .
>
> Why should I deny that there is a mental process? But "There has just taken place in me the mental process of remembering. . . ." means nothing more than: "I have just remembered. . . ." To deny the mental process would mean to deny the remembering; to deny that anyone ever remembers anything.
>
> "Are you not really a behaviorist in disguise? Aren't you at bottom really saying that everything except human behavior is a fiction?" —If I do speak of a fiction, then it is of a *grammatical* fiction.
>
> How does the philosophical problem about mental processes and states and about behaviorism arise? —The first step is the one that altogether escapes notice. We talk of processes and states and leave their nature undecided. Sometime perhaps we shall know more about them—we think. But that is just what commits us to a particular way of looking at the matter. For we have a definite concept of what it means to learn to know a process better. (The decisive movement in the conjuring trick has been made, and it was the very one that we thought quite innocent.) . . .
>
> Try not to think of understanding as a "mental process" at all—for *that* is the expression which confuses you. But ask yourself: in what sort of case, in what kind of circumstances, do we say, "Now I know how to go on." . . .[j]

Instead of allowing himself to become involved in a sterile debate over whether minds and mental states are real, Wittgenstein examined the circumstances in which people have occasion to use words that may seem to designate mental states. He held that if we look closely at these occasions we find that the expressions used have perfectly straightforward, everyday meanings that do not involve any metaphysical issues at all. It is essential to remember that "we are not analysing a phenomenon (e.g., thought) but a concept (e.g., that of thinking), and therefore the use of a word." [k]

Under what circumstances would I say, for instance, that I was thinking about what time it was? Well, first, under what circumstances would I *not* say that I was thinking about what time it was? Suppose "I read this question in some narrative, or quote it as someone else's utterance." Or suppose I am "practicing the pronounciation of these words." In such circumstances I would not say that I was thinking about what time it was. On the other hand, I *would* say I was thinking of what time it was if "I was thinking about my breakfast and wondering whether it would be late today."[1]

The context in which I use the term "thinking" (and conversely, the context in which I do not use the term) reveals what I mean when I ascribe (or refuse to ascribe) thought to people. It turns out that we use the term in different circumstances and hence that thinking is a matter of family resemblance. This throws a new light on Wittgenstein's remark that inner processes need outward criteria. The point is that a mental state gets whatever specific character it has—as a thought or a feeling, a hope or a fear, an intention or an expectation—because of the context in which it occurs.

> Could someone have a feeling of ardent love or hope for the space of one second—*no matter what* preceded or followed this second? —What is happening now has significance—in these surroundings. The surroundings give it its importance. And the word "hope" refers to a phenomenon of human life. (A smiling mouth *smiles* only in a human face.)
>
> Now suppose I sit in my room and hope that N.N. will come and bring me some money, and suppose one minute of this state could be isolated, cut out of its context; would what happened in it then not be hope? —Think, for example, of the words which you perhaps utter in this space of time. They are no longer part of this language. And in different surroundings the institution of money doesn't exist either.
>
> A coronation is the picture of pomp and dignity. Cut one minute of this proceeding out of its surroundings: the crown is being placed on the head of the king in his coronation robes. —But in different surroundings gold is the cheapest of metals, its gleam is thought vulgar. There the fabric of the robe is cheap to produce. A crown is a parody of a respectable hat. And so on.[m]

Hence, when we hear an individual use such an expression as "I hope he'll come" or "I wonder what time it is" we have to look to the rest of his behavior: "The point is: what led up to these words?"[n] That is, we must look to the circumstances in which the words were used. Depending on the circumstances, we may ascribe thought to the individual (or hope, or expectation). Or we may conclude that he is not thinking but merely saying the words mechanically. To say that he is thinking is to say that a whole characteristic pattern of action is going forward—including, but not limited to, certain verbal expressions. That is why we do not ascribe thought to parrots or to gramophones (though they "talk"): Their behavior lacks this characteristic pattern of action. And that pattern—not just an isolated psychic occurrence—is what we *mean* by "thought." Thus the metaphysical question (What is thought? What is mind?) is dissolved. We are left only with such straightforward empirical questions as "Was he thinking or was he just speaking mechanically?" Questions of this type, of course, are answered by reference to "what he tells us and the rest of his behavior."[o]

VOLUNTARY ACTS

Similar considerations apply to the age-old problems clustering around the nature of voluntary acts and around the supposed inaccessibility and privacy of pains and other sensations. As regards the former, Wittgenstein maintained that instead of looking for (and of course failing to find) a psychic cause of a peculiar kind, we should look at the way in which we ourselves and other people use the word "willing" in everyday speech. Under what circumstances does one say, "I willed to raise my arm"? Under what circumstances does one say, "My arm rose"? The differences in circumstances—inner and outer—are the meaning of "willing." One of these differences, and therefore one of the criteria of whether a voluntary act has occurred, is the absence of surprise.

> Examine the following description of a voluntary action: "I form the decision to pull the bell at 5 o'clock, and when it strikes 5, my arm makes this movement." —Is that the correct description, and not *this* one: ". . . and when it strikes 5, I raise my arm"? . . .
>
> So one might say: voluntary movement is marked by the absence of surprise. And now I do not mean you to ask "But *why* isn't one surprised here?" [p]

Thus the "philosophical" problem about the nature of an act of will is dissolved by taking note of the circumstances in which people use words like "I decided" and the circumstances in which they do not use such words.

ARE SENSATIONS PRIVATE?

Philosophers have been puzzled for centuries about how we can know that other people feel pain and have other sensations. Their reasoning goes like this: Only I can know that I feel pain, for my pain is something that goes on inside me and is therefore inaccessible to anyone else. Other people's pain, if indeed they feel pain, is similarly private to them. I can therefore only surmise that they experience pain.

Wittgenstein used a number of strategies to dissolve this puzzlement. The first was simply to point out that if we use the word "know" in the everyday sense the situation is exactly reversed.

> If we are using the word "to know" as it is normally used (and how else are we to use it?), then other people very often know when I am in pain. —Yes, but all the same not with the certainty with which I know it myself! —It can't be said of me at all (except perhaps as a joke) that I *know* I am in pain. What is it supposed to mean—except perhaps that I *am* in pain?
>
> Other people cannot be said to learn of my sensations *only* from my behaviour, —for *I* cannot be said to learn of them. I *have* them. [q]

In a second argument Wittgenstein pointed out that if the situation were what philosophers say it is—if everyone knew only his own pain—it would be wholly irresponsible to infer anything at all about anyone else's experiences. It would be wildly speculative, for instance, for a physician to infer anything about his patient's condition from what the patient says about the pain he feels.

> Suppose everyone had a box with something in it: we call it a "beetle." No one can look into anyone else's box, and everyone says he knows what a beetle is only by looking at *his* beetle. —Here it would be quite possible for everyone to have something different in his box. One might even imagine such a thing constantly changing. —But suppose the word "beetle" had a use in these people's language? —If so it would not be used as the name of a thing. The thing in the box has no place in the language-game at all; not even as a *something:* for the box might even be empty. —No, one can "divide through" by the thing in the box; it cancels out, whatever it is.
>
> That is to say: if we construe the grammar of the expression of sensation on the model of "object and name" the object drops out of consideration as irrelevant.[r]

Wittgenstein's point is that if the philosophical doctrine of private sensations were right, the patient and his physician would be talking only about the word "pain"; they could not be discussing the patient's pain. Since everyone—not only the patient and his physician but even the philosophers themselves—believes he is discussing pain, not "pain," it follows that something is wrong with the doctrine in question.

Finally, Wittgenstein attacked the doctrine of privacy by arguing that the very notion of a private language in which a person talks about his private sensations is meaningless. Although this criticism of private languages is involved and has occasioned much debate, the main line of the argument is fairly straightforward. According to Wittgenstein, since language is a social game it requires more than one player. The notion of a rule is fundamental to language, and a *private* rule is meaningless.

> Why can't my right hand give my left hand money? —My right hand can put it into my left hand. My right hand can write a deed of gift and my left hand a receipt. —But the further practical consequences would not be those of a gift. When the left hand has taken the money from the right, etc., we shall ask: "Well, and what of it?" And the same could be asked if a person had given himself a private definition of a word; I mean, if he has said the word to himself and at the same time has directed his attention to a sensation.[s]

Wittgenstein's Place in Philosophy

In many respects Wittgenstein—not only the Wittgenstein of the *Tractatus* but also the Wittgenstein of the *Investigations*—was a continuator of the analytical tradition. This can be seen, for instance, in his conviction that linguistic confusions are chiefly responsible for philosophical puzzles. But in other respects Wittgenstein revolutionized this tradition. At some important points Wittgenstein was much closer to Dewey than to any of the analytical philosophers—in his instrumentalism, in his emphasis on use, in his insistence that meaning is relative to social context. At other points, Wittgenstein was close to Nietzsche. Like Nietzsche, he believed that philosophy is a form of therapy and that this therapy is successful when it brings us to the painful realization that what we have taken to be an account of the nature of the world is only and can be only an "interpretation."

Thus Wittgenstein did not say that the picture theory of meaning was *false*. He said that it was an interpretation that men have naïvely believed to be true: "A *picture* held us captive. And we could not get outside it, for it lay in our language and language seemed to repeat it to us inexorably." [t] Note that the illusion here lay not merely in supposing that a particular picture represents reality. The illusion was far deeper: It lay in supposing that *any* picture represents, or could represent, reality. What held men captive was the picture of a picture, the belief that language mirrors reality. Thus Wittgenstein quoted the doctrine of the *Tractatus*—"The general form of propositions is: This is how things are"—and commented, "That is the kind of proposition that one repeats to oneself countless times. One thinks that one is tracing the outline of the thing's nature over and over again, and one is merely tracing round the frame through which we look at it." [u]

There are many such "frames," each embedded in a particular language. The ideal of exactness is one. This is why it is so difficult to rid ourselves of the conviction that "there can't be any vagueness in logic." "The ideal, as we think of it, is unshakable. You can never get outside it; you must always turn back. There is no outside; outside you cannot breathe. —Where does this idea come from? It is like a pair of glasses on our nose through which we see whatever we look at. It never occurs to us to take them off." [v]

Thus, like Nietzsche, Wittgenstein was far more radically antimetaphysical than were even such antimetaphysical philosophers as Bergson, Russell, and Dewey; the whole history of philosophy since Descartes can be viewed as a progressive erosion of the domain that philosophers have been willing to allot to metaphysics. Kant denied that we can know what ultimate reality is; but he took it for granted that we can at least know that "things-in-themselves" exist. Schopenhauer and Bergson, who maintained that ultimate reality is inaccessible to reason, thought that in intuition we know it to be will. Though Russell and the positivists curtailed the sphere of metaphysics still further, they held that by a rigorous logical analysis we can get back to "hard data." Even Dewey, despite his instrumentalism, worked out a doctrine of experience that he held to be a correct account of how things are. All these thinkers belonged to the major tradition in holding that philosophy is a cognitive enterprise—that its goal is to ascertain the truth about the universe, even though, in contrast to such earlier thinkers as Descartes and Aristotle, they believed there was little to be ascertained.

In conceiving of philosophy as a therapeutic rather than a cognitive enterprise, Nietzsche and Wittgenstein made a profound shift in orientation. For such thinkers, the existential problem comes to the fore: Men must learn to live in a world in which God is dead; they must learn to get along without Truth, or rather, they must learn to live with the one truth that there is no Truth. This means that, for Wittgenstein as well as for Nietzsche, philosophy was an intensely serious matter: It was not something one "does," in the way in which one might "take up" painting or bird-watching. Indeed, Wittgenstein was as passionately committed to philosophy as Kierkegaard was to God. In the *Investigations* he addressed his pupils as individuals. Though his rhetoric was certainly different from Kierkegaard's or Nietzsche's, he too aimed at edification. He wanted desperately to "cure" his pupils, to convert them, to save them from the "deep inquietudes" [w] from which they—and, it would seem, he too—suffered.

But Wittgenstein and Nietzsche differed in temperament. Nietzsche had certainly experienced "deep inquietudes," but he had seemingly overcome them: He had bitten the head of the snake that had bitten him. Wittgenstein, it would seem, did not accomplish this. Unlike Nietzsche, he could not wave away with a cavalier gesture the paradox of the truth that there is no Truth.[24] Yet neither could he make Kierkegaard's leap of faith. As a result paradox haunts the pages of the *Investigations*. For instance, by making us aware of how language functions, therapy calls our attention to the glasses on our nose. Or, in terms of the picture metaphor, we suddenly see the "frame" and realize that we have been looking only at the picture, not at the landscape itself. But do we ever get an unimpeded view of the landscape? No; all views have frames around them; all views are through glasses. How, then, can we be sure that there is a landscape out there? Nietzsche avoided this difficulty by maintaining that we do not really *need* the notion of a landscape out there; he was quite willing to abandon the idea of an "inaccessible original" and got on satisfactorily with interpretations of interpretations. It is not clear, however, that Wittgenstein was willing to take this step.

FORMS OF LIFE

Consider, for instance, his remarkable—and remarkably Nietzschian—insight that "to imagine a language is to imagine a form of life." [x] Every language, that is, condenses and expresses some social group's characteristic way of doing things, of accomplishing its aims. From the group's language it is possible to "read back" to this mode of life, this way of organizing and carrying out the daily routine. In talking about forms of life Wittgenstein was doubtless thinking primarily about everyday practices like buying apples, constructing buildings and weighing cheese, rather than about world views and value systems. There is no reason, however, why his view of the relation between a language and a form of life

24 See pp. 247–48.

cannot be extended (as Nietzsche extended the notion of interpretation) to differences between cultures—say, to the difference between the Hopi language and "standard, average European." But—this is the present point—cultural (or linguistic) relativism is implicit in the concept of forms of life, whether this be understood narrowly or more broadly. The relativism only becomes more noticeable as forms of life diverge.

Agreements and disagreements that occur *within* a given form of life are not merely expressions of opinion; procedures for distinguishing the true from the false have been established in this form of life and are specified in its language. "'So you are saying that human agreement decides what is true and what is false?'—It is what human beings *say* that is true and false; and they agree in the *language* they use. That is not agreement in opinions but in form of life." [y] But what about disagreements *across* forms of life? Suppose that what is true in one form of life is false in another? What procedures exist to resolve such a conflict? "What has to be accepted, the given, is—so one could say—*forms of life.*" [z] Is it possible to get beyond these given divergencies? This, of course, is where therapy is supposed to come in. Therapy can show us that our conflict is not simply a disagreement about the facts; it is a disagreement about facts-through-frames. If I see a green color-patch where you see a red one, the situation looks hopeless until we suddenly realize that each of us is wearing glasses—your glasses have red lenses and mine have green. Therapy, that is, will show me that I am in my fly-bottle and that you are in yours. But will therapy get us out of our fly-bottles and into a common world? *Can* it get us into a common world, or does it only get us into still another fly-bottle? The *Investigations* leaves this question unanswered.

This difficulty can be put in another way in order to bring out the paradox more forcefully. Wittgenstein's whole method of dissolving philosophical problems consisted in referring back to everyday language. His procedure, he said, was "to bring words [for example, such words as "thinking"] back from their metaphysical use to their everyday use." [a] To talk about everyday language in this way is to suggest that its use leads us into the common world outside of all metaphysical fly-bottles. Now, people who use a language in common (whether everyday or not) will doubtless live in *a* common world—the world of their form of life. But it is not *the* common world; it is common only to the users of this language. Thus everyday language is just another "frame." And worse than that, everyday language is not *one* language; it is a whole family of languages—and of forms of life. Finally, is not Wittgenstein's own language a language, and hence still another "frame"?

Or consider Wittgenstein's view of philosophy as a ladder that we can eventually leave behind. It is easy to understand why he wanted to leave the ladder behind, for in that way one gets rid of the embarrassing frame. But leaving the ladder implies a "complete" cure, and the notion of a complete cure is another frame—very similar, indeed, to the frame of exactness that Wittgenstein himself had exposed. The goal of "complete clarity" (that is, of being freed from fly-bottles) is a survival in the *Investigations* of one of the analytical tradition's deepest convictions—the belief that the end result of linguistic analysis is Truth.

The vestiges of the view of the *Tractatus* survive at many points in the *Investigations*, as in this striking metaphor:

> Where does our investigation get its importance from, since it seems only to destroy everything interesting, that is, all that is great and important? (As it were all the buildings, leaving behind only bits of stone and rubble.) What we are destroying is nothing but houses of cards and we are clearing up the ground of language on which they stand.[b]

The suggestion here is that the inquiries undertaken in the *Investigations* were merely preparatory: Wittgenstein's intent was to demolish all old buildings (false metaphysical theories) in order to provide a secure site for a new and permanent structure (the true theory). This is all very different from a ladder that disappears. Moreover, the procedure by which the old buildings are demolished actually reveals that *all* buildings, new as well as old, are houses made of cards; the bitter truth—carefully avoided in this passage—is that there exist only "bits of stone and rubble."

Thus there is an unresolved tension between the goal of therapy, as inherited from the *Tractatus* and its analytical forebears, and the new method of therapy, as worked out in the *Investigations*. Perhaps the deepest of Wittgenstein's disquietudes arose from this tension. If so, this is a disquietude that Western culture as a whole seems to share.

CHAPTER 9

The Phenomenological Tradition: Husserl and Sartre

The Phenomenological Tradition
Contrasted with the Analytical Tradition

The reader who has just finished the chapter on the analytical tradition will have the sensation in turning to this chapter of entering a different world—a world of pure intuitions, apodeictic certainties, and transcendental egos. But though the world of phenomenology looks very different—indeed, *is* very different—from the sparsely populated world of the analytical tradition, with its hard data and its neutral stuff, some future historian, looking at these two movements from the perspective of several centuries, may well discern more similarities than differences. Just as the disputes between the Stoics and the Epicureans appear to us, from the distance of two thousand years, to have been conducted within the basic framework of post-Aristotelianism and to reflect the profound cultural changes that were occurring in the late classical world, so we may safely hazard the prediction that the historian of the future will view the analytical tradition and the phenomenological tradition as variants of the same basically post-Kantian themes—variants that reflect the great shifts in the patterns of thought and feeling that occurred early in the twentieth century.

Both movements are post-Kantian, not merely in the literal sense that they occurred "after Kant," but in the deeper sense that they started from Kant's distinction between noumena and phenomena, between things as they are in themselves and things as they appear in (or to) consciousness, and developed within this framework. For instance, since both traditions wholly rejected Kant's things-in-themselves (on the grounds that the notion of something that is by definition unknowable is meaningless), they were left not simply with things, which was the pre-Kantian position, but with things-for-consciousness. This position was quite different from the pre-Kantian view, for it required that consciousness be taken account of. Despite major differences in *how* the two traditions dealt with consciousness, they were basically similar in that both developed with a Kantian, "things-for-consciousness" orientation.

The traditions were also similar in that each wanted to eliminate the traces of Cartesian dualism that had somehow survived two centuries of criticism; both thought they were freeing philosophy from unverifiable speculation and bringing it back to the plain facts. Both movements believed that there are public, verifiable truths the human mind can come to know and that the primary business of philosophy is to disclose what these truths are. Both believed that when the false preconceptions that distort our vision are removed and the mind is brought into a right relation to these truths, they will "stand out" for all to see. To put this differently, both the analytical tradition and the phenomenological tradition claimed to be antimetaphysical and empirical in outlook—though they differed, of course, about what "being empirical" consists in and each (rightly) held that the other's claim to be free of assumptions was unjustified.

Thus both movements were reacting against the constructivism and relativism that, as it seemed to them, had "infected" nineteenth- and twentieth-century culture. Here again the starting point was Kantian. Kant had held that the experiential world, including the empirical self, consists in "representations" ordered in accordance with twelve a priori rules and two a priori forms of sensibility. Since Kant believed he had established that these "syntheses" were necessary types of ordering for all human minds, he held the phenomenal world to be public and objective: For even though it is "for" consciousness, all consciousnesses construct it according to the same rules. But how much of what is for consciousness is thus objective? Is the public world a world of "things" or a world of sense data? On this question Kant wobbled—there is a subjectivist as well as an objectivist strain in his *Critique*[1]—and this indecision was inherited by his successors.

1 See pp. 48–49.

Hegel and the Hegelians developed Kantianism in a way that increasingly emphasized the constructivist side of Kant's thought. Mind, they maintained, has a history; it passes through a succession of developmental levels. To each of these levels there corresponds a particular kind of world—the experiential world that is "for" consciousness at this level. Like Kant, Hegel was not thinking in terms of individual minds and their idiosyncracies. The experiential world that is constructed by mind at any particular level is objective and public at that level. Further, though there is a plurality of these experiential worlds, they are arranged in an objective order and each successive level includes, while it transcends, the levels below it. Thus Hegel himself was far from being a relativist or a subjectivist, at least in intent.

But to many philosophers it seemed that constructivism was a camel that could not be stopped once it was allowed to poke its nose inside the philosophical tent. The subsequent course of philosophical thought in the nineteenth and early twentieth centuries seemed to bear this out: Kierkegaard, Nietzsche, and Dewey each in his own way undermined the traditional claims to objective knowledge. Hence there was a natural reaction against constructivism in favor of "realism." For most philosophers, however, it was unthinkable to return to the easy, "pre-critical" realism of Scholasticism or Cartesianism. Kant had made this impossible, and the revival of realism was therefore largely conducted within the framework of his distinction between things-in-themselves and phenomena. Those who did not want to claim a direct, special form of access to things-in-themselves (for instance, access via Schopenhauer's intuition) had to find an objectively real world in the realm of Kantian phenomena.

But how was this to be done? Brentano's[2] psychological studies seemed to provide a clue. Brentano's approach to psychology was not genetic or physiological, but descriptive. However, instead of describing consciousness as consisting in "ideas" or "representations," he described it as intentional in nature. Consciousness, he held, is a direction, not a state: Every act of consciousness "points towards an object." The old description of consciousness as consisting in mental states, or ideas of objects, was a survival of Cartesianism, and it had caused many difficulties for philosophers. For instance, how can we ever know that the mental representations of which we are aware correspond to the objects of which they are alleged to be the representations? Brentano's way of describing consciousness freed philosophy from such epistemological puzzles: To be conscious of a desk is not to contemplate a private, inner representation of the desk; it is simply to be directed toward the desk, to "intend" the desk.

More important in the present connection is the fact that Brentano's view suggested to those opposed to constructivism a way of escaping from the subjectivist strain in Kant's view. If consciousness is a direction rather than a psychic

---

2 Franz Brentano (1838–1917) was a Catholic priest for nearly ten years but resigned his priesthood because he refused to accept some of the fundamental dogmas of the Church. He taught at Würzburg and at Vienna, but his independence of mind cost him both posts, and he spent the last twenty years of his life in Italy and Switzerland. His lectures on "descriptive psychology" were given at Vienna in 1888–89.

state, it does not construct its object; it merely discloses, or displays, it. Hence it seemed possible to agree with Kant that human experience is limited to phenomena (that is, to things-for-consciousness) while denying that the objects thus experienced are constructs. This was a starting point for the phenomenologists, as well as for the analytical philosophers.[3] But if the analysts and the phenomenologists thus not only had similar anticonstructivist motives but also shared the same starting point, how did they come to diverge so radically?

First of all, the whole orientation of the traditions differed. The analysts found British empiricism, especially Hume, congenial. When they asked what the objects of consciousness are, they naturally thought of Hume's impressions, though of course, thanks to Brentano's insight, these impressions were no longer regarded as mental states; they were held to be "neutral stuff" toward which consciousness is directed. That part of Brentano's view that appealed to the analysts was the notion that consciousness is transparent; indeed, to them it was so transparent that they in effect passed through it and fixed their attention exclusively on its objects.

The phenomenologists, for their part, thought of Hegel, not Hume. They believed that Hegel had not realized that consciousness is intentional. Since it seemed to them that he had missed its essential nature, they proposed (and this, of course, was why they called themselves "phenomenologists") to make an improved study of consciousness—to do better than Hegel what Hegel had sought to do. For this reason alone it is obvious that the paths taken by the analytical tradition and by the phenomenological tradition had to diverge: The former regarded the intentionality of consciousness as a reason for ignoring consciousness; the latter regarded this intentionality as a justification for concentrating on consciousness.

Second, the analytical philosophers believed (as has been seen) that each of the real entities of which the universe is composed is itself and not another thing. Since in their opinion explanation consists in the analysis of complexes into their parts, there must be—if completely satisfactory explanations are to be possible—encapsulated entities that are absolutely simple. (Here again Hume's "loose and separate" impressions were their model.) In contrast, the phenomenological philosophers were impressed by the interconnectedness of things—for them experience was a river, not a collection of "loose and separate" sense data.

Third, the analytical philosophers and the phenomenologists differed about the status of the world of everyday experience. The analytical philosophers

3 That the analytical philosophers found Brentano's realistic, anticonstructivist point of view congenial is evident from the care they took to extricate it from the metaphysical monstrosities it seemed at first sight to entail. If to be conscious is to be conscious of an object—if to think is to think about something, if to imagine is to imagine something, if to believe is to believe something—it seems to follow that there must be nonexistent, unreal, fantastic, and false entities to serve as the objects of such intentional acts as lying, fantasizing, imagining, and so on. Because the analytical philosophers took Brentano's account of consciousness seriously, it seemed important to them to show, by means of a logical analysis, that adopting this view did not require them to attribute "subsistence" to (say) that king of France whose nonexistence one happens now to be thinking of. See p. 339.

recognized that there is a puzzle about the relation between the world that physics discloses and the world of ordinary perception—the world of shoes, ships, and cabbages that even physicists encounter in their daily round. But they thought this puzzle could be disposed of by a properly rigorous linguistic analysis. For the most part they were epistemologists and they were not much interested (apparently) in man's existential, or moral, relation to the aseptic world disclosed by physics. Thus Russell held that "when we assert that this or that has 'value', we are giving expression to our own emotions."[4] The phenomenologists were unwilling to write off as "subjective" the experiential world of lovely, hateful, enduring, and transitory things; hence they took their stand on this experiential world—our "life-world," as they called it. In this respect, they were very close to Whitehead. Like him they rejected that bifurcation of nature to which, it seemed, physics had committed modern culture.[5] They shared with Whitehead the sense, so vividly expressed by the Romantic poets, that all things are "interfused" together. Had the phenomenologists read Wordsworth, they would have noted with approval his

> . . . observation of affinities
> In objects where no brotherhood exists
> To passive minds. . . .[a]

For, like him, they

> . . . felt the sentiment of Being spread
> O'er all that moves and all that seemeth still;
> O'er all that, lost beyond the reach of thought
> And human knowledge, to the human eye
> Invisible, yet liveth to the heart;
> O'er all that leaps and runs, and shouts and sings,
> Or beats the gladsome air; o'er all that glides
> Beneath the wave, yea, in the wave itself,
> And mighty depth of waters.[b]

The phenomenologists, that is, shared Wordsworth's sense of the presence in everything of everything else, his feeling that into every here and now are synthesized not only past experiences but anticipated future ones. The phenomenologists believed philosophy should, and could, take account of all this ambience—not merely reduce it to the association of disconnected simples.

To mention a final reason for the radical differences between the phenomenological movement and the analytical movement, the approach of the analytical philosophers was, for reasons already described, primarily linguistic; the approach of the phenomenologists was not. Both movements believed there is a barrier between our minds and things and that it is the business of philosophy to over-

4 See p. 350.
5 See pp. 318–19.

come this barrier. For the analytical philosophers the barrier was sloppy language; hence they focused their attention on clarifying linguistic muddles and confusions. As their standards for clarity became higher, their philosophical language became more sparse, precise, and exact. For the phenomenologists the barrier consisted not in language but in preconceptions—such as the atomistic preconception that dominated much of the thinking of the earlier analytical philosophers. Thus clarity was their aim too, but this was to be achieved by looking at things directly, instead of indirectly through a pair of philosophical spectacles. They felt no particular need to prune language; indeed, their method actually encouraged it to flourish. Their effort to describe the unusual and surprising things they encountered when they *did* succeed in looking at things directly, led them to introduce an increasingly elaborate terminology that repulses philosophers who have experienced Wittgensteinian therapy.

This divergence in attitude toward language and linguistic precision was one of the most obvious differences between the phenomenologists and the analytical philosophers. Their mutual hostility on this account is understandable but unfortunate, since at many points the interests of phenomenology and those of analytical philosophy coincide, and each tradition is a counterfoil to the excesses of the other.

In this chapter two philosophers are presented as representative of the phenomenological tradition. The first is Husserl, who as the founding father of the movement occupied a place even more prominent than that of Russell in the analytical tradition. The second is Sartre, who started out with a fundamentally phenomenological orientation and then modified it in order to accommodate it to his existentialist interests; in doing so Sartre participated in a revolution in phenomenology analogous to, if not so profound as, Wittgenstein's impact on the analytical tradition.

Husserl

The animating force in Husserl's[6] life and thought was a deep need for certainty. In 1906 he wrote in his diary, "I have been through enough torments from lack of clarity and from doubt that wavers back and forth. . . . Only one need absorbs

6 Edmund Husserl (1859–1938) was born in Czechoslovakian Moravia, at that time a part of the Austrian empire. He studied mathematics, physics, and astronomy at the universities of Leipzig, Berlin, and Vienna and wrote his dissertation on the calculus of variations. From early on, however, he was interested in philosophy, and, abandoning his plans to be a teacher of science, he returned to Vienna in 1884 to attend Brentano's lectures (see p. 388, note 3) and to finish his education in philosophy. Subsequently, Husserl taught at Halle, Göttingen, and Freiburg. His production was immense, especially after his retirement in 1928. Though much of his work has been published, even more remains in manuscript—as much as 45,000 pages in the shorthand that Husserl used. All this material is preserved in the Husserl Archives in Louvain and is carefully supervised by faithful disciples.

me: I must win clarity, else I cannot live; I cannot bear life unless I can believe that I shall achieve it."c It was this passion that led Husserl from mathematics to logic and from logic to philosophy, always in search of absolutely secure foundations.

Attitudes toward the quest for certainty vary; indeed, they constitute a major parting of the ways in contemporary culture. Kierkegaard, for instance, fully shared Husserl's passion for certainty; but unlike Husserl he was convinced that men cannot attain certainty by their own efforts. The best that men are capable of, according to Kierkegaard, is an approximation process, and the end result of such a process is as far from certainty as is total ignorance. Hence his leap of faith. Another possible attitude is Dewey's. He was quite satisfied with approximation processes, since he believed they yield all that a man can reasonably ask for—continually improved conditions of life. He held that the quest for certainty is a symptom of a mild neurosis. And there is Nietzsche, who did not believe even in the possibility of approximation processes. He regarded the belief that the truth can be gradually approximated as itself a symptom of neurosis, and he held that the capacity to *enjoy* uncertainty (in distinction from merely accepting it, as with Dewey) is a sign of strength, an expression of man's will to power.

It is interesting in this connection to contrast Husserl's and Nietzsche's use of the same metaphor. In his *Cartesian Meditations* Husserl likened his position to Descartes', pointing out that both he and Descartes not only sought certainty but also found it in the transcendental ego. Unfortunately, however, Descartes went wrong by misinterpreting the transcendental ego.[7] Correct interpretation of the transcendental ego is, then, the critical stage in the quest for certainty:

> When making certain of the transcendental ego, we are standing at an altogether dangerous point, . . . it is as though we were on the brink of a precipice, where advancing calmly and surely is a matter of philosophical life and death. . . . [Descartes stood] on the threshold of the greatest of all discoveries . . . yet . . . he [did] not pass through the gateway that leads into genuine transcendental philosophy.d

Nietzsche too once represented himself as standing at a gateway.[8] But the name of Nietzsche's gateway was "Moment"; and far from passing through to rest on the other side in indubitable certainty, he passed through only to continue forever the path on which he had already been traveling forever. Nietzsche had abandoned the notion of "advance," as well as the notion of "end," as an illusion. Both he and Husserl were aware of precipices, but whereas Nietzsche rejoiced in them, Husserl hoped to get beyond the danger point as quickly as possible—as if, from Nietzsche's point of view, there were a "beyond the danger point."

---

7 For a discussion of the transcendental ego and Descartes' mistake, see pp. 405–09. Here the point is simply to see the difference between Husserl's attitude and Nietzsche's, and for this an understanding of the details of Husserl's doctrine is not necessary.

8 See pp. 254–55.

Every reader's own attitude toward certainty will probably determine his overall assessment of Husserl's version of phenomenology. Those who agree with Dewey and Nietzsche that the quest for certainty is illusory will perceive Husserl's elaborate investigations as a complicated exercise in self-deception. Those who hold, with Kierkegaard, that it is essential to confess that man is "always in the wrong" will view these same investigations as one more demonstration of the utter failure of "objectivity" and of the "speculative point of view." Such people might indeed allow that Husserl's phenomenological method could make useful contributions to psychology and to the social sciences, but only those who share his need for certainty and who also regard this quest as rational will sympathize with what Husserl himself took to be his main contribution to culture.

Criticism of Relativism

Before examining Husserl's account of his method, we should take a look at the case he made for the possibility of "universally valid truth." In an essay published in 1911 Husserl attacked both "the flood of positivism and pragmatism, which latter exceeds the former in its relativism," and historicism, that "romantic philosophy" that rejects "any belief whatever in an absolute philosophy" and offers instead "the relative justification of every philosophy in its own time."[e] The pragmatist argues that what is true is what works; but since what works at one time and in one context may not work at another time and in another context, the pragmatist's argument involves the admission that truth is relative. The historicist also holds that truth is relative—not to what works, but to social or cultural context. What does the historicist's argument amount to?

> He will point to changes in scientific views—how what is today accepted as a proved theory is recognized tomorrow as worthless, how some call certain things laws that others call mere hypotheses, and still others vague guesses, etc. [But] does that mean that in view of this constant change in scientific views we would actually have no right to speak of sciences as objectively valid unities instead of merely as cultural formations? [No; for] it is easy to see that historicism, if consistently carried through, carries over into extreme sceptical subjectivism. The ideas of truth, theory, and science would then, like all ideas, lose their absolute validity. . . . There would be no unqualified validity, or validity-in-itself, which is what it is even if no one has achieved it and though no historical humanity will ever achieve it. . . . It is not necessary to go further. . . . We shall certainly have said enough to obtain recognition that no matter what great difficulties the relation between a sort of fluid worth and objective validity, between science as a cultural phenomenon and science as a valid systematic theory, may offer an understanding concerned with clarifying them, the distinction and opposition must be

recognized. . . . The mathematician will not turn to historical science to be taught about the truth of mathematical theories. It will not occur to him to relate the historical development of mathematical representations with the question of truth. How, then, is it to be the historian's task to decide as to the truth of given philosophical systems and, above all, as to the very possibility of a philosophical science that is valid in itself? . . .

The unconditional affirmation that any scientific philosophy is a chimaera, based on the argument that the alleged efforts of millenia make probable the intrinsic impossibility of [any absolutely valid scientific] philosophy, is erroneous not merely because to draw a conclusion regarding an unlimited future from a few millenia of higher culture would not be a good induction, but erroneous as an absolute absurdity, like $2 \times 2 = 5$. And this for the indicated reason: if there is something there whose objective validity philosophical criticism can refute, then there is also an area within which something can be found as objectively valid. If problems have demonstrably been posed "awry," then it must be possible to rectify this and pose straight problems. If criticism proves that philosophy in its historical growth has operated with confused concepts, has been guilty of mixed concepts and specious conclusions, then if one does not wish to fall into nonsense, that very fact makes it undeniable that, ideally speaking, the concepts are capable of being pointed, clarified, distinguished, that in the given area correct conclusions can be drawn. Any correct, profoundly penetrating criticism itself provides means for advancing and ideally points to correct goals, thereby indicating an objectively valid science.[f]

The arguments presented in this passage are of very different worth. As regards the contention that historical evidence cannot establish that any particular theory T is false, this seems correct. Historical evidence can establish, for instance, that during some particular period of time P_1 people disbelieved T, that during a subsequent period P_2 they believed T, and that during another period P_3 they again disbelieved T. But since no one—not even that "flood of positivists and pragmatists"—equates "T is false" simply with "People disbelieved T at P_1," historical evidence does not show that theories are false. This distinction clearly is important, for people often become muddled about what the "historical argument" shows.

Husserl was also correct in pointing out that an inductive argument that runs from past failures to prospective future failures does not yield the absolutely certain conclusion that there is no absolutely certain truth—for no inductive argument yields more than probability. But past failures (coupled with historical evidence about the special psychological and sociological factors that make T persuasive at P_2) can make this conclusion probable—which is all that most positivists and pragmatists would want to maintain.

But what about the argument that anyone who denies the possibility of absolute truth is involved in contradiction? Is it the case that anyone who criticizes a claim must logically allow the existence of "an objectively valid science"? It is not difficult to reconstruct how Dewey or Nietzsche would have dealt with this contention. They would have looked for the need being expressed in Husserl's rather emotional affirmation of absolute validity. Approaching the matter from a psychological, or even psychoanalytical, point of view, they would have maintained that, appearances to the contrary, Husserl's talk about an "absolutely objective science" was not actually talk about an absolutely objective science, in the way that talk about Bucephalus is presumably talk about Bucephalus. On the contrary, it was expressive or revelatory of Husserl's state of mind (in this case, his fear of uncertainty), in the same way that talk to the effect that "so-and-so is a dirty Red" is not a comment on so-and-so's political opinions but a reflection of the speaker's dislike or fear of so-and-so.

As for Wittgenstein, he would have characterized Husserl's whole discussion as nothing but another example of the "subliming" of logic.[9] He would have pointed out that criticism of an argument no more depends on there being an objectively valid science than criticism of a game of chess depends on there being an objectively valid set of rules for chess-playing—or than criticism of an ambiguous signpost depends on there being an absolutely unambiguous set of directions.

The Crisis of European Man

In addition to arguing that relativism is self-contradictory, Husserl maintained that it has deleterious social consequences. Writing in 1935, when the Nazis had been in power for two years, Husserl saw that Europe was in crisis, and he thought that the gradual decay of men's belief in rational certainty was responsible for that crisis. The revival of this belief therefore seemed to him essential.

Husserl's exposition of the belief in rational certainty led him back to the Greeks. The ideal of rational certainty was their discovery, and Europe's inheritance of it had unified Western culture for centuries. According to Husserl, what the Greeks had actually done was to anticipate the basic insight of phenomenology. The rehabilitation of the ideal of rational certainty could therefore be accomplished by returning to the phenomenological method, which the Greeks had only dimly understood, and perfecting it. For when phenomenology was perfected it would demonstrate that the quest for certainty was not in vain; it would do this by actually establishing a secure foundation for the sciences. Husserl's account of the Greek discovery may not be historically accurate, but it does at least throw light on his view of the nature of phenomenology and shows the context of values and of goals in which he developed his method.

What was it, then, that distinguished the Greeks' "overall orientation" toward the world from that of other peoples, not only primitive races but also "the wise Egyptians, Babylonians," and so on? Whereas the attitude of other groups was

9 See p. 373.

either practical or "mythico-religious," the Greek attitude was "theoretical"—the Greeks were curious about the world; they wanted to understand it.

> There is a sharp cleavage, then, between the universal but mythico-practical attitude and the "theoretical," which by every previous standard is unpractical, the attitude of *thaumazein* [Greek: to wonder], to which the great men of Greek philosophy's first culminating period, Plato and Aristotle, trace the origin of philosophy. Men are gripped by a passion for observing and knowing the world, a passion that turns from all practical interests and in the closed circle of its own knowing activities, in the time devoted to this sort of investigation, accomplishes and wants to accomplish only pure *theoria*. In other words, man becomes the disinterested spectator, overseer of the world, he becomes a philosopher. More than that, from this point forward his life gains a sensitivity for motives which are possible only to this attitude, for novel goals and methods of thought. . . .
>
> With an attitude such as this . . . there arises the distinction between the represented and the real world, and a new question is raised concerning the truth—not everyday truth bound as it is to tradition but a truth that . . . is identical and universally valid, a truth in itself.[g]

This description of the Greek attitude coincides completely with Dewey's.[10] But whereas Husserl praised the disinterested attitude and the spectator point of view, Dewey condemned them. Both philosophers agreed that the spread of this attitude, with the accompanying belief in a "universally valid truth," led in the course of time to "a transformation of human existence and of man's entire cultural life."[h] But whereas Dewey regarded this transformation as an unmitigated misfortune and wanted philosophy to adopt the methods of natural science and to turn to practical problems connected with our traffic with nature, Husserl held that it is the methods of natural science that are responsible for the "crisis of European man," and that the only hope for Europe was a revival of the disinterested attitude and a return to rationality "in that noble and genuine sense, the original Greek sense."[i]

THE RISE OF "NATURALISM"

The root of the crisis, Husserl thought, lay in the fact that the ideal of rationality, the ideal of disinterested theory, had gradually become identified with a set of assumptions that Husserl called "naturalism." Naturalism is the belief that "the extraordinary successes of natural knowledge are now to be extended to knowledge of the spirit."[j] This belief is understandable, for the natural sciences have had enormous success in their own field. Nevertheless, such an extension is an "aberration," because the least amount of attention given to psychic processes as they actually occur in experience (instances of willing, thinking, imagining, and the like) shows them to be utterly different in nature from the

10 See pp. 289–90.

material objects studied in physics. To extend the methods of natural science to the psychic life is to "objectivize" that life; it is to treat psychic processes as if they were material objects existing in the same public space and time as the bodies with which these processes are associated. Since rationality has quite mistakenly come to be associated with this extension and since (as Husserl pointed out) the consequences of the extension are grave, it is not surprising that rationality too has been attacked.

> With this [extension of the methods of the natural sciences to psychic processes] the interpretation of the world immediately takes on a predominantly dualistic, i.e., psychophysical form. The same causality—only split in two—embraces the one world; the sense of rational explanation is everywhere the same, but in such a way that all explanation of spirit,[11] in the only way in which it can be universal, involves the physical. There can be no pure, self-contained search for an explanation of the spiritual, no purely inner-oriented psychology or theory of spirit beginning with the ego in psychical self-experience and extending to the other psyche. The way that must be traveled is the external one, the path of physics and chemistry. . . . This objectivism or this psychophysical interpretation of the world, despite its seeming self-evidence, is a naive one-sidedness. . . . To speak of the spirit as [an] annex to bodies and having its supposedly spatiotemporal being within nature is an absurdity. . . .
>
> There are all sorts of problems that stem from naiveté, according to which objectivistic science holds what it calls the objective world to be the totality of what is, without paying any attention to the fact that no objective science can do justice to the subjectivity that achieves science. One who has been trained in the natural sciences finds it self-evident that whatever is merely subjective must be eliminated and that the method of natural science, formulated according to a subjective mode of representation, is objectively determined. By the same token, it is taken for granted that the subjective, eliminated by the physical scientist, is, precisely as psychic, to be investigated in psychophysical psychology. The investigator of nature, however, does not make it clear to himself that the constant foundation of his admittedly subjective thinking activity is the environing world of life. The latter is constantly presupposed as the basic working area, in which alone his questions and his methodology make sense. Where, at the present time, is that powerful bit of method that leads from the intuitive environing world to the idealizing of mathematics and its interpretation as objective being, subjected to criticism and clarification? Einstein's revolutionary changes concern the formulas wherein idealized and naively objectivized nature (*physis*) is treated. But regarding the question of how formulas or mathematical objectification in general are given a sense based on life and the intuitive environing world, of this we hear nothing. Thus Einstein does nothing to reformulate the space and time in which our actual life takes place.

11 [If "spirit" has any supernaturalistic or religious connotations for the reader, it is a bad translation of *Geist*, the rather vague term that Husserl used; "psychic" would be better—AUTHOR.]

Mathematical science of nature is a technical marvel for the purpose of accomplishing inductions whose fruitfulness, probability, exactitude, and calculability could previously not even be suspected. As an accomplishment it is a triumph of the human spirit. With regard to the rationality of its methods and theories, however, it is a thoroughly relative science. It presupposes as data principles that are themselves roughly lacking in actual rationality. Insofar as the intuitive environing world, purely subjective as it is, is forgotten in the scientific thematic, the working subject is also forgotten, and the scientist is not studied. . . .[k]

In the paragraphs just quoted, as well as in those that follow below, a number of theses can be distinguished. First, there is the contention that the natural sciences are uncritical. For instance, scientists have never so much as asked what sort of entity a spatiotemporal object is; they have simply plunged ahead into investigating the interrelations, causal and otherwise, among such objects. Further, the natural sciences all assume a very naïve form of dualism, according to which the physical world that they study is mind-independent. Second, there is the contention that psychology in particular has been misguided. Having made the mistake of distinguishing sharply between minds and bodies, psychologists have then proceeded to compound this mistake by treating minds as if they were like bodies. Third, a program is sketched for a radically different method that would avoid all these errors. Fourth, it is proposed that the findings of this new method should become the foundation stones for a reconstruction of all the sciences, including physics. It may be said at once that there will be more agreement among philosophers about the two critical theses than about the two proposals for reform and reconstruction.

It is true that . . . there is psychology, which . . . claims . . . to be the universal fundamental science of the spirit. Still, our hope for real rationality, i.e., for real insight, is disappointed here as elsewhere. The psychologists simply fail to see that they too study neither themselves nor the scientists who are doing the investigating nor their own vital environing world. They do not see that from the very beginning they necessarily presuppose themselves as a group of men belonging to their own environing world and historical period. By the same token they do not see that in pursuing their aims they are seeking a truth in itself universally valid for everyone. By its objectivism psychology simply cannot make a study of the soul in its properly essential sense, which is to say, the ego that acts and is acted upon. Though by determining the bodily function involved in an experience of evaluating or willing, it may objectify the experience and handle it inductively, can it do the same for purposes, values, norms? . . . Completely ignored is the fact that objectivism, as the genuine work of the investigator intent upon finding true norms, presupposes just such norms. . . . More and more perceptible becomes the overall need for a reform of modern psychology in its entirety. As yet, however, it is not understood that psychology through its objectivism . . . simply fails to get at the proper essence of spirit; that in isolating the soul and making it an object of thought . . . it is being absurd. . . .

> In our time we everywhere meet the burning need for an understanding of spirit, while the unclarity of the methodological and factual connection between the natural sciences and the sciences of the spirit has become almost unbearable.[1]

CRITICISM OF NATURAL SCIENCE

As regards Husserl's first contention, little need be said. Writers as diverse in other respects as Whitehead and Nietzsche agreed that nineteenth- and early twentieth-century physics assumed a whole mass of highly questionable concepts—from the notion of simple location to that of causality.[12] But the main thrust of Husserl's attack on natural science differed in an important way from that of most other critics. Whitehead, for instance, argued that since the basic concepts of physics had become inadequate, an improved set of concepts was necessary. Whitehead derived such a set from quantum physics, and he hoped it would prove to be "categoreal," that is, applicable also to biology and the social sciences. From Husserl's point of view this proposed reform remained completely "naturalistic" and "objectivistic," for Whitehead never questioned the essential rightness of the experimental method used in biology and psychology as well as in physics. Further, Whitehead did not think of his categoreal scheme as complete and absolutely valid: The complete pattern, he believed, always eludes us; philosophy must remain open-ended. Therefore, from Husserl's point of view, to the other deficiencies of the philosophy of organism must be added "relativism." Husserl was not looking for a revised conceptual scheme that would enable scientists to achieve more reliable, but still always tentative, interpretations of the evidence supplied by the experimental method; he was looking for apodeictically *certain* evidence, and he saw that to find such evidence he needed a method radically different from that of the natural sciences. The experimental method might indeed have a suitable place in scientific research, but only after a secure foundation had been laid by the new phenomenological method. Thus Husserl's critique of the natural sciences was far more drastic than Whitehead's and called for very different measures of reform.

CRITICISM OF PSYCHOLOGY

This brings us to Husserl's criticism of psychology, a science that had gone wrong, he held, because it aped the methods of the natural sciences. As a laboratory science committed to experimentation, it generally focused its attention on measuring bodily changes held to be related in some way to mental states. Pavlov's experiments on the conditioned reflex are a classic example of the kind of psychology Husserl condemned: In such experiments changes in the rate of a dog's salivation are correlated with the change from visual and olfactory stimuli (food actually present) to an auditory stimulus (ringing of a bell, which has previously become "associated" with the presence of food).

12 See pp. 242–43 and 315–18.

In Husserl's view, it is bad enough that physics ignores the fact that its mathematical method is itself the product of the human spirit—bad enough that Einstein revolutionized the concept of objective space and time but said nothing whatever about lived-through space and lived-through time. But it is deplorable that psychology, which is supposed to be the science of the human spirit, makes the same mistake. Husserl considered it ironic that the psychologists who devise and conduct all these experiments forget that they "are a group of men belonging to their own environing world and historical period."

Husserl's manner of criticism may suggest that his approach was what is now called sociology of knowledge. However, Husserl would have held that sociology of knowledge possessed the same fatal defect as historicism—that is, relativism. But sociology of knowledge studies the norms of scientists and Husserl wanted psychology to study, among other psychic activities, the scientists' setting of norms for themselves. What, then, is the difference? Why would he have criticized sociology of knowledge? Sociology of knowledge studies scientific norms from the *outside;* it asks, for instance, how these norms are related to the social class from which scientists are drawn. It is possible to think of an experiment designed to ascertain whether scientific norms change as men from lower social strata infiltrate into the scientific establishment. Husserl would have held this point of view to be as naturalistic as physiological psychology. In contrast, he wanted psychology to observe norm-setting from the *inside,* as one of the ways in which the ego acts. As a universal human phenomenon norm-setting has, he thought, an essential nature that can be grasped if, and only if, we attend to it in the right way—that is, if we use the phenomenological method for studying specifically psychic phenomena. The essence of norm-setting is an absolute that characterizes every actual instance of norm-setting, regardless (for instance) of the social class of the scientists who happen to be setting the norms by which laboratory experiments are devised and conducted. And this essence, when it is uncovered by observation, is precisely one of those fundamental facts on which the sciences should be built. Of course, norm-setting is only one of the activities of the ego; it is simply an example of the investigations that psychology should undertake. The starting point for all investigations must be this special method of phenomenological observation that Husserl had discovered.

The Phenomenological Method

CONTRAST WITH THE NATURAL STANDPOINT

Essential to Husserl's method was what may be called the phenomenological stance. In order to describe it, Husserl contrasted it with what he called "the natural standpoint," that is, the stance toward the world that most people adopt all the time and that all people, even phenomenologists, adopt most of the time.

Our first outlook upon life is that of natural human beings, imagining, judging, feeling, willing, *"from the natural standpoint."* Let us make clear to ourselves what this means in the form of simple meditations which we can best carry on in the first person.

I am aware of a world, spread out in space endlessly, and in time becoming and become, without end. I am aware of it, that means, first of all, I discover it immediately, intuitively, I experience it. Through sight, touch, hearing, etc., in the different ways of sensory perception, corporeal things somehow spatially distributed are *for me simply there,* in verbal or figurative sense "present," whether or not I pay them special attention by busying myself with them, considering, thinking, feeling, willing. . . .

[Further,] what is actually perceived, and what is more or less clearly co-present and determinate (to some extent at least), is partly pervaded, partly girt about with a *dimly apprehended depth or fringe of indeterminate reality.* I can pierce it with rays from the illuminating focus of attention with varying success. . . .

As it is with the world in its ordered being as a spatial present—the aspect I have so far been considering—so likewise is it with the world in respect to its *ordered being in the succession of time.* This world now present to me, and in every waking "now" obviously so, has its temporal horizon, infinite in both directions. . . .

[Moreover,] this world is not there for me as a mere *world of facts and affairs,* but, with the same immediacy, as a *world of values,* a *world of goods,* a *practical world.* . . . I find the things before me furnished not only with the qualities that befit their positive nature, but with value-characters such as beautiful or ugly, agreeable or disagreeable, pleasant or unpleasant, and so forth. . . .

We emphasize a most important point once again in the sentences that follow: I find continually present and standing over against me the one spatio-temporal fact-world to which I myself belong, as do all other men found in it. . . . This "fact-world," as the word already tells us, I find to *be out there,* and also *take it just as it gives itself to me as something that exists out there.* All doubting and rejecting of the data of the natural world leaves standing the *general thesis of the natural standpoint.* "The" world is as fact-world always there; at the most it is at odd points "other" than I supposed, this or that under such names as "illusion," "hallucination," and the like, must be struck *out of it,* so to speak; but the "it" remains ever . . . a world that has its being out there. To know it more comprehensively, more trustworthily, more perfectly than the naive lore of experience is able to do . . . is the goal of the *sciences of the natural standpoint.*ᵐ

Husserl's point in the last paragraph is that, although we often come to suspect (and eventually to reject) this or that particular segment of experience, we simply and unquestioningly accept the world as a whole. This is surely correct, and commonly we do not even come to suspect a particular segment of experience unless and until it conflicts with some other segment (for example, our visual perception of an oar in water as bent conflicts with our tactile perception of the oar as straight). Indeed, most people would probably say that there is something a bit neurotic about doubting any experience until we have reason to do so—that is, until it conflicts with some other experience.

Those who find this position reasonable will experience great difficulty in making the move (which Husserl recommends) from the natural standpoint to the phenomenological stance. For it would seem to follow from what has just been said, both about the way doubt arises and about our ways of dealing with it, that unless we accept the world as a whole we cannot in any meaningful way doubt a part of it. Yet to doubt the world as a whole is precisely what Husserl asks us to do.

"BRACKETING"

Instead now of remaining at this [that is, the natural] *standpoint, we propose to alter it radically.* Our aim must be to convince ourselves of the possibility of this alteration on grounds of principle.

The General Thesis according to which the real world about me is at all times known . . . as a fact-world *that has its being out there,* does *not* consist of course in *an act proper,* in an articulated judgment *about* existence. . . .

[Nevertheless] we can treat the potential and unexpressed thesis exactly as we do the thesis of the explicit judgment. A procedure of this sort, *possible at any time,* is, for instance, *the attempt to doubt everything.* . . .

Rather is [such doubt] *something quite unique. We do not abandon the thesis we have adopted, we make no change in our conviction.* . . . And yet the thesis undergoes a modification—whilst remaining in itself what it is, *we set it as it were "out of action," we "disconnect it," "bracket it."* It still remains there like the bracketed in the bracket, like the disconnected outside the connexional system. We can also say: The thesis is experience as lived (*Erlebnis*), but *we make "no use of it,"* and by that, of course, we do not indicate privation (as when we say of the ignorant that he makes no use of a certain thesis); in this case, rather, as with all parallel expressions, we are dealing with indicators that point to a definite but *unique form of consciousness,* which clamps on to the original simple thesis . . . and transvalues it in a quite peculiar way. *This transvaluing is a concern of our full freedom.* . . .

In relation to *every* thesis and wholly uncoerced we can use this *peculiar* ἐποχή,[13] *a certain refraining from judgment which is compatible with the unshaken and unshakable because self-evidencing conviction of Truth.* . . .

We put out of action the general thesis which belongs to the essence of the natural standpoint, we place in brackets whatever it includes respecting the nature of Being: *This entire natural world therefore,* which is continually "there for us," "present to our hand," and will ever remain there, is a "fact-world" of which we continue to be conscious, even though it pleases us to put it in brackets.

13 [*Epoche* was the term used by the Greek sceptics to designate the attitude that they recommended men to adopt in the face of a world of doubt and uncertainty, an attitude of non-commitment and suspension of judgment—AUTHOR.]

> If I do this, as I am fully free to do, I do *not* then *deny* this "world," as though I were a sophist, *I do not doubt that it is there* as though I were a sceptic; but I use the "phenomenological" ἐποχή which *completely bars me from using any judgment that concerns spatio-temporal existence (Dasein)*.[n]

It is important to understand what Husserl meant by "doubt." Suppose I am now looking at a book that I hold in my hands. I am not to doubt the *experience* of having a book in my hands, but I *am* to doubt that I actually have a book in my hands: It may be that I am dreaming and that my hands are empty. To put this in technical language: I am not to doubt the being of the book; I am to doubt that the book has being in the mode of existence, for it may have being in the mode of a dream. This, then, is phenomenological doubt. To prescribe universal doubt is to prescribe this doubt regarding *all* my experience.

Husserl would not have denied that such an attitude is unusual; indeed, he would have insisted on its rarity—and also on its difficulty. Otherwise phenomenology would not have had to wait so long for its discoverer. But though universal doubt is unusual, it was essential to his whole position that it be psychologically possible. This is presumably an empirical question, but it is not exactly an easy one to settle. And some people will be tempted to reply that, even if it is psychologically possible to doubt everything, to do so would be to fall into a serious psychosis. These people may therefore question whether Husserl himself ever actually carried out his program of bracketing. They will suspect that it was never more than an elaborate bit of play-acting (by which Husserl himself was taken in).

Perhaps it will be possible to make the notion of bracketing more intelligible by emphasizing the aspect of detachment. As soon as we do so we understand why Husserl regarded the ideal of rationality as the Greeks' greatest legacy to Europe. Both Plato and Aristotle had distinguished between the pure theoretical reason that contemplates the world and the practical reason that seeks to change it. Though Plato's and Aristotle's notion of disinterested contemplation was a long way from Husserl's *epoche*, it at least involved a detachment from involvement in the world.

Even more interesting is the parallel that can be drawn with Schopenhauer and Bergson, philosophers whose views were otherwise very different from Husserl's. Schopenhauer's description of the "pure knowing subject" who has freed himself from the influence of his will was not at all unlike Husserl's description of the detachment involved in bracketing. Similarly, for Bergson intuition was a pure and detached state. What was common to all three of these thinkers was their distrust of epistomological theories based on the model of physics. Like Husserl, Schopenhauer and Bergson were reacting against the tendency in nineteenth-century culture to equate all knowledge with the kind of knowledge that is possible in the natural sciences. All three found what they believed to be a superior kind of knowledge in a type of direct and immediate experience, in contrast to the discursive, conceptual form of experience. Of course, whereas Bergson and Schopenhauer (and Plato and Aristotle as well) believed that what is encountered in this deeper form of cognition is a separate realm of metaphysically real existents, Husserl denied this, for he accepted the Kantian prohibition against the possibility of knowledge of things-in-themselves. But the point here is simply that all three thinkers shared the conviction that the individual who suspends the truth-claims of his everyday cognitive processes, far from being (as might be supposed) in a state of not knowing anything, finds himself in the presence of truths of great importance that otherwise wholly escape his attention.

Why, in Husserl's view, are the truths encountered in this phenomenological stance so important? Because whatever survives universal doubt is absolutely certain. Recall that Husserl held it to be his mission in life to resolve the crisis of European man by establishing philosophy as a rigorous science. Phenomenology *is* this rigorous science, inasmuch as its method yields those certain truths that European man has been seeking.

This brings us to another important question: What, according to Husserl, does survive the "attempt to doubt everything"? The general answer is that what survives is consciousness.

> We have learnt to understand the meaning of the phenomenological ἐποχή, but we are still quite in the dark as to its serviceability. . . . *For what can remain over when the whole world is bracketed, including ourselves and all our thinking (cogitare)?* . . .
>
> *Consciousness in itself has a being of its own which in its absolute uniqueness of nature remains unaffected by the phenomenologic disconnexion.* It therefore remains over as a *"phenomenological residuum,"* as a region of Being which is in principle unique, and can become in fact the field of a new science—the science of Phenomenology.[o]

Of course, in maintaining that consciousness is what survives universal doubt, Husserl meant consciousness in Brentano's sense, as that which involves both an act of intending and the intended object of this act. Here is an example: What you now see is a page of white paper with the words "What you now see . . ." printed on it. When we are in the natural standpoint it never occurs to us to doubt such a fact—after all, we see it. But we *can* doubt it—at least Husserl said that we can. Perhaps what you are now seeing are not the printed words "What you now see . . ." but black dots floating before your eyes. However, it is not possible to doubt the experience of having seen printed words on the page. *That* this experience occurred is indubitable. Further, within this experience of printed words on a page it is possible to distinguish the intentional objects (the printed words) from the act of intending them. *What* I experience, when I bracket, is both my experiencing (that is, intending) printed words on a page and also the printed words as experienced (that is, as intended) by me.

It is important that both poles of consciousness-of can be bracketed, for each becomes a special domain for phenomenological investigation. Thus, when we are in the natural standpoint we can certainly reflect on our experience. It is possible, while in the natural standpoint, not only to experience the printed words on the page but also to experience yourself experiencing them—to say, or think to yourself, "I am now reading the words 'What you now see . . . .'" But just as bracketing is needed to bring out the true character of the objects we intend, so bracketing is needed to bring out the true nature of these acts of reflection. In short, "from the natural standpoint nothing can be seen except the natural world." So entrenched are the habits of this standpoint that

> . . . we take all these data of psychological reflexion as real world-events, as the experiences (*Erlebnisse*) of animal beings. . . . We fail to notice that it is from out of these centres of experience (*Erlebnisse*) themselves that through the adoption of the new standpoint the new domain emerges. Connected with this is the fact that instead of keeping our eyes turned toward these centres of experience, we turned them away and sought the new objects in the ontological realms of arithmetic, geometry, and the like, whereby indeed nothing truly new was to be won.[14]
>
> [Thus] the "phenomenological" ἐποχή [is] the necessary operation which *renders "pure" consciousness accessible to us, and subsequently the whole phenomenological region.* . . . So long as the possibility of the phenomenological standpoint was not grasped, and the method of relating the objectivities which emerge therewith to a primordial form of apprehension has not been devised, the phenomenological world must needs have remained unknown, and indeed barely divined at all.[p]

To repeat, there are two correlated domains of investigation—the acts of the ego as it thinks, wills, doubts, fears, believes, hopes, and loves (acts that are revealed in reflection and then held in suspension by bracketing) and the objects of these acts of thinking, willing, doubting, fearing, believing, hoping, and loving (objects that in turn are held in suspension by bracketing). At the outset of his phenomenological investigation, Husserl focused his attention chiefly on the intended entities. When some of these are held for inspection by bracketing, they prove to be "essences." For instance, if you bracket your experience on the page of printed matter, you encounter the essence "page" and also the essences "white," "black," and "rectangular."[15] Essences have the property of being present completely on each occasion that they are present at all. They are therefore apodeictically certain. In contrast, when you attend to the page itself, in distinction (say) from its color or its shape, you find that it is not present all at once (for instance, when one side is present, the other side is not present). Indeed, by its nature an individual object (this particular page), in distinction

---

14 [Here Husserl was presumably thinking of Plato, who, instead of directing his disinterested, contemplative gaze toward consciousness, turned it toward mathematics and thus derived his abstract, otherworldy forms—AUTHOR.]

15 Husserl held that essences are disclosed in a special form of bracketing that he called "eidetic reduction."

from an essence (the essence "page"), is never completely present. It is present in a different mode, a mode of openness. The same is true for other types of intended entities.

Reflection on the way in which objects are present to consciousness led Husserl to devote more attention to the opposite pole of consciousness-of, that is, acts of intending. Bracketing disclosed to him various activities of the ego (such as, in the example given above, synthesis of successive partial presentations of the page); and beneath such relatively accessible activities he found still other, deeper levels of ego activity, all supposedly revealed by rigorous bracketing. We need not follow Husserl into these ramifications and refinements; indeed, he insisted that it was impossible to follow him without extensive practice and training in phenomenological reduction. It will be enough for our purposes to understand the phenomenological method in a general way and to consider its implications for philosophy.

For these purposes let us consider Husserl's account of how his method differs from Descartes'. That there are parallels is obvious, for Descartes too sought certainty and found it in the absolute indubitability of the *cogito*, the "I think." By focusing on the points at which Husserl parted company from Descartes we can begin to understand Husserl's conception of phenomenology.

DESCARTES' DISCOVERY AND HIS MISTAKES

France's greatest thinker, René Descartes, gave transcendental phenomenology new impulses through his *Meditations*. . . . One might almost call transcendental phenomenology a neo-Cartesianism, even though it is obliged —and precisely by its radical development of Cartesian motifs—to reject nearly all the well-known doctrinal content of the Cartesian philosophy. . . .

Every beginner in philosophy knows the remarkable train of thoughts contained in the *Meditations*. Let us recall its guiding idea. The aim of the *Meditations* is a complete reforming of philosophy into a science grounded on an absolute foundation. That implies for Descartes a corresponding reformation of all the sciences, because . . . only within the systematic unity of philosophy can they develop into genuine sciences. As they have developed historically, on the other hand, they lack that scientific genuineness which would consist in their complete and ultimate grounding on the basis of absolute insights, insights behind which one cannot go back any further. Hence the need for a radical rebuilding. . . . With Descartes this demand gives rise to a philosophy turned toward the subject himself. . . .

The *Meditations* were epoch-making in a quite unique sense, and precisely because of their going back to the pure *ego cogito*. Descartes, in fact, inaugurates an entirely new kind of philosophy. Changing its total style, philosophy takes a radical turn: from naive objectivism to transcendental subjectivism. . . . And so we make a new beginning, each for himself and in himself, with the decision of philosophers who begin radically: that at first we shall put out of action all convictions we have been accepting up to now, including all our sciences. . . .

Logic must be included among the sciences overthrown in overthrowing all science. Descartes himself presupposed an ideal of science, the ideal approximated by geometry and mathematical natural science. As a fateful prejudice this ideal determines philosophies for centuries and hiddenly determines the *Meditations* themselves. . . . For him a role similar to that of geometrical axioms in geometry is played in the all-embracing science by the axiom of the ego's absolute certainty of himself. . . .

None of that shall determine our thinking. As beginning philosophers we do not as yet accept any normative ideal of science; and only so far as we produce one newly for ourselves can we ever have such an ideal.

But this does not imply that we renounce the general aim of grounding science absolutely. The aim shall indeed continually motivate the course of our meditations, as it motivated the course of the Cartesian meditations; and gradually, in our mediatations, it shall become determined concretely. . . .

At this point, following Descartes, we make the great reversal that, if made in the right manner, leads to transcendental subjectivity: the turn to the *ego cogito* as the ultimate and apodictically certain basis for judgments, the basis on which any radical philosophy must be grounded.q

Though the method of doubt thus brought Descartes to the very threshold of phenomenology,[16] Husserl claimed that from that point on he went badly wrong. First, he interpreted the "I think" substantivally; second, he interpreted the objects of the "I think's" thoughts realistically, that is, as things-in-themselves. Since he did not have the advantage of Brentano's insight that consciousness is always consciousness-of, he failed to see both that the self is not a thing but a flow of intentional acts and also that things exist only in and for such acts, as objects intended by them.[17]

To put this differently, for Descartes the absolutely certain starting point on which the whole reconstruction of science had to depend was the single item, the self conceived of as a unitary substance. For Husserl, the absolutely certain starting point was a vast realm of intentions and intentional objects—the innumerable consciousnesses-of that come into view as a result of bracketing. Or, to put this in the Cartesian language that Husserl liked, for Descartes the starting point was simply the unitary *cogito* itself; for Husserl it was *ego cogito cogitatum*, an ego and its intended objects. This starting point gave Husserl a much broader base on which to construct his new sciences—a base that included all the manifold believings, rememberings, imaginings, and enjoyings encountered in bracketing and all the manifold objects (people, houses, trees, pages of printed matter, and so on) that can be remembered, thought about, imagined, and enjoyed.

If we follow this methodological principle [of bracketing] in the case of the dual topic, *cogito–cogitatum* (*qua cogitatum*), there become opened to

16 See p. 391.
17 Since this was a discovery Husserl himself did not make until he came to write the *Cartesian Meditations*, he was perhaps too critical of Descartes.

us, first of all, the general descriptions to be made, always on the basis of particular *cogitationes,* with regard to each of the two correlative sides. Accordingly, on the one hand, descriptions of the intentional object as such, with regard to the determinations attributed to it in the modes of consciousness concerned, attributed furthermore with corresponding modalities, which stand out when attention is directed to them. (For example: the "modalities of being," like certain being, possibly or presumably being, etc.; or the "subjective"—temporal modes, being present, past, or future.) This line of description is called *noematic.* Its counterpart is *noetic* description, which concerns the modes of the *cogito* itself, the modes of consciousness (for example: perception, recollection, retention), with the modal differences inherent in them (for example: differences in clarity and distinctness).[r]

Consider, for instance, the object we call a house—a particular house, like the house I live in now. This house can be intended in innumerable different acts: I can look at it now, I can shut my eyes and imagine it, I can remember it, and so on. Corresponding to each of these modes of intending my house there is a uniquely determined essence, or meaning.

Each *cogito,* each conscious process, we may also say, *"means" something or other,* and bears in itself, in this manner peculiar to the *meant,* its particular *cogitatum.* Each does this, moreover, in its own fashion. The house-perception means a house—more precisely, as this individual house—and means it in the fashion peculiar to perception; a house-memory means a house in the fashion peculiar to memory; a house-phantasy, in the fashion peculiar to phantasy. A predicative judging about a house, which perhaps is "there" perceptually, means it in just the fashion peculiar to judging; a valuing that supervenes means it in yet another fashion; and so forth.[s]

By collating all the ways in which the house means (the various meanings of the house) I can grasp what it is to be this house and, generally, what it is to be an object in the spatiotemporal world. I can, for instance, come to see that "the object is, so to speak, a *pole of identity,* always meant expectantly as having a sense yet to be actualized; in every moment of consciousness it is an index, pointing to a noetic intentionality that pertains to it according to its sense, an intentionality that can be asked for and explicated. All this is concretely accessible to investigation."[t] Or I can concentrate on the noetic side and bracket various instances of, say, remembering—remembering the house, remembering the book I read yesterday, remembering the painting I saw two years ago in Paris, and so on. By collating these instances of remembering I can grasp the essential structure of the psychic process of remembering. Natural science studies material objects without knowing what a material object is; psychology studies psychic processes without having the least idea what a psychic process really is. No wonder that these sciences lacked rigor! Husserl believed that phenomenology would provide them with the secure bases that they desperately needed. Descriptions from the side of the *cogitata* (*noema*) reveal the structures of the various kinds of states of affairs intended by the ego and hence provide an absolutely secure foundation for the natural sciences; descriptions from the side of the *ego cogito* (*noesis*) reveal the structure of the ego's intentional acts and hence provide corresponding foundations for empirical psychology.

EVIDENCE

In addition to mistakenly interpreting the "I think" as a unitary substance and the objects of the "I think's" thoughts as things-in-themselves, Descartes made a third mistake, according to Husserl. This was to adopt a geometric model for the rigorous new science that he was seeking. He regarded the *cogito* as an axiom and tried to deduce theorems from it. As Husserl pointed out in a passage quoted earlier, a thinker who aims at apodeictic certainty cannot afford to proceed in this careless way: He must subject the "normative ideal" of logic itself to criticism, not merely take it for granted. The Cartesian proofs of God and of the external world are suspect as long as the rules of evidence that guided these proofs have not themselves been exposed to universal doubt. Obviously, philosophy cannot simply take over the rules of evidence used in logic and in geometry; one of the tasks of philosophy as a rigorous science is to examine those rules of evidence in order to find for them too a secure foundation.

Husserl therefore proposed to be more careful than Descartes. According to his plan phenomenology's ideal of evidence would not be assumed at the outset; on the contrary, it would "be determined concretely in the course of the investigations." Given Husserl's motivation, which he shared with Descartes, it is easy to sympathize with his desire to provide an assumption-free account of the nature of evidence. But is not this enterprise inevitably involved in circularity? Our conclusion that certain evidence is adequate and that certain other evidence is not is the result of a reasoning process. But in order to know that this reasoning process is correct, must we not have been guided by some notion of what constitutes adequate evidence, a notion that was prior to our conclusion regarding what particular evidence is adequate? Husserl thought he could escape the danger of such a regress: The evidence that is disclosed by bracketing and that serves as the foundation of the reformed sciences is not the end result of any process of reasoning or inferring. It is simply present.

> Evidence is, in an *extremely broad sense*, an *"experiencing"* of something that is, and is thus; it is precisely a mental seeing of something itself. . . .
>
> In the broadest sense, evidence denotes a universal primal phenomenon of intentional life, namely . . . the quite pre-eminent mode of consciousness that consists in the *self-appearance*, the *self-exhibiting*, the *self-giving*, of an affair, an affair-complex (or state of affairs), a universality, a value, or other objectivity, in the final mode: "itself there," "immediately intuited," "given originaliter." . . . In the case of most objects, to be sure, evidence is only an occasional occurrence in conscious life; yet it is a possibility—and more particularly, one that can be the aim of a striving and actualizing inten-

tion—in the case of anything meant already or meanable. Thus it points to an essential *fundamental trait of all intentional life*. Any consciousness, without exception, either is itself already characterized as evidence (that is, as giving its object originaliter) or else has an essential tendency toward conversion into givings of its object originaliter. . . .[u]

The term "collating," used above to describe the process by which we come to grasp the nature of such psychic process as remembering and such states of affairs as spatiotemporal objects will be misleading if it suggests that Husserl believed that what occurs is some sort of inferential process. Rather, when we put several instances of remembering side by side we simply intuit the essential nature of the psychic process of remembering, just as when we put several instances of whiteness together we intuit the essence of whiteness. It is simply the fact, he maintained, that in phenomenological observation we come to see clearly and unambiguously the true nature of different modes of being—the mode of being of a spatiotemporal object, the mode of being of a necessary object, the mode of being of a possible object, the mode of being of an ego, and so on. We do not have to deduce these; we do not have to infer them. We simply see them—when we have learned how to bracket our experience properly.

Phenomenology the Science of Being

Phenomenology is thus the science of being; for this reason it serves as the foundation for all the special sciences. But phenomenology is the science of being in a radically different sense from that in which, for centuries, metaphysics had been regarded as the science of being. Beginning with Aristotle, philosophers had held that metaphysics is concerned with an ultimate reality that exists in and for itself. Kant had finally demolished the claims of this traditional metaphysics by showing that things-in-themselves (being-in-itself) are forever inaccessible to human minds. Accordingly, many philosophers concluded that the possibility of any science of being was thereby excluded. Knowledge, they thought, was limited to mind-dependent objects; thus they launched philosophy on the fatal path of relativism.

For Husserl, the beauty of the phenomenological method was that it made possible a new science of being.[18] It disclosed a realm of being that was ultimate, not in the sense that it existed beyond experience, but in the sense that it presented itself with absolute certainty within experience. To study being is not to turn to another reality (things-in-themselves, Platonic forms, *élan vital*); it is to penetrate deeper and deeper into the same—the one and only—reality

18 Given the fact that the term "metaphysics" was closely associated with an alleged being beyond experience, the new phenomenological science of being could better have been called "ontology."

(things-for-consciousness). Hence Husserl liked to think of phenomenology as archaeology. The ruling idea in this metaphor was the notion of getting back to what is genuine, simple, and uncontaminated by later excrescences. In this respect Husserl's view was diametrically opposed to Nietzsche's: Whereas Nietzsche held that there is no text that is immune to interpretation, Husserl believed that, in the phenomenological method, he had found a way of reaching the original manuscript.

DID HUSSERL RELAPSE INTO IDEALISM?

This may seem an odd question, for Husserl's own position was, of course, that he was neither an idealist nor a realist—he was a phenomenologist. In one place, it is true, he described phenomenology as *"eo ipso 'transcendental idealism,'"* but he added that it is idealism "in a fundamentally and essentially new sense."[v] He might just as well have described phenomenology as "realism in a fundamentally and essentially new sense"—better still, he might have pointed out that, whereas both idealism and realism attempt to stake out metaphysical claims on domains beyond experience, phenomenology is a doctrine of, and limited to, experience.

Thus Husserl's position was—at least in intent—radically different from Kant's, despite the fact that some of the elements disclosed by bracketing ("synthesis," for example) sound remarkably Kantian and despite the fact that Husserl used a good deal of Kant's terminology. But for Kant "transcendental" meant "underlying" experience; for Husserl it meant "disclosed in experience by phenomenological analysis."[19] Kant called his investigations "transcendental logic," for he was setting out the logical conditions that make experience of self and world possible. Husserl, in contrast, did not think of his investigations as logic; he supposed them to be empirical and descriptive. What they disclosed was as much a part of the experiential world as are the tables and chairs that are disclosed in the natural standpoint. Thus whereas Kant's categories were a priori, or universal and necessary conditions of there being any experience at all, Husserl's essences were apodeictic—"self-given" in experience, visible to anyone who took the trouble to learn how to bracket.

In Husserl's own estimation his position was very different from Kant's, but to many philosophers—even to sympathetic ones—his position seemed much less sharply differentiated. They detected a movement on Husserl's part from realism to idealism, and many of them deplored it. It is easy to see why they believed Husserl's position had changed, and easy also to understand why they objected. As regards the supposed shift, as Husserl became more and more adept in the practice of bracketing, he uncovered more and more activities of the ego at supposedly deeper and deeper levels.[20] From Husserl's own point of view these

19 According to Husserl, not only the intentional objects but also the underlying intentional acts are disclosed in experience.
20 See pp. 412–13.

activities were all within experience, waiting to be disclosed; but they were so deeply hidden that they became accessible only through the most severe bracketing. But what about readers less adept than Husserl in the art of bracketing who were unable to uncover these deeper activities? If they did not want to cast doubt on the whole method, they had no recourse but to think of these activities as lying outside the phenomenal field all together, that is, as "transcendent" in the Kantian sense.

From the point of view of many phenomenologists this relapse into Kantianism spoiled everything. They objected to Husserl's position on this question because they shared with the analytical philosophers a dislike of constructivism, a desire to see things clearly and unambiguously, and hence a disposition to treat consciousness as transparent.[21] Husserl's method of bracketing had appealed to many phenomenologists precisely because it claimed to present "objects originaliter." It seemed to them that the attribution of activities to the ego reintroduced ambiguity into the epistemological situation, which had seemed so simple and straightforward; it was a return to the slippery Hegelian slope.

Who, then, was correct about Husserl's view—Husserl himself or his phenomenologist critics? This question presupposes, as both Husserl and his critics assumed, that realism and idealism are genuine philosophical alternatives. But practitioners of Wittgenstein's type of therapy would be disposed to reply in the following way: What is "hidden within" experience may, by a shift of metaphor, be thought of as "lurking behind" experience. With this shift the move is made from phenomenalism either to idealism or to realism, depending on the bias of the individual thinker. In either case it is a shift only from one picture frame to another. The question of whether Husserl was an idealist or a realist is thus not answered; it is dissolved.

HOW THE PHENOMENOLOGICAL METHOD WORKS: AN EXAMPLE OF BRACKETING

So far, the account of Husserl's method has been perforce in very general terms. It may be useful therefore to give an example of bracketing and of the results it is supposed to achieve. Consider the relatively simple object of a die that I hold in my hand. In the natural standpoint, I look at it. It is a cube; it has a certain color; it is of a certain size; on one surface there is a dot; on another surface there are two dots, and so on. There is nothing very interesting about it; perhaps I wonder where its mate is or toss it idly in my hand.

Now suppose I bracket this experience. At once everything is immensely more complex. Instead of the unitary, enduring, and unchanging die, there is a rapid and continuous flow of slightly changing colors as I move my hand toward the light; changing sizes as I move it toward my face; changing shapes as I rotate the die; and so on. Further, these appearances are not discrete units; each merges into the others. For instance, as I rotate the die through 180° the look of the

21 See pp. 428–31.

die from one angle includes an anticipation, as it were, of the look of the die from succeeding angles of vision. Each look of the die implicitly contains other looks; the same is true for colors and shapes. This characteristic of experience (which is supposedly revealed only in the *epoche*) Husserl called "shadowing forth."

Further, my experience of the die is not just a matter of my experience at any particular time (say, the two or three seconds during which the die is lying in the palm of my hand). Memories of the die flow into present experiences, and future possible experiences are adumbrated in it. These aspects of intentionality (again revealed only in the *epoche*) Husserl called "horizons." Every individual object has infinitely open horizons; consequently no object can ever be experienced completely—though it can nonetheless be experienced "adequately."

Finally, all these experiences—past, present, and future—are being continuously "synthesized" so as to form, on the one noematic side, the die that I have in my hand and, on the noetic side, the acts that constitute the self that perceives the die. Thus "synthesis," "horizons," and "shadowing forth" are features of the constitutional structure of intentionality. They and other features supposedly revealed in the *epoche* are described in the following passage. It should be noted that the descriptions move back and forth from the noetic to the noematic poles.

> Inquiry into consciousness concerns *two sides* . . . ; they can be characterized descriptively as *belonging together inseparably.* The sort of combination uniting consciousness with consciousness can be characterized as *synthesis,* a mode of combination exclusively peculiar to consciousness. For example, if I take the perceiving of this die as the theme for my description, I see in pure reflection that "this" die is given continuously as an objective unity in a multiform and changeable multiplicity of manners of appearing, which belong determinately to it. These, in their temporal flow, are not an incoherent sequence of subjective processes. Rather they flow away in the unity of a synthesis, such that in them "one and the same" is intended as appearing. The one identical die appears, now in "near appearances," now in "far appearances": in the changing modes of Here and There, over against an always co-intended, though perhaps unheeded, absolute Here (in my co-appearing organism). Furthermore, each continued manner of appearance in such a mode (for example: "the die here, in the near sphere") shows itself to be, in turn, the synthetic unity pertaining to a multiplicity of manners of appearance belonging to that mode. Thus the near-thing, as "the same," appears now from this "side," now from that; and the "visual perspectives" change—also, however, the other manners of appearance (tactual, acoustic, and so forth), as we can observe by turning our attention in the right direction. . . . Always we find the feature in question as a unity belonging to a passing "flow of multiplicities": Looking straightforwardly, we have perhaps the one unchanging shape or color; in the reflective attitude, we have its manners of appearance (orientational, perspectival, and so forth), following one another in continuous sequence. Furthermore, each of these manners of appearance

(for example: the shadowing forth [*Abschattung*] of the shape or color) is itself an *exhibition of* [*Darstellung von*] the shape, the color, or whatever the feature is that appears in it. Thus each passing cogito intends its cogitatum, not with an undifferentiated blankness, but as a cogito with a describable *structure of multiplicities*, a structure having a *quite definite* noetic-noematic composition, which, by virtue of its essential nature, pertains to just *this* identical cogitatum. . . .

Once we have laid hold of the phenomenological task of describing consciousness concretely, veritable infinities of facts—never explored prior to phenomenology—become disclosed. . . .

If we consider the *fundamental form of synthesis*, namely *identification*, we encounter it first of all as an all-ruling, *passively* flowing synthesis, in the form of the *continuous consciousness of internal time*. Every subjective process has its internal temporality. If it is a conscious process in which (as in the perception of the die) a worldly Object appears as cogitatum, then we have to distinguish the *Objective temporality that appears* (for example: the temporality of this die) from the *"internal" temporality of the appearing* (for example: that of the die-perceiving). This appearing "flows away" with its temporal extents and phases, which, for their part, are continually changing appearances *of* the one identical die. Their unity is a unity of synthesis: not merely a continuous connectedness of cogitationes (as it were, a being stuck to one another externally), but *a connectedness that makes the unity of one consciousness*. . . .

Now the same die (the same for consciousness) can be intended in highly diverse modes of consciousness—simultaneously, or else successively in *separated* modes of consciousness—for example: in separate perceptions, recollections, expectations, valuations, and so forth. Again it is a synthesis that, as a unitary consciousness *embracing* these separated processes, gives rise to the consciousness of identity and thereby makes any knowing of identity possible. . . .

Synthesis, however, does not occur just in every particular conscious process, nor does it connect one particular conscious process with another only occasionally. On the contrary, . . . the *whole of conscious life is unified synthetically*. Conscious life is therefore an all-embracing cogito. . . . The *fundamental form* of this universal synthesis, the form that makes all other syntheses of consciousness possible, is the all-embracing *consciousness of internal time*. . . .

The multiplicy of the intentionality belonging to any cogito . . . is a theme not exhausted with the consideration of cogitationes as *actual* subjective processes. On the contrary, *every actuality involves its potentialities*, which are not empty possibilities, but rather possibilities intentionally predelineated in respect of content. . . .

With that, *another fundamental trait of intentionality* is indicated. Every subjective process has a process "horizon," which changes with the alteration of the nexus of consciousness to which the process belongs and with the alteration of the process itself from phase to phase of its flow—an intentional *horizon of reference* to potentialities of consciousness that belong to the process itself. For example, there belongs to every external perception its reference from the "genuinely perceived" sides of the object of perception to the sides "also meant"—not yet perceived but only anticipated. . . . Furthermore, the perception has horizons made up of other possibilities of perception, as perceptions that we *could* have, if we *actively directed* the course of perception otherwise: if, for example, we turned our eyes that way instead of this. . . .

The horizons are "predelineated" potentialities. We say also: We can *ask any horizon what "lies in it,"* we can *explicate* or unfold it, and *"uncover"* the potentialities of conscious life at a particular time. . . . The predelineation itself, to be sure, is at all times imperfect; yet, with its *indeterminateness,* it has a *determinate structure.* For example: the die leaves open a great variety of things pertaining to the unseen faces; yet it is already "construed" in advance as a die, in particular as colored, rough, and the like, though each of these determinations always leaves further particulars open. This leaving open, prior to further determinings (which perhaps never take place), is a moment included in the given consciousness itself; it is precisely what makes up the "horizon." . . .

Thus, as consciousness of something, every consciousness has the essential property, not just of being somehow *able to change into continually new modes of consciousness of the same object* . . . , but of being able to do so according to—indeed, *only according to those horizon intentionalities.* The object is, so to speak, *a pole of identity,* always meant expectantly as having a sense yet to be actualized. . . .^w

WHAT DOES THE METHOD "REALLY" UNCOVER?

Perhaps enough has been quoted to indicate how Husserl practiced his phenomenological method. What are we to make of it? Does the method really uncover apodeictically certain truths about the nature of being?

To begin with, in some cases it is possible, even for those not adept at bracketing, to identify what Husserl is describing in this passage. But, one is tempted to ask, why use the language Husserl chose? As an example, consider Husserl's account of what he called "predelineated possibilities." What does this amount to? Apparently something like this: What I mean by "die" is, among numerous other things, that if I am looking at the one-dot surface, I will see the six-dot surface if I rotate the die through 180°. If on rotating it I were not to see the six-dot surface, I would say, "Something has gone wrong," or "That's a dishonest die," or possibly "Why, that's not a die at all." In a word, to talk about "possibilities" in this case is to point out that, on the basis of prior experience, I believe that the die has another side; this being the case, I often anticipate seeing the other side while I am still looking at this one. To talk about "predelineation" is simply to point out that while I am looking at the one-dot side I anticipate seeing a configuration of six dots, and not, for example, the king of spades or General de Gaulle.

Husserl's description in terms of predelineated possibilities sounds much more impressive than this one, but is it *better*? Is it, for that matter, better than the one Husserl himself gave from the natural standpoint, in terms of a "fringe of indeterminate reality"?[22] Is it better than Whitehead's description in terms of prehendings into unity?[23] Both philosophers seem to be saying that if we attend to the die as we actually experience it, we find that it is not *here* all at once; nor is it *now* all at once. Finally, is Husserl's description of this experience of the interconnectedness of things better than the Romantic poets' description in terms of "affinities" that "passive minds" overlook?[24]

At this point Wittgenstein would have asked, "Better for what?" and he would have urged us to examine the various language games in which these descriptions occur. Thus Whitehead's description is part of a language game designed to expound a new monistic metaphysics; and since Husserl himself eschewed metaphysics, he could have replied that he was uninterested in Whitehead's description. As for the Romantic poets, Husserl might have said with justice that they were not trying, as he was, to lay the foundations for new, rigorous sciences of man and nature; in his view the phenomenological descriptions are necessary for this purpose. But since the sciences to be founded on these descriptions are to be universally valid, the descriptions themselves must be apodeictic. They are not merely "better" for particular purposes in connection with particular language games; they are *true*. Husserl would doubtless have held that the language he used was justified because it was the "correct" description of the entities that bracketing has disclosed.

Thus Husserl differed profoundly from Wittgenstein about the relation between philosophy and language—perhaps the major issue in twentieth-century philosophy. For Wittgenstein, all seeing is "language-ified"; all seeing is relative to "frames"—to presuppositions, assumptions, and values that have become congealed in language. Hence philosophical inquiry is intrinsically linguistic in nature. In Husserl's view, there is a special kind of seeing, wholly free from language, that occurs when we bracket properly. First we see what is the case; then we look around for the right words to describe what we see. Doubtless it is not always easy to find the right words; indeed, Husserl's own difficulty in finding them can be seen in the way in which his descriptions changed from book to book. But the problem of finding the right words is a subsidiary and completely separate task. In Husserl's view, philosophical inquiry itself is not in any sense linguistic.[25]

If bracketing is, as Husserl claimed, a special kind of seeing that discloses objects originaliter, then Wittgenstein's view of the relation between philosophy

22 See p. 400.
23 Also, the essences that Husserl believed come into view as a result of eidetic reduction (for instance, the red color of the die) are descriptions of the same aspects of experience that are described, in Whitehead's terminology, by the phrase "eternal objects."
24 See p. 389.
25 Husserl would, of course, have agreed with Wittgenstein that most philosophical theories—indeed, all philosophical theories before his own—present false and misleading pictures of reality. This is because none of them was assumption-free. But it is one thing to agree that most pictures are false and another thing to say that the picture theory itself is a profound illusion.

and language is mistaken, and his whole program of therapy is undermined. Thus Husserl's phenomenology is, in effect and by anticipation, a direct answer to the *Philosophical Investigations*. But now we have to ask whether Husserl's claims for bracketing are correct. This may seem like a straightforward (if admittedly difficult) empirical question. Are things "self-given" when we bracket or are they not? Suppose Wittgenstein had bracketed and had reported that he did not find anything that was self-given. Husserl could have replied that this was merely evidence that Wittgenstein had failed to bracket successfully, for the procedure requires careful training. And Wittgenstein could have retorted that bracketing is only a particularly subtle sort of frame, that what seemed to be self-given and originaliter to Husserl looked that way only because Husserl identified so closely with his frame that he was wholly unconscious of it.

There is no way of adjudicating definitively between these interpretations. To hope to settle such an issue between Husserl and Wittgenstein by an appeal to the empirical evidence is naïve, for what is "empirical evidence" itself turns out to be at issue. What seems to one party apodeictically certain because it is "there" seems to the other party a projection of the quest for certainty. Here, then, we have reached another fundamental parting of the ways in philosophy. But to speak in this fashion is to side with Wittgenstein rather than with Husserl. For instance, the language just used about their difference being a matter of "interpretation" is language that is congenial to Wittgenstein, not to Husserl. Furthermore, Wittgenstein could accept, and Husserl had to reject, the notion that what is "empirical evidence" remains an open issue; finally, Wittgenstein could agree, and Husserl could not, that there *are* partings of the ways.

Husserl's Influence

To allow these last comments to stand alone would be to create too negative an impression of Husserl's philosophy. Certainly, if his philosophy is judged by its own grandiose aims, its accomplishments are meager. But his influence on contemporary philosophy and on the social sciences has been great. Although he did not lay the foundation for a new ontology, he did found a school of psychology that, following his method more or less closely, has made detailed and often illuminating investigations of such phenomena as bad faith, anxiety, and time sense. And quite apart from the work of what may be called "arm-chair" psychology, phenomenology has had a salutary influence on experiential psychology in calling attention to the importance of "experiential variables," which tend to be overlooked by psychologists with a strongly behavioristic orientation. For instance, it has been pointed out that

> . . . if we are to understand the world of color, we must first look carefully at the colors themselves, not just at their qualities, but at all the ways in

which they appear. They usually appear as surfaces . . . ; but they may also have a filmy quality devoid of surface characteristics, or they may be seen as tridimensional or as lustrous or glowing. These are all different modes of appearance of the same color. . . . The same stimulus applied in different contexts may produce radically different perceptions of color. . . . The surface appe .rance is not a simple function of the wave length or intensity of incoming light; it is a complex function of many variables which contribute to the structuring of the visual world.[x]

Husserl saw that psychologists who attended only to external, physical "stimuli" that could be isolated and then correlated with other similarly isolated "responses," not only missed important variables altogether. In their desire to correlate variables they did not see that they were ignoring context (even "physical" context) and thus creating a highly artificial situation. Because they had uncritically taken over the methods of physics, they blandly regarded the limitations of these methods not as limitations but as the essence of science. Husserl helped to free psychology from the dogma that all sciences should model themselves on physics; he taught psychologists to begin with the experiential field itself rather than with stimuli or hypothetical elements of sensation. In this sense he was far more empirical than many psychologists who prided themselves on their "empiricism."

Similarly, Husserl's influence has caused sociologists to attend to social experience as well as social structure—to the inner *Erlebnis*, the inner flow of men's experience as they live and act in groups of various kinds, to their beliefs and value systems, and to their different ways of perceiving their social realities, in addition to attending to men's overt, "observable" interactions. Here too the result has been to start with problems and to devise means of dealing with them, instead of starting with a method that "predelineates" results in advance.

These achievements, which are of great importance, all flow from Husserl's empirical orientation and his repeated injunction to "return to the things themselves."[26] He was sufficiently freed from metaphysical dualism and from the "scientism" that infected the thinking of many of his contemporaries to take note of many ranges of facts that they ignored. But somehow this empirical approach became entangled in his urgent personal need for absolutes, with the unfortunate result that his experientialism was converted into ontology and the data of observation were dressed up as "objects originaliter." This, not the move from realism to idealism, is the most serious shift in Husserl's philosophy. It shows once again that the central problem for man in contemporary culture (the real crisis of Western man) is to come to terms with his quest for certainty. Perhaps the only absolute that man can have is the knowledge that he cannot have absolutes: It is to recognize with Kierkegaard that one is always in the wrong and yet to abstain from Kierkegaard's leap of faith. This at least was the position of Sartre.

26 *Not* to things-in-themselves.

Sartre

Sartre's[27] central theme is man's situation in a world without God. What *is* such a world? What is such a man? What, above all, is such a man to do in such a world? Thus Sartre's philosophy, like Kierkegaard's, is intensely personal. But his answers to these existential questions are very different from Kierkegaard's. For Sartre, as for Nietzsche, Kierkegaard's leap of faith was an act of cowardice and surrender. One does not *find* an integrating focus and a center for one's life; one must *make* a focus and a center. In Sartre's view it is impossible even to begin to do this until one has purged oneself of the illusions that cloud most men's vision of themselves and of their world. To know the world for what it is, is to experience despair. But this desperate knowledge is a necessary prelude to action. As Orestes says in Sartre's play *The Flies,* "Human life begins on the other side of despair." What counts for Sartre, as for Nietzsche, is what a man does *after* he has bitten the snake that is biting him.

Up to this point it seems that Sartre's orientation, with its focus on existential problems, is very different from that of the phenomenological tradition. But though Sartre is a moralist, he is also, like the phenomenologists, an epistemologist. He too holds that reality consists, not in Kantian things-in-themselves, but in phenomena—that is, in consciousnesses-of. And he agrees with the standard phenomenological doctrine that consciousnesses-of involve not only intentions but also intentional objects. Hence he shares the view, widespread among phenomenologists, that Husserl fell from grace and slipped into idealism.[28] According to Sartre, the ego is an intentional object among other intentional objects. In Husserlian language, it is on the "noematic" rather than the "noetic" side. All that is left on the noetic side is a pure, impersonal spontaneity, a wind blowing toward objects. Thus for Sartre consciousness is as transparent as it was for Russell. But whereas for Russell the transparency of consciousness meant that consciousness could be ignored, for Sartre the "nothingness" of consciousness both creates man's existential dilemma and provides such means as exist for resolving it.

This discovery about consciousness was in fact the starting point for both Sartre the phenomenologist and Sartre the existentialist. For Sartre the phenomenologist, the transparency of consciousness excluded all those "syntheses" that Husserl had emphasized and thus led to an ontology very different from that of Husserl. For Sartre the existentialist the nothingness of consciousness meant

27 Jean-Paul Sartre was born in Paris in 1905. His father died when he was a child and he was brought up in the home of his grandfather, who was a teacher of German. Sartre took his doctor's degree in 1929 and spent the next ten years teaching in a number of different *lycées,* traveling, and studying in Germany. In 1939 at the outbreak of the war he was called up for active service and sent to the Maginot line. He was captured during the fall of France but was released the next year. He spent the rest of the war in Paris, teaching and taking part in the resistance movement. After the liberation, he gave up teaching to devote himself to writing and to politics.

28 See pp. 410–11.

that man is not imprisoned in a ready-made self but is free to become the self of his choice. Whereas the phenomenological method had appealed to Husserl because it seemed to reveal those apodeictic evidences that satisfy men's thirst for certainty, the method appealed to Sartre because it seemed to reveal those harsh existential truths that every man must face and overcome if he is to be an authentic individual, reconciled to living with uncertainty.

In addition to Sartre as both phenomenologist and existentialist, there is Sartre as both literary artist and technical philosopher. This is a most unusual combination. Other philosophers of course have had high literary skills—Plato and Nietzsche, for instance. And other philosophers have carried on a literary career more or less concurrently with a philosophical career—Hume and Russell, for instance. But usually the literary and philosophical writings of most thinkers are quite independent of each other. Generally philosophers give us only the end products of their thinking; it is necessary to reconstruct from the finished philosophical treatise (insofar as this is possible) the vision of the world and of man that was the impetus, the starting point, for this treatise. In studying Sartre we have the advantage of literary works that are intensely personal documents that reveal from inside his own experiences of the world and also philosophical treatises that are relatively neutral and objective accounts (from outside, as it were) of these experiences.

Although the literary works cannot justify the truth-claim that they make for his vision, they can persuade the reader by the vividness of their presentation, by their concreteness, and by the overwhelming conviction of the author that he has *seen* the truth. The philosophical works, making the same truth-claim, attempt to substantiate it by incorporating it in an ontology that has been worked out systematically. For this reason—quite apart from one's evaluation of the truth-claim he has made—Sartre is a most instructive philosopher to read. We shall begin our examination of Sartre with the vision of the human condition as presented in his novels, for judging by the popularity of his writings this vision is shared by many people today. We shall then proceed, by way of his writings on phenomenological psychology, to his ontological formulation of the vision.

The Human Condition

What is the human condition as it is revealed when phenomenological observation strips away the curtain of words, and with it all our presuppositions, theories, and hypotheses? In *Nausea* Sartre presents a dramatic account of one such revelatory encounter with reality, presumably very close to what Sartre himself had experienced.[29]

29 The novel, which is written in the form of a diary, takes place in Bouville, a thinly disguised Le Havre, where Sartre had taught. It is fair to say that Antoine Roquetin, the protagonist, is a thinly disguised Sartre.

> Everywhere, now, there are objects like this glass of beer on the table there. . . . I have been *avoiding* looking at this glass of beer for half an hour. I look above, below, right and left; but I don't want to see *it*. And I know very well that all these bachelors [who are sitting at other tables in the restaurant] can be of no help. . . . They could come and tap me on the shoulder and say, "Well, what's the matter with that glass of beer?" It's just like all the others. It's bevelled on the edges, has a handle. . . . I know all that, but I know there is something else. Almost nothing. But I can't explain what I see. To anyone. There: I am quietly slipping into the water's depths, towards fear.[y]

It is evident that Roquetin is performing—quite unwittingly, of course—what Husserl called phenomenological reduction. But note that whereas Husserl held that it requires long and arduous preparation, Sartre believes that people may happen on it quite by accident, in the midst of other activities, and with literally shocking results to their sense of reality. Further, what Roquetin experiences is quite different from Husserl's apodeictically certain essences. Who is correct? One feels that whereas Husserl merely talked about bracketing and never really left the natural standpoint, Roquetin-Sartre must have actually had the experience of losing the whole world of stable, useful, familiar things, with their complex relations among themselves ("causes" and "effects") and relations with us as instrumentalities of our purposes. To lose this stable, familiar world would surely be terrifying and nauseating—anything but reassuring, as Husserl supposed.

THINGS

What has happened, as Roquetin says, is that "things have become divorced from their names." What he used to see as he sat on a moving streetcar was (say) a house at the end of the street. Because he "knew" that it was a house, it only "seemed" to grow larger as the car advanced down the street. And because he knew that it was built of yellow bricks it only seemed in a particular light to be blue. But all this "knowing" depended on pinning down and fixing the fleeting consciousnesses-of by means of the name "house." Once they became divorced from the name everything changed: What before he had taken as real ("stationary yellow house") was suddenly revealed to be a fiction, a construction, a projection on the appearances that actually displayed themselves to him as the car moved down the street; what before he had believed to be "mere" appearances ("The house looks bluish in this light, but I know it is really yellow") are revealed to be, quite literally, all that there is—in other words, reality.

> Bluish objects pass the windows . . . blue this great yellow brick house advancing uncertainly, trembling, suddenly stopping and taking a nose dive. . . . [It] starts up again, it leaps against the windows. . . . It rises, crushing. . . . It slides along the car brushing past it. . . . Suddenly it is no longer there, it has stayed behind. . . .

> I lean my hand on the seat but pull it back hurriedly: it exists. This thing I'm sitting on, leaning my hand on, is called a seat. They make it purposely for people to sit on, they took leather, springs and cloth, they went to work with the idea of making a seat and when they finished, *that* was what they had made. . . . I murmur: "It's a seat," a little like an exorcism. But the word stays on my lips: it refuses to go and put itself on the thing. It stays what it is, with its red plush, thousands of little red paws in the air, all still, little dead paws. This enormous belly turned upward, bleeding, inflated . . . is not a seat. It could just as well be a dead donkey. . . . It seems ridiculous to call them seats or to say anything at all about them; I am in the midst of things, nameless things. Alone, without words, defenseless, they surround me, are beneath me, behind me, above me. They demand nothing, they don't impose themselves: they are there.[z]

In other words, that this plush red expanse is a streetcar seat is Roquetin's interpretation—an interpretation that imports an immense amount into the experience itself. If this sounds like Nietzsche, it is like Nietzsche, for Roquetin has made the same discovery that Nietzsche the classical philologist made—that there is no original text.

To illustrate this discovery, let us take another example connected with Roquetin: The Marquis of Rollebon, whose biography Roquetin is writing, is as inaccessible as any long-lost classical text, and what one thinks of as ascertaining the facts, as *re*constructing the life of this man, is sheerly constructing it. It is like writing a novel. After working for years on the life of the Marquis, Roquetin has accumulated an immense amount of material—letters, memoirs, secret reports, police reports. He knows more about Rollebon than he knows about any living person. But he comes to realize that he knows nothing at all about him. It is not just a question, he sees, of not being personally acquainted with Rollebon. All the testimony he possesses was written down by people who were personally acquainted with Rollebon. Had Roquetin himself known the Marquis, his knowledge of him would still have been from outside; it would have been only one more "report" to be added to the others.

> What is lacking in all this testimony is firmness and consistency. [The reports] do not contradict each other, neither do they agree with each other; they do not seem to be about the same person. . . .
>
> I am beginning to believe that nothing can ever be proved. These are honest hypotheses . . . but I sense so definitely that they come from me, and that they are simply a way of unifying my own knowledge. Not a glimmer comes from Rollebon's side. Slow, lazy, sulky, the facts adapt themselves to the rigour of the order I wish to give them; but it remains outside of them.[a]

THE SELF

The problem is not merely that the personality of others is inaccessible; the very notion of personality is just another product of words. Just as seathood was only an order, a pattern, that Roquetin imposed on his experience of red plushness in order to unify it, so the enduring personhood he has attributed to Rollebon is an order he imposed on those "sulky" reports. And, as Roquetin realizes, what applies to Rollebon applies equally to Roquetin himself: He too exists only in a momentary present. This is a truth that dawns on him when, after having interrupted his writing for a moment, he tries to resume.

> But as my eyes fell on the pad of white sheets, I was struck by its look and I stayed, pen raised, studying this dazzling paper: so hard and far seeing, so present. The letters I had just inscribed on it were not even dry yet and already they belonged to the past.
>
> "Care had been taken to spread the most sinister rumours. . . ." I had thought out this sentence, at first it had been a small part of myself. Now it was inscribed on the paper, it took sides against me. I didn't recognize it any more. I couldn't conceive it again. It was there, in front of me; in vain for me to trace some sign of its origin. Anyone could have written it. But *I* . . . *I* wasn't sure I wrote it. The letters glistened no longer, they were dry. That had disappeared too; nothing was left but their ephemeral spark.[b]

Roquetin sees that the self he has attributed to himself—the self who is an historian, who has written other monographs, who has spent years on this biography of Rollebon—is a construction, like the construction that he calls "Rollebon." This self is something he has fashioned out of reports, other people's outside views of him, like his outside views of Rollebon. Stripping away all these interpretations, he is left only with fleeting, fugitive consciousnesses-of. In them he finds intentional objects in appalling abundance, including of course those intentional objects called memories. But he finds no enduring "I think," no transcendental ego, no synthesizing activities. Beyond the intentional objects there is only a thin transparency, a distance, a nothingness.

> Now when I say "I," it seems hollow to me. I can't manage to feel myself very well. . . . And just what is Antoine Roquetin? An abstraction. A pale reflection of myself wavers in my consciousness. Antoine Roquetin . . . and suddenly the "I" pales, pales, and fades out.
>
> Lucid, static, forlorn, consciousness is walled-up; it perpetuates itself. Nobody lives there any more. A little while ago someone said "me," said *my* consciousness. Who? Outside there were streets, alive with known smells and colours. Now nothing is left but anonymous walls, anonymous conscious-ness. This is what there is: walls, and between the walls, a small transparency, alive and impersonal. . . . Consciousness . . . is conscious of being superfluous. It dilutes, scatters itself, tries to lose itself on the brown wall, along the lamp-post or down there in the evening mist. But it *never* forgets itself. That is its lot.[c]

The world as we have known it—a world of substantival Cartesian egos and substantival Cartesian objects—has now disappeared. According to Sartre there is only the disgusting, overflowing abundance of existence, plus that transparent nothingness we call "consciousness" that separates us from this abundance. That is all. Words are simply devices by which we protect ourselves from seeing the world as it is; and though all words are therefore inadequate for describing it as it is, if we have to use any word at all, the best one is "absurd."

Never, until these last few days, had I understood the meaning of "existence." . . . And then all of a sudden, there it was, clear as day: existence had suddenly unveiled itself. It had lost the harmless look of an abstract category: it was the very paste of things, this root [at the time Roquetin happened to be sitting in a public garden, looking at the roots of a tree] was kneaded into existence. Or rather the root, the park gates, the bench, the sparse grass, all that had vanished: the diversity of things, their individuality, were only an appearance, a veneer. This veneer had melted, leaving soft monstrous masses, all in disorder—naked, in a frightful, obscene nakedness. ·. . .

The word absurdity is coming to life under my pen; a little while ago, in the garden, I couldn't find it, but neither was I looking for it, I didn't need it: I thought without words, *on* things, *with* things. . . . Without formulating anything clearly, I understood that I had found the key to Existence, the key to my Nausea, to my own life. In fact, all that I could grasp beyond that returns to this fundamental absurdity. Absurdity: another word; I struggle against words; down there I touched the thing. But I wanted to fix the absolute character of this absurdity here. A movement, an event, in the tiny coloured world of men is only relatively absurd: by relation to the accompanying circumstances. A madman's ravings, for example, are absurd in relation to the situation in which he finds himself, but not in relation to his delirium. But a little while ago I made an experiment with the absolute or the absurd. This root—there was nothing in relation to which it was [not] absurd. Oh, how can I put it in words? Absurd: in relation to the stones, the tufts of yellow grass, the dry mud, the tree, the sky, the green benches. Absurd, irreducible; nothing—not even a profound, secret upheaval of nature—could explain it. . . . The world of explanations and reasons is not the world of existence. A circle is not absurd, it is clearly explained by the rotation of a straight segment around one of its extremities. But neither does a circle exist. This root, on the other hand, existed in such a way that I could not explain it. . . . This root, with its colour, shape, its congealed movement, was . . . below all explanation.[d]

This passage shows that the most unlikely people can be bedfellows: Roquetin-Sartre's world is very similar to Hume's. Everything is loose and separate from everything else. There is no reason why the world might be different in whole or in part from what it happens to be, for any reason to the contrary—for reasons belong to one realm and existence to another. The attempt made by philosophers like Whitehead to answer Hume by showing that there is, after all, a rationale in things was wholly rejected by Sartre. He explicitly adopted Hume's radical distinction between "relations of ideas" and "matters of fact," a distinction from which all the Humian conclusions follow. The end of the passage just quoted repeats Hume's reasoning almost verbatim: We see why every point on the circumference of a circle is equidistant from its center, for this property follows logically from the definition of a circle. A circle therefore is not absurd, but a circle does not exist. On the other hand, relations between existing things—say, between being a root and being pink under a dark outer surface—are sheerly accidental. Since all relations among matters of fact ("existence") could be otherwise, existence is absurd.

Hume would have agreed. But far from finding this "obscene" (as Sartre did), he was completely composed.

> Most fortunately it happens, that since reason is incapable of dispelling these clouds, nature herself suffices to that purpose, and cures me of this philosophical melancholy and delirium. . . . I dine, I play a game of backgammon, I converse, and am merry with my friends; and when after three or four hours' amusement, I would return to these speculations, they appear so cold, and strain'd, and ridiculous, that I cannot find in my heart to enter them any further.
>
> Here then I find myself absolutely and necessarily determin'd to live, and talk, and act like other people in the common affairs of life.[e]

How are we to account for these astonishingly different responses to what both Hume and Sartre agreed is the situation in which men find themselves? This divergence is in part caused by their differing attitudes toward certainty. Sartre renounced it with regret; Hume renounced it willingly enough: "Experience is a principle which instructs me in the several conjunctions of objects for the past." In Hume's view, although experience may on occasion lead one astray in the future, it is nonetheless a sufficiently reliable guide. Their differing attitudes toward what Husserl called the natural standpoint also contributed to the divergence of their responses. For Hume "nature" and "natural" were still good words; he wrote off deviant standpoints as "melancholy and delirium." He would have regarded Roquetin as a psychotic personality desperately in need of clinical help, a man whose vision of "obscene abundance" should not be taken seriously. In contrast, the intervening century of constructivistic thinking led Sartre to conclude that the natural standpoint is simply a reflection of bourgeois mentality, one of the many devices that people use "to veil the enormous absurdity of their existence."[f] Accordingly, in his view Hume's decision to "act like other people in the common affairs of life" was not prudence and good sense but an escape, an attempt to avoid the painful knowledge of what the world really is. To Sartre this is how most people have always dealt with their existential problems.

> They have dragged out their life in stupor, and semisleep, they have married hastily, out of impatience, they have made children at random. They have met other men in cafés, at weddings and funerals. Sometimes, caught in the

tide, they have struggled against it without understanding what was happening to them . . . And then, around forty, they christen their small obstinacies and a few proverbs with the name of experience;[30] they begin to simulate slot machines: put a coin in the lefthand slot and you get tales wrapped in silver paper; put a coin in the slot on the right and you get precious bits of advice that stick to your teeth like caramels.[g]

At one point Roquetin visits the picture gallery where the portraits of local notables are hung, the men who had "made Bouville the best equipped port in France for unloading coal and wood." Here is a description of the portrait of Jean Pacôme.

> The slightest doubt had never crossed those magnificent grey eyes. Pacôme had never made a mistake. He had always done his duty, all his duty, his duty as son, husband, father, leader. He had never weakened in his demands for his due: as a child, the right to be well brought up, in a united family, the right to inherit a spotless name, a prosperous business; as a husband, the right to be cared for, surrounded with tender affection; as a father, the right to be venerated; as a leader, the right to be obeyed without a murmur. . . .
> He never told himself he was happy, and while he was enjoying himself he must have done so with moderation. . . . Thus pleasure itself, also becoming a right, lost its aggressive futility. On the left, a little above his bluish-grey hair, I noticed a shelf of books. The bindings were handsome; they were surely classics. Every evening before going to sleep, Pacôme undoubtedly read over a few pages of "his old Montaigne" or one of Horace's odes in the Latin text. Sometimes, too, he must have read a contemporary work to keep up to date.
> He had never looked any further into himself; he was a leader.[h]

Pacôme was a leader because he was perceived by other people as a leader; he had rights because other people accorded him rights. He never had to face any really moral decision: At every critical point he knew what to do, for this was decided for him in advance by society, which decreed what was expected of men of his class and position. He was in fact not a man but a social type. In contrast to people like Pacôme there are a few authentic individuals who have seen through the social self and who have surmounted the moral crisis that this revelation entails; they have experienced doubt and have suffered anguish in their attempt to discover who they are and what they ought to do.

The anguish is suffered because, when a person has seen through the social self, he does not find, neatly tucked away beneath it and waiting to take over, an authentic self—he finds neither the Christian's immortal soul, nor Descartes' substantival *cogito*, nor Husserl's transcendental ego. He finds only the nothingness that is consciousness. This is the discovery of phenomenology as Sartre practiced it; this is the discovery that sets the existential problem as Sartre experienced it.

30 [So much for experience as the "principle which instructs me"—AUTHOR.]

MAN'S FREEDOM IN AN ABSURD WORLD

How is it possible under these circumstances to be an authentic self at all? How can nothingness be anything?

Sartre's answer is that the question is badly posed. Since the only self that a person can be is the social self, he cannot *be* an authentic self at all. Authenticity is not a category of being; it is a category of acting, of becoming. A person is an authentic self in and through choices made on his own initiative, without adopting other people's standards or following their advice. By revealing that we do not "have" a nature and by releasing us from the straitjacket of the social self (and of course the metaphysical self), phenomenology frees us to become anything we choose. It is only nothingness that is free to be anything and everything.

But this perfect freedom is a heavy burden. To see through the social self is to become free to make an authentic self. Yet at the same time it is to lose the rationale for choosing among possible selves. In a world that is intrinsically absurd there is no *reason* for doing any one thing rather than another. Why not, then, do whatever enters one's head, providing only that it is sufficiently idiosyncratic not to be derived from one's social role? Why not indeed? As Roquetin sits in a restaurant eating dinner, he reflects on this idea.

> I feel as though I could do anything. For example, stab this cheese knife into [another diner's] eye. After that, all these people would trample me and kick my teeth out. But that isn't what stops me: a taste of blood in the mouth instead of this taste of cheese makes no difference to me.[i]

What stops Roquetin is the realization that he would only be playing another role—perhaps the role of the phenomenological observer or that of the despairing existentialist. Thus he would not achieve authenticity; or if he did momentarily achieve it he would promptly lose it. He still would be unable to accept himself.

Roquetin never finds a way of resolving this dilemma. At the end of the novel Sartre suggests, in a passage reminiscent of Nietzsche in his account of overman as a creative artist, that the solution may be "a book, a novel." But he puts this idea forward very tentatively; and if we are correct in identifying Sartre with Roquetin he *had* to be tentative, for *Nausea* was itself the novel that, in *Nausea*, is just about to be begun. Sartre could not know until the book was finished whether writing it would "save" Roquetin. As it turned out, it did not. Though Sartre continued to write novels and plays, he apparently came to feel that literary production was too detached a relation to the world. As involvement in the world—*engagement*—proved to be necessary in Sartre's own life, as he himself became more involved in politics, the characters in his later novels seek the solution for their existential problems in commitment rather than in "arid purity."

For instance, one of the chief characters of *Paths to Freedom*, Mathieu Delarue, is presented as a detached man of the Roquetin type who finds it impossible to commit himself to anything—to his mistress, to politics,[31] to World War II (or, alternatively, to protest against the war). Like Roquetin, Mathieu eventually comes to realize that he is completely free—free from obligations public and private, free from constraints of law or custom. And like Roquetin he experiences this freedom as anguish. What is he to do with his freedom? How can Mathieu become an authentic self now that he is freed from that social self in which he had been so long restrained? Late one night, after the outbreak of the war and several days after he should have reported for active duty, Mathieu almost reaches a decision that would indeed be definitive: to kill himself.

> Outside. Everything is outside. . . . Inside, nothing, not even a puff of smoke, there is no *inside*, there is nothing. Myself: nothing. I am free, he said to himself, and his mouth was dry.
>
> Halfway across the Pont-Neuf he stopped and began to laugh: liberty—I sought it far away; it was so near that I couldn't touch it, that I can't touch it; it is, in fact, myself. I am my own freedom. He had hoped that one day he would be filled with joy, transfixed by a lightning flash. But there was . . . only a sense of desolation, . . . an anguish. . . . Outside the world, outside the past, outside myself: freedom is exile, and I am condemned to be free.
>
> He walked on a few steps, stopped again, sat down on the parapet, and watched the water flowing past. What shall I do with all this freedom? What shall I do with myself? . . . Shall I take the train? What did it matter?—go or stay, or run away—acts of that kind would not call his freedom into play. And yet he must risk that freedom. He clutched the stone with both hands and leaned over the water. A plunge, and the water would engulf him, his freedom would be transmuted into water. Rest at last—and why not? This obscure suicide would *also* be an absolute, a law, a choice, and a morality. . . . Deep down within him he felt his heart throbbing wildly; one gesture, the mere unclasping of his hands and *I would have been* Mathieu. . . . Suddenly he *decided* not to do it. He decided: it shall merely be a trial. Then he was again upon his feet and walking on, gliding over the crest of a dead star. Next time, perhaps.[j]

The "next time" comes the following summer, 1940. The French army, Mathieu now included, is retreating in total confusion; Pétain is about to surrender unconditionally; the war is over. In these circumstances, Mathieu and several other soldiers suddenly decide to occupy the belfry of a village church and to attack a German column as it advances. On any utilitarian calculation the decision is obviously absurd; the men are "unbalanced." They will not only lose their own lives; they will cause great suffering for the villagers, who are their compatriots and to whom they are indebted for hospitality. Against these heavy costs they can chalk up only the killing (possibly) of a few Germans who

---

31 Mathieu's friend Brunet constantly urges him to join the Communist Party, which Mathieu resists to his friend's disgust. But though Brunet is a "dedicated" Communist, he has by no means achieved existential commitment: He has simply accepted communism, much as Jean Pacôme had accepted the bourgeois culture in which he had been brought up.

have done them no personal harm. They will not alter the course of events in the slightest degree, or delay the German army.

Mathieu's "project" has become simply to hold out for fifteen minutes, but this is the first project to which he has ever been utterly committed.

> He made his way to the parapet and stood there firing. . . . Each one of his shots wiped out some ancient scruple. One for Lola, whom I dared not rob, one for Marcelle, whom I ought to have ditched, one for Odette, whom I didn't want to screw. This for the books I never dared to write, this for the journeys I never made, this for everybody in general whom I wanted to hate and tried to understand. He fired, and the tables of the law crashed about him—Thou shalt love thy neighbor as thyself—bang! in that bastard's face—Thou shalt not kill—bang! at that scarecrow opposite. He was firing on his fellow men, on Virtue, on the whole world: Liberty is Terror. . . . He looked at his watch; fourteen minutes and thirty seconds. Nothing more to ask of fate now except one half-minute, just time enough to fire at that smart officer, at all the Beauty of the Earth, at the street, at the flowers, at the gardens, at everything he had loved. Beauty dived downwards obscenely, and Mathieu went on firing. He fired; he was cleansed, he was all-powerful, he was free.
>
> Fifteen minutes.[k]

This, then, is Sartre's anguished discovery of man's dreadful freedom in an absurd world. For a formal "account" of these matters, let us turn from the literary works to Sartre's psychological and philosophical writings, in which the nature of the self and the nature of its world are systematically worked out. We shall begin with his account of consciousness, the key concept both for his ontology and for his ethics.

Consciousness and Consciousness of Self

Sartre's method is empirical in the phenomenological sense. That is, he proposes to describe consciousness as it is, without allowing any metaphysical assumptions or Nietzschian interpretations to affect the description. This of course is exactly what Husserl had set out to do, but he went astray in supposing that some kind of synthesizing "I think" is necessary to make possible the multitude of consciousnesses-of. Without it, Husserl thought, there would be no unity by virtue of which all these consciousnesses-of are one's own. But according to Sartre every consciousness already contains self-consciousness. Hence Husserl's transcendental ego is unnecessary—it "has no *raison d'être*."

> But, in addition, this superfluous *I* would be a hindrance. If it existed it would tear consciousness from itself; it would divide consciousness; it would

> slide into every consciousness like an opaque blade. Indeed, the existence
> of consciousness is an absolute because consciousness is consciousness of itself.
> This is to say that the type of existence of consciousness is to be consciousness
> of itself. And consciousness is aware of itself *in so far as it is consciousness
> of a transcendent object.* All is therefore clear and lucid in consciousness:
> the object with its characteristic opacity is before consciousness, but con-
> sciousness is purely and simply consciousness of being consciousness of that
> object. This is the law of its existence.[1]

In other words, consciousness of self (self-consciousness) and consciousness
of objects are not different kinds of consciousness. Consciousness is a unique type
of existence: Every consciousness of an object is *also* a consciousness of self. This
can be shown empirically by the following example. When I am intensely
interested in what I am doing—say, in reading an exciting novel—I never think
of myself as reading; I am fully occupied with the narrative. But if, after I have
put the book aside, someone asks me what I have been doing, I reply without
hesitation, "I was reading a book." Where does this knowledge come from?
Careful introspection reveals that no "I" was actually present in my consciousness
while I was reading the book. Nevertheless I now know that at that time I was
reading. Further, the "I" that is so seldom present is always available, on call.
This too is shown by introspection: I can at any time recall either *what* I
experienced on a particular occasion in the past or the fact that it was *I* who
experienced it.

> If, for example, I want to remember a certain landscape perceived yester-
> day from the train, it is possible for me to bring back the memory of that
> landscape as such. But I can also recollect that *I* was seeing that landscape.
> . . . In other words, I can always perform any recollection whatsoever in
> the personal mode, and at once the *I* appears.[m]

UNREFLECTED AND REFLECTIVE CONSCIOUSNESS

Here then is an apparent paradox—an "I" that is not present in consciousness
but that can nonetheless be brought into consciousness at will. How can the
paradox be resolved? The solution is to distinguish between two *levels* of consciousness rather than to distinguish—as many philosophers in the past, even
Husserl, had done—between two *types* of consciousness. The two traditional types
were, of course, consciousness of objects and self-consciousness. Sartre's two levels
are "unreflected consciousness" and "reflective consciousness." At *both* levels
consciousness is at once consciousness of objects and consciousness of self. This
distinction simply makes explicit Brentano's discovery of intentionality: Every
consciousness involves both an intention and an intentional object. The difference
between the two levels is simply that at the unreflected level the self-conscious
aspect of the consciousness is not "positional." That is, it is not an object in its
own field. At the reflective level, it is.

To repeat, all consciousness is consciousness of itself; that this is true follows from the nature of consciousness' unique kind of existence. But under ordinary circumstances, as when I am reading or looking out of the train window, "this consciousness of consciousness is not *positional*, which is to say that consciousness is not for itself its own object."ⁿ When, later on, I recall that it was I who was reading or who saw that particular landscape, this consciousness of consciousness becomes positional in a second consciousness, just as the book or the landscape had been positional in the first consciousness. Meanwhile, of course, the second consciousness (the reflecting consciousness) contains its own nonpositional consciousness of consciousness.

> There is an indissoluble unity of the reflecting consciousness and the reflected consciousness (to the point that the reflecting consciousness could not exist without the reflected consciousness). But the fact remains that we are in the presence of a synthesis of two consciousnesses, one of which is conscious *of* the other. Thus the essential principle of phenomenology, "all consciousness is consciousness *of* something,"³² is preserved. Now, my reflecting consciousness does not take itself for an object. . . . What it affirms concerns the reflected consciousness. Insofar as my reflecting consciousness is consciousness of itself, it is *nonpositional* consciousness. It becomes positional only by directing upon the reflected consciousness which itself was not a positional consciousness of itself before being reflected. Thus the consciousness which says *I Think* is precisely not the consciousness which thinks. Or rather it is not *its own* thought which it posits by this thetic act. . . . All reflecting consciousness is, indeed, in itself unreflected, and a new act of the third degree is necessary in order to posit it. [But] there is no infinite regress here, since a consciousness has no need at all of a reflecting consciousness in order to be conscious of itself. It simply does not posit itself as an object.º

THE TRANSCENDENT EGO

The upshot is that since there is no transcendental ego the only ego that exists is transcendent,³³ that is, an object that exists in the world and that is encountered there, along with other objects. Let us, then, consider the ego as it is revealed in phenomenological intuition along with such objects as tables, chairs, and trees. Of course, these objects are positional in unreflected consciousness. To describe the ego involves moving from this unreflected level, where consciousness is nonpositional, to the reflective level, where it becomes positional.

Consider, for instance, an unreflected consciousness of Peter being hated. I can turn my reflective consciousness on this hatred, in which case there is now

---

32 [Sartre is quoting Husserl, of course—AUTHOR.]
33 "Transcendental" is used by Sartre to designate what is outside consciousness; "transcendent" characterizes an object that is within consciousness but not wholly within it at any one time. Thus Sartre's criticism of Husserl can be rephrased by saying that Husserl mistakenly supposed the ego to be transcendental, whereas in fact it is transcendent.

a consciousness that it is I that hate Peter. But if I scrutinize the experiential field carefully, what is in my consciousness at this moment is my reflective awareness that I am angry with Peter, or that I am disgusted with Peter. Unlike anger or disgust, hatred is a state that "implicates" the past and the future: If I refused to implicate the future I could not possibly hate Peter now. But I *do* experience hatred of Peter; therefore I do implicate the future. Hence consciousness is not a matter of instantaneous, encapsulated awarenesses. My hatred of Peter is

> ... given *in* and *by* each movement of disgust, of repugnance, and of anger, but at the same time it is *not* any of them. My hatred escapes from each of them by affirming permanence. . . . It overflows the instantaneousness of consciousness. . . . Hatred, then, is a transcendent object. Each *Erlebnis* reveals it as a whole, but at the same time the *Erlebnis* is a profile, a projection (an *Abschattung*). Hatred is credit for an infinity of angry or repulsed consciousnesses in the past and in the future. It is the transcendent unity of this infinity of consciousnesses. Thus, to say "I hate" or "I love" on the occasion of a particular consciousness of attraction or repugnance is to effect a veritable passage to infinity, rather analogous to that which we effect when we perceive *an* inkstand, or *the blue* of the blotter.[p]

In Sartre's view the ego (or more precisely, the *me*) stands to a state like hatred in much the same way that the state of hatred stands to the instantaneous anger or disgust that I now feel. That is, the ego is a transcendent object that appears through the state of hatred but is not limited to that state, just as the state of hatred appears through the momentary repugnance but is not limited to that repugnance. This is why the ego is hard to find: Usually we look for it *in* or *behind* the states; but in fact it is transcendent to them. For the most part we think of the ego as a kind of box (a Cartesian substance) that "contains" or "supports" psychic phenomena. But the ego

> ... is nothing outside of the concrete totality of states and actions it supports. Undoubtedly it is transcendent to all the states which it unifies, but not as an abstract X whose mission is only to unify: rather, it is the infinite totality of states and of actions which is never reducible to *an* action or to *a* state.[q]

NO PRIVILEGED ACCESS TO THE EGO

From this account of the ego some important conclusions follow. In the first place, no one has any special, or privileged, access to his own ego. Indeed,

> ... from this point of view my emotions and my states, my ego itself, cease to be my exclusive property. To be precise: up to now a radical distinction has been made between the objectivity of a spatio-temporal thing or of an external truth, and the subjectivity of psychical "states." It seemed as if the subject had a privileged status with respect to his own states. When two

men, according to this conception, talk about the same chair, they really are talking about the *same* thing. This chair which one takes hold of and lifts is *the same* as the chair which the other sees. There is not merely a correspondence of images; there is only one object. But it seemed that when Paul tried to understand a psychical state of Peter, he could not *reach* this state, the intuitive apprehension of which belonged only to Peter. . . . Psychological understanding occurred by analogy. Phenomenology has come to teach us that *states* are objects, that an emotion as such (a love or a hatred) is a transcendent object and cannot shrink into the interior unity of a "consciousness." Consequently, if Paul and Peter both speak of Peter's love, for example, it is no longer true that the one speaks blindly and by analogy of that which the other apprehends in full. They speak of the same thing. Doubtless they apprehend it by different procedures, but these procedures may be equally intuitional. And Peter's emotion is no more *certain* for Peter than for Paul. . . . There is no longer anything "impenetrable" about Peter; unless it is his very consciousness. But his consciousness is *radically* impenetrable. We mean that it is not only refractory to intuition, but to thought.[r]

Sartre has reached exactly the same conclusion about privileged access that Wittgenstein reached—but by a very different route. For Sartre, the accessibility of Peter's hatred (or love) to both Peter and Paul follows directly from the nature of objects. Objects, whether egos or chairs, are present in intuition, but they are never wholly present in any one intuition or in any finite set of intuitions. If, for instance, Peter and Paul see a chair, it is indubitably the case that they have seen (had the experience of) a chair; but it is not indubitably the case that it was a chair that they saw, for the chair was not wholly present in this momentary experience. Only a "profile" was present, and what appeared in this profile may have been an hallucination, not a physical chair. Similarly, Peter and Paul may both experience Peter's anger. But this anger is a profile, and the psychic state that is appearing in it may not be hatred. Peter may be as mistaken as Paul about what psychic state is appearing in Peter's present anger.

> The transcendent totality [that is, the ego] participates in the questionable character of all transcendence. This is to say that everything given to us by our intuitions of the ego is always given as capable of being contradicted by subsequent intuitions. For example, I can see clearly that I am ill-tempered, jealous, etc., and nevertheless I may be mistaken. In other words, I may deceive myself in thinking that I have *such* a *me*. . . . This questionable character of my ego—or even the intuitional error that I commit—does not signify that I have the *true me* which I am unaware of, but only that intended ego has in itself the character of dubitability (in certain cases, the character of falsehood).[s]

Thus Sartre's conclusion is that states of mind are no more and no less dubitable, and no more and no less accessible, than are any other objects. What would Wittgenstein have made of this argument? He would have said that it is not a question of what is really dubitable or of how much is really accessible.

It is simply a question of how we use the terms "dubitable" and "accessible"—and also, of course, the term "really." That is, it is a question not of ontology but of language games.

The second major conclusion that follows from Sartre's account of the ego as a transcendent object is that it is unknowable. This follows from the fact that "the only method for knowing" any object (the chair, for instance) "is observation, approximation, anticipation, experience." But whereas these methods are adequate for knowing spatiotemporal objects like chairs and planets, they are unsuitable for knowing the ego, which is an "intimate" object. The chair and the planet stay over there, far enough away for us to be able to get a good look at them. But the ego

> ... is too much present for one to succeed in taking a truly external viewpoint on it. If we step back for vantage the *me* accompanies us in this withdrawal. It is infinitely near, and I cannot circle around it. Am I an idler or a hard worker? I shall doubtless come to a decision if I consult those who know me and get their opinion. Or again, I can collect facts concerning myself and try to interpret them *as objectively as if it were a question about someone else.* But it would be useless to address myself directly to the *me,* and to try to benefit from its intimacy in order to know it. For it is the *me,* on the contrary, which bars our way. Thus, "really to know oneself" is inevitably to take toward oneself the point of view of others, that is to say, a point of view which is necessarily false. And all those who have tried to know themselves will admit that this introspective attempt shows itself from the start as an effort to reconstitute from detached pieces, from isolated fragments, what is originally given *all at once,* at a stroke. Also, the intuition of the ego is a constantly gulling mirage, for it simultaneously yields everything and yields nothing. How could it be otherwise, moreover, since the ego is not the real totality of consciousnesses (such a totality would be a contradiction, like any infinite unity enacted), but the *ideal* unity of all the states and actions? [t]

Obviously Sartre is describing, in the neutral and objective language of phenomenological psychology, the truth that nauseated Roquetin when he actually encountered it. Having been brought up to believe in some sort of continuing self-identical ego that "inhabits" all of his consciousnesses, and by inhabiting them makes them his, Roquetin was inexpressibly shocked to discover that this inhabitant does not exist—to discover, first, that what exists (to put Roquetin's discovery in the language of phenomenological psychology) are only states and qualities (for example, the state of being an idler, the state of being a hater) and, second, that these states are not "inner" or directly accessible but only reconstituted by means of observation and inference.

SPONTANEITY

But what about the sense each of us has of generating our states and qualities? If, as it seems to me, I create my states spontaneously, my self is not merely social, not merely reconstituted by what I observe and by what people tell me about myself. Sartre would say in reply that it is necessary to distinguish between true spontaneity and pseudo-spontaneity.

> Everyone, by consulting the results of his intuition, can observe that the ego is given as producing its states. . . .
> We begin therefore with this undeniable fact: each new state is fastened directly (or indirectly, by the quality) to the ego, as to its origin. This mode of creation is indeed a creation *ex nihilo*, in the sense that the state is not given as having formerly been in the *me*. . . . The ego is the creator of its states and sustains its qualities in existence by a sort of preserving spontaneity. . . . It would be interesting to study the diverse types of progression from the ego to its states. Most of the time, the progression involved is magical. At other times it may be rational (in the case of reflective will, for example). But always there is a ground of unintelligibility. . . .
> But this spontaneity must not be confused with the spontaneity of consciousness. Indeed, the ego, being an object, is *passive*. It is a question, therefore, of a pseudo-spontaneity which is suitably symbolized by the spurting of a spring, a geyser, etc. This is to say that we are dealing here with a semblance only. Genuine spontaneity must be perfectly clear: it *is* what it produces and can be nothing else.[u]

Sartre's point here is that although I attribute spontaneity to myself (to the personal me), the only true spontaneity is absolutely impersonal. It cannot be attributed to anything; it simply occurs. Each consciousness is a totally new, totally fresh existence that simply emerges out of nothing; it has no real connection—causal, logical, or moral—with anything that has gone before or with anything that will come after. Each consciousness, then, is quite literally absurd. But how is it that this pure impersonal spontaneity comes to be experienced as personal?

As an example, consider some occasion of there being an experience of hatred of Peter. This hatred of Peter is a consciousness that emerges *ex nihilo* and at the unreflected level. Once it has emerged, however, it can be reflected on; and, if reflected on, I attribute it to my ego: It is I that hate Peter. This attribution is correct. The hatred of Peter belongs to my ego in the sense that, as has been seen, reflection reveals the self-consciousness that has been present all the time, but has not yet been posited, in this hatred of Peter. But though this hatred of Peter belongs to my ego, my ego has not *produced* it, in spite of appearances to the contrary. Indeed, far from producing this hatred, my ego (my social me) is itself being constituted in this and other acts of reflection. This production actually occurs in a direction contrary to that in which it seems to occur. In reality, consciousnesses are first; they emerge out of nothing with an impersonal spontaneity. Then in acts of reflection the ego is constituted. Finally, after the ego is constituted,

> . . . consciousness projects its own spontaneity into the ego-object in order to confer on the ego the creative power which is absolutely necessary to it. But this spontaneity, *represented* and *hypostatized* in an object, becomes a degraded and bastard spontaneity, which magically preserves its creative power even while becoming passive. Whence the profound irrationality of the notion of an ego.[v]

But though the ego is irrational, it serves a very useful purpose: Attribution of production to the ego protects us from realizing the true state of affairs. "Perhaps the essential role of the ego is to mask from consciousness its very spontaneity." [w]

Here again Sartre is describing in the language of phenomenological theory the dreadful, total freedom that Roquetin experienced when he inadvertently saw through the mask. It follows from this absolutely spontaneous and impersonal generation of consciousness that at any moment each of us could be totally different from what he is now. Thus it is no good to think complacently, as I read in the newspaper about some vicious crime, "*I* could never do that!" I *could,* and I might. The social self—that is, the only self that I "am"—is but a construction, a "reconstitution," from past accumulations of consciousness; every new consciousness is a totally new existence without connection with this past accumulation. There are, then, no bounds or limits—either psychological or ontological—to what I may become. As Sartre remarks (note the difference in tone from the cry of anguish in the novels),

> . . . there is something distressing for each of us, to catch in the act this tireless creation of existence of which *we* are not the creators. At this level man has the impression of ceaselessly escaping from himself, of overflowing himself, of being surprised by riches which are always unexpected. . . . It seems to us that this monstrous spontaneity is at the origin of numerous psychasthenic ailments. Consciousness is frightened by its own spontaneity. . . . This is clearly seen in an example from Janet. A young bride was in terror, when her husband left her alone, of sitting at the window and summoning the passers-by like a prostitute. Nothing in her education, in her past, nor in her character could serve as an explanation of such a fear. . . . She found herself monstrously free, and this vertiginous freedom appeared to her *at the opportunity* for this action which she was afraid of doing. But this vertigo is comprehensible only if consciousness suddenly appeared to itself as infinitely overflowing in its possibilities the *I* which ordinarily serves as its unity.[x]

We have now reached, by means of a psychological analysis, the question posed in the novels: "What shall I do?" That is, given my total freedom to become anything (as revealed through phenomenological analysis), what shall I become? Given the lack of psychological or ontological limits on what I *can* become, are there any moral limits on what I *may* become? Before examining this moral dilemma, it will be necessary to discuss briefly Sartre's ontology. What light does an examination of the nature of being throw on the human condition?

Sartre's Ontology

Ontology, as Sartre understands it, is the science of being. It is distinguished from metaphysics, which has traditionally been regarded as the science of being, first in that it is purely descriptive and second in that it rejects things-in-themselves and takes its stand on phenomena. Thus Sartre's ontology eliminates the old dichotomy between appearance and reality. Since the phenomena are not the appearances of some "behind-the-scene" reality, "the being of an existent is exactly what it appears." Nevertheless, Sartre's ontology introduces another dichotomy, for though the phenomena are not relative to a noumenal reality, they are relative to consciousness: "'To appear' supposes in essence somebody to whom to appear." [y]

There are, then, two sorts of being. To Sartre this seemed to follow from Brentano's and Husserl's central thesis that consciousness is consciousness-of. Thus the task of ontology, as the science of being, is to describe these two sorts of being—the being of consciousness and the being of that which appears to consciousness.

BEING-IN-ITSELF

Let us consider first the being of that which appears. What can be said about it beyond the fact that it is that which appears? Sartre pointed out that what appears is never wholly or completely an object for any consciousness-of or any series of consciousnesses-of. That this is the case follows from what Sartre has already said about profiles.[34] This real existent—say, the chair over there at the other end of my room—is the intended object of an infinite number of rememberings, perceivings, imaginings, and other intentional acts. "Our theory of the phenomenon has replaced the *reality* of the thing by the *objectivity* of the phenomenon and . . . has based this on an appeal to infinity." [z] Whereas the traditional versions of realism escaped subjectivity by alleging the chair to be an independently existing entity (a thing-in-itself), Sartre held it to be an intentional object with an infinity of profiles. It follows that being is "transphenomenal"; that is, "the being of that which *appears* does not exist *only* in so far as it appears. The transphenomenal being of what exists *for consciousness* is itself in itself (*lui-même en soi*)." [a]

Since being is transphenomenal it is possible to describe it as it is transphenomenally—as it is in itself, without consciousness. What, then, is being-in-itself? Sartre's answer sounds very much like an account of Parmenides' one. Being is "uncreated." It is not a cause, not even a cause of itself. It is neither passive nor active. It does not undergo change or transformation. One cannot say about the in-itself that it is not yet; and "when it gives way, one cannot even say that

34 See p. 432.

it no longer is." One can say only that "it was and at present other beings are." [b] Finally, the in-itself is contingent.

> Necessity concerns the connection between ideal propositions but not that of existents.[35] An existing phenomenon can never be derived from another existent qua existent. This is what we shall call the *contingency* of being-in-itself. But neither can being-in-itself be derived from a *possibility*. . . . Being-in-itself is never either possible or impossible. It *is*. This is what consciousness expresses in anthropomorphic terms by saying that being is superfluous (*de trop*)—that is, that consciousness absolutely cannot derive being from anything, either from another being, or from a possibility, or from a necessary law. Uncreated, without reason for being, without any connection with another being, being-in-itself is *de trop* for eternity.[c]

To sum up, the in-itself is undivided singleness—it is "massive," "solid," "glued to itself." This is why one can say nothing except that the in-itself is. For everything one says *about* it is true, not of the in-itself in itself, but only of it as it is for consciousness.

BEING-FOR-ITSELF

This brings us to the for-itself, that is, conscious being. How is the mode of being of the for-itself to be characterized? Whereas the in-itself simply *is*, the for-itself "is what it is not and is not what it is." To understand this rather obscure saying it will be helpful to think of such typical human activities as imagining, asking questions, and telling lies. What is necessary for a man to be able to imagine a unicorn? It is necessary first to be able to make a realm of imaginary (in distinction from real) things and then to place the unicorn in that realm. But this realm of imagination is *not;* it is a realm of not-being. As for lying, to lie is to say what is not the case; it is to appear to others what one is not. And to be capable of self-deception is to appear to oneself what one is not. Furthermore, to ask questions—to ask, for instance, "Is that a chair?"—is to raise the possibility of nonbeing. To be a man is to be aware that *everything,* not merely the chair, might be otherwise than it appears to be; it is to be aware that everything might not-be. To be a man in fact is to question what one encounters rather than merely to accept it at its face value.

Other human activities can be brought under this same rubric. Thus men are distinguished from, say, chairs not only by their capacity to imagine, to dissimulate, and to question but by their capacity for role-playing. They may be, for instance, waiters, homosexuals, fathers. But no man's being is exhausted by his being a waiter or a homosexual or a father. The man who is a waiter is not a waiter in the same sense that a tree is a tree, for he is not only a waiter but a son. And since he is a son as well as a waiter, it is correct to say that

---

35 [Compare what Roquetin said about the circle. See p. 423—AUTHOR.]

he is not (merely) a waiter. Or consider the fact that man lives into the future. He does not merely grow older as a chair does; he has a sense of the future as a not-yet-but-may-be. At any given point in his life he is not yet what he may become, and his thought about this not-yet (which, because it is a not-yet, is not) nonetheless affects what he now is and does.

Doubtless all these activities can be said to involve, in some sense or other, negation. But is this more than a series of plays on words? In Sartre's view, it is. According to him, he is calling attention to the fundamental characteristic of the mode of being of the for-itself. To be conscious is to be conscious *of* something; to be conscious of something is to be aware of that something as not oneself and of oneself as not that something. Thus the mode of being of the for-itself is not to be the objects it is conscious of, or as Sartre put it more succinctly but also more ambiguously, the mode of being of the for-itself is not-to-be.

This at least casts some light on the obscurity of Sartre's characterization of the for-itself as being that which "is what it is not and is not what it is." Do we, however, want to play this sort of language game—a game in which the for-itself "secretes" nothingness, "nihilates" the in-itself, and is "a hole of being at the heart of being" d? Whether we want to use this language probably turns on whether we think that ontology is a viable enterprise. But this is too large a question and involves too major a parting of the ways to be dealt with here.

It is possible, however, without raising this question and hence without leaving Sartre's frame of reference, to phrase his point in less picturesque language. It may be said that the mode of being of the for-itself differs from the mode of being of the in-itself precisely by the *of* in "consciousness-of." Consciousness does not make being; it makes meanings. When the for-itself "upsurges," [36] it makes a *world*, a world of things that stand in complex spatiotemporal and causal relations to one another and in instrumental relations to the for-itself. Without the for-itself the in-itself does not "have" meanings or "stand in" relations; it simply *is*. Thus the for-itself lives in a world that it has created and for which, as the creator, it is responsible. Here again, stated this time in terms of ontology, is the source of Roquetin's anguish.

In Sartre's view his discovery that there are two modes of being—being-in-itself and being-for-itself—does away with the various dualisms that have plagued philosophy since its beginning: appearance and reality, attribute and essence, actuality and potentiality, idealism and realism. No one will deny that these issues have plagued philosophy; most philosophers who have aspired to philosophize in the grand manner have tackled them. In this sense Sartre is a philosopher in the Western tradition—in contrast, for instance, to Wittgenstein,

36 Ontology can give no account of why the for-itself upsurges. This would be the task of metaphysics. The most ontology can say is that "*everything takes place as if* the in-itself in a project to found itself gave itself the modification of the for-itself" (*Being and Nothingness*, p. 621). But to say "it is as if" is to say that it is a condition contrary to fact. In fact, the for-itself is as contingent as the in-itself; it simply upsurges, and on each occasion of its upsurge it makes a world.

who proposed not to solve these questions but to dissolve them by linguistic therapy.

It is impossible here to appraise Sartre's proposed solution, but we can at least consider the question of whether his so-called "monism of the phenomenon" overcomes the new dualism that Sartre himself introduced. To many philosophers the in-itself and the for-itself are so different that placing them "under the same heading"[e] is merely a meaningless semantic gesture. However this may be, the discussion presented below will concentrate on those aspects of Sartre's ontology that help illuminate the nature of the human predicament. These are the non-existence of God and the total freedom of the for-itself.

GOD DOES NOT EXIST

Whereas Hume modestly undertook to show only that the existence of God cannot be proved and whereas Nietzsche simply announced God's death, Sartre set out to *prove* the nonexistence of God. One advantage of his ontology, from his point of view, is that it demonstrates that the idea of God is contradictory. God is defined by Sartre as being-in-itself-for-itself. This is merely a translation into Sartrian terms of the formulation of such Christian philosophers as St. Thomas. To define God as the Scholastics did—as his own essence, as a self-cause, or as perfect intelligence—is to say that He is being-in-itself-for-itself.

But as soon as God is defined in this way the contradiction is obvious. An in-itself that is for-itself is divided; this follows from the nature of the for-itself. If divided, it is not an in-itself; this follows from the nature of the in-itself. To be a cause, even a self-cause, is to be sufficiently divided for there to be a distinction between cause and effect. To know something, even only to know oneself, is to be sufficiently divided for there to be a distinction between subject and object. For instance,

> . . . no consciousness, not even God's, can . . . apprehend the totality as such. For if God is consciousness, he is integrated in the totality. And if by his nature, he is a being *beyond consciousness* (that is, an in-itself which would be its own foundation) still the totality can appear to him only as *object* (in that case he lacks the totality's internal disintegration as the subjective effort to reapprehend the self) or as subject (then since God *is not* this subject, he can only experience it without knowing it). Thus no point of view on the totality is conceivable.[f]

This gave Sartre still another way of characterizing the human predicament: Man is not only the being who asks questions; he is the being who wants answers. He does not want to be a chair or a tree—an in-itself that does not question.[37] Because he wants answers, he must be a questioner. And he wants answers that are final and complete. That is, man is the being who yearns passionately to be God. But since "the idea of God is contradictory," it follows that "man is a useless passion."[g]

37 But see note 41, p. 444.

Freedom and Action

According to Sartre man has no substantival self. The only self that "is" is the reconstituted social self. Hence—and this follows from the mode of being of the for-itself—man *is* only insofar as he *acts*. Action, of course, is not simply behaving or having things happen to one. A chair may fall or turn over; so may a man. But a man does not act when he falls down, or when his leg jerks in response to a tap on the knee. Action—as a specifically human trait like imagining, perceiving, lying, and role-playing—involves nihilation, nonbeing. When we imagine a unicorn we create an imaginary realm and place the unicorn in this realm. When we act (in distinction from simply reacting) we create a not-yet world and locate the act that we now do in this not-yet (and hence nonworld) as a step toward the realization of it.

The world that we create when we act may be as small as this evening's dinner, or it may be as large as a flight to the moon. That is, our action may have only trivial or it may have momentous consequences. From the point of view of a Utilitarian like Mill it is the consequences themselves that matter, not whether they have come about as a result of someone's action. From Sartre's point of view (and in this respect he is like Kant) consequences, whether momentous or trivial, are inconsequential. What matters is whether we have acted, for only in action—defined as the free adoption of a project—are we truly men. It is only when I *make* a world that I have being in the mode of the for-itself. Otherwise I have being in the mode of the in-itself, for then I am behaving in accordance with a *given* world instead of nihilating that given world in order to become a self.

> A first glance at human reality informs us that for it being is reduced to doing. . . . Thus we find no *given* in human reality in the sense that temperament, character, passions, principles of reason would be acquired or innate *data* existing in the manner of things. . . . Thus human reality does not exist first in order to act later; but for human reality, to be is to act, and to cease to act is to cease to be. . . .
>
> Furthermore, . . . the act . . . must be defined by an *intention*. No matter how this intention is considered, it can be only a surpassing of the given toward a result to be obtained. This given . . . can not provide the reason for a phenomenon which derives all its meaning from a result to be attained; that is, from a non-existent. . . . Psychologists ought to have asked what could be the ontological structure of a phenomenon such that it makes known to itself what it is by means of something which does not yet exist. . . .[38]
>
> Since the intention is a choice of the end and since the world reveals itself across our conduct, it is the intentional choice of the end which reveals the world, and the world is revealed as this or that (in this or that order) according to the end chosen. The end, illuminating the world, is a state *of* the world

---

38 [Thus a phenomenon (for instance, a movement of my hand and arm through space) becomes the act it is (an offer to shake hands) by its projected end (getting someone to make up a quarrel). Given a different project, the *same* phenomenon might be, say, a threat—AUTHOR.]

to be obtained and not yet existing. . . . Thus my *end* can be a good meal if I am hungry. . . . This meal which [is] beyond the dusty road on which I am traveling is projected as the *meaning* of this road. . . .

Thus the intention by a single unitary upsurge posits the end, chooses itself, and appreciates the given in terms of the end. Under these circumstances the given is appreciated in terms of something which does not yet exist; it is in the light of non-being that being-in-itself is illuminated. . . .

This characteristic of the for-itself implies that it is the being which finds *no help, no pillar of support* in what it *was*. But on the other hand, the for-itself is free and can cause there to be a world because the for-itself is *the being which has to be what it was in the light of what it will be*. Therefore the freedom of the for-itself appears as its *being*. . . . We shall never apprehend ourselves except as a choice in the making. But freedom is simply the fact that this choice is always unconditioned.

Such a choice made without base of support and dictating its own causes to itself . . . is absurd.[h]

Thus Sartre reverses the usual way of thinking about human behavior. Most people (not merely social scientists) assume that a man beats his wife and neglects his children because he is (say) a drunkard, and that he is a drunkard because (say) he grew up in a ghetto, without a "proper" upbringing. Thus most people believe that the state of the world (being a drunkard, having grown up in a ghetto) determines what men do. Sartre holds, instead, that the project that we choose (the not-yet end) determines the actual world we live in. A man chooses to be a drunkard, and because he so chooses he lives in a drunkard's world, a world that includes wife-beating and child-neglect. He could choose to live in a different world—that is, he could drop this project and adopt a new one. And he *may* do so at any time: There is nothing in his past that makes this impossible or unlikely.

The free project is fundamental, for it is my being. . . . [It] is a project concerning not my relations with this or that particular object in the world, but my total being-in-the-world. . . . However we need not understand by this that the fundamental project is coextensive with the entire "life" of the for-itself. Since freedom is a being-without-support and without-a-spring-board, the project in order to be must be constantly renewed. I choose myself perpetually and can never be merely by virtue of having-been-chosen; otherwise I should fall into the pure and simple existence of the in-itself. . . . Since I am free, . . . I can always nihilate this first project and make it past. . . .

No law of being can assign an a priori number to the different projects which I am.[i]

FUNDAMENTAL PROJECTS

Obviously, not every project is "fundamental"—the project of eating dinner at a certain restaurant this evening is not. But presumably there was a fundamental project, an "original upsurge," by which I chose the life (for example, that of a loafer and a carefree wanderer) that has brought me to this dusty road this afternoon. According to Sartre, a special method ("existential psychoanalysis") is necessary for uncovering a primary project of this kind. And in such a project we create a total world—the life of a drunkard, or a wanderer, or a homosexual, as the case may be. Since our choice of this fundamental project is absolutely spontaneous, we are wholly responsible for it. We cannot pass on the responsibility to others or excuse ourselves by blaming the time, the place, or the circumstances.

> Thus there are no *accidents* in a life; a community event which suddenly bursts forth and involves me in it does not come from the outside. If I am mobilized in a war, this war is *my* war; it is in my image and I deserve it. I deserve it first because I could always get out of it by suicide or by desertion. . . . For lack of getting out of it, I have *chosen* it. This can be due to inertia, to cowardice in the face of public opinion, or because I prefer certain other values to the value of the refusal to join in the war (the good opinion of my relatives, the honor of my family, etc.). Any way you look at it, it is a matter of a choice. This choice will be repeated later on again and again without a break until the end of the war. . . .j

There is no way to escape from this freedom. I cannot evade responsibility by asking other people's advice about whether I should enlist or desert, for then I have chosen the people whose advice I solicit and I have chosen to follow their advice. If I kill myself in despair over the agonizing choice I face, I have chosen suicide.

Further, when I choose for myself, I also choose for all other men:

> If . . . existence precedes essence, and if we grant that we exist and fashion our image at one and the same time, the image is valid for everybody and for our whole age. Thus our responsibility is much greater than we might have supposed, because it involves all mankind. If I . . . choose to join a Christian trade-union rather than be a communist, and if by being a member I want to show that the best thing for man is resignation, . . . I am not only involving my own case—I want to be resigned for everyone. . . . If I want to marry, to have children, even if this marriage depends solely on my own circumstances or passion or wish, I am involving all humanity in monogamy and not merely myself. . . . I am creating a certain image of man of my own choosing. In choosing myself, I choose man.k

This sounds rather like Kant's categorical imperative, with its universalization principle.[39] But Kant of course held that the universalization principle shows that certain specific acts—truth-telling and promise-keeping, for instance—are always right and that others are always wrong. Sartre rejected this. In his view, each autonomous individual chooses and makes his own world—be it the world

39 See pp. 72–78.

of the deserter or the world of the volunteer. What is universal for Sartre is only the respect that each free man feels for the free choices of other men. In the sense that one cannot say that it is universally wrong to desert and universally right to volunteer Sartre is a subjectivist. But in one respect at least he is an objectivist. In his view, there is one kind of life that is categorically wrong—or at least "dishonest." This is the life that tries to escape responsibility by retreating into, or never emerging from, the social self. Sartre's argument is that to try to escape responsibility is to involve oneself in a logical contradiction—the contradiction of choosing not to choose.

It is true, Sartre says, that we cannot "pass judgment" either on the deserter who really chooses to desert or on the volunteer who really chooses to fight, for each of these men "sanely and sincerely involves himself and chooses his configuration." But we *can* pass judgment on the deserter who has merely followed the lead of his friends or on the volunteer who has unthinkingly accepted the claim his country makes on him.

> First, one can judge (and this is perhaps not a judgment of value, but a logical judgment) that certain choices are based on error and others on truth. If we have defined man's situation as a free choice, with no excuses and no recourse, every man who takes refuge behind the excuse of his passions, every man who sets up a determinism, is a dishonest man.
>
> The objection may be raised, "But why mayn't he choose himself dishonestly?" I reply that I am not obliged to pass moral judgment on him, but that I do define his dishonesty as an error. One can not help considering the truth of the matter. Dishonesty is obviously a falsehood because it belies the complete freedom of involvement. On the same grounds, I maintain that there is also dishonesty if I choose to state that certain values exist prior to me; it is self-contradictory for me to want them and at the same time state that they are imposed on me. Suppose someone says to me, "What if I want to be dishonest?" I'll answer, "There's no reason for you not to be, but I'm saying that that's what you are, and that the strictly coherent attitude is that of honesty."[1]

SOME DIFFICULTIES WITH THIS VIEW

That there is a logical contradiction may be true. But in an absurd world (it might be argued) it is not illogical to choose a logical contradiction. And absurdity apart, if one chooses a contradiction is one *morally* wrong—or is one merely muddleheaded? Perhaps the argument can be restated in a way that will bring out more clearly what seems to be Sartre's real position. Consider the Pacômes[40] of this world. Obviously Sartre detests them; obviously he wants to be able to justify this disgust, to hold that it is not merely prejudice. His argument is that a Pacôme-like existence is not really human. To be human is to make a world by adopting a project. Pacôme has not made a world; he has accepted

40 See p. 425.

ready-made the world of his social class—a given. He has not chosen capitalism; he *is* a capitalist. Thus the contradiction consists in the fact that Pacôme is a man who is not a man—a for-itself that does not have being in the mode of the for-itself but in the mode of the in-itself.

Note that this is not the expression of a prejudice; it is not even a value judgment. It is (or at least purports to be) the assertion of an ontological truth. But, unfortunately, the argument proves too much. Pacôme is not a capitalist in the way in which a tree is a tree or an inkwell is an inkwell. Sartre of course was quite aware of this; indeed, in another connection he made a point of it.[41] Thus, just as some men yearn for the complex being of the in-itself-for-itself, so others yearn for the simplicity of the being of the in-itself. But in Sartre's view the one desire is as vain as the other. Man is condemned to be free.

It is easy to agree that man cannot *be* simply in the mode of the in-itself. But is it any more possible to be (except in unusual circumstances and then only from moment to moment) in the mode of the for-itself? Consider Brunet,[42] for instance. It is true that Brunet chose to be a Communist. He did not grow up as a Communist; nor did he drift into it, as we might suppose Pacôme slipped, without noticing, into being a capitalist. But the fact that Brunet chose makes no real difference, for once he became a Communist and accepted party discipline he no longer made his world; communism became his "given." Nor does this problem exist only for Communists and for other people who accept an authoritarian code. A man who adopts desertion as his project is only too likely to slip from his freedom into playing the role of a deserter. Similarly, the man whose project is to become a soldier or the man whose project is his own existential freedom is likely to slip from freedom. Doubtless some projects lend themselves more easily than others to slippage into bad faith. But no project, by its very nature as a project, is immune to such slippage.[43]

The trouble is that Sartre's account of the for-itself commits him to holding that freedom is an all-or-none affair, whereas to many people it will seem a matter of degree. The same is true for humanity, and also for responsibility. Consider the question of responsibility. Most people hold that there are degrees of responsibility, corresponding roughly to the legal distinctions between first-degree murder, manslaughter, negligence, and innocence. Regarding the American atomic attack on Japan during World War II, they might say that President

---

41 For example, Mathieu's friend Daniel, a homosexual, wants to *be* a homosexual, that is, to "coincide" with himself: "Just to be. In the dark, at random! To be homosexual just as the oak is oak. To extinguish myself" (*The Reprieve*, p. 101). Similarly, in *Nausea* (p. 234) Roquetin says, "I, too, wanted to *be*."

42 See note 31, p. 427.

43 One of the difficulties for a man who is committed to "commitment" is that in order to get things done in the world he must combine forces with other men—not only join a movement but institutionalize (even bureaucratize) it. And this, it would seem, means surrendering one's freedom and hence becoming a thing. This is the paradox Sartre encountered in his own life; it helps to explain his on-again, off-again relationship with the Communist Party.

Truman and his advisers were "chiefly" responsible, that the scientists who designed the bomb and the aviators who flew the plane were "somewhat" responsible, and that the ordinary citizen, who did not even know that nuclear fission had been achieved, was "not at all" responsible. These are doubtless vague notions, but they represent an attitude toward morality that is profoundly different from Sartre's. In his view, since men are totally free they are wholly responsible: Since everyone of us could have made a world that excluded the atomic attack on Hiroshima, we are all equally responsible for that attack. To some this view will appear extreme.[44]

Further, it could be plausibly argued that total freedom, far from entailing total responsibility, is actually incompatible with responsibility. It might be maintained that to be responsible for an act is to attribute this act to a self that, in some sense or other, has endured from the past into the present that includes this act. An act that is simply the upsurge of a wholly impersonal spontaneity is not owned by anyone.

Sartre's reply would probably be, first, that phenomenological observation fails to disclose any such enduring self and, second, that it does disclose perfect freedom. Further, he would say that the critic's philosophical objections are only a subtle attempt to evade responsibility by closing his eyes to his own freedom. This brings us back to the vision that is so passionately affirmed in the novels and the plays. Is this vision reliable? Sartre of course is committed to it—"Suddenly, suddenly, the veil is torn away, I have understood, I have *seen*."[m] If Sartre's vision of the human condition is veridical, then criticisms of this or that detail of the ontology, though perhaps of some "philosophical" interest, are from an existential viewpoint trivial.

Or is the vision but one more interpretation, an interpretation made by one man at one point in the world's history? If so, our attitude toward Sartre's whole enterprise inevitably shifts—even though it is easy to understand why, given the nature of modern mass-society, a morally sensitive man would experience the world as Sartre experiences it, and as Kierkegaard and Nietzsche experienced it. But is it correct to interpret the vision as an interpretation, instead of seeing it as a "seeing"? To this question there can be no definitive, objective answer;

---

44 Since writing *Being and Nothingness* Sartre has relaxed his assertion that man is totally free. In *Search for a Method*, which is a part of his *Critique of Dialectical Reason*, he suggests that the social order imposes severe restraints on man's freedom to exist in the mode of being of the for-itself. According to Sartre, this is what is wrong with capitalism. It keeps the vast majority of men in such a deprived condition economically and socially that they are unable to exercise their freedom. Marxism, by destroying the class structure, will make true existential freedom possible. But will the existential anguish experienced by Roquetin, Mathieu, and Sartre's other protagonists be relieved even in a Marxist utopia? Anguish seems to have its source in human nature (the for-itself), not in socioeconomic conditions. It is difficult, therefore, to determine whether Sartre's new views are compatible with his existential phenomenology—or, indeed, whether it is important to him that they be compatible. The most that can be said is that Sartre's philosophical development exemplifies his view of freedom: A new upsurge is possible at any moment.

it can be answered only by each individual in terms of his own life and the way he chooses to lead it. To this extent it would appear that Sartre's existential phenomenology is true even if it is false.

With Sartre, who everyone will agree is a contemporary philosopher, we have crossed the vague boundary that separates the history of philosophy from the study of contemporary philosophy. It is time, then, for this particular history to end. What conclusions can be drawn from this long survey? It would seem that the only definite conclusion is that no conclusions are definite. One might well ask, therefore, if this record of philosophy's failure is not a virtual confession of the bankruptcy of philosophy. What is the possible use of so obviously futile a subject?

These questions assume that the business of philosophy is to find answers. But perhaps its business is to *ask* questions, not to answer them. If it is worth men's while to rebuff dogmatism and intolerance and to keep before the mind a sense of possibilities as yet unrealized, then philosophy has an important social use, and its utility lies precisely in what seems to some its futility. Its special competence lies in its seeming incompetence—in the way in which it discourages solutions that are too neat and too easy.

To many men and women today, as to Yeats, things seem to "fall apart." But the history of the Western mind offers a "dusty answer" only to those who are "hot for certainties in this our life." To others with less grandiose expectations it is a study in *reasonableness*. To be reasonable is to be able to distinguish between evidence and emotional appeal even while recognizing that under certain circumstances emotion becomes a form of evidence. It is to be ready to abide by evidence even while recognizing that evidence is always incomplete. Reasonableness involves a search for truth that inevitably fails but that is never wholly defeated. It requires faith in the possibility of correction and gradual advance. To study the history of philosophy is to see reasonableness at work in the world. It is this open-ended, on-going pursuit of truth, rather than any alleged eternal verities trapped in the process, that is our noblest inheritance, and also our best hope for the future.

Notes

Chapter 1 / The Age of Reason

a Antoine Nicholas de Caritat, Marquis de Condorcet, *Sketch for a Historical Picture of the Progress of the Human Mind,* translated by J. Barraclough (Weidenfeld and Nicolson, London, 1955), pp. 173–75, 179, 187–88, 199, and 200–01.

b *Emile* (J. M. Dent, London, 1930), p. 239. The passage is from "The Creed of a Savoyard Priest," Bk. IV.

c *Decline and Fall of the Roman Empire,* Ch. XV.

d *Ibid.,* Ch. XX.

e *The Spirit of the Laws,* translated by T. Nugent and revised by F. V. Prichard (Bohn, London, 1896–97), I, i.

f *Ibid.,* XIV, i.

g *Ibid.,* XIV, ii.

h This condensation is made from the German text in *Immanuel Kants Werke,* edited by E. Cassirer (E. Cassirer, Berlin, 1922), Vol. IV, pp. 169–76.

i   *Ibid.*, Vol. VI, pp. 452–53.
j   *Notes from Underground*, in *The Best Short Stories of Dostoyevsky*, translated by D. Magarshack (Modern Library, New York, n.d.), pp. 107–08, 111–13, 117–18, 129–30, 133, and 136.
k   *Ibid.*, pp. 239–40.
l   *Ibid.*, p. 174.
m   *Ibid.*, p. 108.
n   *Ibid.*, p. 142.
o   *Ibid.*, p. 138.
p   *Ibid.*, p. 163.
q   *Ibid.*, p. 144.
r   *Ibid.*, p. 234.

Chapter 2   /   Kant: Theory of Knowledge

a   *Critique of Pure Reason*, translated by N. Kemp Smith (Macmillan, London, 1929), B xii–xviii. (A refers to text of first edition, B to text of second edition.)
b   *Ibid.*, B 3–4.
c   *Ibid.*, B 1–2.
d   *Ibid.*, B 14–16.
e   *Ibid.*, A 23–25 = B 38–40.
f   *Ibid.*, B 40–41.
g   *Ibid.*, A 26–28 = B 42–44.
h   *Ibid.*, A 51 = B 75.
i   *Ibid.*, A 70 = B 95.
j   *Ibid.*, A 80 = B 106.
k   *Ibid.*, A 79 = B 104–05.
l   *Ibid.*, A 104–06.
m   *Ibid.*, A 107–08 and 111 = B 164–65.
n   *Ibid.*, A 177 = B 218–19.
o   *Ibid.*, A 182–89 = B 225–32.
p   *Ibid.*, A 189–95 = B 233–40.
q   *Ibid.*, B 406–11.
r   *Ibid.*, footnote to B 411.
s   *Ibid.*, A 426 ff. = B 454 ff.
t   *Ibid.*, A 466 and 468 = B 494 and 496.
u   *Ibid.*, A 470–71 = B 498–99.
v   *Ibid.*, A 592–602 = B 620–30.
w   *Ibid.*, A 604–10 = B 632–38.
x   *Ibid.*, A 623–27 = B 651–55.
y   *Ibid.*, A 642–60 = B 670–88.
z   *Ibid.*, A 670–86 = B 698–714.
a   *Ibid.*, A 253–56 = B 306–11.
b   *Ibid.*, B xxiv–xxx.
c   *Ibid.*, B xxvi.

Chapter 3   /   Kant: Theory of Value

a   *Fundamental Principles of the Metaphysic of Morals*, translated by T. K. Abbott (Longmans Green, London, 1927), §1, pp. 9–10.

b   *Ibid.*, §1, pp. 16–17.

c   *Ibid.*, §2, pp. 32–33 and 35–36.

d   *Ibid.*, §1, p. 18.

e   This and the following passage are from *A Treatise of Human Nature*, III, ii, 1.

f   *Fundamental Principles*, translated by Abbott, *op. cit.*, §2, pp. 46–47.

g   K. Vorlander, *Immanuel Kant* (F. Meiner, Leipzig, 1924), Vol. II, p. 331.

h   *Fundamental Principles*, translated by Abbott, *op. cit.*, §2, pp. 52–59.

i   *Ibid.*, §2, p. 46.

j   *Critique of Practical Reason*, translated by T. K. Abbott (Longmans Green, London, 1927), Pt. I, Bk. I, Ch. 3, pp. 188 ff.

k   Compare C. D. Broad, *Five Types of Ethical Theory* (Kegan Paul, London, 1930), pp. 138–39.

l   *Fundamental Principles*, translated by Abbott, *op. cit.*, §3, pp. 65–66.

m   *Critique of Practical Reason*, translated by Abbott, *op. cit.*, Pt. I, Bk. II, Ch. 2, §1, p. 206.

n   *Ibid.*, §5, pp. 220–22.

o   *Ibid.*, §4, pp. 218–19.

p   *Critique of Judgment*, translated by J. H. Bernard (Macmillan, London, 1931), §87, pp. 381–82.

q   *Ibid.*, §86, pp. 372–73.

r   *Religion Within the Limits of Reason Alone*, translated by T. M. Greene and H. H. Hudson (Open Court, Chicago, 1934), Bk. II, §§IA and IB, pp. 54–57.

Chapter 4   /   Reactions Against Kantianism: Hegel and Schopenhauer

a   Wordsworth, *Expostulation and Reply.*

b   Wordsworth, *To My Sister.*

c   Keats, *What the Thrush Said.*

d   Byron, *The Dream.*

e   Wordsworth, *Lines composed on the beach near Calais in the autumn of 1802.*

f   Wordsworth, *Ode. Intimations of Immortality from Recollections of Early Childhood.*

g   Coleridge, *To a Young Ass.*

h   Wordsworth, *Tintern Abbey.*

i   Byron, *Mont Blanc.*

j   Byron, *Childe Harold*, Canto IV.

k   Wordsworth, *Tintern Abbey.*

l   *Faust*, translated by L. MacNeice (Oxford University Press, 1952), p. 23.

m   *The Phenomenology of Mind*, translated by J. B. Baillie (Allen and Unwin, London, 1949), p. 127.

n   *Ibid.*, p. 124.

o   *Ibid.*, p. 125.

p   *Ibid.*, pp. 80 and 113–14.

q   T. S. Eliot, *The Love Song of J. Alfred Prufrock*, in *The Complete Poems and Plays* (Harcourt, Brace & World, New York, 1952), p. 7.

r   *Phenomenology*, translated by Baillie, *op. cit.*, p. 68.

s   *Ibid.*, p. 82.

t   *Ibid.*, p. 117.

u   *Ibid.*, pp. 108–10.

v   *Faust*, translated by MacNeice, *op. cit.*, p. 113.

w   *Phenomenology*, translated by Baillie, *op. cit.*, pp. 72–74 and 79.

x   *Ibid.*, pp. 111–13.

y   *Ibid.*, pp. 81–82 and 85–86.

z   *Ibid.*, pp. 80–81.

a   *Ibid.*, pp. 131–32 and 139–45.

b *Ibid.*, p. 70.
c *Encyclopaedia of the Philosophical Sciences,* translated by W. Wallace (Clarendon Press, Oxford, 1892), Ch. VII, §§86–88.
d *Ibid.*, Ch. VIII, §156.
e *Philosophy of Right,* translated by T. M. Knox (Clarendon Press, Oxford, 1942), §§158, 160–63, and 167–68.
f *Phenomenology,* translated by Baillie, *op. cit.*, p. 75.
g *Ibid.*, p. 89.
h *The World as Will and Idea,* translated by R. B. Haldane and J. Kemp (Kegan Paul, London, 1883), Bk. I, §6.
i *Ibid.*, Bk. I, §12.
j *Ibid.*, Bk. II, §18.
k *Ibid.*, Bk. III, §33.
l Byron, *Stanzas to the Po.*
m *The World as Will and Idea,* translated by Haldane and Kemp, *op. cit.*, Bk. III, §34.
n *Ibid.*, Bk. IV, §54.
o *Ibid.*, Bk. IV, §63.
p *Ibid.*, Bk. IV, §68.
q *Ibid.*
r Quoted in E. Caird, *Hegel* (Blackwood, London, 1903), p. 40.

Chapter 5 / Science, Scientism, and Social Philosophy

a J. Bentham, *Theory of Legislation,* translated from the French of E. Dumont by C. M. Atkinson (Clarendon Press, Oxford, 1914), Vol. I, pp. 1–5 and 42–43.
b *On Liberty,* (J. M. Dent, London, 1910), Ch. I, pp. 72–75.
c *Ibid.*, Ch. II, pp. 79–81, 95, and 102–03.
d *Ibid.*, Ch. III, p. 121.
e *Ibid.*, Ch. V, pp. 151–52.
f *Ibid.*, Ch. V, p. 154.
g *Utilitarianism* (J. M. Dent, London, 1910), Ch. IV, pp. 32–33.
h *The Positive Philosophy of Auguste Comte,* translated by H. Martineau (George Bell, London, 1896), Vol. II, pp. 151–53.
i Keats, *Lamia,* Pt. II, ll. 231–37.
j *Early Writings,* translated and edited by T. B. Bottomore (C. A. Watts, London, 1963), pp. 120–25.
k *Socialism: Utopian and Scientific,* translated by E. Aveling (Scribner's, New York, 1892) p. 43.
l *Ibid.*, pp. 51–53 and 55.
m *Ibid.*, p. 72.
n *The German Ideology,* translated by R. Pascal (International Publishers, New York, 1947), p. 22.
o *Socialism: Utopian and Scientific,* translated by Aveling, *op. cit.*, p. 82.
p *The Communist Manifesto,* edited by F. Engels (Henry Regnery, Chicago, 1954), pp. 34 and 5.
q *Ibid.*, p. 25.
r *Ibid.*, p. 35.
s "Contribution to the Critique of Hegel's Philosophy of Right," in *Early Writings,* translated by Bottomore, *op. cit.*, pp. 43–44 and 52–53.
t *Ibid.*, p. 39.
u *Ibid.*, p. 5.

v   *A Contribution to the Critique of Political Economy,* translated by N. I. Stone (Charles Kerr, Chicago, 1911), pp. 11–12.

w   *Socialism: Utopian and Scientific,* translated by Aveling, *op. cit.,* pp. 3–4.

x   "Contribution to the Critique of Hegel's Philosophy of Right," in *Early Writings,* translated by Bottomore, *op. cit.,* p. 44.

y   *Ibid.,* p. 52.

z   *Socialism: Utopian and Scientific,* translated by Aveling, *op. cit.,* pp. xv–xvi.

a   *Theses on Feuerbach,* in Friedrich Engels, *Ludwig Feuerbach* (International Publishers, New York, 1941), pp. 82–84.

b   *The Origin of Species* (A. L. Burt, New York, n.d.), p. 17.

c   *Ibid.,* p. 20.

d   *Ibid.,* pp. 59–60.

e   *Ibid.,* pp. 83–84.

f   *Ibid.,* pp. 124–25.

g   *Ibid.,* pp. 500 and 504.

h   Compare G. West, *Charles Darwin* (Routledge, London, 1937), pp. 249 ff.

i   *Origin of Species, op. cit.,* p. 505.

j   *The Riddle of the Universe* (Harper & Row, New York, 1900), pp. 13–14.

k   *Ibid.,* p. 349.

l   *The Mechanist Conception of Life* (University of Chicago Press, 1912), p. 3.

m   *Ibid.,* pp. 26–27 and 41.

n   *Ibid.,* p. 31.

o   *The History and Theory of Vitalism,* translated by C. K. Ogden (Macmillan, London, 1914), pp. 208–09.

p   *Ibid.,* p. 204.

q   *The Science and Philosophy of the Organism* (A. and C. Black, London, 1908), p. 41.

r   *The Science of Mechanics,* translated by T. J. McCormack (Open Court, Chicago, 1907), p. 492.

s   *Ibid.,* pp. x and 481–83.

t   *Ibid.,* pp. 5–6.

u   *Ibid.,* pp. 1, 4, and 489–90.

v   *The Grammar of Science* (A. and C. Black, London, 1911), pp. viii, 95–96, vi, and 96.

w   *Ibid.,* pp. 115–16.

x   *Ibid.,* p. 73.

y   *Ibid.,* pp. 15, 37, and 17.

z   Bertrand Russell, "Logical Atomism," in *Contemporary British Philosophy,* edited by J. H. Muirhead (Macmillan, New York, 1924), p. 379.

Chapter 6   /   Kierkegaard and Nietzsche

a   *The Journals of Kierkegaard,* translated and edited by A. Dru (Collins, London, 1958), p. 44.

b   *Ibid.,* p. 96.

c   *Ibid.,* p. 54.

d   *Ibid.,* p. 39.

e   *Ibid.,* p. 89.

f   *Ibid.,* pp. 50–51.

g   *Ibid.,* p. 65.

h   *Ibid.,* p. 149.

i   *Ibid.,* p. 106.

j   *The Point of View for My Work as an Author,* translated by W. Lowrie and edited by B. Nelson (Harper & Row, New York, 1962), p. 76.

k   *Journals,* translated by Dru, *op. cit.,* p. 85.

l   *Ibid.*, p. 70.

m   *Ibid.*, pp. 71–72.

n   *Ibid.*, p. 87.

o   *Ibid.*, p. 224.

p   *Point of View for My Work as an Author*, translated by Lowrie, *op. cit.*, p. 18.

q   *Kierkegaard's Concluding Unscientific Postscript*, translated by D. F. Swenson with notes and introduction by W. Lowrie (Princeton University Press, 1941), p. 276.

r   *Journals*, translated by Dru, *op. cit.*, p. 46.

s   *Concluding Unscientific Postscript*, translated by Swenson, *op. cit.*, pp. 267, 271, and 273.

t   *Ibid.*, pp. 274 and 277–81.

u   *Ibid.*, pp. 302–04.

v   Mark 7 : 20–21, in *The Complete Bible*, translated by J. M. Powis Smith and E. J. Goodspeed (University of Chicago Press, 1939).

w   *Journals*, translated by Dru, *op. cit.*, pp. 181–82.

x   *Either/Or*, translated by W. Lowrie and revised by H. A. Johnson (Doubleday, Garden City, N. Y., 1959), Vol. II, pp. 171 and 173.

y   *Concluding Unscientific Postscript*, translated by Swenson, *op. cit.*, p. 180.

z   *Ibid.*, p. 183.

a   *Journals*, translated by Dru, *op. cit.*, p. 184.

b   *Concluding Unscientific Postscript*, translated by Swenson, *op. cit.*, p. 84.

c   *Either/Or*, translated by Lowrie, *op. cit.*, Vol. II, pp. 347–48 and 354.

d   *Concluding Unscientific Postscript*, translated by Swenson, *op. cit.*, p. 182.

e   *Fear and Trembling*, translated with notes by W. Lowrie (Doubleday, Garden City, N. Y., 1954), pp. 69–72.

f   *Concluding Unscientific Postscript*, translated by Swenson, *op. cit.*, p. 431.

g   *Ibid.*, p. 445.

h   *Ibid.*, pp. 434–35.

i   *Ibid.*, p. 178.

j   *Ibid.*, p. 181.

k   *Ibid.*, pp. 25–26, 29–30, and 32.

l   *Ibid.*, p. 51.

m   *Either/Or*, translated by Lowrie, *op. cit.*, Vol. II, p. 19; *Journals*, translated by Dru, *op. cit.*, pp. 77, 175, 214, and 191; *Concluding Unscientific Postscript*, translated by Swenson, *op. cit.*, p. 318.

n   *The Genealogy of Morals*, translated by F. Golffing (Doubleday, Garden City, N. Y., 1956), p. 255; *Beyond Good and Evil*, translated by M. Cowan (Henry Regnery, Chicago, 1955), pp. 100–01.

o   *Genealogy of Morals*, translated by Golffing, *op. cit.*, pp. 209–10.

p   "On Truth and Lie in an Extra-Moral Sense," in *The Portable Nietzsche*, edited by W. Kaufman (Viking, New York, 1954), p. 44.

q   *Genealogy of Morals*, translated by Golffing, *op. cit.*, pp. 178–79.

r   *Beyond Good and Evil*, translated by Cowan, *op. cit.*, pp. 18–19.

s   *Ibid.*, pp. 3–6.

t   *Ibid.*, p. 15.

u   *Ibid.*, pp. 24–26.

v   "On Truth and Lie," in *The Portable Nietzsche*, *op. cit.*, pp. 42–43 and 46–47.

w   *Genealogy of Morals*, translated by Golffing, *op. cit.*, pp. 217–18 and 225–26.

x   "Notes, 1875," in *The Portable Nietzsche*, *op. cit.*, p. 50.

y   *Genealogy of Morals*, translated by Golffing, *op. cit.*, p. 219.

z   *Beyond Good and Evil*, translated by Cowan, *op. cit.*, pp. 42–43.

a   *Ibid.*, p. 201.

b   *Genealogy of Morals*, translated by Golffing, *op. cit.*, pp. 170–72.

c   *Ibid.*, p. 267.

d   *Ibid.*, p. 268.
e   *Ibid.*, p. 269.
f   *Ibid.*, p. 271.
g   *Ibid.*, pp. 276 and 279.
h   *Beyond Good and Evil,* translated by Cowan, *op. cit.*, pp. 70–71.
i   *Twilight of the Idols,* in *The Portable Nietzsche, op. cit.*, p. 508.
j   *Beyond Good and Evil,* translated by Cowan, *op. cit.*, p. 175.
k   "On Truth and Lie," in *The Portable Nietzsche, op. cit.*, p. 44.
l   *Collected Poems of Thomas Hardy* (Macmillan, New York, 1925), p. 7.
m   *Thus Spoke Zarathustra,* in *The Portable Nietzsche, op. cit.*, pp. 268–72.
n   "Homer's Conquest," in *The Portable Nietzsche, op. cit.*, p. 38.
o   *The Birth of Tragedy,* translated by F. Golffing (Doubleday, Garden City, N. Y., 1956), pp. 59–60.
p   "Homer's Conquest," in *The Portable Nietzsche, op. cit.*, p. 37.
q   *Twilight of the Idols,* in *The Portable Nietzsche, op. cit.*, p. 518.
r   *Thus Spoke Zarathustra,* in *The Portable Nietzsche, op. cit.*, p. 129.
s   *Twilight of the Idols,* in *The Portable Nietzsche, op. cit.*, pp. 553–54.
t   *Beyond Good and Evil,* translated by Cowan, *op. cit.*, p. 230.
u   *Genealogy of Morals,* translated by Golffing, *op. cit.*, p. 157.

Chapter 7   /   Three Philosophies of Process: Bergson, Dewey, and Whitehead

a   *An Introduction to Metaphysics,* translated by T. E. Hulme (Putnam's, New York, 1912), pp. 1–19.
b   *Ibid.*, pp. 21 and 39–40.
c   *Creative Evolution,* translated by A. Mitchell (Henry Holt, New York, 1911), pp. 1–2 and 4–5.
d   *Introduction to Metaphysics,* translated by Hulme, *op. cit.*, pp. 55–56 and 62–64.
e   *Creative Evolution,* translated by Mitchell, *op. cit.*, pp. 94–95.
f   *Ibid.*, p. 127.
g   *Ibid.*, pp. 126 and 98–99.
h   *Ibid.*, pp. 109–11.
i   *Ibid.*, pp. 131–32.
j   *Ibid.*, p. 133.
k   *Ibid.*, pp. 139 and 140–41.
l   *Ibid.*, pp. 144–45.
m   *Ibid.*, pp. 152–54.
n   *Ibid.*, p. 160.
o   *Ibid.*, pp. 165 and 153.
p   *Introduction to Metaphysics,* translated by Hulme, *op. cit.*, pp. 40–43.
q   *Creative Evolution,* translated by Mitchell, *op. cit.*, pp. 136 and 176.
r   *The Two Sources of Morality and Religion,* translated by R. Ashley Audra and C. Brereton (Henry Holt, New York, 1935), pp. 15–18.
s   *Ibid.*, pp. 112, 5, and 121.
t   *Ibid.*, pp. 59–60.
u   *Ibid.*, p. 76.
v   *Ibid.*, pp. 264–65, 257, 285, and 214–15.
w   *Ibid.*, pp. 285, 287, and 289.
x   *Ibid.*, pp. 300–01.
y   *Creative Evolution,* translated by Mitchell, *op. cit.*, pp. 101–02 and 84.
z   *Human Nature and Conduct* (Henry Holt, New York, 1922), pp. 42 and 15.
a   *Ibid.*, pp. 95 and 155–57.
b   *How We Think* (Heath, Boston, 1933), pp. 100–07.

c   *Human Nature and Conduct, op. cit.*, pp. 98–99 and 101.

d   "Democracy and Educational Administration," *School and Society* (April 3, 1937), reprinted in *Intelligence in the Modern World*, edited by J. Ratner (Modern Library, New York, 1939), pp. 400–04.

e   *The Quest for Certainty* (Minton, Balch & Company, New York, 1929), pp. 3–24.

f   *Experience and Nature* (Open Court, Chicago, 1929), pp. iii and 4a-I.

g   *Ibid.*, pp. v and iv.

h   *Ibid.*, pp. 318–20.

i   *Ibid.*, pp. 182–83.

j   *Ibid.*, p. 11.

k   *Quest for Certainty, op. cit.*, pp. 150–59.

l   *Experience and Nature, op. cit.*, p. 185.

m   *Ibid.*, pp. 179 and 184–85.

n   *Ibid.*, p. 319.

o   *Ibid.*, pp. 6–8.

p   *Ibid.*, p. 24, n. 1.

q   *Ibid.*, p. 3a.

r   *Ibid.*, pp. 321–22.

s   *Ibid.*, pp. 161, 156, and 158.

t   *Ibid.*, pp. ii–iii.

u   *Ibid.*, pp. 2, 96, and 21.

v   *Ibid.*, pp. iv–v.

w   *Ibid.*, p. 394.

x   *Ibid.*, pp. 395–96 and 403–04.

y   *Ibid.*, p. 425.

z   *Quest for Certainty, op. cit.*, pp. 258–61.

a   *Experience and Nature, op. cit.*, p. 437.

b   "Autobiographical Notes," in *The Philosophy of Alfred North Whitehead*, edited by P. A. Schilpp (Northwestern University, 1941), p. 5.

c   *Essays in Science and Philosophy* (Philosophical Library, New York, 1947), p. 14.

d   *Process and Reality* (Macmillan, New York, 1929), p. 15.

e   *Modes of Thought* (Macmillan, New York, 1938), pp. 233–34 and 237–38.

f   *Science and the Modern World* (Macmillan, New York, 1925), p. 27.

g   *Modes of Thought, op. cit.*, p. 58.

h   *Process and Reality, op. cit.*, p. 30.

i   *Science and the Modern World, op. cit.*, pp. 29–41.

j   *Process and Reality, op. cit.*, pp. 7–12.

k   *Ibid.*, pp. 4–8.

l   *Ibid.*, pp. 11–14.

m   *Ibid.*, p. x.

n   *Ibid.*, pp. 21–22 and 25–26.

o   *Science and the Modern World, op. cit.*, pp. 71–74.

p   *Ibid.*, p. 24.

q   *An Enquiry Concerning the Principles of Natural Knowledge* (Cambridge University Press, 1919), pp. 1–3.

r   *Ibid.*, p. 16.

s   *Science and the Modern World, op. cit.*, pp. 5–6.

t   *Principles of Natural Knowledge, op. cit.*, pp. 10–11.

u   *Science and the Modern World, op. cit.*, p. 80.

v   *Ibid.*, p. 127.

w   *Ibid.*, pp. 113–15.

x   *Ibid.*, p. 226.

y   *Principles of Natural Knowledge, op. cit.*, p. 13.

z *Science and the Modern World, op. cit.,* pp. 52–55.

a *Ibid.,* pp. 158–59 and 183.

b *Ibid.,* pp. 191, 189–90, and 191.

c *Ibid.,* p. 150.

d *Process and Reality, op. cit.,* p. 70.

e *Science and the Modern World, op. cit.,* pp. 158, 126, and 227–29.

f *Ibid.,* pp. 136–67.

g *Ibid.,* pp. 250–57.

h *Ibid.,* p. 228.

i "Mathematics and the Good," in *The Philosophy of Alfred North Whitehead, op. cit.,* pp. 674 and 677–78.

j "Immortality," in *The Philosophy of Alfred North Whitehead,* pp. 684 and 683–84.

k *Science and the Modern World, op. cit.,* p. 275.

l *Ibid.,* pp. 249–50.

m *Ibid.,* pp. 266 and 264.

Chapter 8 / The Analytical Tradition: Russell and Wittgenstein

a *Leviathan,* in *The English Works of Thomas Hobbes,* edited by W. Molesworth (Bohn, London, 1839), Vol. III, Pt. I, Ch. 4.

b *An Essay Concerning Human Understanding,* edited by A. C. Fraser (Clarendon Press, Oxford, 1894), Epistle to the Reader.

c *Principles of Human Knowledge,* edited by A. C. Fraser (Clarendon Press, Oxford, 1901), Introduction, §24.

d *Principia Ethica* (Cambridge University Press, 1903), p. vii.

e "Logical Atomism," in *Contemporary British Philosophy* edited by J. H. Muirhead (Macmillan, New York, 1924), p. 359.

f *Introduction to Mathematical Philosophy* (Macmillan, New York, 1930), p. 4.

g *Ibid.,* p. 5.

h *Ibid.,* pp. 11 and 14–18.

i *Ibid.,* p. 194.

j *Our Knowledge of the External World* (Open Court, Chicago, 1929), pp. 45–48 and 62.

k *Introduction to Mathematical Philosophy, op. cit.,* p. 168.

l *Ibid.,* pp. 172–77.

m "Logical Atomism," in *Contemporary British Philosophy, op. cit.,* p. 365.

n *Ibid.,* p. 371.

o *Ibid.,* pp. 379–80.

p *Mysticism and Logic* (Longmans Green, London, 1918), p. 98; *Philosophy* (Norton, New York, 1927), p. 2.

q "Logical Atomism," in *Contemporary British Philosophy, op. cit.,* pp. 368–69.

r *Our Knowledge of the External World, op. cit.,* p. 52.

s *Ibid.,* p. 42, n. 1.

t *Ibid.,* p. 5.

u "Philosophy in the Twentieth Century," in *Sceptical Essays* (Allen and Unwin, London, 1935), pp. 61–63.

v *Ibid.,* pp. 65–68.

w *Our Knowledge of the External World, op. cit.,* p. 4.

x *Religion and Science* (Thornton Butterworth, London, 1935), p. 204.

y *Our Knowledge of the External World, op. cit.,* pp. 75–77.

z *An Inquiry into Meaning and Truth* (Norton, New York, 1940), pp. 9–10.

a *Ibid.,* p. 15.

b "My Mental Development" and "Reply to Critics," in *The Philosophy of Bertrand Russell*, edited by P. A. Schilpp (Northwestern University, 1944), pp. 700, 16, and 719.

c *Sceptical Essays, op. cit.*, pp. 11 and 45.

d *Philosophy, op. cit.*, p. 225.

e *Religion and Science, op. cit.*, pp. 175–76, 230–31, and 235–40.

f *Ibid.*, pp. 233–35.

g *The Impact of Science on Society* (Columbia University Press, 1951), pp. 51–59.

h *Religion and Science, op. cit.*, pp. 9, 144, 8, and 7.

i *The Impact of Science on Society, op. cit.*, pp. 44 and 45; *The Problems of Philosophy* (Henry Holt, New York, n.d.), p. 223.

j "A Free Man's Worship," in *Mysticism and Logic, op. cit.*, pp. 56–57.

k *Philosophical Investigations*, translated by G. E. M. Anscombe (Macmillan, New York, 1953), §309.

l *Tractatus Logico-Philosophicus*, translated by C. K. Odgen and F. P. Ramsey (Kegan Paul, London, 1922), 6.54.

m *Philosophical Investigations*, translated by Anscombe, *op. cit.*, §§38 and 127 and preface, §133.

n *Ibid.*, §1.

o *Ibid.*, §3.

p *Ibid.*, §5.

q *Ibid.*, §1.

r *Ibid.*, §§2 and 6.

s *Ibid.*, §§11–19, 23, 26–27, and 49.

t St. Anselm, *Monologium*, translated by S. N. Deane (Open Court, Chicago, 1930), pp. 37–40.

u *Philosophical Investigations*, translated by Anscombe, *op. cit.*, §§65–67, 71, and 116.

v *Ibid.*, §§68–69, 75–76, and 78–79.

w *Ibid.*, §84.

x *Ibid.*, §§87–88.

y *Ibid.*, §47.

z *Ibid.*, §§60 and 63.

a *Ibid.*, §81.

b *Ibid.*, §89.

c *Ibid.*, §§89–91 and 97.

d *Ibid.*, §101.

e *Ibid.*, §§107–108.

f *Ibid.*, §109.

g *Ibid.*, §36.

h *Ibid.*, §436.

i *Ibid.*, §580.

j *Ibid.*, §§305–308 and 154.

k *Ibid.*, §383.

l *Ibid.*, §607.

m *Ibid.*, §§583–84.

n *Ibid.*, §586.

o *Ibid.*, §344.

p *Ibid.*, §§627–28.

q *Ibid.*, §246.

r *Ibid.*, §293.

s *Ibid.*, §268.

t *Ibid.*, §115.

u *Ibid.*, §114.

v *Ibid.*, §103.

w *Ibid.*, §111.

x *Ibid.*, §19.
y *Ibid.*, §241.
z *Ibid.*, §226.
a *Ibid.*, §116.
b *Ibid.*, §118.

Chapter 9   /   The Phenomenological Tradition: Husserl and Sartre

a Wordsworth, *The Prelude*, Bk. II, ll. 384–86.
b *Ibid.*, 401–09.
c Quoted in H. Speigelberg, *The Phenomenological Movement* (Martinus Nijhoff, The Hague, 1965), p. 82.
d *Cartesian Meditations*, translated by D. Cairns (Martinus Nijhoff, The Hague, 1960), §§9–10.
e "Philosophy as Rigorous Science," translated by Q. Lauer, in *Phenomenology and the Crisis of Philosophy* (Harper & Row, New York, 1965), pp. 81 and 77.
f *Ibid.*, pp. 124–28.
g "Philosophy and the Crisis of European Man," translated by Q. Lauer, in *Phenomenology and the Crisis of Philosophy, op. cit.*, pp. 171 and 173.
h *Ibid.*, p. 177.
i *Ibid.*, p. 179.
j *Ibid.*, p. 184.
k *Ibid.*, pp. 184–86.
l *Ibid.*, pp. 186–88.
m *Ideas: General Introduction to Pure Phenomenology*, translated by W. R. Boyce Gibson (Macmillan, New York, 1931), §§27 and 30.
n *Ibid.*, §§31–32.
o *Ibid.*, §33.
p *Ibid.*
q *Cartesian Meditations*, translated by Cairns, *op. cit.*, §§1–3 and 8.
r *Ibid.*, §15.
s *Ibid.*, §14.
t *Ibid.*, §19.
u *Ibid.*, §§5 and 24.
v *Ibid.*, §41.
w *Ibid.*, §§17–19.
x R. B. MacLeod, "Phenomenology: A Challenge to Experimental Psychology," in *Behaviourism and Phenomenology*, edited by T. W. Wann (University of Chicago Press, 1964), pp. 59–60.
y *Nausea*, translated by L. Alexander (New Directions, New York, 1959), pp. 16–17.
z *Ibid.*, pp. 168–69.
a *Ibid.*, pp. 22–23.
b *Ibid.*, p. 130.
c *Ibid.*, p. 227.
d *Ibid.*, pp. 171–74.
e *A Treatise of Human Nature*, edited by L. A. Selby-Bigge (Clarendon Press, Oxford, 1896), Bk. I, Pt. IV, § VII.
f *Nausea*, translated by Alexander, *op. cit.*, p. 150.
g *Ibid.*, p. 94.
h *Ibid.*, pp. 116–17.
i *Ibid.*, p. 166.
j *The Reprieve*, translated by E. Sutton (Bantam Books, New York, 1960), pp. 280–87.
k *Troubled Sleep*, translated by G. Hopkins (Bantam Books, New York, 1961), p. 200.

l   *The Transcendence of the Ego,* translated by F. Williams and R. Kirkpatrick (Farrar, Straus & Giroux, New York, 1957), p. 40.

m *Ibid.,* pp. 43–44.

n *Ibid.,* pp. 40–41.

o *Ibid.,* pp. 44–45.

p *Ibid.,* pp. 63–64.

q *Ibid.,* p. 74.

r   *Ibid.,* pp. 94–96.

s   *Ibid.,* pp. 75–76.

t   *Ibid.,* pp. 86–87.

u *Ibid.,* pp. 77–79.

v *Ibid.,* p. 81.

w *Ibid.,* p. 100.

x *Ibid.,* pp. 99–100.

y *Being and Nothingness,* translated by H. E. Barnes (Philosophical Library, New York, 1956), p. lxvi.

z *Ibid.,* p. lxvii.

a *Ibid.,* p. lxii.

b *Ibid.,* p. lxvi.

c *Ibid.,* p. lxvi.

d *Ibid.,* p. 617.

e *Ibid.,* p. lxiii.

f   *Ibid.,* p. 302.

g *Ibid.,* p. 615.

h *Ibid.,* pp. 476–79.

i   *Ibid.,* pp. 479–80.

j   *Ibid.,* p. 554.

k *Existentialism,* translated by B. Frechtman (Philosophical Library, New York, 1947), pp. 20–21.

l   *Ibid.,* pp. 52–53.

m *Nausea,* translated by Alexander, *op. cit.,* p. 170.

Suggestions
for Further
Reading

The best course to pursue is to turn directly to the various great texts from which the selections in this volume have been drawn. Thus, instead of being content with the extracts given here, read more deeply in Kant's *Critique*, Hegel's *Phenomenology*, and Wittgenstein's *Philosophical Investigations*. Information concerning translations and editions will be found in the bibliographical notes section.

Beyond the masters themselves, here is a short list of books about them and their times that should help to make their theories more intelligible.

KANT

L. W. Beck: *A Commentary on Kant's Critique of Practical Reason* (Chicago, 1960). Places this work "in the context of Kant's philosophy" and of eighteenth-century thought on ethics.

N. Kemp Smith: *A Commentary on Kant's Critique of Pure Reason* (London, 1930). A monumental study.

A. D. Lindsay: *Kant* (London, 1934). A useful introduction for the general reader to Kant's work as a whole.

B. K. Milmed: *Kant and Current Philosophical Issues* (New York, 1961). Discusses the relevance of Kant's views to contemporary disputes over "the distinction between analytical and synthetical statements" and over the presence of "a conceptual factor in all knowledge."

H. J. Paton: *The Categorical Imperative* (Chicago, 1948). Holds that "Kant contrived to say something new about morality" and that his work on moral theory is "indispensable for all who seek to lead a good life intelligently."

C. C. J. Webb: *Kant's Philosophy of Religion* (Oxford, 1926). Maintains that Kant's account of religion contains "important truths" despite its "unhistorical individualism" and an "element of subjectivism."

T. D. Weldon: *Introduction to Kant's Critique of Pure Reason* (Oxford, 1958). An excellent introduction; especially good on the background of the problem of knowledge as Kant saw it and on the complex argument of the transcendental deduction.

R. P. Wolff: *Kant's Theory of Mental Activity* (Cambridge, Mass., 1963). Seeks to establish the "Analytic as a single connected argument beginning with the premise that my consciousness has a necessary unity, and concluding with the validity of the causal maxim."

HEGEL

J. N. Findlay: *Hegel: A Re-examination* (New York, 1958). Holds that Hegel was not a "transcendent metaphysician," a "subjectivist," a "manic rationalist," or a "political reactionary."

W. Kaufmann: *Hegel: Reinterpretation, Texts, and Commentary* (Garden City, N. Y., 1965). A fresh view of Hegel's development; includes a translation of the Preface to the *Phenomenology*, with helpful commentary.

J. M. E. McTaggart: *A Commentary on Hegel's Logic* (Cambridge, 1931). Holds that "the dialectic method is valid" and that in many cases "the categories do stand to one another in the relations in which he asserts them to stand," but that "certain errors vitiate particular stages in the process."

G. R. G. Mure: *An Introduction to Hegel* (London, 1940). A useful introduction; includes a long section on Hegel's philosophical inheritance, especially his debt to Aristotle.

MARX

I. Berlin: *Karl Marx: His Life and Environment* (New York, 1948). An interesting and readable study of Marx's life.

M. M. Bober: *Karl Marx's Interpretation of History* (Cambridge, Mass., 1927). A critical analysis of Marx's theory of economic determinism, showing its one-sidedness as well as "some logical weaknesses."

G. Lichtheim: *Marxism: An Historical and Critical Study* (New York, 1961). "It is the thesis of this study that Marxism is to be understood as a historical phenomenon." Its starting point is the French Revolution and the Industrial Revolution, with their "repercussions in the theoretical sphere."

H. B. Mayo: *Introduction to Marxist Theory* (New York, 1960). Contains a useful annotated bibliography.

R. C. Tucker: *Philosophy and Myth in Karl Marx* (Cambridge, 1961). Holds that Marx was less an economist than a moralist whose premise was "man's self-alienation."

KIERKEGAARD

J. Collins: *The Mind of Kierkegaard* (Chicago, 1953). This work "confines itself to the philosophical aspects of his fundamental dialectic of esthetic, ethical and religious modes of existence upon which his scale of values is founded."

M. J. Heinecken: *The Moment Before God* (Philadelphia, 1956). Maintains that Kierkegaard was right on "what it means to become and to be a Christian."

H. A. Johnson and N. Thulstrup (editors): *A Kierkegaard Critique* (Chicago, 1962). Includes translations of essays that appeared originally in Danish, French, German, Italian, and Swedish.

W. Lowrie: *Kierkegaard* (New York, 1962). A detailed biographical study "written by a lover" of Kierkegaard, including extensive quotations from Kierkegaard's writings.

NIETZSCHE

W. Kaufmann: *Nietzsche: Philosopher, Psychologist, Antichrist* (New York, 1956). Argues that Nietzsche was not a romanticist, not a Darwinist, and not a wayward disciple of Schopenhauer's: "The will to power is the core of Nietzsche's thought but inseparable from his idea of sublimation."

A. H. J. Knight: *Some Aspects of the Life and Work of Nietzsche* (Cambridge, 1933). Emphasizes the importance of Nietzsche's Greek studies, with extensive quotations from Nietzsche's writings.

G. A. Morgan: *What Nietzsche Means* (Cambridge, Mass., 1941). A sympathetic study, holding that Nietzsche had "the courage to experience the myriad anxieties that fester the modern soul and a will to overcome them with a new vision."

BERGSON

H. W. Carr: *The Philosophy of Change* (London, 1914). The author had "the advantage of friendship and personal communication with M. Bergson himself."

J. Chevalier: *Henri Bergson,* translated by L. A. Clare (New York, 1928). Contains an account of the intellectual milieu in France in the second half of the nineteenth century, during which time Bergson's opinions were formed.

A. D. Lindsay: *The Philosophy of Bergson* (London, n.d.). Concentrates on Bergson's "critical rather than his constructive and positive work."

DEWEY

S. Hook (editor): *John Dewey: Philosopher of Science and Freedom* (New York, 1950). Essays on various aspects of Dewey's thought and on his influence.

P. A. Schilpp (editor): *The Philosophy of John Dewey* (New York, 1951). Contains a biography, a bibliography, critical essays by various writers on Dewey's logic, epistemology, psychology, and other topics, and Dewey's replies to these critics.

WHITEHEAD

W. A. Christian: *An Interpretation of Whitehead's Metaphysics* (New Haven, 1959). Attempts to meet "the need for something more advanced than the introductions and more comprehensive than the special studies" already available.

V. Lowe: *Understanding Whitehead* (Baltimore, 1962). "Meant to help people understand Whitehead's philosophy, no prior acquaintance with which is assumed."

I. LeClerc: *Whitehead's Metaphysics* (New York, 1958). Argues that "in developing the system which he elaborated in such detail in *Process and Reality*" Whitehead became involved in problems that were "specifically metaphysical, and not those which characterized his earlier investigations in the philosophy of natural science."

THE ANALYTICAL TRADITION

I. M. Copi and R. W. Beard (editors): *Essays on Wittgenstein's Tractatus* (New York, 1966). These "often conflicting accounts illuminate from quite different perspectives various difficult and obscure corners of the *Tractatus.*"

K. T. Fann: *Ludwig Wittgenstein: The Man and His Philosophy* (New York, 1967). Includes memoirs of Wittgenstein by friends as well as essays on *Philosophical Investigations*.

J. Passmore: *A Hundred Years of Philosophy* (London, 1957). Begins with Mill and ends with a "postscript" on existentialism; especially good on logic and epistemology in Britain, the topics on which it concentrates.

G. Pitcher: *The Philosophy of Wittgenstein* (Englewood Cliffs, N. J., 1964). The focus of this book is about equally divided between the *Tractatus* and the *Investigations*, which are held to differ in fundamental ways.

D. Pole: *The Later Wittgenstein* (London, 1958). A short, well-balanced study.

P. A. Schilpp (editor): *The Philosophy of Bertrand Russell* (Evanston, Ill., 1946). Contains descriptive and critical essays, Russell's reply, an autobiographical sketch, and a bibliography.

J. O. Urmson: *Philosophical Analysis* (Oxford, 1956). A survey of British philosophy between the world wars, beginning with logical atomism, passing on to logical positivism, and ending with the first signs of linguistic analysis.

THE PHENOMENOLOGICAL TRADITION

W. Desan: *The Tragic Finale* (New York, 1960). "Concerned with Sartre the philosopher, pure and not-so-simple," and restricted "entirely to his phenomenological ontology as it appears principally in *Being and Nothingness.*"

J. J. Kockelmans (editor): *Phenomenology: The Philosophy of Edmund Husserl and Its Interpretation* (Garden City, N. Y., 1967). Includes discussions of Sartre, Heidegger, and Merleau-Ponty, as well as Husserl.

N. Lawrence and D. O'Connor (editors): *Readings in Existential Phenomenology* (Englewood Cliffs, N. J., 1967). These twenty-two studies show the range of topics in psychology and the social sciences to which phenomenologists have applied their method.

I. Murdoch: *Sartre: Romantic Rationalist* (New Haven, 1953). Approaches Sartre's philosophy primarily through the novels; maintains that "he has the style of the age."

M. Natanson (editor): *Essays in Phenomenology* (The Hague, 1966). Among these studies are two short pieces by Sartre, "Official Portraits" and "Faces."

H. Spiegelberg: *The Phenomenological Movement: A Historical Introduction* (The Hague, 1965). Discusses in detail the views of leading phenomenologists in Germany and France, with briefer accounts of the movement's developments elsewhere. Contains a glossary of phenomenological terms.

Glossary

Short, dictionary-type definitions of philosophical terms are likely to be misleading, for philosophers use terms in many different ways and with little regard to common usage (on which, of course, dictionary definitions are based). Accordingly, many of the definitions given in this Glossary are accompanied by references to places in the text where the terms in question appear in a concrete context. For terms not defined in the Glossary, consult the Index; for fuller treatment of the terms defined here and of other philosophical terms, see *The Encyclopedia of Philosophy*, edited by P. Edwards (Free Press, New York, 1967). Also available are the *Dictionary of Philosophy*, edited by D. D. Runes (Philosophical Library, New York, 1942), and *Dictionary of Philosophy and Psychology*, edited by J. M. Baldwin (Macmillan, New York, 1925). The *Encyclopedia Britannica* (eleventh edition) contains excellent articles on many philosophical terms, including some of those in this Glossary.

Absolute: A term used, in connection with the degrees-of-truth doctrine, to designate the most real thing of all. Also used, in connection with the doctrine that all finite things are parts of one infinite thing, to designate this all-inclusive whole. Hence that which is unconditioned and free from any limitations or qualifications. See Hegel's discussion of Absolute Spirit, pp. 131–34.

Abstraction: The power of separating, in thought, one part of a complex from the other parts and attending to it separately. Thus to consider the color of an apple in isolation from the apple's other qualities would be to abstract this quality for attention.

A priori: What is known independently of sense perception and for this reason held to be indubitable. For Kant's account of the a priori, see pp. 22–23.

Attribute: See **Substance**.

Axiom: A proposition held to be self-evidently true and so neither requiring nor indeed capable of proof. Hence a first principle from which all proofs start. Those who deny the self-evident truth of axioms hold them to be simply postulates from which such-and-such theorems can be deduced. Thus, according to this view, the axioms of one deductive system may be deduced from another set of postulates in some other deductive system.

Category: Any very general, fundamental concept used for interpreting experience. See, for instance, Whitehead's "categoreal scheme" (p. 320, n. 19). For the meaning of "category" in Kant's philosophy, see pp. 43–45.

Conceptualism: The view that universals are neither independently existing entities nor mere names, but are concepts formed in the mind. See **Nominalism, Realism,** and **Universal**.

Contingent: That which may be and also may not be. Hence an event whose occurrence is not necessarily determined (see **Determinism**) by other events.

Cosmology: The study of the universal world process. Distinguished from ontology (see definition) chiefly by the fact that, whereas the latter asks what reality *is*, cosmology asks how reality unfolds and develops in successive stages.

Deduction: A type of inference (see definition) that yields necessary conclusions. In deduction, one or more propositions (called "premises") being assumed, another proposition (the conclusion) is seen to be entailed or implied. It is usually held that in deduction the movement of thought is from premises of greater generality to a conclusion of lesser generality (from the premises "All men are mortal" and "All Greeks are men," we deduce that "All Greeks are mortal"), but the chief mark of deduction is the necessity with which the conclusion follows from the premises.

Determinism: The theory that denies contingency (see **Contingent**) and claims that everything that happens happens necessarily and in accordance with some regular pattern or law. There are three main types, or versions, of determinism: (1) a *scientific determinism* (in which all events are determined by antecedent events in time), (2) a *logical determinism* (as with Spinoza), and (3) a *teleological determinism* (as with Augustine).

Dialectic: A widely and variously used term. Applied by Kant to the section of the *Critique of Pure Reason* devoted to exposing the claims of rationalistic metaphysics (see p. 33, n. 6); used by Hegel to designate the triadic movement of thought from thesis to antithesis to synthesis (see p. 125); and used by Marx to describe the process by which one social class replaces another (see p. 185).

Discursive: The characteristic of the human intelligence that limits it, in the main, to a step-by-step reasoning—from premises to conclusion, from this conclusion to another, and so on. Hence to be contrasted with the all-inclusive vision of the mystic, with the possible operation of a suprahuman intellect, and with the way in which, according to some writers, axioms (see **Axiom**) and other self-evident principles are comprehended by the mind.

Dualism: Any view that holds two ultimate and irreducible principles to be necessary to explain the world—as, for instance, mind and matter.

Empiricism: The view that holds sense perception to be the sole source of human knowledge.

Epistemology: From the Greek terms *episteme* (knowledge) and *logos* (theory, account). Hence the study of the origins, nature, and limitations of knowledge.

Essence: The that-about-a-thing-that-makes-it-what-it-is, in contrast to those properties that the thing may happen to possess but need not possess in order to be itself. Thus it is held (1) that we have to distinguish between those properties of Socrates that are "accidental" and so nonessential (for example, dying by hemlock) and those properties that are essential (for example, those traits of character and personality that made him the man he was). Further, it is held (2) that we have to distinguish between essence and existence (see definition): It is possible according to this view to define Socrates' essence exhaustively; yet when we have done so, the question still remains whether any such being exists. Holders of this view would maintain that there is only one object in which essence and existence are inseparable; this object is God. For Kierkegaard's attack on the notion of essence see pp. 229–31. According to Dewey, we call "essential" whatever properties happen to interest us; hence the essence of anything varies in different contexts (see p. 293).

Eudaemonism: From the Greek term *eudaimonia*, usually translated as "happiness." Hence the view that the end of life consists in happiness, conceived of as an all-round, balanced, long-range type of well-being, in distinction from pleasure. Contrasted with hedonism (see definition).

Existence: Actuality or factuality. Contrasted with essence (see definition). For Kierkegaard's assertion of the primacy of existence over essence, see pp. 213–16. For Sartre's view of existence, see pp. 440–41.

Experiment: A situation arranged to test a hypothesis. Contrasted with "mere" observation.

Free will: The doctrine of contingency (see **Contingent**) applied specifically to human behavior; the denial that men's acts are completely determined (see **Determinism**). The question of free will is important because many philosophers hold that "ought" implies "can"—that moral judgments of approbation and disapprobation are meaningless unless the acts judged about are free, that is, under the control of the agent, who, had he so chosen, might have done otherwise. The main problems connected with free will are (1) what meaning, if any, can be attached to the notion of a free choice and (2) how the possibility of being otherwise is compatible with either (a) belief in an omnipotent and omniscient Deity or (b) the doctrine of universal causal determinism. For Kant's attempt to reconcile freedom with natural necessity, see pp. 84–88. For Sartre's assertion of man's radical and total freedom, see pp. 442–43.

Hedonism: The view that pleasure is man's good. Contrasted with eudaemonism (see definition). *Ethical hedonism* holds either (1) that a man's own pleasure is the sole end worth aiming at or (2) that other people's pleasure is to be taken into account (see pp. 164–69). *Psychological hedonism* holds that, whatever men ought to aim at, they do in fact aim at pleasure.

Humanism: A variously used term. Employed (1) to describe the type of view that distinguishes man from animals on the ground that man has certain moral obligations.

Also used (2) to contrast a secular type of ethics with a religious ethics. Thus Plato's and Aristotle's ethics could be called "humanistic," in contrast with the ethics of Augustine, on the ground that they hold man himself, rather than God, to be the supreme value. Also used (3) to designate a particular historical movement, beginning in the fourteenth century, that emphasized the study of classical literature and the revival of classical ideals.

Idealism: In general, any view that holds reality to be mental or "spiritual," or mind-dependent. *Subjective idealism* emphasizes the ultimate reality of the knowing subject and may either admit the existence of a plurality of such subjects or deny the existence of all save one (in which case the view is called solipsism [see definition]). *Objective idealism* denies that the distinction between subject and object, between knower and known, is ultimate and maintains that all finite knowers and their thoughts are included in an Absolute Thought (see pp. 131–34).

Induction: A type of inference (see definition) in which (in contrast to deduction [see definition]) the movement of thought is from lesser to greater generality. Thus induction begins, not from premises, but from observed particulars (for example, the observation that A, B, and C all have the property x) and seeks to establish some generalization about them (for example, that all members of the class y, of which A, B, and C are members, have the property x). The main problem connected with induction is the difficulty of determining the conditions under which we are warranted in moving from an observed "Some so-and-so's have such-and-such" to the unobserved "All so-and-so's probably have such-and-such."

Inference: The movement of thought by which we reach a conclusion from premises. Thus we speak of inductive and of deductive inference.

Intuition: Direct and immediate knowledge. To be contrasted with discursive (see definition) knowledge.

Judgment: The movement of thought by which, for example, we assert (or deny) some predicate of a subject, or, more generally, by which we connect two terms by some relation. Thus, when we say "This rose is red" or "New York is east of Chicago," we judge. Following Kant (see pp. 22–23), most philosophers distinguish between (1) *analytical judgments,* in which the predicate concept is contained in the subject concept, and (2) *synthetical judgments,* in which the predicate concept is not so contained; and also between (3) *a priori judgments,* which are universal and necessary, and (4) *a posteriori judgments,* which are not universal and necessary.

Law of nature: See **Natural law.**

Materialism: The doctrine that reality is matter. Whereas idealism (see definition) holds that matter is "really" the thought of some mind or other, materialism holds that minds and all other apparently nonmaterial things are reducible to the complex motions of material particles. For a modern version of materialism, see pp. 199–200.

Metaphysics: The study of the ultimate nature of reality, or, as some philosophers would say, the study of "being as such." To be contrasted, therefore, with physics, which studies the "being" of physical nature; with astronomy, which studies the "being" of the solar system; with biology, which studies the "being" of animate nature; and so on. By "being as such," these philosophers mean, not the special characteristics of special kinds of things (for example, living things), but the most general and pervasive characteristics of all things. For some criticisms of metaphysics utilizing a variety of strategies against it, see pp. 51–58, 288–91, and 375–80.

Monism: The view that everything is reducible to one kind of thing, or that one principle of explanation is sufficient to explain everything. Both Hegel and Marx, for instance, were monists; the former was an idealistic monist, the latter a materialistic monist.

Mysticism: The view that reality is ineffable and transcendent; that it is known, therefore, by some special, nonrational means; that knowledge of it is incommunicable in any precise conceptual scheme; and that it is communicable, if at all, only in poetic imagery and metaphor.

Naturalism: A variously used term. (1) In one meaning, naturalism is a view that excludes any reference to supernatural principles and holds the world to be explicable in terms of scientifically verifiable concepts. In this meaning, naturalism is roughly equivalent to secularism and, like humanism (see definition), can be contrasted with a religiously oriented view like Kierkegaard's (see pp. 213–33). (2) In another meaning, the emphasis is on the unity of behavior; any difference in kind between men and animals is denied, and human conduct and human institutions are held to be simply more complex instances of behavior patterns occurring among lower organisms. It was naturalism in this sense that Husserl criticized (see pp. 395–98).

Natural law: This term may designate (1) a pattern of regularity that holds in physical nature. Thus people talk about the "law" of gravity and hold it to be a law of nature (or a natural law) that bodies attract each other directly with their masses and inversely with the square of their distance. Those who affirm the existence of natural laws in this sense hold that these laws are necessary and universal (not merely empirical generalizations concerning observable sequences) and that they are discoverable by reason. Or the term may designate (2) a moral imperative—not a description of what actually happens in the physical world, but a description of what *ought* to happen in men's relations to one another. In this sense, too, these laws would be regarded by those who affirm their existence as being of universal application and discoverable by reason.

Nominalism: The view that only particulars are real and that universals (see **Universal**) are but observable likenesses among the particulars of sense experience.

Objective: To say that anything is "objective" is to say that it is real, that it has a public nature independent of us and of our judgments about it. Thus the question of whether or not values are objective turns on whether or not values are more than private preferences. If they are private preferences, our value judgments are subjective, and there is no more disputing about them than there is about judgments of taste: My good is what *I* prefer; yours is what *you* prefer. On the other hand, if values are objective, it follows that when we differ about them, at least one of us is mistaken.

Ontological argument: An argument for the existence of God, first formulated by St. Anselm. According to this argument, since perfection implies existence, God necessarily exists. For Kant's criticism of this argument, see pp. 55–56.

Ontology: From the Greek terms *ontos* (being) and *logos* (theory, account). For many philosophers ontology is equivalent to metaphysics (see definition). For instance, to inquire about the "ontological status" of something, say, perception, is to ask whether the objects of perception are real or illusory, and, if real, what sort of reality they possess (for example, whether they are mind-dependent or whether they exist independently of minds), and so on. For the phenomenologists (see **Phenomenology**), however, ontology is the science of being as it is revealed in phenomenological observation, in contrast to metaphysics, which is concerned with things-in-themselves (see pp. 409–14).

Pantheism: From the Greek terms *pan* (all) and *theos* (god). Hence the view that all things share in the divine nature, or that all things are parts of god.

Phenomenalism: A type of view that, like idealism (see definition), holds that what we know is mind-dependent, but that, unlike idealism, holds that reality itself is not mind-dependent. Hence Kant's view that we do not know reality (that is, things-in-themselves) and that our knowledge is limited to the data of inner and outer sense (that is, the sensuous manifold organized by the categories and the forms of sensibility) is a type of phenomenalism.

Phenomenology: The name Husserl gave to his philosophical theory, which is characterized by a method of "bracketing" as a result of which the intentional acts and intentional objects within experience are brought into view (see pp. 399–409). Not to be confused with the much broader and looser term "phenomenalism" (see definition).

Positivism: A term first introduced by Comte to describe his account of the nature of knowledge (see pp. 175–76). Also used, more broadly, to characterize any view that rules out the possibility of metaphysical knowledge and that limits a priori truths to analytical statements (see, for instance, pp. 202–04). *Logical Positivism* (see p. 205), a movement derived from positivism in this broad sense, was chiefly characterized by its assertion of the verifiability principle (see definition).

Primary qualities: Those qualities thought to belong to bodies. To be distinguished from secondary qualities, which are held to be products of the interaction between our sense organs and the primary qualities of bodies.

Rationalism: (1) As contrasted with empiricism (see definition), rationalism means reliance on reason (that is, on deduction, on the criterion of logical consistency). (2) As contrasted with authoritarianism or mysticism (see definition), rationalism means reliance on our human powers.

Realism: (1) As contrasted with nominalism (see definition), realism holds that universals are real, and more real than the particulars of sense experience. (2) As contrasted with idealism (see definition), realism holds that the objects of our knowledge are not mind-dependent but are independently existing entities. (3) As contrasted with idealism in still another sense, realism is the point of view that interests itself in men and institutions as they are, rather than as they ought to be. In this sense, realism is almost equivalent to naturalism (see definition).

Relativism: The view that maintains our judgments to be relative to (that is, conditioned upon) certain factors such as cultural milieu or individual bias. Hence the view that we do not possess any absolute, objective (see definition) truth. The relativist need not hold that all judgments are relative; it is possible, for instance, to hold that the physical sciences yield absolute truth while maintaining that in other fields (for example, ethics and religion) there is no absolute truth.

Scepticism: The position that denies the possibility of knowledge. Here, as with relativism (see definition), it is possible either to have a total scepticism or to limit one's scepticism to certain fields.

Solipsism: From the Latin terms *solus* (alone) and *ipse* (self). Hence the view that everything other than oneself is a state of oneself.

Subjectivism: See **Objective, Relativism,** and **Scepticism.**

Substance: A variously used term. (1) In one meaning, substance is simply that which is real. Thus, because Aristotle held reality to consist of amalgams of matter and form, he called each such amalgam a "substance." (2) In another meaning, substance is about equivalent to essence (see definition). Also (3) substance is contrasted with attribute (or property, or quality) as that which *has* the attributes. Thus substance is the underlying (and unknown) ground in which properties are thought to inhere; it is that about which we are judging when we assert properties of a subject, for example, when we say, "The rose is red." Hence (4) substance is that which, unlike an attribute or property, exists in its own right and depends on nothing else.

Teleology: From the Greek terms *telos* (end, goal) and *logos* (theory, account). Hence the view that affirms the reality of purpose and holds the universe either to be consciously designed (as with the Christian doctrine of a providential God) or (as with Aristotle) to be the working out of partly conscious, partly unconscious purposes that are immanent in the developing organisms.

Universal: A universal is that which is predicable of many. Thus "man" is a universal because it is predicable of Washington, Jefferson, Hamilton, and all other individual men. The main problem about universals concerns their ontological status (see **Ontology**). Are they (1) separate entities distinct from the individuals of which they are predicable, (2) real but not separable, or (3) not real at all, but merely the names of likenesses shared by certain particulars? See **Nominalism** and **Realism**.

Verifiability principle: According to this principle, the meaning of a statement is the method of its verification. A statement that cannot be verified (for example, "God exists") is without cognitive meaning (see p. 205).

Voluntarism: The theory that asserts the primacy of will over intellect as an explanatory principle of human behavior, of God's nature, and of the universe as a whole. For two very different versions of voluntarism, see pp. 147–50 and 440–43.

Index

This is primarily an index of proper names. Thus titles and principal topics of discussion are indexed under the authors. Topics that recur in the work of several philosophers are also indexed as main entries. Page numbers in *italics* refer to quotations; those in **boldface** refer to major discussions.

A 9
B 0
C 1
D 2
E 3
F 4
G 5
H 6
I 7
J 8